Oscar Wilde

Oscar Wilde

by

RICHARD ELLMANN

VIKING

VIKING

Penguin Books Canada Ltd, 2801 John Street, Markham, Ontario, Canada L3R 1B4
Penguin Books Ltd, 27 Wrights Lane, London W8 5TZ (Publishing and Editorial)
and Harmondsworth, Middlesex, England (Distribution and Warehouse)
Viking Penguin Inc., 40 West 23rd Street, New York, New York 10010, USA
Penguin Books Australia Ltd, Ringwood, Victoria, Australia
Penguin Books (NZ) Ltd, 182-190 Wairau Road, Auckland 10, New Zealand

First published in Canada, 1987, by Penguin Books Canada Ltd
First published in Great Britain, 1987, by Hamish Hamilton Ltd

Copyright © 1987 by Richard Ellmann

Copyright © Letters and unpublished material by Wilde: Merlin Holland
and John Murray Ltd.
© Vyvyan Holland 1962,
reprinted from *Selected Letters of Oscar
Wilde*, edited by Rupert Hart-Davis, Oxford
University Press, 1979

Copyright © Letters of Lord Alfred Douglas: Edward Colman

Printed and bound in the United Kingdom by
Robert Hartnoll (1985) Ltd

Canadian Cataloguing in Publication Data
Ellmann, Richard, 1918 –
    Oscar Wilde.
    ISBN 0-670-81420-2
1. Wilde, Oscar 1854-1900 – Biography. 2. Authors,
Irish – 19th century – Biography. I. Title

PR5823.E43 1987   828'.8   C87-094279-4

To Lucy Ellmann

CONTENTS

EXILE

LIST OF ILLUSTRATIONS

1, 2, 3, 5, 8, 28, 35, 40, 57, 58, 59, courtesy of William Andrews Clark Library; 9, 38, courtesy of Library of Congress, Kaufmann Collection; 10, courtesy of Oxford City Library; 11, 13, 30, 32, 53, 54, courtesy of The Hyde Collection; 14, courtesy of Palazzo Rosso, Genoa; 15, courtesy of City of Bristol Museum and Art Gallery; 16, 18, 19, 20, 21, 22, 23, 24, 25, courtesy of Library of Congress; 17, courtesy of University of Glasgow, Birnie Philip Bequest; 29, courtesy of the Reverend Brocard Sewell, O.P., and of the Reverend Bede Bailey, St Dominic's Priory; 31, courtesy of Art Institute of Chicago; 33, Author's collection; 44, courtesy of the International Museum of Photography at George Eastman House; 45, courtesy of Sotheby's London; 47, courtesy of the Hunterian Art Gallery, University of Glasgow, Birnie Philip Bequest; and Weidenfeld Archives; 48, courtesy of The Raymond Mander and Joe Michenson Theatre Collection; 49, 55, Collection Guillot de Saix, H. Roger Viollet, Paris; 50, courtesy of Ashmolean Museum, University of Oxford; 52, courtesy of Yorick; 63, photograph by Jack Oppenheim.

ACKNOWLEDGEMENTS

This book has been under way for a long time, and I have been helped by many people. From the time I began Sir Rupert Hart-Davis, whose edition of Wilde's letters is a landmark in modern scholarship, was prodigal of his assistance; he allowed me to use his invaluable Wilde archive and to tap his profound knowledge of the period. He has also kindly read the manuscript, and I have respected his blue pencil. He has my heartfelt thanks. Dr Mary Hyde (Viscountess Eccles) graciously put at my disposal the largest collection of Wilde materials in private hands, and I owe much to her generosity. The largest institutional collection is at the William Andrews Clark Library of the University of California at Los Angeles; its successive directors, William E. Conway and Thomas Wright, as well as John Bidwell, have never failed to give the utmost help. The Ross Collection at the Bodleian Library has been a principal source. I want to thank Donald J. Kaufmann for letting me use his Wilde collection before he donated it to the Library of Congress.

Merlin Holland has kindly allowed me to quote from published and unpublished Wilde material, and has also offered other kinds of valuable assistance. Edward Colman, the holder of Lord Alfred Douglas's copyrights and his literary executor, has kindly allowed the many quotations from Douglas.

Owing partly to the dispersal of Wilde's papers at a bankruptcy sale, many libraries have important holdings. I mention here the Berg Collection and the Manuscript Room of the New York Public Library (NYPL in the notes), the Houghton Library at Harvard, the Beinecke Library at Yale (and Miss Marjorie Wynne), the Library of Congress (LC), the Trinity College, Dublin Library (TCD), the National Library of Ireland (NLI), the British Library (BL), the Morgan Library, the Rosenbach Museum, the Humanities Research Center at the University of Texas, the Reading University Library, the Dartmouth College Library, the Princeton University Library (especially the Taylor Collection), the Radcliffe College Library, the Eastbourne (Sussex) Area Library, the Bibliothèque Doucet. In many city libraries in the United States the staff unearthed press accounts of Wilde's lecture tour. The archives of the Royal Literary Fund and of Magdalen and Brasenose Colleges at Oxford have been useful.

The manuscript has been read by Catharine Carver, from whose criticisms I have greatly profited; by Lucy Ellmann, who made many improvements; and by Mary Ellmann, with considerable advantage. Maud Ellmann took time from her busy life to help me with the notes. Dr

Paul Cohen, acting director of the Library of the New York Historical Society, hunted down many seemingly untraceable sources. Dr John Stokes and Professor Ian Fletcher have made available to me their extraordinary knowledge of the Wilde period. J. Robert Maguire furnished me with many details of Wilde's relation to the Dreyfus case. R. E. Alton deciphered for the first time the message on Queensberry's visiting card which set off the libel suit. He and Professor Donald Taylor helped with Wilde's sonnet on Chatterton. Professor Barbara Hardy made many valuable suggestions. Malcolm Pinhorn, Quentin Keynes, and Jeremy Mason opened their collections to me. Dr Owen Dudley Edwards was especially kind and helpful. Rosita Fanto, with whom I collaborated on Oscar Wilde playing cards, gave me some useful hints. H. Montgomery Hyde took a benign interest.

Dr Mary Reynolds put me under great obligation by composing the elaborate index for this book.

I have many specific acts of kindness to record from the following: Professor Marcia Allentuck, Anna and Karen Bamborough, Michael Bassan, Dr John C. Broderick, Professor J. E. Chamberlin, Dennis Cole, Professor Morton N. Cohen, Roger Dobson, Robert Ellmann, Professor Charles Feidelson, Bobby Fong, Professor Peter Gay, John Hamill, Barbara Hayley, Sir William and Lady Hayter, Patrick Henchy, Tim Hilton, Michael Holroyd, Dr Roger Hood, Robert Jackson, Jeri Johnson, Professor Alix de Jonge, Professor Emrys Jones, Dr Alon Kadish, Professor John Kelleher, Dr John Kelly, Professor Roger Kempf, Clinton Krauss, Trudy Kretchman, Professor Henry Lethbridge, Professor Harry Levin, Lee Ann Lloyd, Professor J. B. Lyons, W. S. G. Macmillan, Dr Wolfgang Maier, Professor Thomas Mallon, Professor E. H. Mikhail, Professor W. M. Murphy, Milo M. Naeve, Dr Eoin O'Brien, Eileen O'Byrne, Seán Ó Mórdha, Johan Polak, Professor Martin and Mary Price, Ellis Pryce-Jones, Dr Bernard Richards, Michael Rhodes, Julia Rosenthal, Professor Ernest Samuels, Professor George Sandulescu, Dr Keith Schuchard, Professor Ronald Schuchard, G. F. Sims, Professor W. B. Stanford, Dr J. I. M. Stewart, Tom Stoppard, Andrew Treip, Ruth Vyse, Elizabeth Wansborough, Wade Wellman, Terence De Vere White.

I must thank also the universities I have been associated with, Northwestern, Yale, Oxford, and Emory, for facilitating my research.

R.E.

St Giles', Oxford
Ides of March, 1987

INTRODUCTION

Oscar Wilde: we have only to hear the great name to anticipate that what will be quoted as his will surprise and delight us. Among the writers identified with the 1890s, Wilde is the only one whom everyone still reads. The various labels that have been applied to the age – Aestheticism, Decadence, the Beardsley period – ought not to conceal the fact that our first association with it is Wilde, refulgent, majestic, ready to fall.

From as early as 1881, when he was in his late twenties, to the middle of 1895, when he was forty, literary London was put out of countenance by this outrageous Irishman from Dublin (via Oxford), who declared he was a socialist and hinted he was a homosexual, while patently mocking wise saws on all subjects. He declined, in a public and ceremonious manner, to live within his means, behave modestly, respect his elders, or recognize such entities as nature and art in their traditional apparel.

He won admiration, and denigration. Legends sprang up about him, and unsavory rumors too. He was accused of sins from effeminacy to plagiarism. That he was the kindest of men was not so widely known. Instead, at the very moment he was writing his best and *The Importance of Being Earnest* had crowned his career, what the law picturesquely calls sodomy was imputed to him. He was sentenced in the end to two years of hard labor for the lesser charge of indecent behavior with men. So much glory has rarely been followed by so much humiliation.

The hardships of prison life and of subsequent exile in France and Italy, left Wilde a broken man. A spendthrift on his uppers, slighted by old acquaintances, he pursued on his release the life for which he had been jailed. He wrote *The Ballad of Reading Gaol* and after that nothing. In 1900 he died in an obscure Paris hotel. He left behind him a sort of testament, *De Profundis*, in the form of a prison letter to his lover, Lord Alfred Douglas. It skirted penitence and while acknowledging faults (not those cited in the courtroom) vindicated his individuality. Published bit by bit over sixty years, it reawakened the quarrels of old friends, who continued to dispute their sometime place in his life as long as they lived.

Other contemporaries snubbed Wilde as an ex-convict, but entertained him gladly enough in their memoirs. Many a dull chronicle, as in life many a dull table, was posthumously enlivened by this boulevardier. As for the reading public, it never failed in devotion to him, within the English-speaking countries or abroad, where his genius shines through translation.

When Wilde left Oxford in 1878 he called himself a professor of aesthetic, and aestheticism is the creed which is usually attributed to him.

Yet his theme is not as is often supposed art's divorce from life, but its inescapable arraignment by experience. His creative works almost always end in unmasking. The hand that adjusts the green carnation suddenly shakes an admonitory finger. While the ultimate virtue in Wilde's essays is in make-believe, the dénouement of his dramas and narratives is that masks have to go. We must acknowledge what we are. Wilde at least was keen to do so. Though he offered himself as the apostle of pleasure, his created work contains much pain. In the smash-up of his fortunes rather than in their apogee his cast of mind fully appeared.

Essentially Wilde was conducting, in the most civilized way, an anatomy of his society, and a radical reconsideration of its ethics. He knew all the secrets and could expose all the pretense. Along with Blake and Nietzsche, he was proposing that good and evil are not what they seem, that moral tabs cannot cope with the complexity of behavior. His greatness as a writer is partly the result of the enlargement of sympathy which he demanded for society's victims.

His language is his finest achievement. It is fluent with concession and rejection. It takes what has been ponderously said and remakes it according to a new perspective and a new principle. An older generation's reassuring platitudes and tired certainties are suddenly infused with youthful intransigence, a sort of pontifical impudence that commands attention. We have the pleasure of affirming the *ancien régime* and of rebelling against it at the same time. Long live the king, we cry, as we cut off his head.

As for his wit, its balance was more hazardously maintained than is realized. Although it lays claim to arrogance, it seeks to please us. Of all writers, Wilde was perhaps the best company. Always endangered, he laughs at his plight, and on his way to the loss of everything jollies society for being so much harsher than he is, so much less graceful, so much less attractive. And once we recognize that his charm is threatened, its eye on the door left open for the witless law, it becomes even more beguiling.

Some of his interest lies in a characteristic that, along with his girth, he shared with Dr Johnson. He occupied, as he insisted, a 'symbolical relation' to his time. He ranged over the visible and invisible worlds, and dominated them by his unusual views. He is not one of those writers who as the centuries change lose their relevance. Wilde is one of us. His wit is an agent of renewal, as pertinent now as a hundred years ago. The questions posed by both his art and his life lend his art a quality of earnestness, an earnestness which he always disavowed.

BEGINNINGS

CHAPTER I

Toil of Growing Up

*The soul is born old, but grows young. That is the comedy of
life. The body is born young and grows old. That is life's
tragedy.*

LADY BRACKNELL: *Prism! Come here, Prism! Prism!
Where is that baby?*

First Words

Oscar Wilde first emerges for us into articulate being in 1868, when he
was thirteen, in a letter he wrote to his mother from school. Portora Royal
School, in Enniskillen, which prepared pupils for Trinity College, Dublin, was a good school, though to call it 'the Eton of Ireland,' as the
headmaster and Wilde's mother did, was pretentious.[1] In later life Wilde
told D. J. O'Donoghue, the tireless compiler of an Irish biographical
dictionary, that he had spent 'about a year there.' The actual period was
seven years, from age nine to sixteen. Facts were for bending: interviewed
for the *Biograph*, an English annual which published his 'life' in six pages
when he was only twenty-six, Wilde said that he had been privately tutored
at home.[2] Portora was not a resonant name, and it seemed preferable to
have attended no school rather than one that had to be laboriously
identified. 'I have forgotten my schooldays,' says Mrs Cheveley in *An Ideal
Husband*. 'I have a vague impression that they were detestable.' Then, too,
Wilde found it imaginatively seductive to deconstruct his nurture, to
obliterate by whim all those sums and paradigms. No school on earth
produced Oscar Wildes. But Portora, which flourishes still, must be
credited with having prepared not only Wilde but Samuel Beckett.

The letter Wilde wrote from there unfortunately survives only in a
fragment. Still, as a hieroglyph of his adolescence, it is valuable:

September 1868   Portora School

Darling Mama, The hamper came today, and I never got such a jolly
surprise, many thanks for it, it was more than kind of you to think of it.

3

Don't please forget to send me the *National Review* . . . The flannel shirts you sent in the hamper are both Willie's, mine are one quite scarlet and the other lilac but it is too hot to wear them yet. You never told me anything about the publisher in Glasgow, what does he say? And have you written to Aunt Warren on the green note paper?[3]

The rest of the letter is said to have referred to a cricket win over a regimental side, and to 'that horrid regatta.' Accompanying the letter was a sketch, now lost, captioned, 'ye delight of ye boys at ye hamper and ye sorrow of ye hamperless boy.'

The person we think of as Oscar Wilde is assembling here. He is on excellent terms with his darling mother, and keen to be on better ones, perhaps because his elder brother Willie is distinctly a rival for her attention. Oscar will unseat him later. With a precocious sense of the ridiculous he pictures the scene of felicity and misery which the delivery of the hamper had created. His appetite for dramatic presentation is whetted. Other predilections are clear: cricket interests him mildly, rowing not at all. Since the school was situated on the river Erne, the antipathy to regattas must have been unfashionable and individual. His liking for cricket was to flag, and later he would tease his robust biographer, Robert Sherard, by pretending to find the players' attitudes 'indecent' and 'not Greek.'[4] Eventually he dismissed these two team sports as 'bats and boats,' preferring riding, shooting, and fishing.

The letter reveals that his thirteen-year-old tastes in clothing were a dandy's, discriminating between his own scarlet and lilac shirts and the unmentionable colours of Willie's. Wilde was wearing a lilac shirt, with a heliotrope tie, when the two women who halved the pen name of 'Michael Field' came to see him in 1890.[5] His predilection for scarlet and related tints was shared with his mother, who is reported as wearing into her sixties a scarlet dress, and whom a Dublin observer, Lord Rathcreedan, claims to have seen flaunting a red shawl.[6] 'Vermilion' was a word that Wilde liked to draw out lingeringly, in his inflection of tints and shades. (On the other hand, he had a horror of magenta.)[7] In *The Ballad of Reading Gaol*, the last indignity suffered by the condemned man is that he cannot be hanged in his scarlet coat. When it was pointed out to Wilde that the regiment to which the man belonged was the Blues, he offered instant revision:

He did not wear his azure coat
For blood and wine are blue.[8]

More than aesthetic preference lay behind his eagerness to read his mother's new poem in the *National Review*. It bore the patriotic title, 'To Ireland,' and renewed a plea that Lady Wilde had made in her youth, for someone to blow the trumpet of rebellion. A new edition of her poems was to appear from a Scottish publisher, and the new poem would replace the dedication in the first edition of 1864, which read,

Dedicated to my sons Willie and Oscar Wilde

'I made them indeed
Speak plain the word country. I taught them, no doubt,
That country's a thing one should die for at need'

lines of her own with more fervor than style. The young Wilde had a taste for both her poetry and her politics.

He also enjoyed his mother's practical jokes. 'Aunt Warren' in the letter was Lady Wilde's much older sister, Emily Thomazine, who in 1829 had married Samuel Warren, then a captain, and later, like his brother Nathaniel, a lieutenant-colonel in the British Army. Mrs Warren, her Unionist politics befitting an army wife, frowned on her sister, who as a nationalist frowned back. Irking Aunt Warren with green note paper was a shared subversive delight. Emily Warren, except as co-owner with the Wildes of certain properties, does not appear on the scene again. Her husband had died about 1850, and she herself in 1881. Like her older brother, who became a judge in Louisiana, she kept her distance from sister Jane. Yet perhaps a bit of Emily Thomazine Warren survives in Aunt Augusta Bracknell, whose husband's brother is a general with a first name, Ernest, more solemn than Samuel and Nathaniel. Lady Bracknell issues English commands which are promptly disobeyed by Irish hearts.

(Jane) Speranza Francesca Wilde

All women become like their mothers. That is their tragedy.
No man does. That's his.

The mother to whom this boy of thirteen addressed himself was no ordinary person. Lady Wilde had a sense of being destined for greatness, and imparted it. Her son subscribed to her view, and treated her with the utmost consideration and respect, almost as though he were her precursor rather than she is. Four years before she received that letter from school, her husband had been knighted. The title helped because she had always been uneasy about her first name, which was Jane, and had modified her second name, almost certainly Frances, into Francesca, regarding the new name as a brilliant vestige of the Elgee family's origins in Italy, where – according to what she maintained was a family tradition – they had been called Algiati. From Algiati to Alighieri was an easy backward leap, and Dante could not save himself from becoming Jane Elgee's ancestor. (Her son in turn was to claim a visual resemblance to and a spiritual kinship with both Shakespeare and Nero.) What signature to use became a complicated matter. To tradesmen or correspondents of no consequence, she signed herself Jane Wilde, to those she liked she was Francesca or J. Francesca Wilde. But she had another forename as well, altogether of her own devising. This was Speranza. It was part of the motto with which her notepaper was embossed: *Fidanza, Speranza, Costanza.* In her correspondence with Henry Wadsworth Longfellow, translator of Dante, she signed herself Francesca Speranza Wilde.[9]

That she found a certain humor in her *nom de plume* is evident from a cheering letter she sent to the Irish novelist William Carleton: 'In truth I cannot bear this despondency of yours – *unrecognised genius* may name its miseries, deep and poignant, but not yours . . . Let St Speranza, if you will allow my canonisation, work the miracle of your restoration, for your gloom is all imaginary . . .' Carleton responded by praising 'the great Ocean' of her soul.[10]

The rivering waters that formed that great Ocean have been traced. Among her ancestors, if not Dante, there was on her mother's side the Reverend Charles Maturin, whose *Melmoth the Wanderer*, with its mysterious, satanic hero, exercised fascination upon Scott, on Balzac who wrote a sequel to it, on Baudelaire who found in Melmoth an alter ego, and on Oscar Wilde, who would one day take Melmoth as his own name. Lady Wilde's maternal great-grandfather, Dr Kingsbury, was a well-known physician and friend of Jonathan Swift. Her father, Charles Elgee (1783–1821), took up the law, and his father John Elgee (1753–1823) was a rector and archdeacon in the Church of Ireland. Her mother, Sarah, was the daughter of another cleric, Thomas Kingsbury, who besides being vicar of Kildare held the secular post of Commissioner of Bankruptcy. Further back, Lady Wilde's paternal great-grandfather, Charles Elgee (1709–87), was a well-off farmer in County Down; another ancestor on her mother's side was English: a bricklayer (died 1805) who emigrated from County Durham in the 1770s because of the Irish building boom.[11] Given these unexceptionable antecedents, Lady Wilde still opted for her hypothetical Tuscan origins.

Like her son, she enjoyed improving upon reality. She allowed it to be understood that she had been born in 1826. When pressed, she responded airily that her birth had never been recorded, no Registry Office having been required when giants still walked the earth. The parish register that might have refuted her has not been found. 'Indeed,' says Lady Bracknell, 'no woman should ever be quite accurate about her age. It looks so calculating.' Though biographers have sought the date of Lady Wilde's birth in vain, it is possible now gracelessly to reveal, on the basis of her application for a grant from the Royal Literary Fund in November 1888, by which time age rather than youth was to her advantage, that she was born on 27 December 1821, a mere half decade earlier than she had said. Her son Oscar was a match for her: he regularly claimed to be two years younger than he was, even on his marriage certificate; and Lady

Wilde went along with this chronology, congratulating him on winning the Newdigate 'at the age of only 22,' when she knew he was close to twenty-four.

Lady Wilde communicated to her son both her nationalism and her determination to embody it in verse. One version she gave of how she made her debut on the national stage was that she had come upon a book or pamphlet by Richard D'Alton Williams, who was tried for treason, though acquitted, in 1848. Presumably it was the work of his that began with the poem, 'The Nation's Valentine, To the Ladies of Ireland,' which called upon women to 'sing us no songs but of FATHERLAND now.' She was moved, she was fired. 'Then it was I discovered I was a poet.'[12] She did manage a rhetoric close to her master's. But for W. B. Yeats she evolved a different account. 'Walking through some Dublin street, she came upon so great a crowd that she could go no further,' Yeats recalled her telling him. 'She asked a shopman what brought so many people into the street and he said: "It is the funeral of Thomas Davis." And when she answered, "Who was Thomas Davis? I have never heard of him," he said, "He was a poet." '[13] That a poet should be so multitudinously mourned decided her to be a poet too.

Thomas Davis's poetry did in fact convert many to nationalism, including Yeats's friend John O'Leary. But Davis's funeral was in 1845, when Jane Wilde was a good twenty-two rather than eighteen, and she could not have been ignorant of his identity as leader of Young Ireland.[14] Williams's verse and Davis's funeral contributed to the rising sentiment among sensitive Irishmen, Protestants as well as Catholics, that they must take up the nationalist cause. Jane Elgee began to write verse on the coming revolution, on the famine, and on the exodus from Ireland of the famished. These she submitted to Charles Gavan Duffy, editor of the *Nation* (which had been founded in 1842), under the name of 'Speranza.' They were enclosed in letters signed 'John Fanshaw Ellis' in echo of Jane Francesca Elgee. When Gavan Duffy liked and printed her patriotic poems, she submitted some love poetry, which he liked less and did not print. Still his curiosity was awakened and he asked Ellis to come and see him. Ellis responded by asking Gavan Duffy to pay a visit instead to 34 Leeson Street. There, as Gavan Duffy recounts, the smiling maid, on being asked for Mr Ellis, showed him into a drawing room, where he found only George Smith, publisher to the University. 'What! my loyal friend, are you the new volcano of sedition?' asked Gavan Duffy. Smith left the room and returned 'with a tall girl on his arm, whose stately carriage and figure, flashing brown eyes, and features cast in an heroic mould, seemed fit for the genius of poetry, or the spirit of revolution.'[15] The stage-managing was characteristic: as Jane Elgee confided later to the mathematician Sir William Hamilton, she loved 'to make a sensation.' Gavan Duffy wrote to her that one day she would 'win a reputation not second to Mrs Browning.'[16]

Speranza's verses were inflammatory. 'The Young Patriot Leader' was on Thomas Francis Meagher, convicted of treason in 1849 in a trial she attended. The government, however, took more notice of the prose in the *Nation*. Gavan Duffy as editor and leader-writer was put in prison to await trial for sedition. In his absence, Jane Elgee wrote editorials for two successive issues of the paper, which said outright what Gavan Duffy had put circumspectly. In 'The Hour of Destiny,' on 22 July 1848, she announced that 'The long pending war with England has actually commenced,' and a week later in 'Jacta Alea Est' ('The Die is Cast') fiercely exclaimed: 'O! for a hundred thousand muskets glimmering brightly in the light of Heaven.' But she was willing to allow, if England capitulated promptly, 'the golden link' of the monarchy to continue to unite the two nations. These articles inflamed the government if not the populace, and were tacked on to the charges against Gavan Duffy as being his work, even though he was in prison. When the barrister pleading his case, Isaac Butt, said he could defend everything except the 'Jacta Alea Est,' Jane Elgee went to the Solicitor-General, denounced herself as author of the articles, and asked to have the added charge removed from Gavan Duffy's indictment. She was refused. 'I think this piece of Heroism will make a good scene when I write my life,' she boasted to a Scottish friend.[17] When the prosecutor interrogated Gavan Duffy about the articles, a tall woman arose in the gallery to interrupt. 'I, and I alone, am the culprit, if culprit there be.' The judge gavelled her down, but the prosecution dropped this line of questioning.[18] Gavan Duffy was tried four times. Jury after jury being unwilling to convict, he was at last set free. Jane Elgee's intervention was the most effective act in the three great courtroom dramas in which the Wilde family performed. It must have been in her mind forty-seven years later, when she insisted that her son Oscar stand trial rather than run away, anticipating that he too might have a famous victory.

Immoderateness was a policy with her. In December 1848 she wrote, 'I should like to rage through life – this orthodox creeping is too tame for me – ah, this wild rebellious ambitious nature of mine. I wish I could satiate it with Empires, though a St Helena were the end.' 'All virtue must be active,' she declared at another time. 'There is no such thing as negative virtue.'[19] If heroic deeds were not possible, she could at least dress with derring-do. At the Lord Lieutenant's ball on St Patrick's Day, 1859, she vaunted a dress that was 'three skirts of white silk ruched round with white ribbon and hooped up with bouquets of gold flowers and green shamrocks.'[20] In her salon in Dublin, and later in London, she cut a figure in increasingly outlandish costumes, surmounted by headdresses and festooned with outsize and bizarre jewelry.

Her remarks were in keeping with her attire. Oscar Wilde would comment later, 'Where there is no extravagance there is no love, and where there is no love there is no understanding.'[21] In its lower range Lady Wilde's conscious rhetoric could be quite forthright, as when she wrote in an essay on 'The Bondage of Woman', 'We have now traced the history of women from Paradise to the nineteenth century, and have heard nothing through the long roll of the ages but the clank of their fetters.'[22] Her son would turn this round in *A Woman of No Importance*, 'The history of woman is the history of the worst form of tyranny the world has ever known. The tyranny of the weak over the strong. It is the only tyranny that lasts.' His mother did not see history in this way. She interrupted the feminist Mona Caird to say, 'Every woman will give the top of the jug to some man till the end of the chapter.'[23]

In conversation she was iconoclastic. When someone asked her to receive a young woman who was 'respectable,' she replied, 'You must never employ that description in this house. It is only tradespeople who are respectable. We are above respectability.'[24] In *The Importance of Being Earnest*, when Lady Bracknell asks, 'Is this Miss Prism a female of repellent aspect, remotely connected with education?' Canon Chasuble replies, 'She is the most cultivated of ladies, and the very picture of respectability.' 'It is obviously the same person,' says Lady Bracknell. Wilde once announced that his mother and he had decided to found a society for the suppression of virtue, and it says something for their kinship of minds that either of them might have originated the idea.

What Lady Wilde contributed to the Irish scene was a talent for magnifying parochial matters. For her poetry meant oratory. Coulson Kernahan reports her rebuke to a friend of his, 'You, and other poets, are content to express only your little soul in poetry. I express the soul of a great nation. Nothing less would content me, who am the acknowledged voice in poetry of all the people of Ireland.'[25] When she moved to England, after her husband's death, she complained with pomp and dejection, 'I have a habit of looking at souls, not forms. Alas now I only feel the agony and loss of all that made life endurable, and my singing robes are trailed in London clay.'[26] She claimed her aquiline look came from having been an eagle in a previous existence, and to the young Yeats, whom she befriended, she said, 'I want to live in some high place, Primrose Hill or Highgate, because I was an eagle in my youth.'[27]

Yet she did not want to lead the troops like Joan of Arc, only to inspire them as 'a priestess at the altar of freedom.'[28] It was up to men to wage the wars. Women should be free, and the highest form of their freedom was to suffer for a cause.[29] Other forms of freedom did not attract her. She would rebuke George Eliot for having characters in *Middlemarch* say 'By God!' when 'By Jove!' would have been enough. Her own part after her marriage, she said, when 'at last my great soul is imprisoned within a woman's destiny,'[30] was to provide the poetry to go with her husband's prose.

An All Round Man

ALGERNON: *The doctors found out that Bunbury could not live . . . so Bunbury died.*

LADY BRACKNELL: *He seems to have had great confidence in the opinion of his physicians.*

William Robert Wilde, who married Jane Elgee on 14 November 1851, was worthy of her regard. She had testified to it in the *Nation* by an extremely laudatory review of his *The Beauties of the Boyne* in 1849, which may have been the agent of their first meeting. His family, like hers, was resolutely middle-class. His great grandfather was a Dublin merchant, his grandfather, Ralph Wilde, settled as a farmer in Castlereagh; Ralph's son Thomas, a physician, married Amalia Flynn (born about 1776). Two of their three sons became Church of Ireland priests, and only the third, William Robert Wilde (born March 1815), followed his father's profession.

William Wilde had his detractors, but no one in Ireland, or perhaps even in Britain, knew as much as he about the eye and ear. St Mark's Hospital, Dublin, which he founded in 1844, was the first in Ireland to treat afflictions of these organs. His books *Aural Surgery* (1853) and *Epidemia Ophthalmia* (1851) were the earliest textbooks in their fields, and stood up well for years. Even today surgeons use the terms 'Wilde's incision' for mastoid, 'Wilde's cone of light' and 'Wilde's cords.' He displayed great skill in amassing medical data for books about Austria and the Mediterranean coast. When a census of Ireland was undertaken in 1851, Wilde was appointed Census Commissioner to organize the collection of medical information. His statistics on the incidence of deafness and blindness and eye and ear diseases were the first ever compiled in Ireland. He was appointed Surgeon Oculist to the Queen in Ireland in 1863, and the next year was knighted.

However demanding his medical work was, he pursued other interests. He wrote easily, and on many subjects. The skull of Swift came into his hands, and he published a short, valuable book to prove that the great satirist in his last years was not insane but physically ill. William Wilde trained his own eye on Irish archaeological remains, and his ear on folklore. He was the first to find and identify a lake dwelling, he brilliantly and speedily catalogued the great collection of antiquities now in the National Museum of Ireland. From his peasant patients, often in lieu of fees, he collected superstitions, legends, cures, and charms that might have been lost. An attendant wrote them down at the time, and Wilde's widow would edit and publish them in two posthumous volumes that had a great influence on Yeats. The catalogue of antiquities is still in use, and William Wilde's little book of *Irish Popular Superstitions* (1852), dedicated to Speranza, can still engage and amuse.

Like his wife, William Wilde was a nationalist. Discouraged by the failure of the 1848 uprising, both dissociated themselves from the republican Fenianism of the late 1860s. (Speranza expressly disavowed democracy.) William Wilde's nationalism expressed itself in a love for the countryside, past and present. Two of his books deal with Lough Corrib and Lough Mask in the west (1867) and with the Boyne and Blackwater in the east of Ireland (1849). He not only knew the places thoroughly, he could also recreate their history. The legendary battle of Moytura, for example, in which the Tuatha De Danaan defeated the Fomorians near Cong, was so much in his mind that he claimed to have found the grave of one of its heroes, and in 1864 built Moytura House on the supposed site of the battle. When the British Association visited the Aran Islands in 1857, William Wilde was their official guide, and so impressed the Governor of Uppsala, who was among the visiting dignitaries, that he invited the Wildes to Sweden. There, in 1862, he conferred on Wilde the Order of the Polar Star.*

Success promotes malice. Yeats discounts, but cannot keep from relating, 'a horrible folk story' that Sir William once took out the eyes of a man who had come to consult him as an ophthalmologist and laid them upon a plate, intending to replace them, and that the eyes were eaten by a cat. 'Cats love eyes,' said a friend of Yeats. More to the point, tongues in Dublin wagged that Sir William was dirty. Yeats retails the riddle, 'Why are Sir William Wilde's nails so black?' and the answer, 'Because he has scratched himself.' But Bernard Shaw calls this a misconception owing to the fact that Sir William had the kind of porous skin that looks dirty, and Yeats's father, with a portrait painter's exact eye, confirmed that Wilde was 'a neat and well-dressed man,' though the square beard that grew from rather than under his chin was untidy.[32] William Wilde was aware of the danger of infection in hospitals, and, before the advent of Lister, advocated that doctors wash their hands with chlorite of lime.[33] Yet once, at a dinner party in his house, he tasted the soup by dipping his thumb in the tureen and then sucking it. When he asked Lady Spencer, the Lord Lieutenant's wife, why she did not touch her soup, he was told, 'Because you put your thumb in it.'[34]

Sir William was of average height, but Lady Wilde was nearly six feet tall, which led to their being caricatured as a giantess and dwarf. In later years Speranza became so bulgy in the lumbar region that Shaw attributed her condition to gigantism, which he offered, without medical evidence,

---

* Reports circulated later that during his stay in Sweden Wilde had operated on King Oscar's eye, and while the king was temporarily blinded seduced the Queen. The Boccaccian rumor was sufficiently widespread for Crown Prince Gustave on a visit to Dublin to claim waggishly that he was Oscar Wilde's half-brother. The Wildes did meet the royal family once in Uppsala,[31] but the royal archives give no evidence of Wilde's having operated on the king. Nor of the king's having agreed to be godfather to Oscar Wilde.

as a hereditary cause of Oscar Wilde's homosexuality. R. Y. Tyrrell, professor of classics at Trinity, with equal authority pronounced William Wilde to be pithecoid. J. B. Yeats said, however, that 'His figure was spare and exceedingly well-knit. He walked with his elbows . . . very rapidly. He had sharply inquisitive eyes . . . and looked very eccentric . . . a wiry restless man and a contrast to his ponderous wife and her measured speech.'[35] Sir William was reputed to be vain, and certainly relished wearing his Swedish decoration and the uniform that went with it; members of the Irish Academy were instructed to address him as Chevalier. He was accustomed, like his son, to dominate dinner tables;* 'the best conversationalist in the metropolis,' his wife said of him when they married. Dubliners liked to remember that on one occasion another unstoppable talker seized the initiative before Sir William, and Sir William's response was to put his head down on the table and audibly doze.[37]

He never lacked for friends; these were as various as Maria Edgeworth, whom he had known in London, the hilarious Charles Lever, with whom he had been at medical school, and the more severe Sir Samuel Ferguson, who would write his elegy. In their house at 1 Merrion Square, one of the largest and best maintained in the city, the Wildes at first gave dinner parties for a dozen guests, but later held receptions on Saturday afternoons for over a hundred.[38] Writers, university professors, government officials, and visiting actors and musicians thronged to these parties. Under Lady Wilde's aegis musicians played, actors and actresses enacted scenes, and poets recited their verses.

The energy with which Sir William faced the world was not necessarily maintained in private. Between his bursts of activity he was often despondent. His wife reported that she had asked him, 'What could make you happy,' only to receive the answer, 'Death.'[39] Though he was acquisitive of honor, he could be humble. In his book on the Boyne he begins by saying that he is not strictly speaking an archaeologist, having much other work to do, and he defers to the authority of Petrie and others (Sir William had little Irish).

One aspect of Sir William Wilde was known only to his intimates. Before his marriage he had fathered three illegitimate children. He was twenty-three when his first child, a boy named Henry Wilson (the surname slyly implying 'Wilde's son'?), was born in Dublin, in 1838, and since Wilde had been away from Ireland for more than nine months, the child was evidently conceived abroad. Sir William looked after his son,

---

* At dinner one evening, Sir William expatiated to his guests on salmon fishing. Yeats's grandfather, a country rector, heard him out and muttered under his breath, 'He knows nothing about it.' But Oscar Wilde used to tell how one morning Yeats's father, trained as a barrister, came down to breakfast and announced, 'Children, I am tired of the law, and shall become a painter.' 'Could he paint?' Wilde was asked. 'Not in the least, that was the beauty of it.'[36]

educated him, and took him into his surgery as a fellow practitioner. The mother or mothers of the two other children – Emily, born in 1847, and Mary, born in 1849 – are also unknown. The Reverend Ralph Wilde, Sir William's eldest brother, adopted the two girls as his wards, so they kept the name of Wilde.

In the Dublin of this time, the old Regency permissiveness lingered. Sir William's friend Isaac Butt, before Parnell the leader of the Irish party in Parliament, also had illegitimate children, and apparently no one minded. Perhaps Oscar Wilde derived his interest in foundlings, orphans, and mysteries of birth from his experience of his father's extended family, when they all summered together, legitimate and illegitimate children alike, in Glenmacnass, south of Dublin.[40] So Dorian Gray is in love with a young woman of illegitimate birth, whose brother reproaches their mother for her fall. Lady Windermere has been abandoned by her errant mother and a cloud hangs over Jack Worthing's birth in *The Importance of Being Earnest*. Young Arbuthnot's mother in *A Woman of No Importance* is unmarried. More largely, discovering who they really are is the pursuit of most of Wilde's principal characters.

Henry Wilson outlived his father, but Emily and Mary were not so fortunate. In the course of showing off their ball dresses before a party, one went too close to an open fire, caught her crinoline in the flames, and was terribly burned. So was her sister, who tried frantically to rescue her. Their gravestone records them as dying, both on the same day, on 10 November 1871.* Sir William's grief was intense and his groans could be heard outside the house.[41] A simple stone in the garden of Moytura House, bearing the inscription, 'In Memoriam,' may commemorate the death of the two girls as well as that of Isola, legitimate daughter of the Wildes, who had died four years before.

Lady Wilde was conversant with her husband's past, and did not resent it. John Butler Yeats many years later privately attributed her indulgence to the fact that she had herself, before her marriage, been caught with Isaac Butt in circumstances 'that were not doubtful' by Mrs Butt.[42] She certainly admired Butt, once calling him, in print, 'the Mirabeau of the Young Ireland movement, with his tossed masses of black hair, his flashing eyes, and splendid rush of cadenced oratory.' But Jane Wilde needed no such history to make her tolerant of passion. She remarked in her sixties to a young man, 'When you are as old as I, young man, you will know there is only one thing in the world worth living for, and that is sin.' She was, however, to be severely tried by one post-marital episode. A longtime patient of her husband, Mary Travers, began to hint that Sir

---

* However, the *Northern Standard* for 25 November 1871 announced tersely that Emily Wilde, aged 24, had died on the 8th and Mary, 22, on the 21st. Family influence was strong enough to prevent any other Irish paper carrying even this much mention of an event which would ordinarily have commanded headlines.

William had given her chloroform and then raped her. It seemed she had withheld this allegation for two years, but public recognition of the Wildes – Sir William's knighthood, conferred on 28 January 1864, and the fanfare accorded Lady Wilde for her 1863 translation of M. Schwab's *The First Temptation* – roused her to action.

Mary Travers had first become a patient of William Wilde in 1854, when she was eighteen. She dated her 'ruin' as from October 1862, yet she had remained a patient. That same year she had accepted from Wilde the fare to Australia, and failed to embark. Her case was not strong. An allegation of rape after so long an interval would have had no chance of a favorable verdict; instead Mary Travers wrote letters containing dark hints to newspapers and composed a scurrilous pamphlet about the Wildes (as 'Dr and Mrs Quilp') which she cheekily signed 'Speranza.' Lady Wilde was so stung she protested by letter to Mary Travers' father, lately become professor of medical jurisprudence at Trinity College, that his daughter was making 'unfounded' allegations. When Mary Travers discovered this letter of 6 May 1864 among her father's papers, she sued Lady Wilde for libel.

The case was heard over five days from 12 to 17 December 1864. Everyone wondered whether Sir William would take the stand, but since it was not he who was being sued, he did not have to. His failure to do so was of course a point for Mary Travers. The barrister for Miss Travers was the omnipresent Isaac Butt, who was anything but gallant towards Lady Wilde. Why had she taken no notice of the woman's charges that her husband had raped her? he asked. Lady Wilde replied majestically, 'I really took no interest in the matter. I looked upon the whole thing as a fabrication.' Like her younger son, she was more emancipated than the age. The jury upheld the charge of libel: Sir William was not without fault, they found – some of his letters to Mary Travers, produced as evidence, showed considerable fluster – but they placed a low value on Miss Travers' outraged innocence, awarding her a farthing in damages. Sir William was obliged on his wife's behalf to pay £2,000 in costs, a large sum in a year when he was building four houses in Bray and one at Moytura.

It has been said that the case left Sir William Wilde a broken man. The evidence points otherwise. He was not so affluent, but, according to his loyal wife, he had more patients than ever. The *Lancet*, the journal of the British Medical Association, defended him in England, and when *Saunders's News Letter* spoke up for him in Dublin, Mary Travers brought libel proceedings against that journal in 1865, but this time she lost.* Lady Wilde did not trouble to bury the matter. She wrote of it to her friends in Sweden, assured them that Mary Travers was 'certainly mad,' and sent clippings to show how Sir William's colleagues stood behind him. 'All

---

* Mary Josephine Travers died 18 March 1919, aged 83, at Kingston College, an almshouse in Mitchelstown, County Cork.

Dublin has called on us to offer their sympathy,' wrote his wife, 'and all the medical profession here and in London have sent letters to express their entire disbelief of the (in fact) impossible charge.'[43] Sir William showed his indifference by writing his most cheerful book, *Lough Corrib* (1867), after the trial.[44] In April 1873 the Royal Academy of Ireland conferred on him its highest honor, the Cunningham Gold Medal. When the Wildes' two sons reached Trinity College in 1869 and 1871, they could not have helped hearing a ballad commonly sung there, which ran,

> An eminent oculist lives in the Square.
> His skill is unrivalled, his talent is rare,
> And if you will listen I'll certainly try
> To tell how he opened Miss Travers's eye.[45]

But no one brought up in Dublin would take this sort of thing seriously. Oscar Wilde brushed aside the Mary Travers case when he wrote in *De Profundis*, 'I inherited a famous name.' He might have thought twice about it, however, before instituting the prosecution of Queensberry in 1895.

Shaping Oscar Wilde

The wonderful palace – Joyeuse, as they called it – of which he now found himself lord, seemed to him to be a new world fresh-fashioned for his delight.

The marriage of William and Jane Wilde was a contented one. Lady Wilde presented her husband with three legitimate offspring to match his three illegitimate ones. The first, William Robert Kingsbury Wills Wilde, was born on 26 September 1852, and inspired her to write,

> Alas! the Fates are cruel.
> Behold Speranza making gruel.[46]

The second, Oscar Fingal O'Flahertie Wills Wilde, was born on 16 October 1854, when the family was still living at 21 Westland Row, though he always claimed that they had already moved to their better address at 1 Merrion Square West. The third child, Isola Francesca Emily Wilde, was born on 2 April 1857. The naming of the children was carefully done, on the principle enunciated by Lord Henry Wotton in *Dorian Gray*, that 'Names are everything.' Willie, as he was always called, had his father's name with the addition of Kingsbury in tribute to his mother's family, and both boys took the name of Wills from the family of the playwright W. G. Wills. (Sir William dedicated his first book, *Madeira*, 'with gratitude' to two people, one of them a William Robert Wills.) The

15

parents were more venturesome with their daughter, whose first name Isola was meant to suggest Isolde or Iseult, while her second name Francesca perpetuated the Italian connection. But it was the middle child whose naming was most elaborate. On 22 November 1854, Jane Wilde wrote to a Scottish friend:

> A Joan of Arc was never meant for marriage, and so here I am, bound heart and soul to the home hearth by the tiny hands of my little Willie and as if these sweet hands were not enough, behold me – me, Speranza – also rocking a cradle at this present writing in which lies my second son – a babe of one month old the 16th of this month and as large and fine and handsome and healthy as if he were three months. He is to be called Oscar Fingal Wilde. Is not that grand, misty, and Ossianic?[47]

Oscar (she called him Oscár) and Fingal came from Irish legend, but the name O'Flahertie was added in deference to William Wilde's connections with Galway families through his grandmother O'Flynn. O Flaithbherartaigh, the name of the pre-Norman kings of West Connacht, is the most Galwegian of Galway names. The famous prayer of the Galway burgesses was, 'From the wild O'Flaherties good Lord deliver us!' Oscar Wilde misspelt the terrifying name as *O'Flehertie* when he enrolled at school. At Oxford a fellow student recalled that he signed himself 'O. O'F. Wills Wilde' and was known as Wills Wilde (though this can have been true only for a time),[48] and in his contributions to the Trinity classical magazine *Kottabos* he initialed himself 'O.F.O.F.W.W.' When someone supposed, later on, that he had always been Oscar Wilde, he replied, 'How ridiculous of you to suppose that anyone, least of all my dear mother, would christen me "plain Oscar" . . . I started as Oscar Fingal O'Flahertie Wills Wilde. All but two of the five names have already been thrown overboard. Soon I shall discard another and be known simply as 'The Wilde' or 'The Oscar.'[49]* (He did not like it, however, when William Archer referred to him casually in print as 'Oscar.')[51] Eventually, in jail, he would find his simplest cognomen: C.3.3.

Oscar Wilde was christened by his uncle, the Reverend Ralph Wilde, rector of Kilsallaghan, on 26 April 1855 in St Mark's Church. His mother had asked Sir William Hamilton to stand as godfather to the 'young pagan' (as she described him),[52] but Hamilton declined. In a letter of 17 June 1855, his mother described her second son as 'a great stout creature who minds nothing but growing fat.' Willie, then nearly three, she saw as 'light, tall, and spirituelle [sic], looking with large beautiful eyes full of expression. He is twined round all the fibres of my heart, but what do you

---

* When an Englishman said that in the nineteenth century the Mac's had done everything and the O's nothing, Wilde replied, 'You forget. There are O'Connell and O. Wilde.'[50]

think of Mrs Browning's son who at six years old composes the most sublime poetry? Poor child, I should die of apprehension if Willie were like this.'[53] Robert Ross said that Lady Wilde longed for a girl when she bore, instead, a second boy.[54] A London friend of the family, Luther Munday, recalls how Lady Wilde declared that, for the first ten years of Oscar's life, she had treated him as a daughter rather than as a son in dress, habit, and companions.[55] Indeed a photograph of Oscar at the age of about four shows him wearing a dress.

However accommodating it is to see a maternal smothering of masculinity as having contributed to his homosexuality, there is reason to be sceptical. Jane Wilde was addicted to large statements, not meant for scrutiny. Victorian and even Edwardian children of both sexes were put in dresses during their infancy. Her letters do not suggest that she regarded Oscar as anything but a boy. Early in his third year she did give birth to a girl; having the reality, she did not need to force the semblance. Although she has been described by Thomas Flanagan as 'the silliest woman who ever lived,'[56] she had some common sense, and her treatment of her children appears to have been more normal than she was willing to admit. The birth of Isola was a great pleasure to all members of the family. A letter of 17 February 1858 from Jane Wilde remarks, 'We are all well here – Willie and Oscar growing tall and wise, and Baby – you don't forget little Isola I hope – is now 10 months old and is the pet of the house. She has fine eyes and promises to have a most acute intellect. These two gifts are enough for any woman.'[57]

Soon after Isola's birth the Swedish writer, Lotten von Kraemer, then a very young woman, accompanied her father, Baron Robert von Kraemer, the governor of Uppsala, on a visit to the Wildes when the British Association came to Ireland in July 1857. The butler at 1 Merrion Square greeted them, and when they asked for Mrs Wilde gave them an old retainer's wink: 'There isn't daylight in her room,' he said, although it was one o'clock in the afternoon. She appeared eventually, festooned and cordial, very much the poet, and they had just sat down to what was for her breakfast when William Wilde returned to meet his visitors: 'The noble figure is slightly bowed,' wrote Lotten von Kraemer, 'less by years than by ceaseless work . . . and his movements have a haste about them which at once conveys the impression that his time is most precious . . . He carries a small boy in his arm and holds another by the hand. His eyes rest on them with content. They are soon sent away to play, whereupon he gives us his undivided attention.'[58]

Oscar Wilde as a child survives in glimpses. He once ran away and hid in a cave; another time, playing chargers with Edward Sullivan and Willie, he broke his arm.[59] Sir William had bought, in 1853, a hunting lodge, called Illaunroe, on what his son would call 'the little purple island' (attached by a causeway to the mainland) in Lough Fee in the west. Here Willie and Oscar learned to fish. As Wilde told Robert Ross long after,

'The lake was full of large melancholy salmon, which lay at the bottom and paid no attention to our bait.'[60]

When the Wildes moved from 21 Westland Row to 1 Merrion Square in June 1855, they acquired a German governess and a French *bonne*, and staffed their big house with six servants. The children were brought up to speak French and German, and were privately tutored during their early years. In a revealing story Wilde told Reggie Turner, Oscar and Willie were once having their evening bath in the nursery in Merrion Square, in front of the fireplace; their little singlets were hung to warm on the high fender. While the nurse was momentarily out of the room, the two boys noticed a brown spot in one of the singlets which deepened and burst into flame. Oscar clapped his hands with delight, while Willie shouted to the nurse, who came to the rescue by pushing the singlet into the fire. At this Oscar cried with rage at having his spectacle spoiled. 'This,' said Wilde, 'was an example of the difference between Willie and me.'[61]

In the summers the Wilde family would often go to the beautiful country south of Dublin; they stayed at Dungarvan, County Waterford, and Oscar is said to have played on the seashore with a boy called Edward Carson, later to be his cross-examiner as well as the architect of Irish partition.[62] (Michael MacLiammoir commented, 'Yes, that would explain it all. Oscar probably upset Edward's sandcastle.') Perhaps a year or two later they were at Glencree in the Wicklow mountains. They took a farm house, probably Lough Bray Cottage, at the foot of the vale of Glencree, less than a mile from the newly opened Glencree Reformatory. The Reformatory chaplain, the Reverend L. C. Prideaux Fox (1820–1905), visited them. William Wilde expressed his bitter opposition to reformatories, but his wife enjoyed the chaplain's company, and even asked if she could bring her children to his chapel. Father Fox explained there was a tribune in the chapel from which the altar could be seen without contact with the prisoners. Jane Wilde came with her children. She occasionally showed a hankering to turn Catholic, and a letter to her from Sir William Hamilton hopes that the Catholic poet Aubrey De Vere would not 'succeed in converting, or perverting you.'[63] Now she thought of having the children received, and the fact that both boys had been baptized as Protestants did not faze her. Father Fox, himself a convert, wrote, 'It was not long before she asked me to instruct two of her children, one of them being that future erratic genius, Oscar Wilde. After a few weeks I baptized these two children, Lady Wilde herself being present on the occasion.' Oscar would have been perhaps between four and five. At her request, Father Fox bravely called on William Wilde to say what he had done. The doctor, a resolute Protestant, one of whose books is dedicated to the Dean of St Patrick's, cannot have been pleased, but passed the matter off lightly with the remark, 'I don't care what the boys are so long as they become as good as their mother.'[64] Soon afterwards Father Fox was given another post, and never saw the family again.

As often happened with private baptisms, this one was not registered, and doubt has been cast on this first of Wilde's conversions as well as on his last; but there are reasons for believing that Father Fox did as he said. His account of the people living near the Glencree Reformatory is in other respects accurate.* Wilde himself told friends that he had an obscure recollection of having been baptized a Catholic.[65] The incident would seem to have given rise to the second baptism planned by both Algernon and Jack in *The Importance of Being Earnest*, on which Lady Bracknell comments, 'At their age? The idea is grotesque and irreligious! . . . I will not hear of such excess.' But when Oscar Wilde later made some tentative overtures towards Rome, he did not regard the early ceremony as worthy of mention. Father Fox had baptized in vain, but the incident offers an example of Lady Wilde's pleasure in ceremonies in which she had no intention of participating herself. A taste for vicarious spiritual sensations was implanted early.

On the secular plane, Wilde appears to have had an untroubled upbringing. Quite possibly he is himself a model for his fairy tale hero, 'The Young King,' who in boyhood had already 'shown signs of that strange passion for beauty that was destined to have so great an influence over his life. Those who accompanied him. often spoke of the cry of pleasure that broke from his lips when he saw the delicate raiment and rich jewels that had been prepared for him.' Though Wilde would later theorize that one should have no possessions, he was gratified by scarlet and lilac shirts just as at school he made a point of having beautiful large-paper editions of the classical texts that others read in more basic copies. At a time when most schoolboys were concerned with games and grades, Wilde was cultivating his tints and textures. Still, he was not all precocity. His reading was chiefly in historical romances, such as J. W. Meinhold's *The Amber Witch*, and an even greater favorite, the same author's *Sidonia the Sorceress*, which his mother had translated in 1849. Sidonia was one of those gifted, ferocious women who fascinated the Pre-Raphaelites; Burne-Jones did a painting of her; William Morris in later life remained so enamored of her that in 1893, through Wilde, he sought Lady Wilde's consent to the Kelmscott Press's republishing the book, which he praised as 'an almost faultless reproduction of the past, its action really alive.'[66]

What distinguishes Sidonia from run-of-the-mill sorceresses is that she has a power of ironic speech. Brought to trial for witchcraft, she worsts her accusers point for point in a way that Lady Wilde and her courtroom-conscious son could admire. Sidonia was 'a game old devil and fought it out like a brick to the last,' said Morris. The book makes much of a

---

* Another reason, modestly volunteered by a member of the same order, is that Father Fox, before he became an Oblate, was a Quaker, and, whatever Oblates may do, 'Quakers never lie.'

painting of Sidonia which proves to be a double portrait: in the fore-
ground, executed in the style of Lucas Cranach, is a woman golden-
haired and richly gowned, while in the background lurks the ravening
sorceress in the garments she wore at her execution, done in the manner
of Rubens.[67] The search for sources of Wilde's *The Picture of Dorian Gray*
is unending, but here is another analogue to the benign portrait of Dorian
by Basil Hallward, and the malign one of Dorian as drawn by his own soul.

The three Wilde children grew up amid increasing affluence and success.
William Wilde's knighthood in 1864 was the climax, and they all delighted
in it. Oscar's letters to his mother speak of 'Sir William' instead of
'Father,' as if to savor the title. He and his brother were allowed at an early
age to sit at the foot of the dinner table, and so, as Oscar Wilde said, he
heard as a child all the important questions of the day discussed. He and
Willie were not allowed to speak: this childhood training in holding his
tongue, Oscar said, was responsible for his wagging it so successfully in
his maturity.[68]

As the boys approached adolescence, their parents began to think of a
school to replace home tutoring. 'My eldest boy is nearly eleven – very
clever and very high spirited,' Lady Wilde explained on 22 April 1863 to a
Swedish friend, 'and tho' he obeys me he will scarcely obey a governess. I
feel it would be a risk to leave him. But we think of sending both boys to a
boarding school soon.'[69] Evidently Oscar was more tractable than his
brother. In May 1863 Willie was experimentally put in school near
Dublin, at St Columba's College, but in February 1864 both boys were
sent to the Portora Royal School; a railway line from Dublin to Enniskillen
had conveniently been opened in 1859. (It has been conjectured that their
parents packed them off because of the Mary Travers case, but that suit
did not go to trial until December 1864.) The boys were then twelve and
almost ten, Oscar being younger than most entrants at that time.

At Portora Willie threw himself into school activities, and though never
a systematic student, became a popular 'character,' quickwitted, erratic,
and energetic. He was inclined to boastfulness, and ridiculed for it. His
best subject was drawing, which he had practiced with his father. At first
the masters thought that he was the talented son, and the headmaster, the
Reverend William Steele, was to amuse Oscar by suggesting that with
effort he might match Willie's standard.[70] Lady Wilde had been partial
to Willie as her first-born: 'Willie is my kingdom,' she wrote on 22
November 1854, and announced, 'I will rear him a Hero perhaps and
President of the future Irish Republic. *Chi sa?* I have not fulfilled my
destiny yet.'[71] Four years later, on 20 December 1858, she informed
Lotten von Kraemer, 'Willie is a darling child. He is so good and so wise,
but little Isola is rapidly taking her place as pet of the house.' Oscar is
conspicuously unmentioned. By 1865 Lady Wilde was remarking impar-
tially in a letter, 'My two boys have gone to a public school.' In 1869 she

writes, 'My two sons were home for the vacation – fine clever fellows – the eldest quite grown-up looking.'[72] By this time Willie was in his last year at Portora, and clearly being outdone by his brother, who was, for example, fourth in classics when Willie was thirteenth. Probably it was now that Lady Wilde remarked to George Henry Moore (the father of George Moore the novelist), 'Willie is all right, but as for Oscar, he will turn out something wonderful.'[73]

Willie patronized Oscar, who patronized Willie. Oscar was big, languid, and dreamy. Willie was a tolerable pianist, Oscar had no musical talent. But his wit made itself felt: thanks to his mischievous eye, nearly all the boys in the school bore nicknames conferred by him, though good-humouredly enough.* His own nickname, which annoyed him, was 'Grey Crow,' perhaps premonitory of Dorian's surname. Willie was known as 'Blue Blood' because he had protested, when accused of having failed to wash his neck, that its color came not from dirt but from the blue blood of the Wilde family.[74]

Oscar's most marked talent, at first, was his gift for fast reading. 'When I was a boy at school,' he told Eugene Field in 1889, 'I was looked upon as a prodigy by my associates because, quite frequently, I would, for a wager, read a three-volume novel in half an hour so closely as to be able to give an accurate résumé of the plot of the story; by one hour's reading I was enabled to give a fair narrative of the incidental scenes and the most pertinent dialogue.' He told the novelist W. B. Maxwell that he read facing pages of a book at one time, and in a demonstration showed he had mastered the intricacies of a novel in three minutes.[75] Wilde could talk on other subjects while he was quickly turning the pages. At school the more studious pupils assumed that he was a skimmer rather than a scholar. It was true that he did not cram for examinations, and read the prescribed texts for pleasure, along with much that was unprescribed, neglecting what he found boring. Still, in 1866 he was a prizeman in the Junior School, which meant he was excused from the annual examinations, and in 1869 he won a copy of Butler's *Analogy* as a third prize for Scripture. What distinguished him was his excitement over the literary qualities of Greek and Latin texts, and his disinclination to enter into textual minutiae. Not until his last two years at Portora, 1869–71, when he began to make deft and mellifluous oral translations from Thucydides, Plato, and Virgil, did his fellow students realize his talent. The classical work that caught his imagination was the *Agamemnon* of Aeschylus, which he must have studied with a master, J. F. Davies, who published a good edition of the play with commentary in 1868. At a *viva voce* on it, Wilde 'walked away' from all others, including Louis Claude Purser, later the distinguished professor of Latin at Trinity College. The

---

* In later life he called Claire de Pratz '*la bonne déesse*' and Mrs Potter 'Moon-beam.'

Agamemnon stirred Wilde's sensibilities so that he never left off quoting from it.

Purser, Wilde's classmate, wrote down his recollections of Wilde at Portora for Robert Sherard and A. J. A. Symons. These differ from those of others, perhaps because Wilde had changed his ways by 1868, when Purser entered the school. Dr Steele and two of Wilde's other classmates remembered him as being dirty and slovenly, but Purser is firm that he 'was more careful in his dress than any other boy.' Perhaps he was dirty under those scarlet and lilac shirts. According to Robert Sherard, Wilde alone among the boys wore a silk hat on weekdays, though this cannot have been, as Sherard asserts, the Eton topper, which was never worn at Portora. Wilde's refusal to participate in games made him at first unpopular. 'Now and then he would be seen in one of the school boats on Lough Erne,' says another classmate, 'yet he was a poor hand at an oar.' On one occasion when he did participate in a game, which consisted of a 'tournament' in which smaller boys rode on bigger boys' shoulders and tried to unhorse each other, he was thrown and for the second time broke his arm.[76]

Another pupil at the school was Edward (later Sir Edward) Sullivan, who would one day publish an edition of the Book of Kells. When he and Wilde met in the autumn of 1868, Sullivan recalled, Wilde wore his straight fair hair long and had, for all his height, a boyish appearance, which he kept for some years. Outside the classroom he was restless, eager to talk. He was known for his humorous exaggerations of school occurrences. One day he and Sullivan and two other boys went into Enniskillen and happened on a street orator; tiring of the rant, one boy pushed the speaker's hat off with a stick, and they all fled headlong towards the school with some of the indignant audience in rapid pursuit. In his hurry Wilde collided with an aged cripple and knocked him down. By the time he reached Portora, this sorry incident had undergone Falstaffian transformation: an angry giant had barred his path, he had had to fight him through round after round and eventually, after prodigies of valour, to leave him for dead. In 'The Critic as Artist' Wilde would attribute the foundation of social intercourse to whoever 'first, without ever having gone out to the chase, told the wandering cavemen at sunset how he had . . . slain the Mammoth in single combat.' 'Romantic imagination was strong in him,' says Sullivan, 'but there was always something in his telling of such a tale to suggest that he felt his hearers were not really being taken in.'[77]

Like his mother, Wilde undercut his grandiosities with a smile. In later life he described a narrator of his own stamp to Charles Ricketts and others:

Now a certain man was greatly beloved by the people of his village, for, when they gathered round him at dusk and questioned him, he would relate many strange things he had seen. He would say, 'I beheld three mermaids by the sea who combed their green hair with a golden comb.' And when they besought him to tell more, he answered – 'By a hollow rock I spied a centaur; and, when his eyes met mine, he turned slowly to depart, gazing at me sadly over his shoulder.' And, when they asked eagerly, 'Tell us what else have you seen,' he told them 'In a little copse a young faun played upon a flute to the dwellers in the woods who danced to his piping.'

One day when he had left the village, as was his wont, three mermaids rose from the waves who combed their green hair with a comb of gold, and, when they had departed, a centaur peeped at him behind a hollow rock, and later, as he passed a little copse, he beheld a faun who played upon a pipe to the dwellers in the wood.

That night, when the people of the village gathered at dusk, saying 'Tell us, what have you seen today?' he answered them sadly: 'Today I have seen nothing.'[78]

The kingdoms of imagination and observation are embattled. As Wilde said later, 'The impossible in art is anything that has happened in real life.'[79] At Portora during the winter the boys gathered around a stove which stood in 'the Stone Hall,' and here Oscar and Willie were often the raconteurs, Willie – until he left Portora for Trinity in 1869 – being preferred. Sometimes Oscar would vary the entertainment by forcing his double-jointed limbs into weird contortions, in imitation of holy people in stained glass attitudes. Later in life he learned to take on more comfortable roles.

In 1870, at one of these Stone Hall sessions (as Sullivan recalled), the boys were discussing an ecclesiastical prosecution then in the news in England. This must have been the case of the Reverend W. J. E. Bennett, vicar of Frome Selwood, accused of heresy for a book insisting that Christ was physically present in Holy Communion. Because of appeals it was heard three times at the Court of Arches (the Provincial court of appeal of the Archbishop of Canterbury), on 30 April, 18 November 1869, and 20 July 1870. Bennett was found guilty. Wilde was fascinated by the mysterious name of the court, derived from the arched steeple of its original site, and by the case itself. He announced to the other boys that nothing would please him more than to be the principal in such an action, 'to go down to posterity as the defendant in such a case as "Regina versus Wilde."'[80] As his mother's son, he was determined 'to make a sensation,' and at any cost.

While their children pursued their studies, Sir William and Lady Wilde pursued theirs. Sir William published an ethnographic lecture on *Ireland Past and Present* in 1864, and then in 1867 his *Lough Corrib*, which he revised for a second edition in 1872. A first collection of Lady Wilde's poems, published in 1864 (*Poems*), was followed by *Poems: Second Series: Translations* (1867), and by a reissue of both together in 1871. But in

February 1867, Isola, nine years old, the only child still at home, developed a fever. On her partial recovery, she was sent, for a change of air, to stay with her uncle, the Reverend William Noble, at Mastrim (Edgworthtown). 'Then she had a relapse and sudden effusion on the brain,' wrote Lady Wilde to Lotten von Kraemer. 'We were summoned by telegraph and only arrived to see her die [on 23 February]. Such sorrows are hard to bear. My heart seems broken. Still I feel I have to live for my sons and thank God they are as fine a pair of boys as one could desire.' Sir William added, for himself, 'It has left me a mourner for life.' Three years later Lady Wilde declared to her Swedish friend that since Isola's death she had gone to no dinner, soirée, theatre, or concert, 'and never will again.'[81] Oscar was equally distressed; the doctor who attended Isola thought him 'an affectionate, gentle, retiring, dreamy boy,' deeper than his brother Willie. He paid regular visits to his sister's grave,[82] and wrote a poem ('Requiescat') about her; the melancholy which he always afterwards insisted underlay his jaunty behavior may have been first awakened by this early death.

> Tread lightly, she is near
>   Under the snow,
> Speak gently, she can hear
>   The lilies grow.
>
> All her bright golden hair
>   Tarnished with rust,
> She that was young and fair
>   Fallen to dust.
>
> Lily-like, white as snow,
>   She hardly knew
> She was a woman, so
>   Sweetly she grew.
>
> Coffin-board, heavy stone,
>   Lie on her breast,
> I vex my heart alone,
>   She is at rest.
>
> Peace, Peace, she cannot hear
>   Lyre or sonnet,
> All my life's buried here,
>   Heap earth upon it.

Wilde's dandyism and Hellenism became conspicuous at Portora, as did a certain independence of judgment, often of a paradoxical kind. A question he put to one master, 'What is a Realist?', anticipates his later redefinitions of that term.[83] (In 'The Decay of Lying' he would say, 'As a method Realism is a complete failure.') When Dickens died in 1870,

Wilde made a point of expressing his dislike for the dead man's novels, preferring, he said, those of Disraeli, a man who could write a novel and govern an empire with either hand. Wilde would have relished *Coningsby*, in which the old Jewish hero bears the name Sidonia, like the sorceress, and is of mysterious alien origin, with unusual power over others, bent upon shaping the lives and minds of young men. The novel seemed in a line of descent from his great-uncle's *Melmoth the Wanderer*. Disraeli had urged along the Young England movement; Wilde was perhaps beginning to glimpse a movement he would lead of his own, cultural rather than political, of a vaguely neo-Hellenic sort.

Wilde's showing at Portora in 1870 and 1871 was triumphant. When he won the Carpenter prize for Greek Testament in 1870, Dr Steele summoned him to the platform by calling out 'Oscar Fingal O'Flahertie Wills Wilde' to the great amusement of the other pupils, who until then had no idea of his abundant cognomens. Wilde got his own back the following year, according to vague reports, by treating Steele with insolence. In 1871 he was one of three pupils awarded a Royal School scholarship to Trinity College, Dublin, and his name was duly inscribed in gilt letters on Portora's black notice board. In 1895, the year of his disgrace, it was painted out, and the initials O.W. which he had carved by the window of a classroom were scraped away by the headmaster. Now his name has been regilded.

Aesthete among the Classicists

The new Individualism is the new Hellenism.

Oscar Wilde liked surprises, but Trinity College, Dublin, notwithstanding its scholarly distinction, had few to offer him. He had grown up close to its gates and knew its principal scholars from their frequent attendance at his mother's receptions. Then too, his brother Willie was already much in evidence there, the winner of a number of prizes including a Gold Medal for Ethics; Willie would leave the next year, 1872, to study law in the Middle Temple in London. While at Trinity, he played a leading part, as Oscar scorned to do, in the Philosophical Society to which both belonged. The Trinity students included many whom Wilde had known before, such as his old Portora competitor Louis Claude Purser, and his sometime playmate in sandcastle building, Edward Carson. Wilde and Purser were not close, but Wilde recalled wryly later that he and Carson used to walk about arm in arm, or with arms draped around each other's shoulders, schoolboy fashion. Carson denied that he and Wilde had been such friends, claiming rather that he had disapproved of Wilde's 'flippant approach to life.'[84] It seems likely that they were friendly at first and then drew apart, perhaps because Wilde's character altered so much during his Trinity years. He became aesthetic as Carson became political.

Wilde's tutor was the Reverend J. P. Mahaffy, since 1869 Professor of Ancient History. The association was mutually important. Wilde had met Mahaffy at Merrion Square, but could scarcely have seen all the facets of his personality. That it was many-faceted, Mahaffy was not the last to divulge. 'Take me all round,' he was heard to say, 'I am the best man in Trinity College.'[85] His pupil would seek to brag less parochially. Wilde and Mahaffy were of the same height, six feet three inches, but Mahaffy was born an authority figure, and at thirty-two was already known as 'the General,' while Oscar Wilde at sixteen was a delicate and modulated non-combatant. Mahaffy's hair was auburn or ginger and descended into impressive side-whiskers; his forehead was broad, his jaw and mouth firm. A caricature of Wilde at Trinity shows him with side whiskers too, perhaps in emulation of his tutor. If Wilde avoided games, at Trinity as at Portora, Mahaffy had captained the Trinity cricket eleven and shot with the Irish team in an international marksmanship competition at Wimbledon. Wilde, thanks to his mother's tutoring arrangements, was fluent in French and probably competent in German; Mahaffy, having spent his early years in Europe, spoke German easily and was very good in French, Italian and, as a final fillip, Hebrew. He also knew theology, to which Wilde was indifferent, and music, always a closed book to his pupil.

Apart from such interests Mahaffy was a connoisseur of claret and cigars, old silver and furniture, and Wilde might well struggle to reach his tutor's standard as he began to collect exquisite bric-à-brac. Perhaps most impressive of all Mahaffy's accomplishments was his skill in making friends with the great, including several reigning monarchs. This he attributed to his regal mastery of the art of conversation.* Mahaffy wrote a book about that art later, and his old pupil, in reviewing it, candidly regretted that the professor could not write as well as he could speak.[86] Mahaffy boasted that he had taught Wilde the conversational art in which he himself took such pride; but at Portora Wilde had already demonstrated how well he could talk. There was also an important difference between them. The caustic dismissals of the liberal, the innocent, and the ignorant, which were Mahaffy's flourishes, were at variance with Wilde's republican ideals. From Wilde's point of view, Mahaffy lacked charm and style.[87]

Their politics were different, the tutor Tory and Unionist, his pupil anti-Tory and nationalist. When George Russell asked Mahaffy to sign a petition of protest against the knouting of peasants by the Czar of Russia, Mahaffy replied in character, 'Why, my dear fellow, if he doesn't knout them, they'll knout themselves.' Wilde, whose play *Vera* was to express

---

* Mahaffy in the Common Room said, 'I was only once caned in my life, and that was for telling the truth.' The Provost observed, 'It certainly cured you, Mahaffy.'

sympathy with the knouted, may have drawn on Mahaffy's manner and opinions for the character of the unsympathetic Prince Paul in the play. That Mahaffy was a snob was generally recognized, but Oliver Gogarty – a close friend of Mahaffy who himself liked to talk of the lower classes 'with their backs aching for the lash' – defended Mahaffy against the accusation. It was, in Gogarty's attempted palliation, only 'the justifiable arrogance of the well-bred.'[88] Still, a rhyme that circulated in college about Mahaffy registered the justifiable disapproval of the snubbed:

> Yclept Mahoof by those of heavenly birth
> But plain Mahaffy by the race of earth.[89]

Yet Wilde, without fully approving of Mahaffy, felt gratitude to him. In a letter written probably in 1893, he complimented him as 'my first and best teacher' and 'the scholar who showed me how to love Greek things.' His mother reminded him that Mahaffy gave 'the first noble impulse to your intellect and kept you out of the toils of meaner men and pleasures.'[90] Part of the reason was Mahaffy's absolute preference for Greece: 'The touch of Rome,' he wrote, 'numbed Greece and Egypt, Syria and Asia Minor.' Wilde would write of the Roman religion, 'They had not the creative imagination and the power of the Greeks to give life to the dry bones of their abstractions: they had no art; no myths. For 170 years says Varro, there were no statues at Rome.'[91] To Mahaffy the Greeks – he called them the 'Gweeks,' *r*'s not being one of his talents[92] – might be our modern nextdoor neighbours. Wilde followed him when he wrote in 'The Critic as Artist' that 'Whatever in fact is modern in our life we owe to the Greeks. Whatever is an anachronism is due to medievalism.' In defense of Greek wholesomeness, Mahaffy ventured to touch gingerly upon the vexed question of Greek homosexuality. No previous scholar, writing in English for a general audience, had done as much. Mahaffy characterized it as an ideal attachment between a man and a handsome youth, and acknowledged that the Greeks regarded it as superior to the love of man and woman. Unless debased, as he conceded it sometimes was, it was no more offensive 'even to our tastes' than sentimental friendship. In his Commonplace Book Wilde would write, 'The Roman was educated for the family and the state: to be a pater familias and a civis: the refinement of Greek culture comes through the romantic medium of impassioned friendship; the freedom and gladness of the palaestra were unknown to the boy whose early recollections were those of the senate house and the farm.'

That Wilde read Mahaffy on Greek love is proved by an acknowledgement in the preface of *Social Life in Greece from Homer to Menander* (1874) to 'Mr Oscar Wilde of Magdalen College' and to another former pupil, H. B. Leech, for having 'made improvements and corrections all through the book.' One can only speculate about these improvements, but a remark about the unnaturalness of homosexuality sounds distinctly more like Wilde than like Mahaffy: 'As to the epithet *unnatural*, the Greeks would answer probably, that all civilisation was unnatural.'[93] Mahaffy quickly recognized that he had gone too far. When a second edition appeared the year after, he dropped the pages about homosexual love. He also omitted the acknowledgement to his two pupils, perhaps feeling that it was beneath his dignity to be assisted by such young men.

Wilde did not have to depend upon Mahaffy alone for his classical knowledge, since the rival eminence at Trinity, Robert Yelverton Tyrrell, was as good a classicist and a pleasanter man. Tyrrell had just been made Professor of Latin at only twenty-five. His interest was in Latin and Greek, it was said, Mahaffy's in Romans and Greeks. He committed fewer errors in scholarship than Mahaffy, though he ventured less far afield; he did not quarrel so much with other classicists, but he stood up to Mahaffy willingly enough. His wit, like Wilde's, was more jovial than Mahaffy's, and he had a genuine literary inclination which prompted him to found and edit the magazine, *Kottabos*. He published in it some of his own excellent parodies, and Wilde would later contribute to it translations and his own poems. The professor married in Wilde's last year, and Mrs Tyrrell commented long afterwards that she and her husband saw a good deal of Wilde at Trinity, and found him 'amusing and charming.'[94] In 1896 Tyrrell compassionately signed a petition asking for Wilde's early release from prison, when Mahaffy, who before this had boasted of having created Wilde, just as conspicuously refused to affix his name and referred to Wilde as 'the one blot on my tutorship.'

Wilde's excellence as a classicist made itself obvious at Trinity. Portora had prepared him well; he worked conscientiously during his first year, and at the end of it had the satisfaction of beating Louis Purser by being named first of those in the first class. After that he fell back a little, out of indifference to the technicalities of scholarship, and Purser drew ahead. Still, in a competitive examination in 1873, Wilde received one of ten Foundation Scholarships awarded, which entailed many privileges, he had come sixth out of ten successful candidates, and the man behind him in seventh place was William Ridgeway, later Professor of Archaeology at Cambridge.* Wilde crowned his classical career at Trinity by winning the

---

* Wilde's marks in the 1873 scholarship examination were:

Viva Voce Thucydides	8
Viva Voce Tacitus	7, 1/2
Greek Prose Composition	5
Greek Translation	7 [best mark given]
Greek Tragedians	7
Latin Comedians	7
Latin Prose Translation	6
Demosthenes	5

Berkeley Gold Medal for Greek, achieving the highest score in a difficult examination on Meineke's *Fragments of the Greek Comic Poets*. He would repeatedly pawn and redeem the medal in later life.[95]

At Trinity Wilde was already an aesthete. Becoming one was not difficult. The college offered a course in aesthetics; its Philosophical Society dealt with such subjects as Rossetti and Swinburne, and Willie Wilde even gave a paper on 'Aesthetic Morality.' Mahaffy ended his *Social Life in Greece* by invoking the Greek example for 'the aesthetical education of our lower classes.' Wilde would try to educate the upper classes aesthetically as well. The interminable German novel, *The First Temptation, or 'Sicut Eritis Deus'*, by M. Schwab, of which Lady Wilde published a translation in 1863, was the history of an overweening aesthete who turned aesthetics into a religion of beauty and died tragically. In this atmosphere Wilde, at eighteen, thought of becoming a writer. A recorded incident at Trinity is possibly concocted: Wilde read out a poem to a class. A bully sneered. Wilde went up to him and asked by what right he did so. The man laughed again, and Wilde struck him in the face. Soon everyone was outside and the two antagonists squared off. No one gave Wilde a chance, but to general astonishment he proved to have a devastating punch and utterly worsted his opponent.[96]

More reliable and surprising evidence is in the Suggestion Book of the Philosophical Society, in which members might write down random comments about their fellow members.[97] Two adjoining pages of this book deal with Wilde, one overtly and one implicitly. One page has a caricature of him hirsute and hatted, staring indignantly at a policeman who is evidently rebuking him for some midnight (aesthetic?) meeting. Another student, [John B.] Crozier, is quoted as calling the policeman 'The Benevolent Bobby,' while Wilde characterizes him as 'That Prig of a Policeman.' On the second page a heading presumably mocks Wilde as the recent winner of the Berkeley Gold Medal Examination:

A glimpse at
The Aesthetic Medal Examination
U.P.S. 1874

Is Mrs Allen (whose Lylobalsamum has attained such
world-wide reputation) the subject of:–

Ancient History	7
Greek Verse	5
Greek Verse Composition	1 [Purser had 5]
Greek Viva Voce	6
Latin Viva Voce	5, 1/2
Translation from Latin Poets	4
English Composition	6 [highest mark scored by a candidate]
Latin and Greek Grammar	4

29

Ruskin's 'Queen of the "air"'
or Spenser's 'Fair-'airy Queen'?

+ The corruption (hitherto undiscovered) of this
title into 'Fairy Queen' has arisen through
the copyist's avoidance of dittography. Some
MSS exhibit 'Faiërie' which led to the discovery
of the true reading.

N.B. In connexion with this question candidates are
recommended to study her Works of Art (chignons)
to be seen in most barbers' shops and on the heads
of certain fair individuals.

The play on 'airy fairy' implies effete and effeminate. There is gibing at
hairstyles (chignons), and the reference to Lylobalsamum (which would
be slightly misspelt Latin for Lily balsam) suggests that Wilde, in pursuit
of the Pre-Raphaelites, was already extolling the attributes of the lily. The
two pages together appear to confirm that by early 1874, six months before
he went up to Oxford, Wilde was an exponent of aestheticism, and
flaunted his doctrine with a certain style which needed mockery.

The memories of Wilde in Trinity confirm that he was well on his way
towards his later attitudes. Sir Edward Sullivan, fellow migrant from
Portora, mentions that Wilde's favorite reading was Swinburne. 'Dolores'
and 'Faustine' in Swinburne's *Poems and Ballads* (1866) were just the
poems to appeal to an admirer of Sidonia the Sorceress.[98] The impact of
'Hymn to Proserpine' is still being registered in Wilde's poem, 'The
Garden of Eros,' written half a dozen years later, where he says of
Swinburne,

> And he hath kissed the lips of Proserpine
> And sung the Galilaean's requiem,
> That wounded forehead dashed with blood and wine
> He hath discrowned . . .

He found an analogy in the way that Euripides 'was criticized by the
conservatives of his own day much as Swinburne is by the Philistines of
ours,' as he was to write.[99] Perhaps for this reason, in 1876 he translated a
Euripidean chorus into Swinburne's rhythm and vocabulary:

> Without love, or love's holiest treasure,
> I shall pass into Hades abhorr'd,
> To the grave as my chamber of pleasure,
> To death as my Lover and Lord.

Songs Before Sunrise, which appeared during Wilde's first year at Trinity,
offered democratic passion to go with amorous passion. The following
year he obtained *Atalanta in Calydon* (his copy is dated Michaelmas

30

1872).[100] He would praise both books in his 'The Garden of Eros.'* The same poem celebrates William Morris, whose *Love is Enough* he obtained, hot from the press, in the same term at Trinity.[101] He evidently got hold of the Pre-Raphaelites' books the moment they appeared. He would also have read Rossetti's first book of verse in 1870, and would have known Robert Buchanan's article 'The Fleshly School of Poetry' (1871), which berated the Pre-Raphaelites for their sensuality. Reading Swinburne put him on to Baudelaire and Whitman – the latter the subject of a lecture by Professor Edward Dowden at the Philosophical Society in 1871. In his admiration for these writers Wilde had an immediate reason for repudiating the evaluation of poetry in terms of its message, as he did forever after.

According to Sullivan, he was reading also John Addington Symonds' *Studies of the Greek Poets*, the first volume of which was published in 1873. Although Mahaffy disapproved of the book, Wilde admired the style for its Pateresque 'picturesqueness and loveliness of words.' (He later dismissed it as being poetical prose, rather than the prose of a poet.)[102] Its final chapter confirmed the all-importance of the word 'aesthetic.' It was not that Symonds coined it; Baumgartner had done that in 1750. But Symonds, agreeing with Pater, conspicuously related it to the Greeks: 'If their morality was aesthetic and not theocratic, it is none the less on that account humane and real,' he said.[103] 'The Greeks were essentially a nation of artists,' he went on, a remark Wilde remembered. 'When we speak of the Greeks as an aesthetic nation,' Symonds explained, 'this is what we mean. Guided by no supernatural revelation, with no Mosaic law for conduct, they trusted their *aesthesis*, delicately trained and preserved in a condition of the utmost purity.' Wilde was so delighted by Symonds' book that he wrote to him, and a correspondence (mostly lost) now began. In 1878 Symonds had copies of his *Sonnets of Michael Angelo Buonarroti and Tommaso Campanella* sent to twelve persons, including Browning and Swinburne, and Oscar Wilde at Magdalen College, Oxford. The following year Wilde bought a copy of Symonds' *Shelley*, and marked among other passages one on an intimate friendship of the adolescent Shelley with another boy.[104]

Another aspect of Greek thought was not directly touched upon in *The Greek Poets*. But by this time, 1873, Symonds had written his pamphlet, *A Problem in Greek Ethics*, privately printed a decade later, which dealt with homosexuality. In his youth at Harrow he had informed on the headmaster and ruined his life; now he was all indulgence. His silence on the subject in *The Greek Poets* was pointed, since he avoided the customary

---

* It was not long before Wilde sought out Swinburne's acquaintance. His copy of *Studies in Song* (1880) is inscribed:

> To Oscar Wilde from Algernon Ch. Swinburne.
> Amitié et remerciements.

reproof for the practices referred to in the Greek poems. Mahaffy was not as emancipated as that.

As aesthete Wilde found it essential to cultivate more than one art. At Trinity, Sullivan indicates, when Wilde was not living at home, he had rooms in a building known as Botany Bay. These were evidently dingy after Merrion Square, and Wilde made no effort to keep them clean or to receive friends there. Sometimes, however, a visitor called, and would find in the sitting room an easel prominently placed, which held an unfinished landscape in oils by the host. 'I have just put in the butterfly,' Wilde would say, indicating that he was familiar with Whistler's already famous signature.[105] At Oxford he used the same easel for the same purpose. Sullivan also establishes that Wilde continued at Trinity the elaborate style of dressing which he had invented at Portora. He came into Sullivan's rooms one day wearing an outlandish pair of trousers. When Sullivan started to tease him about them, Wilde begged him with mock solemnity not to make them an object of jest. He was planning a trip to Umbria, he explained: 'These are my Trasimeno trousers, and I mean to wear them there.' Happily, his taste in clothing was not so fastidious as to prevent him from smiling (as he told Sullivan) at the recollection of a down-at-heels classical scholar, John Townsend Mills, who had tutored him for the Berkeley Prize. Mills wore a tall hat, which one day was covered with crepe; on Wilde's commiserating with his supposed loss, Mills explained that he was simply covering a hole in the hat.

Wilde can be seen slowly accumulating at Trinity the elements of his Oxford behavior – his Pre-Raphaelite sympathies, his dandiacal dress, his Hellenic bias, his ambiguous sexuality, his contempt for conventional morality. These positions were taken, at least on occasion, with a slight air of self-mockery, just as his delight in Swinburnian passion would continue to be mitigated by that 'chaffable innocence' which his Oxford friend J. E. C. Bodley (who first met him in Dublin during the summer of 1874) ascribed to him.[106] One further change in his behavior – also to persist – was his dallying with the idea of turning Catholic. Much to his father's displeasure, Wilde made friends with some priests in Dublin. The doctrine of papal infallibility had just been declared, and this, and the rise of the Catholic University in Dublin which Cardinal Newman had founded, had given new alarm to members of the (Protestant) Church of Ireland. No doubt Newman's prose style, its beauty just demonstrated again in his *Grammar of Assent* (1870), had as much to do with Wilde's interest as papal infallibility; and a delight in the *forms* of Catholicism, rather than its content, accounted for his newfound admiration, just as it probably explained his mother's arrangement for his Catholic baptism years before. Yet he preferred to ascribe his remaining a Protestant to his father's threat of disinheriting him. His father need not have worried. Wilde was fostering self-contradictory inclinations.

In any event, he had other interests, other ambitions. His reading made the Irish scene parochial, and his excitement over Pre-Raphaelitism – an English movement – was regarded in Dublin as an amiable folly, not to be entertained without derision in that city. The claustral quality of Irish life, which Yeats would describe as 'great hatred, little room,' rendered the possibility of promulgating some new aesthetic evangel at home exceedingly remote. If Wilde was beginning to leave Ireland spiritually, he had still to leave it physically. The particular suggestion may have come from Mahaffy: another excellent pupil of his, Leech, after taking a Trinity degree had gone on to Gonville and Caius College, Cambridge, for a second undergraduate degree. Mahaffy did not think that the study of the classics could be carried out better in England than at Trinity College, but he had a worldly respect for the older English universities, and would send one of his own sons to Oxford, the other two to Cambridge. He knew that Wilde, brilliant classicist though he was, could not be sure of being offered a fellowship in classics at Trinity in preference to his fellow-student Purser. On the other hand, if he should be conspicuously successful at Oxford, he might return to Ireland, as Leech eventually did, to take up a chair.

It was necessary to persuade not only Oscar Wilde but his father. Mahaffy is said to have concerted with Sir Henry Acland, Regius Professor of Medicine at Oxford and a friend of Sir William, for this purpose.[107] But Sir William had his own reason for agreeing, the mistaken hope that the move to Oxford would cause his son to break off his dalliance with Catholicism. England would keep him Protestant. Willie was already in the Middle Temple in London, 'ready,' as his mother said, 'to spring forth like another Perseus to combat evil.'[108] She added, 'His hope is to enter Parliament and I wish it also. He has a good prospect and can be anything if he cares to work,' a qualification which is the first warning of Willie's inadequacies. (He left the Middle Temple in a few months, and was called to the Irish bar on 22 April 1875.) Sir William made no objection to his second son's going off too.

So Wilde was free to respond to the announcement in the *Oxford University Gazette* of 17 March 1874, that Magdalen College would award two Demyships (scholarships) in classics by examination on 23 June. Each paid £95 a year and could be held for five years. Wilde felt confident enough of success not to bother to take the Trinity examinations for his third year. He presented himself at Magdalen on the day, bearing the required testimonial of good conduct and certification that he was under twenty years of age. One of the four other candidates, G. T. Atkinson, who came second to Wilde and was also awarded a Demyship, recalled fifty-four years later how Wilde, older than the others and much more assured in manner, kept coming up to the invigilator for more paper, because he wrote only four or five words to a line. Atkinson remembered Wilde's writing as 'huge and sprawling, somewhat like himself.' Actually it was spidery and lingering. He observed Wilde's colorless, moonlike face with its heavy eyes and thick lips, and his swinging walk. (Edith Cooper, who noted also his china-blue eyes and protrusive teeth, said his face was like 'a rich yet ungainly fruit.')[109] Wilde breezed through his examination and was obviously the best.

Afterwards, he met his mother and brother in London.[110] It was his first important excursion into the city where he would make and break his name. Sir William, feeling ill, did not join them. The examination results were announced to Wilde soon after his arrival, and the family celebration took the form of visits to literary people with whom Lady Wilde had some acquaintance or had corresponded. They called upon Thomas Carlyle, whom Wilde would later characterize as 'a Rabelaisian moralist.'[111] (After Carlyle's death he bought and used his writing table.) Carlyle had sent Lady Wilde a copy of Tennyson's poems during a visit to Ireland, and presented her with another book, inscribed with four lines from Goethe, translated by himself:

> Who never ate his bread in sorrow,
> Who never spent the midnight hours
> Weeping and wailing for the morrow,
> He knows you not, ye heavenly powers.

She would often quote the lines to her son, who responded insouciantly but never forgot them. The Wildes were delighted with their stay, and Lady Wilde wrote to her friend in Sweden, Mrs Rosalie Olivecrona, wife of a professor, 'This is truly a great and mighty city – the capital of the world.'[112] After 9 July they crossed over to Geneva and came back by way of Paris. They stayed at the Hôtel Voltaire on the Quai Voltaire, and Wilde later told Robert Ross that while there he began work on his poem, 'The Sphinx.'[113] Its subject-matter came from reading Swinburne and Edgar Allan Poe, for the poem spanned the gnomic message of 'The Raven' and the imputation of ageless profligacy in 'Dolores.'

On their return to Dublin that summer, they found Sir William Wilde broken in health. Lady Wilde wrote to Mrs Olivecrona on 31 December 1874, 'He is low and languid, and scarcely goes out – he complains of gout, but along with this, he seems fading before our eyes – and has grown so pale and wan and thin and low-spirited that I too have failed like an unstrung instrument, and no poet-music can be struck from my heart.' Sir William had been declining for some time; he reduced his practice and went as often as he could to his beloved Moytura House near Cong. His income declined with his health, and in February 1872 he had to take a £1,000 mortgage on the house at 1 Merrion Square. His sons' expenses in England made it necessary to capitalize some of Lady Wilde's property. In late November 1874 he obtained £1,260 of which he, Lady Wilde, Willie, and Oscar each received £315. In August 1874 he had gathered himself to give the address to the opening session of the Anthropological Section of the British Association in Belfast.

Oscar's concern for his father did not spoil his delight in being admitted to Oxford on such favorable terms. There was general applause among his friends. Mahaffy rose to the occasion by remarking, 'You're not quite clever enough for us here, Oscar. Better run up to Oxford.'[114] Tyrrell was amused and said that Oxford was the place where German philosophies go when they die. But the decision was momentous. Childhood ties were broken, and Wilde's Dublin reputation as scholar and wit would have to be built again in new surroundings. Hellene and aesthete, but Irishman still, Wilde at almost twenty left on the packet boat from Kingstown in October to pit himself against the most ancient university in England.

CHAPTER II

Wilde at Oxford

LADY BRACKNELL: *Untruthful! My nephew Algernon? Impossible! He is an Oxonian.*

First Truancies

For Irishmen, Oxford is to the mind what Paris is to the body. Wilde was as receptive as anyone to this fabled equation. The university, gathering in a disproportionate number of the best talents in the islands, treated them with a mixture of tenderness and rigor, and dispatched them permanently classified as brilliant, clever, or just average, but Oxford average. The students felt affection towards this mighty mother and awe of her power to define their lives.

Wilde had no reason to regard himself as a Lucien de Rubempré coming from the provinces to find in Oxford the great world. Dublin was not Skibbereen. He already knew many Englishmen – talented people were always attending his mother's Saturday afternoons – and his family name was English. Many of his relations lived in England, and so did friends like Henry S. Bunbury,[1] once at Trinity and now resident in Gloucestershire, who would give his name to the errant behavior of Algernon in *The Importance of Being Earnest.* The antiquity of Oxford could not overwhelm a man familiar with cromlechs and barrows. Yet, in Dryden's words, Oxford still seemed to be Athens, and everywhere else Thebes. 'The most beautiful thing in England,' Wilde said of it. Henry James, after a visit the year before Wilde came up, commented on 'the peculiar air of Oxford – the air of liberty to care for intellectual things, assured and secured by machinery which is in itself a satisfaction to sense.' Wilde put it lyrically: he said his stay in Oxford was 'the most flower-like time' in his life.[2]

He matriculated the day after his twentieth birthday, on 17 October 1874, before the Reverend J. E. Sewell, Warden of New College and Vice-Chancellor. For once he gave his age and even his birthplace in Westland Row with irreproachable accuracy, though he underestimated as two the nearly three years he had studied at Trinity College. For the

36

first year he was assigned Magdalen rooms in No 1, 2 Pair Right, in
Chaplain's, the next two years in No 8, Ground Floor Right, in Cloisters,
and the fourth year, most sumptuously, in Kitchen Stairs, 1 Pair Left. His
fellow students constituted a scene more varied and complex than
Trinity's. They had larger expectations, more confidence, more money.
Most of them were younger than he was, a new experience for someone
used to being youngest in his class. Their persistent affection for their old
schools such as Eton, Harrow and Winchester struck him as absurd.
Neither Portora nor Trinity had aroused him to sentimental feeling; he
was free to bestow it entirely upon Oxford.

Still, nostalgia is one thing, and the student world of old Etonians and
Wykehamists another. In his writings Wilde presents himself with a high
polish which has been the envy of young people since. But at the start he
committed his gaucheries. A friend of his at Balliol, J. E. C. Bodley, who
wrote for the *New York Times* in 1882 a malicious but probably accurate
account of Wilde as an undergraduate,[3] said Wilde was naïve, embarrassed, had a convulsive laugh, a lisp and an Irish accent. The first time he
dined in hall, according to Bodley, he happened to be seated next to a
guest from another college – an athlete in his third year and therefore
someone not to be taken lightly. Wilde talked well, and feeling that he had
ingratiated himself, presented the athlete with his card. By the unsurmis-
able rules of Oxford decorum, this was not done. Rebuffed on this
occasion, and no doubt on others, Wilde determined to be beyond rather
than behind the English. His lisp and native intonation disappeared. 'My
Irish accent was one of the many things I forgot at Oxford,' he said, and
the actor Seymour Hicks, among other witnesses, vouched that no trace of
it was audible. In the course of remaking his speech Wilde adopted that
stately and distinct English which astonished its hearers. Max Beerbohm
said that Wilde's was 'a mezzo voice, uttering itself in leisurely fashion,
with every variety of tone.' Wilde's perfect sentences seemed to Yeats to
have been written 'overnight with labour and yet all spontaneous.'[4] In a
poem, 'Ave Imperatrix,' he would speak of 'our English land,' as though
he had been born east of the Irish Sea. He developed a great appetite for
formal wear, and told a friend, 'If I were all alone marooned on a desert
island and had my things with me, I should dress for dinner every
evening.'[5] (Who would cook for him he did not say.) By day, he put aside
his Dublin clothing and became sportier than his friends, as Bodley says,
by donning tweed jackets with even larger checks than theirs, bird's-eye-
blue neckties, tall collars, curly brimmed hats balanced on one ear. His
thick brown hair was cut acceptably short at Spiers' barber shop in the
High. This was only the first phase of his sartorial revolution: it would be
succeeded a couple of years later by a more bizarre dandyism.

Wilde had curiosity enough to become familiar with the various kinds of
life at his new university. He watched cricket. He went out to see the
famous Stevenson training for the three-mile distance, and lyrically

commented, 'His left leg is a Greek poem.'[6] Like his fellow Demy Atkinson, he allowed himself to be persuaded to train in the college barge for Eights Week. Being tall and strong, Wilde was assigned to stroke, Atkinson to bow. Wilde insisted upon keeping a gentlemanly and un-hurried pace. To the coxswain's exhortation to row with a straight back, he remarked to Atkinson, 'I am sure the Greeks never did so at Salamis.' One day the Varsity eight approached the Magdalen barge and signaled for Magdalen to move over quickly. Wilde shrugged off the scoldings of both coxes as he maintained his stately stroke. When dismissed from the crew, he remarked, 'I don't see the use of going down backwards to Iffley every evening.'[7]* Still, he had other moods: he did a little boxing with another Irishman, Barton, later a judge, and he proposed one day that an Oxford friend join him in rowing from Oxford to London. (In 1878 he paddled a canoe with Frank Miles as far as Pangbourne.) His eye for Greek precedent did not extend to sports of the *palaestra*. 'Exercise!' he said to an interviewer, 'the only possible exercise is to talk, not to walk.' 'It is so exhausting not to talk,' a character would say in *Vera*. When asked at a country house later which outdoor athletics he preferred, Wilde replied, 'I am afraid I play no outdoor games at all. Except dominoes. I have sometimes played dominoes outside French cafés.'[9] Ever since *Lucinde* (1799), aesthetes had known from Schlegel that 'the most perfect way of life is pure vegetating.'

The best contemporary record of Wilde's first two years at Oxford is a journal kept by Bodley. It tells how the two young men had first met in Grafton Street in Dublin on 24 August, during Horse Show Week, and quickly discovered that both were going up to Oxford (Bodley to Balliol), and that they had mutual friends, the Tennants. (Wilde would dedicate one of his fairy tales, 'The Star-Child,' to Margot Tennant.) They renewed their acquaintance on 25 October in the Pembroke Common Room, and succeeding entries show a steady intimacy. On 7 November Bodley bet Wilde £10 even money that their friend Rowland Childers would take a first class in Honour Moderations (the examinations at the end of the second year) and that Wilde would not. It was one of Bodley's many errors of judgment.

Wilde's friend was the son of a rich pottery owner. He hoped for a first in history, but got a second. Socially he was more of a success, being a *bon vivant*, and among the friends he made at Oxford was Prince Leopold, Queen Victoria's youngest son, a commoner at Christ Church. They shared an ardent interest in Freemasonry, which, partly because Leopold was Grand Master of the Order, was much in fashion in the 1870s. Bodley had a sharp eye and some journalistic ability, of which Wilde would suffer the sting. They remained good friends.

---

* His disciple Max Beerbohm, asked if he were going down to the river for the boat races, replied, 'What river?'[8]

Bodley's journal is about diversions rather than studies; he and Wilde devoted themselves to being flamboyant rather than workaday. In January, during their second term, the journal makes frequent references to meals at the Mitre and long drives. Wilde's large physique was such that one entertainment (which he shared with Dr Johnson) was to go to the top of a hill and be rolled down it. On 29 January they went to the theatre to hear some Tyrolese yodelers, and their party, spread over two adjoining boxes, indulged in a 'grand ballyrag, hats and umbrellas playing a not inconsiderable part.' Wilde climbed into Bodley's box to say that his brother Willie had come on a visit, and as soon as the performance had ended Willie and Oscar, Bodley and the rest mounted the proscenium and Willie strummed a Strauss waltz on the piano. Ejected by stagehands, they gathered up the yodelers and took off to the Mitre for more singing. Wilde lent his monotone. That their gambols affected their studies is indicated by the fact that Childers, instead of taking his first as Bodley had wagered, had to accept rustication from January to the end of the summer. Bodley tried in vain to intercede with the Master of Balliol, Benjamin Jowett.

Bodley had become a Mason himself in his first term, and was determined to recruit Wilde for the Apollo Lodge – the university lodge – in the second. On 3 February he wrote to him about it, and on 16 February Wilde was voted in. Before the ensuing initiation Bodley and another Mason named Williamson had a long talk with him and showed Wilde the Masonic properties. Bodley's note is perceptive: 'Wilde was as much struck with their gorgeousness as he was amazed at the mystery of our conversation.' The Masonic costume, which included knee breeches along with tail coat, white tie, silk stockings, and pumps, was to have its effect upon Wilde. (To this day the Apollo Lodge, alone of all the lodges in Great Britain, requires this raiment.) He was received into the Apollo Lodge by special dispensation – because he was under twenty-one – on 23 February 1875. After the meeting came a dinner at which, Bodley notes, 'Wilde got very festive, and at my request hedged in John the B[aptist]. "I have heard," he said, that S[aint] J[ohn] the B[aptist] was the founder of this Order [yells of laughter]. I hope we shall emulate his life but not his death – I mean we ought to keep our heads."' (It was his first mention of *Salome.*) The next morning, as Bodley was about to begin breakfast, Wilde appeared and carried him off to the Mitre where he had ordered salmon and devilled kidneys as a sign of gratitude. Wilde's father was a Mason, and had been in 1841–2 Worshipful Master of the Shakespeare Lodge (No 143) in Dublin. His son took to the pomp and quasi-religious ritual of Masonry, and its fashionable secrecy, and rose quickly through the next degrees, being raised to the 2nd on 24 April and to the 3rd (Master Mason) on 25 May.

Bodley's journal reports a series of high-spirited entertainments during their first year. On 21 April he and Wilde lunched together, then drove to

Woodstock. On the way back they were delayed by a heavy rain and were late for dinner, a punishable offense. 'Proctored at nine-fifteen by Shadwell,' Bodley says sadly, but the next day he writes, 'Wilde's plausibility won the heart of Shadwell and he did not take the fine.' On 6 May Bodley's mother came to Oxford, and Bodley telegraphed his sisters, presumably in London, to come too. 'We drove down to the Eights [the boat race] . . . Walking back through the Cherwell walks Wilde talked "Art" to Agnes.' Agnes was more interested in such matters than her down-to-earth brother. The next day they all came by invitation to Wilde's rooms and were escorted up the Magdalen tower. One sister was so excited at the prospect that she declared she would stay there all day. 'Wilde performed prodigies of valour and we succeeded in getting her down.' Another excursion is recorded for 14 May, when Wilde and Bodley, with another student named Goldschmidt, took a 'tub' on the Cherwell before dining at the Mitre.

Free and easy as this life sounds, Wilde did not totally neglect his classical studies except when the exercises were boring. The course included ancient history and philosophy as well as literature. He had an advantage over other students because of his excellent preparation at Portora and Trinity, and could treat his Oxford tutors with some arrogance. (His performance would not be assessed by them but by other examiners at the end of his second and fourth years.) Much of his time went into reading in other fields. He kept up with Swinburne, whose *Essays and Studies* (1875) gave him the idea of uniting 'personality' and 'perfection' that he made much of later. While at Oxford he kept a Commonplace Book in which the range of reference is wide. He read Herbert Spencer and the philosopher of science William Kingdon Clifford; he was on easy terms not only with Plato and Aristotle, as required by his course, but with Kant, Hegel, Jacobi, Locke, Hume, Berkeley, and Mill. He alludes knowledgeably to Alfieri and quotes Baudelaire's '*O Seigneur! donnez-moi la force et le courage / De contempler mon coeur et mon corps sans dégoût!*'* And he characteristically draws together contemporary and classical concerns, as when he announces that 'In modern times Dante and Dürer, Keats and Blake are the best representatives of the Greek spirit.'

The headings in the Commonplace Book invoke abstractions such as Culture, Progress, Slavery, Metaphysics, and Poetry, as if he already saw the need for taking positions on these matters. Questions of art and artistic attitudes are a common theme. He writes about beauty as a believer about God, though his use of French suggests that his veneration of beauty, while more than a flourish, was less than a creed:

* 'O Lord! give me the strength and the courage / To contemplate my heart and my body without disgust!'

La beauté est parfaite
La beauté peut toute chose
La beauté est la seule chose au monde qui n'excite pas le désir*

More committed is his defense of Keats's and Swinburne's 'effeminacy and languor and voluptuousness which are the characteristics of that "passionate humanity" which is the background of true poetry.'

One subject to which he returns again and again is the conflict between progress and authority. He is on the side of those who resist: 'To Dissenters we owe in England Robinson Crusoe, Pilgrim's Progress; Milton: Matthew Arnold is unjust to them because "not to conform to what is established" is merely a synonym for progress.' In fact, 'Progress in thought is the assertion of individualism against authority,' or even 'simply the instinct of self-preservation in humanity, the desire to affirm one's own essence.' Therefore, he concludes, 'Mankind has been continually entering the prisons of Puritanism, Philistinism, Sensualism, Fanaticism, and turning the key on its own spirit: But after a time there is an enormous desire for higher freedom – for self-preservation.' So rebellion has a Darwinian or Spencerian justification.

Although he was keeping the book for his private use, Wilde fell into stylish phrasing. In praise of Euripides, he declares, 'And we who toil in the heated quarries of modern life may perhaps – or is it our fancy – gain some freedom of soul from his genius who was the great humanist of Hellas, the cor cordium of antiquity.' He moves constantly towards epigram, not so rehearsed as later, but already condensing large subjects into small, pungent, and cadenced phrases:

The danger of metaphysics is that men are often turning nomina into numina.

Socrates and Kant brought philosophy back to man: Aristotle and Hegel set out again to reconquer the World . . .

Berkeley annihilated the non-ego: Hume did the same for the ego: and when these were followed up by the resolving of the laws of cause and effect into a mere association of subjective ideas all honest folk thought the world was coming to an end.

Survival of Fittest in Thought
   Nature kills off all those who do not believe in the Uniformity of Nature and the Law of Causation.

However passionately he read in philosophy, the history of science, and literature, the reputation Wilde sought was of being brilliant without zeal.

---

* 'Beauty is perfect / Beauty is capable of all things / Beauty is the only thing in the world which does not excite desire'

On 24 November 1874 he suffered a check in the examination called Responsions, which consisted of questions on Greek and Latin authors and mathematics. Wilde was put down in the college records as 'plucked,' an unseemly result for a Demy. On 18 January the President of Magdalen, Dr Frederick Bulley, formally admonished him, and two months later (18 March) Wilde penitently passed the examination by answering questions on Euripides' *Medea* and *Hippolytus*, Virgil's *Georgics*, and geometry.[10] One of his friends, David Hunter Blair, was convinced that Wilde plugged away secretly in the small hours so as to keep up his air of insouciance.[11] He did not do more than pass the examination given at the end of the first term, but settled down in the second and third to secure mild commendation.

Wilde's fellow Demy Atkinson has left a brief account of the classics teaching at Magdalen at this time. Their tutor was John Young Sargent, who had a reputation for his work in Latin composition. Five students would gather round the fire in Sargent's rooms at five o'clock in the evening. A silver tankard of beer was always warming at the hearth, but not for them. The 'lecture' was delivered drowsily, and listened to in the same way. Wilde did not care much for Latin, having absorbed Mahaffy's contempt 'for any Roman thing,'[12] and never succeeded in becoming adept at Latin prose. But poetry, even in Latin, excited his best efforts, and his compositions won high praise from Sargent, though he was not considered good enough to be put forward for the Hertford scholarship in Latin, the winner of which generally went on to a college fellowship.[13]

So far he had not made much of a mark in his studies, but the first important examination, in Honour Moderations, was still a year away. He was more successful in creating a legend about himself among his fellow students. His aestheticism remained tenacious, not merely on walks with Agnes Bodley, and his attitudes were precious enough to arouse hostility. His fellow students in classics considered him a freak.[14] He scorned and was scorned by the athletes, who according to one story revenged themselves by dragging him to the top of a high hill, and only then releasing him. He got to his feet, flicked off the dust, and commented, 'The view from this hill is really very charming.'[15] Atkinson doubted that the incident ever took place, but as Wilde remarked, 'What is true in a man's life is not what he does, but the legend which grows up around him . . . You must never destroy legends. Through them we are given an inkling of the true physiognomy of a man.'* The spirited defense of his poem which he had insisted upon at Trinity might make one expect a defense of another kind, and Sir Frank Benson in his memoirs vouches

---

* Another story, recounted by Douglas Sladen, is that some students broke into Wilde's rooms, smashed his china, and held his head under the college pump. Hesketh Pearson investigated this report and satisfied himself that it happened not to Wilde but to a disciple of Wilde after Wilde had gone down.[16]

that Wilde came off with more obvious heroism. According to Benson, himself an athlete, Wilde was 'far from being a flabby aesthete,' and 'only one man in the college, and he rowed seven in the Varsity Eight [J. T. Wharton] . . . had a ghost of a chance in a tussle with Wilde.' To prove his point Benson quotes Wharton's respectful comment about Wilde's muscularity and goes on to tell how the junior common room at Magdalen decided one evening to beat up Wilde and break up his furniture. Four undergraduates were deputed to burst into his rooms while the rest watched from the stairs. The result was unexpected: Wilde booted out the first, doubled up the second with a punch, threw out the third through the air, and taking hold of the fourth – a man as big as himself, carried him down to his rooms and buried him beneath his own furniture. He then invited the spectators to sample the would-be persecutor's wines and spirits, and they accepted.[17]

Whatever hostility he provoked, Oxford's bosom was capacious enough to take him to it. Within Magdalen College his closest friends in his first year were three near neighbors. The first was William Walsford Ward, later a lawyer who was halfway through the Greats course (classical literature for two years, ancient history and philosophy for two more) that Wilde also was taking. Wilde called him 'the only man in the world I am afraid of,'[18] perhaps because of his opposition to Wilde's flirtation with Catholicism. There was also a fair, good-looking student named Reginald Richard Harding, later a stockbroker, whom Wilde described as 'my greatest chum.'[19] His letters to both Harding and Ward have survived. They make much use of nicknames, Ward being 'Bouncer' after a character in a comic novel, and Harding 'Kitten,' after the song, 'Beg your parding, Mrs Harding, Is my kitting in your garding?' Wilde was called 'Hosky.' This circle was enlarged to include David Hunter Blair, a serious-minded young man whom Ward enticed downstairs with the promise that Wilde's conversation would be worth hearing. Hunter Blair, a Scottish baronet with a large property at a place called Dunskey, and known therefore as 'Dunskie,' was deeply religious and, though a Mason, was meditating conversion. He became a Benedictine and rector of St Benet's Hall in Oxford. Wilde would compare him to Sir Blaise in Mrs Browning's *Aurora Leigh*, whose style rises to 'So fie! no blasphemy, I pray you.'[20]

Hunter Blair describes Wilde in an autobiographical book (*In Victorian Days*), and is quick to point out that there was no indecorum in his conversation or action. One of his chief interests was in furnishing his rooms. To judge from three of his early Oxford poems, Pre-Raphaelite lilies were always about. On several occasions Hunter Blair went shopping with Wilde, once to help him buy two large vases of blue china, possibly Sèvres, to hold the lilies. These vases may have inspired the remark which reverberated first round the university, then round the country, 'I find it harder and harder every day to live up to my blue china.' *Punch* got hold of it, but not until George du Maurier's drawing in the issue of 30 October 1880. Before that an Anglican sermon was preached in St Mary's, Oxford, against its vicious tendencies: the priest, Dean Burgon, declaimed, 'When a young man says not in polished banter, but in sober earnestness, that he finds it difficult to live up to the level of his blue china, there has crept into these cloistered shades a form of heathenism which it is our bounden duty to fight against and to crush out, if possible.'[21] It remains one of Wilde's most memorable assertions and the earliest to achieve currency. Pater used it as the epigraph to the unpublished part of his last book, *Gaston de Latour.* Its authenticity has been questioned, but Oscar Browning records that when he met Wilde in Oxford in 1876 Wilde was already famous for the remark.[22] No one else could have said it. The *Oxford and Cambridge Undergraduate's Journal* confirms this in a satirical piece on Wilde as 'O'Flighty' on 27 February 1879, which comments, ' "How often I feel how hard it is to live up to my blue china" is a favourite remark of his.' The longing has something of his mother's highspiritedness, which revels in excess and pokes fun at the speaker.

Other purchases were made at Spiers' Emporium in the High Street; Spiers' bill for three of Wilde's years at Oxford has survived.[23] (In those days tradesmen were willing to wait for students to settle their bills, but even Spiers lost patience with Wilde and dunned him in the Vice-Chancellor's Court.) During Wilde's first term he bought two blue mugs and some candle ornaments; a claret decanter and some playing cards are mentioned for the second term. In October of his second year he bought four soda water tumblers, four plain tumblers, and six port glasses. During the spring vacation of 1876 he stayed in college and on 21 March, momentarily disloyal to his blue china, bought a china déjeuner service 'richly gilt.' The following January, 1877, he added six coffee cups and saucers, six Venetian hock glasses, two green Rumanian claret decanters, a water filter, and six ruby champagne tumblers. Clearly the drinks were flowing and the company growing. Hunter Blair remembered Wilde entertaining lavishly even during his first year. Perhaps in imitation of his mother's Saturday afternoons, he used to hold open house on Sunday evening after coffee had been served in the common room. Two bowls of gin and whiskey punch were on a table (his mother had contented herself with coffee and wine), and there were long churchwarden pipes filled with choice tobacco. As in Merrion Square, musical entertainment was often provided: the college organist Walter Parrott sat at Wilde's piano and accompanied the singer Walter Smith-Dorrien. Atkinson says that Wilde made his servant (at Oxford called a scout) wear felt slippers, because a creak caused him 'agony,' and extract corks in the bedroom, for fear that guests might hear the plebeian pop.[24]

Such evenings often ended with Wilde, Ward, and Hunter Blair, like the friends in 'The Decay of Lying,' sitting up until the morning whitened. Hunter Blair recalled that Wilde talked fancifully of the future, until Bouncer Ward tried to pin him down. 'You talk a lot about yourself, Oscar,' said Ward, 'and all the things you would like to achieve. But you never say what you are going to do with your life.' Wilde discouraged such blunt questions and only replied, 'God knows. I won't be a dried-up Oxford don, anyhow.'* He was not being altogether candid, for his mother's letters to him in 1875 and 1876 show that he had not given up hope in this quarter. But in the dead of night at Magdalen he soared above donship: 'I'll be a poet, a writer, a dramatist. Somehow or other, I'll be famous, and if not famous, notorious.' He was modulating his old aspiration, from Portora days, of being tried for heresy at the Court of Arches. 'Or perhaps I'll lead the βίος ἀπολαυστικός [life of pleasure] for a time and then who knows rest and do nothing. What does Plato say is the highest that man can attain here below? καθεύδειν καὶ ὁρᾶν τὸ ἀγαθον – to sit down and contemplate the good. Perhaps that will be the end of me too.' Hunter Blair would have none of this: 'Rot, Oscar. That's just what you won't do. Sitting down and doing nothing will never be in your line. You are much more likely to get up and knock about and do all sorts of queer things.' 'You wait and see, my boy,' Wilde replied. 'I may begin like that, but the end will be very different. These things are on the knees of the gods. What will be, will be.' The words are Hunter Blair's, but the reply is in character. Wilde was always ready to reverse his field. The hurlyburly attracted him, but so did quietism. And beyond both was a quality noted by Yeats, 'the enjoyment of his own spontaneity.'[25]

Between Ruskin and Pater

Who cares whether Mr Ruskin's views on Turner are sound or not? What does it matter? That mighty and majestic prose of his . . . is at least as great a work of art as any of those wonderful sunsets that bleach or rot on their corrupted canvases in England's Gallery.

Wilde was too much an intellectual buccaneer to confine himself to the requirements of Greats. He became interested in the Orientalist Friedrich Max-Müller, then translating the Vedas, and was given breakfast by him at All Souls, as he allowed his mother to know. She

---

* He voiced this sentiment again in his poem 'Humanitad';

> And yet I cannot tread the Portico
>   And live without desire, fear and pain,
> Or nurture that wise calm which long ago
>   The grave Athenian master taught to men,
> Self-poised, self-centered, and self-comforted,
> To watch the world's vain phantasms go by with unbowed head.

allowed her correspondents to know it, too.[26] Max-Müller may have encouraged Wilde's Vedic contempt for mere English getting-on, which Wilde would express more largely later in a strong endorsement of the contemplative philosophy of Chuang-Tsu. But in sorting out the intellectual universe with which Oxford amazed him, the two principal people at Oxford, and the ones he said he most wanted to meet, were John Ruskin and Walter Pater. For an undergraduate with artistic tastes, they were the inevitable poles of attraction. Ruskin, at fifty-five, occupied the respected position of Slade Professor of Fine Art; Pater, at thirty-five, a fellow of Brasenose College, tried in vain to become his successor. Wilde cannot have known in advance how opposed to each other they were: Pater, once Ruskin's disciple, disagreed with his master without naming him; Ruskin loftily ignored Pater's aspirations.

Wilde did not meet Pater in person until his third year at Oxford, but during his first term he came under the spell of his *Studies in the History of the Renaissance*, published the year before. He never ceased to speak of it as 'my golden book,' and in *De Profundis* he described Pater's work as the 'book which has had such a strange influence over my life.'[27] Much of it, especially the celebrated 'Conclusion,' he had by heart. Pater declared that, life being a drift of momentary acts, we must cultivate each moment to the full, seeking 'not the fruit of experience, but experience itself.' Dorian Gray quotes this without acknowledgement. 'Success in life,' said Pater, is to 'burn always with this hard gemlike flame' – Wilde now adopted 'flamelike' as one of his favorite adjectives, and longed, as he said in 'Humanitad,' 'to burn with one clear flame.' We can burn variously, through the passions (of which Pater strongly approved), through political or religious enthusiasms or what he called the religion of humanity, and best of what life offers, through art. To expose one's sensibility as fully as possible was an ideal that attracted Wilde: in 'The Burden of Itys' he would write,

> I would be drunk with life,
> Drunk with the trampled vintage of my youth.

He would, however, indicate his reservations when he had Lord Henry Wotton in *The Picture of Dorian Gray* talk this kind of Paterese to Dorian Gray with evident ill effects.

Ruskin had made England art-conscious by a different approach, in which morality played a major part. Artists could display their morality by fidelity to nature, and by eschewing self-indulgent sensuality. The word 'aesthetic' became a bone of contention between Ruskin's disciples and Pater's. Ruskin sometimes used the term favorably, as when in Michaelmas (autumn) term, 1874, he offered a series of eight lectures, from 10 November to 4 December, on 'The Aesthetic and Mathematic Schools of Art in Florence.' By 'Mathematic' he meant the science of perspective, by 'Aesthetic' everything else. Though his use of the term indicates how much it was part of the university vocabulary, Ruskin was enraged when it was used to mean self-justified amoral art. As early as 1846 he denounced the aesthetic as a slogan that degraded the arts into mere amusements, 'ticklers and fanners of the soul's sleep.' But in 1868 Pater commended the Pre-Raphaelites as 'The Aesthetic School of Poetry,' the vogue of the word having spread. Biding his time to respond, Ruskin declared in 1883 that the growing habit of calling 'aesthetic' what was only 'pigs-flavouring of pigs' wash' argued a 'moral deficiency.'[28] His own art criticism harked back to the medieval period, with its faith and its Gothic, while he argued that the more the Renaissance bloomed, the more it decayed. Wilde would accept this point of view in *De Profundis*. But what he read in Pater was different: for Pater the medieval period was valued only as an anticipation of the Renaissance, and the best of the Renaissance was still going on. As for decadence, Pater did not shrink from welcoming what he called 'a refined and comely decadence.'[29]

Wilde could see that he was being offered not only two very different doctrines, but two different vocabularies. Though both Ruskin and Pater welcomed beauty, for Ruskin it had to be allied with good, for Pater it might have just a touch of evil. Pater rather liked the Borgias, for example. Ruskin spoke of faith, Pater of mysticism, as if for him religion became bearable only when it overflowed into excess. Ruskin appealed to conscience, Pater to imagination. Ruskin invoked disciplined restraint, Pater allowed for a pleasant drift. What Ruskin reviled as vice, Pater caressed as wantonness.

Wilde was as concerned for his soul as for his body, and however titillated he was by Pater, he looked to Ruskin for spiritual guidance. He made a point of attending Ruskin's lectures on Florentine art (in Michaelmas term, 1874) in the University Museum. 'Wilde was always there,' Atkinson recalled, and H. W. Nevinson also remembered him in constant attendance, 'leaning his large and flabby form against the door upon our right, conspicuous for something unusual in his dress, still more in his splendid head, his mass of black [really dark brown] hair, his vivacious eyes, his poet's forehead, and a mouth like a shark's in formlessness and appetite.'[30] Ruskin's lectures as formally printed in Cook and Wedderburn's edition do not of course include the asides with which he punctuated them. He would, as Atkinson writes, give 'a loving exposition of a picture, and then suddenly break off into an appeal to his hearers to fall in love at the first opportunity.' His eloquence led them to clap for him as for no other professor, or even – greatest tribute of all – to forget to clap.

During one of his impromptu exhortations, Ruskin apparently reminded his hearers that the previous spring (1874) he had proposed to them that instead of developing their bodies in pointless games, in 'fruitless slashing of the river,' in learning 'to leap and to row, to hit a ball

with a bat,' they should join him in improving the countryside.[31] Wilde, as
ready to spurn sports as Ruskin, did not need persuasion. Ruskin asked
them to help complete a project he had initiated some months before, of
constructing a flower bordered country road in Ferry Hinksey, where
there was only a swampy lane. It would be like building a medieval
cathedral, an ethical adventure, rather than a Greek and narcissistic
game. In an undergraduate ballad of the period, he was made to say,

> My disciples alack, are not strong in the back,
>   And their arms than their biceps are bigger.
> Yet they ply pick and spade, and thus glorify Slade:
>   So to Hinksey go down as a digger!

Although Wilde found rising at dawn more difficult than most men –
preferring like his mother not to rise till afternoon – he overcame his
languor for Ruskin's sake. Later he bragged comically that he had enjoyed
the distinction of being allowed to fill 'Mr Ruskin's especial wheel-
barrow,' and of being instructed by the master himself in the mysteries of
wheeling such a vehicle from place to place.[32] The road was in the process
of being paved, digging having been finished the previous spring. It was
not much of a road, but for Wilde it was the road to Ruskin, who invited his
sweaty workers to breakfast after their exertions. The work went on in
November to the end of term, after which Ruskin was off to Venice, and
Wilde could again rise late, as the road for its part slowly sank from sight.

The roadbuilding fostered Wilde's conviction that art had a role to play
in the improvement of society. A good deal of his talk at Magdalen was
devoted to the social regeneration of England. Ruskin was apt to anglicize
the afterlife with such remarks as, 'At Paddington station I felt as if in hell,'
and Wilde as disciple told his friends that all the factory chimneys and
vulgar workshops should be taken up and placed on some far-off island.
'I would give Manchester back to the shepherds and Leeds to the
stockfarmers,' he magnanimously announced.[33]

When Ruskin came back from Venice he encouraged Wilde to call, and
they saw each other often. To Wilde the friendship was gratifying and
instructive. 'The dearest memories of my Oxford days are my walks and
talks with you,' he wrote to Ruskin after going down, 'and from you I
learned nothing but what was good. How else could it be? There is in you
something of prophet, of priest, and of poet, and to you the gods gave
eloquence such as they have given to none other, so that your message
might come to us with the fire of passion, and the marvel of music, making
the deaf to hear, and the blind to see.'[34] This acknowledgement of
discipleship suggests, perhaps, that Wilde knew how much in need of
reassurance the great Ruskin was. Bodley's journal describes how on 25
April 1875 he went to see William Money Hardinge, a Balliol friend, very
much the aesthete. As Bodley came in Hardinge broke off playing Weber

on the piano to tell of his tea with Ruskin. The table had been lit with unduly ceremonious wax candles. Ruskin soon began to confide in Hardinge, 'True sorrow does a man good; false sorrow does one harm. I only loved but one woman and I still feel chivalrous towards her and the man who robbed her from me.' To be an intimate of Ruskin was to be admitted to his disappointments as well as his achievements.

Wilde knew about Ruskin's white marriage, as he shows in a letter of 28 November 1879. He tells there of going with him that night in London to see Henry Irving play Shylock, after which he went, without him, to the Millais ball. 'How odd it is,' Wilde remarked.[35] The oddity lay in attending *The Merchant of Venice* with the author of *The Stones of Venice*, and then going on to a ball which celebrated the marriage of the Millais' daughter. Mrs Millais had been for six years Mrs Ruskin, and for three of those years Millais had been Ruskin's special friend and protégé. That Ruskin's marriage had been annulled on grounds of non-consummation was public knowledge, and much of the information that has since filled a dozen books was already well known at Oxford by word of mouth. There was an element of sympathy as well as respect in Wilde's attitude to Ruskin, and greatly as he admired the older man, he could hardly disregard the failings of his life.

Wilde accepted, at least sometimes, Ruskin's conception of Venice as a medieval Virgin who became a Renaissance Venus, specific works of architecture and painting marking the change. In *De Profundis* he spoke of 'Christ's own renaissance which had produced the Cathedral of Chartres, the Arthurian cycle of legends, the life of St Francis of Assisi, the art of Giotto, and Dante's *Divine Comedy*'; and then was unfortunately 'interrupted and spoiled by the dreary classical Renaissance that gave us Petrarch, and Raphael's frescoes, and Palladian architecture, and formal French tragedy, and St Paul's Cathedral, and Pope's poetry, and everything that is made from without and by dead rules, and does not spring from within through some spirit informing it.'[36] Yet at Oxford and afterwards Wilde also followed Pater in speaking with great favor of much in the Italian Renaissance and after. Where Ruskin was all severance, Pater was all blend. The essays in Pater's book deal with subjects from the thirteenth to the eighteenth century, but they all tend to glorify the same thing, male friendship, as found in the medieval Amis and Amile, in Pico della Mirandola and Ficino, in Leonardo and his model for St John, in Michaelangelo and the amorous addressee of his sonnets, and in Winckelmann, murdered on his way to meet Goethe. An atmosphere of suppressed invitation runs through Pater's book, just as an atmosphere of suppressed refusal runs through Ruskin's work. As to homosexuality, Ruskin refused to allow that it was sanctified because practiced in Athens, arguing that 'the partial corruption of feeling' for women and the excessive 'admiration for male physical beauty,' had conduced to the fall of Greece.[37] But Ruskin's own obsesssion with the child Rose La Touche made it difficult to take his pronouncements about normal sexuality seriously. Pater's blandishments were more persuasive. Something of the extraordinary effect of the *Studies* upon Wilde came from their being exercises in the seduction of young men by the wiles of culture. As against the resolute '*Noli me tangere*' of Ruskin, Pater drew from the Renaissance the subversive lesson that we must continue it, hand in male hand.

For Wilde the two stood like heralds beckoning him in opposite directions. If he needed evidence for what he would say later, that 'Criticism is the highest form of autobiography,' he could find it in their unconscious self-revelation. The rhythms with which one denounced were matched by the rhythms with which the other beguiled. One was post-Christian, the other post-pagan. Ruskin was sublime, full of solemn reproof, and fanatical; Pater insidious, all vibration, but cautious. Neither offered a way which Wilde could follow unequivocally or gravely. He liked to refer to Pater as 'Sir Walter,' and came to criticize the style of the *Studies* as too studied, lacking 'the true rhythmical life of words.' When Pater died, Wilde commented, according to Max Beerbohm, 'Was he ever alive?'[38] In later life he disparaged Pater as man, as writer, and as an influence, as Robert Ross noted with some distress.[39] As to Ruskin, Wilde would present another prophet named John as the frenzied, untouchable Iokanaan in *Salome.* He outgrew them both.

CHAPTER III

Rome and Greece

I have suffered very much for my Roman fever in mind and
pocket *and happiness.*

Manningism

Wilde was at home in Oxford now. He was not, however, carefree. His
studies did not trouble him; the state of his soul did. Roman Catholicism
attracted him more powerfully at Oxford than at Trinity, and his letters
frequently betray his anxiety. He knew that Ruskin had spent the summer
before they met in a monastic cell at Assisi, though he refused to be
converted on the grounds that he was more Catholic than the Roman
Catholics. Pater used to visit Roman Catholic churches to admire the
rituals and decorations, and in *Marius the Epicurean* he would praise their
'aesthetic charm,' while treating the dogmas with reserve. Others at
Oxford were less resistant: the apostasies of Henry Edward Manning of
Balliol and John Henry Newman of Trinity, the one all force, the other all
sinuosity, were now historic. More recently, Gerard Manley Hopkins,
also of Balliol, had gone over. For Wilde in Magdalen the issue was
brought home by his friend David Hunter Blair.

The circumstances of Hunter Blair's conversion were spectacular.
During the winter term of 1875 he obtained leave to study music in
Leipzig and from Leipzig proceeded to Rome in time to attend the
ceremony at which Manning was created a cardinal, on 15 March 1875.
Manning was a special hero because of his stern espousal of the doctrine
of papal infallibility, which he had recently defended against Gladstone's
charge that it 'equally repudiated modern thought and ancient history.'
Swept away by enthusiasm, Hunter Blair, ten days after the Manning
ceremony, was himself received into the Church. He was a notable
convert: Archbishop (later Cardinal) Howard confirmed him, Pius IX
himself blessed him and conferred on him the honorary post of papal
chamberlain.

On his return to Magdalen at the end of April, Hunter Blair urged
Wilde and others to follow him. Several Magdalen students did. William

Ward smiled and said nothing; Wilde did not smile and said a good deal. His main impediment was Sir William Wilde's opposition. 'I am sure that if I had become a Catholic,' he said, referring to his Trinity College days, 'he would have cut me off altogether, and that he would do the same today. That is why he rejoiced at my winning a scholarship to Oxford, where I should not be exposed to these pernicious influences. And now my best friend turns out to be a Papist!' Their situations were not to be compared. Hunter Blair had his own property. 'Lucky you, my dear Dunskie, to be as you are independent of your father and free to do what you like. My case is very different.'[1]

Hunter Blair was unimpressed by this financial argument and continued his persuasions. Wilde was tempted: he felt guilty and sinful; he liked what he called 'the perfume of belief',[2] and adorned his third finger with an oval amethyst ring that looked faintly ecclesiastical. He put his own case in describing later the seductiveness of the Roman ritual for Dorian Gray. 'The daily sacrifice, more awful really than all the sacrifices of the antique world, stirred him as much by its superb rejection of the evidence of the senses as by the primitive simplicity of its elements and the eternal pathos of the human tragedy that it sought to symbolise. He loved to kneel down on the cold marble pavement, and watch the priest, in his stiff flowered vestment, slowly and with white hands moving aside the veil of the tabernacle, or raising aloft the jewelled lantern-shaped monstrance with that pallid wafer . . . or, robed in the garments of the Passion of Christ, breaking the Host into the chalice, and smiting his breast for his sins. The fuming censers, that the grave boys, in their lace and scarlet, tossed into the air like great gilt flowers, had their subtle fascination for him.'[3] By June 1875 Wilde's interest in Catholicism was ostentatious enough to astonish his visitors. Among these was the sculptor Lord Ronald Gower, the younger son of the second Duke of Sutherland,* who came to see Wilde, bringing with him Frank Miles, a young portrait sketcher with whom he had become acquainted. Gower described Wilde in his diary for 4 June 1875 as 'A pleasant cheery fellow, but with his long-haired head full of nonsense regarding the Church of Rome. His room full of photographs of the Pope and of Cardinal Manning.'[4] (Wilde had also a Madonna done in plaster.) Gower, himself attracted to Newman earlier, cautioned Wilde about the blandishments of Hunter Blair. Wilde remained more Protestant heresiarch than Catholic zealot.

The summer vacation of 1875 affirmed his indecision. He spent the first part of it in Italy, looking at the paintings which Ruskin's descriptions had made him eager to see. Oddly enough, in view of his adhesion to Hunter Blair, his companions there were his old tutor from Trinity,

---

* Gower, a homosexual, adopted a young man named Frank Hird, leading Wilde to warn a friend about them, 'Gower may be seen but not Hird.'

Professor Mahaffy, in Protestant orders and dead set against Roman Catholicism, and a young man named William Goulding, the son of a wealthy Dublin businessman and also inflexibly Protestant. It may have been to protect himself against Hunter Blair's persuasions that Wilde went with them. His letters home gave his father no anxiety about a possible religious upheaval, and described Etruscan tombs and Titian's *Assumption* ('the best painting in Italy') with equal pleasure. What he did not describe was the turmoil he felt at the sight of so many artistic memorials of Catholic piety. A poem he wrote just after a visit to San Miniato in Florence, about 15 June 1875, conveys his delight in metaphysical sensation on the one hand and the shows of this world on the other.

Wilde's first impulse to write stemmed largely from his awareness of this tension, and much of his work deals with the sale of souls, the attempt to repurchase them, and the states of the negotiators' minds. The early manuscript version of 'San Miniato' differed markedly from the later:

San Miniato
(June 15th)

I

See, I have climbed the mountain side
  Up to this holy house of God,
  Where the Angelic Monk has trod
Who saw the heavens opened wide.

The oleander on the wall
  Grows crimson in the morning light;
  The silver shadows of the night
Lie upon Florence as a pall.

The myrtle-leaves are gently stirred,
  By the sad blowing of the gale,
  And in the almond-scented vale
The lonely nightingale is heard.

II

The day will make thee silent soon
  O! nightingale sing on for love,
  While yet upon the shadowy grove
Fall the bright arrows of the moon.

While yet across the silent lawn
  In golden mist the moonlight steals,
  And from love-wearied eyes conceals
How the long fingers of the dawn

Come climbing up the Eastern sky
  To grasp and slay the shuddering night,
  All careless of my heart's delight,
Or if the nightingale should die.[5]

He praises Fra Angelico, but Fra Angelico among the nightingales, and among the unchastened oleanders and myrtles. The Christian scene is more than faintly subverted by the pagan birds, and by the imagery of love, theft, and murder – arrows falling, moonlight stealing, dawn slaying night. In the battle of sacred and profane for Wilde's soul, the profane is inching ahead. But when the poem was revised for publication in the *Dublin University Magazine* in March 1876, the sacred had taken over all but the last words, and his passive tolerance of nature has given way to a desperate longing for supernatural intervention.

San Miniato

See, I have climbed the mountain-side
  Up to this holy house of God,
  Where that Angelic Monk once trod,
Who saw the heavens opened wide,

And throned upon the crescent moon
  The Queen of heaven and of grace –
  Mary, could I but see thy face,
Death could not come at all too soon.

. . . . .

O! crowned by God with love and flames,
  O! crowned by Christ the Holy One,
  O! listen, ere the searching sun
Show to the world my sin and shame.

The opening lines remain the best, but fall into the abyss with 'Death could not come at all too soon.' Sir William was delighted to see his son's poem. Lady Wilde made no comment about the pietism of the poem, but offered a professional objection: '*Sin* is respectable and highly poetical, *Shame* is not.'[6] Wilde had borrowed the conjunction from an even more professional poet, Tennyson (*In Memoriam*, 48).* In Wilde it becomes stagey, penitential self-preening. He would learn to keep such confessions to himself.

On 19 June the travellers went on from Florence to Bologna and then to Venice. Wilde would remember how 'the pearl and purple of the seashell

---

* 'And [Sorrow] holds it sin and shame to draw / The deepest measure from the chords . . .'

is echoed in the church of St Mark.' On 22 June they stopped briefly in Padua to see the Giottos, of which Wilde, like his master Ruskin, could fully approve, and then travelled late on the 23rd to Verona. Wilde wrote a sonnet about Dante's exile there in 1303–04, which for the first time surrounds a poet with prison imagery, though Dante was not imprisoned in Verona:

> behind my prison's blinded bars
> I do possess what none can take away
> My love, and all the glory of the stars.

These consolations – so facilely offered here – were less dependable than he supposed.

After Verona Mahaffy and Goulding proceeded to Rome; Wilde had spent all his money and had to start for home on the 25th. He had the subject of a new poem, 'Rome Unvisited,'

> And here I set my face towards home,
>   For all my pilgrimage is done,
> Although, methinks, yon blood-red sun
>   Marshals the way to holy Rome.

The poem delighted Hunter Blair,* because it expressed Wilde's desire to meet the Pope as 'the only God-appointed King,' and his hope that, if he could sing as a religious poet, his heart would be free of fears. As he moved physically away from Rome, he moved imaginatively close to it.

The rest of the summer brought secular pleasures. Wilde returned home to Ireland by way of Paris, and spent some weeks in the west of Ireland. He could travel freely between Moytura House near Cong, where the view of Lough Corrib was magnificent, and Illaunroe, the hunting lodge in the middle of a lake. He could row, shoot, fish, ride, and sail as he pleased. In August he returned to Dublin to welcome his friend Frank Miles, who had come on a brief visit to him. Miles at this time made a sketch of Wilde that showed him essaying a small moustache, to be given up not long after.

In August 1875 too, Wilde met the first of a series of beautiful women with whom he would be associated for the rest of his bachelor days. She was Florence Balcombe, third of five daughters of an English lieutenant-colonel who had served in India and the Crimea. Though dowerless, she was, according to Wilde, 'exquisitely pretty.'[8] They met at her house at 1 Marion Terrace, Clontarf. She was seventeen to Wilde's twenty. On 16 August Wilde escorted her to the afternoon service at the Protestant cathedral, St Patrick's. A lively affection for each other developed. At

* It also pleased John Henry Newman, to whom Wilde sent it.[7]

Christmas in 1875, it appears, Wilde presented her with a small gold cross which united their names. The idea of marriage was in the air, there was evidently some mild love-making, but Wilde could not marry while still a student. It is hard to gauge the intensity of his feelings, which he exaggerated and she later minimized. Wilde's affection may have been largely self-regarding. It did not prevent him from dandling on his knee another young woman in Dublin named Fidelia,* or from flirting with one called Eva.† But Florence Balcombe came close to being an official beloved. In September 1876 he sent her a water color he had painted of Moytura House. The love poems he wrote during their period of putative commitment to each other imply tentativeness. Two of them envisage the death of lover or beloved – a convenient way out for half-hearted suitors – as in the poem eventually entitled 'Chanson':

> A ring of gold and a milk-white dove
> Are goodly gifts for thee,
> And a hempen rope for your own love
> To hang upon a tree.

Swinburne is invoked to describe her 'delicate / Fair body made for love and pain,' and Rossetti to name her 'white lily overdrenched with rain.' In 'The Dole of the King's Daughter,' the title character has committed seven sins, which turn out to be the murders of her seven admirers. The poems show more interest in phrasing than feeling, and in complications than consummations.

When Wilde returned to Oxford in the autumn of 1875 for his second year, he had religion as well as love on his mind. Cardinal Manning preached derisively on the Oxford motto, *Dominus Illuminatio Mea*, on 23 November 1875 at the dedication of the new church of St Aloysius in St

---

* The girl's mother wrote to him,

'Dear Oscar, I was very much pained the last time I was at your house when I went into the drawing room and saw Fidelia sitting upon your knee. Young as she is, she ought to have had (and I told her) the instinctive delicacy that would have shrunk from it – but oh! Oscar, the thing was neither right, nor manly, nor gentlemanlike in you. You have disappointed me . . .

'Now to touch another matter – I have been almost amused at the way you have often treated me as though I were a fool – as to kissing Fidelia when you met her – that is, trying to do it out of sight as it were . . . as for instance the last day I saw you – you left me, a lady, *to open the hall door for myself*, you staying behind at the same time in the hall to kiss Fidelia. Did you think for a moment that I was so supremely stupid as not to know that you always kissed F. when you met her, if you had an opportunity?'

† A letter to him from Edith J. Kingsford of Brighton, 11 October 1875, suggests that he has been flirting with her cousin Eva, who is obviously taken with him, and offers to help arrange a match if that is in accord with his intentions, even though Eva's mother will never agree.[9]

Giles'. This was the first Roman Catholic church to be built in Oxford since the Reformation. Wilde inscribed his name among those who listened to the Cardinal denounce Oxford for its spiritual apathy and decay. Now and later Wilde found Manning 'fascinating,'[10] a word more secular than spiritual. Hunter Blair may have expected that this visit would bring Wilde to decision but he did not take into account Wilde's enjoyment of half-choice. Extended discussions of the state of Wilde's soul went on. One night even Hunter Blair lost patience. He hit Wilde on the head and exclaimed, 'You will be damned, you will be damned, for you see the light and do not follow it.' William Ward, who had been listening to their talk, asked, 'And I?' 'You will be saved by your invincible ignorance,' Hunter Blair allowed.[11] Wilde paid a visit to Bodley early in December to confess that he was 'swaying' (in Bodley's words) 'between Romanism (Manningism), and Atheism.' Bodley acidly reminded him that one Irish Papist the more would not disturb the universe. Wilde continued to sway, attending the Reverend Henry James Coleridge's sermons in St Aloysius, writing to Ward that he was 'more than ever in the wiles of the Scarlet Woman,'[12] and backing altarwards with an eye to the exit.

Along with his incipient apostasy to his family religion went the first hint of ambiguity in his relations with men. Atkinson and others noted something effeminate in his swaying walk, and Julian Hawthorne (the son of Nathaniel) remarked in his diary that 'there is a sort of horribly feminine air about him.'[13] His friends in Magdalen were not homosexual, but the artist Frank Miles probably hovered on the edges, as might be inferred from the great interest taken in him by Lord Ronald Gower, with whom he went off to Paris. That other friendships of Wilde at Oxford were equivocal is indicated by a note in Bodley's diary, dated 4 December 1875 – Wilde's second year at the university. It read, 'Called on Wilde, who leaves foolish letters from people who are "hungry" for him and call him "Fosco" for his friends to read. Fitz lent him a fiver and we did not make hay in his rooms.' That Wilde wrote warmly to men is borne out by a letter sent from Magdalen to an unidentified friend:

> My dear Harold: I really never thought to hear from you again. I wish music was not such a siren to you as to make you forget everybody else. Will you come in and see me tonight at 9 o'c or any time when you can escape from 'Sir John' – whom by the bye I believe you like much better than
>
> > Yours scy
> > OSCAR WILDE
>
> I have some men dining tonight with me – not very intellectual – but you will find Vaughan Hughes amongst them.[14]

Whatever uneasiness Bodley may have felt about Wilde's reception of male endearments he decided to disregard, for the next day he played a practical joke on Wilde and on 6 December noted ironically its success: 'Wilde does not like to have the heads of cods and the *London Journal* sent him. The former, he said, he dropped stealthily in the Cherwell, feeling quite like Wainewright (the murderer).' (This is the first sign of Wilde's affinity for criminals, especially artistic ones like Wainewright, about whom he would later write 'Pen, Pencil and Poison.') But there was another incident of a more alarming kind.

It happened in Balliol and involved Bodley's friend (and Ruskin's) William Money Hardinge, whom Wilde knew as one of Ruskin's road-builders. Hardinge was near the end of his course when it was discovered that he had received letters from Walter Pater signed, 'Yours lovingly.' He made matters worse by his 'indecency' in talk and behavior. Although the subject was kept as quiet as possible, it was well known in Balliol, especially among the Ruskin disciples. Alfred Milner (later Viscount Milner), a friend of Hardinge's, had to admit that Hardinge was known as 'the Balliol bugger.' It was the time when 'boy worship' was conspicuous at Oxford.* Hardinge was considered to be giving the college a bad name, and in the spring of 1875, R. L. Nettleship, a classics tutor in the college, was informed. When nothing happened, Leonard Montefiore, an under-graduate, and like Milner a Ruskin roadbuilder, made a formal complaint to the Master of Balliol, Benjamin Jowett, about Hardinge's blasphemy and impiety, the evidence apparently being some homosexual sonnets. Milner and Arnold Toynbee (1852–83) – another roadbuilder – tried to help Hardinge, Toynbee by getting him to destroy his incriminating correspondence, Milner by defending the sonnets as mere literary exer-cises intended to startle. Early in 1876 Jowett was told of the letters and given copies of the sonnets. He was deeply shocked, as much at Pater, with whom he broke off relations, as at Hardinge. Himself a bachelor and a Platonist, Jowett found excuses for Plato's love of men, on the grounds that this was easily transposable by modern readers into love of women. 'Had he lived in our own times he would have made the transposition himself.'[15] But he found no excuses for Hardinge, whom he summoned on the official charge of 'keeping and reciting immoral poetry.' At first Hardinge denied it. In disgust Jowett then offered him the choice of being sent down quietly or facing a proctorial inquiry. He chose to be sent down. Jowett wrote to his father that his son was 'living here in a way which might ultimately harm himself and was already throwing discredit on his college. His conversation and writings are indecent, his acquaintance bad, his work $= 0^2$. Why should he remain at Oxford?' Hardinge's father, a dis-tinguished physician, acquiesced. The only difficulty was that Hardinge

---

* A pamphlet on *Boy Worship*, by Charles Edward Hutchinson though not signed, was published there in April 1880, and led to an animated correspondence in the *Oxford and Cambridge Undergraduate's Journal* over three weekly issues (22 and 29 April, 6 May) until it was halted by the university authorities.

had won the Newdigate Prize for his poem on Helen of Troy, and would in the normal course of events have come back and recited it in the Sheldonian at the June Encaenia (conferment of honorary degrees). Under pressure, he gracefully acknowledged himself to be too ill to come, and Bodley, like others, pretended to accept the reason as true.[16]*

If any confirmation was needed, the incident defined the peril of conduct like Hardinge's at Oxford. Wilde was a close friend of Milner and Montefiore, and knew the risk. At the same time, he began to display an interest in relations between men. André Raffalovich, an unfriendly witness, says that Wilde boasted of having as much pleasure in talking about the subject of homosexuality as others in practising it.[18] Anything might trigger a compromising response. So Violet Troubridge, a young artist friend, showed him a pastel she had done entitled 'Wasted Days,' with a double portrait, of a boy idle in summer and hungry in winter. Wilde was moved to a sonnet, which began,

> A fair slim boy not made for this world's pain,
>   With hair of gold thick clustering round his ears . . .
>
> Pale cheeks whereon no kiss hath left its stain,
>   Red under-lip drawn in for fear of Love,
>   And white throat whiter than the breast of dove –

It was published so in *Kottabos*, 1877, but when he revised it for his volume of poems four years later, he made the boy into a girl:

> A Lily-girl, not made for this world's pain,
>   With brown, soft hair close braided by her ears . . .
> Pale cheeks whereon no love hath left its stain,
>   Red underlip drawn in for fear of love,
>   And white throat, whiter than the silvered dove,

and called it 'Madonna Mia.'

In 1876, Wilde noticed another Oxford student sitting with a choirboy in a private box in a Dublin theatre. Gossipy yet alerted, he wrote to William Ward,

> Myself I believe Todd is extremely moral and only mentally spoons the boy, but I think he is foolish to go about with one, if he *is* bringing this boy about with him.
>
> You are the only one I would tell about it, as you have a philosophical mind, *but don't tell anyone about it like a good boy – it would do neither us nor Todd any good.*[19]

---

* Wilde eleven years later would review one of Hardinge's novels and comment goodhumoredly that its hero was an 'Arcadian Antinous and a very Ganymede in gaiters.'[17]

Still, he refused to take alarm. When early in 1876 he heard that Oscar Browning, who had just lost his teaching position at Eton in December 1875 because of excessive intimacy with such pupils as George Curzon, was in Oxford, Wilde asked to meet him on the ground that 'I have heard you so much abused that I am sure you must be a most excellent person.'[20] Neither now nor later would he hesitate to take risks. He could find learned sanction in Aristotle, for he wrote in his copy of the *Nicomachean Ethics* (inscribed 'Magdalen College 1877 October'), following Aristotle's preface, 'Man makes his end for himself out of himself: no end is imposed by external considerations, he must realize his true nature, must be what nature orders, so must discover what his nature is.'[21]

His hopes of a fellowship in classics were in danger of being dashed if he did not do well in Honour Moderations, which he would have to take in June 1876. In a burst of zeal, he was spending the spring vacation studying in Oxford when he received alarming news from Dublin about his father's health. Sir William's decline had continued. Attacks of asthma and gout were frequent and destructive. He managed to keep up some of his activities, and as late as February 1876 attended an official function, wearing as he loved to do his order of the Polar Star and the uniform that went with it. But the next day he had to take to his bed, short of breath. From the beginning of March he was bedridden. On his return to Dublin Oscar was saddened by his father's condition. He marveled at his mother, for during what were obviously Sir William's last weeks, she permitted an unidentified veiled woman – perhaps the mother of one or more of Sir William's three illegitimate children – to come and sit by the bedside, silent and griefstricken. Sir William died on 19 April, with his family about him. An elegy by his friend Sir Samuel Ferguson bade him farewell,

> Dear Wilde, the deeps close o'er thee; and no more
> Greet we or mingle on the hither shore . . .

and praised his healing power, his kindness, his wonderful acts of preserving and collecting antiquities, his communion with the rural landscape. It was no little life that Sir William had led.

His will proved to be a disaster, for he had spent his money as he made it, and perhaps had conveyed substantial sums to the mothers of his illegitimate children. No 1 Merrion Square and Moytura House were heavily mortgaged, only the Bray houses and Illaunroe were free and clear. Lady Wilde discovered that her marriage jointure was much reduced. Though each had a share – Oscar the Bray houses, Willie the house in Merrion Square, Lady Wilde Moytura, and Henry Wilson and Oscar jointly the lodge at Illaunroe – the income from the estate was not likely to be enough for any of them to live on. Wilde returned to Oxford in a sad and self-pitying mood. He saw financial troubles ahead, perhaps for

60

life, and wondered whether, for the sake of so small a legacy, he had been wise to put off the purification of becoming a Catholic.

He now had to concentrate on studying for his second-year examinations. He knew that an examination on Divinity would come first, but he did not bother to prepare for it. In June he went up to the proctor at the Examination Schools for his paper. The proctor asked, 'Are you taking Divinity or Substituted Matter?' (The substituted matter was for non-Anglicans.) 'Oh, the Forty-Nine Articles,' Wilde replied indifferently. 'The Thirty-Nine, you mean, Mr Wilde,' said the proctor. 'Oh, is it really?' asked Wilde in his weariest manner. (He would talk later of the Twenty Commandments. To miscount was to discount.) 'In examinations,' he would say later, 'the foolish ask questions that the wise cannot answer.'[22] He did not pass.

But the principal examination, in classical literature, went well. He translated adeptly from and into Greek and Latin, and demonstrated his familiarity with a large number of Greek texts. One congenial question was, 'What account do you gather that Aristotle would have given of the nature and office of Poetry? Compare any later definition of Poetry with that which in your opinion he would have given, and explain his point of view.'[23] Wilde had a strong conviction that Aristotle, unlike Plato, offered a theory of art 'from the purely aesthetic point of view' and not from the ethical one. As he wrote long after his time for taking examinations was over, in 'The Critic as Artist,' Aristotle found art's 'final aesthetic appeal . . . in a sense of beauty realised through the passions of pity and awe. That purification and spiritualising of the nature which he calls catharsis is, as Goethe saw, essentially aesthetic, and is not moral, as Lessing fancied.' In this paper Wilde felt confident he had done well. But he was also examined in Logic, a subject he knew less about. He guessed resignedly that he had achieved only a second class, but much depended still on the *viva voce* which would take place a few weeks later.

To while away the time he visited his father's brother, John Maxwell Wilde, vicar of West Ashby in Lincolnshire. His cousin asked him to drill her in geography and history, and he remembered these lessons when he came to write Cecily's in *The Importance of Being Earnest.* Her father liked his nephew Oscar but was scandalized at his financial extravagance in sending telegrams ('Would not the penny post do as well?') and at his religious extremism. After all, two of his uncles were in orders in that Church of England which he spoke so genially of renouncing. Though mild in disposition, John Wilde was strenuous in argument, and when his nephew showed obstinacy, the vicar preached two sermons on a Sunday, the morning one in opposition to Rome and the evening one in favor of humility. Wilde was not improved by either. He left next morning for London, where he called on Frank Miles, bearing a great basket of roses from West Ashby. Miles was fast becoming the favorite artist for society women, and to Wilde's un-Catholic delight was sketching 'the most lovely and dangerous woman in London' (Lady Desart, then well on her way to a divorce).[24]

By the evening of Monday 3 July, he was again in Oxford to brush up Catullus before the *viva* on Thursday. He went to bed reading not Catullus but Swinburne, intending to sleep late; at ten in the morning an insistent rapping at his door roused him. It was the Clerk of Schools asking why he was not at his *viva*. He had nonchalantly mixed up the days. He arrived in a leisurely manner at the Examination Schools at one o'clock. First came his *viva voce* in Divinity. The examiner, the famous W. H. Spooner of New College, reproved him for being late. Wilde replied, 'You must excuse me. I have no experience of these pass examinations.' This reference to the fact that no marks except 'pass' or 'fail' were given was so patronizing that Spooner told Wilde to copy out the twenty-seventh chapter of Acts. After a time, as Wilde was writing away, Spooner relented and said he had done enough. But Wilde continued to write. Spooner said 'Did you hear me tell you, Mr Wilde, that you needn't write any more?' 'Oh yes, I heard you,' Wilde answered, 'but I was so interested in what I was copying that I could not leave off. It was all about a man named Paul, who went on a voyage and was caught in a terrible storm, and I was afraid that he would be drowned; but do you know, Mr Spooner, he was saved; and when I found that he was saved, I thought of coming to tell you.'[25]* Spooner, himself in orders and a nephew of the Archbishop of Canterbury, was as outraged as Wilde could wish. 'I was ploughed of course,' Wilde informed a friend afterwards. He would have to take 'Divers' again.

The *viva* in classics was more to his taste. The questions were not about Catullus, as he had feared, but about Homer and epic poetry, dogs, and women. His examiner led him on to Aeschylus, from whom Wilde had translated a set passage, and asked for a comparison with Shakespeare and then with Walt Whitman, already one of Wilde's enthusiasms. The examiner was pleased with him, but the possibility remained that his papers in Logic would drag him down. After the *viva* was over, Wilde 'swaggered' to his friends that he had got a first, as if he had no doubt at all. That evening he was walking with them past the Examination Schools at eight o'clock and was told that the list of honours had just been posted. Wilde declined to look at it: 'I know I have a first,' he said. 'It's all a bore.' In a letter to Ward afterwards he laughed at his own pretended cocksureness, 'I made them all very ill, absolutely.' As a result, he remained in

* A variant of the story is that Spooner asked Wilde to construe from Greek those verses in Matthew which record the sale of the Savior by Judas for thirty pieces of silver. Wilde construed a few verses correctly and was stopped, 'Very good, that will do, Mr Wilde.' 'Hush, hush,' replied the candidate, raising an admonitory finger, 'let us proceed and see what happened to the unfortunate man.' Wilde once informed Bishop Wilberforce that the chief argument against Christianity was the style of St Paul. In extenuation, he said of the bishop, 'I fear he tempted me.'[26]

trepidation until the next day at noon when, breakfasting at the Mitre, he read the list in *The Times*. 'My poor mother is in great delight and I was overwhelmed with telegrams on Thursday from everyone I know. My father would have been so pleased about it. I think God has dealt very hardly with us.' In a cooler mood he confided to Frank Benson, 'My weakness is that I do what I will and get what I want.'[27]

Wilde went up to London and heard his favorite preacher, Cardinal Manning, at the Pro-Cathedral, on Sunday, 9 July 1876. Next day he travelled to Bingham Rectory in Nottinghamshire to stay with Frank Miles and his family. Miles's mother was an artist, his father a Church of England priest. There were many debates between the rector and Wilde about Roman Catholicism. Canon Miles was dismayed at the Vatican Council's verdict that Mary had been immaculately conceived; Wilde thought it 'very strange' that the English Church should be 'so anxious to believe the Blessed Virgin conceived in sin.'[28] He parted amicably with his hosts, and it was arranged that Frank Miles should come to Illaunroe later in the summer and paint a mural. He did, and it still exists, showing two cherubs, one light and one dark, as fisherboys; the title, 'Tight Lines,' was a fisherman's good luck cry, incongruous with the uncherubic models Miles and Wilde.

Roman Catholicism threads its way through all Wilde's activities. He carried some of Newman's books with him to Ireland, evidently anxious to see how Newman's conversion had come about. His copy of Thomas à Kempis's *Imitation of Christ* is dated 6 July 1876.[29] But in writing to the more sceptical Ward, Wilde said the books were not persuasive. 'About Newman I think that his higher emotions revolted against Rome but that he was swept on by Logic to accept it as the only rational form of Christianity. His life is a terrible tragedy. I hear he is a very unhappy man.' This was common talk about Newman at the time, though mostly dispelled when he was created cardinal in 1879. Wilde remained sceptical of Newman. In 'The Critic as Artist,' he wrote, 'The mode of thought . . . which seeks to solve intellectual problems by a denial of the supremacy of the intellect – may not, cannot, I think, survive. But the world will never weary of watching that troubled soul in its progress from darkness to darkness.'[30] Ward took advantage of his friend's doubts to urge the reasonableness of Protestantism as against Catholicism, but failed to convince Wilde, who declined to worship at the Temple of Reason. He noted however that his mother was close to Ward's views: 'except for the people, for whom she thinks dogma necessary, she rejects all forms of superstition and dogma, particularly any notion of priest and sacrament standing between her and God.' Wilde praises the beauty, as well as the necessity, of the Incarnation, acknowledging doubts about the Atonement. 'But I think since Christ the dead world has woke up from sleep.'[31] (He was later to imagine the world reawakening through art rather than religion.) For the time he continued to read Thomas à Kempis.

Many of his early poems marked stages in his spiritual history. His Catholic friends Hunter Blair and the Irish poet Aubrey De Vere recommended him to the Reverend Matthew Russell, S. J., editor of the *Irish Monthly*, and Russell welcomed seven of his poems, mostly religious, from 1876 to 1878. Another Dublin Catholic magazine, the *Illustrated Monitor*, published two of Wilde's poems in the same period. *Kottabos*, Professor Tyrrell's magazine at Trinity College, published six of his poems between 1876 and 1879, and the *Dublin University Magazine* five others. Reflecting his Greats course, several were translations or bore epigraphs or titles in Greek. What his poems show is not freshness of thought, but a sense of the fascination of his personal pageant, and a not always discriminating love of evocative words. Colours such as gold and white and blue, attributes such as shadowy, the canopy of sky, sun, and moon, and flowers – especially the lily – recur often enough to suggest that he wants them to echo and re-echo. Being a poet is vital to him.

Fortified by his first in Honour Moderations, Wilde on his return to Oxford for his third year in October 1876 took a lofty line with the authorities. On 1 November he was found with three other undergraduates (Fitzgerald and Harter of Oriel, and Ward of Christ Church) at supper in the coffee room of the Clarendon Hotel.* Their names were taken and they were ordered to finish their supper and go to their colleges. The junior proctor reported to his senior, J. R. Thursfield, 'I did this because I was told that they had been about the streets all evening. Their manner to me was as impertinent as it well could be and the chief joke at their command seemed to be getting me to mention the College [Jesus] at which they were to call. In answer to repeated enquiries Where? Where? I told them that Mr Fitzgerald could inform them (He had been to my rooms and was fined £1 for dining at the Mitre).' In fifteen minutes he returned and found them in the same places. 'I ordered them at once to leave the room and go to College. They were, if possible, ruder than before. Wilde strutted about the room with his hat on till I told him that it would be proper for him to remove it . . . One of them calmly lighted a cigar . . . I, of course, made him put it out immediately . . . I will hand them over to you only suggesting that it is a case for a severe penalty and that they shd be gated on the 5th [Guy Fawkes Day].'[32]

Wilde treated the dons with the same insolence. He was now in Litterae Humaniores, which meant ancient history and philosophy, and his tutor for Michaelmas term was William Dennis Allen. It was easy to take offense at Allen's conduct of his teaching. According to Atkinson, the students entered Allen's sitting room and sat down, faced by a mastiff in

---

* The proctorial rules of the time barred students from all houses where drinks or tobacco were sold, and required them to be in their rooms by nine o'clock in the evening.

front of the fire. Allen did not appear in person, but his voice came eerily, and no doubt drearily, from the bedroom, reading out 'notes' through the half-opened bedroom door. On cold days, Allen would sport his oak and go ice-skating, leaving a lame excuse tacked to the closed door. Wilde resolved to treat Allen with equal discourtesy. At Collections in January 1877, with the dons and students assembled in hall for progress reports, the mild President of Magdalen, Dr Bulley, asked, 'How do you find Mr Wilde's work, Mr Allen?' Allen answered angrily, 'Mr Wilde absents himself without apology from my lectures. His work is most unsatisfactory.' 'That is hardly the way to treat a gentleman, Mr Wilde,' said Bulley, seeing a chance to turn insubordination into bad manners. 'But Mr President,' said Wilde, not similarly disposed, 'Mr Allen is not a gentleman.' Bulley ordered him out of the hall.[33]

The main activity of the first term of this third year was not classical study, nor even tergiversation over becoming a Catholic, but a new burst of Masonic interest. On 27 November 1876 Wilde elected to proceed not into the Apollo Royal Arch Chapter but into the Apollo Rose-Croix Chapter, which suited him because, unlike the other, it was High Church.* It had been 'consecrated' only four years before. The earlier degrees he had taken were based on the Masonic allegory of the building of Solomon's temple by the architect Hiram Abif, his subsequent death, its destruction and rebuilding. Now, as he took the eighteenth degree, he learned that the Rose-Croix dealt explicitly with Christ's death and resurrection and offered a ritualized progress towards illumination and a communion rite. The ornate regalia included lambskin apron and red collar, sword and swordbelt, and a jewelled rose-cross. The scene was set in three rooms, one black, one funerary, and one red, with various symbolic implements. Wilde performed as Raphael, his duty being to conduct the candidates during the Perfection (joining) ceremony. This role commanded a resounding if stale rhetoric, 'I come to conduct you from the depths of darkness and the Valley of the Shadow of Death to the Mansions of light.' He was an active proselytizer, sponsoring four new Magdalen students into the order. On 3 March 1877 he wrote to Ward, himself a Mason, 'I have got rather keen on Masonry lately, and believe in it awfully – in fact would be awfully sorry to have to give it up in case I secede from the Protestant Heresy.' Hunter Blair had had to give it up for this reason. But the same letter indicates how complicated were Wilde's spiritual sensations:

I now breakfast with Father Parkinson, go to St Aloysius, talk sentimental religion to Dunlop [one of Hunter Blair's student converts] and

---

* In a burst of enthusiasm in 1878, Wilde took the Mark degree in the University Mark Lodge. The degree, having to do with the design, loss, and rediscovery of an arch in Solomon's temple, had been a separate Masonic order since 1856. Wilde presumably joined because he had friends in it.

altogether am caught in the fowler's snare, in the wiles of the Scarlet Woman – I may go over in the vac[ation]. I have dreams of a visit to Newman, of the holy sacrament in a new Church, and of a quiet and peace afterwards in my soul. I need not say, though, that I shift with every breath of thought and am weaker and more self-deceiving than ever.

If I *could hope* that the Church would wake in me some earnestness and purity I would go over *as a luxury*, if for no better reasons. But I can hardly hope it would, and to go over to Rome would be to sacrifice and give up my two great gods 'Money and Ambition.'

Still I get so wretched and low and troubled that in some desperate mood I will seek the shelter of a Church which simply enthrals me by its fascination.[34]

Wilde had absorbed enough of the Victorian work ethic to be eager to be earnest, though being fascinated was more natural to him. He came later to a benign indulgence of the spiritual mobility over which he fretted when he was young.

In December 1876 Wilde moved into Ward's rooms, his friend having gone down with a second in Greats. The rooms were the best in the college. He could now decorate their paneled splendor more lavishly, and fill them with his piano, his portfolio of pictures, his grey carpet to cover the stained floor. The pictures included photographs of his favorite Burne-Jones paintings: 'The Beguiling of Merlin,' 'The Days of the Creation,' 'The Mirror of Venus,' and 'Christ and Magdalen.'[35] Other Magdalen men twitted him for his lavish décor when they came to his Sunday evenings. During the second term he applied himself to study for the Ireland scholarship in classical learning and taste, but the six weeks of study he devoted, as opposed to the years expended by others, were not enough, and he did not win the scholarship on 5 March 1877. He castigated himself in a letter to Ward, 'I am too ridiculously easily led astray.'[36]

Hellas

To be Greek one should have no clothes: to be mediaeval one should have no body: to be modern one should have no soul.

The only spirit which is entirely removed from us is the mediaeval; the Greek spirit is essentially modern.

Wilde's melancholy fit was broken by the spring vacation of 1877. Ward and Hunter Blair, an ill assorted couple, were travelling to Rome, and urged him to join them there. Wilde, having given up a 'pilgrimage' the previous year on which Gower and Miles invited him, was eager to do so, but he was again short of money, having just paid the membership fee of £42 at his first London club, a new one called St Stephen's. (Whistler and the architect Edward Godwin were founder members.) Hunter Blair determined to make a final effort to bring Wilde into the Roman Catholic Church, and thought the sight of eternal Rome would overcome his temporizing quibbles. To get over the money problem he proposed that, since he was on his way to Mentone to see his family, he should stop off at Monte Carlo and lay £2 on Wilde's behalf. If pagan Fortune smiled on this Christian undertaking, he would realize enough money to pay for Wilde's trip. Soon £60 arrived, ostensibly Hunter Blair's winnings. It seemed that Wilde had no choice but to go. He wrote to a friend, 'This is an era in my life, a crisis. I wish I could look into the seeds of time and see what is coming.'[37]

He qualified his acceptance, however, by arranging with Professor Mahaffy, who was taking two young men to Greece, to accompany him as far as Genoa. Accordingly they met at Charing Cross Station, Mahaffy having with him Goulding as before, and also George Macmillan, recently out of Eton and about to join his family's publishing firm. As they proceeded to Genoa by way of Paris and Turin, Mahaffy as an arch-Protestant attempted to dissuade Wilde from going to Rome in favor of going to Greece. 'No, Oscar, we cannot let you become a Catholic but we will make you a good pagan instead.' Wilde was firm. Then Mahaffy said sternly, 'I won't take you. I wouldn't have such a fellow with me.' Proof against argument, Wilde was not proof against disdain. He agreed to go to Greece. On 2 April Mahaffy boasted to his wife in a letter, 'We have taken Oscar Wilde with us, who has come round under the influence of the moment from Popery to Paganism. He has a lot of swagger about him which William Goulding vows he will knock out of him as soon as he gets him on horseback in Arcadia . . . The Jesuits had promised him a scholarship in Rome, but, thank God, I was able to cheat the Devil of his due.'[38]

Wilde had not, however, forsaken Hunter Blair altogether. Faced with two alternatives, he had chosen both, as he liked to do. He would return from Athens via Rome. The solution was not so clever as it appeared, for it meant being late for term. Still, he thought he could rely upon the indulgence of Dean Bramley, with whom he had had friendly theological debates about Catholicism. How could anyone object to a student of classics going to Greece with Professor Mahaffy? He promised to come back directly from Athens, which they would reach by 17 April. He forbore to mention that he planned to stop in Rome,[39] a detail as certain to displease Bramley as it would please Hunter Blair, and for the same reason. Bramley had been dismayed by the recent conversions in Magdalen.

The Mahaffy party proved as congenial as on the previous trip. In Genoa Mahaffy had to spend several days with his sister and his ailing mother, so the rest of the party were free to go about. Macmillan now took stock of Wilde, and liked what he saw. In a letter to his parents he said that their new companion was 'very nice ... aesthetic to the last degree, passionately fond of secondary colours, low tones, Morris papers, and capable of talking a good deal of nonsense thereupon, but for all that a very sensible, well-informed and charming man.'[40] This is the fullest hint of what being an aesthete entailed in the way of special tastes. Macmillan gives no details of costume, but Wilde sported a new brownish-yellow coat in Genoa.

The colours in Genoa were not secondary during Holy Week but primary, and low tones were hard to come by in the general raucousness. Wilde had in mind a new poem, and he observed with attention the churches decorated with flowers and with images of Jesus in the sepulchre guarded by soldiers. He was equally affected by the ripe oranges, flamboyant birds, and narcissi of the Scoglietto gardens. After visiting these the travellers went on to the Palazzo Rossi to see Guido Reni's *San Sebastian*.* Macmillan, expressing their consensus, called it 'about the most beautiful picture I ever saw.'[41] Wilde glowed about it later. The collation of pagan and Christian spectacles affected the imagery of Wilde's 'Sonnet Written in Holy Week at Genoa,' in which he pretends for the poem's sake that he has already been to Greece and so is in need of having his pagan thoughts checked by Christian ones:

> I wandered in Scoglietto's green retreat,
> The oranges on each o'erhanging spray
> Burned as bright lamps of gold to shame the day;
> Some startled bird with fluttering wings and fleet
> Made snow of all the blossoms, at my feet
> Like silver moons the pale narcissi lay:
> And the curved waves that streaked the sapphire bay
> Laughed i' the sun, and life seemed very sweet.
>
> Outside the young boy priest passed singing clear,
> 'Jesus the son of Mary has been slain,
> O come and fill his sepulchre with flowers.'
> Ah, God! Ah, God! those dear Hellenic hours
> Had drowned all memory of Thy bitter pain,
> The Cross, the Crown, the Soldiers and the Spear.

Phrases such as 'fluttering wings and fleet,' 'life seemed very sweet,' and the waves that 'laughed i' the sun,' are limp. Yet the poem is faithful to

---

* Sebastian, always iconographically attractive, is the favorite saint among homosexuals. André Raffalovich, when admitted to the third order of Dominicans, took the name Brother Sebastian, and Wilde took Sebastian as his Christian name for his alias in France.

Wilde's conception of himself as a soul trembling between two waves not of thought but of feeling, and finally falling back to the Christian out of a surge of pity rather than of awe. The boy-priest (originally 'a little child') adds a further inducement.

Mahaffy was not free to leave Genoa until Good Friday, the day on which they set out for Ravenna. It was a fortunate stop, because the town turned out to be the next subject for the Newdigate, giving Wilde an advantage over other competitors. In his poem he would describe his own entry into the city on horseback:

> O how my heart with boyish passion burned,
> When far away across the sedge and mere
> I saw that Holy City rising clear,
> Crowned with her crown of towers! – On and on
> I galloped, racing with the setting sun,
> And ere the crimson after-glow was passed,
> I stood within Ravenna's walls at last!

A train was actually the mode of transport. He found the fourth-century mosaics most interesting because they showed the Virgin being adored long before the Middle Ages invented mariolatry, and in the letter to Dean Bramley he was concocting he decided to convey this bit of somewhat unpalatable information.[42]

On Easter Sunday, 1 April, they went to Brindisi and the same night took ship for Greece. They woke at dawn to see Corfu before them. On 3 April they travelled to Zante, where on a hill Wilde suddenly came upon a young shepherd with a small lamb slung round his neck, as in a picture of the Good Shepherd.[43] At Katakolo, their next stop, they were joined by Dr Gustav Hirschfeld, director of the German excavations at Olympia, who conducted them to the site on horseback next day. In later life Wilde told Charles Ricketts, 'Yes, during the excavation I was present when the great Apollo was raised from the swollen river. I saw his white outstretched arm appear above the waters. The spirit of the god still dwelt within the marble.'[44] In fact, the head of Apollo, not his arm, had been found, but on dry land, and some days before Wilde got there. Neither Macmillan nor Mahaffy mentions, as they would doubtless have done if they had been eyewitnesses, this rescue of the drowned god. Robert Ross in the preface to the German edition of Wilde's works gives another variant he must have heard from Wilde, that the Hermes of Praxiteles was discovered while he was present, but this happened after Wilde's departure. As Wilde would say in 'The Critic as Artist,' 'To give an accurate description of what has never occurred is not merely the proper occupation of the historian, but the inalienable privilege of any man of arts and culture.'

The next day, 7 April, they rode under pear trees covered with blossom to Andritzena, and then on to the Temple of Bassae. They were touristic enough to have themselves photographed in native costume, to great effect. Two incidents enlivened the trip. Their guide, who owned the horses, objected to their fast pace. When they paid no attention, he approached one member of the party and made threats. We do not know which member it was – there is no reason to assume it was Wilde – but whoever it was recalled he had a revolver, drew it and pointed it at the guide. The guide swallowed his tongue. The other incident, on the way to Tripolitza on 9 April, was the disappearance of 'the General,' Professor Mahaffy. It was feared he had fallen into the hands of brigands, and the others searched for hours and then appealed to the police. Mahaffy was found at last. He had been looking for his greatcoat which had been torn off his pack as he negotiated a short cut.[45]

After having visited Argos and Nauplia, they took ship to Aegina and Athens. The sight of Athens on 13 April made a great impression upon them, and was described in print by both Mahaffy and Macmillan. Wilde, if a novel in which he appears can be relied upon, spoke of it as 'the city of the early morning – rising in the cool, pale, steady light of dawn, a new Aphrodite from out the lapping circle of the waves.' For him the Parthenon was 'the one temple as complete, as personal, as a statue.' Wilde missed the Elgin marbles, however, and a few years later in his lecture to art students would call Lord Elgin a thief.[46] Apart from the absence of the marbles, Greece had been all that he hoped, and Rome must prove an anticlimax.

Wilde made a final excursion with his friends to Mycenae, where Mahaffy's name earned them access to Schliemann's recently discovered treasures. It was now 21 April, and Wilde was already seventeen days late for term. He sailed to Naples, and experienced on the way a terrifying storm. (The Atlantic would distress him in 1882 by not providing such a good one.) He hurried on to Rome and joined Hunter Blair and Ward at the Hotel d'Inghilterra. Now he hurried no more. A professor of humanities from Glasgow, G. G. Ramsay, showed them around the city, and at dinner they usually had the company of two Englishmen, both papal chamberlains – H. de la G. Grissell (to reappear late in Wilde's life) and Ogilvie Fairlie.

But Hunter Blair had something grander in store for Wilde, a meeting with the Pope. Wilde had in several poems expressed his sympathy with Pius IX, 'the prisoned shepherd of the Church of God,' and regretted that, because Victor Emmanuel had marched into the papal states in 1870, 'in evil bonds a second Peter lay' ('Sonnet on Approaching Italy'). Pius IX received them in a private audience, and expressed to Wilde the hope that he would follow his '*condiscipulus*' (so popes talk) into the city of God. On the way back to the hotel Wilde was too awestricken to speak, and once there he locked himself in his room. When he emerged he had completed a sonnet, perhaps 'Urbs Sacra Aeterna,' which Hunter Blair liked, feeling, as often before, that his long struggle for Wilde's soul was successful at last. Wilde sent a copy to Pius IX.[47] Hunter Blair more effectually sent a copy to Father Coleridge, editor of *The Month*, where the poem appeared in September 1876 under the title 'Graffiti d'Italia.'

But poems are not so good as prayers. As before, Wilde's soul was elusive. There was Ward to keep it Protestant. There was Greece to keep it Hellenic. And even without Ward, Wilde did not behave like one of the faithful. Some hours later, on the very day he had been received by the Pope, the carriage in which he and his friends were riding came to the basilica of St Paul Without the Walls, and Wilde could not be dissuaded by Hunter Blair from stopping at the Protestant Cemetery nearby. There, before the grave of Keats, 'the holiest place in Rome,' he prostrated himself on the grass. It was a humbler obeisance than he had offered to the Pope, and irritated Hunter Blair because of its confusion of aesthetic and religious postures. To submit to a poet as one should to a prelate was to undermine the meaning of submission. And the poem, 'The Grave of Keats,' which Wilde now wrote, medleyed Guido's *San Sebastian* with a hero of literature:

> The youngest of the martyrs here is lain,
> Fair as Sebastian, and as early slain.*

Hunter Blair did not give up, but he began to see where it would end. He refused to read any more sonnets: 'I don't want to see them,' he said. 'It is useless to talk of your weakness and want of principle – truly a strange reason for turning your back on what alone will make you strong . . . and as for your want of faith and enthusiasm, you cannot pretend to believe that God, who has given you grace to see His truth, will not also keep you firm when you choose to embrace it.' Pagan Greece was having some of the subversive effect upon Papal Rome that Mahaffy desired. Wilde was pleased to see Greek statues in the Vatican, as later he would note that the Greek chorus survived in the servitor answering the priest at Mass.[49] There was a creed older than Christendom to which the divided Wilde had also pledged allegiance.

During his week or ten days in Rome, not all Wilde's time was spent in the company of his Oxford friends. He made the acquaintance of a gifted

---

* Wilde glossed the poem with a prose note a few weeks later: 'As I stood beside the mean grave of this divine boy, I thought of him as of a Priest of Beauty slain before his time; and the vision of Guido's St Sebastian came before my eyes as I saw him at Genoa, a lovely brown boy, with crisp, clustering hair and red lips, bound by his evil enemies to a tree and, though pierced by arrows, raising his eyes with divine, impassioned gaze towards the Eternal Beauty of the opening Heavens.'[48]

Father Russell, to whom Wilde submitted the poem and note, suggested that, before publication in the *Irish Monthly*, at least one of the two references to 'boy' might be changed to 'youth'. Wilde did not oblige him.

young woman of twenty, Julia Constance Fletcher, who was said to have been romantically engaged to an earl, Lord Wentworth, only to jilt or be jilted by him at the last moment.[50] She and Wilde rode in the Campagna together. Miss Fletcher was determined to become a novelist, and observed Wilde attentively as a possible character. Within a few weeks of their encounter she turned out a three-volume novel entitled *Mirage*, published (under the pseudonym of George Fleming) the same year, and with enviable speed processed Wilde in it under the name of Claude Davenant. Many novels star him later, but this was the first. He would reciprocate by dedicating 'Ravenna' to her. She describes him well:

> That face was almost an anachronism. It was like one of Holbein's portraits, a pale, large-featured individual: a peculiar, an interesting countenance, of singularly mild yet ardent expression. Mr Davenant was very young – probably not more than one or two and twenty; but he looked younger. He wore his hair rather long, thrown back, and clustering about his neck like the hair of a medieval saint. He spoke with rapidity, in a low voice, with peculiarly distinct enunciation; he spoke like a man who has made a study of expression. He listened like one accustomed to speak.

Other characteristics are caught to the life. At one point Davenant almost falls off his horse from absentmindedness, so enwrapt is he in what he is saying. He flaunts one of his poems, a Pre-Raphaelite ballad with varying refrains, such as Wilde used in 'The Dole of the King's Daughter' the year before. When asked what it means, Davenant replies, 'Ah, but I never explain things' in his 'most languid tone.'[51] Both mystery and languor had become part of the aesthetic presentation.

To Constance Fletcher, Wilde-Davenant was 'an early Christian brought down to date – and adapted – like a restored Church.' His religious formula was 'a Venus re-baptised into a Virgin, and the halo was newer than the smile.' The influence of aesthetes from Gautier to Pater was detectable in all this, and also in Davenant's advice to the heroine to accept existence, multiply emotions, heighten and intensify the quality of sensations.[52] Lord Henry Wotton was to sing the same tune to Dorian, but in a tone of moral irony.

What Constance Fletcher's novel helps to make clear is that in the course of his spring travels, Wilde had found topographic symbols for his inclination on the one hand towards 'earnestness and purity' and on the other towards self-realization and beauty. Earlier the ethical Ruskin and the aesthetic Pater had epitomized these urges; but now the inclinations could be envisaged as Papal Rome and pagan Greece as well. Whatever Hunter Blair might say, Wilde could see that to deny either impulse would be to contract his nature, which might otherwise remain happily binary; he would be the contemplative or 'Theoretikos' (the title of another sonnet), 'neither for God nor his enemies.' (He borrowed this idea from Pater's phrase, 'Neither for Jehovah nor for his enemies,' in an essay on Botticelli.) In the sonnet, 'Vita Nuova,' which Father Russell first published in the *Irish Monthly* in 1877, the poet walks by 'the unvintageable sea' and feels despair,

> When lo! a sudden brightness! and I saw
> Christ walking on the waters! fear was past;
> I knew that I had found my Perfect Friend.

Christ had become a kind of boy lover. When after an interval Wilde republished the poem in a book, he changed the lines in a way that Father Russell could not have stomached:

> When lo! a sudden glory! and I saw
> The argent splendour of white limbs ascend,
> And in that joy forgot my tortured past.

The order of rhymes has been sacrificed so that Jesus can turn into Hylas. Wilde had begun to find better lines in pagan than Christian imaginings.

CHAPTER IV

An Incomplete Aesthete

Modern pictures are, no doubt, delightful to look at. At least, some of them are. But they are quite impossible to live with; they are too clever, too assertive, too intellectual. Their meaning is too obvious, and their method too clearly defined. One exhausts what they have to say in a very short time, and they become as tedious as one's relations.

Joys of Rustication

Voyages to Greece were not common in the Seventies of the last century. That they were necessary to a classical course in Oxford was more than Magdalen was ready to concede. Wilde returned to find that his request for ten days' leave had not sat well with the authorities. Bramley, as college dean and a devout Anglican who believed in eternal punishment, was already concerned that a gifted student in their principal course might prove an apostate to his religion. The trip to Rome, even if diluted with another one to Greece, was not reassuring. It was during just such a stopover in Rome two years before that Hunter Blair had become a Roman Catholic, and his friendship with Wilde was well known. But the immediate reason for collegiate severity was one that Wilde never acknowledged: he had asked for ten days' leave, and after ten days he was not there. The six-week Easter term began on 4 April 1877, no Oscar Wilde had appeared by the 26th. On that day the Magdalen officers lost patience with his effrontery, and resolved 'that Mr Wilde having absented himself during this term up to the present time without permission, be not allowed to reside for the Easter and Trinity Term, and that he be deprived of the emoluments of his Demyship for the half-year ending Michaelmas 1877; and that he be informed that unless he return punctually on the appointed day of October Term, 1877, with an amount of work prescribed by his tutor satisfactorily prepared, the officers will consider whether he shall retain his Demyship.'[1] The official language, barely concealing official fury, peremptorily put Wilde at the mercy of Allen, his hated tutor.

Two or three days after this grim edict, Wilde arrived. Kind and childlike by nature, inclined to like and be liked, he was, as Charles Ricketts said, staggered and then indignant at his rustication. Long afterwards he complained to Ricketts, 'I was sent down from Oxford for being the first undergraduate to visit Olympia.'² There was no recourse. He examined the statutes carefully, and then had them examined by the Clerk of Schools to see if the fellows of Magdalen were within their rights. They were. To his distress, they also reassigned his beautiful rooms during his absence.

One way of mitigating the injustice of rustication was by taking a few days in town. Wilde went to London and stayed with his sympathetic friend Frank Miles. The London season was a brisk one. Wilde apparently went to hear Richard Wagner conduct the Spinning Wheel chorus in *The Flying Dutchman*, and also to hear Anton Rubinstein play what Wilde carelessly miscalled in print the *Sonata Impassionata.*³ (He got it right in 'The Critic as Artist.') He felt more comfortable with the visual arts, and the event of the season was the opening of the new Grosvenor Gallery by Sir Coutts Lindsay. With artist friends such as Miles and Gower, Wilde had no trouble being invited to the private showing on 30 April 1877, and he was not one to shirk the official opening next day, when the Prince of Wales, Gladstone, Ruskin, Henry James, and other dignitaries were also present.

The occasion was intended to be memorable. Lindsay's gallery offered to present the contemporary art scene more fairly and vivaciously than the jealous Royal Academy. The year before, Sir Charles Dilke had complained on the floor of the House that the Academy excluded from its exhibitions certain important painters, chiefly Pre-Raphaelites. Lindsay intended his new gallery to present not only paintings of this school and others, but to constitute in itself a work of art. Accordingly a new Palladian façade was imposed upon the front of 135–37 New Bond Street (now the Aeolian Hall). Whistler, with whom Wilde had struck up an acquaintance, was commissioned to do a frieze on the coved ceiling of the West Gallery, showing in silver, against a subdued blue ground, the moon in its phases and the accompanying stars. The gallery walls, as Wilde approvingly noted, were 'hung with scarlet damask above a dado of dull green gold.' Henry James's fastidious eye observed that these strong colours, especially 'the savage red,'⁴ distracted the eye from the paintings, and Ruskin made the same objection, but Wilde rejoiced in the lavishness of the spectacle.

Part of this spectacle was himself. No ordinary clothing would serve for what he recognized to be his London début, so he was pranked out in a new coat even more astonishing than the yellow-brown one which had dazzled the Genovese. A contemporary diarist reports the answer he gave when questioned about this acquisition.⁵ He had had a dream, he said, in which a ghostly personage appeared in a coat of a shape and colour that somehow reminded him of a violoncello. On waking he hastily sketched out what he had seen and brought the drawing to his tailor. The coat was cut to meet the dream specifications: in some lights it looked bronze, in others red, and the back of it (Wilde was proud of his back) resembled the outline of a cello.

That anyone should care what a young man of twenty-three was wearing confirms that Wilde was becoming a wonder. It was his first rehearsal of the role of art-critic at exhibitions, in which Frith was to paint him ironically a few years later, dominating a crowd.* The attention he drew by his cello coat he was able to hold by his wit and enthusiasm. He felt so enamored of his newly revealed ability that he decided, virtually on the spot, to 'take up the critic's life.' As a start, he memorialized the opening and his presence at it by writing his first published work in prose, 'The Grosvenor Gallery,' for the *Dublin University Magazine.* The editor, Keningale Cook, balked at a number of Wilde's comments and manner-isms, but Wilde stood his ground. 'I always say I and not "we",' he informed Cook, insufferably, and insisted that he and all his artist friends were agreed that Alma-Tadema could not draw. He added some passages in the proofs and then arrogantly prevented Cook from leaving them out: 'Please have all my corrections attended to. Some of them are merely "style" corrections, which, for an Oxford man, must be always attended to.'[6] He emphasized his precocity by a sentence speaking of 'those of us who are yet boys,' and, oblivious to rustication, he signed the article, 'Oscar Wilde, Magdalen College, Oxford.' If he had dropped the panoply of 'Fingal O'Flahertie Wills' from his name, his being what Lady Bracknell calls 'an Oxonian' was by no means to be lost upon his editor or readers.

Wilde's article on the exhibition may be compared with one by Henry James. The new gallery was particularly well-disposed towards the Pre-Raphaelites, and James like Wilde praised Burne-Jones. James feared, however, that he detected in this painter a want of 'manliness.'† By chance both critics described the first important painting in the show, one by G. F. Watts entitled 'Love and Death.' James attempts exactitude but not exuberance:

* Wilde's riposte came in 'The Critic as Artist,' with reference to Frith's *Derby Day*: 'It seems that a lady once gravely asked the remorseful Academician . . . if his celebrated picture of "A Spring-Day at Whiteley's," or "Waiting for the Last Omnibus," or some subject of that kind, was all painted by hand?' To which Gilbert replies, 'And was it?'

† This objection was made also to Pater. On 3 May 1877 the *Oxford and Cambridge Undergraduate's Journal* attacked Pater's idea of enjoying moments 'simply for those moments' sake,' on the grounds that 'we have a manhood within us, and . . . there is a man's work for us to do not only in the world that is beyond Oxford, but also in Oxford itself . . .'

On a large canvas a white draped figure, with its back to the spectator, and with a sinister sweep of garment and gesture, prepares to pass across a threshold where, beside a rosebush that has shed its flowers, a boy figure of love staggers forth, and, with head and body reverted in entreaty, tries in vain to bar its entrance.

Wilde is moved by the same subject to go overboard. He lushly perceives

a marble doorway, all overgrown with white-starred jasmine and sweet briar-rose. Death, a giant form, veiled in grey draperies, is passing in with inevitable and mysterious power, breaking through all the flowers. One foot is already on the threshold, and one relentless hand is extended, while Love, a beautiful boy with lithe brown limbs and rainbow coloured wings, all shrinking like a crumpled leaf, is trying, with vain hands, to bar the entrance.

Judicious, cautious James finds that the painting 'has a certain graceful impressiveness'; aesthetic, incautious Wilde ranks it with Michelangelo's 'God Dividing the Light from the Darkness.' When they come to the beautiful boy, Wilde is all atremble, James all aslant.

James appears to less advantage when he comes to Whistler. As yet he was unprepared for the innovations of this painter, and it would take him the better part of twenty years to acknowledge his greatness. He dismissed him contemptuously now. Wilde had reservations also, but fewer. Whistler's connections were with both the poeticized paintings of the Pre-Raphaelites and with the anti-anecdotal work of the French Impressionists. Wilde, as yet committed only to anecdotal painting, praises Whistler for his traditional portrait of Carlyle, but balks at the more venturesome one of Henry Irving, and is not even patronizing towards the 'symphonies in colour.' The more unconventional they are, the less he likes them. When he comes to the 'Nocturne in Black and Gold: The Falling Rocket,' the most daring of all, Wilde banters about it like a simple-minded realist: it 'is worth looking at for about as long as one looks at a real rocket, that is, for somewhat less than a quarter of a minute.' He grants, however, as James did not, that Whistler has great power when he chooses to exercise it. Keningale Cook expressed anxiety that Whistler would be offended, but Wilde confidently assured him, 'I know he will take them [Wilde's remarks] in good part, and besides they are really clever and amusing.' (He has also a footnote to the article, obviously based on conversation with Whistler, saying eruditely that Whistler was not aware, when he executed his famous peacock ceiling, that there was an ancient one like it in Ravenna.) Whistler did not trouble himself about Wilde's banter, especially when it was sweetened with praise, but he did take seriously Ruskin's unsweetened remark in *Fors Clavigera* about 'Falling Rocket,' that he had 'never expected to hear a coxcomb ask two hundred guineas for flinging a pot of paint in the public's face.'[7] The libel suit that resulted split the English art world, breaking up established friendships. Wilde contrived to remain on good terms with Ruskin and Burne-Jones on the one hand, and with Whistler on the other, in the circumstances an acrobatic feat.

In the course of a few pages Wilde cultivates the art of self-advertisement as well as that of criticism. He comments readily on his travels in Greece and Italy. There is no want of back-scratching. Both Ruskin and Pater come in for favorable mentions: Ruskin because of Millais' long since finished portrait of him, which was *not* in the exhibition, Pater because of his description of colour in his essay on Botticelli as 'a spirit upon [things] by which they become expressive to the spirit.' Wilde applies this comment to Burne-Jones and manages to quote it twice. (He had still another quotation from Pater in the article, but Keningale Cook deleted it.) As Wilde circles through the rooms, he comments knowingly that Millais' portraits of the Duchess of Westminster and her children are remarkably like the originals. (He had met her as Lord Ronald Gower's sister.) Gower wins his commendation, too, for two sculptures *not* in the exhibition, but then hanging in the Royal Academy.

Though Wilde allowed himself occasional stringencies about other exhibited artists, he declares in the *Dublin University Magazine* his Irish conviction that 'this dull land of England, with its short summer, its dreary rains and fogs, its mining districts, and factories, and vile deification of machinery, has yet produced very great masters of art . . .' He continues the tribute in his last sentence when he unites the artists with the writers to praise 'that revival of culture and love of beauty which in great part owes its birth to Mr Ruskin, and which Mr Swinburne, and Mr Pater and Mr Symonds, and Mr Morris, and many others, are fostering and keeping alive, each in his own peculiar fashion.' He has not yet proclaimed an English renaissance, but is almost ready to do so.

After his stylish week in London, Wilde went home to Dublin. His mother was disgusted with the stupidity of the Magdalen officers, and Mahaffy raged at what seemed derogation of his valuable companionship in Greece. He might well do so, for the previous year, in somewhat similar circumstances, he had been censured by his Trinity colleagues for extending his first trip to Greece into term time. Only Willie Wilde was so callous as to ask his brother Oscar what the reason for being sent down had 'really' been, since the ostensible one seemed to him only a dodge.[8] He was perhaps beginning to suspect that his brother had unusual propensities. Wilde took what action he could: he wrote a persuasive letter to Magdalen, and on 4 May the authorities modified their previous decision to the extent of reducing his fine from £47/10/0 to £26/15/0, provided that the work prescribed by his tutor was satisfactorily done. The condition did not please Wilde.

The indignity at least helped him to clarify his aims. He would be an art critic, as he had informed Cook, and he would also be a poet. For the latter he needed poems first, and influential friends second, and he composed and cajoled during the summer. His method, so disingenuous as to be naïve, was to dispatch a poem with a charming letter, referring to his youth and Oxford connections. (Matthew Arnold as a young man had done the same, with Sainte-Beuve.) He sent Gladstone a sonnet in Miltonic style which protested against the massacre of the Christians in Bulgaria in May 1876, as Gladstone had protested in prose, and mentioned in the accompanying letter that he was 'little more than a boy.'* Since, he said, young men love to have their works published for others to read, perhaps Gladstone, if he liked it, would recommend the sonnet to the *Nineteenth Century* and the *Spectator*.[10] Gladstone responded cordially enough to be sent more sonnets, which Wilde sent off at the same time to the *Spectator*, using Gladstone's name with permission. The *Spectator* declined them. Yet Wilde's letter to Gladstone about the first sonnet is not mere toadying: he explains the two lines,

> And was thy Rising only dreamed by Her
> Whose love of thee for all her sin atones?

as meaning that Mary Magdalene was the first to see Christ after his Resurrection; he then adds, in worldly fashion, 'Renan says somewhere this was the divinest lie ever told.' He enclosed more appropriately his poem, 'Easter Day,' in which he is Protestant enough to compare unfavorably the splendor of the Pope with the poverty of Jesus.

He sent others his sonnet on Keats. He was of the opinion that the medallion portrait of Keats placed beside the grave in February 1876 was not like the poet, and in writing to Lord Houghton, whom he had met with Mahaffy in Dublin, made this point. Unfortunately he did not trouble first to read Houghton's life of Keats, for in his reply Houghton, after referring politely to the poem, insisted that its description of Keats as an unhappy warrior was unwarranted. 'Keats,' he said, 'was anything but unhappy, and he was recognised with unusual rapidity.' As for the medallion, Houghton insisted that the likeness was a good one. A similar letter from Wilde to W. M. Rossetti elicited no rebuff, but Rossetti took a long time to reply, and then said that while he agreed with the proposal that Keats should have a statue, there was no hurry, since in the fullness of time all the deserving poets would have all the statues they deserved.[11]† Wilde's tentatives were not brilliantly successful, but they served at

---

* When someone complained about the Miltonic echo in his sonnet, Wilde replied, 'What the critic calls an echo is really an achievement. I set myself to write sonnets like Milton's which should be as good as Milton's.'[9]

† Wilde said in a review of Rossetti's life of Keats on 27 September 1887 that it was 'a great failure.'

least to bring his name forward and sometimes to prompt further correspondence.

When the *Dublin University Magazine* appeared in July with his review of the Grosvenor Gallery, he sent Pater a copy. In many ways the article was a declaration of his congruence with Pater, whom he had still not met. Its references to paintings of boys included the telltale sentences: 'in the Greek islands boys can be found as beautiful as the Charmides of Plato. Guido's "St Sebastien" in the Palazzo Rossi at Genoa is one of these boys, and Perugino once drew a Greek Ganymede for his native town, but the painter who most shows the influence of this type is Correggio, whose lily-bearer in the cathedral at Parma, and whose wild-eyed, open-mouthed St John in the "incoronata Madonna" of St Giovanni Evangelista, are the best examples in art of the bloom and vitality and radiance of this adolescent beauty.' Pater caught the signal, and recognized the ability. He wrote promptly, on 14 July, to thank Wilde for his 'excellent article' and to ask him to call as soon as he returned to Oxford. 'I should like much to talk over some of the points with you, though on the whole I think your criticism very just, and it is certainly very pleasantly expressed. It shows that you possess some beautiful, and for your age quite exceptionally cultivated, tastes, and a considerable knowledge also of many beautiful things. I hope you will write a great deal in time to come.'[12]

Vaunting this approval, Wilde copied out Pater's letter for his friends Ward and Harding. He followed up his initial overture in prose by sending Pater a sonnet, perhaps several, for when, rustication over, they met in late October, Pater asked him with a smile, 'Why do you always write poetry? Why do you not write prose? Prose is so much more difficult.'[13] But he praised a poem of Wilde's, 'Magdalen Walks.' Wilde soon came over to Pater's view, and wrote to Ernest Radford, 'For myself, prose so fascinates me that I prefer to sit at its organ, than to play on the pipe or reed.' He said to Michael Field, 'There is only one man in this century who can write prose.' Next to Pater, he found 'Carlyle's stormy rhetoric, Ruskin's winged and passionate eloquence,' to be the product of enthusiasm rather than art. Prose in previous centuries was also defective. Jacobean prose was 'too exuberant,' Queen Anne prose 'terribly bald and irritatingly rational.' (His own was sometimes hirsute.) But Pater's essays remained 'the golden book of spirit and sense, the holy writ of beauty.'[14]

Pater and Wilde were not slow to become friends. Bodley came in one day to see Wilde and, finding him laying the table for luncheon, said he would stay and join him. Wilde replied, 'No, no! Impossible to have a Philistine like you. Walter Pater is coming to lunch with me for the first time.' Bodley, alarmed at Hardinge's fall from grace for receiving those letters from Pater signed, 'Yours lovingly,' thought the intimacy ominous. He said later that it had turned Wilde into an 'extreme aesthete,' in context almost a euphemism for homosexual.[15]

The intimacy flourished. Pater lent Wilde a copy of *Trois Contes*, just published in Paris. In this work of 'the sinless master whom mortals call Flaubert,' as Wilde described him in a letter,[16] were the stories of St Julien, Herodias and St John. These particularly impressed Wilde, who thereafter began to compose his sceptical revisions of Biblical narratives. He borrowed from Flaubert also the Greek form of John's name (Iokanaan). (Pater would get into trouble later for lending Flaubert's books to undergraduates.) In January 1878 Pater thanked Wilde for his photograph; and on numerous occasions went for walks and had tea with him.

What tea with Pater was like is suggested by the entry of 5 May 1878 in the diary of Mark Pattison, Rector of Lincoln College: 'To Pater's to tea, where Oscar Browning who [was] more like Socrates than ever. He conversed in one corner with 4 feminine looking youths "part dawdling" there in our presence, while the Miss Paters and I sat looking on in another corner. Presently Walter Pater, who, I had been told was "upstairs" appeared, attended by 2 more youths of similar appearance . . . [Pattison's dots]'.*

Although this account may offer a contrary impression, Pater was generally cautious, and more so since the publication in 1873 of his *Studies in the History of the Renaissance.* 'Yes,' said Wilde to Ricketts later, 'poor dear Pater has lived to disprove everything he has written.' Wilde reminisced about him to Robert Ross some years later, 'Dear Pater was always frightened of my propaganda.'[18] Another of his memories was of visiting Pater to find him brooding over an article that ridiculed his essay on Charles Lamb. Wilde said to Vincent O'Sullivan, 'Just imagine! Pater! I could not conceive how one could be Pater and yet be susceptible to the insults of the lowest kind of journalist.' Secretly he thought, and would venture to say later, that Pater's prose was too far from actual speech. Pater, for his part, considered Wilde's prose too close to speech. Robert Ross felt that Pater disliked Wilde personally while admiring his cleverness, and Vincent O'Sullivan confirmed that Pater talked to him of 'the strange vulgarity which Mr Wilde mistakes for charm.' At Oxford Wilde never attended Pater's lectures, as he did Ruskin's, but in 1890 he went with Ross to hear Pater on Mérimée. As was his custom, Pater the lecturer

---

* Pater's behavior with young men is also reflected in a letter written in all innocence in 1907 to Thomas Wright, Pater's biographer, by Ed Dugdale, a barber in Spiers & Son's haircutting saloon. Dugdale wrote that, as a young man of twenty-two, he was chosen from among several other barbers by Pater; while he was arranging his client's hair, Pater 'suddenly stooped down and gazed intently at my slippered feet; without saying a word, he took up one of my feet and placed it upon his knee, and stroked it and observed it from every angle possible. Evidently he admired some curves or lines which the foot exhibited. He invited me to come to his rooms at BNC [Brasenose College], but being then unacquainted with the great reputation of this great man . . . I did not avail myself of what would now appeal to me as a high privilege.'[17]

spoke in a low tone, never glancing at the audience. Afterwards he said to Wilde and Ross, 'I hope you all heard me.' Wilde replied, 'We overheard you.' 'You have a phrase for everything,' said Pater reprovingly.[19] But in Wilde's fourth and final year in the Greats course Pater was his great enthusiasm, as Ruskin had been in the first year. Thereafter he would often begin letters to him, according to Thomas Wright, 'Homage to the great master.'[20]

Wilde knew that in June of 1878 he must take the Schools Examinations on which the class of his degree depended. The academic year (1877–1878) began with money troubles, for when he failed to submit the required work to his tutor, the college withdrew the remission of half his fine. It required all his eloquence to persuade the officers not to keep to that decision. The President's Minute Book at Magdalen reads:

> 15 October 1877: Resolved. That the officers having considered the reasons given by Mr Wilde for not having prepared the work assigned to him by his tutor, in accordance with the Orders of April 26, and thereby are so far satisfied that they will inflict no further penalty than that already imposed, of the loss of the emoluments of his Demyship for the half-year ending Michaelmas 1877.

Wilde had never been thrifty, had overspent before Sir William Wilde died, and continued to do so now, when the income available was much smaller. As early as the autumn of 1876, he wrote to his mother that he thought he must give up all hope of a college fellowship because he could not afford it even if elected, and must seek instead some sort of 'paid work' – a desperate alternative. (He could not marry Florence Balcombe for the same reason.) Speranza was not one to allow her son the luxury of hopelessness, and she wrote back:

> I should be sorry that you have to seek a menial situation and give up the chance of the fellowship. But I do not see that, for so far, your state is one that demands pity or commiseration – from May last, (just five months) you have received in cash for your own private personal expenses £145 and the rents of Bray, and the sale of your furniture may bring you over the year till spring. Then you can sell your houses for £3,000, £2,000 of which will give you £200 a year for ten years. A very wonderful provision to my thinking – I wish I could have £200 a year for ten years – of course, like all of us, you will have to live on your house? money – but £2,000 is a splendid sum to have on hand – and with your college income in addition I do not think you will need to enter a shop – or beg your bread – I am very glad indeed you are so well off as in any case you are certain of £300 a year for the next ten years . . .[21]

Wilde continued to complain of his straitened circumstances, though his Bray houses brought him in some money in rent and eventually more

Lady Wilde in youth
(*Courtesy of the William Andrews Clark Library*)

Sir William Wilde as a young man, from a drawing by J. H. Maguire, 1847
(*Courtesy of the William Andrews Clark Library*)

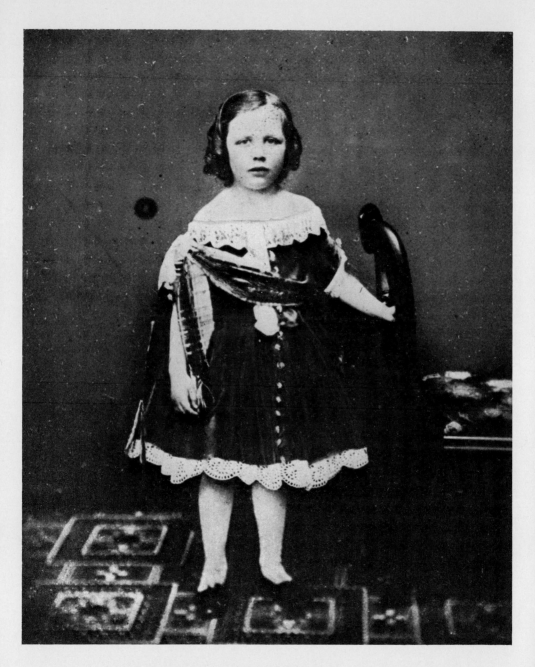

Wilde as a child (*Courtesy of the William Andrews Clark Library*)

Lady Wilde ("Speranza"),
painted by J. Morosini

Wilde's half-brother,
Henry Wilson (*Courtesy of
the William Andrews
Clark Library*)

Florence Balcombe, Wilde's early love

A gathering at Magdalen College, Oxford. Wilde is standing at right.
(*Library of Congress, Kaufmann Collection*)

Ruskin's crew of roadbuilders at work in Ferry Hinksey, on the edge of Oxford
(*Oxford City Library*)

Wilde (left) in the Prince Rupert costume he wore to a fancy-dress ball 1 May 1878
(*Courtesy of The Hyde Collection*)

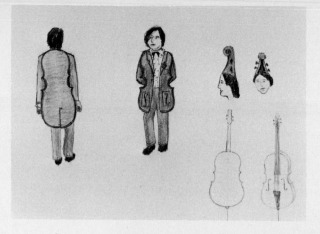

Wilde's cello coat, worn to the
opening of the new Grosvenor
Gallery, 1 May 1877,
as imagined by Lucy Ellmann

In Greek costume during a trip
to Greece, April 1877
(*Courtesy of The Hyde Collection*)

Two of Wilde's favorite paintings:
San Sebastian (above), by Guido Reni
(*Palazzo Rosso, Genoa*), and *Love and
Death* (right), by George F. Watts
(*City of Bristol Museum and Art Gallery*)

through sale. He was nevertheless always in debt. In November 1877 he twice suffered the fashionable Oxford indignity of being called up before the Vice-Chancellor's Court, which had the power to enforce trades-men's unpaid debts, on the 16th and the 30th. The first case was for £20 owed to a tailor, Joseph Muir of 20 High Street, for such items as a 'Super Fancy Angola Suit.' Wilde had to pay the debt plus almost £3 more for court costs. The second case was for £5/18/6 still owed to M.G.H. Osmond, Jeweller, at 118 St Aldates, out of a former debt of £16, largely for Masonic regalia. On this occasion he was ordered to pay the debt plus twenty-five shillings in costs. The archives of the University have a letter from Wilde protesting the amount:

> *Monday*   Magdalen College, Oxford
>
> Dear Sir I desire to have the enclosed bill taxed [inspected] as I consider it a most extortionate and exorbitant claim. The balance of the bill for which the tradesman summoned me was I think £5.10: certainly a good deal under six – and it appears to me that if nearly £3 costs are allowed on a £5 bill, the Vice-Chancellor's Court must be conducted on a system which requires the investigation of the University Commission: I trust that this monstrous claim will not be allowed. I remain your obedient servant
>   OSCAR WILDE[22]

Clearly he has mixed up the court costs for the first bill with those for the second. It is hard to imagine any other undergraduate of the time making this mistake, let alone accusing the Vice-Chancellor's Court of embezzlement.

Another blow had come after his half-brother Henry Wilson's early death on 13 June 1877. Wilde had dined with Wilson only a few days before, and had not sensed how alarmed his half-brother was by poems published in Catholic magazines. He and Willie expected to be the sole heirs, but Wilson left £8,000 to St Mark's Hospital, with £2,000 going to Willie and £100 to Oscar, and that only if he remained a Protestant. As to Illaunroe, which Wilson and Oscar Wilde owned jointly, Wilson's share was made over conditionally upon Wilde's not becoming a Catholic for five years. Otherwise it would go to Willie.[23] Oscar persuaded Willie to give up his reversionary interest for £10, but his sense of the Catholic Church as an unaffordable luxury deepened.

Vindication

The mind of a thoroughly well-informed man is a dreadful thing. It is like a bric-à-brac shop, all monsters and dust, with everything priced above its proper value.

Neither now nor later did Wilde allow his uncertain future to interfere with present enjoyments. His mother's idea that he might live comfortably on the £200 annual interest from his inherited capital was not his. Whether or not money came in, he spent it. Some went to enable him to dress magnificently. Not only were there the cello coats and the Super Fancy Angola suits, but on 1 May 1878 he dazzled an all-night fancy dress ball, given by Mr and Mrs Herbert Morrell at Headington Hill Hall for 300 guests, by wearing a Prince Rupert costume with plum-colored breeches and silk stockings. This finery pleased him so well that he bought it from the hiring firm and wore it playfully in his rooms. Those rooms in turn were filled with exquisite objects, not only blue china but Tanagra statuettes brought back from Greece, Greek rugs bought with the help of William Ward, photographs of his favorite paintings, and his famous easel sporting its unfinished painting. He would explain the easel by owning that he sometimes felt the need to 'find expression through the veiling medium of colour. Some artists feel their passion too intense to be expressed in the simplicity of language, and find in crimson and gold a mode of speech more congenial because not quite so translucent.' So, as Wilde informed the *Biograph*, he might some day become an artist.

His décor included also the talismanic lily, sanctified by Ruskin in *The Stones of Venice* as one of the most beautiful and most useless things in the world. Gilbert and Sullivan were to parody lily love in *Patience* in 1881. Some have assumed that this cult began later. But Wilde himself said that he filled his rooms at Oxford with lilies. A friend of his, Douglas Sladen, recalls in *Twenty Years of My Life*, 'At one time he banished all the decorations from his rooms, except a single blue vase of the true aesthetic type which contained a "Patience" lily.'[24] This testimony connects with that to be found in a novel, *Second Thoughts* by Rhoda Broughton, published in May 1880 but written during the two preceding years.

Rhoda Broughton had come to live in Oxford at this time, and had put Wilde off by her skill in combats of wit. She was therefore not invited to his 'Beauty Parties,' but her friend, the novelist Margaret Woods, was, so Rhoda Broughton was well informed of aesthetical goings-on. In *Second Thoughts* she introduced a 'long pale poet' named Francis Chaloner, who is 'flaccid limbed,' has an 'early Byzantine face,' and wears the hair of his 'Botticelli head' very long.[25] Given the still sparse population of aesthetes in Oxford at the time, Wilde seems definitely meant. The poet escorts the heroine to 'a great white lily standing in a large blue vase,' the same one that Sladen observed. The décor of Chaloner's rooms sounds like an exaggeration of Wilde's; here too are unfinished pictures on easels, one a portrait of Venus, the other of Heracles' page Hylas (also a subject of the sculptor Roderick Hudson in Rhoda Broughton's friend Henry James's novel), as if to point up the sexual ambiguity of aesthetic young men. Wilde's Pateresque patter, and Rhoda Broughton's repartee, are rendered in Chaloner's question, 'Do you never wish for a larger life? more utterly human? more rhythmical? Fuller?', and the heroine's reply, 'Never!' Chaloner writes poems about 'sweet-sick' subjects, and thinks they 'should be read . . . to the low pale sound of the viol or virginal, with a subtle perfume of dead roses floating about, while the eye is red with porphyry vases and tender Tyrian dyes.' Wilde's delayed rejoinder came in a review of 28 October 1886, where he said, 'In Philistia lies Miss Broughton's true sphere, and to Philistia she should return.'

As this early satire indicates, the figure of the aesthete, once the Pre-Raphaelite, was being reconstituted at Oxford in the late 'seventies. On 26 April and again on 3 May 1877, the *Oxford and Cambridge Undergraduate's Journal* took official note of the movement, first praising it faintly as a civilizing influence, then recanting to dispraise it for seeking 'insidiously' to obtain not open but '*implicit* sanction' for 'Pagan worship of bodily form and beauty,' and for renouncing 'all exterior systems of morals or religion' in the name of liberty and nature. The *Journal* was of two minds about it.

Wilde was aware that aestheticism had a history which long preceded the coinage in 1750 of the word 'aesthetic' by the philosopher Baumgartner. In an article of 4 September 1880, he pointed out that in Plato's *Symposium* the host, Agathon, was 'the aesthetic poet of the Periclean age.'[26] The proponent of the lily called attention to the title of Agathon's lost play, 'The Flower.' (Wilde confused *Antheus* with *Anthos*.) Not only Plato, but also Aristophanes, had portrayed Agathon in 'brilliant colours,' said Wilde. Actually the latter, in his *Thesmaphoriazusae*, mocked aesthetic effeminacy more sharply than Rhoda Broughton by having Agathon go among the women in drag.

If the classical world was divided about its 'aesthetic poet,' the nineteenth century was equally so. Aestheticism had been given a sanction by Kant when he spoke of art as disinterested, and as creating a second nature through human agency. Such ideas were absorbed by Théophile Gautier, a favorite of Wilde, and expressed in his celebrated preface to *Mademoiselle de Maupin*. Against conventional notions, Gautier announced that art was completely useless, amoral, and unnatural. His novel illustrated his views by nonchalantly presenting a heroine with bisexual tastes, which in the end she lavishly gratifies. The theme of variable sexuality was set by Gautier's heroine for the rest of the century. Wilde particularly liked a later manifestation of it in Rachilde's *Monsieur Vénus*.[27]

Yet Mademoiselle de Maupin had scarcely begun to make her way in the world when the movement she authorized was subjected to an equally powerful attack. Within six years Soren Kierkegaard published his *Either/Or*, in which he anatomized aesthetic man. Unlike ethical man, aesthetic man is so caught up in a succession of moods, to each of which he surrenders wholly, that he loses touch with the personality he wished to express. For fear of losing the mood, he cannot afford to reflect, nor can he attempt to be more than what he for that mood-moment is. He moves from sensation to sensation, much in the manner that Pater was later to extol. Kierkegaard seems to be refuting Pater before Pater wrote.

Wilde did not know Kierkegaard's book, but he knew an up-to-date assault on aestheticism in W. H. Mallock's *The New Republic*, which he pronounced to be 'decidedly clever' when he read it in 1877, soon after its publication.[28] Mallock contrasted aesthetic man, whom he calls 'Mr Rose' (based upon Walter Pater), with ethical man, 'Mr Herbert' (based upon Ruskin), and gives Herbert the victorious part. Their views are instructively divergent: for Herbert the modern age is degenerate, for Rose it is the best age of all, since it commands all the possibilities of sensation that earlier ages have discovered, along with its own. Indeed, it is implied that the Renaissance has never ended, but has expanded in modern times. Against Herbert's eloquent insistence upon restraint and moral improvement, Rose delights in a poem which he says was written by an eighteen-year-old undergraduate. In its equal treatment of pagan and Christian, it reads like a parody of Wilde's 'Sonnet Written in Holy Week at Genoa.' The poet recounts three 'visions' he has had in one night's sleep, the first of white-limbed Narcissus, the second of Venus rising from the sea, the third of the lean Thomas Aquinas in his cell. When the first two flee, the poet turns, with diminished enthusiasm, to the saint and Christ. As in Gautier, the object of sexual interest is variable, though Mallock presents Rose as a pornographic brooder rather than an active lover. It was a charge that Wilde would echo later when he accused Pater of detachment, meaning that he lacked the courage to act.

Oxford aestheticism, as developed by Wilde, proved to be of a peculiarly knowing kind. Self-parody was coeval with advocacy. Wilde could see by the time he reached Oxford, that the movement was going out as much as it was coming in. Though he adopted some of its interests, such as tints and textures, he did so always with something of his mother's high-spiritedness, poking fun at his own excess. His literary preferences were at first towards something quite unaesthetic and earnest, such as Mrs Browning's *Aurora Leigh*, which he praised inordinately as 'much the greatest work in our literature.'*[29] (Ruskin said it was greater than Shakespeare's *Sonnets*.) A copy Wilde presented to his friend William Ward contains passages marked with great approval.[30] He knew as well as Mallock or Kierkegaard that aestheticism was limited. In a letter to a

---

* Eventually he wished it had been written in prose.

young woman enclosing a photograph of Burne-Jones's water color, *Spes*, he wrote, 'In so many of Burne-Jones's pictures, we have merely the pagan worship of beauty: but in this one I seem to see more humanity and sympathy than in all the others.'[31] The parade of these divergent qualities, with a view to their ultimate reconciliation, was the method of Wilde's early poems, and can be found in two that he was writing during this last full year at Oxford. One was 'The Sphinx [or Sphynx],' begun – he said – in 1874, and the other his poem for the Newdigate Prize, 'Ravenna.'

They are very different works, but both are set pieces, revolving around a fixed object and brooding upon it. That they come from the same period, though 'The Sphinx' would not be finished for a long time, is perhaps indicated by their sharing the poet's juvenescence:

> . . . one who scarce has seen
> Some twenty summers cast their doublet green
> For Autumn's livery . . .
>   'Ravenna'

An extant page of the 'Sphinx' manuscript has a rough drawing by Wilde of some affrighted dons, and, for what it is worth, the speaker describes himself as a student.[32]

Both poems interweave a state of mind with a historical or legendary past. 'The Sphinx' is in the true aesthetic mode, foisting upon the stone monster a medley of pagan and Christian legends, the homosexual Adrian and Antinous in close conjunction with heterosexual Isis and Osiris, Venus and Adonis, and Mary and Jesus incongruously in the offing. But the student who embroiders this fantasy is gradually revolted by it, and drives the Sphinx away:

> False Sphinx! False Sphinx! By reedy Styx old Charon, leaning on his
>   oar,
> Waits for my coin. Go thou before, and leave me to my crucifix,
>
> Whose pallid burden, sick with pain, watches the world with wearied
>   eyes,
> And weeps for every soul that dies, and weeps for every soul in vain.

The final line indicates that the speaker, like Wilde, was still having difficulties accepting the doctrine of the Atonement, and it throws doubt on the speaker's devotion to the religion he is professing.

In 'Ravenna' the young man recalls his journey there the year before, and muses elegiacally upon its fallen greatness. Collapse was always one of Wilde's themes. As in 'The Sphinx,' the 'fond Hellenic dream' (which Wilde introduces as if to justify his Grecian travels) is evoked only to be rejected when the vesper bell is rung. Wilde put aside his Catholic inclinations to work into the poem the triumphal return of Victor

Emmanuel to Rome in 1871, when the king ousted Pius IX from the Quirinal Palace. Hunter Blair, on reading the passage, remonstrated that Wilde had once called the dethroned Pope, 'the prisoned shepherd of the Church of God,' but Wilde replied with disarming candour: 'Don't be angry, Dunskie. You must know that I should never, never have won the Newdigate if I had taken the Pope's side against the King's.'[33] The poem is a clever hodgepodge of personal reminiscence, topographical description, political and literary history. It contains apostrophes to Dante and Byron. The latter is called 'a second Anthony, / Who of the world another Actium made,' but Wilde has to check his own rhetoric by lamely noting that Byron did not succumb to Egyptian wiles but went to fight for Grecian liberty. As to Ravenna, the city is alternately regarded as doomed and evergreen, and the poet, to finish off, promises inconclusively to love it for ever. Wilde seems to have had *Childe Harold* as his model, and at a Newdigate remove the poem has something of Byron's easy energy, even when uttering such clichés as

> We see Death is mighty lord of all,
> And king and clown to ashen dust must fall . . .

By the end of March 1878 Wilde had finished 'Ravenna,' and handed it in, anonymously as required, on the very day (the 31st) that he had entered the city a year before. After that he fell ill, of an unspecified malady, and spent some days in bed in Magdalen, enjoying the luxury of being brought flowers by his friends. He then convalesced for a few days in Bournemouth. But physical sickness had perhaps revived his never quelled anxiety about the state of his soul. In 1877, when Newman had come back to Trinity College, Oxford, for the first time in thirty-two years, to receive an honorary fellowship, Wilde had dreamed 'of a visit to Newman, of the holy sacrament in a new Church, and of a quiet and peace afterwards in my soul.'[34] But what particularly stirred him in 1878 may well have been the memory of what was advisedly called 'a positive sin.'

It was at Oxford that an event occurred that was to alter his whole conception of himself. Wilde contracted syphilis, reportedly from a woman prostitute.* As a doctor's son, he had been inclined to minimize

* My belief that Wilde had syphilis stems from statements made by Reginald Turner and Robert Ross, Wilde's close friends present at his death, from the certificate of the doctor in charge at that time (see p. 547), and from the fact that the 1912 edition of Ransome's book on Wilde and Harris's 1916 life (both of which Ross oversaw) give syphilis as the cause of his death. Opinion on the subject is however divided, and some authorities do not share my view of Wilde's medical history. Admittedly the evidence is not decisive – it could scarcely be so, given the aura of disgrace, shame, and secrecy surrounding the disease in Wilde's time and after – and might not stand up in a court of law. Nevertheless I am convinced that Wilde had syphilis, and that conviction is central to my conception of Wilde's character and my interpretation of many things in his later life.

illness, so this came as an especially crushing blow. In the 1870s medical authorities followed Sir Jeremy Hutchinson's advice that anyone contracting the disease should wait two years before marrying, and undergo a course of mercury treatment. The main physical effect of mercury on Wilde was to turn his slightly protrusive teeth black, so thereafter he usually covered his mouth with his hand while talking. (Mercury did not cure the disease, though it was reputed to do so.) But the mental effect was profound. Like his father he had been subject to fits of melancholy; now there was a new warranty for them.

The awareness of his vulnerability was related to a sense of doom which he said in *De Profundis* was pervasive in his works. It had distant connections with a sense of doom that he had most poignantly encountered in adolescence, in Aeschylus's *Agamemnon*. That play had never been far from his thoughts, and in 1877 he published in *Kottabos* his translations of some speeches of Cassandra and the Chorus from it. His accompanying note emphasized 'doom': 'Agamemnon has already entered the House of Doom, and Klytaemnestra has followed close on his heels – Kasandra is left alone upon the stage . . . She sees blood upon the lintel, and the smell of blood scares her . . . ['I have slipped in blood. It is an evil omen,' Wilde's Herod would say.] Her second sight pierces the palace walls; she sees the fatal bath, the trammelling net, and the axe sharpened for her own ruin and her lord's.' Wilde did not confuse his own doom with Agamemnon's, but the sense of a strange fatality hanging over him did not leave his consciousness.

His poems offer some evidence of his feelings. In 'Taedium Vitae' he speaks of 'that hoarse cave of strife / Where my white soul first kissed the mouth of sin.' This may have been the poem advertised by a bookseller as addressed to the woman from whom Wilde contracted syphilis.[35] In 'The Sphinx' the speaker, a student, says in an impassioned moment,

> Are there not others more accursed, whiter with leprosies than I?
> Are Abana and Pharphar dry that you come here to slake your thirst?

This allusion is to the leprosy about which in the Old Testament Naaman, the Syrian captain, consults the prophet Elisha. On being told to bathe in the Jordan, Naaman indignantly replies, 'Are not Abana and Pharphar, rivers of Damascus, better than all the waters of Israel?' (II Kings 5) Wilde's interest in Naaman continued; he gave his name to the executioner in *Salome*.* An unused line for 'The Sphinx' addresses her as 'You

---

* If the imagery of Naaman may be taken as an index, Wilde seems to have contracted his illness before he met Constance Fletcher, for in her novel *Mirage*, Davenant (Wilde) suddenly asks like Naaman, 'Are not Abana and Pharphar, rivers of Damascus, better than all the waters of Israel?' (II:175) The question makes little sense in *Mirage*, but more in 'The Sphinx.' Presumably Wilde, beset with guilty thoughts, startled Miss Fletcher with the question. In *The Duchess of Padua*, Guido echoes the line when he says, 'Are there no rivers left in Italy?'

mirror of my malady.' The portrait of Dorian Gray was another such mirror. Its composition was contemporary with his being 'grievously ill, of a "nervous fever,"' which Lionel Johnson suspected to be the result of 'Tiberian excess.'[36]

Upset as he was, Wilde came as close now to becoming Catholic as he ever would until his deathbed. The month after he was confined to his bed, April 1878, he went to speak confidentially to the fashionable priest of the day, the Reverend Sebastien Bowden, at the Brompton Oratory in London. Bowden was known for his conversions among the well-to-do. What was said can be divined from the letter Bowden wrote to Wilde afterwards:

My dear Mr Wilde,

Whatever your first purpose may have been in your visit yesterday there is no doubt that as a fact you did freely and entirely lay open to me your life's history and your soul's state. And it was God's grace which made you do so.

You would not have spoken of your aimlessness and misery or of your temporal misfortune to a priest in a first interview unless you hoped that I should have some remedy to suggest, and that not of man's making. Be true to yourself then, it was no power or influence of mine (which is nonsense to speak of) but the voice of your own conscience urging you to make a new start, and escape from your present unhappy self, which provoked your confession. Let me then repeat to you as solemnly as I can what I said yesterday, you have like everyone else an evil nature and this in your case has become more corrupt by bad influences mental and moral, and by positive sin; hence you speak as a dreamer and sceptic with no faith in anything and no purpose in life. On the other hand God in His mercy has not let you remain contented in this state. He has proved to you the hollowness of this world in the unexpected loss of your fortune and has removed thereby a great obstacle to your conversion; He allows you to feel the sting of conscience and the yearnings for a holy pure and earnest life. It depends therefore on your own free will which life you lead. As God calls you, He is bound, remember, to give you the means to obey the call.

Do so promptly and cheerfully and difficulties disappear and with your conversion your true happiness would begin. As a Catholic you would find yourself a new man in the order of nature as of grace. I mean that you would put from you all that is affected and unreal and a thing unworthy of your better self and live a life full of the deepest interests as a man who feels he has a soul to save and but a few fleeting hours in which to save it. I trust then you will come on Thursday and have another talk; you may be quite sure I shall urge you to do nothing but what your conscience dictates. In the meantime pray hard and talk little.

Yours very sincerely,
H. SEBAST[n] BOWDEN[37]

At last Wilde had been brought to the point of decision. Although Bowden's letter has been available for some time, what Wilde did in response to it has not been known. But André Raffalovich, himself a convert, was told by Father Bowden what happened next. On the Thursday, when Wilde was to be received into the Church, there arrived at the Brompton Oratory, instead of Wilde, a large package. On being opened this proved to contain a bunch of lilies. It was Wilde's polite way of flowering over his renunciation.[38] What he would say later of Dorian Gray was true of himself: 'It was rumoured of him that he was about to join the Roman Catholic communion; and certainly the Roman ritual had a great attraction for him . . . But he never fell into the error of arresting his intellectual development by any formal acceptance of creed or system, or of mistaking, for a house in which to live, an inn that is but suitable for the sojourn of a night in which there are no stars and the moon is in travail . . . no theory of life seemed to him to be of any importance compared with life itself.'* A few years later, asked by Asquith what his religion was, Wilde replied, 'I don't think I have any. I am an Irish Protestant.'[39] He adopted mercury rather than religion as the specific for his dreadful disease. Perhaps now the parable of Dorian Gray's secret decay began to form in his mind, as the spirochete began its journey up his spine toward the meninges.

It was perhaps soon after this that Wilde exhibited the obverse of his penitence. His turn had come to read the lesson in the Magdalen chapel, with Prince Leopold present. Wilde leafed over the pages and began in a languorous voice, 'The Song of Solomon.' Dean Bramley swooped down from his stall, and thrusting his beard into Wilde's face, cooed out, according to Atkinson, 'You have the wrong lesson, Mr Wilde. It is Deuteronomy 16.' In later life, as Ainslie recalled, Wilde was facetiously opposed for membership in the Crabbet Club on the grounds that as a Magdalen Demy he had read the lessons in a surplice. Wilde admitted the offense but pleaded in extenuation, 'I always read the lessons with an air of scepticism, and was invariably reproved by the President after Divine Service, for "levity at the lectern."'[40]

In June Wilde took the examinations for Final Schools. A future scholar named Horton, who was present, observed him 'with his flabby face and ruffled hair striding up to the desk for fresh paper after the first hour; then handing in his book half an hour before time was up. He was a genius, and for him to pose was second nature.'[41] Whatever his demeanor, he expected a fourth not a first, as he confided to his friends. But some of the questions played into his hands. For example, he was asked about 'the geographical position and military importance of the following places: –

---

* Lord Henry Wotton is more cynical: 'Religion consoles some. Its mysteries have all the charm of a flirtation, a woman once told me, and I can understand it. Besides nothing makes one so vain as being told that one is a sinner.'

Potidaea, Heracleia, Plataea, Naupactus, Mantieneia [*sic*].' It was as if he were being quizzed on his travels with Mahaffy, and he knew all the answers. (In 'Ravenna' he had written, 'O Salamis! O lone Plataean plain!') Another question that suited him was, 'What causes led Aristotle to insist on the superiority of the speculative to the practical life?' His Commonplace Book shows that he had been pondering this question:

> If Philosophy aims at some good to man it comes too late in the day for that: for while religions preside over the birth of nations, philosophy often follows them to their grave. It is not till the twilight comes that the owl of Athena begins its flight.
>
> So in Aristotle the philosophic life is the contemplative life: He expressly disavows any philanthropic aim to Sophia . . .
>
> It is good says Aristotle for its own sake because it is an 'arete of the soul': the fact of its existence is the reason of its existence.
>
> Bacon's scornful words are its glory. Like a virgin consecrated to God, it bears no fruit. Its duty is to comprehend the world not to make it better.
>
> Its sphere is the Universal – the Universal law of the Mind's movement. It examines not what ought to be but what is. It is the possession of real wisdom, not the love of wisdom.

He adduced Plato for support, 'The end of life is not action but contemplation, not doing but being,' and added, 'to treat life in the spirit of art is to treat it as a thing in which means and end are identified. To witness the spectacle of life with appropriate emotions . . .' He is delighted when Euripides – a favorite of his – makes a character say, 'Stand off and view my sorrow as a painter might.'

In 'The Critic as Artist' Wilde would flesh out this skeleton. Of course his equation of art and contemplation extends Aristotle and Plato in a way those philosophers would scarcely approve:

> Society often forgives the criminal. It never forgives the dreamer. The beautiful sterile emotions that art excites in us, are hateful in its eyes, and so completely are people dominated by the tyranny of this dreadful social ideal that they are always coming shamelessly up to one at Private Views and other places that are open to the general public, and saying in a loud stentorian voice, 'What are you doing?' whereas 'What are you thinking?' is the only question that any single civilised being should ever be allowed to whisper to another . . . But someone should teach them that while, in the opinion of society, Contemplation is the gravest sin of which any citizen can be guilty, in the opinion of the highest culture it is the proper occupation of man . . . To Plato, with his passion for wisdom, this was the noblest form of energy. To Aristotle, with his passion for knowledge, this was the noblest form of energy also . . . To us, at any rate, the Bios Theoretikos is the true ideal.

When he was asked by the examiners what Aristotle would have thought of Whitman, he must have divorced Whitman's cult of 'myself' from any considerations except that of self-development.

While the scripts were being read by the examiners, Magdalen held a commemoration ball. Wilde was there, evidently with another grand coat on, for Margaret Woods recalled a conversation with him about it. He did not dance well, so they stood talking away from the dance floor. He suddenly swung round and said to her, 'Isn't it sad for me, when I love beauty so much, to have a back like this?' She recognized that it was a cue to praise his back, and the coat that covered it, but she found herself replying unhelpfully, 'You should join the Volunteers. They will soon straighten it for you.' Wilde's boyish vanity was wounded.*[42]

But it would soon receive a surfeit of gratifications. First came the results of the Newdigate, on 10 June. It had been judged by the Public Orator (T. F. Dallin), the Professor of Poetry (J. C. Shairp), and three members of Congregation whose names are unrecorded. On 11 June the President of Magdalen noted in his Minute Book: 'The Newdigate Prize has been awarded to Oscar O'F Wilde, Demy of Magdalen . . . The last time the College gained the Newdigate was in 1825 by R. Sewell. By obtaining this prize Mr Wilde becomes entitled to the following bequest by Dr Daubeny, who died on December 13, 1867: "I desire my Executor to retain my Marble Bust of the young Augustus, and give it as a Prize to the first Member of Magdalen College after my decease who shall gain the Newdigate Prize Poem."' The bust was duly presented. Meanwhile the public announcement had earned Wilde a great deal of praise. A congratulatory letter came from Aubrey De Vere in Dublin. But the most ecstatic praise came of course from Lady Wilde, who saluted her son 'To the Olympic Victor' and wrote:

> 1 Merrion Square, North
> Tuesday – one o'c

Oh, Gloria, Gloria! thank you a million times for the telegram. It is the first pleasant throb of joy I have had this year. How I long to read the poem. Well, after all, we have *Genius* – that is something attorneys can't take away.

Oh, I do hope you will now have some joy in your heart. You have got *honour* and *recognition* – and this at only 22 [23] is a grand thing. I am proud of you – and am happier than I can tell – This gives you a certainty of success in the future – You can now trust your own intellect, and know what it can do. I should so like to see the smile on your face now. Ever and ever with joy and pride

> Your loving Mother[43]

---

* He still praised highly her novel, *A Village Tragedy*, in a review of November 1887.

The letter discloses that she accurately recognized his spiritual malaise, which involved anxiety over his future as well as compunction over his past. As she predicted, his spirits were lifted with the award of the Newdigate. The winner had the duty of reading it aloud at Encaenia, but the Professor of Poetry, Shairp, had the duty to suggest improvements before the official ceremony. Wilde listened to all Shairp's suggestions and respectfully took notes, but left the poem as it was.[44] His public reading on 26 June, for which Mahaffy and Willie Wilde came over, went well. *The Oxford and Cambridge Undergraduate's Journal* reported next day, 'The Newdigate was listened to with rapt attention and frequently applauded.'* Magdalen asked Wilde to stay on for a few days until the Magdalen Gaudy, where they 'said nice things about me. I am on the best terms with everyone including *Allen*! who I think is remorseful of his treatment of me.'[45]

Now came his second great achievement. The examiners in Final Schools summoned him for his *viva voce* on his written papers, and instead of questioning spent their time complimenting him. They discussed further his view of what Aristotle would have thought of Whitman. He had feared that his technical work, as opposed to his essays, would bring him down, but his tutor Sargent told Hunter Blair that Wilde's examination as a whole was the best of his year. The same had been true of his Honour Moderations examination two years earlier. He was awarded a rare double first. The news made almost as much impact as the Newdigate, not least in Magdalen. 'The dons are "astonied" beyond words – the Bad Boy doing so well in the end!' Wilde wrote to William Ward.[46] With minimal prompting from Wilde the college on 7 November 1878 remitted to him the amount that had been deducted from his Demyship the previous year. Since he had yet to pass the Divinity examination, without which he could not take his degree, his Demyship was extended for a fifth year.†

Where all this would lead was not clear. No fellowship had been offered him. A career in poetry or criticism looked financially bleak. There remained the course that his mother was always urging upon both him and Willie, to marry an heiress.‡ Unfortunately Florence Balcombe could not qualify, and no one else was in his mind. But if he had no marital prospects or career prospects, he had evidence, as his mother said, that he could not fail.

---

* The *Journal* would later think better of its praise, issuing a vicious review of the printed text on 30 January 1879.

† As was customary, however, he had to leave his college rooms, and he seems to have moved into lodgings with a Mrs Brewer at 76 High Street.

‡ His brother Willie was giving the game away by his eagerness. Ethel Smyth describes how he persuaded her into an engagement after only a few hours of acquaintance. She found strange his request to keep the arrangement quiet for the moment. He was probably similarly committed to someone else. She shortly broke it off but kept his ring.[47] He was unsuccessful with other young women as well.

And so Wilde created himself at Oxford. He began by stirring his conscience with Ruskin and his senses with Pater; these worthies gradually passed into more complicated blends of Catholicism, Freemasonry, aestheticism, and various styles of behavior, all embraced fervently but impermanently. Initially, his letters reveal, he tried to resolve his own contradictions and berated himself for being weak and self-deceiving. But gradually while at Oxford he came to see his contradictions as a source of strength rather than of volatility. His contemporaries, 'the dullard and the doctrinaire,' might have their world of decision-making and conformity, but in having it they had to deny another world of secret impulse and furtive doubt. His paradoxes would be an insistent reminder of what lay behind the accepted or conventional. 'A truth in art is that whose contradictory is also true,' he would declare in 'The Truth of Masks.' This was the great lesson which his immersion in various movements had taught him, first about art, then about life. He would be neither a Catholic nor a Freemason; aesthetic one moment, he would be anaesthetic the next. This conclusion jibed with what was perhaps involuntary, his oscillation between the love of women and of men.

As a result, Wilde writes his works out of a debate between doctrines rather than out of doctrine. In 'Hélas!', the poem which he would preface to his first book of verse, he indicates that in yielding to pleasure he has given up his austerity, that the heights as well as the depths still attract him. In his first play, *Vera*, the heroine plans to kill the Czar, but instead saves his life, as if she had suddenly been made aware of her own contradictory impulse and decided not to resist it. When Wilde writes a 'Sonnet to Liberty' about political revolutionaries, he disparages them in the octave but at the end of the sestet is suddenly impelled to say, 'God knows it I am with them, in some things.' *The Picture of Dorian Gray* is a critique of aestheticism, which is shown to bring Dorian to ruin; yet readers have been won by Dorian's beauty and regretful, rather than horrified, at his waste of it, so that he has something of the glamor of a Faust rather than the foulness of a murderer and drug-addict. And Wilde, feeling that the book had too much moral, subverts it with a preface which expounds sympathetically some of that aesthetic creed by which the book shows Dorian to be corrupted. In *Salome* Wilde allows the tetrarch Herod to pass from sensual delectation as he watches Salome dance the dance of the seven veils, to spiritual revulsion as he watches her kiss the dead lips of Iokanaan, and finally to outraged conscience as he orders the guards to kill her. Lady Windermere has to discover that in all her puritanism she is capable like other people of doing something utterly adverse to her principles. In *An Ideal Husband* Lady Chiltern has to reconcile herself to the fact that behind every ideal husband is a real secret. In *The Importance of Being Earnest* Wilde parodies his own tendency to look for contradictions by having serious Jack turn out to be frivolous Ernest. 'The wise contradict themselves,' Wilde declares in his 'Phrases and Philosophies for the Use of the Young,' and in *De Profundis*, which he wrote in prison, Wilde offers himself as a penitent but within this guise begins to turn into a martyr, to be released and reborn and justified. In his last work, *The Ballad of Reading Gaol*, the hero of which has slit his wife's throat with a razor, Wilde suddenly turns upon the *hypocrite lecteur* to say that we are all murderers of the thing we love.

This sudden perception of a truth opposed to the home truth we are all prepared to acknowledge, and just as plausible, was Wilde's answer to what he called the 'violence of opinion' exhibited as he saw by most of his contemporaries. He traced his own detachment from that violence to Oxford, where he said he had learned 'the Oxford temper,' though it was really his own temper. By the time he left the university he could see that life's complexity could not easily be codified into thirty-nine or even forty-nine articles, into ten or twenty commandments, into pluses and minuses awarded to this person or that creed. Wilde was a moralist, in a school where Blake, Nietzsche, and even Freud were his fellows. The object of life is not to simplify it. As our conflicting impulses coincide, as our repressed feelings vie with our expressed ones, as our solid views disclose unexpected striations, we are all secret dramatists. In this light Wilde's works become exercises in self-criticism as well as pleas for tolerance.

ADVANCES

CHAPTER V

Setting Sail

There is nothing like youth. The middle-aged are mortgaged to Life. The old are in life's lumber room. But youth is the Lord of Life. Youth has a kingdom waiting for it. Everyone is born a king, and most people die in exile, like most kings. To win back my youth . . . there is nothing I wouldn't do – except take exercise, get up early, or be a useful member of the community.

Looking for Work

Summer diminished Wilde's euphoria. He had an anxious time over his Bray houses, which unwittingly he and an estate agent with whom they were listed sold at almost the same moment to different purchasers. The unsuccessful bidder sued to invalidate the sale, but Wilde, in his first appearances in a law court, on 8, 11, 17 July 1878, was able to win a verdict with costs. He had, however, incidental expenses which, since he regarded them as heavy, must indeed have been so. His vacation came to an end with bitter news. Shortly before he was to return to Oxford, he learned, though not from her, that Florence Balcombe, now twenty years old, had accepted a proposal of marriage from Bram Stoker. (They were married on 4 December 1878.) Stoker, later the author of *Dracula*, was at this time known as an enterprising Irish civil servant and drama critic, seven years older than Wilde. He had often come to 1 Merrion Square, and at Trinity had put Wilde up for the Philosophical Society. Two years before he had promoted an Irish tour by Henry Irving, and in October – without Wilde's knowing – he agreed to become business manager of the Lyceum Theatre which Irving had just taken over. On the strength of this new position, Stoker was better than Wilde for Florence Balcombe, who had aspirations to become an actress. In any case, Wilde, though he now almost had his degree, evidently did not feel he was in a position to marry. His obligatory two years' wait after syphilis had been diagnosed was not over. He wrote to her a proud and eternal farewell. He was leaving Ireland, he announced, 'probably for good,' so they would never see each other again. He asked her to give him back the gold cross he had presented to her two years before. Because it bore his name conjoined with hers, she could never wear it, and he would keep it in memory of two years during which 'the currents of our lives' had flowed together, 'the sweetest of all the years of my youth.' His sense of disappointment was still keen two and a half years later, when, on 3 January 1881, he sent her anonymously a crown of flowers for her stage début. 'She thinks I never loved her, thinks I forget. My God, how could I?' he wrote to Ellen Terry as intermediary.[1] Yet his letters to Florence Balcombe in 1878, after her engagement, sound distressed, not shattered. She probably provided the occasion for five poems expressing dejection. In London later on they would become friends again.

His friends the Oswald Sickerts, with whom he stayed at Neuville near Dieppe early in October, saw no sign of depression. Their fifteen-year-old daughter Helena, whom Wilde called Miss Nelly, testified later to his joyfulness and wholehearted laughter. He took pleasure in quoting his poem 'Ravenna' to her, and seeing her interest in verse, presented her with a copy of Matthew Arnold's poems. Her two brothers, aged seven and five, found him a delightful playmate. He told them all preposterous stories and when Helena showed scepticism, he would reply, with mock sadness, 'You don't believe me, Miss Nelly. I *assure* you . . . well, it's as good as true.'[2]

He left Neuville for Oxford, and prepared to pass in November the Divinity examination which had proved a stumbling-block two years before. This being no great matter after his double first, he whiled away the time in sociability. It was now that he became friendly with a paler poet, Rennell Rodd, four years younger than he was. Rodd, later raised to the peerage as Lord Rennell of Rodd for his work in the diplomatic service, was Wilde's successor as Oxford aesthete. As he acknowledged in his autobiography, Wilde liberated him from convention in thought and action. Rodd was also spurred on to win the Newdigate in 1880. Wilde took his disciple everywhere, to Windsor to visit Lord Ronald Gower, who pronounced him 'full of artistic desires, unable to develop them at Balliol,'[3] and to London, to meet Whistler, in whose friendship Rodd was eventually to take Wilde's place. Rodd was the prime mover in a little magazine of verse published in Oxford by Blackwell's from 1880 to 1882, entitled *Waifs and Strays*, to which he persuaded Wilde to contribute. Yet almost from the first their friendship was discountenanced by Rodd's family, and Rodd himself seems to have been both stimulated and made uneasy by Wilde, foreseeing that his friend's iconoclasm might lead to trouble.

On 22 November Wilde passed his Divinity examination, and took his degree of Bachelor of Arts six days later. Soon afterwards he was off to London. The departure from Oxford's age-old surroundings and assured friendships was not easy for him. In March he went back for a visit and in years to come did not lack pretexts for frequent returns. In the early Nineties his love affair with Alfred Douglas reintroduced him to under-graduate life. Not long before his death, casting about for a humorous epithet by which posterity might remember him, he canonized himself as 'the infamous St Oscar of Oxford, Poet and Martyr.'[4] Oxford had replaced Dublin as his provenance.

Not to be at Oxford was unpleasant enough for him to take steps to reconnect himself. Unfortunately Magdalen, where he was at last in favor, had no vacancy in classics. (Herbert Warren, destined to be the college's next President, had been elected to the last fellowship to fall vacant in classics, in 1877.) The years 1878 and 1879 happened to be unusually lean ones in all the colleges so far as classics fellowships were concerned. Three were offered, at Trinity, Jesus, and Merton. Wilde is known to have applied for that at Trinity, which entailed a six hour examination extend-ing over two days. His behavior at the examination was recalled by another candidate, Lewis Farnell, later a distinguished Oxford classicist though also unsuccessful in this instance. After Wilde had looked at the first part, which was in philosophy and contained such lazy questions as, 'What is the relation between metaphysic and ethic? metaphysic and religion? metaphysic and art?', he stood up and stretched before the hall fire. He then turned to his fellow applicants to say, 'Gentlemen, this paper is really the work of a very uncultured person. I observe the word "metaphysic" [without the *s*] in every question. That word is never heard in polite society.'[5] He was right about metaphysics, but the examiners, whether or not they heard of his fastidiousness, did not elect him.

His efforts continued. On 28 May 1879 he had written to A. H. Sayce, Oxford Professor of Comparative Philology, whom he had come to know through Mahaffy, to ask about the possibility of an archaeological studentship at Oxford. On 8 December he pursued the matter:

> I think it would suit me very well – as I have done a good deal of travelling already – and from my boyhood have been accustomed, through my Father, to visiting and reporting on ancient sites, taking rubbings and measurements and all the technique of *open air* archaeologica – it is of course a subject of intense interest to me – and I should give myself to it with a good deal of enthusiasm. Your support would of course be invaluable – I hear there are many competing.[6]

Too many, or the wrong ones – Wilde did not get it.

He kept up his interest in Greek. Faithful as always to the *Agamemnon* of Aeschylus, he proposed to Frank Benson that the play be put on at Oxford in the original Greek. He claimed to have distributed the parts, chosen the costumes, and arranged the scenery for the production that took place the next year.[7] His friend Rennell Rodd was the scene painter. Benson played Clytemnaestra, and W. L. Courtney the Watchman, when the play was produced on 3 June 1880 in the Hall of Balliol. Wilde was in the audience, along with Browning, Tennyson, and Andrew Lang. In the same year he confided to the *Biograph* that he planned to publish two or three essays about 'Greek matters.' One was probably an essay he wrote for the Chancellor's Essay Prize in 1879. (By a quirk of the Oxford statutes he was still eligible, in spite of having gone down, to compete for this prize.) The subject, 'Historical Criticism in Antiquity,' seemed cut out for him; the essay he offered was longer than anything he would ever write in the discursive mode, and did not escape an uncharacteristic tediousness.

The praise he gave to ancient historians for secularizing history by refusing to accept myths and legends he would not have given later;* he did it now, no doubt in part with an eye to his chances. The subject had a ticklish corner: what to do when Christianity took over from paganism? Wilde was veering away from his former devoutness, but bore in mind that his examiners were probably in orders. So he qualified his praise of the historian Polybius by adding an orthodox sigh: 'But the turning of all men's hearts to the East, the first glimmering of that splendid dawn which broke over the hills of Galilee and flooded the earth like wine, was hidden from his eyes.' When he quotes a sceptic like Herbert Spencer, he is quick to remind his readers that even Spencer covertly acknowledged the existence of a reality subsuming both spirit and matter.

Otherwise, the organization of this essay was rickety, a defect which Wilde attempted to override by frequent references to his structural 'plan.' The range of reference, to Fichte, Hegel, Vico, Comte, Montesquieu, and De Toqueville, was impressive. But in only a few paragraphs does he appear to be writing in character. His praise of Polybius, unusual for the time, showed his independence, and testified to a fellow feeling for Polybius's idea of a universal history. 'He indeed of all men,' he said, 'is able, as from some lofty tower, to discern the whole tendency of the ancient world, the triumph of Roman institutions and of Greek thought which is the last message of the old world and, in a more spiritual sense, has become the Gospel of the new.' The catholicity of Christianity was in his mind, but Wilde seems also to be thinking of his own place at the end of a romantic century, and of his aspiration towards a synthesis, heralded by his essay on the Grosvenor Gallery, that would reconcile Pater, Ruskin, Morris, Swinburne, Symonds, and the painters of the time.

In fifth-century Athens Wilde finds an analogy to the Victorian age. 'The new age is the age of style. The same spirit of exclusive attention to form which made Euripides often, like Swinburne, prefer music to

---

* In 'The Decay of Lying' he declares, 'The ancient historian gave us delightful fiction in the form of fact; the modern novelist presents us with dull facts under the guise of fiction.' Elsewhere he said, 'History never repeats itself. The historians repeat each other. There is a wide difference.'

meaning and melody to reality, which gave to the later Greek statues that refined effeminacy, that overstrained gracefulness of attitude, was felt in the sphere of history.' The reference to effeminacy is characteristic; Wilde never fails to seek out dangerous ground. Similarly, he calls attention to the overthrow of the Peisistratid tyranny 'not by the love of freedom, but, as Thucydides insisted, by the jealous love of tyrant and liberator alike for Harmodius, then a beautiful boy in the flower of Greek loveliness.' He cannot resist his own suspect cadences.

The examiners may have disagreed with the ideas or disliked the lack of structure in the essay. They took the unusual course of not awarding the prize. Wilde's response is not recorded. But he continued various attempts to make use of his classical learning. He wrote to George Macmillan, his old travelling companion in Greece, that he would gladly translate Herodotus for the latter's publishing house, and would like also to edit a play – preferably *Hercules Furens* or *The Phoenician Maidens* – of Euripides on whom he had been working 'a good deal lately.'[8] He did not carry out either of these projects. He also sketched an essay on Greek women, in which he awarded the palm to Nausicaa, Andromache, Penelope, and Helen. The beauty of Nausicaa was such that Sophocles, himself beautiful, played the role in a drama. Wilde did not publish this essay.

On 4 September 1879 he wrote anonymously for the *Athenaeum* the greater part of a long review of Volumes X and XI of the *Encyclopaedia Britannica*, in which R. C. Jebb had contributed essays on Greek history and literature. Jebb, the Irish-born scholar at Cambridge, famous for his work on Sophocles, was a *bête noire* of Mahaffy, who had conducted a long controversy with him in 1876 and 1877, and Wilde shared his old tutor's dislike. In his historical essay, Wilde said, Jebb had wrongly stated that Themistocles was ostracized for intriguing with the Persians, a misunderstanding of ostracism, which was a punishment never inflicted on any definite accusation and least of all for high treason. More centrally, Jebb had no inkling of the enormous interests at stake at Marathon and Salamis, and no general views on the relation of Greek history to modern. But the literary essay was worse still: Jebb failed to mention Menander or Agathon, 'the aesthetic poet of the Periclean age,' or 'Hero and Leander,' treated Polybius as a 'mere chronicler,' and presented Theocritus only as a pastoral poet. In so doing, Wilde said, Jebb ignored the 'Pharmaceutria,' which 'for fiery colour and splendid concentration of passion is only equalled by the Attis of Catullus in the whole range of ancient literature.' Wilde's attack was, as E. R. Dodds commented, 'an early example of the romantic reaction against the orthodox Victorian assumption that the hallmark of all the best Greco-Roman literature was its serenity and balance. Jebb was throughout his life an exponent of this view. Wilde is quite justified in citing against it the "Pharmaceutria" of Theocritus and Catullus's "Attis," two splendid poems which no one could call serene or balanced.'⁹ Wilde was perhaps too captious for the *Athenaeum*, for he was never to review in its pages again.

Still probing for a chink in the wall, Wilde during this period of confusion applied for a post as inspector of schools. It was a position which had been dignified by Matthew Arnold's having held it. In a letter written probably early in 1880 to Oscar Browning, Wilde remarks that rents in Ireland are 'as extinct . . . as the dodo or moly,' and asks him for a testimonial.¹⁰ 'Any education work,' Wilde says, 'would be very congenial to me,' and assumes that Browning's name would carry weight with the authorities. He shows here an unaccustomed naïveté, for Browning's forced resignation from Eton in suspicious circumstances made his recommendation of doubtful value. Wilde was turned down. He disapproved of contemporary methods of education. 'People say that the schoolmaster is abroad,' he would say in 'The Critic as Artist,' and add, 'I wish to goodness he were.' He thought that 'the man who is so occupied in trying to educate others . . . has never had any time to educate himself.' 'Nothing that is worth knowing can be taught,' he insisted, and urged that the true goal should be self-culture. In pursuit of this he remembered fondly how he himself had been educated at home for most of his childhood, and would offer his own children the same privilege. Such opinions could hardly have won over the electors of an inspector of schools.

His failure in these applications, and his sense that his money from the sale of the houses at Bray was slipping through his generous fingers, did not cause him great concern. He had increasing confidence. So did his mother, envisaging a career in Parliament for him as once she had envisaged it for Willie, who by this time was back in Ireland, idling. A letter from Wilde to Reginald Harding admitted that he had not 'set the world quite on fire as yet,'¹¹ but in a way he had begun to do so. London, though slow to welcome newcomers, had welcomed him. He had met Gladstone, Asquith, Balfour, Rosebery and others, who soon learned the pleasure of his company. On meeting Disraeli, Wilde said, 'I hope you are very well,' only to have that eminence rejoin, 'Is one ever very well, Mr Wilde?'¹² His antics were sometimes remarkable. The artist Louise Jopling recalled opening the door to him, to find him with a large snake twisted around his neck. He assured her that its poison sac had been extracted. But it was his tongue, not his reptilian collar, that won attention. This was not always favorable. Frank Benson, meeting him at a theatre, heard someone say, 'There goes that bloody fool Oscar Wilde.' Wilde brightly remarked, 'It's extraordinary how soon one gets known in London.' More solemnly, he remarked to the wife of Julian Hawthorne, 'I should never have believed, had I not experienced it, how easy it is to become the most prominent figure in society.'¹³ London offered him the opportunity to carry out the project he had set for himself earlier; as he wrote in *De Profundis*, 'I remember when I was at Oxford saying to one of my friends . . . that I wanted to eat of the fruit of all the trees in the garden of the world, and that I was going out into the world with that passion in my soul. And so, indeed, I went out, and so I lived.'[14] Amid that orchard the tree of life, with its 'blind lush leaf,' stood next to the tree of knowledge, with its 'staring fury.'

The residue of £2,800 for his Bray houses enabled Wilde to set himself up in London, sharing bachelor quarters with Frank Miles. In conversation with the actress Elizabeth Robins he found a lofty precedent: 'Shakespeare wrote nothing but doggerel lampoon before he came to London and never penned a line after he left.'[15] In the early months of 1879, he and Miles found a place at 13 Salisbury Street off the Strand. The house, Wilde said, was 'untidy and romantic.' According to Lillie Langtry, it had old staircases, twisting corridors, and dim corners. The family that ran it was Dickensian in its eccentricities.[16] Wilde promptly named it Thames House, since they had a view of the river. There were three floors; Miles and his studio occupied the top; Wilde the floor below; and on the ground floor a Bluecoat schoolboy named Harry Marillier was allowed to keep his books and to study. One day Wilde ran into Marillier on the stairs and asked him who he was. The boy spoke of his school and his study of Greek, and Wilde invited him upstairs. What he saw amazed Harry: a long sitting room was done entirely in white panelling, utterly at variance with the dishevelled character of the house; there was blue china, and lilies were everywhere. Edward Poynter's portrait of Lillie Langtry stood on an easel at one end of the room like an altar. Wilde had brought down from Oxford his Damascus tiles, some drawings by Blake and Burne-Jones, his Greek rugs and hangings, his Tanagra figures, and had bought some expensive furniture.[17] Harry needed no persuasion to bring Wilde coffee in the mornings in exchange for help with his Greek.

Frank Miles was in many ways a congenial fellow-tenant. Two years older than Wilde, he had decided early on an artistic career. His representation of clouds had roused Ruskin to comment, 'With his love for his mother and his ability to paint clouds he must get on.' He had encouraged him as 'the coming Turner.'[18] Miles won the Turner Prize at the Royal Academy in 1880. That he was almost color-blind, as he confessed in secret to Lillie Langtry, restricted his success in any medium except drawing, but he could do skilful likenesses, making his women sitters prettier than they were but still recognizable. Heinrich Felberman, editor of the magazine *Life*, appointed Miles his artist-in-chief, and ran a series of society portraits by him. His drawings were often reproduced under titles such as, 'I've Been Roaming,' 'The Widow's Mite,' 'The Young Blind Girl,' 'Pity,' or 'The Gardener's Daughter,' and were sold in editions of many hundreds as Victorian pin-ups. The Prince of Wales purchased Miles's portrait of 'The Flower Girl.'

Miles was tall, blond, good-looking and affable. His father, rector of Bingham in Nottinghamshire, was well to do, and fond of his mildly gifted and apparently highminded son. But highminded did not quite describe Miles, as Wilde had reason to know. There was his puzzling intimacy with Lord Ronald Gower, who took Miles abroad and also invited him often to his house in Windsor. More suspect was his intimacy with young girls. A violet seller named Sally, who had been painted by Lord Leighton, Marcus Stone, and W. F. Britten, was among those taken into his house by Miles.[19]

The world knew nothing of this. Thames House offered a kind of salon. The P.B.s (Professional Beauties) whom Miles sketched were frequent visitors, along with artists such as Whistler and Burne-Jones, actors and actresses, even the Prince of Wales. There was one guest who was specially prized.

Beauties on the Stage

Poets know how useful passion is for publication. Nowadays
a broken heart will run to many editions.

Lillie Langtry, arising from Jersey like Venus from the foam, if we can tolerate Wilde's opulent metaphor, was a breathing myth. Her first official appearance was at a party at Lady Sebright's house, 23 Lowndes Square, in May 1876. There her classic features – 'the grave low forehead, the exquisitely arched brow; the noble chiseling of the mouth, shaped as if it were the mouthpiece of an instrument of music; the supreme and splendid curve of the cheek; the augustly pillared throat* which bears it all' – as Wilde with careful rapture described them, instantly overwhelmed the assembled guests.[21] She was like an unprepared actress suddenly given a new part to play. Whistler and Millais asked to paint her, Frederick Leighton to do her head in marble; and Frank Miles on the spot made two sketches of her and handed her one as an oblation. The actors Henry Irving and Squire Bancroft, also among the guests, were not behind-hand in their praise, nor was George Lewis, the astute solicitor. Just when London needed a new Professional Beauty, Lillie Langtry suddenly was there.

Soon she was posing for the portrait which Millais, also from Jersey, entitled 'The Jersey Lily,' although in it she holds a Guernsey one. G. F. Watts painted her with a more demure rubric, and a Quaker bonnet, as 'The Dean's Daughter' (her father combined the functions of cleric and rake). She posed in a yellow gown for Edward John Poynter, whose portrait Wilde acquired and displayed on the easel at the end of his sitting room. He had photographs of her as well. When she refused, from fatigue rather than artistic preference, to sit for Edward Burne-Jones, he stood

* Graced with the three *plis de Vénus*, according to Lady Randolph Churchill.[20]

outside her window and serenaded her cruelty towards artists until she relented and agreed to pose. The serenaders must have tripped over each other, for there is an account of Wilde singing in the same place his apologies for having annoyed her with the remark, 'I will predict, accurately, all human behavior except that which governs the human heart. Man is constant in his infidelity and woman puts him to shame because she is, by nature, fickle.' He compared her to Helen of Troy, and said, like Yeats after him, 'Yes, it was for such ladies that Troy was destroyed, and well might Troy be destroyed for such a woman.'[22] Max Beerbohm, writing much later, called her Cleopatra, or more archly, Cléopatre.

Wilde had met her soon after the Sebright party. His friend Bodley, judged unworthy to lunch with Pater, was again left out; after Wilde and he saw *Our Boys* at the Vaudeville Theatre in 1876, Wilde excused himself with the enthusiastic explanation, 'I am going to meet the loveliest woman in Europe.'[23] The introduction took place in Frank Miles's studio. In *The Days I Knew* Mrs Langtry described the tall young man, with his profusion of brown hair worn long, and his face 'so colourless that a few pale freckles of good size were oddly conspicuous. He had a well-shaped mouth, with somewhat coarse lips and greenishhued teeth. The plainness of his face, however, was redeemed by the splendour of his great, eager eyes.' She took in his 'large and indolent hands,' with pointed fingers and 'perfect shaped filbert nails,' like his father's not always clean. 'He had one of the most alluring voices that I have ever listened to, round and soft, and full of variety and expression.' She welcomed him as a friend.[24] For him, her beauty was 'a form of genius.' He was engaged in the same storming of London by his wits that she was achieving by her looks. Then too, they were both weary, Wilde of being an overage undergraduate, Mrs Langtry of being wife to a nondescript Irish yachtsman, and both eager to perform on a larger stage. She complaisantly allowed her two young admirers, Wilde and Miles, to dedicate themselves to her interests. Miles predicted to Ronald Gower that he and Wilde, by pencil and pen, would make Lillie Langtry 'the Joconde and the Laura of this century.'[25] His drawings of her were reproduced and circulated, and Wilde wrote, with comparable fanfare, half a dozen poems. Once he went to Covent Garden to purchase some lilies to give to her and was waiting for a hansom when an unkempt child, fascinated by the mass of flowers, exclaimed, 'How rich you are!' Wilde told the story to Ruskin, who was enchanted by it.[26]

After he moved to London in December 1878 Wilde's friendship with Lillie Langtry flourished. She liked having him about. Though indiscreet by nature and conviction, he was perhaps thinking of her when he said to André Raffalovich, 'A woman's name should be like the secret name of Rome, never mentioned.'[27] He mentioned Lillie Langtry's a good deal. Near the end of his life he talked of her in such a way as to allow Vincent O'Sullivan to wonder if he had been one of her lovers.[28] That he was close to being so appears to be confirmed by two poems. In one, 'Humanitad,' he refers to her Greek features when he speaks of 'the arched splendour of those brows Olympian,' and declares, 'of thy too perilous bliss / My lips have drunk enough – no more, no more . . .' The other poem, which he published after his marriage under the unconfiding title of 'Roses and Rue,' bore in manuscript the title, 'To L.L.,' and eventually regained it under Robert Ross's editorship. The various versions of this poem and some attendant poems describe something like the following incidents: the lover and his beloved had met often by a garden seat. One day in June, probably 1879, their relationship became more intense when he 'stooped and kissed her.' But a shower interrupted these overtures, and she ran towards the house, only allowing him to catch up and kiss her once more just before they went inside. She was wearing an amber-brown dress, with two little bows that rose from her shoulders, and she looked at him with her grey green eyes. (Some said Lillie Langtry's eyes were blue, some grey.) The lover must have offered an apology for his lack of worldly accomplishments. Unencouragingly, the beloved said, 'You have wasted your life. You have only yourself to blame that you are not famous.' The rejected lover rushed off through the garden gate, turning back to see her hand waved in farewell. It was a subject for a Grecian urn. In his poem Wilde insists, in an unexpected way for an aesthete, upon his sincerity rather than his art:

> I had wasted my boyhood, true:
>> But it was for you.
> You had poets enough on the shelf,
>> I gave you myself.

The versification is so bad as to hint that the sentiment was genuine. The related poem, 'Glokokris Eros' ('The Flower of Love'), finds another mode of self-defense:

> I have made my choice, have lived my poems, and, though youth is
>> gone in wasted days,
> I have found the lover's crown of myrtle better than the poet's crown
>> of bays.

Whatever his preference, he seems, except perhaps for a brief interlude, to have contented himself with the poet's crown of bays, so far as Lillie Langtry was concerned. It was a period, 1879–80, when Mrs Langtry had caught the eye of the most important lover in England, the Prince of Wales. Edward constituted himself her protector, refusing invitations to parties unless she was invited, so insuring that she was at once respected and available. Two contretemps, however, he could not prevent: in October 1880 Edward Langtry went bankrupt and all the

Langtry possessions were sold up. About the same time or a little earlier, Lillie Langtry conceived a child. To prevent gossip, she spent the months of obvious pregnancy in Jersey, and only returned to London in the summer of 1881, leaving her daughter, Jeanne (not by her husband), to be discreetly brought up on the island. Wilde was almost certainly among the few who knew the delicate line Mrs Langtry was treading between social prestige and opprobium, and he delighted in her success in braving out the role of virtuous wife on the London proscenium. He used the incident as the basis for his first successful play, *Lady Windermere's Fan* (1891), where Mrs Erlynne returns from the Continent to find her abandoned daughter grown up. When he offered her the part, Mrs Langtry scoffed at the notion that she could play a woman with a grown-up daughter. (She was then thirty-nine.)[29] So Wilde took the play away, and gave Mrs Erlynne the speech, 'Besides, my dear Windermere, how on earth could I pose as a mother with a grown-up daughter? I have never admitted that I am more than twenty-nine, or thirty at the most. Twenty-nine when there are pink shades, thirty when there are not.'

Aside from her beauty, Lillie Langtry had a good deal of shrewdness. Recognizing her own shortcomings, she was glad to have Wilde's help in rectifying them. He talked to her about the classics, and brought her in 1881 to King's College, London, to hear the lectures of Sir Charles Newton, the discoverer of Halicarnassus. This became a morning ritual: the students would wait outside the building until the cab bringing her and Wilde arrived, and cheer them in. He told her about Ruskin, and even brought them together, though Ruskin drove her out of the room in tears with one of his diatribes against Jezebels. 'Beautiful women like you hold the fortunes of the world in your hands to make or mar,' he called after her retreating form.[30] Wilde tutored her in Latin, and while it is tempting to believe that if the lessons began with Caesar, they ended with Ovid, a letter referring to them, probably written in 1879, gives nothing away:

Sunday   Beaconsfield, Milehouse, Nr Plymouth

Of course I'm longing to learn more Latin but we stay here till Wednesday night so I shan't be able to see my kind tutor before Thursday. Do come and see me on that afternoon about six if you can.

I called at Salisbury Street about an hour before you left. I wanted to ask you how I should go to a fancy ball here, but I chose a soft black Greek dress with a fringe of silver crescents and stars, and diamond ones in my hair and on my neck, and called it Queen of Night. I made it myself.

I want to write more but this horrid paper and pen prevent me so when we meet I will tell you more: (only don't tell Frank)

LILLIE LANGTRY[31]

Evidently she was accustomed to following his taste in dresses, though capable of striking out for herself. Wilde's fascination with her Queen of Night costume is probably behind the line in his poem, 'The New Helen,' when he considers that perhaps she is Semele:

> Or didst thou rule the fire-laden moon?

He suggested that she wear a more extreme version still. As he told Graham Robertson, 'The Lily is so tiresome, she won't do what I tell her. I assure her that she owes it to herself and to us to drive daily through the Park dressed entirely in black, in a black victoria drawn by black horses, and with "Venus Annodomini [a good pun on Anadyomene]" emblazoned on her black bonnet in dull sapphires. But she won't.'[32] What all this came to was that he accustomed the imperfectly educated but teachable Mrs Langtry to conversation, and helped not only to publicize but also to create her as he was creating himself.

Another of the three surviving letters from her to Wilde apologizes for having forgotten the brougham, and says that since she cannot forgive herself she must ask him to forgive her. The wording is confident and shows who had control. Evidently he received many slights, and losing her favor was forbidden her house. At one such time she appeared in the theatre, where he and Frank Miles had taken their seats; and on seeing her Wilde burst into tears and had to be helped out by Miles.[33] Given her obligations to the Prince of Wales and other more favored lovers, Mrs Langtry – as she says in *The Days I Knew* – found Wilde occasionally in the way. Still, he was wonderful company, and rumour had it that each day he carried a lily in his hand to her, a custom from which W. S. Gilbert profited in *Patience*. It seems likely that Wilde did so sometimes, because Frank Miles was an ardent gardener and cultivated lilies and narcissi in particular, as if in tribute to Mrs Langtry and to Wilde, respectively. Wilde was also ostentatiously writing his poem, 'The New Helen,' for her, and insisted that he had to find equivalents for artist's sittings the better to inspire his muse. So once Edward Langtry, the Menelaus to Lillie's Helen, came home in the early morning hours to trip over Wilde huddled on the doorstep, waiting for a glimpse of Mrs Langtry as she alighted from her carriage after some even later engagement. Even if Wilde had only to go around the corner to huddle, for at this time they were living near each other, it was a fine bit of stage business, and perhaps more heartsick than that.

'The New Helen' insists upon the mythological character of Lillie Langtry. Wilde had always a great appreciation of women as spreaders of havoc, Salome, the Sphinx, and, in 'Charmides,' Athena, being among them. He wrote 'The New Helen' to a late nineteenth-century prescription, begotten by Gautier upon Swinburne upon Pater upon Wilde. The object was to link the living woman with both pagan and Christian prototypes. So while, she is mostly Helen:

> Where hast thou been since round the walls of Troy
>   The sons of God fought in that great emprise?

she is keenly aware of the new dispensation, and like Aphrodite has been hiding from

> The face of Her, before whose mouldering shrine
>   To-day at Rome the silent nations kneel;
> Who gat from Love no joyous gladdening . . .

But she is, like Mona Lisa, closer to Christianity still, even to the point of heresy:

> And at thy coming some immortal star,
>   Bearded with flame, blazed in the Eastern skies,
> And waked the shepherds on thine island-home.

He borrows from the Litany of the Blessed Virgin some of his epithets:

> Lily of love, pure and inviolate!
>   Tower of ivory! red rose of fire!

So he salutes her both for her experience, as Helen of Troy, and for her innocence, as the embodiment of 'spiritual love.' Though he begs her to be 'kind to me, / While yet I know the summer of my days,' he defers to 'the red lips of young Euphorion,' as a subject must to the Prince of Wales. Lillie Langtry liked the poem enough to print it in its entirety in her autobiography, a compliment Wilde would have appreciated.

A problem more pressing for Mrs Langtry than to arise 'from the depths of sapphire seas' to please her poet friend was to make ends meet. The Prince was generous, but volatile, and not to be depended upon for a monthly stipend. Miles, the eager gardener, proposed that she go in for horticulture. Wilde was quick with a reproof, 'Would you compel the Lily to tramp the fields in muddy boots?'[34] Miles proposed that she should become a landscape gardener, an idea also discarded. Whistler urged her to become an artist. Wilde insisted that she should become an actress. Having beauty already, he said, she could quickly develop technique. She saw it as a way of becoming her own mistress rather than someone else's. Her friends rallied, and Henry Irving offered her a big part for which she decided she was not ready. A good job on *Life*, where Frank Miles's drawings were featured, was also offered and refused.[35] Wilde introduced her to Henriette Labouchere, the wife of the MP and editor of *Truth*,

Henry Labouchere. Mrs Labouchere had been an actress, and was now coaching prospective players. She trained Mrs Langtry to take a part with her in a two-character play lasting a half-hour, *A Fair Encounter*, on 19 November 1881. From this the pupil quickly graduated to playing Kate Hardcastle in *She Stoops to Conquer* on 15 December 1881, and then on 19 January she had a small part in Tom Taylor's *Ours*. The Prince of Wales favored her performances with his presence, and in no time she was an established actress. Although never so proficient on the stage as she was beautiful, Lillie Langtry did well enough. Wilde, as much as anyone, kept her up to the mark.

His insistence that she become an actress reflected his own delight in the theatre. He was a regular theatregoer, and the possibility of writing a play was beginning to take hold of him. He longed to have a great performer speak lines he had written, and when the fiery Polish actress, Helen Modjeska, came to London in 1880 to play in *Heartsease* (an adaptation of *La Dame aux camélias*), he was one of the first to seek her acquaintance. For the moment he had nothing to show her, and she found the phenomenon of Wilde astonishing. 'What has he done, this young man,' Mme Modjeska asked, 'that one meets him everywhere? Oh yes he talks well, but what has he done? He has written nothing, he does not sing or paint or act – he does nothing but talk. I do not understand.'[36] (Wilde said in his own behalf, 'Talk itself is a sort of spiritualised action,'[37] and he praised the criminal Wainewright because 'The young dandy sought to be somebody, rather than to do something.')* Modjeska was at first resistant to his overtures, and declined an invitation to his house by saying, 'Mr Borenta is unwell and cannot possibly accompany me. It is true that an old woman like me [she was forty] ought not to be afraid to pay visits to young men – but it is always better to avoid danger *et je tiens beaucoup rester un ange*.'[38] But she was gradually won over, and by late 1880 she was glad to avail herself of Wilde's abilities by having him translate a hundred-line poem she had written, 'Sen Artysty; or The Artist's Dream.' Clement Scott then published it in *Routledge's Christmas Annual* for 1880. And probably soon afterwards, she came to tea at last, with Lillie Langtry and the painter Louise Jopling. Wilde sounded her out about acting in a play he was writing. When they left, he ceremoniously presented each of the three women with a long-stalked Annunciation lily.[39]

Two other actresses for whom he also hoped some day to write parts were Ellen Terry and the great Bernhardt herself. Sarah Bernhardt arrived in London in May 1879. Histrionic gestures were expected of her admirers, and perhaps the most successful was that of Pierre Loti, who the year before had had himself carried in to her, wrapped in a large and

---

* In Henry James's *The Tragic Muse* the aesthete Gabriel defends himself against a similar charge by saying, 'O having something to show's such a poor business. It's a kind of confession of failure.'

expensive Persian carpet. Wilde could not match this extravagance, but he did well enough. He went to Folkestone with his friend, the actor Norman Forbes-Robertson, as a quasi-official delegation to meet her boat. Forbes-Robertson had only a gardenia to hand her, and someone was heard to say, 'They will soon be making you a carpet of flowers.' Wilde, sensing his cue, said, *'Voilà!'* or its English equivalent, and cast an armful of lilies at her feet.[40] Bernhardt was charmed. She soon inscribed her signature on the white panelling of Thames House as one of Wilde's guests, and one night she offered to show how high up the wall her foot could kick.

She seemed to have lived the life of sensations as fully as a disciple of Pater could wish. With a bankrupt's nonchalance, she urged her young friends, 'Money's meant to be spent. Spend it, spend it!'[41] Wilde had no need of particular exhortation, but he could recognize a daemonic element in her. He described how, when he took tea with her, she was 'lying on a red couch like a pallid flame.'[42] Robert Sherard fancied that Wilde had copied from Bernhardt her golden voice, but beside hers (in spite of elocution lessons from the actor Hermann Vezin), his was only gilded. Mme Bernhardt paid him a compliment too. 'Most men who are civil to actresses and render them services have an *arrière-penseé*,' she said. 'It is not so with Oscar Wilde. He was a devoted attendant, and did much to make things pleasant and easy for me in London, but he never appeared to pay court.'[43] To be praised for lack of inclination was scarcely praise.

Still, if he wanted an impulse to write for the theatre, she gave it to him. On 2 June 1879 she opened in *Phèdre* as if to challenge the supremacy of Rachel, whose *succès fou* in the same play twenty-four years before in London was legendary. Wilde was of course at the first night. It was 'not until I heard Sarah Bernhardt in *Phèdre*,' he commented, 'that I absolutely realised the sweetness of the music of Racine.'[44] He wrote a sonnet to her, which Edmund Yates published in *The World* on 11 June. As with Lillie Langtry, he traced Bernhardt to ancient Greece – his ultimate tribute – but found appropriately infernal imagery for her:

> Ah, surely once some urn of Attic clay
>   Held thy wan dust, and thou hast come again
> Back to this common world so dull and vain,
> For thou wert weary of the sunless day,
>   The heavy fields of scentless asphodel,
>   The loveless lips with which men kiss in hell.

He had said that Lillie Langtry's head could be found only on silver coins of Syracuse, and now he enlisted Mrs Langtry's aid in searching among the Greek coins in the British Museum for Sarah Bernhardt's profile.

Mrs Langtry put up with this rival with good grace, even when it was rumoured that the Prince of Wales had temporarily defected from her arms to those of Bernhardt. She was rewarded by Bernhardt's gracious prediction of a stage future for her, '*Avec ce menton elle ira loin.*'[45] Wilde probably had this in mind when Lady Bracknell says to Cecily, 'The chin a little higher, dear. Style largely depends on the way the chin is worn. They are worn very high, just at present.' Wilde formed a lifetime ambition of having Bernhardt act in one of his plays.*

The most agreeable of the actress friends he made in these years was Ellen Terry. She pleased him by encouraging Mrs Langtry's stage ambitions, and condoning the lapses in her acting of which Mrs Langtry was sensibly aware. Her own career had been arrested for four years because of marriage to Watts and then a love affair with Edward Godwin, during which she bore two children; but Irving brought her back in 1878 to be his leading lady at the Lyceum. Wilde was swept away by her performance as the queen, Henrietta Maria, in his quasi-kinsman W. G. Wills's play, *Charles I*, on 27 June 1879. Her appearance in the second act inspired his sonnet, written at the theatre, with its lines,

> In the lone tent, waiting for victory,
> She stands with eyes marred by the mists of pain,
> Like some wan lily overdrenched with rain . . .

He never found a better display for his ubiquitous talisman of the lily. Close to cliché as it was, it struck Ellen Terry, at least, as exactly what she was trying to represent. He would soon follow up this advantage by sending her, in September 1880, a privately printed copy bound in dark red leather, with her name in gold letters, of his first play. 'Perhaps some day I shall be fortunate enough to write something worthy of your playing' was his tactful accompanying note. Ellen Terry did not respond by the immediate offer to play the heroine that he hoped for, and Henry Irving, another recipient, offered only polite thanks. Another actress, the American Genevieve Ward, to whom an ornate copy also went, proved pleasant

---

* He dreamed, as Ricketts recalled, of having her perform in a play he would write about Queen Elizabeth. '"She would look wonderful in monstrous dresses covered with peacocks and pearls!" He thought of having "Princess Elizabeth and her lover, the Lord High Admiral Seymour, watched by the pathetic Catherine Parr and the sinister Lord Protector [Wilde believed that Elizabeth had borne a child by Seymour]; the Queen and Essex and the tragic passion of Lady Shrewsbury." He would often relate the quaint episode when the Scottish Ambassador undertook to bring Elizabeth, disguised as a page, to the court at Holyrood to see Mary Stuart. I am still astonished that this subject, and the tremendous death scene of the Queen, have remained untouched, though I have heard him say with mock seriousness "Of course the death of Elizabeth gave great encouragement to the revival of our literature."'[46]

but uncooperative, as had Madame Modjeska. But Wilde had forcefully answered Modjeska's and Lillie Langtry's complaint of idleness. Neither his hobnobbing with players nor the enactment of a new role in English culture exhausted his capacity. It was as a playwright that he claimed his place.

Irishman among the Muscovites

A Russian who lives happily under the present system of government in Russia must either believe that man has no soul, or that, if he has, it is not worth developing.

Agitators are a set of interfering, meddling people, who come down to some perfectly contented class of the community and sow the seeds of discontent among them. That is the reason why agitators are so absolutely necessary.

The play that Wilde had circulated with such fanfare was *Vera; or, The Nihilists*. His sub-title introduced a current problem into a tale of old Russia. Having disengaged himself from both Roman Catholicism and Freemasonry, the first public yet subversive, the second secret but respectable, he moved on to a similar perplexity in the political sphere. As he hunted success among foreigners, he expressed in his writing a sense, largely dormant at Oxford, of himself as Speranza's son, eager to free his country from the yoke of the English whose favor he needed.

In verses and in conversation he gave evidence of mounting political emotions. His sonnet to Ellen Terry praised her pathos in the queenly role for making him briefly forget 'my life Republican.' In another 'Sonnet to Liberty,' he expressed his dislike of agitators,

> Not that I love thy children, whose dull eyes
> See nothing save their own unlovely woe,
> Whose minds know nothing, nothing care to know –

but found in roaring Democracies, reigns of Terror, and great Anarchies congenial images of his own wildness. Yet, as if to renounce such sanction, he concludes equivocally but honestly,

> and yet, and yet,
> Those Christs that die upon the barricades,
> God knows it I am with them, in some things.

115

Wilde was like his mother in hating mob rule and excess, and in admiring personal heroism and feeling fellowship with the oppressed. Rennell Rodd recorded how, at this time, when a flood forced many people out of their houses in Lambeth, Wilde took him to see if they could be of help. There was an old bedridden Irish woman in a tenement whom Wilde so cheered with his stories, and with some money, that she cried out to him, 'May the Lord give you a bed in glory.'[47] His politics were grounded in such sympathies.

He was not satisfied with paternalism. In conversation with young Violet Hunt, he declared himself: 'I am a Socialist.' By socialism he did not mean any specific variety, but a general hatred of tyranny. He would say later that Socialism is 'beautiful,'[48] and that 'Socialism is enjoyment,' a definition that he knew might be applied to aestheticism as well, an ultimate rapprochement of these two being dimly apprehended. In his play, nihilism, socialism, and democracy are compounded. Prince Paul in *Vera* appears to be speaking for the author when he says, 'in good democracy, every man should be an aristocrat.' And Alexis, in a grandiloquent speech Wilde inserted in the play in 1883, is made to say, 'I do not know if I be king or slave: but if a slave what should I do but kneel, and if a king – where should kings sit, but at the feet of some democracy casting their crowns before it!'[49]

The politics of *Vera* reflected this aristocratic socialism. The general reputation of the czars for cruelty served him well, although the Czar of Russia at that time, Alexander II, had at least, while carrying out the customary tortures, emancipated the serfs. Wilde felt himself to be the voice of a large scale liberation. As he wrote to the actress Marie Prescott about *Vera*, 'I have tried in it to express within the limits of art that Titan cry of the peoples for liberty, which in the Europe of our day is threatening thrones, and making governments unstable from Spain to Russia, and from north to southern seas. But it is a play not of politics but of passion.'[50] He was eager to have it both ways. The time of the prologue was supposed to be 1795, and that of the four acts following 1800. He could rely on his audience's vagueness about Russian history, and perhaps his own as well, since the assassination of the reactionary Paul I took place not in 1800 but in 1801, and Alexander I, who followed him, was only ostensibly liberal. To avoid any idea of transcription, Wilde boldly rechristened these czars Ivan and Alexis. He was offhand about anachronisms such as trains and freed serfs, and to talk of Nihilists in 1800 was also precipitate, since Turgenev only coined the term in 1861 in *Fathers and Sons*. Wilde would admit the provenance later: 'The Nihilist, that strange martyr who has no faith, who goes to the stake without enthusiasm, and dies for what he does not believe in, is a purely literary product. He was invented by Tourgénieff and completed by Dostoieffski.'[51] His Nihilists in the play are united in their detestation of torture and martial law, and they insist that whatever is, is wrong.

If Wilde was cavalier about Russian history, he grounded his plot upon actual events. Wilde, like Walter Sickert, William Morris, and Shaw, was a friend of Sergei Mikhailovich Kravchinski, better known as Stepnyak – a Russian revolutionary of noble birth who assassinated General Mezentsev, chief of the Russian secret police.[52] But the play's source is another episode, not obscure in the newspapers in 1878, though time has obliterated it. On 24 January of that year a twenty-two-year-old woman shot the Chief of Police of St Petersburg, General Fyodor Fyodorovich Trepov, in an assassination attempt. She was the daughter of an officer of the Line, and belonged to the gentry, but had been a revolutionary since the age of seventeen. Trepov had infuriated her by imprisoning 'her lover, a Nihilist,' as *The Times* reported, and by ordering that one of their woman friends who was in prison be flogged. The case aroused international attention. The *Pall Mall Gazette* of 14 December 1889 said that 'her pistol shot rang like a bugle across Europe.' In the end the jury acquitted her of the crime in spite of her having confessed it, and Trepov was forced to resign his post. As the woman was leaving the courtroom, the police tried to re-arrest her, but her student friends prevented them. One student, said to be her brother-in-law, fired on the crowd and then turned his gun on himself.

The young woman's name was Vera Zassoulich, and Wilde took her over, along with her fierce revolutionary and amorous passions, for his heroine, Vera Sabouroff (originally called Katinski). He embroidered the facts by situating them in Moscow rather than in St Petersburg, and having the old Czar as the object of assassination. The brother-in-law turned into Vera Sabouroff's brother. Her Nihilist lover is retained, but is transformed into the Czarevich. Wilde shadowed forth experiences of his own in fobbing off the proctors and other authorities, by a comparable scene of soldiers pounding on the door in pursuit of Nihilists, only to be cajoled by Alexis into thinking that he and his masked associates are actors rehearsing a tragedy together.

While he borrowed the Nihilists' oath from 'The Catechism of a Revolutionary,' by S. C. Nechayev and Mikhail Bakunin, for the ritualistic opening of the Nihilists' meetings Wilde drew upon an unexpected English source. His friends in the Oxford Rose-Croix would have been astounded to read the beginning of Act I:

President: What is the word?
First Conspirator: Nabat. [This means 'Tocsin,' and was the actual name
                  of a revolutionary newspaper of the time.]
President: The answer?
Second Conspirator: Kalit.
President: What hour is it?
Third Conspirator: The hour to suffer.
President: What day?

Fourth Conspirator: The day of oppression.
President: What year?
Fifth Conspirator: The year of hope.
President: How many are we in number?
Sixth Conspirator: Ten, nine, and three.

For this exchange Wilde took over a theatrical Masonic ritual, 'Opening of a Lodge,' and turned the Worshipful Master into the President, the Senior Warden into the First Conspirator, and the Junior Warden into the Second. The President's questions are roughly those used in the ritual, although the Conspirators' replies are altered to suit their violent purposes.

While the play had a political subject, most of it was devoted to impugning revolutionary tenets. Alexis assumes the throne but remains a Nihilist, a royalist Nihilist bent upon reform; Vera is torn between revolutionary fervor and amorous submission. 'Why does he make me feel at times as if I would have him as my king, Republican though I be?' Why, indeed. The most interesting character is Prince Paul Maraloffski, the Prime Minister, who on being banished by the Czar throws in his lot with the Nihilists, disbelieving equally in both sides. Paul it is who stamps the play as Wilde's and no one else's. He is an Irishman in court and cabal, blasting shibboleths with his wit. 'He would stab his best friend,' says someone, 'for the sake of writing an epigram on his tombstone.' After reading the bill of rights of the Nihilists, which proclaims: 'Nature is not a temple, but a workshop: we demand the right to labour,' Paul comments, 'Ah, I shall surrender my own rights in that respect.' On reading another clause, 'The family as subversive of true socialistic and communal unity is to be annihilated,' he comments, 'I agree completely with Article 4. A family is a terrible encumbrance especially when one is not married.' Prince Paul is the first of that series of aristocratic dilettantes in whom Wilde delights even while punishing them for being detached and heartless. Paul is fond of saying '*Parbleu!*,' though he is happily free of such archaisms as 'methinks' and 'methought' in which Vera Sabouroff – her rhetoric lagging behind her politics – indulges.

The promotion of Vera Zassoulich's modest attempt to kill the Leningrad Chief of Police into Vera Sabouroff's mission to kill the Czar of All the Russias makes for a number of operatic scenes. In the final one Vera has to decide between her political and her amorous passions. The old Czar has been killed. She has planned to kill the new one for the sake of Russia; in an unexpected turn, she alters her resolution out of love and kills herself instead, saying 'I have saved Russia.' Prolonging the Czar's life proves a nobler course than abbreviating it. She exhibits her bloody dagger to the Nihilists so they will be deluded into thinking she has carried out her original purpose. Of the two causes for which Vera Sabouroff may be said to die, she no longer believes in Nihilism, but she does believe in love. In the complex exaltation of this ending, as Wilde insisted, his political play was more than political.

Granted that *Vera*, in spite of Prince Paul's efforts to save it, was a wretched play, it did not fall disastrously below the standard set by drama in a century when, as Stendhal said, plays could not be written. Wilde loftily submitted it to the chief theatrical personages in London, and to the actress Clara Morris in New York. Mrs Bernard Beere accepted the part. She had made her début at the Opéra Comique in the Strand four years before. *Vera* was scheduled for performance at the Adelphi Theatre on the afternoon of 17 December 1881.[53]

London Life

*Extraordinary thing about the lower classes in England –
they are always losing their relations. They are extremely
fortunate in that respect.*

Oscar Wilde was not the only member of his family in London. His mother and brother despaired of Dublin, Lady Wilde because tenants were failing to pay rents on her properties, and Willie because no Irishwoman with ready money was prepared to take him on as a husband. The house at 1 Merrion Square was sold by Willie early in 1879, and he and his mother arrived in London on 7 May of that year, in pursuit of Oscar. For a few days they used his address at 13 Salisbury Street, then installed themselves at 1 Ovington Square, then at 116 Park Street off Grosvenor Square, and eventually moved to 146 Oakley Street, Chelsea.

In surroundings less imposing than Merrion Square, Lady Wilde was not slow in starting up a London salon. On Saturday afternoons at first, then on Wednesday afternoons as well, she presided over a tea table where informed guests knew better than to try to drink the tea. The gatherings were preposterous yet picturesque, and those who attended came to laugh but stayed to marvel. Although Oscar Wilde was the principal drawing card, Willie did his bit as well, and Lady Wilde moved people purposefully about. She had grown heavier over the years, and sailed among her guests with swelling canvas. Her black wig was often topped with an imposing headdress, and her costumes, in the style of the 1860's, had large bodices and many flounces surmounted by strings of beads and pendants. Now almost sixty, she was not eager to exhibit either her wrinkles or her lack of a housekeeper, so the curtains were drawn at three in the afternoon, the gas jets were covered with red shades, candles flickered in the corners, and the guests peered at each other in the dim light.

Yet she was a *grande dame*, and could be depended upon for flashes of her familiar rhetoric. Her assumption was that all her guests were famous or about to become so. On meeting Helena Sickert, Walter's younger sister, who was still at school, she looked at her sharply and then pronounced, 'A highly intellectual countenance! I shall hear of you in the literary world.' Oscar, standing by, laughed and said, 'Oh come now, Mother! That's too bad.' She was equally unabashed in her introductions. 'Miss X,' she would say, 'allow me to present Mr Y, who has painted that picture the whole of London is talking about, which will be exhibited at the Grosvenor Gallery next season, and Mr Y, I must tell you that Miss X is going to be a London prima donna. You should hear her sing that aria from *Lohengrin*!'[54] That Mr Y could not paint or Miss X sing was no reason to stint praise. Perhaps they would be able to some day. Wilde parodied her in a Pickwickian passage of *Dorian Gray*, which out of filial piety he later removed: ' "Sir Humpty Dumpty – you know – Afghan frontier. Russian intrigues: very successful man – wife killed by an elephant – quite inconsolable – wants to marry a beautiful American widow – everybody does nowadays – hates Mr Gladstone – but very much interested in beetles: ask him what he thinks of Schouvaloff." ' Lady Wilde was a guileless and goodhearted show-off. Her house became a place to meet people, and guests such as Bernard Shaw and Yeats, newcomers to London, were grateful to her.

The death of her husband had freed her for the literary life, and she was the most industrious of the three Wildes in London. She began by finishing her husband's memoir of an antiquarian and illustrator named Gabriel Beranger. Her son Oscar had contemplated this task but willingly relinquished it to her. Then she turned to the notes she had made in Sweden when she and Sir William visited the governor of Uppsala in 1859, and put them together into a volume entitled *Driftwood from Scandinavia*. Next she gathered together, as he had intended, Sir William's vast collection of unsorted stories and legends which his country patients had written down for him in lieu of a fee, rewrote them as necessary, and published them in two important books of Irish folklore. (Yeats among others borrowed for his plays from them.) They show her to be warm and humorous. She filled two further volumes with the essays she had published over the years (many of them in the *Nation* in Dublin) on social and cultural subjects, which featured determined views on everything from George Eliot to hairstyles. Besides these she wrote some more verse, often with Oscar's dubious help over particular lines, and published it in magazines. These books brought in a little money, but she had trouble paying the rent, and was grateful when through Oscar's efforts in enlisting distinguished supporters she received in 1888 a grant of £100 from the Royal Literary Fund, and then on 24 May 1890 a Civil List Pension of £70 a year from the Prime Minister of the nation against which she had once sponsored a revolution. It was given 'in recognition of the services rendered by her late husband Sir William Wilde, M.D., to statistical science and literature.'* She took an active part in London literary life, especially among its Irish members, and was delighted to become along with Willie and Oscar a charter member of the Irish Literary Society.

The situation of Willie Wilde was more problematic. Back in Ireland, though admitted to the Irish bar, he was a personage in pubs. Asked what he was working at, he would reply, 'At intervals.'[56] His relations with Oscar were troubled, one reason being that they resembled each other closely in appearance, and superficially in manners. Willie did not mind but Oscar, feeling his uniqueness at risk, minded a great deal. They were both over six feet, Willie by four inches, Oscar by three, both inclined to be fat, both languid. 'Scratch Oscar and you will find Willie,' Max Beerbohm remembered someone saying. But Beerbohm could tell the brothers apart very well. Willie, he said, was 'very vulgar and unwashed and inferior.' In more extended comment, he said of Willie, '*Quel monstre!* Dark, oily, suspect yet awfully like Oscar: he has Oscar's coy, carnal smile and fatuous giggle and not a little of Oscar's *esprit*. But he is awful – a veritable tragedy of family likeness.'[57] Willie began to wear a beard, and claimed that Oscar paid him to do so. Lady Wilde devoted herself to keeping the brothers on good terms with each other, and for some periods was successful. But Willie's inferiority appeared in every department of his life. To be a man about town on Oscar's model required more capacity than he had. He kept trying regardless. If Oscar was a poet, Willie fancied he could be one too, and brought with him to London a poem he had published in *Kottabos* on the strength of which he hoped for entrée into literary circles. It was a sonnet, of sorts, on a subject – Salome – that was later to obsess his brother. Willie could recite it well enough to persuade his hearers for a moment that it was not drivel:

> And every soul was mine, mine utterly,
> And thrice each throat cried out aloud my name.
> 'Ask what thou wilt,' black-bearded Herod said.
> 'God wot a weird thing do I crave for prize;
> Give me I pray thee, presently, the head
> Of John the Baptist.' 'Twixt my hands it lies.
> Ah, mother, see the lips, the half-closed eyes,
> Dost think he hates us now that he is dead?

But not for long. If Oscar wrote plays, Willie tried his hand at drama too. Two of his plays, printed in Dublin, were entitled *French Polish* and

---

* Those whose names were listed in support of the grant were Lords Lytton and Spencer, Sir Theodore and Lady Martin, Swinburne, Mahaffy, Oliver Plunket, Sir George Otto Trevelyan, Sir John Lisback, Professors A. N. Sayce and Edward Dowden. Only Gladstone refused to sign.[55]

Evening Stream. Since Oscar had told the *Biograph* in 1880 that he was hesitating between a career as a painter and one as a writer, Willie had aspirations to become a sculptor as well as a journalist. Oscar's comments on his efforts were severe: 'Willie's sculpture shows palpable signs of death, but no hopes of living.'[58]

Yet Willie carved out a fragile place for himself in London. His knack for drawing was shown in some illustrations he made for his father's books, but he did not persevere. His piano playing led him to compose his own 'improved' endings for Chopin's *Preludes* – an enterprise that might have made a better man quail.[59] Journalism was the least demanding occupation he could find, and for some years he was successful at it. He liked nothing better than to puff Oscar in a gossip column. Once in a while, as when he reported on the Parnell Commission (some of whose sessions Oscar also attended), he wrote well, perhaps because he passionately accepted his mother's verdict that 'Parnell is the man of destiny. He will strike off the fetters and free Ireland, and throne her as queen among the nations.' The Wildes triumphed vicariously in Parnell's vindication. But in general the life was too easy for Willie. At a night club called the Spoofs in Maiden Lane he would hold forth on the delightfulness – meaning the idleness – of the journalist's profession. A. M. Binstead in *Pitcher in Paradise* renders a bit of Willie's talk which Jimmy Glover certifies to be representative; it was delivered at great speed, unlike his brother's stately rhythms:

> The journalistic life irksome? Dear me, not at all. Take my daily life as an example. I report at the office, let us say at twelve o'clock. To the Editor I say, 'Good morning, my dear Le Sage,' and he replies, 'Good morning, my dear Wilde, have you an idea today?' 'Oh yes, Sir, indeed I have,' I respond. 'It is the anniversary of the penny postage stamp.'
>
> 'That is a delightful subject for a leader,' cries my editor, beaming on me . . .
>
> I may then eat a few oysters and drink half a bottle of Chablis at Sweeting's . . . I then stroll towards the park. I bow to the fashionables, I am seen along incomparable Piccadilly . . . But meanwhile . . . I try to recall all that I ever heard about penny postage stamps. Let me see? There is Mr So-and-so the inventor, there is the early opposition, the first postal legislation, then the way stamps are made, putting the holes in the paper; the gum on the back; the printing . . . I think of all the circumstances as I stroll back along Pall Mall. I might go to the British Museum and grub up a lot of musty facts, but that would be unworthy of a great leader writer, you may well understand that.
>
> And then comes the writing. Ah! here is where I earn my money. I repair to my club. I order out my ink and paper. I go to my room. I close the door . . . Three great meaty, solid paragraphs each one-third of a column – that is the consummation to be wished. My ideas flow fast and free. Suddenly someone knocks at the door. Two hours have fled. How time goes! It is an

old friend. We are to eat a little dinner at the Café Royal and drop into the Alhambra for the new ballet. I touch the button, my messenger appears. The leader is despatched to 141, Fleet Street in the Parish of St Bride, and off we go arm in arm.[60]

There were times when he ran out of postage stamps to write about, and on these occasions, particularly when the editor asked him to turn out a short story, he consulted his brother. Oscar spun off half a dozen tales during breakfast.

Still, Lady Wilde and Willie could hope to impinge only upon parts of London life, while Oscar had set himself to be the center of it. He had by this time a large acquaintance, in which royalty was not lacking. The Prince of Wales asked to meet him, fetching up an epigram for the purpose, 'I do not know Mr Wilde, and not to know Mr Wilde is not to be known.'[61] On 4 June 1881 the Prince came to a thought-reading séance, predictably attended by Lillie Langtry, at the house shared by Miles and Wilde. He obviously enjoyed the witty company. The two young men had now changed their address from 13 Salisbury Street to the newly fashionable Tite Street, Chelsea. Miles had long since asked Edward Godwin, as the architect whose views they found most congenial, to redesign a house, as he had already done for Whistler with 'The White House.' A design was prepared as early as June 1878, but the Works and General Purposes Committee objected to it, as they had objected to the original design for Whistler's house. A modified plan was submitted on 30 September, and in July 1880 the house was at last ready for occupancy. The design was of interlocking rectangles. The brickwork was red and yellow, the roof was covered in green slates, and the windows had balconies. It was an aesthetic creation, and the young men happily installed themselves. Wilde, profiting from the fact that two women named Skeates had occupied it before them, or from the presence of Shelley House (occupied by a descendant of the poet) around the corner, renamed it Keats House.

Among Wilde's friends of this period Whistler and Rennell Rodd, along with Lillie Langtry and Miles, were the most conspicuous. Wilde's Oxford acquaintance with Rodd had continued. Rodd failed to get a first in Greats, and Wilde offered consolation:

Keats House

Dear Rennell,
    My best congratulations. Greats is the only fine school at Oxford, the only sphere of thought where one can be, *simultaneously*, brilliant and unreasonable, speculative and well-informed, creative as well as critical, and write with all the passion of youth about the truths which belong to the august serenity of old age.

I wish you had got a First – that my compeers should not *all* be sluggish and syllogistic Scotchmen. Still, a Second is perhaps for a man of culture a sweeter atmosphere than the chilly Caucasus of an atheistical First.

Come back very soon.

Truly yours,
OSCAR WILDE[62]

During the summer of 1879 Wilde and Rodd took a trip together. Rodd, his parents and sister, and Wilde all stayed in the Hôtel Meunier in Laroche, Belgium, in July. It happened that other residents at the hotel took particular note of them. One was a boy of eight, Paul de Reul, the son of a Belgian geologist, poet and novelist named Xavier de Reul. Paul de Reul remembered distinctly the impression Wilde made. He wrote later that Wilde was '*grand et blême, face glabre, cheveux longs, noirs et plats, il se vêtait de blanc, blanc des pieds à la tête, depuis le large et haut chapeau de feutre jusqu'à la canne, un sceptre d'ivoire, au pommeau tourné, avec lequel j'ai joué bien souvent. Nous l'appelions Pierrot.*'* Pierrot would walk to the valley of the Bronz, and in a place called the Tombs because the grass there is covered with flat stones, read his poems aloud with a dragging voice and monotonous cadence which struck the boy as funny. Another resident in the hotel was a Dutch poet, Jacques Perk (1858–81), who wrote a poem which described Wilde beside a beautiful woman,

> A son côté debout, comme elle de jeunesse
> Etincelant, en l'adolescent Anglais,
> D'intelligence plein, de gaité, d'allégresse,
> Au coeur poète, qui hait tout ce qui est mauvais.†[63]

From Laroche Wilde and Rodd went on to Tournai, where they saw and remembered the tomb of a knight on which was inscribed, '*Une heure viendra qui tout paiera* [An hour will come when all will pay].' Rodd wrote a poem about it, and Wilde, in an 'Envoi' to Rodd's second book of poems two years later, spoke of 'an old grey tomb in Flanders with a strange legend on it, making one think how, perhaps, passion does live on after death . . .'[64] He chose to deflect the ominousness of the augury.

The next year, 1880, Rodd published his first book, *Songs in the South*, and after inscribing it, 'Rennell to Oscar, July 1880,' added an inscription not less startling for being in Italian:

---

* '. . . tall and pallid, clean-shaven, with long, straight, black hair; he dressed in white, white from head to foot, from the tall, broad, felt hat to his cane, an ivory sceptre with a round top, which I played with often. We called him Pierrot.'

† 'Standing at her side, youth / Sparkling in the English adolescent, as in her, / Full of intelligence, of gaiety, of joy, / At heart a poet, who hates everything that is bad.'

Al tuo martirio cupida e feroce
Questa turba cui parli accorera;
Ti vertammo a veder sulla tua croce
Tutti, e nessuno ti compiagnera.*

Wilde's life is as full of tragic prolepses as an Ibsen play. Rodd continued to be alarmed by Wilde, and by some of Wilde's poems. Particular lines were certain to offend. In substance he gave the same warning as the dead knight. Wilde refused to alter the lines. As Rodd says in his memoirs, though sensitive to his friends' complaints of Wilde's influence, he 'took a certain defiant pride in their criticism,'[65] a response easily borrowed from Wilde's imperiousness.

So during the summer of 1881 they traveled together again, this time along the Loire. Wilde wrote George Lewis's twelve-year-old son a playful description: 'I was with a delightful Oxford friend and, as we did not wish to be known [presumably to keep Rodd's friends from suspecting that their intimacy was so constant], he travelled under the name of Sir Smith, and I was Lord Robinson. I then went to Paris – a large town, the capital of France – and enjoyed myself very much.' It was perhaps now that they went also to Chartres, and certainly they were at Amboise, of which Wilde was to write the next year:

> We were staying once, he and I, at Amboise, that little village with its grey slate roofs and steep streets and gaunt, grim gateway . . . And above the village, and beyond the bend of the river, we used to go in the afternoon, and sketch from one of the big barges that bring the wine in autumn and the wood in winter down to the sea, or lie in the long grass and make plans *pour la gloire, et pour ennuyer les philistins*, or wander along the low, sedgy banks, 'matching our reeds in sportive rivalry,' as comrades used in the old Sicilian days.[66]

Rodd, like Hunter Blair, is at some pains to indicate that Wilde's relation to him was not sexual. Still, in all the forms of attachment, the relationship of arrogant master and timid disciple bore a resemblance to love.

Love did not enter into Wilde's relationship with James McNeill Whistler. Whistler demanded admiration bordering on sycophancy and gave in return domination bordering on enmity. To Wilde, gazing down at him, Whistler was short but formidable. During the early period of Wilde's residence in London, Whistler had to endure an enforced absence. His minimally successful libel suit against Ruskin, heard on 25 November 1878, in which he was awarded a farthing damages and no costs, had led to bankruptcy; he fled to Venice from September 1879 until November 1880, and there executed a series of etchings brilliant enough

---

* 'At thy martyrdom the greedy and cruel / Crowd to which thou speakest will assemble; / All will come to see thee on thy cross, / And not one will have pity on thee.'

to enable him to return. Though he could not wrest his old abode, The White House, away from the art critic Harry (or 'arry, as Whistler called him) Quilter, he found another house in Tite Street, and so was a neighbor of Miles and Wilde. In 1879 Wilde was still obscure, in 1880 he was famous. For the time the two suited each other. Whistler was twenty years older, American on his mother's side (not 'a great Virginia gentleman,' as Wilde called him to Robert Sherard,[67] but a North Carolina one). He had spent several years in France, and was well acquainted with the principal artists and writers there. Wilde aspired to be the same. Whistler lived a life made up of seemingly firm friendships which regularly ended in brief, conclusive quarrels. To be his friend was to court dismissal; Wilde managed it successfully for half a dozen years. He received the master's barbs in good part, one of his most attractive characteristics being his enjoyment of jokes against himself.

Although Wilde's approbation of Whistler's paintings in the first Grosvenor Gallery exhibition had been equivocal, his taste being then almost exclusively 'Pre-Raff,' he made up for it by his review, in a Dublin newspaper on 5 May 1879, of a later exhibition.[68] This time he praised 'The Gold Girl' as 'very wonderful.' He even approved some of the 'nocturnes.' He no longer questioned that Whistler was the greatest painter in London, although in defiance of Whistler he clung to an admiration for Burne-Jones. Whistler was as irreverent towards Ruskin's favorite, Turner, 'that old amateur,' as towards Burne-Jones and the other Pre-Raphaelites. J. and E. Pennell quote him as saying, 'Rossetti, well, you know, not a painter, but a gentleman and a poet. As for the others dangling after him, with them it was all incapacity and crime.'[69] Wilde, a welcome guest at Whistler's studio, could marvel at such judgments while the master chatted away at work. Together, Wilde and Whistler constituted a London spectacle. As Ellen Terry commented long afterwards, 'The most remarkable men I have ever known were Whistler and Wilde . . . There was something about both of them more instantaneously individual and audacious than it is possible to describe.'[70]

Whistler's friendly hand was always extended in a bullying way. An invitation to take a trip with him is peremptory and has his customary edge of being funny at the recipient's expense:

Sunday Night

Now Oscar you have simply to get on your disguise again and come off with me *tomorrow* to Jersey.

I shall be down at the studio tomorrow – and shall send for you at about 12 – we can make our final arrangements and probably leave by the 5 o'clock train –

[Butterfly signature]
[Pen drawing of woman's head on blotting paper enclosed]

126

The 'disguise' must have been some new coat that Wilde was showing off. Still, the letter shows they understood each other, as does this one:

> Oscarino! – I have unwittingly broken the seal of the enclosed – *Mille pardons* –
> I have read nothing – but the first word – 'Electra' – and know not who it is from – so you must tell me when we meet –
>
> > [Butterfly signature]

Another letter of this period commends to Wilde (then in Paris), or rather foists upon him Whistler's disciple – the artist Walter Sickert:

> No, Oscar! – I can spare him longer if needs must – behave well to him – and attempt not to palm off wine of inferior quality upon my ambassador!
> Remember, he travels no longer as Walter Sickert – of course, he is amazing – for does he not represent the Amazing One – and his tastes are for the nonce necessarily of the most refined – even the Louvre holds for him no secrets . . .
> What more shall I say? – He can explain to you the Amazing Catalogue – and for the rest has he not my blessing and his return ticket?[71]

That Whistler humorously exaggerates his vanity does nothing to undercut it.

Both men being clever and eager to talk, a rivalry developed in which Wilde, the kinder hearted, was usually worsted. Douglas Sladen describes a reception in 1883 at the house of Louise Jopling, in Beaufort Street. Wilde and Whistler arrived separately but early, and were obviously disconcerted to see almost no one else there. Sladen reproduces their badinage in a way that sounds genuine:

> 'Jimmy, this time last year, when I was in New York, all we men were carrying fans. It should be done here.'
> [No reply from Whistler.]
> 'I hear that you went over to the Salon by Dieppe, Jimmy. Were you economising?'
> 'Don't be foolish. I went to paint.'
> 'How many pictures did you paint?'
> 'How many hours did it take?'
> 'You went, not I. No gentleman ever goes by the Dieppe route.'
> 'I do, often,' said Mrs Jopling. 'It takes five hours.'
> 'How many minutes are there in an hour, Oscar?'
> 'I am not quite sure, but I think it's about sixty. I am not a mathematician.'
> 'Then I must have painted three hundred.'[72]

Sladen claims that it was at this party that Wilde remarked of something a woman had said, 'How I wish I had said that,' and Whistler replied, 'You

will, Oscar, you will'; but a more likely account says it was a remark of
Whistler to Humphry Ward, art critic of *The Times*, which aroused
Wilde's envy. Ward had been calling one of Whistler's pictures good,
another bad, until the artist said, 'My dear fellow, you must never say this
painting is good or that bad. Good and bad are not terms to be used by you.
But you may say "I like this" or "I don't like that", and you will be within
your rights. Now come and have a whisky: you're sure to like that.'[73] Wilde
had no hesitation in borrowing what he needed, partly because he usually
touched it up. As he wrote in a review of Wills's *Olivia* on 30 May 1885, 'It
is only the unimaginative who ever invents. The true artist is known by the
use he makes of what he annexes, and he annexes everything.' Whistler,
on the other hand, was too vain to realize that his own theories of art were
derived largely from Gautier.

The two men enjoyed each other's company for somewhat different
reasons. What Wilde did not know was that Whistler, the future author of
The Gentle Art of Making Enemies, was temperamentally inclined to make
new enemies of old friends. There were many examples. When, later on,
the breach occurred, Wilde could not understand it. For if he had
borrowed, he had also given. He had sung Whistler's praises, had
entertained him verbally and at table, had been in every way generous and
loyal. But Wilde always had a measure of innocence, and never more so
than when dealing with someone who was cruel, because cruelty was not
in his own nature. He was prepared to believe that disciples might be
treacherous to the master, but not that the master might prey on the
disciples.

The personalities of Tite Street were increasingly the talk of London.
They became fair game for parodist playwrights at the end of the
Seventies. A first attempt to caricature them in December 1877 was *The
Grasshopper*, a burlesque of the opening of the Grosvenor Gallery, in
which a dance of three persons was reputed to be Whistler, Miles, and
Wilde. Then came *Where's the Cat?*, adapted from a German source by
James Albery, which opened at the Criterion Theatre on 20 November
1880. It contained lines such as, 'I feel like – like a room without a dado,'
spoken by a character called Scott Ramsay, a writer. Herbert Beerbohm
Tree played the role with Wilde's mannerisms, and the play was a success.
Wilde made a point of not seeing it. At last, three months after the
opening, Ellen Terry was able to persuade him to share her box. He
observed then that the play was poor. F. C. Burnand, the editor of *Punch*,
in adapting *Un Mari de la campagne* for the Bancrofts, decided to twit
Wilde and aestheticism. He called his play *The Colonel* and submitted it to
the Bancrofts, who decided against it. But it was produced by another
company at the Prince of Wales Theatre in February 1881 and scored a
hit. Even Queen Victoria was persuaded by the Prince of Wales to see it,
and a command performance was held at Balmoral. J. Fernandez in the
London production, and W. G. Hawtrey in the provinces, both played an

aesthete called Lambert Stryke with Wilde's mannerisms. The vogue of aestheticism was ripe to be succeeded by the vogue of anti-aestheticism.

A more lasting work was in process of being composed, Gilbert and Sullivan's *Patience*. Gilbert's plan had been at first to dramatize his ballad, 'The Rival Curates,' who outvie each other in mildness until one on compulsion is obliged to play the opposite role. But he quickly perceived that the cultural climate required rival aesthetes, although Max Beerbohm insisted that they were already out of date. By November 1880 Gilbert had written half the libretto, which was kept as secret as possible to discourage imitators. Then *Patience* opened on 23 April 1881. Wilde had been informed that it took him off, and he wrote to George Grossmith, who was playing Bunthorne:

> Keats House
> Tite Street,
> Chelsea

Dear Grossmith,
  I should like to go to the first night of your new opera at Easter – and would be very much obliged if you would ask the Box Office to reserve a three guinea box for me, if there is one to be had; on hearing from the office I will forward a cheque for it.
  With Gilbert and Sullivan I am sure we will have something better than the small farce of the Colonel. I am looking forward to being greatly amused.

> Very truly yours,
> OSCAR WILDE

Gilbert wanted his aesthetes to be composites, though he could scarcely ignore Wilde as the most conspicuous representative. Still, he made the two characters different; Reginald Bunthorne is fleshly and Archibald Grosvenor spiritual. Wilde was an example of both. Perhaps to deflect attention from Wilde, Grossmith played Bunthorne as Whistler, black curls interrupted by a white lock of hair, moustache, tuft, eye-glass, with the famous Whistler 'Ha Ha.'[74] Although Rossetti's ethereality, Swinburne's sensuality, and Ruskin's Gothicizing were amalgamated, in one aesthete or the other, both Bunthorne and Grosvenor have aspects that come unmistakably from Wilde as the most articulate standard-bearer of aestheticism at the time.

The maidens' hopeless love for Bunthorne came naturally out of Wilde's gatherings in Keats House, at which Professional Beauties were in constant attendance. Bunthorne wears his hair long like Wilde, and writes a poem which is described as 'a wild, weird, fleshly thing.' Though Wilde had not preempted all the lilies of the Pre-Raphaelites, his obsession with the flower is probably reflected in Bunthorne's words, 'It is the wail of the poet's heart on discovering that everything is commonplace. To understand it, cling passionately to one another and think of faint lilies.' It was Wilde too who had 'walked down Piccadilly with a poppy or a lily in his medieval hand' – rather a Renaissance hand – or rather, was said to have done so. He would say later that 'To have done it was nothing, but to make people think one had done it was a triumph.'[75] Bunthorne is described as 'such a judge of blue-and-white and other kinds of pottery,' and though Wilde was not alone in his collection of blue china and had been preceded by Rossetti and Whistler, he had made the best remark about it.

As for Grosvenor, he claims to be a 'trustee for Beauty,' an extrapolation of Wilde's possessiveness about it. His reference to 'Francesca da Rimini, mimini piminy,' may draw Jane Francesca Wilde, as well as Rossetti, into the circle. The preference for secondary colours, for the greenery yallery in which the once crimson walls of the Grosvenor Gallery were now painted, caught others in its net, but Wilde with them. *Patience* conferred upon the aesthetic movement a single identity, but could do so because of Wilde's exaggerations. Max Beerbohm is probably right in saying that *Patience* prolonged the aesthetic movement. But it was only a parry to Wilde's thrust.

In his libretto Gilbert profited from a relentless sequence of caricatures by George du Maurier in *Punch*. As an art student du Maurier had lived with Whistler in Paris. The sight of his old friend with Wilde probably stirred du Maurier early in 1881 to conceive two aesthetic types, the poet Maudle and the painter Jellaby Postlethwaite. Week after week these caricatures appeared, never mentioning Whistler, too distinguished to be an easy target, but constantly involving Wilde. Great fun was made of his flowing locks, his lilies, his rondeaux and other French forms, the Grosvenor Gallery, blue china, poems entitled 'Impressions.' His name became Oscuro Wildegoose, Drawit Milde, the Wilde-eyed poet, 'Brother Jonathan' Wilde, Ossian Wilderness. At least once Maudle's face was obviously Wilde's. If by no means always clever, this parody was goodhumored, and Wilde was too aware of the usefulness of publicity to quarrel with *Punch*. He made a point of always greeting du Maurier graciously. Once, at a showing of Whistler's work, the painter came up to them as they stood talking together and asked, 'Which of you two discovered the other?' Du Maurier wished he had replied, 'We have both invented you,' but Whistler had slipped away. He did however include this bit of repartee in the original text of *Trilby*.[76] But, as Burne-Jones understood, the merits of du Maurier and Wilde were not of a kind. When du Maurier's friend Hamilton Aidé praised du Maurier's caricatures to the skies, Burne-Jones cried, 'You may say what you like, but there is more wit in Wilde's little finger than in the whole of du Maurier's wretched little body!'

Wilde's wit proved to be more than a match, also, for the librettist of *Patience*: they met at a supper party at the Haymarket Theatre, and Wilde held the table with his brilliant talk for perhaps half an hour. Gilbert seized the first opportunity to say, 'I wish I could talk like you,' and then added, self-righteously, 'I'd keep my mouth shut and claim it as a virtue!' Wilde retorted, 'Ah that would be selfish! I could deny myself the pleasure of talking, but not to others the pleasure of listening.'[77] He finished off Gilbert and Sullivan in *The Importance of Being Earnest*, where the stage direction says of Jack and Algernon, 'They whistle some dreadful popular air from a British opera.'

So Wilde found ways to act and speak in full knowledge that they could and would be mocked. To be derided so was part of his plan. Notoriety is fame's wicked twin: Wilde was prepared to court the one in the hope that the other would favor him too.

The Drifter Apotheosized

We live in an age when men treat art as if it were meant to be a form of autobiography.

Wilde's *Vera* had circulated in privately printed form for seven months when he decided that the moment had come to issue a book of his poems. By this time he had published in magazines thirty out of the sixty-one poems he wished to include. He was particularly eager to balance his many short poems with extended lyrics, and Rennell Rodd came upon him one day, a book of botany open before him, choosing mellifluous flowers to plant in one of the three longest, 'The Burden of Itys.'[78]* The floral surge with which the poem began is botanically a little suspect:

> This English Thames is holier far than Rome,
>   Those harebells like a sudden flush of sea
> Breaking across the woodland, with the foam
>   Of meadow-sweet and white anemone
> To fleck their blue waves . . .

The meadow-sweet blooms in June and the anemone in April, while the harebell, unlike the bluebell, does not grow in oceanic profusion.

Rodd had set him an example by publishing his first book of poems with a small house, David Bogue, and in April 1881 Wilde wrote to Bogue expressing a similar wish. The contract signed on 17 May made Wilde responsible for all the costs of publication; Bogue was to receive, accordingly, only a small share (something over ten per cent) of the profits. The

---

* Wilde was soon to be done with nature. He told Margot Asquith, 'I hate views – they are only made for bad painters,' and added, 'Let us go in – the sound of a cuckoo makes me sick.'[79]

131

binding, specified by Wilde, was to be white parchment, and the printing on Dutch hand-made paper. He followed the examples of Morris, Rossetti, and Swinburne in wanting the cover and typography to be distinctive. The initial printing was 750 copies, but they were grouped into three 'editions' of 250 each, released during the first year. In Boston a firm called Roberts Brothers brought out three American 'editions' in 1881. In England the demand went on, so that there were two further printings in 1882, after which the book was not reprinted until 1892.

The earliest plan of the book shows that Wilde intended to place on the title page, just beneath the terse title *Poems* and the author's name, an epigraph saying,

> *Mes premiers vers sont d'un enfant, mes seconds d'un adolescent.**[80]

It was a plea for indulgence, though at twenty-six he was a somewhat retarded adolescent. Wisely he decided at last to omit this epigraph, as well as a quotation from Keats intended for the page following:

> I have not the slightest feeling of humility towards the public or to anything in existence but the Eternal Being, the Principle of Beauty, and the Memory of great men.

Not much would be gained by flouting his audience, and Wilde substituted for the quotation a sonnet, 'Hélas!', which he called the 'Proem' to the volume. It was a serious, if flamboyant, attempt to explain himself. He told Yeats, who asked to anthologize 'Requiescat,' that 'Hélas!' was his most characteristic poem:

Hélas!

To drift with every passion till my soul
Is a stringed lute upon which all winds can play,
Is it for this that I have given away
Mine ancient wisdom and austere control?
Methinks my life is a twice-written scroll
Scrawled over on some boyish holiday
With idle songs for pipe and virelay
Which do but mar the secret of the whole.
Surely there was a time I might have trod
The sunlit heights, and from life's dissonance
Struck one clear chord to reach the ears of God:
Is that time dead? lo! with a little rod
I did but touch the honey of romance –
And must I lose a soul's inheritance?

* 'My first verses are those of a child, my second those of an adolescent.'

The sonnet reflected the state of mind he had experienced at Oxford, of which he had complained in his letter of 3 March 1877, that he shifted 'with every breath of thought and am weaker and more self-deceiving than ever.' But maturity consists of finding justification for affirming what, in immaturity, one felt apologetic about. Sighing in French is not quite the same as sighing in English, nor is poeticizing about drifting the same as drifting.

'Hélas!' was a poem that came down naturally from Oxford. The word 'drift' and the image of touching honey with a little rod both reached Wilde through his golden book, Pater's *Studies in the History of the Renaissance.* In the 'Conclusion' which constitutes the final chapter, Pater argued that just as physical life was now known to be a concurrence of forces rather than a group of objects, so the mind must be regarded as a fluid process rather than an adhesion to fixities and definites. William James and Henri Bergson were soon to depict consciousness as a river or stream; for Pater it is, more intensely, a whirlpool. There is nothing 'but the race of the mid-stream, a *drift* of momentary acts of sight and passion and thought.' Drifting is not blameworthy but inevitable. To drift more splendidly we should rely on 'great passions,' so as to get 'as many pulsations as possible into the given time.' 'Not the fruit of experience, but experience itself, is the end.'

The closing image for 'Hélas!', like the opening one, was furnished by Pater, in his penultimate essay on Winckelmann, where he quotes Jonathan's appeal to Saul, 'I did but taste a little honey with the end of the rod that was in mine hand, and lo! I must die.' For Pater this statement epitomizes 'the artistic life, with its inevitable sensuousness,' and can be contrasted with Christian asceticism and its antagonism to touch. In translating this sentiment into his poem, Wilde introduces a compunction foreign to Pater. He recognizes a counter force which would bring him towards the 'august heights' (an earlier version of 'the sunlit heights'): this is a restraint which has both classical and Christian components, and is his 'soul's inheritance.' To be so torn, as Wilde is in this poem, between cadence and decadence, austerity and laissez-faire, has its flamboyance. And as Jonathan was saved, so Wilde, for all his alases, has hope of being saved too, because though he has practiced self-indulgence, it was never without remorse.

By placing this poem first Wilde acknowledged a division in himself, a division pervasively developed and sporadically reconciled in his book. He liked to attribute it to his parents, his father an antiquarian, his mother a libertarian, one with a passion for the past, the other for the future. But he also acknowledged that 'for the aesthetic mind' Catholicism was more attractive than Protestantism, although in his case the lure of the former was checked by his interest in the Greeks. It might be thought that he had a double nature, but he actually claimed to have a triple one: 'I am certain,' he told Mrs Julian Hawthorne, 'that I have had three separate and distinct souls.'[81] For in addition to his counter urges, he had a third urge to contemplate the other two. His title page bore an emblem, designed on his instructions, which showed a papal tiara above a Masonic rose, both enclosed in an egg-shaped oval along the sides of which is printed the rubric, '*Sub hoc signo vinces* [Under this sign thou shalt conquer].' The tiara and the rose invoke the two dispensations, Catholic and pagan, as well as their possible reconciliation in Freemasonry. It was a triple conflict which he knew to be more inclusive than that of the prominent nineteenth-century poets he admired, from Keats to Morris. For he had the same impulse toward paganism in 'The Garden of Eros' as Swinburne in 'Hymn to Proserpine,'

> The new Sign grows dim and grey before its conqueror.

But the victory of paganism is checked by his question in 'The Garden of Eros':

> why must I still behold
> The wan white face of that deserted Christ?

Similarly, the Pope is 'The gentle shepherd of the Fold' in 'Rome Unvisited,' but in 'Humanitad' Pius IX, with whom Wilde had had an audience at the Vatican, is depicted, in sharp contrast to the patriot Mazzini, as 'an old man who grabbled rusty keys,' 'alone with God and memories of sin,' and the Church, once 'the wondrous Temple' in 'Rome Unvisited', turns into 'That murderous mother of red harlotries.' 'The Burden of Itys' declares challengingly, 'This English Thames is holier far than Rome,' and prefers English poppies to the Italian Popes, while 'Italia' laments that

> Rome's desecrated town
> Lies mourning for her God-anointed King!

He had turned away from Catholicism with as much éclat as he had turned towards it.

As if to contradict 'Hélas!', where he admits and regrets having given away his ancient wisdom, 'Humanitad' insists that he has renounced Venus for Athena:

> For I am Hers who loves not any man
> Whose white and stainless bosom bears the sign Gorgonian.

In accord with this sentiment Wilde wrote his most ambitious poem, 'Charmides,' which he considered his best. Pater's essay on Winckelmann declared that 'Greek religion too has its statues worn with kissing,' and spoke of Winckelmann's 'handling' of 'pagan marbles . . . with no sense of shame.' These phrases coalesced in Wilde's mind with a story he remembered from Lucian, of a young man who embraced a statue of Aphrodite. He decided to alter the goddess to Athena, because being virginal she would feel particularly violated and vindictive. Charmides is hot enough:

> And nigher came, and touched her throat, and with hands violate
>
> > Undid the cuirass, and the crocus gown,
> > And bared the breasts of polished ivory,
> > Till from the waist the peplos falling down
> > Left visible the secret mystery
> > Which to no lover will Athena show,
> > The grand cool flanks, the crescent thighs, the bossy hills of snow.
>
> . . . . .
>
> > And then his lips in hungering delight
> > Fed on her lips, and round the towered neck
> > He flung his arms, nor cared at all his passion's will to check.
>
> > Never I ween did lover hold such tryst,
> > For all night long he murmured honeyed word,
> > And saw her sweet unravished limbs, and kissed
> > Her pale and argent body undisturbed,
> > And paddled with the polished throat, and pressed
> > His hot and beating heart upon her chill and icy breast.

Athena revenges herself by luring Charmides to drown himself. His body floats to shore, where a nymph falls in love and, after seeking ineffectually to awaken him, dies of unrequited passion, giving Wilde full scope to describe male beauty. Aphrodite intervenes and arranges for the two, purged of sacrilege and necrophilia, to enjoy each other in the fields of Acheron:

> > And all his hoarded sweets were hers to kiss,
> > And all her maidenhead was his to slay.

Charmides' love for a statue and the nymph's for a corpse, lend the poem a certain gaminess. Wilde lingers like Keats over sweets, and like Swinburne over sours, but what animates the poem is the imagery of psychosexual transgression.

Like Gautier, Wilde opens his book to unusual as well as usual forms of love. His book is polymorphously perverse. He is fond of Heracles' page, Hylas, and at first Charmides is mistaken for Hylas,

> that false runaway
> Who with a Naiad now would make his bed
> Forgetting Herakles.

Hylas appears also in 'The Garden of Eros.' Narcissus, his love turned inward, is also much in evidence. In 'The Burden of Itys' Wilde presents Antinous and Salmacis, one Hadrian's catamite, the other a herm-aphrodite. Sensuality appears in figuring non-sexual things, as when in 'Humanitad' Wilde speaks of Wordsworth living 'blamelessly' yet daring 'to kiss the smitten mouth of his own century!' He is eager to make clear that these are songs of experience:

> Those who have never known a lover's sin
> Let them not read my ditty.
>   ('Charmides')

Charmides' life takes up the anguished reference to 'my sin and shame' from 'San Miniato,' but for him they become 'A fiery pulse of sin, a splendid shame.'

The book moves gradually towards 'Humanitad,' the last long poem. It is a winter poem, where 'The Burden of Itys' was spring and 'The Garden of Eros' summer. The young pagan proves as unhappy as any Christian; he longs to make the spirit and body one, but finds such union elusive. Wilde anticipates here what he would say in 'The Soul of Man under Socialism,' that we are obliged to 'live each other's lives and not our own / For very pity's sake.' We are brought to a new Calvary, in which the whole Christian parable is enacted in each man, a point Wilde was to prove on his pulses. Christ does no more than prefigure what all men discover, that everyone is both victim and oppressor,

> The spear that pierces and the side that bleeds,
> The lips betraying and the life betrayed . . .

But just as we re-enact the Crucifixion, we may re-enact the Resurrection.

> Nay, nay, we are but crucified, and though
>   The bloody sweat falls from our brows like rain,
> Loosen the nails – we shall come down I know,
>   Staunch the red wounds – we shall be whole again,
> No need have we of hyssop-laden rod,
> That which is purely human, that is Godlike, that is God.

Here the mitre and the rose come together; Catholicism blends with paganism in the same sense of mutual suffering and sin, with the promise of eventual unity of being, when opposites will be joined. Insofar as Wilde had a creed, this was it. It had the merit of being unacceptable to many of his readers. But with a sense of the tentativeness with which such a blend could be adopted, he remarked some months later, 'My next book may be a perfect contradiction of my first.'[82] Contradictoriness was his orthodoxy.

Praise and Blame

The primary aim of the critic is to see the object as it really is not.

As with *Vera*, Wilde solicited approval for his new book among writers and friends. Lillie Langtry of course had her copy, inscribed, 'To Helen formerly of Troy, now of London.' Robert Browning, Matthew Arnold, Swinburne, and John Addington Symonds had theirs. Wilde's letter to Arnold has survived in part, and shows how he mingled compliments to the recipient with modesty about his own achievement:

[June–July 1881]   Keats House, Tite Street

Dear Mr Arnold, Will you accept from me my first volume of poems <. . .> of the constant source of joy and wonder that your beautiful work was to all of us at Oxford <. . .> for I have only now, too late perhaps, found out how all art requires solitude as its companion, only now indeed know the splendid difficulty of this great art in which you are a master illustrious and supreme. Still, such as it is, let me offer it to you, and believe me in all affectionate admiration, truly yours

OSCAR WILDE

Arnold's reply was not discouraging, though it played safe:

July 9th [1881]   Pains Hill Cottage, Cobham, Surrey

Dear Mr Wilde, Your volume and note were put into my hands as I was leaving the Athenaeum last night. I have but glanced at the poems as yet, but I perceive in them the true feeling for rhythm, which is at the bottom of all success in poetry; of all endeavor, indeed, which is not fictitious and vain, in that line of expression. I shall read the work attentively when I get a moment of that of which we all have too little – leisure. I see you have found out the force of what Byron so insisted on: – that one must shake off London life before one can do one's best work.

    Your note was very kind – too kind – expressions about me and what I have done. I have not much to thank the public for; but from my fellow-workers, both in poetry and prose, I have met with kindness and recognition such as might satisfy any man.

> Sincerely yours,
> MATTHEW ARNOLD

Arnold, having himself sung of wandering between two worlds, 'one dead, the other powerless to be born,' could conceive sympathy for a young man wavering between half-rejected Catholicism and half-rejected aestheticism, with a longing for a *tertium quid* which would satisfy his leanings in both directions. Swinburne, without having read it all, was favorably impressed, he said, by such a poem as 'Les Silhouettes.' No such sympathy was forthcoming from the reviewers in the *Athenaeum*, *Saturday Review*, and *Spectator. Punch* said it was 'Swinburne and water.' Wilde was accused of all the available vices, from plagiarism to insincerity to indecency, heavy charges against a first book.

The evidence offered was less than cogent. It was true that Wilde had still to create an individual style, and in the end he would do so in prose not verse. Plagiarism was often that homage of half-quotation which every English poet has rendered to his predecessors, and merely 'stealing from thieves,' as Le Gallienne said. His insincerity was the result of his representing difficult hesitations instead of pleasantly easy certainties. His indecency was a calculated risk, to portray his sensuality as frankly as he could. He belonged to 'the fleshly school of poetry,' and acknowledged it. The mildness of his indecency was hinted by *Punch*,

> The poet is Wilde,
> But his poetry's tame.[83]

Against the hostility Wilde had some support from friends. Rodd thought the book full of 'brilliant writing.' Wilde asked Oscar Browning to review it, and Browning complied, at some cost to himself, with a notice in the *Academy*. Browning's welcome conclusion was that 'England is enriched with a new poet,' but on the way to it he objected to 'the irregular pulsations of a sympathy which never wearies. Roman Catholic ritual, stern Puritanism, parched Greek islands, cool English lanes and streams, Paganism and Christianity, despotism and Republicanism, Wordsworth, Milton, and Mr Swinburne, receive in turn the same passionate devotion.'[84] For Wilde the book's originality lay just here, in his openness to contraries. John Addington Symonds' letter to Wilde about the *Poems* also objected to some cultural confusion, but in general Symonds praised sincerity where others had failed to find any. His letter has survived only in draft:

Dear Mr Wilde – If length of days beget forgetfulness, you might well be excused for having forgotten me . . . It is years since we exchanged letters.

These years I have spent in sickness, the seclusion of these mountains, and studies. You have employed them otherwise, upon a wider stage playing a part more brilliant & . . . taking of life I hope not only the delights of youth but at least as much of solid satisfaction to the soul (she cares but little for time place & opportunity) as I can say my soul has gathered. The occasion for now writing is that I have read your book of poems. I should not write to you about them if they had not raised deep interest & sympathy. I feel the poet's gift in them; their inequality is noticeable. Those wh. I presume to have been written latest . . . seem to me the deepest and sincerest the most free from riot of luxuriant adolescence. These in their direct & poignant utterance have, if I mistake not, the right ring, the poet's quality. With regard to the earlier portions of the book – Impressions of Travel & pieces written at Oxford – I feel that they represent a stage already rather overlived by you. As such there is a somewhat painful contrast between their airy insouciance, their Keatsian openness at all pores to beauty, & the intensity of personal experience of the later, so murderous to the play of mere fancy, so gripping on reality. Then again though a poet should have the license of uttering diverse notes on even the most established subjects, do you not think that confusion of a cult for the Prisoner of the Vatican with the cult for Swinburne's Mazzini rather too pronounced? The volume has you see stirred the embers of a jaded man much versed in books. How few such volumes of new poems there are! Arise & shine! This [is] really what I want to say, & why I write. The spontaneity with wh. some while ago you sought me, gives me perhaps the right to seek you now with senile urgency, & ask you how you mean to put your gifts henceforth to use? Boy, if the world gives you time, answer me this, as to one who will hear with sympathy waits to hear the word & with eagerness. There are things in Humanitad (wh. seems to me a middle stage between the earlier manners & the latest manner of the poet) strains wh., if properly developed might be trumpets to our time.[85]

Symonds paid the compliment of taking him seriously, and calling him 'Boy.'

What became clear with *Poems* was that Wilde could hope for little or no indulgence, or even justice. Rennell Rodd's warnings were well-founded. The poetical scene in 1881 was not so bright that these poems required so much excoriation, but it was becoming evident that the critics were laying for Wilde, and that nothing but utter originality would silence them. One of the most galling responses was that of the Oxford Union. Its secretary wrote to Wilde asking for a copy for the library there, and Wilde inscribed one,

> To the Library of the Oxford Union
> my first volume of poems,
>   Oscar Wilde
> Oct 27 '81

When the acquisition was announced, Oliver Elton – later a historian of English literature – rose to denounce it. With the assistance of Henry Newbolt he compiled a list of supposed borrowings from other poets. His speech was received, as Newbolt recalled, with attention at first, and finally with great cheers and hisses:

> It is not that these poems are thin – and they *are* thin: it is not that they are immoral – and they *are* immoral: it is not that they are this or that – and they *are* all this and all that: it is that they are for the most part not by their putative father at all, but by a number of better-known and more deservedly reputed authors. They are in fact by William Shakespeare, by Philip Sidney, by John Donne, by Lord Byron, by William Morris, by Algernon Swinburne, and by sixty more, whose works have furnished the list of passages which I hold in my hand at this moment. The Union Library already contains better and fuller editions of all these poets: the volume which we are offered is theirs, not Mr Wilde's: and I move that it be not accepted.[86]

The proceedings had a Swiftian lunacy. There was a spirited debate, with six speaking against acceptance and four including the Librarian, speaking in favor. In the division the vote was 128 for acceptance and 188 against, but a poll of the membership was requested by the Librarian. The following week the president announced that 180 had voted for acceptance and 188 against. Then Wilde's friend George Curzon intervened, 'with a voice of scorn,' as Wilde afterwards remembered, and 'made some pointed observations . . . on the unfortunate circumstance of Mr Wilde's volume of poems having to be returned by the Society, after having been solicited as a present by the library committee.' The secretary had no alternative but to return the book with apologies, and Wilde responded with acerbic calm:

> 9, Charles Street,
> Grosvenor Square

> Dear Sir: Pray assure the committee of the Oxford Union that, while regretting that they had not ascertained the feeling of the Society with regard to my art, I quite acquit them of any intention to be discourteous towards me, and that I readily accept an apology so sincerely offered.
>
> My chief regret indeed being that there should still be at Oxford such a large number of young men who are ready to accept their own ignorance as an index, and their own conceit as a criterion of any imaginative and beautiful work. I must also for the sake of the good fame and position of the Oxford Union express a hope that no other poet or writer of England will ever be subjected to what I feel sure you as well as myself are conscious of, the coarse impertinence of having a work officially rejected which had been no less officially sought for.

Pray be kind enough to forward to my private address the volume of my poems, and Believe me yours truly

OSCAR WILDE[87]

The issue was not to be completely resolved until a year later, when the Librarian's motion on 18 October that Wilde's *Poems* be bought for the Coffee and Smoking Room was defeated. But there was a further response. The *Oxford and Cambridge Undergraduate's Journal* for 17 November 1881 shows that the sentiment against the book was in part a sentiment against Wilde, presumably the person whose 'evil life' is being discussed:

It would be well for some undergraduates if they would not allow their heads to be turned by the whirl and excitement of University life. Many seem to forget how great an effect on after years a well or ill-spent University career may have. It is better for a man not to 'come up' at all than, when he has come up, to be 'sent down' and for the rest of his life to be ashamed to confess his connection with the University. If a man leads an evil life in the University, even though he may not suffer for his acts at the time, yet his character will not have escaped the notice of his colleagues, who afterwards will always have it in their power to call his remembrance to the past. We would like to see men bear this fact in mind, and show more *esprit de corps* as members of this old University, so as not to allow themselves to act in such a way as to trail her honour in the dust.

Of such college spirit Inquisitions are made.

Wilde's letter to the Oxford Union speaks of 9 Charles Street as his personal address, and this also reflected a change in his fortunes which was a direct result of the publication of *Poems*. Frank Miles's father, the canon, had twitted Wilde for being incomprehensible; he now found him painfully clear. He wrote to his son about the evil tendency in the poems; then, concluding that Frank Miles had not shown his two letters to Wilde, he wrote to Wilde directly on 21 August, to say that his wife had cut out *the poem* as being painful and dangerous. Though it could have been one of several poems, 'Charmides' was presumably the offender, with its monstrous coupling and knowing asides. Wilde had departed from 'Revealed Truth' and the tendency of his verse was anti-Christian. Copulation with statues, though imaginary and unrequited, was out of bounds. So was kissing 'the mouth of sin' in 'Taedium Vitae.' 'As to morality I can't help saying Frank ought to be clear – he has, I believe, often argued with you. Our first thought of course must be of him and his good name and his profession. If in sadness I advise a separation for a time it is not because we do not believe you in character to be very different to what you suggest in your poetry, but it is because you do not see the risk we see in a published poem that, which makes all who read it say to themselves, "this is outside the province of poetry," "it is licentious and may do a great harm to any soul that reads it."[88]

Canon Miles did not suspect that his son had darker proclivities than the poetic lechery of his fellow tenant. Wilde casually mentioned to Robert Sherard what had happened not long before in Keats House. Miles had been 'fooling with a young girl,' and three policemen armed with a warrant came and pounded on the front door. 'Open in the name of the law,' they shouted. Wilde waited until Miles had a chance to get safely over the roof. He then unlocked the door and explained to the angry constables that Miles was away on the Continent, so he had assumed friends were playing a practical joke on him by posing as policemen. His bland assurance convinced the London police as once the Oxford proctors, and they took themselves off, bamboozled and mollified.[89]

Canon Miles followed his letter to Wilde with one to his son enjoining him to separate from his friend. Frank Miles told Wilde what his father had said. A model of Miles, Sally Higgs, daughter of a fishmonger, was present and described Wilde's rage. He demanded to know if Miles was going to obey his father in the name of morality. Miles, financially dependent, said that much as it distressed him, he had no alternative. 'Very well then,' said Wilde, 'I will leave you. I will go now and I will never speak to you again as long as I live.' (Wilde has Dorian Gray threaten Basil Hallward, 'on my word of honour I will never speak to you again as long as I live.') He tore upstairs, flung his clothes in a large trunk, and, rather than wait for help, tipped it over the banister. It crashed down on a valuable antique table and smashed it into fragments. He swept out of the house, slammed the door, hailed a cab, and was gone.[90]

For Miles the sequel was not happy. His father died, and he began to go to pieces. A late letter from him to Mrs George Boughton, the artist's wife, is written in an almost illegible scrawl: 'Tell George I have given up his idea and Oscars – and Jimmy [Whistler] long long ago – that art is for art's sake and if it is good [if some] unfortunate accident happens of its doing some harm to somebody why it is the artist's fault.'[91] And so, still advocating virtue, Miles faded from Wilde's scene. He had to be taken to Brislington asylum near Bristol in 1887, and died there four years later.

Wilde had once outraged Hunter Blair by falling back into Protestantism, but he had outraged the Protestant canon even more. His verse had larger purposes than to flatter his public, and he was beginning to experience the victimization he had once imagined for Keats. He knew perfectly well that his ideas were shocking to the English, provincial in their conventionality, piety, and conservatism, as he, an Irishman, was not. He had no intention of changing. They must change.

CHAPTER VI

Declaring His Genius

My whole life was but a schoolboy's dream. Today my life begins.

We have really everything in common with America nowadays, except, of course, language.

New Prospects

The rage of Wilde's departure from Frank Miles's house was succeeded in calm by the search for new lodgings. He could not afford a house of his own like the one he had happily shared for over a year in Tite Street. At first he went to stay with his mother at 1 Ovington Square, and then moved to two furnished rooms on the third floor at 9 Charles Street (now Carlos Place) off Grosvenor Square. These were oak-paneled and decorated with old engravings in black frames. A retired butler and his wife ran the house and prepared meals when asked. The real inconvenience came from having to separate himself from most of his cherished bric-à-brac and furnishings. He may have left some of these at Miles's house for a time, because at least once he used his old Tite Street address after his abrupt departure from it; and Miles, unhappy at having been his friend's evictor, may have obliged him in small ways.

Otherwise the rift with Miles had no effect but to confirm that friends could betray. The hypocrisy pervading England found its expression when a molester of small children could take a high moral line with him. Wilde was fortified in his conviction that he was a *poète maudit*, subject to all the hazards of that species. But he continued to cherish also his quite different role, that of the man of the world, and for this he required the company and indulgence of a leisured, moneyed class to whom, as to him, language was a form of action, and no negligible one.

To sustain this second position he needed not Frank Miles but money, and money was scarcer than ever. His slender patrimony dwindled. The record of his landed property suggests his predicament: on January 1881 he mortgaged his cherished hunting lodge, Illaunroe, on Lough Fee, and on 25 October 1882 he sold another bit of his Dublin property to one of his Maturin relations. Poetry was not lucrative. His main hope of improving his fortunes was Mrs Bernard Beere's oncoming production of *Vera*. Willie Wilde, now doing dramatic criticism, warned his brother that Mrs Beere could never play the role of Vera adequately, but Oscar was more than pleased to have her try. The production would release him from the charge that Modjeska and others had levelled, that he had done nothing. It would publicly justify his way of life.

He was sufficiently encouraged to think about writing another play. As early as 1880 he had announced in the *Biograph* his intention of writing a five-act tragedy in blank verse. At first this was to be entitled *The Duchess of Florence*; eventually it was relocated as *The Duchess of Padua*. Accustomed to his own oscillations, Wilde designed this play to be as aristocratic as *Vera* was republican. It would be in the Jacobean tradition of Webster, as *Vera* was in the tradition of melodramatic realism in Sardou. The new play too would include an assassination, this time not of the little father of all the Russias but of a treacherous uncle like those in *Richard III*, *Hamlet*, and *Women Beware Women*. Though Wilde had his subject well in mind, he would not write the scenario until late in 1882, and the writing of the play extended into the following year. His friend Forbes-Robertson urged him to write more plays, assuring him that nothing would be easier for him than to turn out half a dozen in record time; but Wilde could not bestir himself so easily and after his first two wrote no more until the 'nineties.

While he waited impatiently for Mrs Beere's rehearsals to begin, he was unexpectedly approached from another quarter. A cablegram, knowledgeably addressed to him at his mother's house, proved to be from the producer Richard D'Oyly Carte in New York. Since September Carte had had *Patience* running in New York with as much success as in London. Another part of his enterprise was to manage lecture tours, and he snatched at a suggestion, possibly from Sarah Bernhardt (who was credited by Wilde with having initiated the idea), to give Americans a chance to see and hear the leading exponent of aestheticism. Carte expected *Patience* to give a fillip to Wilde's lectures, and the lectures to give a fillip to *Patience*.

He was particularly willing to bring over the purported model for Bunthorne because Americans had little direct information about the type, and no history of the mockery of it such as du Maurier's. Of course the United States had a subculture which was dissatisfied with money and power, but this had no single and famed exponent. Neither the shirt-sleeved Whitman, nor the bearded Longfellow, nor the tense Emerson could remotely be thought of as Gilbert's model. The only traces of aestheticism to have reached America were women's gowns hung from the shoulders in flowing folds, Queen Anne furniture, Morris wallpaper,

Japanese screens – all just beginning to be known. Wilde might gather the strands together and give them the force of a program.

The first idea was for Wilde to present readings, in the manner of Dickens. The cable from Carte's office read:

> Responsible agent asks me to enquire if you will consider offer he makes by letter for fifty readings, beginning November first. This is confidential. Answer.

It did not take Wilde long to consider. The next day, 1 October, he cabled back, 'Yes, if offer good. Chelsea, Tite Street.' The offer was good: Carte would cover Wilde's expenses and would share equally with him the net profits. Wilde did not agree until December. A retired army colonel named W. F. Morse, who was managing the lecture business for Carte, corresponded with Wilde about the details. It became apparent that the tour could not be arranged so quickly, and that Wilde would need more time to prepare. He proposed some topics, and Morse in turn tried these out with booking agents around the country. From the beginning it was understood that Wilde was to be paraded as a figure in English society and not only as a writer. Morse expressly dissociated himself and Carte from Wilde's doctrine, but thought it modish enough to be worth a tour. All this Morse conveyed in letters to booking agents, as in this one, to a Philadelphia possibility:

> R. D'Oyly Carte's Opera Companies,
> Central Office, 1267 Broadway,
> New York   Nov. 8 1881
>
> Dear Sir,
>
> I have lately had a correspondence with Mr Oscar Wilde, the new English Poet, with reference to a tour in the U.S. during the winter. My attention was first drawn to him for the reason, that while we were preparing for the opera 'Patience' in New York, his name was often quoted as the originator of the aesthetic idea, and the author of a volume of poems lately published, which had made a profound sensation in English society. It was suggested to me, that if Mr Wilde were brought to this country with the view of illustrating in a public way his idea of the aesthetic, that not only would society be glad to hear the man and receive him socially, but also that the general public would be interested in hearing from him a true and correct definition and explanation of this latest form of fashionable madness . . . He advises me that he has prepared three lectures or essays, one of which is devoted to a consideration of 'The Beautiful' as seen in everyday life, another, illustrative of the poetical methods used by Shakespeare, and the third, a Lyric Poem . . . Now, should he come, I should like to place him for a public reading or lecture in your city. He will be first announced, advertised, and worked up in N.Y. City (where he will

145

probably speak three or four times) following which lectures he desires to visit other parts of the country. Can you find a place for him, for one or more nights, in the list of entertainments which you have in charge, at a moderate fee, or upon a basis of shares with me in the venture . . .

Very truly yours,
R. D'OYLY CARTE
per W. F. Morse[1]

The answers Morse received narrowed Wilde's repertoire at once. A lyric poem was not wanted. Even 'Charmides,' his favorite among the poems and perhaps the one he intended to recite, could not compare with the death of Little Nell read by Dickens in America fifteen years before. Nor did the idea of still another lecture on Shakespeare rouse the provinces. What America wanted, it became clear, was 'The Beautiful.' In December, Wilde accepted this proposal. Evidently he asked that the tour should start at the beginning of 1882, so that he would still be in London for the opening of *Vera*.

But *Vera* was not to open. Two assassinations had recently appalled the world, that of Czar Alexander II on 1 March and that of President Garfield on 19 September. Any hope Wilde may have entertained that these murders would make his play even more attractively topical was checked. There was a sudden burst of pro-royalist sentiment, as when Victoria attended a performance of *The Colonel* (the satire on aestheticism) and was cheered by the audience. (She received the leading actor, Bruce, afterwards.)[2] Actors begged off playing the republican parts. The prospect of *Vera* may have come to the attention of the Russian government, for the *New York Times*, on 26 December 1881, said that Lord Granville (then Foreign Secretary) had received a communication on the subject. One newspaper reported that as Wilde was now one of the 'European powers,' he could not give offense to a crowned head. The Prince of Wales himself or those sensitive to his wishes may have intervened, for he was married to the sister of the new Czarina, and could scarcely be expected to look with favor on an abortive assassination attempt, even on the stage. Some official pressure seems to have been applied, for in the last days of November, just as rehearsals for *Vera* were to begin, with Wilde's friend Dion Boucicault as director and Mrs Beere in the title role, they were cancelled.[3] It was a foretaste of Wilde's later difficulties over *Salome*, no less infuriating because the censorship was unofficial.

This blow gave Wilde a new impulse for his American tour, since in a republic there could scarcely be squeamishness over the lopping of crowned heads. On the other hand, the assassination of Garfield, and the trial of Guiteau for the crime, would occupy the American press for many months to come. Wilde was not discouraged: he announced before he left that he would arrange for the production of *Vera* and publish a second book of poems as well as carry the benevolent and challenging message of aestheticism to America. A letter survives addressed to an unknown recipient:

> Keats House
> Tite Street
> Chelsea, London

Dear Sir:

At the suggestion of my friend, Mr Dion Boucicault, I beg to forward you a copy of a new and original drama on Russia. The note through which the passion of the play is expressed is democratic – and for that reason it's unthinkable to act it in London. It is yet the tragedy, the essence of the play is human. There are two fine men's parts for character acting – the old Prince Metternich sort of statesman full of epigram and unscrupulousness, and the Czar.

The hero is a young enthusiast, and the heroine who gives the name to the play is conceived in all the many moods of passion that a study of Sarah Bernhardt could suggest.

I shall be very happy if you approve of the play, to correspond on the subject of its production.

> Your obedient servant,
> OSCAR WILDE[4]

He prepared carefully for his tour. What to wear came first of all. Wilde concocted a costume for his tailor to make. C. Lewis Hind saw him emerge from a furrier's, wearing 'a befrogged and wonderfully befurred green overcoat' and a Polish cap. Next week *The World* carried a letter from Whistler,

> OSCAR, – How dare you! What means this unseemly carnival in my Chelsea!
>
> Restore these things to Nathan, and never let me find you masquerading the streets in the combined costumes of a degraded Kossuth and Mr Mantalini!*
>
> [Butterfly symbol][5]

A heavy coat made sense in the American if not the English climate. As to lecturing, Wilde was aware, as he had been at Trinity and Oxford, that he had no talent for oratory. He repeatedly confessed as much in America. What he had to do was to cultivate a way of charming rather than coercing his audience. He felt incapable of ornate gestures or heavy emphasis, but told his friend Hermann Vezin, who gave him elocution lessons, 'I want a

---

* Lajos Kossuth, the Hungarian revolutionary who lived in England from 1851 to 1859, wore a Polish cap; and Mr Mantalini, husband of a milliner in Dickens's *Nicholas Nickleby*, wore a gorgeous morning gown.

natural style, with a touch of affectation.' 'Well,' said Vezin, 'and haven't you got that, Oscar?'[6] The sustained and mellifluous period, his particular talent, might go down well enough with Americans jaded by obvious showmanship.

Wilde had yet to prepare a lecture, and probably was waiting to measure the cultural temperature before doing so. In other ways he was provident: he knew the English art and literature of his time extremely well, he was also acquainted with most of the distinguished people in the arts and in politics, Disraeli and Gladstone as well as Browning, Tennyson, Swinburne, Rossetti, Millais, Alma Tadema, Burne-Jones, Whistler. As for the United States, he had read Poe, Whitman, Hawthorne, Holmes, Lowell, Howells, Longfellow, and James, and would later make a point of reading more local figures such as Cable, Fawcett, and Father Ryan. He was determined to meet important people, and wrote letters to many friends asking for letters of introduction. One, addressed to James Russell Lowell, United States Minister in London, is an example:

> 9, Charles Street
> Grosvenor Square.

Dear Mr Lowell,

I am sailing for America on Saturday by the Arizona to give a course of lectures on the modern artistic movement in England. Might I so far presume on our slight acquaintance as to ask you for some letters of introduction. I know what a passport to all that is brilliant and intellectual in America your name is.
　　Believe me

> Truly yours
> OSCAR WILDE

Lowell responded by writing Oliver Wendell Holmes on 21 December 1881,

Dear Doctor Holmes, – a clever and accomplished man should no more need an introduction than a fine day, but since a stranger can no longer establish a claim on us by coming in and seating himself as a suppliant at our fireside, let me ask you to be serviceable to the bearer of this, Mr Oscar Wilde, the report of whom has doubtless reached you and who is better than his report.

> Faithfully yours,
> J. R. LOWELL[7]

He reviewed Wilde's poems rather favorably in an unsigned notice for the *Atlantic Monthly* in January 1882.

A great many people on both sides of the Atlantic were alerted to Wilde's impending voyage. Whistler, probably informed that Wilde was going to tout the Pre-Raphaelites, remarked to him, 'If you get sea-sick, throw up Burne-Jones.'[8]* The press began to present the tour as an event of importance, to be frowned on or smiled at, if not often simply welcomed. In England the newspapers were divided: the *Pall Mall Gazette* carried in December a series of letters, gradually increasing in unpleasantness, against aestheticism. One correspondent, who manfully signed himself 'Titus Manlius,' and was probably on the editorial staff, sent in a letter entitled 'Bunthorne and Bunkum.' It contained among other gratuitous slurs, 'Probably no one laughs (in his sleeve) at and despises these mock-hysterical aesthetes more than does the Great Prophet himself – who, by the way, is not much of a prophet in his own country, Ireland, and not much of a poet in this.' A leading article on 28 December disparaged and dismissed Wilde's movement.

Still, Wilde had friends in the English press, notably Henry Labouchere of *Truth* and Edmund Yates of *The World*. They could be relied upon for a kind word, and Labouchere in particular announced on 22 December 1881 in the opening pages of *Truth*:

> Mr Oscar Wilde is going to the United States at the end of this week in the *Arizona*, having made arrangements to bring out his Republican play 'Vera' there, and during his stay he will deliver a series of lectures on modern life in its romantic aspect. The Americans are far more curious than we are to gaze at all those whose names, from one cause or another, have become household words, and in this I think they are wiser than we are, for it is difficult to realise the personality of anyone, without having seen him. Mr Wilde – say what one may of him – has a distinct individuality, and, therefore, I should fancy that his lectures will attract many who will listen and look.

He continued to endorse Wilde's tour as it proceeded. So in a considered three-page article on 2 February 1882, 'The Aesthete on His Travels,' Labouchere quoted from favorable notices of Wilde's reception, and suggested that hyper-aestheticism might be useful as an antidote to America's hyper-materialism. Wilde had reason in St Louis to call Labouchere 'the best writer in Europe, a remarkable gentleman.'[9]

Morse continued to solicit lecturing engagements for Wilde, citing his parents' titles and talents, his Oxford education and prizes, his poems, his identification with the aesthetic movement. The title of Wilde's lecture was no longer unguardedly 'The Beautiful,' but had become 'The Artistic Character of the English Renaissance'; the final form was 'The English Renaissance.' For this title Wilde had gone back to his favorite book of

---

* Ever since the libel suit against Ruskin, in which Burne-Jones had testified on Ruskin's side, Whistler had always said that Burne-Jones knew nothing about painting.

Pater. Though *Studies in the History of the Renaissance* was ostensibly about the Italian Renaissance, it had included the researches of Winckelmann in the eighteenth century, and implied that a renaissance was available to those looking intensively for artistic pulsations in the modern world. Wilde used renaissance with eloquent vagueness, allowing room in it for Ruskin, Pater, the Pre-Raphaelites, Whistler, and himself.

How to link them was a question. In presenting himself as a spokesman for aestheticism, Wilde was assuming a greater than customary responsibility. Up to now he had espoused attitudes rather than theories, and encouraged a cult rather than a movement. Like Polybius he would now have to bring system to what was unsystematized. The Pre-Raphaelites were not of much help; they had never been good at formulating general principles, and in 1882, their locks grizzled and their youth over, they were even less likely to do so. Still, Wilde was enthusiastic for them all, and he began to think out a lecture which would endorse them and overlook their divergences. He planned to write the lecture on the *SS Arizona*, on which he embarked on 24 December 1881. But by the time the ship docked on 2 January, he did not have it ready. The enterprise had become more ambitious: he must not only formulate the movement of which he was supposedly the leading exponent, but also, like Dorian Gray, 'gather up the scarlet threads of life, and . . . weave them into a pattern.'[10]

Poet and Press

HESTER (smiling): *We have the largest country in the world, Lady Caroline. They used to tell me at school that some of our states are as big as France and England put together.*

LADY CAROLINE: *Ah! You must find it very draughty, I should fancy.*

The *Arizona* docked in New York harbor on the evening of 2 January 1882. It was too late to clear quarantine until the following morning. The press, avid to see Wilde, could not wait. Enterprising reporters 'came out of the sea,' as Wilde picturesquely noted, their pens still wet with brine. In fact, they chartered a launch to bring them aboard. Wilde was in the captain's cabin and emerged to greet them clad in the great green coat that hung down almost to his feet. It was subjected to close inspection: the collar and cuffs were trimmed with seal or otter, and so was the material for the round cap, variously described as a smoking cap or turban. Beneath the coat could be discerned a shirt with a wide Lord Byron collar, and a sky-blue necktie, vaguely reminiscent of the costume of a modern mariner. He wore patent leather shoes on his small feet.

Wilde had been thinking of 'the cloud of misrepresentation that must have preceded' him,[11] but he was not prepared for the reporters: there were so many, and they would ask anything. Nor were the reporters prepared for him. Rather than the Bunthorne they expected, a man arrived who was taller than they were, with broad shoulders and long arms and hands that looked capable of being doubled into fists. He might be lionized but not buffaloed. A chastened *New York Evening Post* reported merely that he had 'a large, white, flat face.' On his finger was a great seal ring bearing a Greek classical profile. The same hand held a lighted cigarette, which he appeared not to inhale. His voice astonished the representative of the *New York Tribune* by being anything but feminine, burly rather. Another thought Wilde spoke in hexameters; the *New York World* heard him accenting every fourth syllable in a kind of singsong: 'I came from *Eng*land because I *thought* America was the best *place* to see.'[12] Singsong or syncopation, it was distinctive.

What had he thought of the crossing? Wilde did not anticipate that his every word would be quoted, usually in distorted form, and merely observed that it had been uninteresting. The reporters were bent upon finding a headline, and they besieged other passengers until one told them that Wilde had remarked during the voyage, 'I am not exactly pleased with the Atlantic. It is not so majestic as I expected. The sea seems tame to me. The roaring ocean does not roar.' These wry comments from the poet who had written of the 'unvintageable sea'* were propelled into large type: 'Mr Wilde Disappointed with the Atlantic,' and promptly cabled to England. The *Pall Mall Gazette* printed a poem, 'The Disappointed Deep,' and a letter printed in Labouchere's *Truth* began, 'I am disappointed in Mr Wilde,' and was signed, THE ATLANTIC OCEAN. Admittedly it was better copy than what Wilde had actually said, which was that on his ship from Athens to Naples in 1877 he had experienced a cyclone which was 'the grandest sight I ever saw,' and made him long for another storm that might 'sweep the bridge from off the ship.' Playfulness in transatlantic passengers was something new to journalistic experience, and they expressed their confusion by attempting to out-do *Punch* and *Patience*.

Their launch had outstayed its time, but the reporters hung on to ask Wilde about his cultural mission. What was this aestheticism he had crossed the sea to promulgate? Wilde laughed, disconcerting them again, for Bunthorne had no sense of humor. Then he braved them by saying, 'Aestheticism is a search after the signs of the beautiful. It is the science of the beautiful through which men seek the correlation of the arts. It is, to

---

* In *De Profundis* Wilde would testify to 'a strange longing for the great simple primeval things, such as the Sea, to me no less of a mother than the Earth.'[13]

speak more exactly, the search after the secret of life.' (He would divulge in his lecture what the secret of life was.) One reporter, more knowledge-able perhaps than the rest, challenged Wilde: was it not true that the movement (the existence of which he allowed) had fostered only idiosyn-cratic responses rather than a correct and consistent taste for the beauti-ful? Wilde replied politely, 'Well, you might say that it has. But then all movements develop characteristics in the individuals taking part in them. Really a movement that did not do so would be of little worth.' So far he had come through this trial fairly well.

The next day the reporters were back as the passengers disembarked. Wilde declined to define aestheticism again, but did not shirk the challenge: 'I am here to diffuse beauty, and I have no objection to saying that.' He interrupted this cloudy utterance himself, 'I say, porter, handle that box more carefully, will you?' It contained his American wardrobe and copies of his *Poems* intended as presents. The beautiful, he went on, might well appear in the commonplace. Puffing a cigarette, both hands deep in the pockets of a green dressing gown, he said, 'Beauty is nearer to most of us than we are aware. The material is all around us but we want a systematic way of bringing it out.' A reporter pointed to a large grain elevator on the Jersey side of the river, and asked, 'Could that have aesthetic value?' Wilde glanced across but with new caution replied that he was too nearsighted to see the object in question. 'Might beauty then be in both the lily and Hoboken?' persisted the reporter. 'Something of the kind,' Wilde agreed, 'it's a wide field which has no limit, and all definitions are unsatisfactory. Some people might search and not find anything. But the search, if carried on according to right laws, would constitute aestheticism. They would find happiness in striving, even in despair of ever finding what they sought. The renaissance of beauty is not to be hoped for without strife internal and external.' 'Where then is this movement to end?' 'There is no end to it; it will go on forever, just as it had no beginning. I have used the word renaissance to show that it is no new thing with *me*. It has always existed. As time goes on the men and the forms of expression may change, but the principle will remain. Man is hungry for beauty . . . There is a void; nature will fill it. The ridicule which aesthetes have been subjected to is the only way of blind unhappy souls who cannot find the way to beauty.'

The beauty to be diffused was not contraband. On being obliged to pass through customs, Wilde said, or was reputed to have said (no contempo-rary account records it), in response to the customs officer's question, 'Have you anything to declare?', 'I have nothing to declare except my genius.' He may well have said it, for after a day in the harbor he could see the importance of having an epigram at the ready. Again the English press felt obliged to take note of him. The overwrought *Pall Mall Gazette* published not only two 'Idylls of the Dado,' on 4 and 9 January, but on the latter date a leader entitled, 'A Postscript to Bunthorne,' saying that du

Maurier had invented the aesthetes, and 'an ingenious young gentleman from Ireland' had amused himself by posing as the typical aesthete, so that now he is 'the hero of the hour' and 'his sayings are telegraphed all over the world' to be printed in 'the gravest journals.' The *Gazette* was gravely indignant.

Now began a series of entertainments. Wilde was treated, as he could brag with justification in letters home, as a *petit roi*. The Brevoort being full, Morse put him up at the Grand at 31st Street and Broadway. His whereabouts were to be secret so he could finish writing his lecture. But Wilde made no difficulties about accepting the round of luncheons, afternoon receptions, dinners, and evening receptions that were offered him. New York newspapers somewhat restrained their derision for the moment because of the obvious pleasure he was giving to a series of distinguished hosts and hostesses. The first party was from three to six o'clock on 5 January at the house of Mr and Mrs A. A. Hayes, Jr, at 112 East 29th Street. Hayes, a travel writer, and his wife were already aesthetically attuned, with rooms done gracefully in a Japanese style. Wilde made his entrance wearing a tightly buttoned Prince Albert coat, and holding in his hand a pair of light kid gloves. He wore as on the ship a broad collar with a light blue scarf encircling it. His hair was long but not excessively so. Soon he was posed in the opening between two large parlors, a gigantic Japanese umbrella behind him, its long handle protecting him on the left and a partition dividing the parlors on the right. Daylight was shut out by heavy dark curtains, and in the Caravaggesque gaslight, Wilde, expatiating, looked (a reporter wrote) 'like a heathen idol.' The décor perhaps put him in mind of Whistler and his Japanese effects, for he assured the company that Whistler was 'the first painter in England, only it will take England 300 years to find it out.'[14]

The reception over, Wilde accompanied Mr and Mrs Hayes and nine other guests to the Standard Theatre where *Patience* was being played. They arrived some minutes after the curtain had risen, just as Lady Jane was about to inform Patience what love is. At first Wilde kept to the back of the box, out of sight, but self-effacement was not his way, and eventually he moved forward. When J. H. Ryley came on stage as Bunthorne, the whole audience turned and stared at Wilde. Bunthorne was made up as Whistler in England, as Wilde in America. Wilde now smiled at one of his women companions and commented patronizingly, 'This is one of the compliments that mediocrity pays to those who are not mediocre.' (In *The Duchess of Padua*, he would write more flatly, 'The most eccentric thing a man can do / Is to have brains, then the crowd mocks at him . . .') The party was invited backstage after the first act, and when the opera was over fifty people waited outside to catch a glimpse of Wilde. But he had already been shown to a side exit so as to escape unobserved.

There were some writers, such as Clarence Stedman, who made a point of not accepting invitations to parties that Wilde might attend.

Stedman had been warned off Wilde by Edmund Gosse, who had informed him shortly before that Wilde's volume of poems was 'a curious toadstool, a malodorous parasitic growth,' parlayed into a third edition by the author's aristocratic friends. At his first meeting with Wilde not long before, when Wilde expressed pleasure at the encounter, Gosse said, 'I was afraid you'd be disappointed.' 'Oh no,' Wilde replied, 'I am never disappointed in literary men. I think they are perfectly charming. It is their works I find so disappointing.'[15] As an indirect result of that slight, Stedman in turn wrote to Thomas Bailey Aldrich, the editor of the *Atlantic Monthly*, 'This Philistine town is making a fool of itself over Oscar Wilde . . . He has brought hundreds of letters of introduction.'[16] Two of these letters had been to Stedman himself, from James Russell Lowell and George Lewis. Aldrich would avoid Wilde similarly in Boston. John Burroughs, the naturalist, received Wilde but had his reservations, summing him up as 'a splendid talker, and a handsome man, but a voluptuary. As he walked from you, there was something in the motion of his hips and back that was disagreeable.'[17]

The social side of Wilde's tour was initially triumphal. He had a letter of introduction from Lord Houghton to 'Uncle' Sam Ward, who was Julia Ward Howe's brother and the uncle of the novelist F. Marion Crawford. Ward, sixty-eight years old, was a lobbyist, a man of the world, and a great lubricator of the wheels of society. He took up Wilde enthusiastically, addressing him in letters as 'My dear Charmides,' and brought him to meet General Grant in Long Branch. Wilde for his part quoted some of Ward's own poems, and so convinced Ward that in aesthetic matters the young man 'knew his business.' He departed from his habit of dining out by entertaining Wilde at a sumptuous dinner in his own flat at 84 Clinton Place. Lilies of the valley occupied the center of the table, and two calla lilies tied with a red ribbon were placed directly in front of Wilde's plate. Guests wore lilies of the valley in their buttonholes. To make matters worse, Ward had written a song called 'The Valley Lily,' which another guest, Stephen Masset, had set to music and now sang. Wilde politely called for an encore. The press was duly informed and announced, 'It was the unanimous verdict that Mr Wilde was the best raconteur since Lord Houghton's time. He talked glibly and knowingly of Sir William Harcourt, Gladstone, and the leaders of the opposing political factions in England and on the continent.' Most of the guests stayed on very late to listen. Ward was delighted and, indomitable poetaster, wrote for Wilde a poem which began,

> 'Father, what is the aesthetic?'
> Asked a child.
> Puzzled, he said, 'Ask the hermetic
> Oscar Wilde.'
> 'Oscar, what is the aesthetic?'

> Asked the girl.
> ''Tis,' beamed Oscar, 'this pathetic
> Suppliant curl.'

Labouchere obligingly published it in *Truth*. Ward also sent a copy to Longfellow. He recommended Wilde to his sister Julia Ward Howe by writing, 'I think him a sincere fellow with sweetness and dignity of manner and character, and forgive him his fantastic penchants which he will outgrow.' To Wilde he offered another poem:

> Go it, Oscar! You are young,
> Owning a conviction,
> To which you have wisely clung –
> Beauty is no fiction!

Wilde presented him with his *Poems*, inscribed, *'L'art pour l'art, et mes poèmes pour mon oncle.* Sam Ward from Oscar Wilde, affectionately.' Wilde recognized that he strained Ward's loyalty, and strolled into Ward's room one day to sigh to him and Marion Crawford, 'Where will it all end? Half the world does not believe in God, and the other half does not believe in me.' Only towards the end of a year of frequent meetings did Ward show the slightest disaffection: 'It irks me to go about as the courier of an elephant. I don't want to be eternally in the papers as his dry nurse.'[18] Still, the friendship held.

While merrymaking was pursued more assiduously than speechwriting, Wilde did not lose sight of his goal, that a New York actress should stage *Vera*. From what he had heard, the likeliest prospects were Mary Anderson and Clara Morris. Two days after his ship docked, he went to see Mary Anderson in *Romeo and Juliet*. His comments afterwards were polite only: the *New York Times* quoted him on 6 January, 'She is a very beautiful woman, but there are traditions about dress in Shakespearean performances that detract much from the pleasure I think of witnessing those plays. Miss Anderson did excellently well, however, but I should prefer to see her in other plays than those of Shakespeare. Why, Modjeska delighted London audiences until she made her appearance as Juliet. Then she seemed to lose her hold upon her audiences, and they were never satisfied with her after that, no matter what she undertook.' For the moment he put Mary Anderson aside in favor of Clara Morris, but, as if to share his favors, accompanied Clara Morris and her husband on 14 January to see Mary Anderson in *Pygmalion and Galatea* at the Booth Theatre.

Miss Morris was known for her intensity. Wilde and she were guests at a reception for Louisa May Alcott at the house of D. G. Croly, 172 East 38th Street, on 8 January. Catching sight of her in the anteroom, Wilde at once took her hand in both of his. 'I have heard much of you from Sarah Bernhardt,' he said; 'Sarah told me, *"Elle a du tempérament; c'est assez dire."* ' Miss Morris was unwon by this half-hearted compliment from her eminent rival, but at subsequent meetings with Wilde she came to like him. On 11 January she and Wilde were among a few guests for luncheon at Kate Field's Cooperative Dress Association, and this time he persuaded her to let him leave his play for her to read. She would not decide about it for some weeks; but the very next afternoon he saw her act for the first time as Mercy Merrick in *The New Magdalen* at the Union Square Theatre, and did not stint his praise either backstage or to a reporter afterwards. He was quoted as having said, 'Miss Morris is the greatest actress I ever saw, if it be fair to form an opinion of her from her rendition of this one role. We have no such powerfully intense actress in England. She is a great artist, in my sense of the word, because all she does, all she says, in the manner of the doing and of the saying constantly evoke the imagination to supplement it. That is what I mean by art. She would be a wonderful actress in London. I don't think however that a play as worn as *The New Magdalen* would be the proper work in which to present her. She is a veritable genius.'

In the wake of this tribute, Clara Morris read *Vera* carefully. In early February, however, she decided it was not for her. Wilde did not quite give her up. He decided to let D'Oyly Carte try to arrange a production, and urged him to make a further effort with Clara Morris; 'I am however quite aware how *difficile* she is,' he wrote Carte on 16 March. Failing her, he proposed Rose Coghlan, an English actress who played mostly in the United States. Carte complained that *Vera* would be obscure to Americans knowing nothing of Russia, and Wilde promptly composed a prologue to alleviate the difficulty. Several further letters urged Carte on, but to no avail. Clara Morris was booked for another play. Though thwarted for the moment, Wilde decided to protect the play by having it copyrighted in the United States, and continued to look about for an actress.

The main thing, however, was his lecture. He finally wrote it out and had it typed. 'If I am not a success on Monday I shall be wretched,' he wrote to Mrs George Lewis in London. By the time he appeared on the stage of Chickering Hall on 9 January, a week after his arrival, he could hardly fail. Tickets were sold out, even for standing room, and the receipts were $1,211. Colonel Morse introduced Wilde with a sentence or two, and the speaker then opened his manuscript which he carried in an expensive morocco case. His audience could now take stock of his attire, which was not at all what he had been wearing to the receptions, and was far more daring than anything in the lecture. ('The costume of the nineteenth century is detestable,' says Lord Henry Wotton in *Dorian Gray*. 'It is so sombre, so depressing.') Its most conspicuous feature was knee breeches, which showed off his well turned legs and feet. Some thought they recognized this as court dress, and probably no one knew that it was the costume of the Apollo Lodge at Oxford to which Wilde belonged. His stockings were also noted. 'Strange,' he said later, 'that a pair of silk stockings should so upset a nation.'[19] Helen Potter, later to impersonate Wilde in public performances, scrutinized him with professional concentration:

> Costume. – A dark purple sack coat, and knee-breeches; black hose, low shoes with bright buckles; coat lined with lavender satin, a frill of rich lace at the wrists and for tie-ends over a low turn-down collar, hair long, and parted in the middle, or all combed over. Enter with a circular cavalier cloak over the shoulder. The voice is clear, easy, and not forced. Change pose now and then, the head inclining toward the strong foot, and keep a general appearance of repose.
>
> This disciple of true art speaks very deliberately, and . . . the closing inflection of a sentence or period is ever upward.[20]*

The essay which he read out was in contrast to his costume. Having won his audience's attention by ostentation, he held it by surprising gravity. What he offered was not the rarefaction and preciosity of early Pater, but a reconsidered aestheticism. Instead of being languid it was energetic. By beautifying the outward aspects of life, he would beautify the inner ones. To disarm those who expected him to say what beauty was, he quoted Goethe in support of defining beauty by example, not by philosophical hairsplitting. The English Renaissance was, he said, like the Italian Renaissance before it, 'a sort of new birth of the spirit of man.' Under this rubric he could discuss the desire for a more gracious and comely way of life, the passion for physical beauty, the attention to form rather than content, the search for new subjects of poetry, for new forms of art, for new intellectual and imaginative enjoyments. The new Euphorion was, as Goethe had foreseen, the product of mating Hellenism and romanticism, Helen of Troy and Faust.

Wilde dealt largely with large matters. The French Revolution had compelled art to respect the facts of physical life, but those facts had proved suffocating. Against the dominion of facts the Pre-Raphaelites had gathered to make their protest. That the British public was unaware of these eminent artists had no bearing on the matter. 'To know nothing about their great men is one of the necessary elements of English education.' Nor did the fact that these artists were frequently the objects of satire detract in any way from their worth. He amplified what he had said at the performance of *Patience*: 'Satire, always as sterile as it is shameful and as impotent as it is insolent, paid them that usual homage which mediocrity pays to genius . . . To disagree with three fourths of the

---

* See Appendix B for Helen Potter's indication of his speech patterns.

British public on all points is one of the first elements of sanity.'[21]

Some characteristics of the English Renaissance were difficult to document among most of the artists he named. He asserted without much justification that they celebrated form at the expense of content, being unconcerned with moral lessons or weighty ideas. (Pater in *Plato and Platonism* had pointed out that for Plato form was everything, matter nothing.) They were right, he said, because not new ideas, or old moral preoccupations, but the discovery of Parian marble, had made Greek sculpture possible, as the discovery of oil pigments had made possible the Venetian school, and of new instruments had made possible the development of modern music. The Pre-Raphaelites were in reaction against empty conventional workmanship. It was the capacity to render, not the capacity to feel, which brought true art into being. And once in being, art conferred upon life a value it had not heretofore had. Its creations were more real than the living. As Swinburne had once remarked in Wilde's hearing at dinner (at Lord Houghton's), Homer's Achilles was more real than England's Wellington. Wilde was piecing together his later discovery that life imitates art.

Although at moments he implied like Pater that his renaissance was a recurrent phenomenon in history, at moments he insisted that the present awakening of the spirit was more thoroughgoing than its predecessors. Although it lacked the 'divine natural prescience of beauty' in Greece and Rome, it had a 'strained self-consciousness' which he did not disparage. It was essentially a western phenomenon, even if some of its decorative patterns came from the east. He hoped that the western spirit, so anxious and disquieted, might find rest in comely surroundings which could foster a fuller existence. Hence the importance of decorative art. 'You have listened to *Patience* for a hundred nights and have listened to me for only one,' he said. 'You have heard, I think, a few of you, of two flowers connected with the aesthetic movement in England, and said (I assure you, erroneously) to be the food of some aesthetic young men. Well, let me tell you the reason we love the lily and the sunflower, in spite of what Mr Gilbert may tell you, is not for any vegetable fashion at all. It is because these two lovely flowers are in England the most perfect models of design, the most naturally adapted for decorative art.' On this note the lecturer drew towards his ringing conclusion. For his final sentence he adopted a mannerism of Pater's, the interjection, 'Well!': 'We spend our days looking for the secret of life. Well, the secret of life is art.' He had disclosed it at last.

Paumanokides

It is a vulgar error to suppose that America was ever discovered. It was merely detected.

The audience applauded warmly. Not all of them were pleased, some had been bored, but all recognized that they had been in the presence of something unaccustomed. Sam Ward praised Wilde for avoiding rhetorical tricks – a generous response to what others called a monotone. Wilde had lectured to them as much through rhythm and manner as through argument, heaping up cadences to make them imagine the beauty he did not define. The lecture was itself a diffusion of beauty, though a glib one. Afterwards there was a reception, and as Wilde moved into the drawing room, an orchestra struck up 'God Save the Queen,' an honor rarely accorded an Irishman. Perhaps it was here that a woman asked him how to arrange some decorative screens, and he replied, 'Why arrange them at all? Why not let them occur?'[22] Following the reception, Wilde was taken to a club. There some of the young men are supposed to have importuned him to sample earthly examples of that beauty which he had been diffusing on a more ethereal level. Wilde seems to have gone along to nighttown, and perhaps did what they proposed.[23]

He felt that he had started off well, and wrote to Mrs George Lewis, 'I am sure you have been pleased at my success! The hall had an audience larger and more wonderful than even Dickens had. . . . I have several . . . secretaries. One writes my autographs all day for my admirers [he would say later that this one had had to go to the hospital with writer's cramp], the other receives the flowers that are left really every ten minutes. A third whose hair resembles mine is obliged to send off locks of his own hair to the myriad maidens of the city, and so is rapidly becoming bald . . . Loving virtuous obscurity as much as I do, you can judge how much I dislike this lionizing, which is worse than that given to Sarah Bernhardt I hear.'[24] What he had succeeded in presenting was not so much precepts as a personality. That personality became the subject of vivid contention as he zigzagged impossibly across the country.

Wilde's next lecture was scheduled for the Horticultural Hall in Philadelphia on 17 January. But he had another errand to carry out first. When he arrived at the Aldine Hotel in that city on the 16th, he was asked by a new batch of reporters which American poet he most admired. He replied without hesitation, 'I think that Walt Whitman and Emerson have given the world more than anyone else.' Longfellow, admirable as he was, was too close to European sources to have much effect in Europe. Wilde actually valued Poe, 'this marvellous lord of rhythmic expression,'[25] above the others, but Poe was dead. 'I do so hope to meet Mr Whitman,' Wilde confided. 'Perhaps he is not widely read in England, but England never appreciates a poet until he is dead. There is something so Greek and sane about his poetry, it is so universal, so comprehensive. It has all the pantheism of Goethe and Schiller.' Two of his friends, J. M. Stoddart and George W. Childs, both publishers, were planning parties in Philadelphia for Wilde, and both invited Whitman to come from Camden, New Jersey, and attend them. Whitman declined both invitations, but asked Mrs Childs to give Wilde 'my hearty salutations and American welcome.' On 18 January, however, perhaps after reading Wilde's encomium in the press, he sent Stoddart a card, 'Walt Whitman will be in from 2 till 3½ this afternoon, and will be most happy to see Mr Wilde and Mr Stoddart.'[26]

Stoddart, the publisher of the Savoyard operas, had become acquainted with Wilde in New York and had gone to the theatre there with him one evening. Now they drove companionably to Camden (Wilde Londonized it later to Camden Town). At this time Whitman was living with his brother and sister-in-law. The room they entered was one which Wilde praised for its fresh air and sunlight as the most impressive room he had entered in America. On the table stood an austere pitcher ('cruse' was Wilde's term) of water. How the two worthies addressed each other rapidly became the subject of comic speculation. A parody by Helen Gray Cone in the *Century* magazine for November 1882 was close enough to the mark:

Paumanokides:

Who may this be?
This young man clad unusually with loose locks, languorous,
                    glidingly toward me advancing,
Toward the ceiling of my chamber his orbic and expressive
                    eye-balls uprolling?

Narcissus:

O clarion, from whose brazen throat,
    Strange sounds across the seas are blown,
Where England, girt as with a moat,
    A strong sea-lion, sits alone!

In humbler prose, Wilde initiated the conversation by saying, 'I come as a poet to call upon a poet.' Whitman replied, 'Go ahead.' Wilde went on, 'I have come to you as one with whom I have been acquainted almost from the cradle.' He explained that his mother had purchased a copy of *Leaves of Grass* when it was published; presumably this was in 1868 (Wilde put it two years earlier), when William Michael Rossetti edited a selection of Whitman's poems. Lady Wilde read out the poems to her son, and later, when Wilde had gone up to Oxford, he and his friends carried *Leaves of Grass* to read on their walks. Whitman, in pleased response, went to the cupboard and took out his sister-in-law's bottle of homemade elderberry wine. Wilde drained without wincing the glass that Whitman had filled, and they settled down to consume the rest of the bottle. 'I will call you Oscar,' said Whitman, and Wilde, laying his hand on the poet's knee, replied, 'I like that so much.' To Whitman Wilde was 'a fine handsome youngster.' Wilde was too big to take on his lap like other youngsters who visited the sage, but could be coddled if not cuddled.[27]

The bottle emptied, Whitman proposed that they go to his den where they could be on what he called 'thee and thou terms.' The den was filled with dusty newspapers preserved because they mentioned Whitman's name, and Wilde would complain later to Sherard of the squalid scene in which the poet had to write. It was hard to find a place to sit down, but by removing a stack of newspapers from a chair, Wilde managed to. They had much to talk about. Whitman was eager to know about Swinburne, who had long ago been his English advocate and had written the tribute, 'To Walt Whitman Across the Sea.' Wilde knew Swinburne well enough to promise to relay Whitman's message of friendship to him. Whitman presented Wilde with two photographs, one for himself and one for Swinburne, and Wilde promised to send him in return a copy of a photograph he had just had taken by Napoleon Sarony in New York. (There had been some twenty poses.) Wilde spoke of the young writers and artists who were forming a new renaissance. Whitman uneasily asked after Tennyson, whose 'verbal melody almost always perfumed, like the tuberose, to an extreme of sweetness,' he greatly admired. 'Are not you young fellows going to shove the established idols aside, Tennyson and the rest?' Wilde would later deride Tennyson as 'the Homer of the Isle of Wight'; he tried to reassure Whitman now. 'Not at all. Tennyson's rank is too well fixed and we love him too much. But he has not allowed himself to be a part of the living world and of the great currents of interest and action. He is of priceless value and yet he lives apart from his time. He lives in a dream of the unreal. We, on the other hand, move in the very heart of today.'[28] Whitman could nod his approval of that last sounding phrase.

Wilde pressed his advantage to ask what Whitman made of the new aesthetic school. Whitman replied with an indulgent smile befitting his sixty-three years, 'I wish well to you, Oscar, and as to the aesthetes, I can only say that you are young and ardent, and the field is wide, and if you want my advice, go ahead.' With comparable politeness Wilde questioned Whitman about his theories of poetry and composition. Prosody was not a subject on which Whitman had ever been articulate, except in relentlessly extolling free verse. He responded with wonderful ingenuousness, 'Well, you know, I was at one time of my life a compositor and when a compositor gets to the end of his stick he stops short and goes ahead on the next line.' He went on unabashed, 'I aim at making my verse look all neat and pretty on the pages, like the epitaph on a square tombstone.' To illustrate he outlined such a tombstone with his hands in the air. Wilde treasured the remark and the gesture, and re-enacted them to Douglas Ainslie some years later.[29] But Whitman concluded with impressive simplicity, 'These are problems I am always seeking to solve.'

So far all had been good cheer and substantial agreement. Wilde risked more dangerous ground when he declared, 'I can't listen to anyone unless he attracts me by a charming style, or by beauty of theme.' At this the older poet remonstrated, 'Why, Oscar, it always seems to me that the fellow who makes a dead set at beauty by itself is in a bad way. My idea is that beauty is a result, not an abstraction.' This time Wilde took his turn in being concessive: 'Yes, I remember you have said, "All beauty comes from beautiful blood and a beautiful brain," and after all, I think so too.'

He shifted to a subject certain to be congenial, Whitman's courage in flouting convention and resisting hostile criticism. The parallel with the hostile reception his own poems had received was apposite. For the moment Whitman's example seemed to prove that America was freer than England, though only five months later a sixth edition of *Leaves of Grass* would be unexpectedly withdrawn because of a threat of prosecution for two of its poems. Wilde said, 'You cannot conceive how doubly and trebly bound literature and art are in England. The poet or artist who goes beyond is pretty sure of a hard time. And yet there is a most determined class of the best people in England, not only among the young but of all ages, both men and women, who are ready and eager for anything in art, science or politics that will break up the stagnation.' He pleased Whitman by praising the American masses as superior to the masses in England and Europe. The sentiment was not original, Whitman commented later, but it showed that Wilde had his wits about him.

After two hours of talk Whitman said, 'Oscar, you must be thirsty. I'll make you some punch.' 'Yes, I am thirsty.' Whitman made him a 'big glass of milk punch,' Wilde 'tossed it off and away he went,' as Whitman recalled afterwards. But as he departed the old poet called out after him, 'Goodbye, Oscar, God bless you.' On the ride back to Philadelphia with Stoddart, who had played silent partner in these eager confabulations, Wilde unwontedly kept still, full of emotion at what he called 'the grand old man.' Stoddart, to lighten his mood, remarked that the elderberry wine must have been hard to get down. Wilde brooked no such criticism: 'If it had been vinegar I should have drunk it all the same, for I have an admiration for that man which I can hardly express.' The next time he was interviewed by a reporter, he said of Whitman, 'He is the grandest man I have ever seen, the simplest, most natural, and strongest character I have ever met in my life. I regard him as one of those wonderful, large, entire men who might have lived in any age and is not peculiar to any people. Strong, true, and perfectly sane: the closest approach to the Greek we have yet had in modern times.'

It was like an eighteenth-century city poet praising a homespun shepherd. To Wilde, who shared Poe's concern with 'the fabric and cut of the garment,' the verse of Whitman was all subject and no form. As he said of Whitman later, 'If not a poet, he is a man who strikes a strong note, perhaps neither prose nor poetry but something of his own that is grand, original and unique.' To Whitman Wilde had the supreme virtue of being young, and 'so frank and outspoken and manly.' With him Wilde had discarded his affectations: 'I saw behind the scene,' Whitman said. He defended Wilde against criticism, 'I don't see why such mocking things are written of him. He has the English society drawl, but his enunciation is better than I ever heard in a young Englishman or Irishman before.' To one of his young friends, Henry Stafford, Whitman bragged, perhaps to make Stafford a little jealous, that 'Wilde had the *good sense* to take a great fancy to *me*.'[30] He particularly liked and quoted a remark Wilde made later in some Boston drawing room: 'If I may presume to speak for them – to include myself among them – I should say, it is not your praise, your laudations, that we, the poets seek, but your comprehension – your recognition of what we stand for and what we effect.'

True to his promise, Wilde wrote off at once to Swinburne to convey Whitman's friendly respect. A reply dated 2 February by Swinburne must have been composed and sent at once:

Dear Mr Wilde,

I am sincerely interested and gratified by your account of Walt Whitman and the assurance of his kindly and friendly feeling towards me: and I thank you, no less sincerely, for your kindness in sending me word of it.

As sincerely as I can say, that I shall be freshly obliged to you if you will – should occasion arise – assure him in my name, that I have by no manner of means either forgotten him or relaxed my admiration of his noblest work – such parts, above all, of his writings, as treat of the noblest subjects, material and spiritual, with which poetry can deal. I have always thought it, and I believe it will hereafter be generally thought, his highest and surely most enviable distinction that he never speaks so well as when he speaks of great matters – liberty, for instance, and death. This of course does not imply that I do – rather it implies that I do not – agree with all his theories or admire all his work in anything like equal measure – a form of admiration which I should by no means desire for myself and am as little prepared to bestow on another: considering it a form of scarcely indirect insult.[31]

Wilde copied out Swinburne's letter, omitting only a few words that slightly lowered its effect, and sent it on to 'My dear dear Walt' on 1 March. He promised to see Whitman again, and did so early in May. This time Stoddart was not present, and the two could talk more freely. Their conversation has not survived, but their parting has. Wilde would later tell George Ives, a proselytizer for sexual deviation in the 'nineties, that Whitman had made no effort to conceal his homosexuality from him as he would do with John Addington Symonds. 'The kiss of Walt Whitman,'

Wilde said, 'is still on my lips.'[32] He would expand upon this theme a little later when signing John Boyle O'Reilly's autograph book in Boston. Under an inscription by Whitman Wilde wrote of him, 'The spirit who living blamelessly but dared to kiss the smitten mouth of his own century.' (He was quoting lines he had applied to Wordsworth in his poem 'Humanitad.')[33]

Now that Swinburne, Wilde, and Whitman had all testified to their mutual respect, they felt compelled to reconsider. Swinburne in particular soon denounced Whitman, whom he had once so highly praised, for formless rant. For good measure, he derided 'the cult of the calamus, as expounded by Mr John Addington Symonds to his fellow-calamites.' Swinburne preferred the whip to the yawp. Whitman dissociated himself from Wilde's movement in *November Boughs* (1888): 'No one will get at my verses who insists upon viewing them as a literary performance . . . or as aiming mainly towards art and aestheticism.' When Wilde reviewed this book, recognizing that this sentence was aimed at him, he suggested that the value of Whitman's verse lay 'in its prophecy not in its performance . . . As a man he is the precursor of a fresh type. He is a factor in the heroic and spiritual evolution of the human being. If Poetry has passed him by, Philosophy will take note of him.' Some of the rapture had cooled. Whitman took account of the slight ambivalence when he said to his disciples of Wilde's allegiance, 'He has never been a flarer, but he has been a steady light.'[34]

CHAPTER VII

Indoctrinating America

Every man of ambition has to fight his century with its own weapons. What this century worships is wealth. The God of this century is wealth. To succeed one must have wealth. At all costs one must have wealth.

Aestheticism Defined, and Imperiled

The meeting with Whitman was a reminder to Wilde that he had so far skirted the problem of defining his principles. Another reminder came from Rennell Rodd in England, who had read with amusement of his friend's exploits in New York and Camden:

> Well, you seem to be having amazing fun over there. We all feel a little jealous. And then your statements are amazing, of course, but you mustn't assert yourself so positively. When you come back, you see you've no one to contradict you! Which is bad for you! We were surprised to read, that Mr Wilde declined to eat, on hearing the ladies were upstairs [at Robert Stewart Davis' house on 16 January 1882]. It was never so known in Israel.
>
> I saw yr Mother the other day, and we jubilated over you. Also Mrs Bigelow writes of you. But to speak seriatim, as she might say. I wish I could have been with you when you went to see Walt Whitman. It must have been charming. When he said, 'You must be thirsty Oscar' – why I wld have drunk beer – even.
>
> Jimmy and I are just off to try and detect a forgery of a picture of his, by of course you know who. Here he is so no more
>
> Yrs ever
RENNELL
>
> Why dont you tell them more of Jimmy and I say mention Me! (This plaintively) Mention us all.
>
> Irving has sent you a note which he is immensely *pleased with*[1]

The idea of mentioning Rennell Rodd had been in Wilde's mind for some time. He had brought with him Rodd's book, *Songs of the South*, and promised to try to find an American publisher for it. Being much with Stoddart in Philadelphia, Wilde proposed that he publish Rodd's poems with an introduction by Wilde. Stoddart attached more importance to the introduction than to the verse, as did Wilde, who thought it a good chance to express the principles of the aesthetic school. He had sketched out some thoughts during his ocean crossing, and in February wrote them down and sent them to Stoddart. The book, renamed by Wilde *Rose Leaf and Apple Leaf*, was announced for October 1882. In gratitude Rodd said he would dedicate it to Wilde.

Stoddart's cordiality was characteristic of Wilde's reception by Philadelphia, which proved to be as warm as New York's. But unknown to him, his troubles were about to begin. He was staying at the Aldine, the same hotel as another lecturer managed by D'Oyly Carte. This was Archibald Forbes, a self-assured Scot who as a journalist had covered several wars and liked to reveal the courage he had displayed on front after front. He carried himself like a soldier, wore a bristling moustache, and had married the daughter of the Quartermaster-General of the United States Army. Oxford did not overawe him, since he had lectured there on 13 March 1878. Accustomed to sporting all his medals on the lecture platform, Forbes found Wilde's knee breeches at Chickering Hall particularly repellent, and was not pleased by the attention bestowed upon his rival by the press. He wrote maliciously to a woman friend, 'Oscar Wilde is here . . . He wears knee breeches, but alas no lily. He lectures here tonight. He can't lecture worth a cent, but he draws the crowds wonderfully and he fools them all to the top of their bent, which is quite clever.'[2] According to a Forbes fancy, Wilde had received an offer for £200 a week from P. T. Barnum, who had just bought Jumbo the African elephant from the London Zoo, to lead Jumbo about carrying a lily in one hand and a sunflower in the other. (Barnum did have enough interest in Wilde to occupy a front seat at Wilde's second New York lecture in May.) Not so fancifully, Forbes described Wilde's indignation at a barber who had come to cut his hair and had failed to bring curling tongs.

Nursing his resentment, Forbes traveled on the same train as Wilde from Philadelphia to Baltimore. Colonel Morse's plan was for Wilde to attend Forbes's lecture, 'The Inner Life of a War Correspondent,' after which they would go to a reception at the house of Charles Carroll, always identified as a descendant of Carroll of Carrollton. But on the train Forbes stung Wilde with stupid jokes about the commercializing of aestheticism, provoked perhaps by some bragging about Wilde's receipts. Wilde took offense and instead of stopping at Baltimore went on to Washington. Carroll of Carrollton was offended in turn, and Morse wired to Wilde to go back to Baltimore. Wilde refused, and settled into his Washington hotel. Forbes took out his anger in his lecture by inserting a new passage contrasting his clothing, when he was summoned after a hundred-and-fifty mile ride into the presence of the Czar, with Wilde's.

'Now I wish it understood that I am a follower – a very humble follower – of the aesthetic ecstasy, but I did not look much like an art object then. I did not have my dogskin knee breeches with me nor my velvet coat, and my black silk stockings were full of holes. Neither was the wild, barren waste of Russia calculated to produce sunflowers and lilies.' This vulgarity was printed verbatim by the newspaper at Forbes's request. Wilde realized that he had given his adversary the headlines and needlessly offended Baltimore society. To make matters worse, he, or his business manager, was said in a newspaper article to have responded to an invitation from the Wednesday Club in Baltimore by asking a $300 fee because the reception was not in a private house. (Wilde said this had been done by an incompetent man provided by Colonel Morse.) Avarice did not advance the aesthetic cause.

Wilde maneuvered to extricate himself. His first effort was disingenuous and made matters worse. On 21 January he told the *Washington Post* that he had never intended to be present at Forbes's lecture: 'Our views are wide apart. If it amuses him to caricature me in the manner which he did last night, well and good. It may serve a purpose, and judging from the fact, as stated, that his audience came to see me, it is answering one very good purpose. It is advertising Mr Forbes at my expense.' It was Forbes's turn to be enraged. He wrote to Wilde claiming that he had heard from Wilde's own lips that his tour was purely mercenary. (Matthew Arnold would commit the same indiscretion to a reporter when D'Oyly Carte brought him over to lecture the following year.)Wilde had belittled his motives once too often. Forbes's own purpose was possibly higher.

Wilde recognized that he must try to compose their differences, and wrote a mollifying letter. Unfortunately he had done little more than glance at what Forbes had written to him, and Forbes, suspecting Wilde's contempt, threatened to publish their correspondence in the press if Wilde failed to make a proper apology. The dispute was jeopardizing Wilde's entire tour. 'The whole tide of feeling is turned,' he wrote in alarm to Carte on 24 or 25 January. In this difficulty he had the clever idea of appealing to his solicitor George Lewis in London, knowing that Lewis was solicitor and friend to Forbes as well. Lewis obliged him by cabling to Forbes, 'Like a good fellow don't attack Wilde. I ask this personal favour to me.'[3] Forbes ceased his public pronouncements, but a series of anonymous cables to the (London) *Daily News* were so scurrilous as to convince Wilde they emanated from Forbes. On 2 February 1882 one such cable said of his Boston lecture, 'After he had spoken for fifteen minutes, many went out. Whenever he paused to drink water the audience broke into uproarious applause lasting several minutes. This occurred so often that Mr Wilde paused, and glared upon the audience until silence was restored. His impressions of Boston are said to be unpleasant.' And on 2 March a cable stated that at the Century Association in New York, 'Many members of the club refused to be presented to him at all . . . One veteran member . . . went about saying, "Where is she? Have you seen her? Well, why not say 'she'? I understand she's a Charlotte-Ann!"' Combining the accusation of effeminacy with charlatanism probably justified the suspicion that Forbes was behind these jeers; in an auto-biography published several years later he was still belligerent. Now that Forbes was ostensibly keeping silent, Wilde was able to return to Baltimore and make amends; he was pleased to see Mrs if not Mr Carroll of Carrollton in his audience, and attended, without fee, a reception at the Wednesday Club. But he wrote to Carte, 'Another such fiasco as the Baltimore business and I think I would stop lecturing.'[4]

The attack by Forbes was partly responsible for a subtle shift in the attitude of the press. Reporters had come to Wilde at first with what appeared to be friendly eagerness, which he reciprocated, only to read waspish reconstructions of his remarks. His courteous attempts to re-spond to their often mindless questions left many openings. Wilde had reason to remember Ruskin's warning to him about journalists, 'Every-thing will be said about you. They will spare nothing.'[5] For a time, Wilde complained, he saw nothing of America but newspapers. One of the worst was the *New York Tribune*, whose editor-in-chief, Whitelaw Reid, ignored Wilde's letters of introduction from George Lewis and Edmund Yates, and allowed his writers to keep up a year-long attack on Wilde as 'a penny Ruskin' and a pretentious fraud. The *Washington Post* was another enemy: a drawing of Wilde holding a sunflower was juxtaposed with one of a 'citizen of Borneo' holding a coconut on its front page. Colonel Morse unwisely, and without consulting Wilde, wrote to protest against the 'gratuitous malice,' and the newspaper replied with a smirking editorial claiming that the comparison was just. Some Chicago papers then announced that the whole affair was a publicity stunt, and that Wilde had corrected proofs of the attack and passed the caricature before it was published. Nastiness could not go much further. If a few newspapers took his side, the greater number did not fail to perceive that better copy lay in making him look foolish. The *New York Times* courteously quoted his rejoinder, 'If you survive yellow journalism, you need not be afraid of yellow fever.'[6] He would later get his own back with the splendid comment, 'In old days men had the rack; now they have the Press.'[7] But even now he quoted Gautier in a visiting book: '*Avis aux critiques: C'est un grand avantage de n'avoir rien fait, mais il ne faut pas en abuser.** Oscar Wilde March 20 '82.'

The English reaction to his trip was equally harsh. A message from Whistler, Rodd, and others on 4 February was funny yet wounding, since Wilde in America was proclaiming Whistler's greatness and Rodd's excellence:

---

* 'Warning to critics: It is a great advantage to have done nothing, but one not to be exploited.'

Oscar! We of Tite Street and Beaufort Gardens joy in your triumphs, and delight in your success, but – we think that, with the exception of your epigrams, you talk like Sidney Colvin* in the Provinces, and that, with the exception of your kneebreeches, you dress like 'Arry Quilter.

Signed J. McNeill Whistler, Janey Campbell, Mat Elden, Rennell Rodd

New York papers please copy.[8]

Lady Wilde could of course be depended upon to see things in a favorable light. She wrote to her son on 23 January, 'Your letter and all the papers were delightful. Since then people have been sending me extracts, and I think your reception seems a triumph. Especially when God Save the Queen was played for you [on 12 January]!' But even she added, 'Mahaffy writes to me, "Oscar should have consulted me – great mistake."' Swinburne wrote to Clarence Stedman, who was determinedly hostile to Wilde in New York, 'The only time I ever saw Mr Oscar Wilde was in a crush at our acquaintance Lord Houghton's. I thought he seemed a harmless young nobody, and had no notion he was the sort of man to play the mountebank as he seems to have been doing. A letter which he wrote to me lately about Walt Whitman was quite a modest, gentlemanlike, reasonable affair, without any flourish or affectation of any kind.'[9]

Then there was Courtenay Bodley. Nastier than Swinburne's contempt was a long article in the *New York Times* on 21 January 1882 which though anonymous could only have been written by this old friend of Wilde at Oxford.† Its tone was surprisingly unpleasant. In it Bodley described uncharitably some ineptitude on Wilde's part as a freshman, his encounters with the proctors, his delight in Freemasonry and his dalliance with Rome. He denied that Wilde did any digging with Ruskin, his wardrobe being too fine for that. His aestheticism was represented as a belated development, and he made light of Wilde's success in the Newdigate. Wilde had lost a chance for a fellowship because he assumed 'a guise which sturdier minds still look upon as epicene,' a compromising word to use of an old friend. His poems, Bodley said, were derivative.

---

* The critic Sidney Colvin's attitude towards Wilde at this time is not known, but in a letter to D. S. MacColl of 27 July 1914 he spoke of 'Oscar Wilde-ism' as 'the most pestilent and hateful disease of our time.'

† The attribution of the article to Bodley is proved not only by internal evidence – references to Masonic costume, Willie Wilde, and other matters which only Bodley knew, but also by a letter from Bodley's mother to him on 20 February 1882, in which she says, 'I don't suppose Mr O. O. F. Wilde will like your strictures on his Oxford life very much, but so far as I know anything of him it is very correct, I remember him best as a perfectly unsophisticated young man talking to me in the Botanical Gardens and afterwards escorting me and the girls to Magdalen Tower; do you remember poor Beta declaring she never could or would get down again! it was not in his mind then, the *Osth* – knee breeches tail coat and lily and sunflower – What a mass of unmanly absurdity.'[10]

Unfriendly rivalry carried Bodley to his conclusion: 'he has considerable ability, and he has seen fit to use it in obtaining a cheap notoriety; he is good-hearted, has been amusing, and probably retains some sense of humor. Will American society encourage him in the line he has taken, which can only lead to one end, or will it teach him not unkindly a needed lesson and bid him return home to ponder it in growing wiser?' There was no doubt that Wilde's friends were put out by his reported behavior in America, but Bodley's attack must still have come as a surprise to Wilde and prepared him to say later, 'It is always Judas who writes the biography.'

This swelling disfavor was also aroused in Wilde's second momentous meeting, which took place in Washington. It was the exact contrary of his encounter with America's principal poet. As yet he knew only slightly the novelist Henry James, who had been visiting in Washington for a month. They were both guests at a reception at the house of Judge Edward G. Loring, where Wilde appeared in kneebreeches and with a large yellow silk handkerchief. General McClellan was there, and Senator Hale, and other dignitaries. Although James wrote that no one had paid any attention to Wilde, Loring's daughter reported to a friend that Henry James was 'so boring,' and Wilde 'so amusing.' James was, however, unexpectedly pleased when Wilde told a reporter that 'no living English-man can be compared to Howells and James as novelists.'[11]* James had just published *Portrait of a Lady* and *Washington Square*. He had already mentioned Wilde to Mrs Henry Adams, but she refused to receive James's 'friend' on the grounds that he was 'a noodle.'[12] Out of politeness and curiosity James resolved to call on Wilde at his hotel and thank him.

It was not a successful visit. James remarked, 'I am very nostalgic for London.' Wilde could not resist putting him down. 'Really?' he said, no doubt in his most cultivated Oxford accent. 'You care for places? The world is my home.'[13] He felt himself to be a citizen of the world. He was accustomed to say, when asked his plans, 'I don't know. I never make plans, but go whither my feelings prompt.' To James, master of the international theme, this was offensive. James winced. He had his own view, as an American living abroad, of floating citizens of the world. To this expert in deracination no quality more impugned the value of aestheticism than its rootlessness. By the end of the interview James was raging. Wilde offended him by saying, among other preciosities, 'I am going to *Bossston*; there I have a letter to the dearest friend of my dearest friend – Charles Norton from Burne-Jones.' James knew both men well, too well to enjoy this playful name-dropping.

We must imagine Henry James revolted by Wilde's kneebreeches,

---

* Howells said to Vincent O'Sullivan, who had linked the names of Wilde and Andrew Lang, 'It is a different thing. Lang simply lives by literature. Wilde would have invented literature if it had never existed.'

contemptuous of the self-advertising and pointless nomadism, and nervous about the sensuality. He informed Mrs Adams that she was right. ' "Hosscar" Wilde is a fatuous fool, tenth-rate cad,' 'an unclean beast.' The images are so steamy as to suggest that James saw in Wilde a threat. For the tolerance of deviation, or ignorance of it, were alike in jeopardy because of Wilde's flouting and flaunting. James's homosexuality was latent, Wilde's was patent. It was as if James, foreseeing scandal, separated himself from this menace in motley. Mrs Adams knew what he meant, and spoke of Wilde's sex as 'undecided.'[14] Some eight years later James would briefly relent and even join in sponsoring Wilde (unsuccessfully) for the Savile Club, but he always insisted that he was not one of Wilde's friends. (He was more generous to Robert Ross.) He recalled their Washington conversation more benignly in *The Tragic Muse*, where the aesthete Gabriel Nash is always on his way 'somewhere else,' and confides, 'I rove, drift, float.' For his part, Wilde had no idea of the hostility he had aroused in James. He remarked in Louisville on 21 February that he had met a Daisy Miller, and 'the sight of her has increased my admiration for Henry James a thousand fold.'[15]

Yet his abrasive encounters and his battle with the press gave him a new confidence. They could attack him, but they could not take their eyes off him. Derision was a form of tribute, and if it went on long enough, could not fail to be so interpreted. He could moreover appeal, over the heads of the journalists, to the people. This he did.

New England: A Latter Day Pilgrim

To be either a Puritan, a prig or a preacher is a bad thing. To be all three at once reminds me of the worst excesses of the French Revolution.

Whatever Henry James thought or Mrs Henry Adams said, they could not spoil Wilde's reception in Washington. He entranced Frances Hodgson Burnett, later the author of *Little Lord Fauntleroy*, by telling her that Ruskin considered her a true artist and read everything she wrote. In return she presented him to other writers. W. H. Hurlbert, editor of the *New York World* and by now Wilde's friend as well as Sam Ward's, introduced him to political society as well. Senators James G. Blaine, Thomas F. Bayard, and George H. Pendleton were all three hospitable. Wilde's remarks were widely quoted. Before he left he urged Washington to display more sculpture. 'I think you have taken quite enough motives from war,' he said, 'you don't want any more bronze generals on horseback, I dare say. Suppose you try the motives that peace will give you now.'[16] (Henry James liked the phrase about 'bronze generals' and took it over.) Then he was off, by way of Albany, to Boston, to see American culture at its best.

Letters of introduction to Charles Eliot Norton and Oliver Wendell Holmes, as well as to Sam Ward's sister Julia Ward Howe, led to dinner parties and other receptions. Mrs Howe invited him more than once, and a reply from Wilde to one such invitation compliments and charms her:

> My dear Mrs Howe: I shall be with you at seven o'clock, but there is no such thing as dining with *you* 'en famille' – when you are present, the air is cosmopolitan and the room seems to be full of brilliant people; you are one of those rare persons who give one the sense of creating history as they live.
>
> No, 'en famille' is impossible – but to dine with you one of the great privileges. Most truly yours,
>
> OSCAR WILDE[17]

He amused her at one gathering by saying that the words 'vermilion' and 'balcony' were pronounced too prosaically, and should have more emphasis on the *r* of the one and the *c* of the other.

Wilde was eager to see Longfellow, with whom his mother had occasionally corresponded, and who was quoted by the *Boston Evening Traveller* for 30 January as having said, 'Well, Mr Wilde has written some good verses, he cannot be an ignorant man.' Wilde knew that Sam Ward had brought Lord Ronald Gower to meet Longfellow, and came armed with a recommendation from Ward. At first there was reluctance because the poet was in failing health, but Wilde persisted and was at last invited to breakfast. He arrived in a blinding snowstorm and left in a hurricane, as he said later, 'quite the right conditions for a visit to a poet.' He was moved by the sight of the old poet. Longfellow told him laughingly of going to England and being invited to Windsor. The Queen said some kind things to him, and Longfellow replied that he was surprised to find himself so well known in England. 'Oh, I assure you, Mr Longfellow,' said the Queen, 'you are very well known. All my servants read you.' 'Sometimes,' said Longfellow, 'I will wake up in the night and wonder if it was a deliberate slight.' Wilde, in telling the story to Vincent O'Sullivan, said, 'It was the rebuke of Majesty to the vanity of the poet.' Another vestige of their conversation is Wilde's question, 'How do you like Browning?' and Longfellow's answer, 'I like him well, what I can understand of him.' Wilde, doing his best to be agreeable, exclaimed, 'Capital!' and promised to repeat this putative epigram. His enthusiasm had its limits. 'A fine old man,' he said. 'Longfellow was himself a beautiful poem, more beautiful than anything he ever wrote.' He would say to Chris Healy later, 'Longfellow is a great poet only for those who never read poetry.'[18] Longfellow was to die in March, two months later, and Emerson in April. When Wilde returned to Boston for a second lecture on 2 June, he memorialized them in the peroration of his lecture:

And, lastly, let us remember that art is the one thing which Death cannot harm. The little house at Concord may be desolate, but the wisdom of New England's Plato is not silenced nor the brilliancy of that Attic genius dimmed; the lips of Longfellow are still musical for us though his dust be turning into the flowers which he loved.

His Boston and Cambridge activities were crowded together. He had lunch with another distinguished Bostonian, the orator Wendell Phillips, who talked of lecture tours and remarked that anyone could move a large audience; but speaking to nearly empty benches was a different matter, a truth Wilde was to confirm as his own audiences became more attenuated. Besides the Brahmins whom he met, there were two Irishmen with whom he felt more at home: Dion Boucicault, as an old friend, received Wilde kindly, and his presence helped with aggressive interviewers. Boucicault's outrage at the treatment meted out to Wilde by the American press was a comfort, as was his offer, which Wilde did not take up, of a couple of thousand pounds to make him independent of Carte and Morse.[19] The other Irishman was the poet, wit and rebel John Boyle O'Reilly, now part owner of the Boston *Pilot*, and always passionately interested in visitors from his native land. With O'Reilly Wilde pressed another aim, to arrange American publication of his mother's poems: 'I think my mother's work should make a great success here,' he wrote to O'Reilly, 'it is so unlike the work of her degenerate artist son. I know you think I am thrilled by nothing but a dado. You are quite wrong but I shan't argue.'[20] He went with O'Reilly on 28 January to see *Oedipus Tyrannus* at the Globe Theatre.

On the night of 31 January, when Wilde was to speak in the Music Hall in Boston, snow fell again. The house was full, nonetheless. (Julia Ward Howe was among the audience.) Full, that is, except for the first two rows, which remained mysteriously empty until just before the speaker was to appear. Then suddenly down the center aisle came sixty Harvard students, dressed in the high aesthetic line with breeches, dinner jackets, Whistler locks of white hair, hats like Bunthorne's, each bearing in a stained glass attitude a sunflower. Their leader lounged, limp and listless and vacant-eyed, to a seat. There was great merriment as the stage door opened to admit the lecturer.

But Wilde was able to mock his mockers. Tipped off in advance, he had donned conventional dinner jacket and trousers, and hinted at iconoclasm only in the unusually wide cravat which reached nearly to his shoulders on either side. Arriving late, he had to climb some stairs at the back of the stage, so that the audience first caught sight of his upper torso, and then to their dismay saw that his legs were trousered in the usual manner.[21] Wilde had also written a new opening paragraph. He began evenly, 'As a college man, I greet you. I am very glad to address an audience in Boston, the only city in America which has influenced thought in Europe, and which has given to Europe a new and great school of philosophy.' He then glanced as

173

if by chance at the fantastic semicircle in front, and said with a smile, 'I see about me certain signs of an aesthetic movement. I see certain young men, who are no doubt sincere, but I can assure them that they are no more than caricatures. As I look around me, I am impelled for the first time to breathe a fervent prayer, "Save me from my disciples." But rather let me, as Wordsworth says, "turn me from those bold, bad men."' By this time his audience was almost won. The students tried to recover their advantage by applauding heartily every time he drank from a glass of water, but this was small revenge.

Wilde proceeded imperturbably with his standard lecture. Only near the end he once again took notice of the students as he described how he and his Oxford contemporaries had worked under Ruskin in North Hinksey. 'These charming young men might be inclined to follow our example; the work would be good for them, though I do not believe they could build so good a road.' He had visited Harvard that day, he said, 'and I beg to assure the students before me that there is more to the movement of aestheticism than kneebreeches and sunflowers.' He had particularly liked the gymnasium, and urged them to combine athletics and aesthetics by placing a statue of a Greek athlete in that building. (In fact, he presented a plaster cast of the Hermes of Praxiteles to them 'by way of casting coals of fire on the Harvard students,' as Robert Ross said. When Ross was in Cambridge in 1892, the cast was still there. It has since vanished.)[22] At this point, Wilde commented later, 'the young men lapsed into acquiescence at last. I could sympathize with them, because I thought to myself that when I was in my first year at Oxford I would have been apt to do the same. But as they put their head in the lion's mouth, I thought they deserved a little bite.' It was one of the great moments of his tour, certified as a triumph by no less an authority than the *Boston Evening Transcript* on 2 February.

Wilde's attitude of connoisseurship towards life and the aromatic manner of his expression, rather than his doctrine, prevented his slipping easily into American hearts. His invocations of beauty managed to sound faintly subversive, faintly unhealthy. His tour was a series of more or less successful confrontations in which his flagrant and unconventional charm was pitted against conventional maleness and resultant suspicion. His costume polarized opposition. Sometimes he thought of giving it up, but the obvious disappointment of his audiences made him don it again. The attacks on him were sometimes gratuitous, like that of Ambrose Bierce in an article of 31 March. But the first that found its target was an earlier one, on 4 February, by T. W. Higginson in the *Women's Journal.* Higginson was a highly respected bore. He had much to answer for in literary terms, since he had judged unworthy of publication the strange poems showed him by an unknown Amherst woman; only after Emily Dickinson's death would he penitently help to edit them. Higginson took the occasion of Wilde's visit to denounce both him and Whitman, as if the end of the alphabet needed pruning. Colonel of a black regiment in the Civil War, Higginson accused Whitman of pretending to military experience when he had been only a hospital nurse. As a former Unitarian minister, he was even more indignant with Wilde's Charmides for undressing Athena's bronze statue. 'Nudities do not suggest the sacred whiteness of an antique statue,' he said with some inaccuracy, since Greek statues were painted, 'but rather the forcible unveiling of some injured innocence.' With military and clerical ferocity, Higginson berated Wilde for writing prurient poems instead of helping to work out the Irish problem in his own country. Higginson was especially agitated because his Newport neighbor Julia Ward Howe, whom he all but named, had entertained this pornographic poet in her home.

Higginson was made to taste the grapes of Mrs Howe's wrath. She wrote a letter to the *Boston Evening Transcript* on 16 February, denying the colonel's right to decide who should be received socially. Judges as eminent as Higginson had admired Wilde's poems. Wilde was willing to learn as well as teach. 'To cut off even an offensive member of society from its best influences and most humanizing resources is scarcely Christian in any sense.' She received Wilde's thanks for her 'noble and beautiful' letter.[23] Higginson was silenced, but the *Pall Mall Gazette* on 18 March ironically endorsed Mrs Howe's courage in trying to improve Wilde. For the moment he was paying in America for the heterosexual overtones in his poems as later in England he would pay for the homosexual overtones in his prose.

A comparably painful incident occurred on 7 February, three days after Higginson's article had appeared, in the city of Rochester. There the Rochester students, trying to outdo their Harvard counterparts, drowned out Wilde's words with hoots and hisses. Wilde folded his arms and gazed calmly at his tormentors until the din abated, then resumed. Half way through the lecture, by prearrangement, an old black man, in formal dress and one white kid glove to parody Wilde's attire, danced down the center aisle carrying an immense bunch of flowers and sat in a front seat. The police tried to quiet the guffawing crowd, but only made matters worse, and many of the audience had left before the lecturer could desperately finish.[24]

Yet this wound also brought its balm. The poet Joaquin Miller, whom Wilde had dined with in New York on 5 February, wrote a letter to him on the 9th expressing shame at the behavior of 'those ruffians at Rochester.' The letter was published next day by Hurlbert in the *New York World* and Wilde replied to Miller in a letter of 28 February which the *World* printed on 3 March. It was a fiery answer to all his enemies, especially Higginson: 'Who, after all, that I should write of him, is this scribbling animalcule in grand old Massachusetts who scrawls and screams so glibly about what he cannot understand? . . . Who are those scribes who, passing with purpose-less alacrity from the police news to the Parthenon, and from crime to criticism, sway with such serene incapacity the office which they so lately swept?' Insouciant as he appeared, and innocent as he felt, Wilde was increasingly conscious of the malice released against him. 'What a tempest and tornado you live in!' his mother wrote to him on 19 February. He was undaunted. 'I have no complaints to make,' he complained to one journalist. 'They have certainly treated me outrageously, but I am not the one who is injured, it is the public. By such ridiculous attacks the people are taught to mock where they should reverence.' If the press's opposition was uncomfortable, its approval would have been much worse. 'Had I been treated differently by the newspapers in England and in this country, had I been commended and endorsed, for the first time in my life I should have doubted myself and my mission.' Then, more grandly, 'What possible difference can it make to me what the *New York Herald* says? You go and look at the statue of the Venus de Milo and you know that it is an exquisitely beautiful creation. Would it change your opinion in the least if all the newspapers in the land should pronounce it a wretched caricature? Not at all. I know that I am right, that I have a mission to perform. I am indestructible!'[25] (As the Duke remarks in *The Duchess of Padua*, 'popularity / Is the one insult I have never suffered.') He appealed to a famous precedent: 'Shelley was driven out of England but he wrote equally well in Italy.' To be treated like Keats and Shelley was not too bad, but he was surprised that a British visitor should be treated so much worse in America than Americans in England.

Dealing with the press was not all hard work. Arriving at his hotel in Boston, he found a card from a reporter said to represent a string of western newspapers, asking urgently for an interview. Wilde donned a dressing gown for the interview. In came a very young gentleman 'or rather a boy, and as I saw him I judged that he was nearly sixteen. I asked him if he had been to school. He said he had left school some time since. He asked my advice as to his course in journalism. I asked him if he knew French. He said no. I advised him to learn French, and counselled him a little as to what books to read. In fact I interviewed him. At last I gave him an orange and then sent him away. What he did with the orange I don't know; he seemed pleased to get it.'[26]

Beautifying America

As to modern newspapers with their dreary records of politics, police-courts and personalities, I have long ago ceased to care what they write about me – my time being all given up to the gods and the Greeks.[27]

From Boston Wilde proceeded to New Haven and then with intermediate stops to Chicago. He was accompanied by a business manager, J. S. Vail, and by a black valet, W. M. Traquair, to take care of his wardrobe. State by state he worked his way patiently through the Middle West to Nebraska, from where at the end of March he went to California for a two-week tour at a reputed fee of $5,000. Then he returned in crisscross fashion through Kansas, Iowa, and Colorado to New Jersey and, as his first tour came to an end on 12 May, to Virginia. He had planned to lecture only until April, but his fame encouraged more bookings. For a time he talked of returning to London, and then, in July, of proceeding to Japan. He broached to Whistler the possibility of their visiting and writing a book together about Japan, but silence was Whistler's only response. A young painter Wilde met in Des Moines, named Spencer Blake, was abruptly invited instead and as abruptly agreed to accompany him as private secretary, following which they would go to Australia, back to London, and then back to America in the autumn of 1883.[28] This plan fell through. Wilde could have financed the expedition by writing articles about Japanese art, and in Australia by lecturing, but no one offered him a series of regular bookings like Carte's in the United States. Colonel Morse proposed that he make a second tour of America following his lecture in Charlottesville, and Wilde deferred, without as yet quite abandoning, the voyage to the Far East.

He closed with Morse's offer* and on 13 May was in central and eastern Canada; a month later he came down to the American South, beginning with Memphis and covering most of the Southern states. Then he went north and in mid-July was still lecturing, even though the customary lecture season was well over, in watering places in Rhode Island, New York, and New Jersey. The tour persisted, though at a retarded pace, well into August. In late September he was off on a third round, for three weeks, to a few spots in New England and eastern Canada, his last lecture being on 13 October in St John, New Brunswick. Then he returned to New York and stopped lecturing.

His lecture schedule was a heavy one, as indicated in the table overleaf.

---

* He had some new clothing made to his order, by a New York tailor named Wirtz. Two new suits were designed by Wilde, one of black velvet and the other the shade of a lake glistening in the moonlight, '*couleur du lac au clair de la lune*,' which turned out to be mouse color. The black suit had 'a plain black velvet doublet fitting tight to the body, without any visible buttons, after the style of Francis I. The lower part of the sleeves was of embossed velvet, with embroidered field-flower designs and fitting tight to the arm. The upper part of the arm is to be in large puffs of the same material, only of a larger pattern, and the body of plain velvet. The sleeves are of two designs of brocaded velvet edges with a delicate ruffle of *mousseline de soie*. Around the neck is a narrow frill in three rows of the same material as that which edges the sleeves. The breeches are to come to the knee and to be tight fitting, with two small buttons at the bottom. The stockings are to be of black silk and the shoes cut low and secured with a silver buckle. It may be interesting to know that the following are the dimensions of the costume in inches: trousers, 30 inches; bottom of doublet, 45¼; waist 38½; and breast 36½. The puffs at the upper part of the sleeves 32 inches, at the bottom 11 inches, the collar being 17 inches in size.' (*New York World*, 4 May 1882)

Wilde's Itinerary, 9 January – 13 October 1882
(Places where he stopped but did not lecture are in brackets)

I. From 9 January to 11 May 1882

9 January 1882	Chickering Hall, New York City, 'The English Renaissance'
17	Horticultural Hall, Philadelphia
23	Lincoln Hall, Washington, DC
25	Lincoln Hall, Baltimore
27	Albany Music Hall
31	Boston Music Hall
1 February	Peck's Opera House, New Haven
2	Hartford Opera House
3	Brooklyn Academy of Music
6	City Opera House, Utica
7	Opera House, Rochester
8	Academy of Music, Buffalo
9	[Niagara] (Prospect House in Ontario)
13	Central Music Hall, Chicago
16	Old Academy, Fort Wayne, Indiana
17	Music Hall, Detroit
18	Case Hall, Cleveland
	[Cincinnati]
20	Columbus
21	Masonic Temple, Louisville
22	English's Opera House, Indianapolis
23	Opera House, Cincinnati
25	Mercantile Library Hall, St Louis
27	Opera House, Springfield, Illinois
1 March	Dubuque, Iowa
2	Rockford, Illinois
3	Aurora, Illinois
4	Racine, Wisconsin
5	Grand Opera House, Milwaukee
6	Joliet
7	Jacksonville, Illinois
8	Decatur, Illinois
9	Peoria, Illinois
10	Bloomington, Illinois
11	Chicago Central Music Hall
15	Academy of Music, Minneapolis
16	Opera House, St Paul
17	Opera House, St Paul (St Patrick's Day speech)
	[New York]
20	Academy of Music, Sioux City, Iowa
21	Boyd's Opera House, Omaha
27	Platt's Hall, San Francisco

28	Oakland Light Cavalry Armory, Oakland, California
29	Platt's Hall, San Francisco
30	San José, California
31	Sacramento, California
1 April	Platt's Hall, San Francisco
3	California Hall, San José
4	Mozart Hall, Stockton
5	Platt's Hall, San Francisco
10	Leavenworth Opera House, Kansas
11	Salt Lake Theatre, Salt Lake City, Utah
12	Opera House, Denver
13	Tabor Grand Opera House, Leadville, Colorado
14	Colorado Springs, Colorado
15	Denver
17	Coates Opera House, Kansas City, Missouri
18	Tootle's Opera House, St Joseph, Missouri
19	[Leavenworth, Kansas]
20	Opera House, Topeka, Kansas
21	Liberty Hall, Lawrence, Kansas
22	Corinthian Hall, Atchison, Kansas
24	Lincoln, Nebraska
25	Fremont, Iowa
26	Des Moines, Iowa
27	Iowa City
28	Cedar Rapids, Iowa
29	Rock Island, Iowa
2 May	Dayton, Ohio
3	Comstock Opera House, Columbus, Ohio
4	Harrisburg, Pennsylvania
8	Freehold
9	Newark
10	[Philadelphia]
11	Wallack's Theatre, New York
12	Lee Avenue Baptist Church, Williamsburg, Virginia

II. From 13 May to 26 August 1882

15 May	Queen's Hall, Montreal
16	Grand Opera House, Ottawa
18	Music Hall, Quebec
20	Queen's Hall, Montreal
22	Opera House, Kingston, Ontario
23	City Hall Auditorium, Belleville, Ontario
25	Grand Opera House, Toronto, Ontario

26	Stratford Opera House, Brantford, Ontario
27	Pavilion of the Horticultural Gardens, Toronto
29	City Hall Auditorium, Woodstock, Ontario
30	Grand Opera House, Hamilton, Ontario
31	Wesleyan Ladies' College, Hamilton
2 June	Globe Theatre, Boston
	New York
11	Grand Opera House, Cincinnati
12	Leubrie's Theatre, Memphis
14	[Vicksburg]
16	Grand Opera House, New Orleans
17	Fort Worth, Texas
19	Pavilion, Galveston
20 or 21	Turner Opera Hall, San Antonio
23	Gray's Opera House, Houston, Texas
26	Spanish Fort, Louisiana
	New Orleans
27	[Beauvoir (visit to Jefferson Davis)]
28	Frascati Amusement Park, Mobile, Alabama
29	McDonald's Opera House, Montgomery, Alabama
30	Columbus, Georgia
3 July	Rolston Hall, Macon, Georgia
4	De Give's Opera House, Atlanta
5	Savannah Theatre, Savannah
6	Augusta, Georgia
7	Academy, Charleston, South Carolina
8	Wilmington, Delaware
10	Van Wyck's Academy of Music, Norfolk, Virginia
11	Richmond Theatre, Richmond, Virginia
14	Opera House, Vicksburg
15	Casino, Newport, Rhode Island
17	[New York]
28	Long Branch
29	[At Peekskill with Henry Ward Beecher]
2 August	Babylon, Long Island
5	Long Beach
7	Long Beach Hotel, Long Beach
9	Gould Hall, Ballston Spa, New York
10	Congress Hall Ballroom, Saratoga, New York
11	Pavilion Hotel, Sharon Springs
12	Cooper House, Cooperstown, New York
14	Spring House, Richfield Springs
15	Hotel Kaaterskill, in Catskill Mountains
16	Long Beach Hotel, Long Beach
17	Mountain House, Cornwall

18	Tremper House, Catskills
19	Grand Hotel, Catskills
21	Octagon House, Seabright, New Jersey
22	West End Hotel, Long Branch
23	Palisades Mountain House, Spring Lake
24	Coleman House, Asbury Park
25	Atlantic City
26	Hotel Stockton, Cape May

III. From 26 September to 13 October 1882

25 or 26 September	Low's Grand Opera House, Providence, Rhode Island
28	Music Hall, Pawtucket, Rhode Island
29	North Attleboro, Massachusetts
3 October	Bangor, Maine
4	City Hall Auditorium, Fredericton, New Brunswick
5	Mechanics' Institute, St John, New Brunswick
6	Academy of Music, Amherst, Nova Scotia
7	YMCA, Truro, Nova Scotia
9	Academy of Music, Halifax, Nova Scotia
10	Academy of Music, Halifax
11	Market Hall, Charlottetown, Prince Edward Island
12	Ruddick's Hall, Moncton, New Brunswick
13	Mechanics' Institute, St John, New Brunswick
14 October– 27 December	[New York (Fifth Avenue Hotel, The Brunswick, The Windsor, and 48 W. 11th Street)]

It had been an extraordinary journey. If America did not bend the knee to its conqueror, half the United States and half of Canada had been lectured to, and the unlectured halves had been obliged to take notice. News of his appearances continued to occupy the British press as well, so that his mother could write him on 18 September, 'You are still the talk of London – the cabmen ask me if I am anything to Oscar Wilde – the milkman has bought your picture! and in fact nothing seems celebrated in London but you. I think you will be mobbed when you come back by eager crowds and will be obliged to shelter in cabs.' In America his poems received the compliment of being pirated and sold at ten cents a copy. Popular songs were published with such titles as 'Oscar Wilde Forget-Me-Not Waltzes,' 'The Flippity Flop Young Man,' and 'Oscar Dear!' Young women posed with sunflowers as hats or sang 'Twenty lovesick maidens we' as he approached. The humorist Eugene Field got himself up as Wilde. Lily in hand, gazing languidly at a book, he drove through Denver on 15 April in an open carriage. Wilde, on being informed, only

181

commented, 'What a splendid advertisement for my lecture.'[29] His opinion was constantly sought in connection with plans for new art schools and galleries, and young artists looked up to him, as he could not help boasting to Mrs Lewis, as a god.* Wilde grew more defiant and solemn about his mission. On being asked in Omaha on 23 March about his plans for future work, he laughed, lit a cigarette, threw himself back in his chair, and replied precisely: 'Well, I'm a very ambitious young man. I want to do everything in the world. I cannot conceive of anything that I do not want to do. I want to write a great deal more poetry. I want to study painting more than I've been able to. I want to write a great many more plays, and I want to make this artistic movement the basis for a new civilisation.'[30]

It was as if he had taken to heart the advice he was quoted as having given in Boston, 'The supreme object of life is to live. Few people live. It is true life only to realise one's own perfection, to make one's every dream a reality. Even this is possible.' Wilde was playing in a mild version the roles of both Lord Henry Wotton and Dorian Gray, seducer and seduced.

At first Colonel Morse spaced the lectures well apart, but after the first few cities he arranged a series of one-night stands, with few intervals. On learning that matinées were agreeable to Wilde, Morse added some of these. Wilde protested mildly at giving six lectures a week, then accustomed himself to it. Though sometimes unpunctual, he was conscientious in fulfilling his engagements, and once, in Saratoga, chartered a special locomotive so as to reach Richfield Springs on time. The famous preacher Henry Ward Beecher, his reputation clouded by being named co-respondent in a divorce case, was summering near New York, and Wilde paid him a visit.†

By 15 June the total receipts of his tour were $18,215.69. After expenses of $7,005.06 were deducted, Wilde received a half share of the $11,210.63 that remained.[31] It was a substantial sum. There were moments during these lucrative travels when America whizzed past his train with bewildering rapidity, so that one of his letters to Stoddart is headed 'Somewhere and sometime – I am not sure where or when.' But he gave no sign of confusion to the relentless interviewers, and in each town he usually managed not only to lecture but to visit the art gallery and art school, and to meet the local worthies at receptions and dinners. That Wilde was as delightful a visitor as America would ever have, never became common knowledge, but he impressed thousands of persons. For

---

* An old artist was not so reverential: George Inness, talking to students in the Art Students' League in New York in May, refused to allow Wilde to break in.

† He was not impressed by Beecher. At a dinner of the Royal Literary Fund in London later, someone said, 'We were just saying, Mr Wilde, how impossible it is to compare a man like Dr Talmadge with a person like Henry Ward Beecher.' 'Indeed yes,' said Wilde, 'it would be like comparing the pantaloon with the clown.'

instance, a letter from a young man named Babb to his mother (preserved as Babb's son James later became director of the Yale University Library) told of a visit by Wilde to Illinois College in Jacksonville: 'He has a splendid diction and his descriptive powers are worthy of the highest praise. His sentences are mellifluous and sparkle with occasional gems of beauty. Munroe Browning and I had the pleasure of calling upon him at the Dunlop House. He is very cordial – extended us his hand both on entering and departing his room. His conversation is very pleasant – easy, beautiful, and entertaining. He said that if he were a young man in this country the West would have great charms for him.'[32] The impact of such a personality on the young must have been appreciable even if not measurable. For the rest of his life people would come up to Wilde to say they had heard him lecture.

Early in his travels Wilde discovered that he would need another lecture besides 'The English Renaissance.' Eastern newspapers had shown no scruple about filling their columns with his remarks, almost verbatim, and since these were copied by other papers, Wilde's audiences were well primed with his views before he uttered them. His Philadelphia friend, Robert S. Davis, was perhaps the first to encourage Wilde to take up a second subject; on 20 January he rather officiously outlined how a lecture on 'Modern Aestheticism Applied to Real Life' might deal, successively, with the home, the costume, and the recognition of merit in art products. Wilde was attentive, but not immediately persuaded. He persisted with 'The English Renaissance' until his arrival in Chicago in February. There he had to speak twice, and when he learned that the Chicago papers already had 'The English Renaissance' in type, from the report in the *Buffalo Courier*, he hastily put together two new lectures, which he gave from that time on. One, first delivered on 11 February, eventually became known as 'The House Beautiful' (a dreadful phrase perpetuated by Pater). The other, first given two days later, was 'The Decorative Arts.' Both these lectures differed from the first, since instead of being historical, they offered practical applications of aesthetic doctrine.

'The Decorative Arts' was more closely tied to 'The English Renaissance,' drawing heavily upon Ruskin and Morris for its examples. Wilde described the recent rise of handicrafts in England, and the advantage of having work made by delighted craftsmen rather than by unfeeling machines. He moved fluently from point to point, not worrying much about organization, trusting to what quickly became dependable patter. Modern dress was ignoble, as could be seen in sculptures: 'To see the statues of our departed statesmen in marble frock coats and bronze, double-breasted waistcoats adds a new horror to death.' There must be schools of art, and these must be in more immediate relation with trade and manufacturing than now. Art should portray the men who cover the world with a network of iron and the sea with ships. Beside each art school should be a museum like the South Kensington Museum in London where artists and craftsmen could come to see excellent work in their fields. Bad art is worse than no art: 'I have seen [in the Philadelphia School of Design] young ladies painting moonlights upon dinner plates and sunsets on soup plates.' The subjects for art need not be searched far afield: 'The most graceful thing I ever beheld was a miner in a Colorado silver mine driving a new shaft with a hammer; at any moment he might have been transformed into marble or bronze and become noble in art forever.' Modern jewelry is vulgar because the individual craftsman is ignored; modern wallpaper is so bad that a boy brought up under its influence could allege it as a justification for turning to a life of crime. Heavy crockery cups should be abjured in favor of the tiny porcelain ones from which he had seen Chinese navvies drinking. Finally, education must be changed: children should not be drilled in 'that calendar of infamy, European history,' but learn in a workshop how art might offer a new history of the world, with a promise of the brotherhood of man, of peace rather than war, of praise of God's handicraftsmanship, of new imagination and new beauty.

'The House Beautiful' was even more prescriptive. Wilde metaphorically walked through the house, commenting on the mistakes he had observed. The entrance hall should not be papered, since it was too close to the outdoors; wainscotting was better. It should not be carpeted but tiled. Secondary colours should be used on walls and ceilings of rooms. Large gas chandeliers should be replaced by side brackets. Windows must be small to avoid glaring light. Ugly heating stoves must give way to Dutch porcelain stoves. No artificial flowers. Blown glass rather than cut glass. Queen Anne furniture. He passed on to the house's inhabitants and the subject of dress. Women should eschew furbelows and corsets, and emulate the drapery on Greek statuary. As for men, the only well dressed men he had seen in America were the Colorado miners with wide-brimmed hats and long cloaks. Kneebreeches like his were more sensible than trousers. After such instructions Wilde passed on to the relation of art to morals. Instead of saying there was none, he argued that art had a spiritual ministry; it could raise and sanctify everything it touched; and popular disapproval should not impede its progress.

This was not altogether fool; most of it was unexceptionable. Wilde increasingly depended upon disseminating his personality rather than his principles. He became adroit at incorporating refreshing responses to local features. In Chicago he complained that the newly built water tower was 'a castellated monstrosity, with pepper box turrets and absurd portcullises,' but he appeased Chicagoans a little by acknowledging that 'the mighty symmetrical, harmonious wheel' inside the tower came up to the highest aesthetic standards. While objecting to machine-made articles, he allowed that machinery could in some ways free people for better use of time. But as he said in Omaha, 'The evil that machinery is doing is not merely in the consequences of its work, but in the fact that it makes men themselves machines also. Whereas we wish them to be artists, that is to say men.' 'If ever America produces a great musician,' he said, 'let him write a machinery symphony.' Then he added, in less delphic mode, 'But first they must abolish the steam whistle.'[33] Asked to comment on the scenery of San Francisco, he said it was 'Italy without its art.' He praised the House of the Seven Gables in Salem, and occasional buildings elsewhere; he complimented Charles Pratt in Baltimore for contributing a million dollars to a public library. In New Orleans he talked of his uncle, Dr J. K. Elgee, once active in Confederate politics in Rapides parish there. The Hudson River on the way to Albany received his approval. Niagara Falls aroused more acid comment: 'Niagara will survive any criticism of mine,' he allowed. 'I must say, however, that it is the first disappointment in the married life of many Americans who spend their honeymoon there.' His particular complaint was against its monotonous outline of 'endless water falling the wrong way.'[34] But when he took the trip under the falls, he grew respectful: 'I do not think I ever realized so strongly the splendour and beauty of the mere physical forms of nature as I did when I stood by the Table Rock. A wonderful thing is the calm directly underneath the falls, the rapids not showing themselves for a long distance under the river.' He was finding in the falls the passionless contemplation he sometimes attributed to art. 'Another thing that interested me very much,' he said, 'was the curious repetition of the same forms, of the same design almost, in the shape of the falling water. It gave me a sense of how completely what seems to us the wildest liberty of nature is restrained by governing laws.' He edged over into grandiloquence when he was invited to write in the Prospect House private album at Niagara, and said: 'The roar of these waters is like the roar when the mighty wave of democracy breaks on the shores where kings lie couched at ease.'[35] He commented ironically on this view in *Vera* when the Czarevich says, 'far off I hear the mighty wave Democracy break on these cursed shores,' only to have Prince Paul reply, 'In that case you and I must learn to swim.'

An unexpected result of his tour was that he rediscovered himself as an Irishman. Having erased his Irish accent at Oxford, he had tended also to minimize the difference between English and Irish. The first response of his compatriots was accordingly adverse. The *Irish Nation* in New York carried an article at the beginning of his tour, on 14 January 1882, with the disapproving headlines:

Speranza's Son
Oscar Wilde Lecture on What He
Calls the English Renaissance
————

The Utterness of Aestheticism
————

Phrasing about Beauty while a
Hideous Tyranny Overshadows
His Native Land

Talent Sadly Misapplied

Speranza's son, as he proceeded across the continent, found unexpectedly that he had potential allies among Irish-Americans, who paid no attention to his aesthetics but liked his nationality. On St Patrick's Day he was in St Paul, Minnesota, and was introduced by a Father Shanley who called him the son 'of one of Ireland's noblest daughters – of a daughter who in the troublous times of 1848 by the works of her pen and her noble example did much to keep the fire of patriotism burning brightly.' Wilde was moved to describe the Irish race as once the 'most aristocratic in Europe,' and Ireland as once Europe's university. 'Rhyme, the basis of modern poetry, is entirely of Irish invention,' he boasted. 'But with the coming of the English,' he told the crowd, 'art in Ireland came to an end, and it has had no existence for over seven hundred years. I am glad it has not, for art could not live and flourish under a tyrant.' Yet the artistic impulse in Ireland was not dead; it persists 'in every running brook' and in the pervasive esteem for great Irishmen of the past. When Ireland, which he liked to call 'the Niobe of nations,' as Byron had called Rome, regains her independence, her schools of art will revive also.[36]

He responded quickly to the murder of Lord Frederick Cavendish by the Invincibles in the Phoenix Park on 6 May. Cavendish had once dined with the Wildes at Merrion Square. To a reporter who asked his attitude, Wilde replied, 'When liberty comes with hands dabbled in blood it is hard to shake hands with her.' Then he added, 'We forget how much England is to blame. She is reaping the fruit of seven centuries of injustice.'[37] For these comments Wilde received unaccustomed praise from editorial writers. He generally insisted upon his republicanism, as on 21 February in Louisville, 'Yes, I am a thorough republican. No other form of government is so favorable to the growth of art.' Britain should be a republic too, as he had indicated in 'Ave Imperatrix.' 'Of course, I couldn't talk democratic principles to my friend the Prince of Wales. That you understand is simply a matter of social tact.' (It was less tactful to vaunt his royal connections.) But to a reporter in San Francisco in April he said his political creed was really in his sonnet, 'Libertatis Sacra Fames,' where he so much detested demagogues as to prefer dictators to them.[38] He also vindicated the Irishry in a fourth lecture, 'The Irish Poets of 1848,' which he delivered first in San Francisco and then in a few other places. He could remember some of the oldest of these poets coming to his house, such as Smith O'Brien and John Mitchel and Charles Gavan Duffy. He praised these, and the poet he described as the greatest of them, Thomas Davis, as well as James Clarence Mangan, who would be the favorite of Yeats and Joyce. He mentioned the poets of the present day,

Ferguson, Waller, De Vere, 'Eve,' and finally came to his mother, whose photograph he carried with him. 'Of the quality of Speranza's poems I perhaps should not speak – for criticism is disarmed before love – but I am content to abide by the verdict of the nation.'[39] When he went south to stay a night with Jefferson Davis,* he made out an analogy between the Southern Confederacy and the Irish; both had gone forth to the battle and fallen, and their pursuit of self-rule made them akin. He was quoted as saying, 'The principles for which Jefferson Davis and the South went to war cannot suffer defeat.' To Mrs Howe he wrote with more candor, 'How fascinating all failures are!'[41] But he had found admirable qualities in the North too, when talking with General Grant, who had had the misfortune to succeed.

At moments Wilde had opportunities to further the cause of art directly. In Chicago a young sculptor named John Donoghue sent him a little bas-relief of a seated girl which was intended to illustrate Wilde's poem, 'Requiescat.' Wilde went to see Donoghue, and found him 'in a bare little room at the top of a great building, and in the center was a statuette of the young Sophocles leading the dance and . . . song after the battle of Salamis, a piece of the highest beauty and workmanship, waiting there in the clay to be cast into bronze. It was by far the best piece of sculpture I have seen in America.' Donoghue reminded him, he said, 'of the old Italian stories of the struggles of genius. Born of poor people, he felt a desire to create beauty. Seeing some workmen modelling a cornice one day, he begged some clay of them and went home and began to model. A man who saw what was in him gave him money for a year in Paris.' But now he was starving upon 'a radish and a crust, the stoic's fare.'[42] Wilde talked about Donoghue in this style to such purpose that commissions poured in to the artist, and Donoghue was able to move to Paris and set up a studio there. When his benefactor needed help later, however, Donoghue did not offer any.

Wilde lent his efforts to further other careers. He had an etching done in New York by James Edward Kelly, which showed him holding the hand of a young boy, possibly Kelly's son. He wisely used the head alone in publicity notices. In April he sat for a portrait by Theodore Wores in San Francisco.[43] On 2 May he praised Frank Duveneck as America's finest painter. He bought a watercolor of the seashore from John C. Miles in St John, New Brunswick. On 2 June he praised the landscape painting of Homer Watson and called him the 'Canadian Constable,' a label which, though not altogether appropriate, usefully stuck to Watson. Wilde would

---

* He would say later that in the South, whenever one mentioned anything, people would reply, 'You should have seen it before the War.' He had never felt what ruin war could bring about until one night in Charleston he turned to someone and said, 'How beautiful the moon is!' and had for reply, 'You should have seen it, sir, before the war.'[40]

secure commissions for Watson and also order a painting for himself later. In Toronto Wilde sat for a bust, now lost, by F. A. T. Dunbar. He said Louis Fréchette was Canada's best poet. In New Orleans he admired the novels of George Washington Cable and the poems of Father Ryan.[44] He gave the Canadian artist Frances Richards a letter to Whistler, and sat some time afterwards for a portrait by her. He paid several visits to a New York painter named Robert Blum, whose portraits he admired. To one female model he suggested she wear his favorite colors, café au lait and sage green, with a yellow tea rose; to another he remarked that Blum's delicious tints gave him a sensation similar to eating a yellow satin dress.[45] Wilde made no attempt to parade his benefactions. Some of his most important effects on people he would never know. For instance, Mrs Joseph Pennell, later to become a most faithful disciple and friend of Whistler, first heard of the painter from Wilde during his tour. Natalie Clifford Barney, then six years old, was placed on Wilde's lap and attributed her decision to become a writer to this formative experience.

Unlike Whistler, Wilde sought no enemies, and managed to be kind even to the incompetent. When people sent him manuscripts he always read and commented on them. On receiving from Anna Morrison Reed a book of poems entitled *Gethsemane*, he wrote to the author on 31 March,

Dear Madam,   I have read with much pleasure your charming little volume with all its sweet and simple joy in field and flower, its sympathetic touching of those chords of life which Death and Love make immortal for us. Pray accept my thanks for your courtesy, and believe me yours truly,

OSCAR WILDE

He urged his hostess in Cincinnati, on hearing that she sometimes wrote verses, to publish them. 'Perhaps,' she answered, 'in heaven, instead of holding receptions, I may get out a book.' 'No, no,' said Wilde, 'there'll be no publishers there.' But his sense of propriety sometimes got in the way of kindness, and it was in America that he annoyed the English actor Charles Brookfield by remarking on his keeping his gloves on at a tea party. Brookfield never forgave him.[46]

His chief effort was on behalf of his friend Rennell Rodd. The volume *Rose Leaf and Apple Leaf* was in Wilde's hands by late July, and he arranged for a small advance to be paid to the author. Wilde was pleased with the way that Stoddart had carried out his suggestions, and said the book was 'a *chef d'oeuvre* of typography.' The edition of 175 copies had parchment covers, like his own *Poems*, with the title printed in red and black. The verses were printed on one side of the paper only, with blank, apple-green pages interleaved. (The paper, found in a Philadelphia warehouse, had originally been intended for printing currency.) On the title page Wilde's artist friend Kelly had sketched the seal of a ring given Wilde by his mother. The preface, entitled 'Envoi,' was written in Wilde's florid manner, praising Rodd but also setting forth the program of what he called 'the modern romantic school.' He differentiated this from Ruskin's search for noble moral ideas, and by implication from the Pre-Raphaelites with their reminiscence and anecdotalism. Wilde's school modelled itself rather on Whistler and Albert Moore, whose works were meaningless except as design and color. Formal perfection was the goal, along with the expression of personality. Beyond faith and scepticism, the new poets tested forms of belief and tinged their nature 'with the sentiment that still lingered about some beautiful creeds.' They subscribed to no intellectual or metaphysical or didactic purpose, subordinating everything to 'the vital informing poetic principle.' They preferred impressions to ideas, brief flights to sustained ones, exceptions to types, situations to subjects. Sincerity did not enter in, for it was 'merely that plastic perfection of execution without which a poem or a painting . . . is but wasted and unreal work.'*

Rodd received a copy of his book at the beginning of October. At first glance he liked its sumptuousness and wrote to compliment Stoddart. Then he looked again. Though he had wanted to dedicate the book to Wilde, he did not anticipate that his friend would take over an inscription Rodd had written in Wilde's copy of the English edition:

TO
OSCAR WILDE –
'HEART'S BROTHER' –
THESE FEW SONGS AND MANY SONGS TO COME.

It was much more 'effusive' than he intended. Nor did he like the program in the preface, for it claimed him as 'a sort of disciple' and identified him 'with so much for which I had no sympathy.' Wilde had also revealed their secret travels on the Continent together. What he could not realize, as he flouted conventions of dress and thought himself, was that Rodd, then just beginning a promising career in the Foreign Office, could not afford to be thus paraded. Rodd wrote trying to withdraw the dedication, but it was too late. Copies had got out, and a mocking notice in the *Saturday Review* on 4 November 1882 was as embarrassing as Rodd had feared. The anonymous reviewer described the book's format with thoroughgoing sarcasm,

---

* The description was less suited to Rodd's poems than to two 'Impressions' by Wilde which his friend Robert Stewart Davis published in his Philadelphia magazine, *Our Continent*, on 15 February. The first, 'Le Jardin,' was written in response to a promise of a guinea a line for a poem mentioning a lily and a sunflower. The second, 'La Mer' ('A white mist drifts across the shrouds, / A wild moon in this wintry sky / Gleams like an angry lion's eye / Out of a mane of tawny clouds'), was probably written during the crossing from England. Each of these poems is sheer description, deliberately devoid of any significance beyond itself.

made sport of the supposed great departure from Ruskin's didacticism, and quoted derisively from Wilde's 'Envoi': 'Among the "many young men" who follow Mr Wilde, "none is dearer to myself" than the beloved of Mr Wilde and of the Muses, Mr Rodd.' This notice led Swinburne to write to a friend the same day, 'Have you read the *Saturday* on Oscar Wilde's young man, the Hephaestion of the all-conquering Alexander? Really these fools are enough to make one turn Wesleyan and contribute in future only to *The Methodist Magazine*.'[47] Wilde had wanted to please Rodd, but only succeeded in frightening him.

Some of Wilde's activities in America were perilous enough. On 19 September a broker named H. K. Burris brought him to see Wall Street, until a threat of being set upon by unaesthetic employees made them retreat hurriedly through a back exit.[48] In Moncton, New Brunswick, in mid-October Wilde came near to being arrested, and in New York, in December, he came near to being fleeced. The Moncton episode arose out of an invitation from the Young Men's Christian Association to lecture for them on a certain day. Wilde's agent proposed another day, but not having received a reply, closed with another offer. A sheriff's writ was prepared against him. Fortunately local friends went bail and brought pressure on the YMCA so that the case was dropped.[49]

As for the New York misadventure, Wilde was approached on the street on 14 December 1882 by a young man who claimed to be the son of Anthony J. Drexel of Morgan's bank, whom he said Wilde had met. Wilde did not recall either father or son but invited the young man to lunch. 'Drexel' had just won a lottery and asked Wilde to accompany him in getting his money. The place proved to be a gambling den, and 'Drexel's' prize was the right to play a turn at house expense. He courteously announced that he would play for Wilde, won, and gave Wilde his winnings. Wilde then threw the dice for himself, and after a first success began to lose heavily. He had soon written checks for over $1,000 at which point he stopped play. 'Drexel' left with him, and said he felt Wilde had been badly treated, and promised to 'See about it.' Wilde bethought himself, rushed to his bank, and stopped payment on the checks. He then went to the 30th Street Police Station, and told the sympathetic captain that he had been 'a damned fool.' On being shown photographs of some notorious confidence men, he identified 'Drexel' as 'Hungry Joe' Sellick, one of the cleverest of his kind. The captain wanted Wilde to start proceedings, but he did not do so. Perhaps as a reward from Sellick, his uncashable checks were mailed in to the police station a few days later and then returned to Wilde. But he did not recover the cash he had lost. He wrote lugubriously to John Boyle O'Reilly, 'I have fallen into a den of thieves.'[50] The *New York Tribune* rejoiced in his plight, and took to poetry to register amusement:

> And then, with the air of a guileless child,
>   Oh, that sweet, bright smile and those eyes aflame,
> He said, 'If you'll let me, dear Mr Wilde,
>   I'll show you a ravishing little game.'

Another unfortunate investment of Wilde's was buying a share in Kelly's Perpetual Motion Company, from which he expected a fortune.[51] As a counter to his sense of latent doom, he believed in his lucky star.

Wilde came twice more into close quarters with danger. On 4 July in Atlanta, he first experienced the terrors of prejudice against blacks. His agent Vail had bought three sleeping car tickets to Savannah, for Wilde, himself, and the valet Traquair. The Pullman agent pointed out that company rules did not allow blacks in sleeping car berths. Wilde said that Traquair had traveled with him all over the South, and insisted he be allowed to stay. The agent then said that the next train stop was Jonesboro, and that if people in Jonesboro saw a black in the car they would mob him. Wilde had no choice but to give in.[52]

The other incident was one of those foretastes of later events which often occurred in Wilde's life. On 23 April, he arrived in Lincoln, Nebraska, where he was to lecture the next evening. On the morning of the 24th, Wilde was introduced to a young teacher at the University of Nebraska. This was George E. Woodberry, later to achieve prominence in the field of comparative literature. Wilde had heard of Woodberry as a friend of Charles Eliot Norton, and was glad of his companionship. Together they drove out 'through mulberry and damp air' to the Lincoln penitentiary, where Woodberry, like Wilde, first entered prison confines. Woodberry wrote Norton of being 'much oppressed at the horrible things I saw,' and though he supposed that Wilde bore it better, Wilde wrote in letters to England that the bareness of the place had horrified him too. He exhibited a childlike faith in physiognomy. On being shown photographs of some of the convicts, he commented, 'O, what a dreadful face. And what did he do?' Warden Nobes did not hesitate to tell of the criminals in the most graphic manner. 'Oh, here's a beast, an animal,' exclaimed Wilde of one picture, 'nothing of the man left.' He would write Helena Sickert afterwards, 'They were all mean looking, which consoled me, for I should hate to see a criminal with a noble face.' He was then ushered into the whitewashed cell of a convict named Ayers of Grand Island, who was due to be hanged on 20 June. 'Do you read, my man?' asked Wilde. 'Yes, sir.' 'And what?' 'Novels part of the time. I am now reading *The Heir of Redclyffe* [by Charlotte M. Yonge].' Wilde left the cell with his party, and then could not resist a comment like one of Wainewright's: 'My heart was turned by the eyes of the doomed man, but if he reads *The Heir of Redclyffe* it's perhaps as well to let the law take its course.' To Helena Sickert he wrote more seriously that novels were 'a bad preparation for facing either God or Nothing.'[53]

Further on they came to the dark cell where refractory prisoners were placed. At Nobes's invitation Wilde and Woodberry stepped into the cell, and heard the solid door clang noisily behind them until they stood in the punitive darkness. These disagreeable sensations were mitigated by a visit to another convict's cell where Wilde caught sight of two neat rows of books. He ran over the titles rapidly, until he came upon Shelley first, and then, to his surprise, Dante, in Cary's translation. 'Oh dear,' he said, 'who would have thought of finding Dante here?' And he wrote to Helena Sickert, 'Strange and beautiful it seemed to me that the sorrow of a single Florentine in exile should, hundreds of years afterwards, lighten the sorrow of some common prisoner in a modern gaol.'[54] He would remember to read Dante when in prison himself fourteen years later.

Under the influence of this experience, he confided in Woodberry more than in most of the people he met. They spoke of Ruskin, and Wilde said, 'Like Christ he bears the sins of the world,' but then contrasted himself as 'always, like Pilate, washing his hands of all responsibility.' In reply to Woodberry's obvious desire that he should not dissociate himself so sharply from moral considerations, Wilde said, 'I was never touched by anything not tangible and visible but once, and that was just before writing "Ave Imperatrix."' He insisted that 'Poetry should be neither intellectual nor emotional' (that is, neither didactic nor autobiographical). When Woodberry pointed out that Wilde's own poems did not carry out his principles, 'Well,' said Wilde, 'those poems are not the best.'

Yet, disapprove as he might, Woodberry was won: 'I have seen no man whose charm stole on me so secretly, so rapidly, and with such entire sweetness. His poems are better than his theories, and he better than his poems.' 'He is the first artistic man I have ever seen – the first man in whom the artistic sense is mastering. He is of the type of Richard II in Shakespeare in his feeling for dramatic situations disjoined from ends or facts, purposes or feelings I mean – in life.' Wilde lectured at the Presbyterian Road Church in Lincoln, and Woodberry said, 'The nearest I have come to going to church for a long while was in attending your lecture.' (He was in fact losing his job because of religious doubts.) Wilde replied, 'Oh, Mr Woodberry, that is the most bitter thing that has been said to me,' and Woodberry wrote to Norton, 'But was it not irony that he, apostle of the beautiful, should be associated in my mind forever with my first view of crime and of misery in music, and with the Presbyterian church?'[55]

Still, Wilde had much to sustain him. In Louisville he happened to quote Keats's 'Sonnet on Blue' in his lecture, and unwittingly delighted a woman in the audience who proved to be Keats's niece, the daughter of his brother George. Mrs Emma (Keats) Speed invited Wilde to look at some of her uncle's manuscripts she owned, and enjoyed his company so much that she later sent him the manuscript of this sonnet as a gift.[56] At Julia Ward Howe's in Newport in July, Wilde amazed the company by outtalking the two great Boston conversationalists, Thomas Appleton and Oliver Wendell Homes. He was not displeased by a subsequent rumor in a gossip column, unfounded though it was, that he was going to marry Mrs Howe's daughter Maud, so it was left for Mrs Howe to say that 'if ever there were two people in the world who had no sympathy in common, they were the two.' Wilde did allow that he had fallen in love five times in the course of his tour, and on each occasion would have been entangled if his business manager had not insisted that he proceed to the next stop. After seeing Miss Alsatia Allen of Montgomery, Alabama, he pronounced her 'the most beautiful young lady in America,' a judgment that the *Saratoga Weekly Journal* of July–August 1882 found worth repeating. But he told Sam Ward he had lost his heart in San Francisco.[57]

There were informal occasions such as a tea in a San Francisco studio to which he was invited by some young artists. They had decorated the room with great care, even to painting roses and rose leaves on the skylight, and to stationing near the door the effigy of a woman in hat and veil whom they called Miss Piffle. A Chinese friend came over especially to prepare and serve the tea. Wilde entered, glanced at the guests, the bowing Chinese, the roses on the skylight, and said, 'This is where I belong. This is my atmosphere. I didn't know such a place existed in the whole United States.' He praised the tea and the teacups, and in strolling around to admire other features of the studio almost fell against Miss Piffle. As he stepped back with an apology, something gave away the identity of the mannequin. Having concocted himself, Wilde had a fellow-feeling for her. Without changing his tone, he began to talk with her about San Francisco. He replied to her imaginary remarks with such wit and gaiety that she seemed actually to be contributing.[58]

Wilde surveyed his American adventures with a mixture of vanity, wonder, and irony. In his running commentary to friends at home, he described some of the striking moments: the audience in Salt Lake City, where each Mormon husband sat surrounded with a coven of wives, for example, or the splendid renaissance of art he detected in the town he was then at, which happened to be Griggsville, Illinois. He would later improve upon this. One of his best adventures, also to be much embroidered, took place at Leadville, high up in the Rocky Mountains. Wilde had prepared himself by wearing, under his usual green overcoat, a pair of baggy trousers, and he wore a miner's black slouch hat. During the 10,000 foot climb he left his railway car to join the engineer in the cab, and when he proved to be an Irishman, they had a particularly pleasant talk. But as he arrived he felt faint, and a physician was summoned. His ailment was diagnosed as merely 'light air,' and his reception then went forward. The mayor, H. A. W. Tabor, known as the Silver King, invited him to visit the Matchless Mine. Wilde was let down in a bucket; once at the bottom, he found two ceremonies had been laid on. One was that he should open a new shaft, named 'The Oscar' in his honor, with a silver drill. 'I had hoped that in their grand simple way they would have offered me shares in "The Oscar,"' he commented later, 'but in their artless untutored fashion they did not.' Then there was supper at the bottom of the mine. 'The amazement of the miners when they saw that art and appetite could go hand in hand knew no bounds,' he reported. They cheered when he lit a cigar; when he downed a drink without a grimace they called him 'a bully boy with no glass eye.' As for the dinner, 'The first course was whiskey, the second whiskey, the third whiskey, all the courses were whiskey, but still they called it supper,' a delusion he did not attempt to disturb. 'In the evening I went to the Casino,' Wilde would reminisce. 'There I found the miners and the female friends of the miners, and in one corner a pianist – sitting at a piano over which was this notice: "Please don't shoot the pianist; he is doing his best." I was struck with this recognition of the fact that bad art merits the penalty of death, and I felt that in this remote city, where the aesthetic applications of the revolver were clearly established in the case of music, my apostolic task would be much simplified, as indeed it was.'[59] In *The Duchess of Padua* the Duke comments with nuanced cruelty about the shouting demonstrators,

> I fear
> They have become a little out of tune,
> So I must tell my men to fire on them.
> I cannot bear bad music!

Asked later whether the miners had not been rough and ready, Wilde defended them, as later he would often defend ordinary people, 'Ready, but not rough. They were polished and refined compared with the people I met in larger cities farther East . . . There is no chance for roughness. The revolver is their book of etiquette. This teaches lessons that are not forgotten.' At his lecture the audience had amused the lecturer more than he had amused them: 'I spoke to them of the early Florentines, and they slept as though no crime had ever stained the ravines of their mountain home.' 'Unluckily' he described one of Whistler's nocturnes in blue and gold. 'Then they leaped to their feet and in their grand simple style swore that such things should not be. Some of the younger ones pulled their revolvers out and left hurriedly to see if Jimmy was "prowling about the saloons."' He saw a performance of *Macbeth* in which Lady Macbeth was played by a convicted poisoner. (It was like Sibyl Vane, in love, playing Juliet in *Dorian Gray*.) Because the miners mined for silver, Wilde read them passages from the autobiography of that eminent silversmith, Benvenuto Cellini. 'I was reproved by my hearers for not having brought him with me. I explained that he had been dead for some little time which elicited the inquiry, "Who shot him?"' Wilde described his visit to Leadville so amusingly that his achievement in bringing art to that city may go unnoticed. There was no challenge that he failed to take up. He boasted smilingly to Whistler, 'I have already civilised America – *il reste seulement le ciel!*'[60]

The whole tour was an achievement of courage and grace, along with ineptitude and self-advertisement. Wilde succeeded in naturalizing the word aesthetic, even if Americans dropped the initial *a*. However effeminate his doctrines were thought to be, they constituted the most determined and sustained attack upon materialistic vulgarity that America had seen. That the attack was itself a bit vulgar did not diminish its effect. And Wilde presented not only a theory of art, but of being, not only a distinguished personality but an antithesis to getting-on without regard for the quality of life. The newspapers may have been unfair, but they paid him his due in attention. From now on the conception of artist was to take on heroic properties; to victimize him might cost one dear.

But Wilde was not yet ready to go home.

The Dream Theatre

The spectator is to be receptive. He is the violin on which the master is to play.

To the surprise of his family and friends, Wilde stayed on in America for almost two and a half months after he stopped lecturing in mid-October. He moved from the Fifth Avenue Hotel to the Brunswick, then to the Windsor, finally going downtown to 61 Irving Place at the corner of 17th Street and then to 48 West 11th Street in Greenwich Village.[61] His mother, grateful for some money he had sent her, wrote to him, 'I thought you had sailed away to Japan – what a long time you are in New York.' She added, 'You have fought your way splendidly.'[62] The obvious reason for his delayed departure was an attack of malaria, which he described to *Andrew's American Queen* on 23 December as 'an aesthetic disease but a deuced nuisance.' (In 1895 he still had quinine in his medicine cabinet, so malaria had probably recurred.) Two other things also detained him. One was the impending arrival of Lillie Langtry, who after a brief apprenticeship in London had organized her own company and was to tour America. Throughout his travels he had claimed her as a sympathizer with his movement who lived in a house surrounded by aesthetic objects, and had praised not only her beauty but her 'wonderfully musical and well-modulated voice.' 'Even my own poor sonnets when recited by her make me quiver with delight. I shall write them to her until she is ninety,' he commented to the same journal on 18 November 1882. In Moncton he was asked by an interviewer if he had discovered her, and neatly evaded the question by saying, 'I would rather have discovered Mrs Langtry than have discovered America,' a remark which went the journalistic rounds.[63]

She was due to arrive on the *SS Arizona* on 23 October. Wilde rose just in time to catch the launch which left the pier at 4.30 a.m. The *New York Times* for the following day commented on his appearance:

He was dressed as probably no grown man in the world was ever dressed before. His hat was of brown cloth not less than six inches high; his coat was of black velvet; his overcoat was of green cloth, heavily trimmed with fur; his trousers matched his hat; his tie was gaudy and his shirtfront very open, displaying a large expanse of manly chest. A pair of brown cloth gloves and several pimples on his chin completed his toilet. His flowing hair and the fur trimming of his coat were just of a shade, and they gave him the appearance of having his hair combed down one side of him to his heels and up the other side.

Wilde carried an armful of lilies, and presented them with appropriate fanfare.

Mrs Langtry had a week to go before opening as Hester Grazebrook in Tom Taylor's *An Unequal Match* at the Park Theatre on Sunday, 29 October. During these days Wilde made himself useful to her. He took her to Sarony for histrionic photographs.* Hearing that she was also planning to play Rosalind in *As You Like It*, he persuaded her not to wear long-legged boots in the part as Rose Coghlan had been doing. In reply, she disputed with him about how he should wear his curled locks.[65] She took up with a wealthy American, Freddy Gebhardt, and once when Wilde was visiting her she suddenly flung a costly necklace at him. She explained, 'When I saw Freddy just now, he took that out of his pocket and flung it at me across the table, saying, like the surly bear he is, "If you want that you can keep it." So I felt I must positively fling it at somebody else.' Wilde may not have been amused. Another bit of their conversation was reported. She asked him why he thought of going to Australia, and he replied, 'Well, do you know, when I look at the map and see what an awfully ugly-looking country Australia is, I feel as if I want to go there to see if it cannot be changed into a more beautiful form.'[66]†

Early on the day of her opening, Mrs Langtry was escorted by David Belasco to see a new type of movable double stage which had just been

* He spoke afterwards of her having had her photograph taken 'with Niagara Falls as a kind of unpretentious background.'[64]

† Wilde made Australia rather than Scotland the butt of his regional jokes. In February 1889, he published 'Symphony in Yellow' in the *Centennial Magazine* in Australia, and was quoted in an Australian magazine as having said: 'So they are desirous of my beauty at Botany Bay. I have inquired concerning this Botany Bay. It is the abode of anthropophagi, the abode of lost souls, whither criminals are transported to wear a horrible yellow livery. Even they are called "canaries." So I have written for them a Symphony in Yellow – they will feel the homely touch. I rhyme "elms" with "Thames." It is a venial offence in comparison with theirs. A symphony with sympathy – how sweet! Suppose I were to add a stanza:

invented by Steele Mackaye. Shortly afterwards she received the dreadful news that the Park Theatre was on fire. The performance was off, but fortunately Wallack's Theatre was available a week after. Wilde attended the opening with Steele Mackaye on 6 November, and afterwards, at the suggestion of his friend Hurlbert of the *New York World*, went to the composing room of that newspaper in his kneebreeches and wrote there a review of the performance. Entitled simply, 'Mrs Langtry,' it began as a paean in praise of her beauty, which he said could be found only in ancient Greece, but insisted that her performance was an artistic fusion of 'classical grace' and 'absolute reality.' Wilde attributed the new movement in English art, that following the Pre-Raphaelites, to the inspiration of Mrs Langtry's face. He liked her dresses immensely, the scenery hardly at all, but thought she made the latter unimportant.[68] It was as much as he could say about a play that was obviously mediocre, but it attempted to link beauty and art very closely in her person, and she could not fail to be pleased by it. After some days she was off on tour, and became a subject of scandal in the press for diffusing beauty among American men in quite a different way from Wilde's.

But Wilde had another interest. In his review of Lillie Langtry he had mentioned the new stage curtain at the Madison Square Theatre – this was a covert compliment to the man who had commissioned it, Steele Mackaye. Mackaye was perhaps the greatest innovator of his time, and had completely remodeled the old Fifth Avenue Theatre into the Madison Square Theatre. A safety curtain was one of his new ideas, another was folding seats, another was the movable double stage which Lillie Langtry had examined. Mackaye like Wilde was eager to bring about a renaissance, and specifically a theatrical one. Although forty years old, he looked almost as young as Wilde. He had studied with Delsarte, and the old master had designated him as his successor in teaching a new conjunction of gesture and word. In New York Mackaye opened a Delsarte school and eventually the first American School of Acting. He gave Wilde lessons in the Delsartian system using *Hamlet*.[69] He wrote a great many plays, but seems to have recognized that his principal talent was for production and stage devices. The one thing he had no skill at all with was money. He was as lavish in entertainment as Wilde, and after having run the Madison Square Theatre from 1879 to 1881 had been forced to give it up because of financial difficulties.

Now Mackaye evolved an even grander scheme, a dream theatre. By 16 June he had a design for it, and determined that it should be situated at

---

And far in the Antipodes
    When swelling suns have sunk to rest
A convict to his yellow breast
    Shall hug my yellow melodies.'[67]

In *Lady Windermere's Fan* a character from Australia is given the name Hopper.

33rd Street and Broadway, attached like the Savoy Theatre in London to a hotel. All that was necessary was to secure a million dollars. Among the potential backers was George Childs, Wilde's rich friend from Philadelphia. Mackaye met with his sponsors several times during August and September, but he could not quite bring them to open their wallets.

Wilde was greatly concerned in these negotiations, because he and Mackaye had joined their hopes together. Mackaye planned to inaugurate the new theatre with Wilde's *The Duchess of Padua*, and, after some changes which he felt were necessary, with *Vera*. These might well be followed by *The Cardinal of Avignon*, a Shelleyesque play of which Wilde had written the scenario. For the *Duchess* they hoped to secure Mary Anderson. Wilde culminated months of delicate coaxing by discussing the play with her in Long Branch. She remembered his telling her, 'The stage is the key that has opened the world of art to you.' 'I cannot write the scenario till I see you and talk to you. All good plays are a combination of the dream of a poet and that practical knowledge of the actor which gives concentration to action . . . I want you to rank with the great actresses of the earth . . . having in you a faith which is as flawless as it is fervent I doubt not for a moment that I can and will write for you a play which, created for you and inspired by you, shall give you the glory of a Rachel, and may yield me the fame of a [Victor] Hugo.' On 8 September, still breathing perfect confidence, he arranged to meet her and settle the scenario: 'I think I have so conceived it that we shall simultaneously become immortal in one night.'[70] All that was necessary was to settle the terms. Wilde wanted an advance of $5,000 and a royalty on performances. But Miss Anderson's stepfather and business manager, Hamilton Griffin, whom Wilde dubbed 'the Griffin,' was stern in her interests. Wilde expected to have her acceptance by mid-September, but on the 20th he was complaining to Mackaye, 'No news from the Anderson – from the Griffin none. O art and Kentucky, how ill your alliance is! She is sweet and good (he is a padded horror), if I could see her I could arrange it all.' But he was confident that the Kentucky-born actress would eventually consent. 'Do not yet despair,' he told Mackaye, 'you and I together should conquer the world. Why not? Let us do it!'[71]

He arranged, while still lecturing, to meet Mary Anderson and the Griffin in Boston at the Hotel Vendome on Sunday 23 September. They indicated that Miss Anderson would produce the play, and proposed to open on 22 January. Wilde warned that Mackaye felt the scenery and costumes would cost $10,000, but Miss Anderson indicated she was ready to spend 'any money' on it. (In *The Duchess of Padua* Wilde would speak of 'a prize / Richer than all the gold the Griffin guards / In rude Armenia.') Wilde saw his opening and said that Steele Mackaye might be induced to direct, provided that he had absolute control of everything. 'They agree,' he jubilantly informed his friend. He and Mackaye would produce the *Duchess*, and after that *Vera*, 'and then the world is at our feet!' On 4

October Mackaye let Wilde know that Mary Anderson and Griffin had decided to defer *The Duchess* until September 1883 when they would try for a long run.[72] On the 12th Mary Anderson wrote to Wilde, formally accepted Mackaye as director, and agreed to take Booth's Theatre. The final agreement was signed early in December as a result of an ultimatum from the Griffin of 1 December, offering Wilde £1,000 on signature, and £4,000 more conditional upon Mary Anderson's acceptance of the completed version of the play, due 1 March 1883. She would produce it within a year. 'Mere starvation wages,' Wilde told the writer Edgar Saltus that night at Delmonico's.[73]

Meanwhile Mackaye, though he had had to put off his dream theatre for lack of funds, continued to work on Wilde's behalf. He approached the actress Marie Prescott early in November and urged her to play *Vera*. Miss Prescott wrote with great respect to Wilde on 9 November, and arranged for him to breakfast with her and her husband, William Perzel, two days later. She felt that *Vera* would suit her, but asked him to rewrite the long scene in Act II and some of Alexis's speeches in Act I. The only remaining questions were financial. This time Wilde held out, as he had not with Mary Anderson, for permanent control of the acting rights, besides a sizable advance. Wilde mentioned to Saltus that some changes had been asked of him, 'But who am I to tamper with a masterpiece?'[74] Actually he consented. When in December Perzel and Wilde failed to agree on terms, Wilde imperiously demanded the play back. But Miss Prescott on 9 January 1883 proposed new terms that mollified him, $1,000 down and $50 for each performance. She would stage the play in the autumn of 1883. To this Wilde agreed. On 11 February 1883 the play was announced in the newspapers, and soon after, Miss Prescott's $1,000 arrived. He had now, or seemed to have, a contract for a play in either pocket. He celebrated by lending Mackaye $200.

By arranging the production of his plays Wilde was not in any way unfaithful to his principal motive of 'civilizing America.' The lecture method was necessarily a limited one. At the Lotos Club on 28 October he was called upon to speak, and described the drama as a school for developing artistic taste. He also took his chance to comment formally on the unpleasant way in which American newspapers had treated him, one of the worst of the unnamed offenders being the toastmaster on this occasion at the Lotos Club, Whitelaw Reid of the *New York Tribune*. Wilde said to Vincent O'Sullivan later, 'Praise makes me humble. But when I am abused I know I have touched the stars.' When Wilde left the country on 27 December, seen off by Modjeska and Norman Forbes-Robertson, the *Tribune* relentlessly quoted him, or claimed to quote him, as admitting that his American tour had been 'a failure.'[75]

But in what sense had it failed? It was true, as Wilde would have said himself, that the country still kept the same shape on the map as when he had first arrived. Otherwise, however, there were many indications of success. Oscar Wilde was now an unforgettable name throughout the United States and Canada, and scarcely less than that in Great Britain; he had arranged for productions of his two plays, he had earned and spent a lot of money; he had disseminated his theories and annoyed, bored, amused, and converted large numbers of people by them. He had made people heartily sick of the words 'beauty' and 'beautiful.' Perhaps the knee breeches, though they had shown off his handsome legs, had been a mistake; if so, they were the kind of mistake Wilde would always make, outraging the people he wanted to please and then contriving to please most of them nonetheless.

Apart from his effect upon Americans, Wilde's tour had an effect upon him. 'How changed you will be,' his mother had written him in some trepidation. He could better estimate his own value after withstanding his critics. He had learned a good deal about playing up to audiences, and had also come to recognize the range of possibility implicit in the aesthetic movement. The aesthete was not the shadow of a man. Wilde had put on quite a few pounds to prove it. Perhaps the aesthete might rather be the type of the only entire man, for to be an artist was to add constantly to one's image of oneself, and not to be an artist was to be merely a creature of habit. So far Wilde had said only in perorations what later he would argue more substantially, that in art lay not only life's secret but also life's future, discovering and satisfying fresh needs and pleasures, initiating a new civilization.

CHAPTER VIII

Countering the Renaissance

And when that day dawns, or sunset reddens, how joyous we shall all be! . . . The very aspect of the world will change to our startled eyes. Out of the sea will rise Behemoth and Leviathan . . . Dragons will wander about the waste places, and the phoenix will soar from her nest of fire into the air. We shall lay our hands upon the basilisk, and see the jewel in the toad's head.

An Irishman in Paris

On his return to London Wilde was in excellent spirits. He had lots of stories to tell, and many people to listen. George Lewis was to be thanked for intervening in the dispute with Archibald Forbes, Edmund Yates of the *World* and Labouchere of *Truth* for treating his tour kindly when the temptation to deride it had been so widely unresisted. His mother and brother could rejoice in his reminiscences and his stunning international fame. As a movement aestheticism had been rendered passé: Wilde would use the word and its cognates in a more gingerly fashion from now on. But the dying movement's vivacious leader was more likely than ever to be consulted on all subjects related to it.

Of course Wilde, dressed for the occasion in a red suit, went to call on Whistler, and was welcomed, though with ironies that prompted him to say, as he often did, 'Jimmy, you're a devil.' He greatly admired the second set of etchings Whistler had done in Venice – 'such water paintings as the gods never beheld,' he wrote to Waldo Story.[1] The meeting was somewhat impaired by the raised eyebrows of Rennell Rodd, who liked neither the suit nor the manner. Wilde looked to him like Heliogabalus or Sardanapalus, and was as unwilling to listen as Rodd had long ago jocularly predicted. When Rodd tried to protest against the highhanded manner in which *Rose Leaf and Apple Leaf* had been exploited by Wilde, he got no satisfaction; Wilde regarded himself as the aggrieved party. In January or February Rodd wrote him a long-meditated letter ending their friendship. Wilde's comment was, 'The only schools worthy of founding

201

are schools without disciples.' As for Rodd's stinging letter, 'What he says is like a poor little linnet's cry by the roadside, along which my immeasurable ambition is sweeping forward.' He would not always be so contemptuous of linnets' cries. Rodd, measurable in his ambitions, hereafter shunned his company. From now on he was for Wilde 'the true poet, and the false friend.'[2] The break with Rodd, who had largely replaced Wilde in Whistler's affection, augured ill for his subsequent relations with that artist.

In London Wilde went back to Charles Street. But he had no intention of settling back at once into London life. After his flamboyant tour in America, with black valet and white manager, plush hotel rooms and sumptuous invitations to the wealthiest homes, this would have been anticlimactic. To dramatize his return he must first go somewhere else and finish *The Duchess of Padua*. A year before he had written to Archibald Forbes that with his American earnings he hoped for a few months in Venice, Rome, and Athens. But, keyed up for conquest of another nation, he needed one whose language he could speak fluently, so went to Paris. He had been there several times before; his mother had translated two books of Lamartine and had been thanked by the great man himself. Wilde was at home in French literature, and venerated in particular Balzac, Gautier, Flaubert, and Baudelaire.

He crossed the Channel at the end of January 1883. After a few days at the Hôtel Continental he moved to the Hôtel Voltaire on the Left Bank. He had furnished himself as usual with letters of introduction from friends and with copies of his *Poems*. The American journalist Theodore Child, who wrote for the *World*, was among the first to give a dinner for him, and others followed. The artist Jacques-Emile Blanche did a painting of a young woman reading Wilde's *Poems*.

One person who assisted him in settling into Paris was a young Englishman, scarcely twenty-one, named Robert Harborough Sherard. He was to become Wilde's biographer several times over, with *The Story of an Unhappy Friendship*, *The Life of Oscar Wilde*, *The Real Oscar Wilde*, and numerous other less sustained accounts. Though the information is needed, perhaps few men have been so peculiarly served by a biographer. Sherard was bumptious, wrongheaded, uncomprehending. That Wilde put up with him at all was due to Sherard's possession of three compensatory merits: he was young, blond, and idolatrous. Not precisely handsome, he was '*beau laid*.' Within four months he asked permission to dedicate to Wilde a book of poems called *Whispers*, and Wilde praised it and consented to receive the dedication, this time without having, as with Rennell Rodd, to write it himself. Sherard's wording was 'To Oscar Wilde, Poet and Friend, Affectionately and admiringly Dedicated.' Oscar Wilde's indulgence did not weigh with his brother Willie, who in a *Vanity Fair* review announced that whispers were what the poems were and what they should have remained. Oscar reviewed a later book of Sherard more generously, saying that he has 'come through "early poems," a three-volume novel, and other complaints common to his time of life.'[3]

Sherard was a great-grandson of Wordsworth. Wilde twitted him about this ancestry. His father, whose surname was Kennedy, was an Anglican priest who had taken his family with him to the Continent and then to Guernsey, where they shared a house with Victor Hugo and became friendly with him. Sherard went up to New College, Oxford, in 1880, but during his first year was sent down for non-payment of debts. He made his way to Paris with the intention of becoming a writer, changed his name from Kennedy to Sherard, and had published a novel before he and Wilde met. Truculent by disposition, he was not disposed to like Wilde on the basis of what he had heard about him. When his friend Maria Cassavetti-Zambaco (a beautiful Greek who had been the model for Vivian in Burne-Jones's *The Beguiling of Merlin* and for Galatea in his Pygmalion and Galatea series) invited him to dinner to meet Wilde, Sherard almost refused. When he entered the room the appearance of Wilde confirmed his forebodings: there were no knee breeches, but the costume was Count d'Orsay, with cuffs turned back over jacket sleeves, tight trousers, colored handkerchief, *boutonnière*, heavy rings, and an elaborate coiffure. His mother wrote that his trousers and sleeves were so tight as to be remarked on the Boulevards. It was all Sherard could do to avoid bursting into mocking laughter; to keep in countenance he joined dour Paul Bourget and grave John Singer Sargent. Wilde did not at first take to Sherard either. 'I fancied, because of your long blond hair, that you were Herr Shulz on the violoncello.' He later found a kindlier comparison: 'It is the head of a Roman emperor of the decadence – the head of an emperor who reigned but for one day – a head found stamped upon a base coin.'[4]

Only when they sat down to dinner did Sherard suspect that his preliminary estimate of Wilde as a fraud or pretender would not do. There was no doubt who ruled the table that night. Wilde probably made use of some of the conversational gambits that he had begun to write down in his notebook, such as:

> Artiste en poésie, et poète, deux choses très différentes: cf. Gautier et Hugo.
>
> Pour écrire il me faut du satin jaune.
>
> La poésie c'est la grammaire idéalisée.
>
> Il me faut des lions dans les cages dorées: c'est affreux, après la chair humaine les lions aiment l'os, et on ne leur [le] donne jamais.*

---

* 'Artist in poetry, and poet; two very different things: cf. Gautier and Hugo.

'To write, I must have yellow satin.

'Poetry is idealized grammar.

'I must have lions in golden cages: it's frightful – after eating human flesh lions like bones, and they're never given them.'

He initialed these 'O.W.' to distinguish them from remarks he had heard from others, such as one from a waiter at the Hôtel Voltaire, '*L'art, c'est le désordre*,' which contradicted all he had been saying about the subject in America. A concierge at the Louvre said to him, '*Les maîtres anciens, c'est la momie, n'est-ce pas?* [The old masters – just mummies, right?]' Wilde did not accept this verdict, and told the assembled dinner guests how he often sat for hours before the statue of the Venus de Milo in the Louvre. His friend Godwin had a cast of this statue in the center of his drawing room, with a censer smoking before it. At this rapturous point Sherard saw his opening, and interjected rudely, 'I have never been to the Louvre. When that name is mentioned, I always think of the Grands Magasins du Louvre, where I can get the cheapest ties in Paris.' To his surprise, Wilde took the remark with good grace: 'I like that, that is very fine,' he said, and after dinner sought Sherard out to invite him for dinner the next night. 'When you bluntly disclaimed all artistic interests,' he explained later, 'I discovered that you had scientifically thought out a pose that interested me.'[5] Vulgarities were tolerable when they issued from fair heads. And Wilde was testing out a cultural scene which he knew to be far different from what he had experienced in America.

When Sherard went to the Hôtel Voltaire the next night, in late February 1883, he found Wilde occupying a suite of rooms on the second floor overlooking the Seine. He began to praise the view, but Wilde stopped him, with a deflation even more final than Sherard's of the Louvre the night before: 'Oh, that is altogether immaterial, except to the innkeeper, who of course charges it in the bill. A gentleman never looks out of the window.' (To avoid saying 'I,' Wilde had concocted his mythical gentleman who never made an expected gesture.) As for Sherard, prevented from looking out, he looked in. Wilde wore a white wool dressing gown, his writing costume, as Balzac had worn a monk's cowl. Balzacian also was Wilde's ivory cane, its head covered with turquoises.* His imitations did not stop there: he would later pose for Will Rothenstein in a red waistcoat, in imitation not of Balzac but of Gautier.

The interior displayed other flourishes. On a table were sheets of ornate paper on which Wilde was writing *The Duchess of Padua*. The mantelpiece was surmounted by a reproduction of Puvis de Chavannes's painting of a slender nude girl sitting on a shroud in a village graveyard, her eyes full of wonder at her own resurrection. When Sherard admired it, Wilde at once presented it to him, writing on the mat an aesthetic motto, '*Rien n'est vrai que le beau*.' He told Sherard to have it framed in grey with a narrow line of vermilion, a word which – as both Sherard and Julia Ward

* In a review of a book of Balzac, he said, 'A steady course of Balzac reduces our living friends to shadows and our acquaintances to the shadows of shades; who would care to go out to an evening party to meet Tomkins, the friend of one's boyhood, when one can sit at home with Lucien de Rubempré? It is pleasanter to have the entrée to Balzac's society than to receive cards from all the duchesses of Mayfair.'[6]

Howe noticed – Wilde pronounced so slowly that a missing *l* could be heard.

Wilde was in funds, and with his accustomed generosity took Sherard to an elegant restaurant, Foyot's in the rue de Tournon. He explained his affluence to his friend by saying, 'We are dining with the Duchess,' meaning that he was drawing on Mary Anderson's advance for his play. In later meetings he would be equally free with his money, quoting Proudhon's '*La propriété, c'est le vol,*' as his authority for spending not only on his guest and himself, but on various Left Bank hangers-on. (One of these was Petit Louis, who wanted to return to his native Brittany and enlist in the Navy. Wilde bought him a suit and gave him his fare.)[7] The question of whether to order red or white wine led Sherard to remark that white wine should really be called yellow, an idea that Wilde liked and appropriated. In recompense, Sherard's locks were no longer blond to him but 'honey-coloured.' Sherard at first stiffly addressed his host as 'Wilde,' but Wilde would not accept this: 'You mustn't call me Wilde. If I am your friend, my name to you is Oscar. If we are only strangers, I am Mr Wilde.' Sherard gave in, and confessed that he had felt hostility when they first met. 'That was very wrong of you, Robert,' Wilde said, explaining that the freemasonry of writers took pleasure in each other's works.[8]

Sherard rebelled a little still. When Wilde talked of lecturing on beauty in America, and of insisting that beauty might be found in the commonest things, Sherard behaved like the New York reporter who had asked if beauty was in Hoboken. He dug his cigar butt into the coffee in his saucer and said 'Do you see any beauty in this?' Wilde was not fazed: 'Oh, yes, it makes quite an effective brown,' but something in his look led Sherard to desist from further mockery. After dinner they walked past the place where the palace of the Tuileries had been burnt down twelve years before, under the Commune. Wilde commented, 'There is not there one little blackened stone which is not to me a chapter in the bible of democracy.' The remark could hardly have pleased his friend more. Sherard had a passion for the French Revolution and dated all his letters according to the revolutionary calendar. On discovering this, Wilde always addressed letters to him as 'Citoyen Robert Sherard.' Challenged as to his own political views, he admitted to 'an elegant Republicanism.'[9]

The two men met again next day, and almost every day thereafter during Wilde's stay. A good deal of affectionate talk went on: Sherard fell into phrases like 'My dearest Oscar,' and they appear to have kissed each other's lips in a social manner.[10] Sherard was thinking of marrying, and found Wilde unsympathetic. ('I have heard strange things about men's wives,' says Simone in *A Florentine Tragedy*.) The infidelity of wives, Wilde enlightened his friend, was almost universal. If Sherard should marry, his advice was, 'Act dishonourably, Robert. It's what soon or later she'll certainly do to you.' (In Sherard's case this proved true.) As they passed a statue of Henri IV Wilde was ruminating about a subject he would later discuss with Louis Latourette: 'Still another great Frenchman who was a cuckold! All the great men of France were cuckolds. Haven't you observed this? All! In every period. By their wives or by their mistresses. Villon, Molière, Louis XIV, Napoleon, Victor Hugo, Musset, Balzac, kings, generals, poets! Those I mention, a thousand more that I could name, were all cuckolds. Do you know what that means? I will tell you. Great men, in France, have loved women too much. Women don't like that. They take advantage of this weakness. In England, great men love nothing, neither art, nor wealth, nor glory ... nor women. It's an advantage, you can be sure.'[11]*

The acolyte Sherard asked Wilde how a husband should behave if he discovered his wife was unfaithful, and Wilde sketched out a scene: 'Pretend to ignore the liaison and delight in watching them. It will get interesting as the time draws near for his departure after you three have been spending the evening together. You should yourself be more and more marital and you close the seánce by giving him his *congé* with some such remarks as, "Well, goodbye. We young married folks, you know ... ," and to the adulterous wife, "*Au lit*, darling, *au lit*." Then some minutes later you go in your pyjamas to the window of the nuptial thalamos and there of course Don Juan is standing on the other side of the road gazing at and sighing toward the place where Cressid lay that night. There you attract his attention and wave your hand towards him to imply that he must be on his way, while you hasten to the matrimonial delights that are awaiting you.'[13] It was clear that Wilde was moving towards the unexpected domination of lover by husband which he would display in *A Florentine Tragedy*.

Yet if he cynically opposed marriage, he did not display sangfroid over fornication; one evening he went to the Eden Music Hall and picked up a well-known prostitute, later to be murdered, called Marie Aguétant. The next day he commented as lesser men might have done, 'What animals we all are, Robert.' 'You wake in me each bestial sense, you make me what I would not be,' was the way he put this in 'The Sphinx.' 'The Harlot's House,' in which the dance of marketed love is also the dance of death, and is mitigated only by the approach 'like a frightened girl' of unsoiled dawn, was also a literary regurgitation of his disgust. It was, as he said of André Raffalovich's verse, 'Herrick after the French Revolution.'[14] Sherard was alarmed that Wilde might have been robbed, but Wilde replied impatiently, 'One gives them all that one has in one's pockets,' as if the worst of the experience had not been financial.

Young Sherard was increasingly dazzled by his new friend. They talked

* In later life Wilde told Augustus John about his friend Ernest La Jeunesse, who spoke in a falsetto. His publisher crudely maintained that it was because of impotence. La Jeunesse, hearing of this, reciprocated by making a long but ultimately successful play for the publisher's wife.[12] It was, Wilde said, 'The Greatest Repartee in History.'

a good deal about literature, especially – of English writers – Swinburne and Carlyle. Wilde could quote long passages from *The French Revolution*. But much of their conversation turned on a quartet more appropriate to the current Parisian scene: Gérard de Nerval, Poe, Chatterton, and Baudelaire. Their pervasive gloom suited the early 1880s. Wilde and Sherard retraced together Nerval's routes in Paris, and Wilde would recite love-and-death lines such as 'Les Cydalises':

> Où sont nos amoureuses?
> Elles sont au tombeau.*

The same theme fascinated him in Baudelaire. He preferred 'Une Charogne,' with its brutal union of the dead carcass and the beloved,

> – Et pourtant vous serez semblable à cette ordure,
>   A cette horrible infection,
> Etoile de mes yeux, soleil de ma nature,
>   Vous, mon ange et ma passion!†

Another favorite was 'Le Vin de l'assassin,' in which a murderer boasts of having killed his wife. For formal reasons, Wilde liked 'La Musique,' with its contrast of being riven by music like a ship in a storm, or of being becalmed in despair.[15]

Wilde wished to meet French writers and artists, and was invited to an evening reception at Victor Hugo's house. There a Polish princess tried to awaken his interest, but he preferred to talk about Swinburne with Auguste Vacquerie, the radical editor of *Le Rappel*. Vacquerie had assumed, from the way that Swinburne, on a visit to Paris, had jumped about 'like a carp,' that he must be a drinker. Wilde was quick to explain that Swinburne was possessed of a temperament so delicate that merely to look at a glass of wine would put him into a Bacchanalian frenzy, and that he actually drank almost nothing. Some of his anecdotes about Swinburne so amused Vacquerie that he took Wilde over to meet Victor Hugo, but Hugo was taking his usual postprandial doze and even Wilde could not wake him up. On leaving Wilde ebulliently quoted 'Napoléon II' from Hugo's *Chants du crépuscule* (no. 5):

> Il cria tout joyeux avec un air sublime:
> – L'avenir! l'avenir! l'avenir est à moi!

He forgot the poet's reply to the ill-fated emperor,

---

* 'Where are our lovers? / They are in the tomb.'
† 'And yet you will come to resemble this filth, / This horrible infection, / Star of my eyes, sun of my being, / You, my angel and my passion!'

Non, l'avenir n'est à personne!
Sire, l'avenir est à Dieu!*

Wilde could scarcely have been unaware of an element of doltishness in his young friend Sherard, but treated him with faultless consideration. One day he spent hours going about Paris in search of a copy of Delvau's biography of Nerval on the ground that, furnished with this, Sherard could write a knowledgeable article for the English press and make a little money. Sherard never rose to this task, though Delvau's book, an expensive one, was duly found and bought for him. His artistic interests were limited; he was doubtful, for example, about Impressionist painting. Wilde did his best to convert him to the painting of Degas, to whose garret studio in the rue Fontaine St Georges he and Whistler had recently climbed by ladder. 'Nothing is worth painting,' he assured Sherard, 'but what is not worth looking at.'[16]† Neither then nor later did Sherard show any sign of catching on. But Wilde was at last coming to admire the work of the Impressionists, especially Degas, Monet, and the Pissarros.‡

Sherard did, however, observe Wilde closely, and one must be grateful for the pages in which he describes him. Wilde was now dressing like a Frenchman of the period, with certain variations. He wore the standard silk hat and redingote. But the cuffs turned up from the sleeves of his jacket were unusual, as was his furlined overcoat, veteran of his American lecture tour. When Sherard ventured to commend Wilde for having given up his American costume, Wilde found the remark 'tedious,' by which he always meant irritating. But he agreed in substance, 'All *that* belonged to the Oscar of the first period. We are now concerned with the Oscar Wilde of the second period, who has nothing whatever in common with the gentleman who wore long hair and carried a sunflower down Piccadilly.'[18] *Punch* also noted the change, and in the issue of 31 March 1883 carried a mock-advertisement: 'To be sold, the whole of the Stock-in-Trade, Appliances, and Inventions of a Successful Aesthete, who is retiring from business. This will include a large Stock of faded Lilies, dilapidated Sunflowers, and shabby Peacocks' Feathers, several long-haired Wigs, a collection of incomprehensible Poems, and a number of impossible

* 'With sublime look he cried joyfully: – The future! the future! the future belongs to me!' 'No, the future belongs to no one! / Sire, the future belongs to God!'

† Wilde noted down a remark by Degas that interested him, '*Il y a quelque chose plus terrible encore que le bourgeois – c'est l'homme qui nous singe* [There's something even more awful than the bourgeois – it's the man who apes us].'

‡ Degas, a man with a scorching tongue, commented to Sickert about Wilde, '*Il a l'air de jouer Lor' Byron dans un théâtre de banlieue* [He has the look of someone playing Lor' Byron in a suburban theatre].'[17] As to Whistler, Degas said to him, 'Whistler, you behave as though you have no talent,' and when Whistler was preening himself on a new flat-brimmed hat, Degas said to him, '*Oui; il vous va très bien; mais ce n'est pas ça qui nous rendra l'Alsace et la Lorraine* [Yes; it suits you very nicely; but that's not how we'll get back Alsace and Lorraine].'

Pictures. Also, a valuable Manuscript Work, entitled *Instruction to Aesthetes*, containing a list of aesthetic catchwords, drawings of aesthetic attitudes, and many choice secrets of the craft. Also, a number of well-used Dadoes, sad-coloured Draperies, blue and white China, and brass Fenders . . . No reasonable offer refused.'

Wilde would later praise the forger Wainewright for having 'intensified his personality' by the wearing of disguises.[19] For him too clothing was a way of carrying each phase to its apogee, whether it confounded and irritated the onlookers or not. He liked also the romantic notion that the soul could be perpetually reborn. He did not accept the suggestion that his present attire was more conventional – it was only more subtly un-conventional. A new wardrobe was needed for each new country.

He also changed his hairstyle. Instead of wearing it long, he resolved to wear it in a Roman fashion, and took his hairdresser from the rue Scribe to the Louvre to show him a marble bust. (He later said it was a bust of Nero, but Louise Jopling heard him say Antinous.)[20] The hairdresser obliged, and Wilde kept this Imperial style for a few more months.* ('Curly hair to match the curly teeth,' someone jeered.[22]) 'I hope your hair curls naturally, does it?' asks Cecily of Algernon, who replies, 'Yes, darling, with a little help from others.' He did not, however, make any effort to disguise his face, and in seeming defiance of his theories refused to wear a mask at a masked ball at Alma-Tadema's. He was complacent about his own features, and later vaunted them to his intimates.

Wilde always spoke of his stay in Paris as one during which he had worked well. When he was simply enjoying himself, he would call himself to order. 'I ought not to be doing this. I ought to be putting black upon white, black upon white.' When he did write, he pretended to outdo Pater in fastidiousness. 'I was working on the proof of one of my poems all the morning,' he said to Sherard, 'and took out a comma.' 'And in the afternoon?' 'In the afternoon? Well, I put it back again.'[23] Finding himself among writers to whom nature poetry was meaningless, he took up the old manuscript of 'The Sphinx' (he spelt it 'Sphynx'), which he had begun in

---

* Wilde's hairdresser delighted him with his conversation, from which Wilde noted down:

'J'aime assez les applaudissements, mais enfin j'ai trouvé que le public ne peut pas découvrir les fautes: dans les arts, monsieur, on peut toujours dissimuler; moi-même j'ai fait des fautes: mais je les ai toujours caché . . . Quand je vais dans un nouveau pays j'observe les coiffures; je sais bien qu'il y a des gens qui s'occupent avec les bâtiments publics mais je me fiche de tout ça: pour moi rien n'existe que les coiffures . . . mais pour être coiffeur il faut être physionomiste aussi.'

['I quite like applause, but actually I've found that the public can't spot mistakes: in the arts, sir, you can always dissimulate; I myself have made mistakes: but I have always hidden them . . . When I travel in a new country I always look at hairstyles; I know well enough that there are people who busy themselves with public buildings but I don't care about all that: for me, nothing counts but hairstyles . . . but to be a hairdresser, one must be a physiognomist too.'][21]

1874, with new enthusiasm. He would be the Robinson Crusoe of decadence. Instead of researching in books of botany for names of flowers, he looked in dictionaries for bizarre words with which to rhyme his exotic subject. Sherard was taxed to provide one with *ar*, and when this was not at once forthcoming, was asked reproachfully, 'Why have you brought me no rhymes from Passy?' 'Lupanar' Wilde had already used, but Sherard came up with 'nenuphar', which was promptly adopted.

> Or did huge Apis from his car leap down and lay before your feet
> Big blossoms of the honey-sweet and honey-coloured nenuphar?

A trisyllabic rhyme for 'catafalque' proved harder, but Wilde settled for Amenalk:

> And did you mark the Cyprian kiss white Adon on his catafalque?
> And did you follow Amenalk, the God of Heliopolis?

There was no doubt that Paris, Poe-ridden since Baudelaire and Mallarmé, was the proper atmosphere for invoking and exorcising this spirit of evil. 'It ['The Sphinx'] will destroy domesticity in England,' he remarked. The rhymes were sought as deliberately as Poe advised in 'The Philosophy of Composition.' A rhyming dictionary was a great help to the lyre, he said. Although the stanza form is that of *In Memoriam* but made into two lines instead of four, the effect of the long lines is to suggest the unfolding of a ceaseless sinister scroll.[24] Even the stanza form seems part of the over-ripeness of the monstrous image that dominates the poem. But the decadence is not primitive. 'It is not in the desert that his Sphinx proposes her riddles,' says Vincent O'Sullivan, 'but in a room – a room in an hotel.'[25] Wilde was indifferent to all life that was not social life.

The Fate of *The Duchess*

I have no store
Of gryphon-guarded gold.

Most of his energy went into *The Duchess of Padua.* He did not finish it by 1 March as the contract with Griffin had stipulated, but by 15 March 1883. After sending it off, he wrote to Mary Anderson on 23 March to overcome any doubts she might have. 'I have no hesitation in saying that it is the masterpiece of all my literary work, the *chef d'oeuvre* of my youth.' In this out and out romantic play, young Guido Ferranti, son of the former Duke of Padua, has sworn to kill his father's murderer, all unaware that this is the present duke. The duke is no simple villain, Wilde said to Miss

James McNeill Whistler
(*Library of Congress*)

Caricature of Wilde as a pig,
by Whistler (*University of
Glasgow, Birnie Philip Bequest*)

Wilde photographed in New York, by Napoleon Sarony, January 1882 (*Library of Congress*)

Wilde, painted during
the months in 1883 when
he sported a coiffure of
Neronian curls

*The Young Sophocles Leading
the Chorus After the Battle of
Salamis,* by John Donoghue
(*Art Institute of Chicago*)

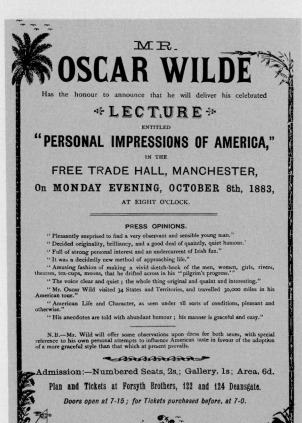

MR.
OSCAR WILDE

Has the honour to announce that he will deliver his celebrated

❖ LECTURE ❖

ENTITLED

"PERSONAL IMPRESSIONS OF AMERICA,"

IN THE

FREE TRADE HALL, MANCHESTER,

On **MONDAY EVENING, OCTOBER** 8th, **1883,**

AT EIGHT O'CLOCK.

PRESS OPINIONS.

"Pleasantly surprised to find a very observant and sensible young man."

"Decided originality, brilliancy, and a good deal of quaintly, quiet humour.'

"Full of strong personal interest and an undercurrent of Irish fun."

"It was a decidedly new method of approaching life."

"Amusing fashion of making a vivid sketch-book of the men, women, girls, rivers, theatres, tea-cups, moons, that he drifted across in his "pilgrim's progress.'"

"The voice clear and quiet ; the whole thing original and quaint and interesting."

"Mr. Oscar Wild visited 34 States and Territories, and travelled 30,000 miles in his American tour."

"American Life and Character, as seen under all sorts of conditions, pleasant and otherwise."

"His anecdotes are told with abundant humour ; his manner is graceful and easy."

N.B.—Mr. Wild will offer some observations upon dress for both sexes, with special reference to his own personal attempts to influence American taste in favour of the adoption of a more graceful style than that which at present prevails.

Admission:—Numbered Seats, 2s.; Gallery, 1s; Area, 6d.

Plan and Tickets at Forsyth Brothers, 122 and 124 Deansgate.

Doors open at 7-15 ; for Tickets purchased before, at 7-0.

Flyer for Wilde's lecture
on America, 1883

Constance and Cyril Wilde, November 1889 (*Courtesy of the William Andrews Clark Library*)

John Gray (*Courtesy of the
Reverend Brocard Sewell, O.P.,
and of the Reverend Bede Bailey,
St Dominic's Priory*)

Reginald Turner (*Courtesy of
The Hyde Collection*)

Robert Ross (*Courtesy of
The Hyde Collection*)

Lillie Langtry and Sarah Bernhardt,
1887 (*Library of Congress*)

Etching of Wilde and a child, possibly the artist's son, by James Edward Kelly, 1882 (*Author's collection*)

On the Isle of Wight, summer 1885

Anderson, but a cynic and a philosopher, a type first used in *Vera* and to
appear again in later plays. Guido is like Vera in oscillation between desire
and revulsion: when the moment for assassination comes, he cannot bring
himself to carry it out. Like most of Wilde's protagonists, he is ingenuous
and merciful. The new turn in this play is that the hapless duchess, in love
with Guido, imagines that he wishes the duke dead for the sake of their
love. She therefore kills her husband, not from hatred of him but from
love of Guido. The surprise is that Guido is shocked by her having
committed the crime which he had barely avoided. When he tells her he
hates her, she betrays him to the guards as the murderer. His supreme
moment comes as he magnificently takes the guilt upon himself, and like
Stendhal's Julien Sorel awaits execution. Remorseful, the duchess comes
to help him escape, but he has decided to die for her. When she protests, 'I
am a guilty woman,' he defends her with eloquence:

> Guilty? – let those
> Who know not what a thing temptation is,
> Let those who have not walked as we have done,
> In the red fire of passion, those whose lives
> Are dull and colourless, in a word let those,
> If any such there be, who have not loved,
> Cast stones against you.

This is a theme to which Wilde's plays regularly return, the pervasiveness
of sinful passion, and its pardonableness. Guido is also aesthete enough to
feel that his life has not been wasted:

> What, Beatrice, have I not
> Stood face to face with beauty; that is enough
> For one man's life.

In his letter to Mary Anderson, Wilde pointed to the sensational
moments in the role she would be playing. The first act would culminate
in her entrance as the duchess. The duchess's character would be
compounded first of pity and mercy, then, these being overcome by
passion, of remorse, and then of passion and remorse together. There
were, as he pointed out, comic bits to relieve the pathos. But as with his
later plays, he insisted that the supreme dramatic virtue was an intellectual
basis. Unlike Dumas *fils' La Dame aux Camélias*, which lacked intellect
and simply played upon the audience's sympathy for a woman 'who is
dying young (and has a dreadful cough!)', Wilde held that his own play
showed passion as a kind of daemonic possession for which the possessed
may ask and receive mercy.[26]

The correspondence with Mary Anderson was somewhat one-sided.
She sent him some newspapers with notices of her current productions.

But otherwise there was silence, and at the end of April Wilde, funds almost gone, cabled to her. A return cable arrived from Victoria, British Columbia, as he was sitting with Sherard. He opened it, read it without emotion, tore a tiny strip off the blue form, rolled it into a pellet, and put it into his mouth. Then he passed the cable over and said, 'Robert, this is very tedious.' Mary Anderson had given a definite no. 'We shan't be able to dine with the Duchess tonight,' he said. 'It is rather a case of Duke Humphrey. But what do you say to a *choucroute garnie* at Zimmer's?'* Sherard had been a guest for weeks because Wilde had insisted that 'Friends always share,' but now he rose to the occasion and asked Wilde, 'Will you not be my guest for once, at a little place on the other side of the water, where they don't do you too badly?' Wilde agreed, and Sherard, who knew Paris well, led him by a circuitous route to a side door of the Café de Paris. When they were inside Wilde fell in with the joke, saying, 'Quite a nice little place!' Their conversation did not touch on *The Duchess*, but they went to the Folies-Bergère afterwards, and Wilde, finding himself stared at, insisted that they leave well before the curtain. This was the only sign that he was upset.[28]

Mary Anderson's letter arrived some days later. It offered no comfort:

Dear Mr Wilde:
 . . . The play in its present form, I fear, would no more please the public of today than would 'Venice Preserved,' or 'Lucretia Borgia.'
 Neither of us can afford failure now, and your Duchess in my hands would not succeed, as the part does not fit me. My admiration of your ability is as great as ever. I hope you will appreciate my feelings in the matter . . .[29]

It was a major reverse, but Wilde's *amour propre* was not to be underestimated. Of his major talent he had no doubts, and Miss Anderson's were irrelevant. He could prove it any night he chose by charming people who thought they disliked him. Fortunately, he still had his arrangement with Marie Prescott for *Vera*. He had rewritten Act II at her request, and also the love scene at the end of Act IV. She asked him to write in a part for a child, and he complied. The actress was pleased with the revisions. She was grateful to him for sending a samovar, which Sarah Bernhardt had presented to him as an item of Slavic décor. The rehearsals would begin at Long Branch, and she asked him to come by 18 August to attend the final rehearsals.

* (To dine with Duke Humphrey means to go without dinner.) Wilde once dropped in unexpectedly on the Sickerts and asked if he could join them for a meal, as he was going to some house nearby. Mrs Sickert explained that they had just had midday dinner, but could give him, as the Scots say, 'an egg to tea.' Wilde, when the egg had been served, stared disconsolately at it, as if he had never seen one before. Oswald Sickert laughed.[27]

Les Décadents

'I believe in the race,' she cried . . . 'It has development.'
'Decay fascinates me more.'
'What of art?' she asked.
'It is a malady.'

Wilde's theatrical efforts did not interfere with his social life in Paris. This time he met mostly older writers and artists, as eight years afterwards he would meet younger ones. He gave a clever speech about his American tour to some American artists and journalists who entertained him at dinner. At the house of the painter Giuseppe de Nittis he talked with Degas, Cazin, and the Pissarros, on the way out remarking, with Whistlerian vanity, 'I was quite amazing.' The power and vitality he exuded seemed to have been extraordinary even for him. He brought Sherard along to the Vaudeville Theatre to see Bernhardt in the title role of Sardou's *Fédora*. It was extraordinarily close to his own *Vera*, though independently conceived, for Sardou also had scented a good subject in the Nihilists of Turgenev and Dostoevsky, dashed with aristocracy and seasoned with love. As the princess Fédora, involved in a Nihilist plot and victim of a series of misapprehensions, Bernhardt was able to span several octaves of emotion as she loved, grieved, hated, dissimulated, conspired, confessed in anguish, and committed suicide. It was as silly a play as *Vera*, but with a slicker sense of theatre. Clearly Wilde had no hope of producing *Vera* in Paris, with or without Bernhardt, and *The Duchess of Padua*, in blank verse, did not lend itself to translation or production.

Whatever consternation he may have felt he suppressed. Between the acts of *Fédora* Wilde and Sherard were ushered into the little salon next to her dressing room, as Sarah Bernhardt changed costumes behind the curtains. She put her head through them long enough to welcome Wilde with her warmest smile. Her current lover, Jean Richepin, was less pleased. Some days later they were invited to her house on the avenue de Villiers at the corner of the rue Fortune. On the way Wilde bought a mass of wallflowers from a streethawker. Sherard thought them vulgar, but Sarah, stretched on a cluster of many-coloured cushions by the fireplace, received them with pleasure. As an old friend from London, Wilde commanded more deference here than in the greenroom. Alexandre Parodi, who had written *Rome Vaincue*, Sarah's first triumph, addressed him respectfully as 'Maître'.[30]

It was perhaps on this occasion that Wilde had a conversation that he himself recorded with Coquelin, who asked him what *The Duchess of Padua* was about. Wilde replied: *'Mon drame? du style seulement. Hugo et Shakespeare ont partagé tous les sujets: il est impossible d'être original, même dans le péché: ainsi il n'y a pas d'émotions, seulement des adjectifs extraordinaires. La fin est assez tragique, mon héros au moment de son triomphe fait un*

213

épigramme qui manque tout à fait d'effet, alors on le condamne à être académicien avec discours forcés. * Coquelin shifted to ampler topics:

Coquelin: *Qu'est-ce que c'est la civilisation, Monsieur Wilde?*
Ego: *L'amour du beau.*
Coquelin: *Qu'est-ce que c'est le beau?*
Ego: *Ce que les bourgeois appellent le laid.*
Coquelin: *Et ce que les bourgeois appellent le beau?*
Ego: *Cela n'existe pas.*†[31]

The actor seems to have enjoyed rather than resented the enigmatic responses.

Sarah Bernhardt told them of her latest protégé, Maurice Rollinat, whom she had presented to the world the previous November as a talented poet and tragedian, an inspired musician, a marvellous artist, and 'one of the curiosities of Paris.' Rollinat had just published his second book of poems, *Les Névroses*, and was being talked about as a second Baudelaire. Wilde contrived to meet him at the house of the hospitable painter Giuseppe de Nittis. De Nittis painted picturesque street scenes of Paris. His house was full of *japonaiseries*, which reflected a taste he shared with his friend Edmond de Goncourt. (Goncourt's most recent novel, *La Faustin* [1882], was dedicated to de Nittis.) Wilde, his back to a tapestried wall, talked with Degas, Cazin, and the Pissarros, taking stock of Rollinat himself, in his mid-thirties, with fiery eyes and a nervous and impassioned manner. Albert Wolff, writing in *Le Figaro* on 9 November 1882, had described him as the very figure of the artist. On being asked to recite a poem, after dinner, Rollinat obliged with 'Le Soliloque de Troppmann' from his *Les Névroses*. This required gesturing and grimacing, for Troppmann was a monster who first killed a husband, his grandson, and then his wife and their five children. The soliloquy described in detail his thoughts as he tricked the mother and children into his house and carried out his plan. What made the poem impressive was its total absence of compunction, as if evil had its assured place in the scheme of things. (The same

---

* 'My drama? It's all about style. Between them, Hugo and Shakespeare have used up all the subjects: it is impossible to be original, even in sin: so there are no emotions, just extraordinary adjectives. The ending is quite tragic – my hero at his moment of triumph makes an epigram which falls flat, so he's condemned to make forced speeches as an Academician.'

† 'C: What is civilisation, Mr Wilde?/E: The love of the beautiful./C: What is the beautiful? / E: What the bourgeois call the ugly. / C: And what the bourgeois call the beautiful? / E: That does not exist.'

method is used in 'Pen, Pencil and Poison.') Wilde registered the poem's power, and invited Rollinat to dinner.*

Rollinat in turn invited Wilde, and in a letter accepting Wilde wrote, at three o'clock in the morning, that he had just reread from Rollinat's book the poem 'La Vache au taureau.' The poem describes two young country people, a boy and a girl, who watch the mating of a cow and bull, and silently recognize that that night they will be repeating the same process. The description of copulation was strong, and moved Wilde to write with genuine enthusiasm, *'c'est un chef d'oeuvre. Il y a dedans un vrai souffle de la Nature. Je vous en félicite. Depuis le* De Natura *de Lucretius, le monde n'a rien encore lu de pareil: c'est l'hymne la plus magnifique que la Vénus des Champs a jamais reçu, car c'est le plus simple.'†* What drew Wilde particularly was Rollinat's affinity to Baudelaire. This was evident throughout *Les Névroses*, in which the opening poem, *'Le Fantôme du crime'* (dedicated to Edmond Haraucourt, whose own recent volume was avowedly *'poèmes hysteriques'*), offered

> Le meurtre, le viol, le vol, le parricide

as Baudelaire's *'Au Lecteur'* had offered

> La sottise, l'erreur, le péché, la lésine.‡

Rollinat's subjects also included suicide, disease, hypochondria, cadavers, embalming, live burial, spectres, madness, diabolism, and putrefaction, with Poe presiding as dark angel. Sherard was convinced that Rollinat was taking drugs and in need of help. 'If you saw a man throw himself into the river, would you go after him?' he felt prompted to ask

---

* His conversation impressed Wilde enough for him to write it down. On a page headed *Rollinat* are the following notes:

Il n'y a qu'une forme pour le beau mais pour chaque chose chaque individu a un formule: ainsi on ne comprend pas les poètes [There is only one form for the beautiful but for each object everyone has a formula: for this reason, poets cannot be understood].

Je ne crois pas au progrès: mais je crois à la stagnation de la perversité humaine [I don't believe in progress: but I do believe in the stagnation of human perversity].

Il me faut les rêves, le fantastique: j'admire les chaises Japonaises parce qu'il[s] n'ont pas etaient [sic] faites pour s'asseoir [Dreams and the fantastic are necessary to me: I admire Japanese chairs because they have not been made to sit on].

– his idea of music continuing the beauty of poetry without its idea.[32]

† '. . . it's a masterpiece. There is a true breath of Nature in it. I congratulate you on it. Not since the *De Natura* of Lucretius has the world ever read its like: it is the most magnificent hymn ever received by Venus of the Fields, because it is the simplest.'

‡ 'Murder, rape, theft, parricide' (Rollinat); 'Stupidity, error, sin, meanness' (Baudelaire).

Wilde, apparently indifferent to Rollinat's addiction. 'I should consider it an act of gross impertinence to do so,' Wilde replied.[33]

The spokesman for the English Renaissance had stumbled into Paris *en pleine décadence*. Decadence characterized two new reviews which had just begun their short lives in 1882, *Le Chat noir* and *La Nouvelle rive gauche*. Jean Lorrain, who would dedicate one of his stories to Wilde, began in 1882 to take up the theme of homosexuality, first in relation to women ('Modernité,' 2 September 1882, in *Le Chat noir*) and then to men ('Bathylle,' 1 July 1883, in the same review). Whether or not Wilde saw these, he must have discussed the subject with his new friend Paul Bourget, who was occupied in writing a book on decadence in contemporary literature. Then there was Verlaine, whom Wilde met once at a café. It was a bad time for him; his lover Lucien Létinois had died of malaria a year before. Wilde was put off by Verlaine's seedy appearance, but recognized his genius. Like Lorrain, Verlaine was beginning to publish poems about homosexuality, and may have recited to Wilde his recent poem, 'Langueur,' which begins, '*Je suis l'Empire à la fin de la Décadence.*' Besides writing about sexual aberration and decay, in November 1882 Verlaine had published 'Art Poétique,' a poem which dismissed all verse not musical and nuanced as mere *littérature*. Artistic composition, it seemed, entailed moral decomposition. For Wilde, who had been celebrating the 'sunlit heights,' it was a dizzy delight to find himself in the decadent depths. No wonder 'The Sphinx' oozed into existence.

He was eager to meet a pillar of French letters, the surviving brother Edmond of the *frères* Goncourt. He sent him a letter with a book,

> Monsieur,
> Daignez recevoir mes poèmes, témoignage de mon admiration infinie pour l'auteur de *La Faustin*.
> Je serai bien content de penser qu'il y aura une place, peut-être, pour mes premières fleurs de poésie, près de vos Watteau, et de vos Boucher, et de ce trésor de laque, d'ivoire, et de bronze, que dans votre *Maison d'un Artiste* vous avez pour toujours immortalisé.*

The approach was successful, since a letter from Wilde to Théodore Duret says he will accompany Duret to Goncourt's on the following Wednesday, and adds praise for another Goncourt novel: '*il est, pour moi, un des plus grand maîtres de la prose moderne, et son roman de* Manette Salomon *est un chef-d'oeuvre.*'[34]

---

* 'Dear Sir,
    Pray accept my poems as testimony of my infinite admiration for the author of *La Faustin*.
    I shall be very happy to think that my first poetic flowers may perhaps find a place near your Watteaus and your Bouchers, and the treasure in lacquer, ivory and bronze which you have forever immortalized in your *Maison d'un Artiste*.'

Manette Salomon, along with *La Faustin*, was an offshoot of the aesthetic movement: both dealt with art and its relation to life. Manette, a Jewish model, dominates her lover and (expressing Goncourt's misogyny) destroys his talent. *La Faustin* was closer to what Wilde was looking for, especially since the artist is an actress, modelled on Bernhardt and Rachel. Here the conflict of life and art is bald enough: La Faustin is better at playing at love than at loving. This point is driven home to her English lover, Lord Annandale, in a deathbed scene. As Annandale grimaces with pain, La Faustin unthinkingly reproduces his grimace, then realizes that he has seen her mimicry. He summons his last strength to cry out to his attendants in English, with 'all the implacability of the Saxon race,' 'Turn out that woman!' She frantically kisses his hands, but he repulses her, '*Une artiste . . . vous n'êtes que cela . . . la femme incapable d'aimer.*' And shunning her imploring look, he repeats even more peremptorily, 'Turn out that woman!' (A helpful footnote explains that the English phrase means, '*Mettez cette femme dehors!*') This ending, the most memorable part of the novel, stayed with Wilde as a model for a curtain speech. In 'The Sphinx,' he concludes with the adjuration, 'Get hence! Get hence!' and in *Salome* Herod, turning to see Salome kiss the head with necrophilic passion, cries to the guards, '*Tuez cette femme!*'

What could not have failed to draw Wilde's attention was that the aesthetic movement, which he had celebrated in the United States for lofty idealism, had a much more dubious aspect which was being enthusiastically developed in France. In the American lectures he had naïvely argued that we must aestheticize our lives by surrounding ourselves with beautiful objects. Here was a novel which showed that such aestheticizing might become unwholesome. *La Faustin* contributed to the story of Sibyl Vane in *The Picture of Dorian Gray*; Sibyl loses her powers as an actress by falling in love, reversing La Faustin's behavior. More precisely, both possibilities are mustered by La Faustin: she feels the need to be in love in order to play Phèdre, but warns her lover that, if she should leave the stage, he would cease to love her in six months. A contrary impulse makes her renounce her career for his sake, only to find that without it life is drab. A husband may be good, but a theatre audience is better. Wilde found in such tensions between life and art a source of dramatic excitement, and developed them variously in the next fifteen years.

There was something else in *La Faustin* which he found fascinating. Lord Annandale has a friend, the Hon. George Selwyn, who had exerted a baleful influence upon his youth, leading him towards unspecified '*salissantes débauches,*' from which his love for La Faustin has rescued him. Selwyn pays a visit to the lovers, and Annandale explains to La Faustin that his friend is '*un sadique*', '*un homme aux amours . . . aux appetits des sens déréglés, maladifs* [a sadist . . . a man whose love affairs and appetites are disordered, sick].' As if to confirm this view, Selwyn, watching a hen yard with La Faustin, points out two homosexual cocks who remain apart from the other fowl of both sexes. La Faustin is shocked and hopes for an end to his visit; it comes rather suddenly when he receives a letter headed, 'Chaumière de Dolmancé.' The name means nothing to her, but everything to the two men, who know that Dolmancé is the philosopher in *La Philosophie dans le boudoir*, one of the most terrible of Sade's fantasies. Goncourt seems to raise the spectre of sadism gratuitously, then to drop it; it has no importance in the plot; neither Annandale nor Selwyn is in the least believable. But the sense of ministering to the '*dérèglement de tous les sens*' (as Rimbaud called it) must have encouraged Wilde to conceive of Dorian's evil influence as also a titled Englishman, though Lord Henry echoes mildly the gamey appetites suggested by Goncourt. Dorian's bizarre loves derive from *La Faustin* as well as from *A Rebours*, a book influenced by it, and one which pays tribute to Goncourt's novel explicitly and implicitly.

Wilde's visit to Edmond de Goncourt's 'grenier d'Auteuil' took place on 21 April 1883. Keeper of journals and recorder of malice, Goncourt wrote down some of Wilde's conversation. It amused him, especially when Swinburne was discussed. There was another encounter with Goncourt on 5 May. Returning from dinner at de Nittis's, Goncourt wrote in his journal of having seen Wilde again, disparaging him as homosexual (*au sexe douteux*) but quoting some of his reminiscences of America.

To listen to heralds of decadence after heralding a renaissance was invigorating for Wilde. What he had said in America was too wholesome to be stomached in Paris – even Sherard's gross rebuke about the Venus de Milo had demonstrated that. On the other hand, Parisian decadence, pretending candor, was edged with absurdity, like his own contribution, 'The Sphinx.' Three months in Paris stopped him speaking so glibly about a renaissance but perhaps – and this was a slowly acquired intimation – it would go down with a dash of decadence. Such a blend had been foreshadowed, but forsaken, by Pater. Wilde had more courage.

Meanwhile, decadent rather than renascent, Wilde was running out of his American money, though he lent some to Sherard, who wanted to return to London. Wilde followed him there in mid-May.

CHAPTER IX

Two Kinds of Stage

LORD CAVERSHAM: *Damme, sir, it is your duty to get married. You can't be always living for pleasure. Every man of position is married nowadays. Bachelors are not fashionable any more. They are a damaged lot. Too much is known about them. You must get a wife, sir.*

Wilde Nubile

Wilde stayed for a time with his mother at 116 Park Street, Grosvenor Square, getting together enough money to resume being host as well as guest. An obliging money lender, probably one named E. Levy whom he had dealt with before in the United States, lent him £1,200. Wilde also exerted himself, with uncertain success, to call in a debt from Steele Mackaye. He wrote Mackaye on 17 May 1883,

> 116 Park Street, Grosvenor Square
> My dear Steele,
>   Will you kindly let me have the $200 I lent you. I have had a great many expenses over here, and bills of my Oxford days (black and white spectres of dead dissipations!) have crowded on me as thick as the quails in the desert, and not as nice. Norman [Forbes-Robertson] told me he saw you in New York looking brilliant, I have been in Paris and written my play for Mary Anderson. I am greatly pleased with it, it is the strongest work I have ever done, and got capital comedy in it, and wonderful picturesque effects. I hope all your people are well and have not forgotten me. I will expect to hear soon from you.
>
> > Very sincerely yours
> > OSCAR WILDE[1]

The letter was noticeably silent about Mary Anderson's failure to be as pleased with *The Duchess of Padua* as its author. Nor did he mention its lack of progress in London. Julia Frankau's sister, Mrs Aria, got Henry Irving to read it. 'Oscar has certainly read *The Merchant of Venice*,' she remarked. Irving replied, 'I expect so, and thought little of it.'

219

Wilde was unequivocally high-spirited when he reported his reception in England. He wrote to Sherard, 'The splendid whirl and swirl of life in London sweeps me from my Sphinx,' as if the Sphinx were muse as well as poem. 'Society must be amazed, and my Neronian coiffure has amazed it. Nobody recognizes me, and everybody tells me I look young: that is delightful, of course.' The *World* took note of his new style in amiable doggerel:

> Our Oscar is with us again, but, O,
>   He is changed who was once so fair!
> Has the iron gone into his soul? O no!
>   It has only gone over his hair.[2]

Wilde could feel he had earned a respite from work by his sporadic application in Paris. Still, of his two plays only *Vera* had the certainty of being staged, and that was not until August. He had several months in which to meditate the wisdom of his mother's urgings that he and Willie improve their financial position by marriage. Willie was only too ready, yet women either laughed him off or lost interest as his enthusiasm waned. His brother Oscar moved slowly too, though not for the same reason. The stirrings of varied impulses, the kisses of Walt Whitman and Sherard, made him delay.

There was no doubt however that marriage would silence the gossip. If he felt ennobled by victimization, he liked better not being victimized, a point not always recognized by students of his character. *Punch* had recently called him a 'Mary-Ann,' Bodley had spoken of him in the *New York Times* as 'epicene,' and if Wilde could not yet have read the entry in Goncourt's 1883 *Journal* picturing him as '*au sexe douteux*,' he could guess that others took this view. A wife would save him from the moralists, and a rich one from the moneylenders. He would no longer need to make laborious conquests of those who would have been unresistingly at his feet if they had not been put off by rumor. Married, he might confront society without having to affront it. Stability, uxoriousness, and routine might prove boring – Pater had warned that failure is in forming habits – but Wilde could at least imagine playing the role of husband as debonairly as that of bachelor.

The idea of marriage was in the air. Florence Balcombe had been the first prospect, in a dreamy future, until Bram Stoker carried her away in the importunate present. Then Lillie Langtry had occupied Wilde's thoughts, though scarcely as a potential wife, since she was still married and as hard up as he was. The second woman he seriously thought of marrying, at the beginning of the 1880s, was Violet Hunt, daughter of the landscape artist Alfred William Hunt and the novelist Margaret Hunt, and destined to be a novelist herself. Wilde described her as 'the sweetest violet in England.' They had met in London when she was not yet seventeen. 'I feel like a young conqueror,' he said as they talked intensely together. 'We will rule the world – you and I – you with your looks and I with my wits. But you will write too, surely, you who have inherited the literary art from your dear mother, you who have assisted at two tragedies and a triumph.' (The tragedies were Rossetti and Swinburne, the triumph Robert Browning.) In July 1881 she wrote to congratulate him on his poems which proved 'you quite deserve your four Burne-Jones drawings!' He responded that she made up for the 'Slander, Ridicule, and Envy' the poems had awakened. In her autobiography, *The Flurried Years* (1926), Violet Hunt recalled how one day, speaking of maps of Africa, Wilde said 'Oh, Miss Violet, think of a map drawn of a whole continent, and beside the names of an insignificant city or two a blank and: *Hic sunt leones!* Miss Violet, let you and me go there.' To which she replied, 'And get eaten by lions?' His more serious proposal was perhaps made in 1880. She does not mention it in her autobiography but, according to Douglas Goldring in *South Lodge*, constantly boasted of it in later life.[3] The same practical sense which made her fear lions made her reluctant to marry one. She later lived, unmarried and undevoured, with Ford Madox Ford.

There were two other prospects. One was the charming Charlotte Montefiore, whose brother Leonard had been up at Balliol when Wilde was at Magdalen. (He died in September 1879, aged only 26.) Wilde seems to have proposed to her, but was refused, probably in 1880 or 1881. That evening he sent her a note, 'Charlotte, I am so sorry about your decision. With your money and my brain we could have gone so far.'[4] She tore it up but remembered it. The other prospect was better. It had begun in May 1881, perhaps soon after the refusals of Violet Hunt and Charlotte Montefiore. Wilde went with his mother to call on a woman belonging to the Atkinson family whom the Wildes had known in Dublin. His hostess introduced her granddaughter, Constance Lloyd, three years younger than Wilde (she was born 2 January 1858). Constance was 5'8" tall, according to her brother; she had long wavy chestnut colored hair, prominent eyes, a good figure.[5] She was interested in music, painting, embroidery, could read Dante in Italian (and did), was logical, mathematical, shy yet fond of talking. Wilde paid her marked attention. On leaving the house he said to Lady Wilde, 'By the by, Mama, I think of marrying that girl.'[6] Constance's father had died in 1874; she did not live with her remarried mother – their relationship was strained from her childhood – but, since the age of twenty, with her grandfather, a Queen's Counsel named John Horatio Lloyd.* Lloyd had a mansion at 100 Lancaster Gate, and a niece, Emily Lloyd (Constance's aunt), to look after it for him. The understanding between Wilde and Constance was slow in

---

* Wilde, according to Constance's brother, was unsympathetic when Constance tried to describe the unhappiness of her upbringing. He could not be bored with people who went back to their childhoods for their tragedies.[7]

forming. Lady Wilde invited her to one of her Saturday afternoons, and
Oscar was there. Emily Lloyd invited Wilde to tea at Lancaster Gate on 6
June 1881. Constance wrote of the visit to her brother, Otho, who had
known Wilde slightly when they were both up at Oxford. 'O.W. came
yesterday at about 5.30 (by which time I was shaking with fright!) and
stayed for half an hour, begged me to come and see his mother again soon,
which little request I need hardly say I have kept to myself. [Emily Lloyd
did not encourage her niece to go about unchaperoned.] I can't help liking
him, because when he's talking to me alone he's never a bit affected, and
speaks naturally, excepting that he uses better language than most
people.' Otho must have regaled her with some Oxford misadventure of
Wilde, for she added, 'I'm glad they didn't duck him though *you* would
have enjoyed it!'[8]

Wilde became a frequent visitor: Lloyd, as well as Constance and her
brother Otho, took a liking to him. Aunt Emily, however, kept her
distance. While Wilde was in the States in 1882 and in Paris for the first
months of 1883, Constance attended an art school, and inclined towards
an aesthetic style of dress. Their relations began to encourage the
connection: in December 1882, Charles Hemphill (Serjeant-at-Law and
later Baron), whom the Wildes had known as a fellow-resident of Merrion
Square, called on Lady Wilde and 'praised Constance immensely.' She
wrote knowingly to her son in the States, 'I had nearly in mind to say I
would like her for a daughter-in-law, but I did not. It was Constance told
him where we lived. I thought the visit looked encouraging.'[9] For her part,
she had Constance and Otho to an at-home on 28 February 1883, and
sang the praises of Oscár.

Wilde had no sooner returned from Paris in May than he invited
Constance to come to his mother's house on the 16th. She came,
chaperoned by Otho, and heard him remonstrate with Switzerland for
being 'that dreadful place – so vulgar with its big ugly mountains, all black
and white like an enormous photograph.' He preferred everything small,
he said, but well-proportioned to give the effect of height. Constance and
Otho attended a reception at Lady Wilde's next day, where Oscar failed to
turn up; but on the 19th he appeared at the Lloyds' with his hair cut short.
Invitations continued on both sides. Constance had agreed to come to
Lady Wilde's on the 24th, but was tempted away to the Isle of Wight. In
apologizing she invited the Wildes for the 28th. Lady Wilde accepted,
urged her to come to her own reception on the 26th, and said of the
missed occasion, 'Oscar talked like Plato, divinely, but said at intervals
that women were not to be trusted, and that you had broken your promise.'

Otho Lloyd was rather baffled by Wilde's interest in his sister, but put it
down to her intelligence. Constance, who had once been engaged, only to
have her fiancé break off, did not confide in him. At the beginning of June
Wilde and his mother visited the Lloyds, and Constance merely remarked
to Otho that in her long conversation she and Wilde had not agreed on a

single thing. On the 3rd, at Lady Wilde's, Oscar invited them both to the Exhibition of Fisheries next day. Constance put him off till the 7th. When they got there, they saw little of the fish, because Wilde was talking the whole time, concluding as they parted, 'I hope that you have enjoyed your stay as much as I have mine.' When they reached home Constance was relieved to find only an aunt about, and said, 'O how delightful it is to see you, Aunt Carrie, after spending three hours and a half with a clever man.'

By this time Otho had decided that anyone but Wilde would have been assumed to be in love. On 30 June he and Constance attended, as Wilde did, a reception for a member of a society advocating the rights of women. Constance, herself unsure what Wilde intended, emboldened herself to remark, 'You know everybody says, Mr Wilde, that you do not really mean half of what you say.' Wilde threw back his head and laughed. A few days later, on 6 July, at Lady Wilde's, Wilde as usual was devoting himself to Constance when his mother reproved him for not speaking to other guests. He moved away, but Otho noticed he followed Constance with his eyes. By this time Constance's mother felt that something would come of the relationship. A week later Wilde asked particularly for Constance to come to Lady Wilde's that day, because it would be his last chance of seeing her before he went to America. It was his most declarative statement to date, and of course she went. But he had one concern more pressing than matrimony on his mind.

Verbal Arts

The Nihilist, that strange martyr who has no faith, who goes to the stake without enthusiasm, and dies for what he does not believe in, is a purely literary product. He was invented by Tourgénieff and completed by Dostoieffski.

If Constance Lloyd was timidly taking her place in his mind, his Nihilist heroine Vera Zassoulich was boldly established there. Much depended upon Marie Prescott's success with his play. Wilde did not greatly admire her as an actress, but she had the merit, exceptional among readers of *Vera*, of liking the play tremendously. During the early months of 1883 they corresponded about it intensively. There were still some points about the finances to be settled, but Marie Prescott went ahead with the arrangements. Rather to his dismay, she booked for four weeks at the Union Square Theatre beginning on 29 August, when the heat in New York was bound to be intolerable. Wilde protested: she explained vigorously that no other theatre was available, that she could not afford to start the play in high season, that it must open in New York so that theatre managers elsewhere would book it in repertory, and that she would bring it back to New York at Christmas. Since she was taking the entire financial risk, she had her way.

He did try to impress on her his conception of the play. When she suggested cutting some of the comic lines, he responded with one of his essential tenets, rephrased later in 'The Truth of Masks': 'Now, one of the facts of physiology is the desire of any very intensified emotion to be relieved by some emotion that is its opposite. Nature's example of dramatic effect is the laughter of hysteria or the tears of joy. So I cannot cut out my comedy lines. Besides, the essence of good dialogue is interruption.'[10]* Miss Prescott's replies, longwinded but not stupid, pointed out that Vera wishes to kill the object of her love. This theme appears in many of Wilde's works, from 'Humanitad' and *The Duchess of Padua* to *The Ballad of Reading Gaol.* The supposed narcissist was at bottom swayed by self-disserving desires.

Wilde had many practical suggestions. There was the samovar from Sarah Bernhardt. His design for Miss Prescott's vermilion dress in the last act delighted her: 'No dress is so becoming to me.' (In *The Duchess of Padua* even a package has to be wrapt in vermilion silk.) She should not wear petticoats, he instructed, and she revealed that she never did. Would he not reconsider the heavy fur coat prescribed for Vera in Act I? Wilde presumably agreed, in view of the August opening. He wrote out his letters to her carefully, and preserved some of his best *mots*, such as this one: 'Success is a science; if you have the conditions, you get the result. Art is the mathematical result of the emotional desire for beauty.' With an eye to publicity, he explained that *Vera* was at once 'a Titan cry of the people for liberty,' and yet a play about passion rather than politics. He told Constance Lloyd later that it was about politics rather than passion. Since it could be read either way, amorous passion would please frivolous New York and political passion please serious Constance. Marie Prescott printed one of his letters in the *New York Herald* as part of the publicity for the play.[11]

The 20th August being slow to come, Wilde had to find other resources until he became a successful playwright. His marital plans he had to defer for the moment. Fortunately in the spring Colonel Morse, D'Oyly Carte's former lecture manager, turned up in London, representing J. M. Stoddart, the Philadelphia publisher, as agent for the *Encyclopedia Americana* and other books. Wilde called on him in mid-June and asked if he could arrange a lecture tour of the British Isles for an old client. Morse agreed to undertake it as a sideline. The lecture fees were paltry, ten to twenty-five guineas a lecture, or at best half the receipts; but Wilde would have money coming in as well as going out. He offered two lectures, one

* Coleridge says in *Table Talk* that 'Plato . . . leads you to see that propositions involving . . . contradictory conceptions are nevertheless true; and which, therefore, must belong to a higher logic – that of ideas. They are contradictory only in the Aristotelian logic, which is the instinct of the understanding.'

bantering, 'Personal Impressions of America,' and one messianic, 'The House Beautiful.'

The first lecture would be given in London at Prince's Hall, Piccadilly, so as to warm the provinces to the idea. While arrangements were being made, Wilde was invited by Eric Forbes-Robertson to lecture to the students of the Royal Academy and accepted. Whistler, envying an invitation which he would have liked to have had an opportunity to refuse, was quick with suggestions for what Wilde might say as his St John. Some of these Wilde developed, though he knew, as Whistler had perhaps forgotten, that many of Whistler's attitudes had been formed by Gautier's Preface to *Mademoiselle de Maupin*, and others by the writings of Baudelaire and Mallarmé. Whistler's originality lay principally in the tartness of his expression, rather than in the content. Wilde's lecture, posthumously printed in somewhat garbled form, indicates that he was still clinging to Ruskin for some of his theory even as he proclaimed the supremacy of Whistler in practice. So after insisting like Whistler that art moved apart from history – a view he would later upset – Wilde urged the students to master their own age the better to ignore it. He also used Ruskin's terms to underline the relation of corruption in human surroundings to decay in art. The Whistler and Gautier dogmas were chiefly negative: art is not national, no age has ever been artistic, nor any people (he would modify this later); art history is useless; art offers no message. Anything can be beautiful, he told them, 'even Gower-street . . . when dawn was breaking . . . A policeman . . . was not, under ordinary circumstances, a thing of beauty or a joy forever, but he saw one in a mist on the Thames Embankment, lit up with dusky light . . . Michael Angelesque in appearance.' When it was objected that Whistler's paintings 'looked as well upside down as right side up, why shouldn't they?' he asked. 'Either way they gave delight.'[12] The students were pleased, the press approbatory, and Whistler jealous. If the hostile Herbert Vivian can be trusted, Whistler checked Wilde's gratification by asking what he had said, and, as Wilde reeled off the points, Whistler rose at each to take a bow as if he himself had originated everything. He would say later, when they were no longer friends, that Wilde 'not only trifled with my shoe, but bolted with the latchet.' Yet half the talk stemmed from Ruskin, and Vivian cannot have reported the bowing altogether accurately.

Whistler could not have been too offended at the supposed borrowings since he went to Wilde's second lecture, at the Prince's Hall on 11 July 1883. The *World* said on 18 July that Whistler was seen there, 'jumping about like a cricket.' This was the lecture on 'Impressions of America,' a mixed bag of comments on scenery, people, art, theatre, done with great wit. Wilde appeared twenty minutes late, impenitent, in evening dress, a white flower in his buttonhole, shirt cuffs overlapping the sleeves, a heavy seal hanging from his watch chain, a large diamond in the shirt front. He transformed the pedestrian circumstance of having lectured in Griggsville, Illinois: 'I was asked to lecture on art at Griggsville, named after its founder – Griggs – I telegraphed them "First change the name of your town." This they declined to do. How dreadful it would have been if I had founded a school of art there – fancy "Early Griggsville." Imagine a school of art teaching "Griggsville Renaissance."' He described his trip to Niagara Falls – 'a melancholy place filled with melancholy people, who wandered about trying to get up that feeling of sublimity which the guide books assured them they could do without extra charge' – and the desolate prairie, 'the alkali plains, which conveyed the impression that Nature had given up the job of decorating the country, so vast its size, in absolute despair.' In Salt Lake City he admired the beauty of the Mormon children, and told how he asked whether the theatre was large enough for him to lecture in, and received the reply, 'Oh, yes, it will hold nine families.'

He approved the luxury of the Pullman Car, while regretting its lack of privacy. On the train, 'Boys ran up and down selling literature, good and bad, and everything one could eat or not eat, but what harrowed my feelings most acutely was to see a pirated copy of my own poems selling for 10 cents. Calling these boys on one side I told them that though poets like to be popular they desire to be paid, and selling editions of my poems without giving me a profit is dealing a blow at literature which must have a disastrous effect on poetical aspirants. The invariable reply that they made was that they themselves made a profit out of the transaction and that was all they cared about.' His narrative rambled about the country, from journalism to politics, machinery to art. He was never addressed as 'Stranger,' as people assumed foreigners in America always were; 'When I went to Texas I was called "Captain," when I got to the centre of the country I was called "Colonel," and on arriving at the borders of Mexico, as "General."' These he did not mind, but he had been much distressed at being called 'Professor.' He complained of the noise and hurry: 'I only saw one reposeful American – a wooden figure outside a tobacco shop.'

The audience seemed pleased and most reports were favorable. Labouchere in *Truth* on 18 July was surprisingly grudging, and complained that Wilde had used the word 'lovely' forty-three times, 'beautiful' twenty-six times, and 'charming' seventeen times. If the statistics were correct, he must have departed from his script to caress these favorite adjectives. The next day *Truth* carried a three-column leader entitled, 'Exit Oscar.' It scanned his career acidly: in Oxford he was 'the epicene youth,' and 'No one laughed at him more than he laughed at himself.' On his tour in the United States he was 'an effeminate phrase-maker,' 'lecturing to empty benches.' The hall in London was only half-full, he said. Wilde commented, 'If it took Labouchere three columns to prove that I was forgotten, then there is no difference between fame and obscurity.'[13] Impervious to Whistler and Labouchere, he went on to lecture at Margate and Ramsgate on 26 July, Southampton on the 27th,

Brighton on the 28th, Southport on the 31st. From that town on 1 August he travelled to Liverpool to welcome Lillie Langtry on her return from the United States. Modest in talent, and increasingly immodest in her offstage activities, she had been able to achieve a success of sorts, and would soon embark on a second tour.

The Tragedy of *Vera*

'I knew I should create a great sensation,' gasped the Rocket, and he went out.

On 2 August 1883 Wilde sailed on the *SS Britannic* for New York for the production of his first play. His hopes were high and the crossing went pleasantly. As part of the shipboard entertainment, Wilde read to general approbation his 'Ave Imperatrix,' the poem which saluted imperial might, regretted the English dead, and predicted a republic in the future. Several English passengers, including a friend of George Curzon's named Broderick, sought out his company. 'Wilde has been the life and soul of the voyage,' he wrote to Curzon. 'He has showered good stories and bons mots, paradoxes, and epigrams upon me all the way, while he certainly has a never failing bonhomie which makes him roar with laughter at his own absurd theories and strange conceits . . . I don't know that I have ever laughed so much as with and at him all through the voyage.'[14] When the ship docked on 11 August, Wilde was not left without an interview. At the Brunswick Hotel the *New York Times* reporter found him more conventionally dressed, with ordinary trousers, but the dandiacal effect remained in a cutaway velvet coat, patent leather boots, a Byronic collar and a scarf with a diamond pin. His hair was cut, another point, yet Neronian still. He spoke to the reporter of his English friends on shipboard, 'They are on their way to the West to shoot buffaloes,' and added in moody afterthought, 'if there are buffaloes and – if they can shoot them.' He spoke of having written *The Duchess of Padua* during his absence: 'Of course I shall mount it handsomely. The best of pictures require suitable frames.' He would visit Newport, to see Mrs Howe, and Peekskill, to see Henry Ward Beecher. Was the rumour true that Wilde had brought with him the scenery for *Vera*? 'Not even a cornfield,' he replied. What he had brought was some vermilion cloth for Marie Prescott.[15]

The rehearsals for *Vera* began on 13 August and the play opened to a packed house on the sweltering night of 21 August. At the end of the second act came cries of 'Author!' and at the end of the third Wilde appeared before the curtain and made a short speech, probably to say that the play was about passion rather than politics, or vice versa. It was just as well he delayed no longer, because everyone found the fourth act too long and Marie Prescott's vermilion gown in that act caused consternation to go with perspiration. There were many friends of Wilde or Marie Prescott in the audience, among them the actor Wilson Barrett, and they praised the play. The reviews were generally less than favorable. Apart from the *New York Sun*, which proclaimed it a masterpiece, and the *New York Mirror*, which spoke of it as 'really marvelous,' the other papers were adverse. The *New York Tribune* dispraised the piece more mildly than usual on 21 August, and allowed editorially on 26 August that Wilde was or could be a changed man. Mrs Frank Leslie blamed the vermilion gown for the adverse reception. The *New York Times* reviewer devoted a pompous column to analysis and rejection of nihilism, before discussing the play, in a style that suggested Wilde's epigrams had not been lost on him: 'We do not doubt the sincerity of Mr Oscar Wilde, who, nevertheless, has given us cogent reason to doubt his sincerity.' 'He has accomplished as little as possible, but we have been willing to believe that he could accomplish more.' Bearing in mind the interview with Wilde the week before, the reviewer granted that 'Ave Imperatrix,' mentioned in it, was a fine poem, and that Wilde's aesthetic theories were not devoid of merit. But the nihilist speeches were boring, and there were other defects. Condemnation was not total: 'Yet there is a great deal of good writing in *Vera*, and Mr Wilde exhibits cleverness and wit in a character like Prince Paul.' In sum, 'It comes as near failure as an ingenious and able writer can bring it.' And, although he himself said nothing, Wilde disliked the performance.

Marie Prescott was distressed by the written response to what the audience seemed to have enjoyed. She bravely addressed a letter to the editor of the *New York Times* naming a dozen reputable theatre people who had praised this 'noble' play. The letter served only to goad the *Times* to more scathing criticism of her and Wilde. She was characterized as having only a 'pulpit eloquence.' (The *Boston Pilot*, always sympathetic to Wilde, also blamed the failure on 'an inferior actress, who can only scold on the stage and off it.') At last the *Times* brought out an even heavier gun in the editorial section. Wilde was 'very much of a charlatan and wholly an amateur,' and the play was valueless.[16]

However unfair this dismissal in 1883 may have been, box office returns fell off sharply, and the theatre was too expensive to keep open. Marie Prescott and her husband devised a final stratagem: a newspaper story announced that Wilde, as soon as he returned from Coney Island – where insouciantly he had gone – would be asked by them to play a part, presumably Prince Paul, or failing that, to speak after each performance. He declined. On 28 August *Vera* was withdrawn. A reporter went to see Wilde, who was smoking a cigar. For once he shunned the press: 'Ah, but I am eating my breakfast, don't you see.'[17] Marie Prescott said she would take the play on tour, beginning 15 October, along with another play called *Czeka*. In December she was playing it in Detroit.

Wilde went off to Newport and Saratoga and stayed a month in the United States. He came back to London to find himself the butt of caricatures in *Punch* and *Entr'Acte*. The latter portrayed Willie consoling his dejected brother. Wilde still believed in the value of *Vera*. If he had reservations about Miss Prescott's acting, he could not express them. In a season of inferior plays, *Vera* cannot have been greatly below the average. The newspapers were resolved to mock and underrate him; Wilde was depressed by *Vera*'s failure but held his tongue.

There was nothing for it but to go on lecturing. Colonel Morse had been able to arrange a great many bookings, chiefly at Mechanics Institutions; by 18 August he had sixteen or seventeen, and during the 1883–4 season he secured, by his own count, over 150 bookings for Wilde.[18] The first was on 24 September at Wandsworth, where twelve years later Wilde would languish in prison. For these lectures he did not wear his velvet breeches or silk stockings. But his evening dress sported a black tie of curious cut, and from between his waistcoat and the bosom of his shirt peeped a salmon-colored silk handkerchief. He spoke now without notes, in his usual deliberate manner. On 11 October he took time off from lecturing to go with Lillie Langtry to Liverpool to see Henry Irving and Ellen Terry off on a tour of the States that would prove more equable than his own. On 25 October he lectured in Derby. But there was something more important, an audience of one.

Prenuptial Maneuvers

Once a week is quite enough to propose to anyone, and it should always be done in a manner that attracts some attention.

In mid-October, Wilde came to London between lectures, and Lady Wilde invited Constance to her reception so they could meet. The next day Wilde came to the Lloyds', and described his tour. 'He is lecturing still,' Otho commented, 'going from town to town, but in the funniest way, one day he is at Brighton, the next he will be at Edinburgh, the next at Penzance in Cornwall, the next in Dublin; he laughed a good deal over it and he said that he left it entirely to his manager.' The topic of *Vera* came up, and Wilde seemed much mortified by its failure. He brought a privately printed copy to Constance, and asked for her opinion. She promised to write from Dublin where she was about to go on a visit. It was a pleasant coincidence that her stay there would coincide with two lectures in Dublin by Wilde.

On 11 November Constance wrote to Wilde from her grandmother's house in Ely Place:

You ask me to let you know what I think of your play, and tho' I have no pretensions to being a critic and do not even know what constitutes a good play, I must, I suppose, give you some answer. I was much interested in 'Vera' and it seems to me to be a very good acting play and to have good dramatic situations. Also I like the passages on liberty and the impassioned parts, but I fancy that some of the minor parts of the dialogue strike me as being slightly halting or strained. I am speaking however only from aesthetic impressions and not from knowledge, so please don't let any remarks of mine weigh upon your mind. I cannot understand why you should have been so unfortunate in its reception unless either the acting was very inferior or the audience was unsympathetic to the political opinions expressed in it. The world surely is unjust and bitter to most of us; I think we must either renounce our opinions and run with the general stream or else totally ignore the world and go on our own regardless of all, there is not the slightest use in *fighting* against existing prejudices, for we are only worsted in the struggle – I am afraid you and I disagree in our opinions on art, for I hold that there is no perfect art without perfect morality, whilst you say that they are distinct and separable things, and of course you have your knowledge to combat my ignorance with. Truly I am no judge that you should appeal to me for opinions, and even if I were, I know that I should judge you rather by your *aims* than by your work, and you would say I was wrong. I told the Atkinsons that you would be here some time soon and they will be very pleased to see you: I shall be here [breaks off]¹⁹

Her aesthetics might not altogether conform, yet her admiration for him was steadfast; the letter displayed spirit as well as modesty. Set an impossible task, she discharged it skillfully. It also indicated her tolerance of his views when opposed to her own. She was intelligent, she was capable and independent.

When Wilde checked in to the Shelbourne Hotel in Dublin on 21 November, he found a note asking him to come round to Ely Place. By now he could see that he was being received as Constance Lloyd's suitor, and the unfamiliar situation ruffled him. Constance reported to her brother Otho that Wilde, 'though decidedly extra affected, I suppose partly from nervousness . . . made himself very pleasant.' His attention was mostly given to her. When he lectured for the first time on 'The House Beautiful' on 22 November, Constance Lloyd was of course an appreciative member of the audience. (So was W. B. Yeats, then eighteen.) After the lecture Wilde came to tea at the Atkinson house in Ely Place, and again addressed himself mostly to her. The following night he took a box for a nondescript play at the Gaiety Theatre, and gave it to the Atkinson family while he kept another engagement. It was perhaps an augury of his later absences from the conjugal home, but Constance made no complaint. She attended his 'Impressions of America' lecture as well, on the 24th, but preferred his highminded to his bantering mood. She could never quite compass his strain of near-nonsense. They talked again of *Vera*, and she read the play once more and this time announced to Otho, and presumably to Wilde, that she thought it 'very fine.'[20] Wilde had told her that 'he wrote it to show that an abstract idea such as liberty could have quite as much power and be made quite as fine as the passion of love.' *Vera* however is not so republican as that. At any rate, it was the curtailment of his liberty in the name of his love which was about to rule him.

The fifth day of his stay in Dublin, Sunday, 25 November, was the climactic one. Wilde was alone with Constance in the drawing room where, as she well knew, her father had thirty years before proposed to her mother. Her relations had left them together, and hinted by their chaffing that they had guessed a declaration was about to be made. It came, and Constance was enraptured. She wrote to her brother, 'Prepare yourself for an astounding piece of news! I am engaged to Oscar Wilde and perfectly and insanely happy.' She only worried a little over the response of some of the family. There was no doubt about her grandfather Lloyd: his pleasure in Wilde's company had long been cordial. Her grandmother Atkinson was also a Wilde partisan and thought Constance extremely lucky. She had nothing to fear from her mother, who liked Wilde immensely. The only opposition might come from her aunt Emily Lloyd whose views of marriage were as strict as Lady Bracknell's, and who treated Constance as a guest on sufferance after years of putting her up in Lancaster Gate.[21]

Meanwhile her suitor was writing to her grandmother and mother, and to her brother Otho, who replied on 27 November, 'I am pleased indeed: I am sure that for my own part I welcome you as a new brother ... If Constance makes as good a wife as she has been a good sister to me, your happiness is certain; she is staunch and true.'[22] So she proved to be.

What Wilde said to Constance Lloyd could only have been passionate. He had no intention of proceeding at less than full sail. One of the lesser yet still genuine pleasures of this momentous change in his way of life was that it afforded him a new verbal situation. Because of the catastrophe to come, his love letters do not survive. But incantatory rhythms and idealistic phrasing came readily to him. His mind had other recesses, from which he drew 'The Sphinx' and later *The Picture of Dorian Gray* and *Salome*; they were left dark as he brought to light his simpler self.

A few letters of Constance to her accepted lover have been kept. One makes clear that he told her something of his sexual past. She responded, 'I don't think I shall ever be jealous. Certainly I am not jealous now of any-one: I trust in you for the present: I am content to let the past be buried, it does not belong to me: for the future trust and faith will come, and when I have you for my husband, I will hold you fast with chains of love.'[23] The confession, to judge from the tone of her absolution, can have been only partial – no light loves and no untoward ones. Syphilis was not mentioned, for Wilde thought himself cured. It seems likely that he mentioned Florence Balcombe and, since he wrote quickly to give her the news of his engagement, Mrs Langtry. Constance recognized that neither of these was a present rival.

To Mrs Langtry Wilde began tactfully by congratulating her on her success in *Peril*. 'You have done what no other artist of your day has done,' he said, 'invaded America a second time and carried off new victories. But then, you are made for victory. It has always flashed in your eyes and rung in your voice.' Then he went on to tell her that

> I am going to be married to a beautiful girl called Constance Lloyd, a grave, slight, violet-eyed little Artemis, with great coils of heavy brown hair which make her flower-like head droop like a blossom, and wonderful ivory hands which draw music from the piano so sweet that the birds stop singing to listen to her. We are to be married in April. I hope so much that you will be over then. I am so anxious for you to know and to like her.
>
> I am hard at work lecturing and getting rich, though it is horrid being so much away from her, but we telegraph to each other twice a day, and I rush back suddenly from the uttermost parts of the earth to see her for an hour, and do all the foolish things that wise lovers do.[24]

Her brother characterized Constance's violet eyes more prosaically as blue-green. The description of her as an Artemis was not altogether just, as Constance Lloyd tried to make clear to him: 'I am so cold and undemonstrative outwardly: you must read my heart and not my outward semblance if you wish to know how passionately I worship and love you.'[25] Worship was perhaps more than Wilde wanted, yet her letters to him were open: he was 'my hero and my god.' Like Dorian Gray's Sibyl Vane, she said repeatedly, 'I am not worthy of him.' Constance had been kept down, first by her cruel mother, then by her reproachful aunt, so that Wilde became a Perseus to whom she would be bound in gratitude and love.

Wilde was pleased for a time to match her, heartbeat for heartbeat. Mrs Belloc Lowndes and other observers thought him head over heels in love with her. He shifted to a playful mode in writing to the sculptor Waldo Story, in whom he confided that she was 'quite perfect except that she does not think Jimmy [Whistler] the only painter that ever really existed: she would like to bring Titian or somebody in by the back door: however, she knows I am the greatest poet, so in literature she is all right: and I have explained to her that you are the greatest sculptor: art instruction cannot go further.'[26]

The two lovers spent some days together at Christmas, when Wilde had a respite from what he called 'civilising the provinces' by his lectures. These were ecstatic hours. The week ended in Constance's tears at his departure and subsequent apology for being silly. In January perfection was not so rampant. Wilde had sent Constance a marmoset, called 'Jimmy' for its whistling. Jimmy died. Constance felt tragic, and remembered some other ill-fated gift: 'Is it my fault that everything you give me has an untimely end?' To add to her misery, Wilde had misaddressed a telegram to her: 'How much do you think of me that you did not even remember that I was not at home? Your telegram was forwarded to me this morning . . . I am too gloomy to write.'[27] Wilde made it up, but Constance guessed that he occupied her thoughts more than she did his. That pattern would continue.

Marriage had its financial as well as its emotional side. As Constance had guessed, there was opposition, though not from Emily Lloyd. It came from her grandfather, who pronounced himself in favor of the marriage, but asked Wilde to answer two questions, what were his means and what were his debts. ('And now I have a few questions to put to you, Mr Worthing,' says Lady Bracknell.) Like Algernon, Wilde had 'nothing but his debts to depend upon.' He acknowledged that he owed Levy £1,200, but said he had already paid off £300 by lecture fees. A conference was held at a lawyer's office. Wilde offered to write the lawyer a sonnet, as proof of his capacity as author, but feared this would be of no use.[28] He and Constance could not marry till at least March, since Wilde was booked for lectures until then, and then had to wait till Lent was passed. John Horatio Lloyd proposed that the marriage be deferred a bit longer until Wilde had paid off another £300 of his debt. So the ceremony, originally planned for April, would not take place until 29 May. Constance had £250 a year, and when her grandfather died she would have £900 a year. The young couple represented their need of money to lease and furnish a house, and Constance was given £5,000 in advance from her grandfather's estate, to count against her eventual share.

The friends and relations of Wilde and his intended wife responded with surprise and pleasure to the news of the engagement. Whistler gave them a luncheon party in mid-December; at first Emily Lloyd, who countenanced the marriage, forbade Constance to attend, on the grounds that an unmarried woman should not appear in society without a chaperone. Eventually she was prevailed upon to give way. Lady Wilde and Willie were in the highest excitement. Willie wrote on 27 November, 'My dear old Boy, This is indeed good news, brave news, wise news, and altogether charming and amazing in the highest and most artistic sense.' He sent his love to 'Alcibiades and Lady Constance.' He and Oscar were affectionate, like two boys together. Lady Wilde wrote at once also, the same day, and her letter implies that the couple had been moving towards an understanding for some months:

My dear Oscar, I am extremely pleased at your note of this morning. You have both been true and constant, and a blessing will come on all true feeling.

But one feels very anxious: so much yet – all the services and the [word indecipherable]. It always seems so hard for two lovers to get married. But I have hope all will end well . . . What lovely vistas of speculation open out.

What you will do in life? Where live? Meantime you must go on with your work. I enclose another offer for lectures. I would like you to have a small house in London and live the literary life and teach Constance to correct proofs and eventually go into Parliament.

May the Divine Intelligence that rules the world, give you happiness and peace and joy in your beloved.

La Madre[29]

The notion of entering Parliament had occurred to Wilde as well, and was still being dandled on 28 February when Lady Wilde wrote to someone else about it as her son's idea. With more result, he began negotiating for a lease on a house at 16 Tite Street, near where he and Miles had lived some years before. The lease would begin on 24 June. Wilde asked Whistler to superintend the redecoration. 'No, Oscar,' came the reply, 'you have been lecturing to us about the House Beautiful; now is your chance to show us one.'[30] Wilde then turned to Godwin, whom Beerbohm described as 'the greatest aesthete of them all,' and Godwin agreed to redo the house for them. Constance's income and the £5,000 proved insufficient to defray the considerable expense. A letter from Wilde's solicitor and friend George Lewis, of 15 May 1884, indicates that Wilde was borrowing £1,000 on what remained of his father's estate. In spite of John Horatio Lloyd's anxiety about prudent domestic management, the marriage began under the shadow of debts, and remained there. Lloyd himself improved as the marriage impended, but he rescued the necessitous lovers by dying on 18 July, thus freeing his legacy.

Marriage

LORD ILLINGWORTH: *The Book of Life begins with a man and woman in a garden.*

MRS ALLONBY: *It ends with Revelations.*

On 29 May 1884 at St James's Church the bride was lovely, and the groom said to look more than ever like George IV. A telegram arrived 'From Whistler, Chelsea, to Oscar Wilde, St James's Church, Sussex Gardens: Fear I may not be able to reach you in time for the ceremony. Don't wait.' Because of the illness of Constance's grandfather, the wedding was kept small and somewhat secret. The bridesmaids – cousins of Constance – were not told where or when the wedding would be till a week before. The plan was to allow only invited guests, furnished with cards, but the rector opened the church doors. Only near relatives were invited afterwards to Lancaster Gate. Lady Wilde embraced Constance with some effusiveness; Wilde kissed her 'calmly and coolly,' according to the *Canterbury Times*. 'A happy little group of *intimes* saw them off at Charing Cross,' reported the *World* on 4 June, and the crusty *New York Times*, probably depending once more upon Bodley as a London correspondent, added on 22 June in a burst of generosity, 'and few married couples ever carried better wishes with them.' They told of the bride's dress, designed by Wilde: it was of 'rich creamy satin' with 'a delicate cowslip tint; the bodice, cut square and somewhat low in front, was finished with a high Medici collar; the ample sleeves were puffed; the skirt, made plain, was gathered by a silver girdle of beautiful workmanship, the gift of Mr Oscar Wilde; the veil of saffron-coloured Indian gauze was embroidered with pearls and worn in Marie Stuart fashion; a thick wreath of myrtle leaves, through which gleamed a few white blossoms, crowned her fair frizzed hair; the dress was ornamented with clusters of myrtle leaves; the large bouquet had as much green in it as white.' Equally overdressed were the bridesmaids, with Wilde again as couturier. It was a wedding in the high aesthetic mode.

The Wildes crossed the Channel and arrived in Paris; at the Hôtel Wagram they took three rooms on the fourth floor overlooking the Tuileries. On the second day Wilde met Robert Sherard, who somewhat resented the radiant happiness of the newly married couple. Wilde made matters worse by taking Sherard aside for a walk. He began with superlatives about his bride, and got as far as 'It's so wonderful when a young virgin . . .' when Sherard steered him away from confidences. Wilde was willing to sacrifice some of the nuptial intimacy for the delight of describing it. That he should so readily turn private acts into public was disturbing to Sherard's sexual jealousy, and a questionable augury.[31] Wilde was reading Stendhal's *Le Rouge et le noir*, another book in which the hero tries to act always deliberately, never *à l'improviste*.

On 9 June 1884 Wilde was stretched out on a sofa amid a heap of books in the hotel when a reporter from the *Morning News* knocked on the door. Wilde protested that he was 'too happy to be interviewed,' but let him in all the same. 'You are reading?' said the reporter. 'Yes, I am dipping,' Wilde replied. 'I never read from the beginning, especially with novels. It is the only way to stimulate the curiosity that books, with their regular openings, always fail to rouse. Have you ever overheard a conversation in the street, caught the fag end of it, and wished you might know more? If you overhear your books in that way, you will go back to the first chapter, and on to the last naturally, as soon as the characters bite.'

Observing *Le Rouge et le noir* among the books, the reporter asked, 'You go to Stendhal again and again?' 'Yes. And he is one of the few. For my part, I think the most exquisite thing in reading is the pleasure of forgetfulness. It is so nice to think there are some books you cared for so much at a certain epoch in your life and do not care for now. There is to me a positive delight in cutting an author and feeling I have got beyond him.' 'And do you extend that observation to persons?' 'Undoubtedly,' Wilde replied. 'So we all do, only I would make it a positive satisfaction instead of a regret. Why should we not joyfully admit that there are some people we do not want to see again? It is not ingratitude, it is not indifference. They have simply given us all they have to give.'

The reporter, remembering the several months Wilde had spent in France the previous year, asked, 'You do not feel that way about Paris?' 'No,' said Wilde. 'It is not easy to exhaust the message of Paris, especially when Sarah Bernhardt is playing. I have seen *Macbeth* over and over again. There is nothing like it on our stage, and it is her finest creation. I say her creation deliberately, because to my mind it is utterly impertinent to talk of Shakespeare's *Macbeth* or Shakespeare's *Othello*. Shakespeare is only one of the parties. The second is the artiste through whose mind it passes. When the two together combine to give me an acceptable hero, that is all I ask. Shakespeare's intentions were his own secret: all we can form an opinion about is what is actually before us.'

He was unstinting in his praise of the actress: 'There is absolutely no one like Sarah Bernhardt. She brings all her fine intelligence to the part, all her instinctive and acquired knowledge of the stage. Her influence over Macbeth's mind is just as much influence of womanly charm as of will – with us they only accentuate the last. She holds him under a spell: he sins because he loves her: his ambition is quite a secondary motive. How can he help loving her? She binds him by every tie, even by the tie of coquetry. Look at her dress – the tight-fitting tunic and the statuesque folds of the robe below. The whole piece is admirably done.' Wilde praised Richepin's prose translation, and went on, 'The very ghost is Elizabethan. Remember, in Shakespeare's day ghosts were not shadowy, subjective conceptions, but beings of flesh and blood, only beings living on the other side of the border of life, and now and then permitted to break bounds. The ghosts of the Porte Saint-Martin are men: you could pinch them and run them through and through. They are not mere things of gauze, like our English stage figures of the kind, elaborated, apparently, from some programme of the Psychical Society.'

The reporter turned the conversation to *Le Maître de forges*, a current dramatization of Georges Ohnet's novel about an aristocratic woman married to a rich but low-born ironmaster, whom she treats with arrogance until his cold politeness brings her to adoring subjection. Wilde had not attended the Paris performance, but had seen it in London. 'And London is not shocked?' asked the reporter. 'Oh, London is improving,' said Wilde, 'and besides, it will take anything from the French. Of course, if an English writer had done anything of the sort there would have been one loud shriek.' 'So you might wish yourself a Frenchman – if you mean to go on writing plays?' 'In one respect certainly,' said Wilde, 'for the sake of the interpretation. What a gulf there is between the character as you conceive it and the character as it comes out on the stage. I admit, after what I said just now, that the author has no right to complain where the result is artistic, but with us that is so often not the case. I speak from experience. I shall never forget the two hours and a half I passed in the playhouse in New York on the first night of my piece.'[32]

A few days later Wilde wrote from Paris to a friend what the *New York Times* (possibly through Bodley again) called on 8 June 'a silly and thoroughly characteristic letter.' In it Wilde proclaimed that 'he has not been disappointed in married life.' The negative phrasing may suggest that he had been thinking the unthinkable. The *Times* paraphrase went on: 'He feels confident of his ability to sustain its labours and anxieties, and sees an opportunity in his new relation, of realizing a poetical conception which he has long entertained. He says that Lord Beaconsfield taught the peers of England a new style of oratory, and that he intends to set an example of the pervading influence of art on matrimony.' This was a heavy burden of theory for Constance Wilde to bear. For the moment the aestheticizing of marriage only meant her being pliantly dressed up, and commissioning the Tite Street house to be done up in extraordinary fashion by Godwin. (Wilde's only self-transformation was to have his hair cut short and waved instead of curled.) But latent was a darker possibility, that some place would have to be found in this marriage for low aesthetic as well as for high aesthetic, for sphinxes and gamey savors as for stately conversations and rapturous orthodox couplings.

The outward events of the wedding trip were entertaining enough. The young couple went to the Salon to see Whistler's paintings; they visited an exhibition of Meissonnier; they saw a light opera called *Lili*; and best of all, they watched Sarah Bernhardt play, or as Constance Wilde said, 'storm' the part of Lady Macbeth. Besides Mme Bernhardt only two other French friends are mentioned. At breakfast with Catulle Mendès, Wilde remarked, 'There is no modern literature outside France.'[33] Paul Bourget came to meet Constance, and Vernon Lee (pen name of Violet Paget) remembered his comment, *'J'aime cette femme – j'aime la femme annulée et tendre.*'[34] Another friend in attendance was John Donoghue, the Chicago sculptor whom Wilde had helped. John Singer Sargent had the couple to dinner, and Henrietta Reubell, a wealthy American who had a salon and was a friend of Henry James, entertained them. She committed the barbarism of asking the name of Constance Wilde's dressmaker so that she might order an identical dress – to the horror of Constance's designer-husband. After Paris the young couple spent a week in Dieppe.

An important element of the honeymoon was recorded in the *Morning News* interview. It was not an event, but a book, a book which was to be for Wilde in the 'eighties what Pater's *Studies in the History of the Renaissance* had been in the 'seventies. Joris-Karl Huysmans's *A Rebours* had been published just two weeks before, in mid-May, and shook up the literary scene. Whistler rushed to congratulate Huysmans the next day on his 'marvellous book.' Bourget, at that time a close friend of Huysmans as of Wilde, admired it greatly; Paul Valéry called it his 'Bible and bedside book' and this is what it became for Wilde. He said to the *Morning News*, 'This last book of Huysmans is one of the best I have ever seen.'[35] It was being reviewed everywhere as the guidebook of decadence. At the very moment that Wilde was falling in with social patterns, he was confronted with a book which even in its title defied them. The book's hero, Des Esseintes, was dandy, scholar, *débauchée*, his appetites and pleasures *raffinés* beyond all example. When Dorian Gray reads a book resembling Huysmans's novel, 'The hero, the wonderful young Parisian . . . became to him a kind of pre-figuring type of himself. And indeed, the whole book seemed to him to contain the story of his own life, written before he had lived it.' Wilde could regard it as the exfoliation of Pater's theory of self-development, for Des Esseintes 'spent his life trying to realize in the nineteenth century all the passions and modes of thought that belonged to every century except his own, and to sum up, as it were, in himself, the various modes through which the world-spirit had ever passed, loving for their mere artificiality those renunciations that men have unwisely called virtue, as much as those natural rebellions that men still call sin.' In short, 'It was a poisonous book.' Wilde drank of it as a chaser after the love potions of matrimony.

Part of the book's attraction was the author's reserved attitude. Huysmans could not be said to endorse his hero, for each chapter was a little parable of spent passion for books, perfumes, jewels, or sexual pleasures. While each burst of energy is deflated, and Huysmans withholds sympathy, the sense of the hero's *jusqu'au-boutisme* almost redeems the absurdity and prevents his being altogether discredited. Certain sections had a staggering effect upon Wilde. One was Huysmans's description of Gustave Moreau's paintings of *Salome*, another the description of English Pre-Raphaelite paintings as evoking not the month of April, as Wilde had said in America, but of October. The art which Wilde had thought of as part of his renaissance turned up as part of Huysmans's decadence. Again the possibility of uniting the two movements must have occurred to him. He had always been both *comme il faut* and *à rebours*, too, Apollonian gentleman and Dionysian subverter. There was a singular passage in Huysmans's book: Des Esseintes recalls a sexual exploit which, being homosexual, was different from all others he had experienced, and in memory dominated them. For some months he had taken up with a young man. According to André Raffalovich's hostile witness, Wilde was particularly fascinated by this part of *A Rebours*.[36] The book as a whole revived those months which Wilde had spent the year before among the decadents, months when he had written 'The Harlot's House' and much of 'The Sphinx.' It summoned him towards an underground life totally at variance with his aboveboard role as Constance's husband.

The ambiguous nature of Paris as helmsman of Wilde's *bateau ivre* on its wedding trip was mildly reflected in notes for poems which he jotted down in that city. One, entitled 'Impression de Paris: Le Jardin des Tuileries,' wholesomely described children running about his chair as he sat in the gardens:

> And sometimes in shrill flight they flee,
>   And sometimes rush, a boisterous band,
> And, tiny hand on tiny hand,
>   Climb up a black and leafless tree.
> Ah, cruel tree! if I were you
>   And children climbed me, for their sake,
>   Though it be winter, I would break
> Into spring blossoms white and blue.

On his return he touched up these lines and contributed them to a benefit volume for a hospital, entitled *In a Good Cause.* His friend Laura Troubridge made an illustration of it, complaining the while that the poem was not to her taste. Still, it suggested some of the transfigurative imagery that Wilde was soon to use in his fairy tales.

On the same page with these jottings were others in keeping with another mood:

> The moon is like a yellow seal
>   Upon a dark blue envelope,
> And down below the dusky slope
>   Like a black sword of polished steel
>
> With flickering damascenes of gold
>   Flows the dark Seine . . . .

Imagining his *lune de miel* as a seal upon a dark blue envelope essays that approximation of modern idiom which Wilde occasionally attempted. Swords and damascenes of gold on the other hand hark back to a familiar heroic diction. Yet the image of the Seine as a dark sword calls up a Baudelairean Paris, in which Wilde saw himself for a moment as experienced among intriguers rather than innocent among children. He was occupying himself with two impulses, one associative and the other deviant.

He was constitutionally incapable of being single-minded for long. While he was in love with Constance, he could not help regarding himself in love with her. He could say with Rousseau's Narcissus, '*Je m'aime aimant.*' Or, as he would conjecture in 'The Portrait of Mr W.H.,' 'Perhaps, by finding perfect expression for a passion, I had exhausted passion itself. Emotional forces, like the forces of physical life, have their positive limitations.' These limitations he would gradually experience.

From double-natured Paris, the double-natured Wilde returned with Constance on 24 June 1884. The Thames was not so chthonic as the Seine, and for a time Wilde embraced the domesticity that lay in wait for him on its banks. There were moments of doubt, however. Not long after his return, he was approached by a friend who said, 'Hullo, Wilde. I hear you've got married.' 'Yes,' he answered dejectedly, 'gone deuced cheap, too!'[37] For Constance, her first season after marriage, as she tried to keep up with her husband's dizzy pace, was painful.

CHAPTER X

Mr and Mrs Wilde

LANE: *I have often observed that in married households the champagne is rarely of a first-rate brand.*

Matrimonial Wear and Tear

Not much time was required for Constance Wilde to perceive that her modest income could never float so brave a venture as the Oscar Wilde argosy. 'Enough is as good as a meal; too much is as good as a feast,' said her husband. 'Those who pay their bills are soon forgotten,' he added, or, phrasing it more formally, 'It is only by not paying one's bills that one can hope to live in the memory of the commercial classes.'[1] On their return from the wedding trip Constance announced to her brother that she thought of taking a job. This prospect was dashed by her becoming pregnant in September. Most of her time went in seconding her husband's wishes for splurging guineas rather than saving pennies. The £50 presented by an aunt of his to start them off in married life went for the purchase of two Apostle spoons, much to the aunt's disgust.[2] It was Wilde who determined how they should live, on what Whistlerian avenue and in what Godwinian style. Never a fluent talker, Constance seemed almost mute beside her husband. Asked how he had happened to fall in love with her, Wilde said, 'She scarcely ever speaks. I am always wondering what her thoughts are like.' In his story, 'The Happy Prince,' the swallow falls out of love with a reed for several reasons, one being, 'She has no conversation.' At a reception Constance happened to pass by, looking pretty; he observed her admiringly, then murmured half to himself and half to Louise Jopling, 'If only I could be jealous of her!'[3] The sentiment had been aroused easily enough by Mrs Langtry and Florence Balcombe, but then neither of them had had any idea of worshipping him.

Still, Constance could be lively in private, and she was intelligent and well-informed. She spoke French and Italian fluently, and was well read in the two literatures. At Wilde's urging Constance learned German so they could enjoy reading new books in the language together. She and her husband could sympathetically share misadventures as well. Immediately on their return, the young couple stayed for two nights at the Brunswick Hotel, in Jermyn Street. With their depleted resources the two guineas a night they had to pay seemed a good deal. They went to call on Emily Lloyd and Constance's dying grandfather at 100 Lancaster Gate, hoping that Emily would invite them to stay. She was not forthcoming, however, and finally Constance had to ask directly. Emily allowed them to remain for a few days until they found other accommodation. They soon moved from Lancaster Gate to 7 Great College Street, Westminster, and some days later back to Wilde's familiar lodgings at 9 Charles Street near Grosvenor Square. They had perhaps expected that Tite Street would be ready for occupancy shortly after their return. It was not.

The redecoration of 16 Tite Street prolonged itself over seven more months, so they could not move in until January 1885. Godwin had ambitious plans, and the builders were slow and inept in carrying them out. Wilde dropped the first firm, owned by a man named Green, without paying his bill, and with Godwin's help found another builder, Sharpe. Sharpe charged even more exorbitantly than Green. Meanwhile Green sued for his unpaid bill, and when Wilde ignored him, had the furniture seized. Wilde counterclaimed, and the case was proceeding towards trial until, the day before it was to be heard, the solicitors on both sides agreed to a settlement. After having paid Green, Sharpe, Godwin and the solicitor, Wilde, confident in his star, remained ebullient.

With Godwin, if not with the builders, he stayed on the best of terms. Godwin had succeeded in winning acceptance for his theories not only of house decoration but of scenery and of dress, and Wilde found occasion to praise him in several of the reviews that he now began to write. Both men intended that the house in Tite Street should set a new standard in interior design. Gone were the Morris wallpapers and other vestiges of Pre-Raphaelite décor. In came the new era of white high-gloss enamel, varied by golds, blues, greens. Godwin's plans[4] give some sense of what the house looked like, though it is clear from Wilde's correspondence, and from the testimonies of visitors, that considerable changes were made in the course of the Wildes' ten-year occupancy.

The house was on four floors with a basement, or lower ground floor, where the kitchen was. The door to the house was white, with a brass knocker and letterbox flap, and a window of frosted glass. Godwin's plan envisaged an entrance hall painted grey to the height of the dado (5′6″) and white above, with a yellow ceiling. A small lamp of beaten iron hung from the ceiling, and on the walls were two large engravings in white frames, one of *Apollo and the Muses*, the other of *Diana and Her Nymphs Bathing*, as if in tribute to husband and wife. The hall colors were apparently changed: Alexander Teixeira de Mattos (the second husband of Willie Wilde's second wife) remembered it as orange below and blue frieze above. But earlier the grey was changed to white, the color remembered by Laura Troubridge's fiancé, Adrian Hope, a relative of

Constance. Hope is probably accurate, since the dining room, also originally intended to be grey, was actually painted in various tones of white and off-white, and had white curtains embroidered with yellow silk.

One unusual feature of the dining room was a sideboard about nine inches wide, which was built round much of the room and was used to serve from. The dining room table Hope irreverently described as dirty brown, remembering also the maroon napkins with deep fringes, and delicate china, especially the yellow cups. On the floor was a green-blue Morris carpet with a white pattern. The other room on the ground floor was the library, executed in a style variously described as Turkish, Moorish, and North African. Over the doorway and along the sides of the room ran a heavy beam and an architrave bearing, in gilt, red, and blue, an inscription from Shelley:

> Spirit of Beauty! Tarry still awhile,
>   They are not dead, thine ancient votaries,
> Some few there are to whom thy radiant smile
>   Is better than a thousand victories.

The library had a high dado painted dark blue, with pale gold on the walls above it and on the ceiling. Along two sides of the room was a low divan, in front of which were ottomans, lanterns, and hangings, an Eastern inlaid table and – no chairs. The window appears to have been covered at first with a wooden grating, eventually with a glass bead curtain to cut off the unpleasant view at the back, as well as the light. It was in this room that Wilde smoked, conducted *têtes-à-têtes*, and did most of his writing.

The white staircase had a curtain in front of it; the stairs were covered with gold yellow matting and led to the drawing rooms on the second floor. These were separated by folding doors. The larger one was to the rear, with dark green walls and pale green ceiling, the fireplace and woodwork painted brown pink. On either side of the fireplace, filling the room's corners, were two three-cornered divans, very low, with cushions. On the mantelpiece was a small green bronze figure of Narcissus. There were also a Chippendale table, a curule armchair, and three white-lacquered straight back chairs. A portrait of Wilde by Harper Pennington was hung on one wall, and in a corner there was also the bust of Augustus Caesar which Wilde had received after the Newdigate. The ceiling originally had two gold dragons at opposite corners painted by Whistler; these gave way at some point to large Japanese feathers inserted into the plaster, also at Whistler's suggestion. Hung on the green walls were small white-framed lithographs by Whistler and Mortimer Menpes, a drawing by Beardsley (later), and the framed manuscript of Keats's sonnet given to Wilde in America. There were also red crayon sketches of some of Mrs Wilde's friends. The front drawing room had flesh-pink walls but the cornice was gilded dull lemon gold and the ceiling covered with Japanese leather, which Wilde somehow acquired. Above the fireplace was displayed the bronze plaque of a young girl by John Donoghue, illustrating Wilde's poem 'Requiescat.'

On the floor above were two bedrooms, Mrs Wilde's in front, with pink walls and applegreen ceiling. It contained an artistically shaped bath. Wilde made a point of never entering her room without permission. As he said in a review, 'men must give up the tyranny in married life which was once so dear to them, and which, we are afraid, lingers still, here and there.'[5] The back bedroom, originally Wilde's, had dark blue walls and a pale blue ceiling. It contained a large plaster cast of the Hermes of Olympia. Eventually this room became the children's bedroom. The third floor originally contained Wilde's study, executed in shades of red, the woodwork in his favorite vermilion. The front room on the third floor was all white except for the yellow ceiling. Eventually these rooms became night and day nurseries. On the top floor were the servants' quarters.

While the House Beautiful was in process of construction, Wilde and Constance were always being invited out, often by people who had looked at him askance before. Respectability was achieved overnight, as he had anticipated, though it had never been his ideal any more than his mother's. On meeting Olive Schreiner, he asked her why she lived in the East End. 'Because the people there don't wear masks.' 'And I live in the West End because the people there do.' He announced also, 'A gentleman never goes east of Temple Bar.'[6] A weekly magazine called the *Bat* lamented the aesthete's decline:

> At last he went and cut his hair –
> The soil proved poor and arid
> And things are much as once they were –
> He's settled down and married!
>   (9 February 1886)

The same magazine, observing him at a matinée of *The Lady of Lyons* on 23 March 1886, when Mrs Langtry was playing Pauline, reported, 'there was Oscar Wilde subdued, meditative, married.' But Wilde was neither settled down nor subdued. He was still outraging the world with his talk, even while amusing it. He played the married man with a flair which suggested that for him it was an adventure rather than a quiescence.

What dandyism he continued to practice he was able to impose, to her discomfort, upon Constance. How could she refuse instruction from the adviser to Lillie Langtry? Her natural shyness consorted ill with the boldness required of her. At his request she had to bedeck herself, a half-convinced martyr to his evangel of dress reform. Sometimes her dresses suited her: when Anna de Brémont, an American woman who had married a putative count, met her for the first time, Constance was wearing a Greek costume of cowslip yellow and apple-leaf green. Her hair, 'a thick mass of ruddy brown, was wonderfully set off by bands of yellow ribbon supporting the knot of hair on the nape of the neck and crossing the wavy tresses above her brow.' Her boyish face, her full dark eyes, had their effect. But when the young couple came for tea to Laura Troubridge's house in July 1884, Miss Troubridge noted in her diary, 'She dressed for the part in limp white muslin with *no* bustle, saffron coloured silk swathed about her shoulders, a huge cartwheel Gains-borough hat, white and bright yellow stockings and shoes – she looked too hopeless and we thought her shy and dull – he was amusing of course.'[7] Yet Constance persisted, and showed considerable variety. She attended a meeting on Rational Dress in the Westminster Town Hall in March 1886, and when she rose to propose a motion showed herself to be clad in cinnamon-colored cashmere trousers and a cape with the ends turned under to form sleeves. The *Bat*, in its worldly way, found this attire strictly irrational, and said so on 30 March 1886. On 6 November 1888 she addressed an audience of women at the Somerville Club on the subject, 'Clothed and in Our Right Minds.' The lecture was reported in the *Rational Dress Society Gazette* for January 1889.

Another observer, Louise Jopling, being an artist was much more willing than Laura Troubridge to see departures from French fashions. One Sunday morning when Mrs Jopling had invited the Wildes to visit her, she saw them arrive in resplendent style. Wilde was dressed in a brown suit with innumerable little buttons that gave it the appearance of a glorified page's costume. Constance wore a large picture hat with white feathers, and a dress of equal flourish. 'As we came along the King's Road,' Wilde reported, 'a number of rude little boys surrounded and followed us. One boy, after staring at us, said, "'Amlet and Ophelia out for a walk, I suppose!" I answered, "My little fellow, you are quite right. We are!"'[8] As always, he was amused by his own finery, as well as by the reactions it elicited.

Wilde and Constance were on excellent terms with Lady Wilde and with Willie. When Willie, who had become dramatic critic of *Vanity Fair*, took a vacation in August 1884, Oscar filled his post. Lady Wilde maintained her salon, and her own standards of dress. A young German artist unfortunately named Herbert Schmalz (later changed to Car-michael) visited her in May 1886 and recorded his impressions. In the double drawing room into which Schmalz and his wife were shown, they had to grope their way because, though it was early afternoon, thick curtains were drawn over the windows; the only light was supplied by candles. The atmosphere was made more mysterious by pastilles burning on the mantelpiece, and large mirrors placed between floor and ceiling, with curtains over the edges, so that, when the room was crowded, it was impossible to see how far it extended.

Lady Wilde received her guests wearing a lavender silk dress over a crinoline with a piece of crimson velvet about a foot deep around the skirt.

Hanging loosely around her waist was a Roman scarf, bright green in color, with stripes of scarlet, blue, and yellow. The dress was cut low at the neck, and on her breast she wore a large miniature about six inches by four. Her hair was dressed in ringlets, surmounted by a high headdress of lace. Incongruous as the costume was, Schmalz said, 'she managed to look more weird and imposing than ridiculous.'

As they arrived a little American girl, with a face like a cherub, was reciting a poem imitating birds and another imitating the echoes of a charcoal burner's voice dying away. When she had finished, Oscar Wilde went up to Schmalz and his wife to say, 'Is she not charming? So like a dear little rose-bud, bespattered with dew.' After a time the visitors decided to leave. 'As I said goodbye to Lady Wilde,' Schmalz recalled, 'she gazed at me like a Sphinx for a little, then said, "I hear you have a large picture in the Royal Academy. And are you not very young to have passed that dreaded council?"

'"I hope you like it, Lady Wilde," I answered.

'"I have not seen it," she replied, "but Oscar shall guide me to it. Oscar shall guide me to it."'

At the door Wilde stopped them. '"Ah, Schmalz! leaving Mamma so soon?"'

'"Yes, I have a picture I must get on with."

'"Might one ask, what subject?"

'"A Viking picture."

'"But, my dear Schmalz,"' said Wilde (slowly gathering himself for a witticism), '"why so far back? You know, where archaeology begins, art ceases."'*

To the young couple, as they went out into the broad daylight of the Brompton Road, it seems they had 'just awakened from some unearthly dream.'[10]

From Speech to Print

It is only the shallow people who do not judge by appearances.

When autumn came, Wilde started his lecturing again. The subjects he offered were 'The Value of Art in Modern Life,' a recasting of what he had been saying in America and after, and a new lecture on 'Dress.' In this he commended a recent revival of the sense of beauty in England, and only regretted that so far it had not extended to what people wore. To promote

---

* In his lecture to art students, Wilde had clarified his attitude: 'All archaeological pictures that make you say, "How curious," all sentimental pictures that make you say, "How sad," all historical pictures that make you say, "How interesting," all pictures that do not immediately give you such artistic joy as to make you say, "How beautiful," are bad pictures.'[9]

radical change he urged that children be taught drawing before they were taught their letters, to imbue them with a sense of the contours of the body. The child would learn that the waist was a beautiful and delicate curve, and not, as the milliner placed it, an abrupt right angle suddenly occurring in the middle of a body. The enemy of proper dress was fashion. 'A fashion is merely a form of ugliness so unbearable that we are compelled to alter it every six months.' French influence was pernicious, and had been so since the time when William the Conqueror landed to find that the English were wearing a dress at once beautiful and simple, and promptly changed it. In the second quarter of the seventeenth century English dress had again been delightful, and Charles II chose that moment to reimport French fashions.

What Wilde proposed was that clothing should be hung from the shoulders rather than from the waist. This would be healthier, and better still, Grecian. 'In Athens there was neither a milliner, nor a milliner's bill. These things were absolutely unknown, so great was the civilisation.'[11] Bustles, stays, corsets must go, and high heels, that tilt the body forward. He thought better ways of dressing could be learned not only from the Greeks, but from the Assyrians and Egyptians. The trousers worn by Turkish women won his approval. Men must change their attire too. Wilde illustrated his own theories. He announced himself as now opposed to the old knee breeches, because like the 'dress improver' they were too tight for comfort. He had substituted closefitting light trousers, above which he wore a broad rolling collar, a high dark waistcoat, and a black stock with a pendant bunch of seals. He opposed the stovepipe hat and favored a broadbrimmed one (perhaps influenced by the Leadville miner's hat) to keep the rain out of the eyes. He spoke in favor of doublets and cloaks. Such ideas, though elegantly phrased and illustrated, did not command instant allegiance. Moreover, people simplified what he said to the point of absurdity.

His new lecture on 'The Value of Art in Modern Life' rested on three principal tenets. The first was that ornament consisted not of super-fluities, but of their purgation. 'I have found that all ugly things are made by those who strive to make something beautiful, and that all beautiful things are made by those who strive to make something useful.' He had come a long way from Gautier's dictum that all art is useless. The second was that bad art arises from taking nature as the ideal. The true painter is not a specialist painting Scottish cattle in an English mist or English cattle in a Scottish mist. His examples of genuine painters were Corot and the Impressionists, by whom he meant Monet and Camille Pissarro, whose shows at Durand Ruel in March and May had evidently won him.[12] He conspicuously failed to celebrate the Pre-Raphaelites who had occupied a central place in his American lectures. The third tenet was that artistic value cannot be measured by its quotient of didacticism. He bowed to Ruskin as one of the greatest men ever produced in England, before he took issue with his old master for estimating a picture 'by the number of noble and moral ideas that he found in it.' His greatest praise was reserved for Whistler as perhaps the first artist not only in England but in all of Europe. Whistler 'had rejected all literary titles for his pictures; indeed, none of his works bore any name but that which signified their tone, and colour, and method of treatment. This, of course, was what painting ought to be; no man ought to show that he was merely the illustrator of history.'[13] Highminded as these views were, they did nothing to infiltrate renaissance with decadence in the way that he had begun to envisage. They were all a bit too sunny. To engage his whole mind, Wilde felt a need for shadows.

The itinerary of Wilde's lectures took him to many places in England, Ireland, and Scotland, from 1 October 1884 to the end of March 1885.* In Edinburgh for the last of them, he called on his old friend Hunter Blair, now a monk, and suddenly sank to his knees and said, 'Pray for me, Dunskie, pray for me.'[14]

Wilde's initial lecture on dress was reported in the press, and a controversy about it began in the *Pall Mall Gazette*. He contributed letters there, defending and expanding his original position, in October and November 1884. Audience interest in dress and home decoration was unfortunately limited, and in the face of shrinking attendance he had no choice but to supplement his lecturing income with some ignoble journalism. Eventually the lectures stopped altogether. Perhaps as a result of his eloquence about dress he became early in 1885 a contributor to the *Pall Mall Gazette*, which in 1882 had been hostile to him. His articles here were unsigned, as was customary, though the custom was one he hated. He also wrote signed articles for the *Dramatic Review* and later for other journals.

---

* Wilde's lectures in the British Isles at this time included: *October 1884*: 1st, lecture on 'Dress' at Ealing; 6th, Liverpool; 8th, Manchester; 9th, 'The Value of Art in Modern Life' and 'Dress' at the Exhibition Hall, York; 14th, 'Dress' at Lesser Victoria-Room, Clifton (near Bristol). *November*: 5th, 'The Value of Art in Modern Life' in Town Hall, Stoke-on-Trent. *December*: 4th, on 'Beauty, Taste and Ugliness in Dress,' at Albert Hall, Leeds; 7th, Glasgow; 11th, Southport; 13th, 'Dress' at Carlisle; ?19th, Glasgow; 20th, two lectures, 'Dress' and 'The Value of Art in Modern Life,' at Queen Street Hall, Edinburgh; ?21st, Crystal Palace.

There followed 21 Irish engagements, December 1884–January 1885, including: *January 1885*: 5th, 'Dress' and 'The Value of Art in Modern Life', at Gaiety Theatre, Dublin; 14th, Clonmel; 17th, Dundalk.

Then: *January 1885*: 21st–22nd, College Hall, Sheffield; 23rd, Huddersfield; 24th, King's Lynn; 25th, Lincoln; 26th, Halifax; 28th, Gainsborough; 29th, Harrogate; 30th, Chesterfield; 31st, York. *February*: 1st, Scarborough; Darlington and Falkirk; 27th, Chesterfield; Stockton, Newcastle, Maryport, Cockermouth, Ulverston, Sunderland, Leicester. *March*: 7th, Leamington; Cheltenham; 10th, Wolverhampton; 11th, Walsall; 12th, Leicester; 14th, Northampton; Colchester, Ipswich, Yarmouth, Norwich, Bury St Edmunds, Cardiff, Swansea; 31st, Newport; Appleton, Birmingham, Peterborough, Edinburgh.

The review was a form that Wilde enjoyed. He made it into a form of chat. Most of the works he dealt with had only an ephemeral interest; instead of reproving them for this he described them pleasantly and usually made them more entertaining than they were. His random comments were best of all. A book on *Dinners and Dishes* enabled him to say that 'the two most remarkable bits of scenery in the States are undoubtedly Delmonico's and the Yosemite Valley.' *Daniel Deronda* was 'that dullest of masterpieces.' While praising the poems of young Marc-André Raffalovich beyond their merits, he noted that they were 'unhealthy and bring with them the heavy odours of the hothouse.' But this, he resumed, 'is to point out neither their defect nor their merit, but their quality merely.' He did however object to Raffalovich's treating the first word of his title, *Tuberose and Meadowsweet*, as if it were a trisyllable, when it should be a disyllable. Raffalovich, as a foreigner not eager to be found guilty of a mispronunciation, wrote to the editor to say that Shelley had committed the same offence, to which Wilde responded cheerfully with a contrary example from the same poet. Raffalovich, a rancorous man, was not pleased.

Several writers had ceased to interest Wilde, Mrs Browning and Symonds among them. Only three aroused his critical antagonism. Rhoda Broughton was one. She was related to the Le Fanus whom he had known in Merrion Square, but her Irish blood had if anything made her impatient with his aestheticism. Reviewing her novel, *Betty's Visions*, Wilde commented that 'whatever harsh criticisms may be passed on the construction of her sentences, she at least possesses that one touch of vulgarity that makes the whole world kin.' George Saintsbury may not have annoyed Wilde personally, as Miss Broughton had, but Wilde was irritated by his pretensions in writing a book about prose style when his own abounded in solecisms. So Saintsbury could say without a quiver, 'constantly right in general,' or 'He saw the rise, and in some instances, the death of Tennyson, Thackeray, Macaulay, Carlyle, Dickens.' The third target was Harry Quilter, well known for his art criticism. Quilter had fulminated in newspaper leaders against the aesthetic movement, and defended Ruskin's views against Whistler's. He dared to buy, he even dared to reconstruct, Whistler's White House in Tite Street, which Godwin had designed and Whistler adorned. Wilde dealt merrily with Quilter as a 'jolly' art critic: 'With the present tendencies of decorative art in England Mr Quilter . . . has but little sympathy, and he makes a gallant appeal to the British householder to stand no more nonsense. Let the honest fellow, he says, on his return from his counting-house tear down the Persian hangings. '(Wilde was busy putting them up in his own Tite Street house.) 'Mr Quilter is quite earnest in his endeavours to elevate art to the dignity of manual labour.'

On larger questions, Wilde was slowly moving towards more complex answers. He is surprisingly willing to consider afresh issues that aestheticism might appear to have already resolved. Perhaps because he so much admired George Sand, as did his mother, he treats her arguments in the famous battle with Flaubert over form and content with unexpected sympathy. He agrees with her that form is not the aim, only the effect. He allows validity to her view that truth and goodness (neither invoked often in his criticism) must accompany beauty, his only reservation being that she puts too high a value on good intentions. Since Wilde is often thought to be an advocate of art for art's sake, that he abjures it here is important; he says it 'is not meant to express the final cause of art, but is merely a formula for creation.' The artist in composition must think only of artistic criteria, but his motive in writing, and the purpose of artistic work, in general, are not to be restricted. Wilde was going far beyond Whistler and Gautier in recognizing the limitations of the old aestheticism they had promulgated.

One subject that embarrasses him is dealt with in 'The Scenery of Shakespeare's Plays,' and several other reviews. Wilde set himself to defend recent efforts by Godwin and others to produce Shakespeare's plays, and neo-Greek plays such as Todhunter's *Helena in Troas*, with archaeological accuracy. He argued that Shakespeare himself had a keen historical sense, and was always filling in by verbal description what was lacking in the scenery and costume of his plays. But realism was a subject that Wilde had pondered since the days at Portora when he asked a master what it meant, and he knew its pitfalls. So he is uneasy, at once endorsing accuracy of detail and acknowledging that the real desideration is unity of artistic effect. He proposes that this unity is best achieved by accuracy of detail, so that perfect accuracy may make for perfect illusion, so long as it is subordinated to the general motive of the play. He distinguishes between fussy archaeology and archaeology used for artistic effect, yet is haunted by the opposite idea, that 'the truest poetry is the most feigning.' In rewriting and retitling the essay later for *Intentions* he calls it 'The Truth of Masks, A Note on Illusion,' when its subject was in fact 'The Truth of Replicas, A Note on Realism.' Reprinting it in *Intentions* he suddenly turned upon himself, realizing that the essay was incompatible with others in the same volume, and added an important palinode:

> Not that I agree with everything that I have said in this essay. There is much with which I entirely disagree. The essay simply represents an artistic standpoint, and in aesthetic criticism, attitude is everything. For in art there is no such thing as a universal truth. A truth in art is that whose contradictory is also true. And just as it is only in art-criticism, and through it, that we can apprehend the platonic theory of ideas, so it is only in art-criticism, and through it, that we can realise Hegel's theory of contraries. The truths of metaphysics are the truth of masks.

Even so qualified, or reversed, the essay did not please him, and he recognized that one day he must discard it from the volume altogether.[15]

Writing about other people's books and plays and lectures, and talking about art, could not satisfy for long the ambition of which he had boasted to Sherard at the time of Rennell Rodd's disaffection. Nothing else was available at the moment, and he and Constance must eat, and eat as well as possible. He abounded in vitality and expectation. He renewed his attempt to get a position as inspector of schools, using Curzon, Mahaffy, and Sayce as references; nothing came of it. For the moment he could not hope, after the fiasco in New York, that any actress could be persuaded to undertake either of his plays. Still he stayed close to the theatre, and persuaded Constance to play a minor part in *Helena in Troas*.

Meanwhile his home life had assumed more definite form. He was often away from Tite Street giving lectures. He consoled Constance with letters, written in his best Olympian:

Dear and Beloved, Here I am, and you at the Antipodes. O execrable facts, that keep our lips from kissing, though our souls are one.

What can I tell you by letter? Alas! nothing that I would tell you. The messages of the gods travel to each other not by pen and ink and indeed your bodily presence here would not make you more real: for I feel your fingers in my hair, and your cheek brushing mine. The air is full of the music of your voice, my soul and body seem no longer mine, but mingled in some exquisite ecstasy with yours. I feel incomplete without you.

Ever and ever yours   OSCAR
Here I stay till Sunday.[16]

The easy assonance of ecstasy and exquisiteness might have disquieted some wives, but Constance had no complaint. Her pregnancy occupied her and her husband delighted her. She does not seem to have guessed that he felt a growing distaste for her swollen body. This has been related in the unreliable testimony of Frank Harris, whose made-up speeches for Wilde rarely ring true. Yet it seems plausible from the sequel that Wilde did say the substance of what Harris relates:

When I married, my wife was a beautiful girl, white and slim as a lily, with dancing eyes and gay rippling laughter like music. In a year or so the flowerlike grace had all vanished; she became heavy, shapeless, deformed. She dragged herself about the house in uncouth misery with drawn blotched face and hideous body, sick at heart because of our love. It was dreadful. I tried to be kind to her; forced myself to touch and kiss her; but she was sick always, and – oh! I cannot recall it, it is all loathsome . . . I used to wash my mouth and open the window to cleanse my lips in the pure air.[17]

It was unfortunate, given a husband so easily disgusted, that Constance had their two sons in rapid succession. Cyril was born on 5 June 1885. His godfather was an explorer, Walter Harris. After eight months Constance became pregnant again, the second child being born on Guy Fawkes Day, 5 November 1886. The parents changed the birthdate to 3 November. Wilde had hoped for a girl, as his mother had hoped for one at the time of his own birth – another Isola, perhaps. But it was a boy, christened androgynously Vyvyan. Ruskin, asked to stand as godfather for him as he had done for a son of Burne-Jones and a daughter of Alfred Hunt, declined on the grounds of age, so Mortimer Menpes, a disciple of Whistler, then in good standing with the artist, was asked and consented.

The two years of childbearing tended to separate the parents. Eager to promote dress reform, Wilde had to make do during his wife's pregnancies without a model. Loving dinner parties as others might love hunting, and performing at them so prodigiously, he had to accept for himself many invitations intended for both. At their own parties, Constance became conspicuous for little practicalities, which she would often voice in the middle of one of her husband's grand flights, that she had heard rehearsed many times. Jean-Joseph Renaud, a French writer who translated some works of Wilde, was occasionally at dinner, and recalled how Constance would sometimes complain, 'But Oscar, yesterday you told that story differently,' or, impatient with his embellishments, would brusquely interrupt and finish the story herself. Mrs Claude Beddington tells of a dinner when someone asked Wilde, 'Where have you been this past week?' He answered that he had been at 'an exquisite Elizabethan country house, with emerald lawns, stately yew hedges, scented rose-gardens, cool lily ponds, gay herbaceous borders, ancestral oaks, and strutting peacocks.' 'And did she act well, Oscar?' asked Constance in a small voice.[18] He had gone to a play.

Little by little Wilde, though he remained fond of Constance, lost enthusiasm for playing husband. He did not feel this way about being father, for his boys delighted him. His partiality for Cyril was already patent, but he loved and watched over both of them. His disaffection from his wife seems implicit in the eagerness of his return to the society of young men, especially in Oxford and Cambridge.

Perilous Connections

The proper basis for marriage is a mutual misunderstanding.

One of these was Harry Marillier, the boy who had brought Wilde his coffee at the house in Salisbury Street and had received in return tutoring in Greek. At the beginning of November 1885 Marillier, who was at Peterhouse in Cambridge, wrote to Wilde and urged him to come see a performance of the *Eumenides* at the beginning of December. Wilde was charmed by the invitation, and in accepting it advanced the date of their meeting. He invited Marillier to visit him in London, and afterwards bewailed that he had had to leave his friend, probably for a lecture engagement:

> Harry, why did you let me catch my train? I would have liked to have gone to the National Gallery with you, and looked at Velasquez's pale evil King, at Titian's Bacchus with the velvet panthers, and at that strange heaven of Angelico's where everyone seems made of gold and purple and fire, and which for all that, looks to me ascetic – everyone dead and decorative! I wonder will it really be like that, but I wonder without caring. *Je trouve la terre aussi belle que le ciel – et le corps aussi beau que l'âme.** If I do live again I would like it to be as a flower – no soul but perfectly beautiful. Perhaps for my sins I shall be made a red geranium!
>
> And your paper on Browning? You must tell me of it. In our meeting again there was a touch of Browning – keen curiosity, wonder, delight.
>
> It was an hour intensely dramatic and intensely psychological, and, in art, only Browning can make action and psychology one. When am I to see you again? Write me a long letter to Tite Street, and I will get it when I come back. I wish you were here, Harry. But in the vacation you must often come and see me, and we will talk of the poets and forget Piccadilly! I have never learned anything except from people younger than myself and you are infinitely young.
>
> OSCAR WILDE

The French quotation was from Gautier's *Mademoiselle de Maupin*, which Wilde characterized in a review of this time as 'that golden book of spirit and sense, that holy writ of beauty.'[19] Since Pater had lent it to Wilde at the inception of their close friendship, it was perhaps indicative that he should cite it to Marillier at a comparable moment of waxing interest.

On 27 November 1885 they met again, at Cambridge. Marillier belonged to a group that called itself 'cicadas' and he had secured the invitation for Wilde to come to see the *Eumenides* as their common guest. Another 'cicada' was J. H. Badley, later to found Bedales School; it fell to Badley to entertain Wilde for breakfast in his rooms. A dish of *oeufs à l'Aurore* placed before Wilde moved him to say with pleasure that it was like 'the standard of the Emperor of Japan,' the allusion if not the enthusiasm being lost on Badley. They talked of poetry: Badley's favorite was Shelley, a choice Wilde would not allow because Shelley was 'merely a boy's poet.' 'Keats is the greatest of them,' he assured the young man. Wilde observed that Badley did not smoke, and asked him why. 'An inherited aversion,' said Badley, 'though I have no doubt that I'm missing thereby what is good in moderation.' 'Ah, Badley,' Wilde rejoined,

* 'I find the earth as beautiful as the sky – and the body as beautiful as the soul.'

'nothing is good in moderation. You cannot know the good in anything till you have torn the heart out of it by excess.' He would give the same advice to André Gide later on.

It was during his visit to Cambridge for the *Eumenides*, that Wilde was prompted to entertain his young friends with a story. His having a child perhaps made the story take the form of a fairy tale, though Cyril was as yet too young to listen. He would call it later 'The Happy Prince,' and it was so well received by the Cambridge students that on returning to his room he wrote it down. 'The Happy Prince' turns on the contrast, used in some of his later writings too, of an older, taller lover with a younger, smaller beloved. In this case the roles are played by members of different species and even different orders of existence, for the prince is a statue and the beloved a swallow.

In the story the swallow is at first in love with a reed, who is female, but he renounces her in favor of the prince. The Prince passes his entire life in the palace of Sans-Souci, but has a keen sympathy for the oppressed and destitute. On his pedestal above the city he sees and laments its wretchedness and sorrow, tears falling from his sapphire eyes. He begs the swallow to take, one by one, the ruby from his sword pommel, and the sapphires from his eyes, to alleviate three of the worst cases, a sick boy, a struggling playwright, and a little match-girl. The swallow, though pressed for time (he is waited for in Egypt), carries out the commissions, then comes to take leave and asks to kiss the Prince's hand. 'No, no,' says the prince, 'you must kiss me on the lips, for I love you.' As he does so, the Prince's heart breaks, and so does the swallow's – their love is perfected, and disinfected, in death. They are transfigured and borne off to God's hand. The self-cancelling nature of their love, which dies in its expression, conforms with a notion of Wilde and Pater about the limit of every energy. In *De Profundis*, Wilde explained that he had always known that the garden had another half besides the beautiful one, and that in 'The Happy Prince' he had given expression to it.

The day after Wilde told this story, half a dozen of the 'cicadas' went down to the station to see him off. They clustered round his carriage window as he kept up a stream of epigrams, timed to culminate as the train drew out of the station. But something went wrong, and the train, having started, backed in again. The students were still on the platform, but Wilde, rather than risk anticlimax, closed his window and remained absorbed in his newspaper until the train drew out again. From London he wrote to Marillier:

> Does it all seem a dream, Harry? Ah! what is not a dream? To me it is, in a fashion, a memory of music. I remember bright young faces, and grey misty quadrangles, Greek forms passing through Gothic cloisters, life playing among ruins, and, what I love best in the world, Poetry and Paradox dancing together!

Wilde's strongest and most invitational letter to Marillier came early in 1886. By now he was imparting a doctrine rather than recalling a mood, and the doctrine is one that might well evoke thoughts of sin without commitment, as if to exonerate those thoughts before they became blameworthy.

> You too have the love of things impossible – ἔρως τῶν ἀδυνάτων – *l'amour de l'impossible* (how do men name it?). Sometime you will find, even as I have found, that there is no such thing as a romantic experience; there are romantic memories, and there is the desire of romance – that is all. Our most fiery moments of ecstasy are merely shadows of what somewhere else we have felt, or of what we long some day to feel. So at least it seems to me. And, strangely enough, what comes of all this is a curious mixture of ardour and of indifference. I myself would sacrifice everything for a new experience, and I know there is no such thing as a new experience at all. I think I would more readily die for what I do not believe in than for what I hold to be true. I would go to the stake for a sensation and be a sceptic to the last! Only one thing remains infinitely fascinating to me, the mystery of moods. To be master of these moods is exquisite, to be mastered by them more exquisite still. Sometimes I think that the artistic life is a long and lovely suicide, and am not sorry that it is so.
>
> And much of this I fancy you yourself have felt: much also remains for you to feel. There is an unknown land full of strange flowers and subtle perfumes, a land of which it is joy of all joys to dream, a land where all things are perfect and poisonous.

After such knowledge what virtue? Wilde had combined at last poison and perfection, qualities he found also in Baudelaire,[20] decadence and renaissance. 'Rappacini's Daughter' of Hawthorne, as well as Huysmans's *A Rebours*, was also in his mind. He wanted to exhibit for Marillier an image of life as delicious decline rather than wholesome growth. A latter-day Faust, he knew in advance that every pleasure would discontent him at last, and saw himself as the prey to the very moods he sought to experience. To fall victim to himself was to bring one's experience to the utmost bound; unfortunately it was like committing suicide, as Dorian Gray would discover.

The Poet and the Painter

One cannot extort affection with a knife. To awaken gratitude in the ungrateful were as vain as to try to waken the dead by cries.

Wilde's urge to find a new life for himself was adumbrated in his correspondence with Marillier and reinforced by tension with Whistler. This increased also in 1886. Their relationship had always been nervous.

Whistler, twenty years older, could never quite accept that Wilde, however imperfect his early writings, had genius too; but he had put up with Wilde's praise for almost ten years contentedly enough. Wilde liked to joke at his own expense, and Whistler was glad to joke at Wilde's expense too. His advantage was that he talked to score, while Wilde talked merely to enthrall. A Whistler breakfast served generous helpings of gall along with the coffee. Over the years there had been many humiliations. One day at the Lambs Club Wilde showed Whistler a poem he had written, probably an impressionistic one such as 'Le Panneau' or 'Les Ballons.' Whistler returned it to him without a word. Wilde was obliged to ask, 'Well, do you perceive any worth?' 'It's worth its weight in gold,' said the artist. The poem was written on the thinnest of tissue paper. Then there had been a meeting of the Hogarth Club which they both attended in November 1883; Wilde was quoted in *Punch* as having compared Mary Anderson, whom he had seen again in *Romeo and Juliet*, with Sarah Bernhardt. According to *Punch*, he said, 'Sarah Bernhardt is all moonlight and sunlight combined, exceedingly terrible, magnificently glorious. Miss Anderson is pure and fearless as a mountain daisy. Full of change as a river. Tender, fresh, sparkling, brilliant, superb, placid.' On reading this Wilde telegraphed to Whistler, '*Punch* too ridiculous. When you and I are together we never talk about anything except ourselves.' To this came the reply, also by wire, 'No, no, Oscar, you forget. When you and I are together, we never talk about anything except me.' The telegrams were published by mutual consent in the *World* of 14 November. A third one is said to have contained Wilde's reply: 'It is true, Jimmy, we were talking about you, but I was thinking of myself.'[21] The narcissists outdid each other.

Whistler tended to come out on top in these exchanges, but that was because he was ready to kill as well as wound. He had begun to cherish a resentment of Wilde ever since the speech to the art students of the Royal Academy. Although at the time he had offered his suggestions freely enough, he disliked hearing Wilde credited with ideas he regarded as his own. Worse still, Wilde had a way of not sticking to Whistler's script. He was as apt to correct the master as to copy him. So Whistler decided to do something unprecedented for him, and give a lecture himself. Archibald Forbes, that old enemy of Wilde, was consulted, and introduced Whistler to Mrs D'Oyly Carte. She arranged for him to lecture in the Prince's Hall where Wilde had delivered his 'Impressions of America' to the audience that included Whistler. He would give the same lecture later in Oxford and Cambridge, and to several groups in London, including the Royal Academy art students whom Wilde had addressed. To make clear the singularity of the occasion, Whistler scheduled the lecture at the unheard of time of ten o'clock, on the evening of 20 February 1885. An elaborate seating plan was drawn up so as to leave nothing to chance, and he had a dress rehearsal the day before.

A good deal of what became known as 'Mr Whistler's Ten o'Clock' was devoted to scoffing at Wilde. The phrasing was heavy with Biblical inversions: 'lamented not,' 'attracted him not,' 'questioned not.' Whistler chortled from the outset, 'Art is upon the town!' and went on to declare with distaste, 'The voice of the aesthete is heard in the land.' He was not to be identified with aestheticism. Without naming him he took Wilde to task for a series of offenses, beginning with dilettantism about dress reform. What the aesthete wanted, he said, was costume, but 'costume is not dress.' As for Grecian wear, Whistler mocked it, 'Haphazard from the shoulders hang the garments of the hawker – combining in their person the motley of many manners with the medley of the mummers' closet.' He disagreed with Wilde (and so with Ruskin) over the idea that once society decayed, art had to decay too. 'It is false, this teaching of decay. The master stands in no relation to the moment at which he occurs.' Art moved in sublime indifference to social change. The rest of the world might grow as melancholy as it wished, but Art went on rejoicing in its own creation. It had no concern with social betterment, indeed, it was so capricious as to prefer the artistic opium eaters of Nanking to the artless do-gooders of Switzerland. He then delivered himself of two snubs, one to humanity, 'There never was an artistic period, there never was an artistic nation.' The other was directed to Nature. 'To say to the painter, that Nature should be taken as she is, is to say to the player, that he may sit on the piano.' Nature was tolerable only insofar as it was susceptible of artistic improvement.

Wilde retorted with two articles, in the *Pall Mall Gazette* for 21 and 28 February 1885. His tone was less ruffled than Whistler had hoped, mixing banter and approval for 'the fine Virginia gentleman' whom he still thought of as his friend. The lecture was a masterpiece, he declared. Having said that, he felt free to say other things. He can hardly have expected to please by echoing the alliterative *m*'s of Whistler's reference to Wilde's 'motley of many manners' in his altitudinous description of the five foot four inch Whistler as 'a miniature Mephistopheles mocking the majority.' He disagreed with Whistler's onslaught upon humanity: 'the arts are made for life and not life for the arts.' To encourage people to ignore the environment – the vulgar objects in their rooms, or the unattractive clothes they felt obliged to wear – was to encourage ugliness. Wilde agreed that 'all costumes are caricatures. The basis of Art is not the Fancy Ball. Where there is loveliness of dress, there is no dressing up.' His innovations were not to be dismissed as stagey. He might have replied in Charles Ricketts's words that Whistler, 'with his yellow tie, wasp-waist, beige-coloured overcoat, wand-like stick and flat-brimmed top hat' gave the impression 'of a Hungarian band-master'.[22]

Wilde went on to make clearer his radical differences from Whistler. Art, he insisted, did have a relation to society and was the product of a certain milieu. It rose or fell as society progressed or decayed, and could be renewed only if society were renewed. Whistler had asserted that only painters can judge painting. Wilde insisted that only artists could judge art, but the supreme artist is not the painter (in whose work Whistler had found 'poetry') but the poet, in whose work the painter's images or the musician's sounds or ideas are enclosed. 'And so to the poet beyond all others are these mysteries known; to Edgar Allan Poe and to Baudelaire, not to Benjamin West and Paul Delaroche.' His report concluded with the tribute, 'For that he is indeed one of the very greatest masters of painting is my opinion. And I may add that in this opinion Mr Whistler himself entirely concurs.'

Whistler took neither praise nor mockery in good part. 'I have read your exquisite article in the *Pall Mall*,' he wrote to Wilde, leaving the word 'exquisite' to cut both ways, though he had used the word favorably himself. That Wilde should fancy his title to the name Poet as good as Whistler's to the name Painter was only one of the irritations: 'Nothing is more delicate, in the flattery of "the Poet" to "the Painter," than the naïveté of "the Poet," in the choice of his Painters – Benjamin West and Paul Delaroche!' Wilde scuttled beyond his grasp:

> Dear Butterfly, By the aid of a biographical dictionary I discovered that there were once two painters, called Benjamin West and Paul Delaroche, who recklessly took to lecturing on Art.
>
> As of their works nothing at all remains, I conclude that they explained themselves away. Be warned in time, James; and remain, as I do, incomprehensible: to be great is to be misunderstood. *Tout à vous*
> Private   OSCAR
> Jimmy! You must *stamp* your letters – they are dear at twopence – and also do send them in proper time. 2.30 on Monday. *Ciel!*[23]

The antagonists were sharpening their weapons for a clash which did not come until more than a year later. It was precipitated by Whistler's discovery that a committee devoted to art reform and opposed to the Royal Academy was to number among its members Harry Quilter and Oscar Wilde. He wrote at once:

> Gentlemen, I am naturally interested in any effort made among Painters to prove that they are alive, but when I find, thrust in the van of your leaders, the body of my dead 'Arry, I know that putrefaction alone can result. When, following 'Arry, there comes an Oscar, you finish in farce, and bring upon yourselves the scorn and ridicule of your *confrères* in Europe.
>
> What has Oscar in common with Art? except that he dines at our tables and picks from our platters the plums for the pudding he peddles in the provinces. Oscar – the amiable, irresponsible, esurient Oscar – with no more sense of a picture than of the fit of a coat, has the courage of the opinions – of others!

With 'Arry and Oscar you have avenged the Academy.
  I am, Gentlemen, yours obediently,

[Butterfly emblem]

Again Whistler sent his letter to the *World*, where Edmund Yates reliably published it on 17 November 1886. It could hardly have been more savage. To attack the dandy's clothes was injury enough; to link him with Quilter, whom Wilde had so recently reviewed with contempt in the *Pall Mall Gazette*, exacerbated the injury. Whistler knew it would. He also appeared to begrudge Wilde those Sunday morning breakfasts where he had been his guest: in other words, if Whistler was short, as Wilde had said, then Wilde was fat. Still, no one ever outdid Wilde in hospitality, as Whistler knew well enough.

Whistler sent a copy of his letter to Wilde with a line, 'Oscar, you must really keep outside "the radius"!' The note suggests that he thought Wilde would put up with his insults. He was right. Wilde salvaged a little by replying on 24 November in the *World*, 'Atlas, this is very sad! With our James "vulgarity begins at home", and should be allowed to stay there. –*A vous*, OSCAR WILDE.' Whistler replied privately, or claimed he had, '"A poor thing," Oscar – but, for once, I suppose, "your own"!' Wilde swallowed this insult as well. We can be sure he did because on 29 November of the following year, 1887, he helped Whistler receive visitors to the Suffolk Gallery where Whistler was exhibiting some of his paintings; they were back on good terms except that Wilde was drawing off some of Whistler's admirers, a situation Whistler could not brook.[24] It was a tribute to Wilde's good company that Whistler waited so long before depriving himself of it.

The Murder of Whistler

One should never make one's début with a scandal. One should reserve that to give an interest to one's old age.

Faced with this hostility, Wilde might well relish the company of worshipful young men. His unconsummated attachment for Marillier had whetted his appetite for a love more perfect or at least more poisonous. Shortly before his death Wilde told Reggie Turner how he went shopping with his wife at Swan & Edgar's in Piccadilly Circus, and saw the painted boys on the pavement. 'Something clutched at my heart like ice,' he said.[25] Curiously his 'ideal husband' in the play of that name uses the same figure: 'I never knew what terror was before. It is as if a hand of ice were laid upon one's heart.' Ice was to turn to fire.

For more than two years Wilde had restlessly performed his roles as

258

husband and father. Whistler dubbed him '*le bourgeois malgré lui*,' a label Wilde was determined not to accept. He required stronger seasoning than an adoring wife and adorable sons could provide. He was conscious of regions of his personality that he had not yet explored, on Aristotle's principle of total self-realization as the goal of every organism. Wilde was not comfortable reposing in his previous phases. He was fond of quoting Pater's admonition, 'Failure is to form habits,' and Emerson's remark, 'I am always insincere, as knowing that there are other moods.' His letter to Marillier had said, 'To be master of these moods is exquisite, to be mastered by them more exquisite still.' Self-exfoliation might come through self-abandonment. He vaulted from stance to stance, putting on new selves as he put on new clothes.

Though never one to keep a secret, he had always been attracted by a secret life. Both *Vera* and *The Duchess of Padua* offered concealed identities and hidden propensities. This secret life was related to contrary impulses which he found within himself, a 'voracious Irony' (as Baudelaire called it) which led him to say in 'Humanitad' that we are both 'The lips betraying and the life betrayed,' every man his own Judas. He wanted to offer and withdraw himself at the same time, as his letter to Marillier said: 'I would go to the stake for a sensation and be a sceptic to the last.' That this policy might lead to the stake, or at least to calamity, he had always understood, from the days when he told his Portora schoolfellows that he longed to be the defendant in 'Regina versus Wilde.'

He was well aware of the dangers of being homosexual, though he had consorted freely with those who were. His delight in young male bodies and in intense friendships with men was patent. Yet he had till now managed not to commit himself about physical as once about spiritual things. This was his state of mind when he met Robert Ross at Oxford in 1886. Ross, with 'the face of Puck' (as Wilde said), and short stature, looked like a boy. He had been beaten for reading Wilde's poems. What must have astonished Wilde was that Ross, so young and yet so knowing, was determined to seduce him. For an 'antinomian,' as Wilde described himself, there could be no objection on moral grounds. Wilde acceded, perhaps out of curiosity or caprice. He was not attracted to anal coition, so Ross presumably introduced him to the oral and intercrural intercourse he practiced later. First as lover and then as friend, Ross was to keep a permanent place in Wilde's life.

The young man was a grandson of the governor general of Canada, and a son of Canada's Attorney General. After his father's early death the family moved to London, and he was put under the guardianship of his elder brother, Alexander. When Ross and Wilde met, he was being prepared by the well-known London crammer W. B. Scoones for admission to King's College, Cambridge. Their affair was carried on sporadically when Ross went up to King's in the autumn of 1888. There he entered with zest into college life: though small, he rowed bow in the college boat, and in his first term he helped start an iconoclastic publication called *The Gadfly*. His tutor was appropriately Wilde's old friend Oscar Browning. Ross, deeply affected by Wilde, annoyed his fellow Kingsmen with his version of Wilde's aesthetic manner, including long hair. He also wrote an article in the *Granta* on 1 March 1889 attacking the choice for a new dean (E. H. Douty). There followed an unpleasant event: a junior tutor named A. A. Tilley, one of the dean's supporters, egged on a group of undergraduates to grab Ross as he came out of hall and dump him in the college fountain. (This was on 8 March 1889.) The joke turned sour when Ross caught pneumonia and a mental disturbance diagnosed as brain fever. The *Granta* on 15 March carried a rhyme about it,

> With joy and exultation
> Still shall the tale be told
> How six men nobly set on one
> In the brave days of old.

Browning tried unsuccessfully to have Tilley dismissed, and Ross and his brother contemplated legal action. But the other students declined to testify against Tilley, and Ross's only satisfaction was that Tilley was obliged to apologize publicly to him in hall.[26]

Ross left Cambridge in the winter term. He had quarreled with his mother and sister by disclosing his homosexuality, and was not welcome at home. At his brother's suggestion he went to Edinburgh in the autumn of 1889 and took a job on Henley's *Scots Observer*. He would later run an art gallery and write art criticism. His self-written epitaph was, 'Here lies one whose name was writ in hot water.' Wilde's verdict was that Ross was 'wasting a youth that has always been, and always will be, full of promise.'[27]

What endeared him to Wilde was his wit, his ease, his loyalty, his buoyancy. They liked each other, and for a time their friendship was passionate. It marked a transformation of Wilde's life. The effect can be measured by comparing two versions of a passage in *The Picture of Dorian Gray*. Dorian has won a bad reputation for unspecified acts, then commits himself irrevocably to an evil life by stabbing the painter of his portrait. In the first version, published in *Lippincott's Magazine*, Wilde wrote, 'It was the 7th of October, the eve of his own thirty-second birthday, as he often remembered afterwards.' When the novel was republished in book form, he altered the date and Dorian's age, 'It was on the ninth of November, the eve of his own thirty-eighth birthday, as he often remembered afterwards.' Altering Dorian's age would be gratuitous if Wilde had not begun to feel that the first reference was too close to actuality, since October 1886 had marked his own thirty-second birthday, and his thirty-third year had been dislocated by the beginning of his affair with Ross.

Both Ross and Wilde told friends that their homosexual encounter had been Wilde's first. Ross said to his close friend Christopher Millard (Wilde's bibliographer) that he felt responsible for Wilde's two sons because he had led their father into homosexual activity. Arthur Ransome stated in his study of Wilde, on the basis of Ross's information, that the incident had happened in 1886. 'Who do you think seduced me?' Wilde asked Reggie Turner, who could not guess. 'Little Robbie,' Wilde confided.[28] Ross turned seventeen on 25 May 1886, and this age is one that Wilde returns to in his writings as if it meant something special to him. It is the age of Dorian's first love, Sibyl Vane, and also the age of Shakespeare's boy lover, Willie Hughes, as Wilde reconstructs that relationship in 'The Portrait of Mr W.H.' Wilde seems to have his initiation by Ross in mind when he canonizes him in a letter as 'St Robert of Phillimore' (Phillimore Gardens being where Ross's family lived), 'Lover and Martyr – a saint known in *Hagiographia* for his extraordinary power, not in resisting, but in supplying temptations to others. This he did in the solitude of great cities, to which he retired at the comparatively early age of eight.'[29]

Ross earned the canonization partly because of his devout Catholicism, a subject they joked about. Wilde twitted Ross in a pseudo-religious story recalled by Ada Leverson. 'There was a certain saint, who was called Saint Robert of Phillimore. Every night, while the sky was yet black, he would rise from his bed and, falling on his knees, pray to God that He, of His great bounty, would cause the sun to rise and make bright the earth. And always, when the sun rose, Saint Robert knelt again and thanked God that this miracle had been vouchsafed. Now, one night, Saint Robert, wearied by the vast number of more than usually good deeds he had done that day, slept so soundly that when he awoke the sun had already risen, and the earth was already bright. For a few moments Saint Robert looked grave and troubled, but presently he fell down on his knees and thanked God that, despite the neglectfulness of His servant, He had yet caused the sun to rise and make bright the earth.'[30]

That Dorian Gray should kill a painter, who in the original draft (as Wilde told the translator Jean-Joseph Renaud)[31] was clearly and libelously Whistler, makes the book more a record of Wilde's personal feelings than might appear. His homicidal impulse toward Whistler ran concurrently with his homosexual impulse towards Ross, also shadowed in the novel. One fantasy remained a fantasy and, for fear of a libel action, the image of Whistler was removed from the text. The other was realized. For Wilde homosexual love roused him from pasteboard conformity to the expression of latent desires. After 1886 he was able to think of himself as a criminal, moving guiltily among the innocent. His wife was the most innocent of all. ('For the invert,' says Proust in *Sodome et Gomorrhe*, 'vice begins . . . when he takes his pleasure with women.') Up to that time Wilde could think of himself as misunderstood; now he had to promote misunderstanding. Instead of challenging Victorian society by words, he engaged it by deeds as well.

Constance was the mother of their children, and he had no intention of giving them up. She was as loving as ever, in a way he could no longer enjoy. He had to find a pretext for their remaining sexually apart. Her brother Otho said there was a virtual divorce, meaning that sexual relations ceased.[32] According to Otho, Constance suspected her husband's reorientation only once, and that was not until 1895, when she came back to the house unexpectedly. Since she continued to live with him, she must have been told something absolutely convincing. A likely conjecture is that he confessed to having caught syphilis at Oxford, perhaps telling her that he had suffered a recurrence of the disease after a long remission. Celibacy was the only answer.

One day Louise Jopling showed Constance a photograph taken at a party at which Constance had not been present. Mrs Jopling had posed with her arms around Oscar Wilde's neck. Constance's response was strange. She showed no sign of jealousy, only looked at the picture for a moment and said, with unexpected sadness, 'Poor Oscar!'[33] The serious embrace of women was forbidden him.

EXALTATIONS

CHAPTER XI

Disciple to Master

Personality is a very mysterious thing. A man cannot always be estimated by what he does. He may keep the law and yet be worthless. He may break the law, and yet be fine. He may be bad, without ever doing anything bad. He may commit a sin against society, and yet realize through that sin his own perfection.

New Anatomies

At Oxford Wilde had made the problem of becoming or not becoming a Roman Catholic the nub of much of his verse. He was now able to make his experience of marriage and counter-marriage the center of his career in prose. Homosexuality fired his mind. It was the major stage in his discovery of himself. Much of what he had sponsored up to now, beauty as understood by the Pre-Raphaelites or embodied in Lillie Langtry, ceased to interest him. The earnestness with which he had lectured both in America and in England did not go with his changed outlook. Although he kept much of his admiration for old idols like Ruskin and Pater, he could now see that Ruskin was too innocent, and Pater too hesitant, to serve him as models. They were also too serious. Ironic frivolity, with dark insinuation, was the compound through which he now sought to express himself.

To the rest of the world he appeared to be lying fallow, or, to use the metaphor of the *Pall Mall Gazette* on 16 September 1887, 'Oscar's star has been low in the horizon since he cut his hair and became "Benedick the married man."' But during these years he began to think and talk the narratives and dialogues which he would almost casually write down in the next decade. 'Talk itself is a sort of spiritualised action,' he said on 4 May 1887.[1] There were more fairy tales, then short stories, and then dialogues, all closely bound to his experience though held at some distance in fictional and dramatic forms.

His audiences were his own children, especially Cyril, women, who had always been eager to listen to him, and a new group with whom he flirted

265

by spellbinding them. Among them Ross had a permanent but not exclusive place. Harry Marillier and the Cambridge group faded out, but other young men interested in the arts and each other were not hard to find. For a time Wilde was friendly with André Raffalovich, the young poet and novelist from Paris who had heard him lecture in the United States in 1882, and had himself emigrated to London two years later. Raffalovich had a good deal of money and entertained lavishly. Wilde came to lunch with Pater and Maxwell at his house, and attended evening parties where Mrs Jopling, Comyns Carr, Henry James, George Moore, and many others congregated. Raffalovich was said to be so ugly that his mother had sent him to London because she could not bear to look at him. Still, Wilde did not complain about his looks until later. At the beginning, Raffalovich recalls, Wilde remarked to him, 'You could give me a new thrill. You have the right measure of romance and cynicism.' They met often enough for Wilde to caution the young man, 'You know, you and I, Sandy, we must be most careful of the people we are seen with. I am so conspicuous and you are not *le premier venu.*' A particular reason for behaving circumspectly after September 1889 was the Cleveland Street scandal, which drove Lord Arthur Somerset out of England because of alleged offenses with telegraph boys at a homosexual brothel. Wilde and Raffalovich talked openly about sexual matters, and Raffalovich was struck by Wilde's evident excitement over Rachilde's *Monsieur Vénus*, in which a lesbian dresses her lover as a man – a costume which eventually leads to the lover's death in a duel. Wilde delighted in telling the story to his friends. Such conversations eventually led to a rupture with Raffalovich; it was unwittingly precipitated by Constance's remark, 'Oscar says he likes you so much – that you have such nice improper talks together.' Raffalovich took offense, or says he did.[2]

He began his role of incubus in Wilde's life by a novel, *A Willing Exile*, published in 1890. It made Wilde's circle sound as obnoxious as *Dorian Gray* made it sound fascinating. Raffalovich represented the Wildes as Cyprian and Daisy Brome:

> Mrs Brome, of course, knew many men. Cyprian was, or seemed to be, intimate with countless young or youngish men; they were all curiously alike. Their voices, the cut of their clothes, the curl of their hair, the brims of their hats, the parties they went to: Daisy could not see much difference between them . . . Affectation characterised all these men, and the same sort of affectation. They were all gushers, professional gushers . . . Married (some were married) or unmarried, they gushed alike, only some were ruder than others, and some were duller than others . . .
>
> Cyprian's cult for his own looks . . . increased instead of diminished. He lived with people who talked much about beauty . . . He had acquired the habit of comparing himself to every one he met and of debating who was better looking, he or the other . . . He had two flowers (or rather, bunches of flowers) sent him every day, one before lunch, and the other before

dinner. His clothes much occupied him; he was never tired of discussing male fashions, and sometimes Daisy, after having been away an hour, would find him and a chum still pursuing their analysis of another man's garments.[3]

Having accustomed himself to hostile trumpeting, Wilde did not bother about Raffalovich's penny whistle.

Relations were easier with Richard Le Gallienne, who at seventeen heard Wilde lecture in Birkenhead in 1883, and instantly found his own literary calling in Wilde's example. By the late Eighties the handsome poet, whom Wilde called the angel Gabriel in Rossetti's *Annunciation* and Swinburne called 'Shelley with a chin,' was a friend and frequent guest. He stayed with the Wildes for three days, and was presented with a copy of *Poems* inscribed 'To Richard Le Gallienne, poet and lover, from Oscar Wilde. A summer day in June '88.' To which he responded with a poem entitled, 'With Oscar Wilde, A Summer-Day in June '88,' printed on handmade paper with a silk-sewn paper cover and the further inscription, 'This copy of verse I have made for my friend Oscar Wilde, as a love-token, and in secret memory of a summer day in June '88. R. Le G.' Le Gallienne accepted Wilde's praise with pleasure but had the prudence to remark to a friend in 1888 that two letters from the master were 'very rich.' In a letter of a slightly later date, 1 December 1890, Wilde, after fulsomely evaluating Le Gallienne's latest book, went on, 'I want so much to see you: when can that be? Friendship and love like ours need not meetings, but they are delightful. I hope the laurels are not too thick across your brow for me to kiss your eyelids.'[4]

Another exceptionally handsome young man was Bernard Berenson, who came to Wilde with an introduction, and was at once invited to stay in Tite Street. He found Wilde exhausted by society, whose luncheon parties he would return from in the late afternoon. 'What was it like?' Berenson asked. 'Oh, terrible.' 'Then why did you stay so long?' The people fascinated him, Wilde said. 'There is something about them that is irresistibly attractive. They are more alive. They breathe a finer air. They are more free than we are.' Wilde found Berenson equally irresistible, and made advances which were resisted. 'You are completely without feeling, you are made of stone,' he informed him.[5]

Not content with the company of possible or actual lovers, Wilde prided himself on leading a life not double but multiple. He could be with Parnell and Gladstone one night, with Wilson Barrett and Ellen Terry the next, with young men the next. And Constance, with his children, was always there, to neglect or not. She had her own interests, on which he looked benevolently. These led her to political meetings. Ross, who felt that Constance disliked him, was inclined to depreciate her spirit and indi-viduality. The newspapers of the time give evidence to the contrary. She had things to say, worthy if not exhilarating, and overcame her shyness to say them. On 16 April 1888 she addressed a conference sponsored by the Women's Committee of the International Arbitration and Peace Association. 'Children should be taught in the nursery to be against war,' she declared. 'It has been suggested that toy soldiers and toy guns should be kept from the children. I do not think much good can be done that way. It is impossible in London for children not to see soldiers, and, seeing them, to like their bright clothes and upright bearing. At the same time, a wise mother can instill into the child a dislike of war.'[6] She published, in 1889 and 1892, two books of children's stories. During 1888 and 1889 she edited the *Gazette* of the Rational Dress Society. The speech she gave on 6 November 1888 advocated lighter clothing and divided skirts instead of petticoats. (When presented to the Queen in 1887, however, the dress she wore was an exact copy of the fashion at the time that Victoria had ascended the throne.)* She brought her husband along to a Hyde Park demonstration in support of the dock strike on 1 September 1889. When Lady Sandhurst campaigned on a feminist platform for a seat on the London County Council, Constance took an active part. Her candidate had a majority, but was disqualified, being a woman.[7]

On 24 May 1889 W. T. Stead reported in the *Pall Mall Gazette*, 'I was astonished and delighted to note yesterday at the conference of the women's Liberal Foundation how very much Mrs Oscar Wilde has improved in public speaking, and I shall not be surprised if in a few years Mrs Wilde has become one of the most popular among "platform ladies."' He also commended her 'tasteful and elegant costume of some golden brown material.'

In 1885 and later Constance and Oscar Wilde were moving into larger circles, together or separately. Wilde had stopped lecturing: to the extent that Britain could be made beauty-conscious, he had done the job. To the extent that America could be satirized, he had done that too. The message had worn thin from repetition. His last reported lecture took place in March 1888, and was on a new subject, the poet Chatterton. In some ways Chatterton, whom Wilde had read carefully, was a better model for him than Keats, because of his criminal propensities, and a better model than the forger Wainewright, because of his artistic power. Wilde sought eagerly for analogues to his own new mode of life, and found one in a young man who used his genius to forge Jacobean plays. The lecture notes show how Wilde rehearsed the events of Chatterton's short life, and proposed a justification for them:

> Was he [a] mere forger with literary powers or a great artist? The latter is the right view. Chatterton may not have had the moral conscience which is

---

* The *Lady's Pictorial* for 8 January 1887 noted another occasion on which Mr and Mrs Wilde appeared wearing matching costumes, in the same shade of Lincoln green.

truth to fact – but he had the artistic conscience which is truth to Beauty.
He had the artist's yearning to represent and if perfect representation
seemed to him to demand forgery he needs must forge. Still this forgery
came from the desire of artistic self-effacement.

He was the pure artist – that is to say there was something in him of 'the
yearning of great Vishnu to create a world' –

He concluded the lecture with an unpublished poem which illustrates the
complexity he relished in this new hero:

> With Shakespeare's manhood at a boy's wild heart
> Through Hamlet's doubt to Shakespeare near allied
> And kin to Milton through his Satan's pride.
> At death's sole door he stooped and craved a dart
> And to the dear new bower of England's art
> Even to that shrine Time else had deified,
> The unuttered heart that seared against his side,
> Drove the fell point and smote life's seals apart.
> Thy nested homeloves, noble Chatterton,
> The angel trodden stair thy soul could trace
> Up Redcliffe spire, and in the world's armed space
> Thy gallant swordplay: these to many a one
> Are dear for ever – as thy grave unknown
> And love-dream of thine unrecorded face.[8]

(The 'homeloves' were Chatterton's mother and sister; 'swordplay' is a
reference to the poet's political satire. His face was 'unrecorded': there
are no known portraits.) Wilde was working out new variations of his poem
'Humanitad'; the young man destroying himself by his own lasting song
was like the nightingale in his new fairy tale, 'The Nightingale and the
Rose,' who puts her breast against the thorn until, by her death agony, a
rose is born. Mallarmé had written in his 'Plainte d'automne' that 'the
literature from which my spirit asks pleasure will be the dying poetry of the
last instants of Rome,' and there was something of this delight possible in
the threnodic contemplation of 'the marvellous boy.' Wilde could share
with Chatterton Hamlet's doubt and Satan's pride, a sense of forging a life
as Chatterton did, as well as a sense that he might one day be his own
victim, a sacrifice to himself.

A Miller's Thumb

The poor reviewers are apparently reduced to be the reporters
of the police-court of literature, the chroniclers of the doings
of the habitual criminals of art.

Lecturing gave way to journalism, the only other means readily available
to supplement Constance's income. However outside the law Wilde had
begun to think himself, he was not yet pursued by the policeman, but only
by the policeman's brother – the bill collector. In his work for W. T.
Stead's *Pall Mall Gazette*, which was his principal outlet, he made a virtue
of necessity and wrote much better than he had to. The articles were a way
of organizing his attitudes towards literature, art, nature, and life; they
exhibit a freshness not often present in his earlier work, as if to suggest
that running foul of the law in his sexual life was a stimulus to thought on
every subject. At last he knew where he stood. His new sexual direction
liberated his art. It also liberated his critical faculty.

From 1886 on, but especially in 1887 and 1888, Wilde wrote a series of
about a hundred reviews, many of them dealing with more than one book.
After that profusion the reviews came to a virtual end, with almost the
same abruptness as the lectures. Journalism was for Willie. For Oscar it
had served its purpose.

Many of the reviews are of such inconsequential works that close
criticism was not required, and in these Wilde offers patience and
indulgence. He can be simply funny, as when he mentions James
Aitchison's *The Chronicle of Mites*:

> *The Chronicle of Mites* is a mock-heroic poem about the inhabitants of a
> decaying cheese who speculate about the origin of their species and hold
> learned discussions upon the meaning of evolution and the Gospel
> according to Darwin. This cheese-epic is a rather unsavoury production
> and the style is at times so monstrous and so realistic that the author should
> be called the Gorgon-Zola of literature.

At other times he is legislative, if only for a moment: 'Indeed, properly
speaking, there is no such thing as Style; there are merely styles, that is
all.' His old mannerism, 'That is all,' appeared more often, to puff up what
might look casual. He had not yet achieved any large statement of
principles, but isolated sentences showed where he was going: 'Every
century that produces poetry is, so far, an artificial century, and the work
that seems to us the most natural and simple product of its kind is probably
the result of the most deliberate and self-conscious effort. For Nature is
always behind the age. It takes a great artist to be thoroughly modern.'[9]

A sense of his role as arbiter in English letters, made him reconsider old
admirations. When he turned to Whistler now, it was in a quite different
tone from that he had adopted in the days of discipleship. Then, on

28 February 1885, he had praised the artist as an orator who combined 'the mirth and malice of Puck with the style of the minor prophets.' On 26 January 1889 he found the combination infelicitous:

> Mr Whistler, for some reason or other, always adopted the phraseology of the minor prophets . . . The idea was clever enough at the beginning, but ultimately the manner became monotonous. The spirit of the Hebrews is excellent but their mode of writing is not to be imitated, and no amount of American jokes will give it that modernity which is essential to good literary style. Admirable as are Mr Whistler's fireworks on canvas, his fireworks in prose are abrupt, violent and exaggerated.

Wilde had received Whistler's taunts in the old days with saintly mildness, now it was Whistler's turn to feel the lash. The painter waited to strike.

With the same independence, Wilde reviewed a book by a man who had once been his follower as well as Whistler's, and had remained Whistler's: Rennell Rodd. In 'L'Envoi' to *Rose Leaf and Apple Leaf* in 1883 Wilde had been full of admiration; now he looked at a subsequent volume of Rodd with a harsher eye:

> Mr Rodd looks at life with all the charming optimism of a young man, though he is quite conscious of the fact, that a stray note of melancholy, here and there, has an artistic as well as a popular value; he has a keen sense of the pleasurableness of colour, and his verse is distinguished by a certain refinement and purity of outline; though not passionate he can play very prettily with the words of passion, and his emotions are quite healthy and quite harmless.[10]

The review was fair, but Wilde had once been more than fair in his estimate of Rodd. Rose leaf and apple leaf had withered.

Another writer whom he did not spare was his old teacher J. P. Mahaffy, two of whose books Wilde reviewed on 9 November and 16 December 1887. Wilde might have treated Mahaffy nostalgically, but the erect pen has no conscience. For his part, Mahaffy had disapproved of Wilde's grand tour of the United States after their grand tours together of Greece and Italy; worse than that, he had become absurdly Tory in his sympathies, and contemptuous of Irish home rule just when through Parnell's advocacy and Gladstone's support home rule was becoming a distinct possibility. So while his former pupil was almost prepared to stomach Mahaffy's absurd manual, *The Principles of the Art of Conversation*, regretting only 'the arid and jejune character of the style,' Wilde was much more severe with the other book, *Greek Life and Thought: From the Age of Alexander to the Roman Conquest*. (It was a sequel to *Greek Social Life and Thought*, which Wilde had helped with.) The publisher was Macmillan, which meant that it had passed through the hands of their old traveling companion in Greece, George Macmillan. But the implied reunion was cheerless: Wilde complained of the disagreeable provinciality and violent Unionism of Mahaffy. 'There is always something peculiarly impotent about the violence of a literary man,' he said. He gathered vehemence as he proceeded, and summed up in the manner of Matthew Arnold: 'In fact, not merely does Mr Mahaffy miss the spirit of the true historian, but he often seems entirely devoid of the temper of the true man of letters. He is clever, and, at times, even brilliant, but he lacks reasonableness, moderation, style and charm.' Instead of solicitously touching up the manuscript, the pupil was now lecturing the master.

As for Swinburne, whose poetry had delighted his youth, Wilde was now much more quizzical. One of his last and best reviews, in the *Pall Mall Gazette* on 27 June 1889, is of *Poems and Ballads* (Third Series). He recapitulates the poet's career, and conveys, with a surer sense of his own individuality, a growing disapprobation:

> Mr Swinburne once set his age on fire by a volume of very perfect and very poisonous poetry. Then he became revolutionary, and pantheistic, and cried out against those who sit in high places both in heaven and on earth. Then he returned to the nursery, and wrote poems about children of a somewhat over-subtle character. He is now extremely patriotic, and manages to combine with his patriotism a strong affection for the Tory party. He has always been a great poet. But he has his limitations, the chief of which is, curiously enough, the lack of any sense of limit. His song is nearly always too loud for his subject. His magnificent rhetoric, nowhere more magnificent than in the volume that is before us, conceals rather than reveals. It has been said of him, and with truth, that he is a master of language, but with still greater truth it may be said that language is his master . . .
>
> Of course we must not look to these poems for any revelation of human life. To be at one with the elements seems to be Mr Swinburne's aim. He seeks to speak with the breath of wind and wave . . . He is the first lyric poet who has tried to make an absolute surrender of his personality, and he has succeeded. We have the song, but we never know the singer . . . Out of the thunder and splendour of words he himself says nothing. We have often heard man's interpretation of Nature; now we know Nature's interpretation of man, and she has curiously little to say. Force and Freedom form her vague message. She deafens us with her clangours.

Even Pater does not escape scot-free. Wilde commends his *Imaginary Portraits*, but qualifies his praise of Pater's celebrated style. It seems clear that he now felt that Pater's unwillingness to speak out, from caution and timidity, had a deadening effect upon spontaneity:

> Asceticism is the keynote of Mr Pater's prose; at times it is almost too severe in its self-control and makes us long for a little more freedom. For indeed, the danger of such prose as his is that it is apt to become somewhat laborious . . . The continual preoccupation with phrase and epithet has its

drawbacks as well as its virtues. And yet, when all is said, what wonderful prose it is.[11]

Whitman and Longfellow are found wanting, and if Balzac and Flaubert are idolized, English writers, including the most famous, are given less than their due of deference: 'George Eliot's style was far too cumbrous, and Charlotte Brontë's too exaggerated' (January 1889). 'Dickens has influenced only journalism; Thackeray . . . found no echoes; nor has Trollope . . . As for George Meredith, who could hope to reproduce him? His style is chaos illumined by brilliant flashes of lightning. As a writer he has mastered everything, except language; as a novelist he can do everything, except tell a story.' (January 1888.) (These last sentences were to go into 'The Decay of Lying.') He was more considerate of the verse of his new friend William Ernest Henley, though he objected strongly to poems not written in formal meter. Among other writers, he speaks with greater sympathy of W. S. Blunt and Michael Field, and with some acuteness of W. B. Yeats. So Wilde wheeled about in the literature of his time, lending an ear here and boxing one there.

Two other issues aroused strong feelings in Wilde. One was Charles Stewart Parnell, who had been severely attacked by *The Times* in a series of articles on 'Parnellism and Crime.' He was accused of inciting and condoning political murder, with letters to prove the point. Wilde and his brother were on their compatriot's side, and attended meetings of the Parnell Commission appointed to hear the charges. Willie wrote articles in the *Daily Chronicle* that were highly regarded. In February 1889 came the exposure of Richard Pigott as the forger of the letters supposedly written by Parnell. Like Chatterton, though without his talent, Pigott shortly afterwards committed suicide. Parnell was vindicated and his supporters triumphant. Then at the end of December Captain O'Shea instituted his suit for divorce, naming Parnell as co-respondent. The case was not defended. Parnell came crashing down, and died in 1891. Even heterosexuals were not immune from public obloquy. It was an example of secular heroism and martyrdom that Wilde could cherish.

The other issue much on his mind was socialism. Wilde attended meetings of the Fabian Society in 1888, and had become acquainted with Bernard Shaw several years before. Shaw, who had come to England from Ireland a year after Wilde, in 1875, used to attend Lady Wilde's after-noons. On 4 May 1886, when the Haymarket Riots took place in Chicago, Shaw sought signatories for a petition in support of the anarchists involved, and among London men of letters only Wilde lent his name at once.* 'A very handsome thing to do,' said Shaw (in a letter), 'Wilde being

---

* Wilde told an interviewer in the spring of 1894, 'We are all of us more or less Socialists now-a-days . . . I think I am rather more than a Socialist. I am something of an Anarchist, I believe, but, of course, the dynamite policy is very absurd indeed.'[12]

a snob to the marrow of his being, having been brought up in Merrion Square, Dublin.' On 14 September 1886, at the house of Fitzgerald Molloy, Wilde listened sympathetically to Shaw's talk of a new magazine that would bring socialist ideas to the country. At length Wilde said, 'That has all been most interesting, Mr Shaw, but there's one point you haven't mentioned, and an all-important one – you haven't told us the *title* of your magazine.' 'Oh, as for that,' said Shaw, 'what I'd want to do would be to impress my own personality on the public – I'd call it *Shaw's Magazine*: Shaw – Shaw – Shaw!' He banged his fist on the table. 'Yes,' said Wilde, 'and how would you spell it?'[13] Though he said of Shaw, 'He has no enemies, and none of his friends like him,' he showed a benign interest in his work.

As early as 15 February 1889 Wilde indicated his socialist sympathies in a review of a book edited by Edward Carpenter, *Chants of Labour: A Song-Book of the People*. He began by finding socialism a new motif for art:

> Mr Stopford Brooke said some time ago that Socialism and the socialistic spirit would give our poets nobler and loftier themes for song, would widen their sympathies and enlarge the horizon of their vision, and would touch with the fire and fervour of a new faith lips that had else been silent, hearts that but for the fresh gospel would be cold. What Art grows from contemporary events is always a fascinating problem, and a problem that is not easy to solve. It is, however, certain that Socialism starts well equipped . . . [she] is not going to allow herself to be trammelled by any hard-and-fast creed . . . And all of this is well. For to make men Socialists is nothing, but to make Socialism human is a great thing.

He praised the Socialists for their conviction that art could help in the building up of 'an eternal city.' Then he was content to end on a lighter note, 'However, they must not be too sanguine. The walls of Thebes rose up to the sound of music, and Thebes was a very dull city indeed.' The article showed how he was drawn to socialism – he would give it full support two years later – and also how he wanted it to be democratic and humanitarian rather than authoritarian in its procedures.

Turning Ladies to Women

MISS PRISM: *A misanthrope I can understand – a woman-thrope, never!*

The skill and buoyancy of Wilde's reviews did not escape attention. Bernard Shaw commented on the high quality of Wilde's journalism. More to the point, Thomas Wemyss Reid, who had been editor of the *Leeds Mercury*, came to London in February 1887 to be general manager of the publishers, Cassell & Company, and recognized that Wilde's talent could be put to use. The firm had started a magazine the previous October under the name, *The Lady's World: A Magazine of Fashion and Society*. Reid asked Wilde to look at the back issues and see whether he could think of improvements, since there was a growing interest in such publications as feminism took firmer hold.

Wilde recognized that here at last was a possibility of a reputable livelihood, and in April he answered Reid in a long and carefully written letter that would have impressed any publisher. It began:

> Dear Mr Wemyss Reid, I have read very carefully the numbers of the *Lady's World* you kindly sent me, and would be very happy to join with you in the work of editing and to some extent reconstituting it. It seems to me that at present it is too feminine, and not sufficiently womanly. No one appreciates more fully than I do the value and importance of Dress, in its relation to good taste and good health: indeed the subject is one that I have constantly lectured on before Institutes and Societies of various kinds, but it seems to me that the field of the *mundus muliebris*, the field of mere millinery and trimmings, is to some extent already occupied by such papers as the *Queen* and the *Lady's Pictorial*, and that we should take a wider range, as well as a high standpoint, and deal not merely with what women wear, but with what they think, and what they feel.

Wilde proposed to reduce the discussion of dress, and relegate it to the end of each issue. He thought there could be articles on the education of women, and on all the things that women do with their time. There should also be a serial story. Out of his wide acquaintance, he named a number of women, such as Olive Schreiner, Violet Fane, the Queen of Rumania (Carmen Sylva), and others distinguished for their titles or their personalities, such as the Princess Christian.

Wemyss Reid liked these plans, whose only fault was in being ahead of their time. He proposed that Wilde's salary should begin on 1 June 1887 but Wilde asked that it begin on 1 May, since he had already begun to solicit contributions. The agreement was signed on 18 May. According to Ross, the salary was fixed at £6 a week. Wilde began to conduct a voluminous correspondence in pursuit of contributions. He asked Queen Victoria for one of her poems, but the indignant regal response was that she had never written one. He had eclectic tastes and tried women of very diverse interests; the magazine took on a miscellaneous look which it never lost. He soon found that many women resented the title, *The Lady's World*, as pretentious and repressive. In particular, Mrs Craik, the author of *John Halifax, Gentleman* and other novels, urged him to change it to *The Woman's World*. At first the firm's directors refused; in September Wilde urged them more strongly:

The present name of the magazine has a certain taint of vulgarity about it, that will always militate against the success of the new issue, and is also extremely misleading. It is quite applicable to the magazine in its present state; it will not be applicable to a magazine that aims at being the organ of women of intellect, culture, and position.[14]

When the November 1887 issue – the first under Wilde's editorship – appeared, it was victoriously entitled *The Woman's World*, and had the words, 'Edited by Oscar Wilde,' prominently displayed on its pink cover. The new approach of the magazine won approval, and in the second issue a page of encomiums from many newspapers was included. Wilde was regarded with favor, a situation he could not allow to last indefinitely, so that his editorship would come to a stop. His assistant, Arthur Fish, has left a record of the editor's behavior. At first Wilde took the work seriously, and arrived at 11 a.m. on his appointed days; but gradually he came later and left earlier, so that his visit was 'little more than a call.' W. E. Henley, who was also editing a magazine for Cassell's, asked Wilde, 'How often do you go to the office?' 'I used to go three times a week for an hour a day,' Wilde replied, 'but I have since struck off one of the days.' 'My God!' said Henley, 'I went five times a week for five hours a day, and when I wanted to strike off a day they had a special committee meeting.' 'Furthermore,' Wilde went on, 'I never answered their letters. I have known men come to London full of bright prospects and seen them complete wrecks in a few months through a habit of answering letters.'[15] Wilde's own contributions to *The Woman's World*, headed 'Literary and Other Notes,' were gracious, informative and amusing, his name attached to them was a selling point; unfortunately he soon found them a nuisance to write, and would advise his assistant, 'Dear Mr Fish, I have not been at all well and cannot get my notes done. Can you manage to put in something else? I will be down tomorrow. Yours truly, O.W.' Wemyss Reid jogged Wilde to keep the notes going, but they appeared in only twelve of the twenty-odd issues (until October 1889) he edited.

This was the period when Wilde had not yet begun to go everywhere by cab. He took the tube from Sloane Square to Charing Cross, then walked up the Strand and Fleet Street to his office on Ludgate Hill, at the Belle Sauvage Yard. He was the best dressed man in Cassell's. Arthur Fish says that in bad weather Wilde was often depressed, a fact he would register by his step as he approached. But in a good mood, especially in springtime, he would answer letters energetically, consider the makeup of the magazine, and sit chatting in an arm chair for a long time. He disliked Cassell's rule against smoking, and the duration of his stay was governed by his ability to survive without a cigarette. In general he was easy to work for, and the only time Fish remembered his becoming angry was when John Williams, the chief editor at Cassell's (and later Wilde's successor as editor of *The Woman's World*), brought in the manuscript of a book by a comic midget, Marshall P. Wilder, entitled *People I Have Smiled With*. Wilder had dared to write, 'The first time I saw Oscar he wore his hair long and his breeches short; now, I believe, he wears his hair short and his trousers long.' Wilde could not bear being a butt, especially of someone with a similar name whom he and his mother had entertained. 'Monstrous! Perfectly monstrous!' he cried, and the offending passage was removed.[16]

The Woman's World did have an intellectual quality that *The Lady's World* had lacked. Wilde began his first issue with an article by Lady Archibald Campbell about the theatricals she had staged with Godwin's help over the past several years. There were articles on feminism and woman's suffrage, with women taking both sides of these questions. The table of contributors was somewhat unexpected. The third issue, of January 1888, started off with a long poem, 'Historic Women,' by his mother; this, which included a eulogy of the Queen, was duly sent to Queen Victoria, whose lady-in-waiting, Lady Churchill, reported that Her Majesty had liked it very much. In November 1888 Lady Wilde contributed 'Irish Peasant Tales,' part of the book she was putting together from notes thrown into an old shoebox by Sir William Wilde. (She had two other pieces from it in the *Pall Mall Gazette* on 1 and 21 May 1888.) It was in fact a little difficult keeping her in check, and when in November 1887 Wilde had reviewed an anthology of poetry entitled *Women's Voices* without mentioning his mother's voice, she was quick to let him feel the weight of her tongue.

Dear Mr Editor,
    Miss Leonard wrote to me to say that she can supply an article on French matters if you wish, as her father sends her all the latest news –
    Why didn't you name *me* in the review of Mrs Sharp's book? Me, who hold such an historic place in Irish literature? and you name Miss Tynan and Miss Mulholland!
    The Hampshire Review gives me splendid notice – *you* – well, 'tis strange – I have lent the W.W. by O.W. to Mrs Fisher. Lady Archie is the best of the women essayists. George Fleming begins interesting – and is good – but women in general are a wretched lot.
    Did you read Willie on soda water – it is so brilliant – Arnold was delighted.
    Come for a talk on Sunday evening. I have so little time left now – for I must certainly drown myself in a week or two – Life is quite too much trouble –

                                                La tua
                                    La Madre Dolorosa[17]

Filial as he was, Wilde had some compunction about praising his mother too obviously, but smoothed her down by quoting, in a review of a volume of fairy tales edited by W. B. Yeats, a long and flattering comment Yeats had made about her collection. He seems to have encouraged his wife to contribute to *Woman's World*, and Constance wrote two straightforward articles, on 'Children's Dress in This Century' and on 'Muffs' (February 1889). The old friend to whom he had dedicated his Newdigate poem, Constance Fletcher, was conscripted for a serial, which went on interminably issue after issue, complete with Scots dialiect.* Contributions by men were not forbidden, but only a few male authors actually wrote, among them Oscar Browning, who had a poem on Bournemouth, and Arthur Symons, with a maudlin poem and then a more interesting essay on Villiers de l'Isle Adam. *The Woman's World* suffered from its editor's loss of interest in it. Contributions flagged, the circulation fell. Wilde gave it up in 1889 to the Cassell functionary Williams who was to make it more 'practical.'

Ingenious Fictions

Art takes life as part of her rough material, recreates it, and refashions it in fresh forms, is absolutely indifferent to fact, invents, imagines, dreams, and keeps between herself and reality the impenetrable barrier of beautiful style, of decorative or ideal treatment.

Another aspect of his experience was ripe for exploitation. The theme of betrayal, whether by friend or lover, would run through his work from *Vera* to *The Ballad of Reading Gaol* and *De Profundis*. By now he had experienced betrayal at the hands of Miles, Rodd, Bodley, and Whistler, and he obliquely portrayed his sense of being wronged in the ironical story, 'The Devoted Friend.' The treacherous miller, while offering the loftiest animadversions upon the nature and sanctity of friendship, treats his friend, Little Hans, abominably: 'Real friends should have everything in common,' he says, and 'At present you have only the practice of friendship. Some day you will have the theory also.' Little Hans has to bear the brunt of this false friendship – he is a minuscule version of the unselfish giant who wrote the story. It is clearly related to 'The Nightingale and the Rose,' written at about this time, which presents a case of unappreciated self-sacrifice; that theme is reversed in a prose poem 'The Master,' in which a young man complains that, though he too has worked miracles, he has *not* been crucified like Jesus. Victimization as something to be sought after rather than endured was a characteristic touch.[19]

* Wilde's attitude towards dialect he expressed elsewhere: 'The amount of pleasure one gets out of dialect is a matter entirely of temperament. To say "mither" instead of "mother" seems to many the acme of romance. There are others who are not quite so ready to believe in the pathos of provincialisms.'[18]

'The Remarkable Rocket,' which dates from the same period, is an exploration of vanity. Wilde, though often accused of vanity, did not approve of it. The vainest man he knew was Whistler, who called himself, with a pretense of jocularity, 'the amazing one.' Wilde in their warmer days had overlooked his vanity. A later review showed some falling away: 'Mr Whistler always spelt art, and I believe still spells it, with a capital "I."' The rocket in Wilde's story insists 'you should be thinking about me. I am always thinking of myself, and I expect everyone else to do the same. That is what is called sympathy.' And again, 'you forget that I am very uncommon and very remarkable ... The only thing that sustains one through life is the consciousness of the immense inferiority of everybody else, and this is a feeling I have always cultivated.' The association of Whistler with rockets went back to the vernissage of the Grosvenor Gallery in 1877, where Wilde had seen (his review said) 'a rocket of golden rim, with green and red fires bursting in a perfectly blank sky,' and another rocket 'breaking in a pale blue sky.' Eight years later he had written of the 'fireworks' in Whistler's prose and painting alike.[20] Now the 'remarkable' rocket, with all its fizzing, is a dud.*

With these stories Wilde established himself as a story teller. If the characters are lacking, interest is not. The plots tumbled out of him, though they were anything but impromptu in the themes they sustained. At the time that he was celebrating personality, Wilde bewailed an excess of selfhood. His generosity led him to mock the hypocrisy which often went with it in others. Friendship and love were displayed through absence, faith through faithlessness, life in the pointlessness of death. There were usually sudden explosions of something into nothing or of nothing into something beyond price.

Among all his stories of this time, the best, and dearest to him, was 'The Portrait of Mr W.H.' It too trod the high wire between being and not-being. Published in July 1889, it was being written, as a letter to Wemyss Reid indicates, by October 1887. The subject was Shakespeare, and takes for granted that Shakespeare was attracted to boys. Frank Harris, as heterosexual as a man can be, tried to dissuade Wilde from

---

* Wilde told E. F. Benson that he was busy with a small volume of ethical essays – moral tracts they might be called – designed to be given as presents at Christmastime. The Bishop of London had kindly consented to write a preface. The first of these was 'The Value of Presence of Mind,' and took the form of a parable. A play was being performed to full houses. One night during that tremendous scene in which the flower-girl of Piccadilly Circus rejects with scorn the odious proposals of a debauched Marquess, a huge volume of smoke and fire poured out of the wings. The audience rose in panic and stampeded to the exits. Then on stage there appeared the noble figure of the young man who was the true lover of the flower girl. His voice rang out – the fire was already under control, the chief danger was from panic. Let them all go back to their seats, and recover their calm. So commanding was his presence that they returned to their places. The young actor then leaped lightly over the footlights and ran out of the theatre. The rest were burned to a crisp.[21]

writing it up, because he could see Shakespeare only in his own womanizing image. If Wilde paid any attention, he did so by writing a story instead of an essay.

In 'The Portrait of Mr W.H.' he dazzlingly offered a theory, withdrew it, and half offered it again, in fiction within fiction that anticipates Borges. The anonymous narrator hears from his friend Erskine about Cyril Graham's theory of Shakespeare's *Sonnets*. Graham, an effeminate young man who at school would always take the female leads in Shakespeare's plays, is convinced that Mr W.H. is a boy actor. His first name, Will, is hidden in the punning sonnets cxxxv and cxliii, and his last name, Hughes, is in xx,

A man in hew, all *Hews* in his controwling.

The sceptical Erskine points out the lack of any evidence that Will Hughes ever existed. Graham goes away in disappointment, but returns later with the missing evidence. It is an Elizabethan chest, against one side of which he has found clamped a portrait of a young man, the masks of Tragedy and Comedy before him, and bearing the rubric, 'Master Will. Hews.' Erskine's doubts vanish until he discovers the portrait is forged, accuses Graham, and Graham shoots himself. He leaves Erskine a letter which insists that the theory is true and that Erskine must give it to the world. The narrator is moved, and comes to the conclusion that Graham was right, and that the *Sonnets* are an attempt to persuade Hughes to act in the sonneteer's plays – an unexpectedly wholesome conclusion. The narrator writes to Erskine with new evidence, but feels suddenly a Wildean indifference. 'Emotional forces, like the forces of physical life, have their positive limitations.' If he has over-persuaded himself, he has persuaded Erskine. Two years later a letter tells the narrator that by the time it is received, Erskine will have committed suicide to prove the truth of Graham's theory. The narrator is too late to stop him. But it turns out that Erskine has actually died of consumption. He has bequeathed the portrait of Willie Hughes to the narrator. At the end, the narrator tells how he looks at it and thinks 'there is really a great deal to be said for the Willie Hughes theory of Shakespeare's *Sonnets*.' Between forgery and genuineness, fiction and fact, there hangs only a hair.

Wilde was using an old theory, but the story was his own. It arose from that sense of a secret life which had drawn him to Chatterton who, with another forger, MacPherson, is mentioned in the story. A fine touch is twinning the forgery of suicide with that of the painting, in an elegant variation of the pattern suggested in his letter to Harry Marillier of dying for what one does not believe in. Erskine cleverly pretends to die for what he believes in. Wilde could see analogies with his own forgery of personalities as a Mason, a Pre-Raphaelite, a Roman Catholic, a *débauchée*, a dandy. Like Willie Hughes, he had played many parts, and like the narrator, Erskine, and Graham, with varying degrees of conviction.

Nowhere, except in *The Importance of Being Earnest*, did Wilde achieve quite this mixture of reality and make-believe, of a world poised on a word. 'You must believe in Willy Hughes,' he said to Helena Sickert, 'I almost do myself.'[22] He had almost believed in Catholicism as an equally attractive fiction.

The story came closer to him still. He imagined Shakespeare, a married man with two children like himself, captivated by a boy as he had been captivated by Ross.* Wilde wrote to Ross, 'indeed the story is half yours, and but for you it would not have been written.' Excited by his idea, Wilde went to call upon the artists Charles Ricketts and Charles Shannon, whom he had not previously met, in May 1889. He read the story to them, and asked Ricketts to illustrate it with a painting of Willie Hughes in the manner of Clouet. On the frame he wanted the motto, *ARS AMORIS, AMOR ARTIS*, in which he said there was an entire philosophy. Confident that his homoerotic hosts would be sympathetic, he expatiated upon Shakespeare's love for the boy actor: 'The Renaissance brought with it a great revival of Platonism. Plato, like all the Greeks, recognised two kinds of love, sensual love which delights in women – such love is intellectually sterile, for women are receptive only, they take everything, and give nothing, save in the way of nature. The intellectual loves or romantic friendships of the Hellenes, which surprise us today, they considered spiritually fruitful, a stimulus to thought and virtue – I mean virtue as it was understood by the ancients and the Renaissance, not virtue in the English sense, which is only caution and hypocrisy.' He held that Shakespeare's dedication of the *Sonnets* to their 'onlie Begetter' was pure Platonism. Yet the sonnets were unhappy: 'Shakespeare felt that his art had been created in him by the beauty of his treacherous friend.' Hence the Latin motto. He contrasted Greek art, 'the expression of joy,' with modern art, 'a flower of suffering.' Even Keats, though 'almost Greek,' had 'died of sorrow.'

Ricketts fulfilled his commission for a portrait of Willie Hughes. On receiving it Wilde wrote to him, 'It is not a forgery at all – it is an authentic Clouet of the highest artistic value. It is absurd of you and Shannon to try and take me in – as if I did not know the master's touch, or was no judge of frames!' He loved confusing still further the borders of life and art. Unfortunately the 'Clouet' disappeared at the time of his trials, when his effects were auctioned off.

Balfour and Asquith, to whom Wilde told the story of Willie Hughes,

---

* Wilde once explained, at Lady Archibald Campbell's, why he thought he looked like Shakespeare. He ended a brilliant monologue by saying he intended to have a bronze medallion struck of his own profile and Shakespeare's. 'And I suppose, Mr Wilde,' said Lady Archibald, 'your profile will protrude beyond Shakespeare's.'[23] It was Lady Colin Campbell who described Wilde as 'a great white caterpillar.'

advised him not to print it, lest it corrupt English homes. He sent it, however, to the *Fortnightly Review*, assuming that Frank Harris would be amused by it in its fictional form. But Harris was abroad, and his assistant rejected it rudely, so Wilde sent it to *Blackwood's*, where it was published. The effect was considerable. Harris said, with Ross as corroborator, 'It set everyone talking and arguing . . . It gave his enemies for the first time the very weapon they wanted.' The story was guarded – more guarded than a longer version which Wilde wrote later – and while it raised the question of Shakespeare's passion for the actor, it deflected it towards a professional friendship. Wilde only played with fire; he was not Prometheus. He remarked to Ross, 'My next Shakespeare book will be a discussion as to whether the commentators on *Hamlet* are mad or only pretending to be.'[24]

His reputation as an author dated from the publication of *The Happy Prince and Other Tales* in London in May 1888. The *Athenaeum* compared him to Hans Christian Andersen, and Pater wrote to say that 'The Selfish Giant' was 'perfect in its kind,' and the whole book written in 'pure English' – a wonderful compliment. The stories suffer from florid figures ('the long grey fingers of the dawn clutching at the fading stars') and Biblical pronouns. The incidents often begin with disfigurement and end, like 'The Happy Prince,' in transfiguration. Wilde presents the stories like sacraments of a lost faith. Most of the characters are brought to recognition of themselves, and a recognition of ugliness and misery. Wilde celebrates the power of love as greater than the power of evil or the power of good. Going from a castle to a hovel leads to suffering and love. For the most part Wilde subdued his desire to assault his readers with unfamiliar sensations, though there are references to the young king's kissing a statue of Antinous, and allusions to the beauty of boys. Their occasional social satire is subordinated to a sadness unusual in fairy tales – the other side of the boisterousness which Wilde was simultaneously expressing in 'Lord Arthur Savile's Crime' and other short stories.

The fairy tales move slowly. Wilde's natural motion was swifter, and he was able to embody it successfully in two pieces of discursive prose which seem more natural expressions of his genius. One was 'Pen, Pencil and Poison,' which Frank Harris published in the *Fortnightly Review* in January 1889, and the other was 'The Decay of Lying,' published the same month in the *Nineteenth Century* and later greatly revised. With these two essays, especially the second, Wilde discovered his own genius. Much of what he had thought and written about Chatterton and Cyril Graham and Erskine went into the first essay, which dealt with Thomas Wainewright the forger. While all illegality impressed him, forgery was a crime which perhaps seems closest to Wilde's social presentation of himself. Robert Ross spoke of his inveterate artificiality. He was now in league with the underworld of people who pretended to be what they were not, like some group of Masons without the law. He said of Wainewright, 'His crimes seem to have had an important effect upon his art. They gave a strong personality to his style, a quality that his early work certainly lacked.'

The calm discussion of Wainewright's phases of artistry and criminality was more appropriate than the emotional defence of Chatterton. Wainewright did not offer for contemplation a beautiful soul, and he was in no sense pathetic. Instead he was 'a forger of no mean or ordinary capabilities, and ... a subtle and secret poisoner almost without rival in this or any age.' Like the character in Rollinat's 'Le Soliloque de Troppmann,' the writer is as free of moral compunction as the murderer. Wilde associated Wainewright with Baudelaire, whom he always described as poisonous and perfect. Among his quaint tastes Wainewright had 'that curious love of green, which in individuals is always the sign of a subtle artistic temperament, and in nations is said to denote a laxity, if not a decadence, of morals.' (The remark heralded the green carnation.) When a friend reproached Wainewright with a murder, he shrugged his shoulders and gave an answer that Wilde relished: 'Yes; it was a dreadful thing to do, but she had very thick ankles.' Wilde concludes that 'the fact of a man being a poisoner is nothing against his prose,' and that 'there is no essential incongruity between crime and culture.' It is too early to judge his value as a writer, Wilde says, but he is inclined to believe that Wainewright's criminal craft revealed a true artist.

Decadence Mocked

The past is what man should not have been.
The present is what man ought not to be.
The future is what artists are.

After 'Pen, Pencil and Poison,' Wilde began to write his first and most successful dialogue, 'The Decay of Lying,' and finished it by December 1888. The impulse to write it came, as with 'The Portrait of Mr W.H.,' from a conversation with Robert Ross, the beloved disciple. Not the least of its effects was that it bound Wilde to Yeats, one of the first to hear it, and it was Yeats who would translate Wilde into fully twentieth-century terms.

They had probably met at Lady Wilde's, but in his *Autobiographies* Yeats sets this first meeting at the house of William Ernest Henley, about September 1888, when Henley and Wilde first became friends. (Bearing out a remark Wilde made on this occasion, 'The basis of literary friendship is mixing the poisoned bowl,' Henley would throw his stick at Wilde later.) At twenty-three Yeats was amused by the contrast of Henley, industrious and imperial, with Wilde, indolent and subversive. He was also amazed by Wilde's 'perfect sentences' which allegorized the victory of imagination over all impeding circumstances. Wilde's 'hard brilliance, dominating self-possession' were more than a match for Henley's lively intelligence. 'I envy those men who become mythological while still living,' Yeats said to Wilde, half in compliment, and received the reply, 'I think a man should invent his own myth.' It was an injunction which Yeats would remember all his life. He was delighted also by Wilde's praise of Pater's *Studies in the History of the Renaissance* in that un-Pater-like company: 'I never travel anywhere without it; but it is the very flower of decadence; the last trumpet should have sounded the moment it was written.' 'But,' said a dull man, 'would you not have given us time to read it?' 'Oh no,' replied Wilde, 'there would have been plenty of time afterwards – in either world.' Wilde was at once admiring Pater and making him faintly ridiculous, freeing himself by professing outlandish bondage. After his departure Henley commented, 'No, he is not an aesthete. One soon finds he is a scholar and a gentleman.'[25]

If Yeats took note of Wilde, Wilde took note of him. He invited him to Christmas dinner in 1888, pretending that Yeats had no family in London, a pretense Yeats was glad not to embarrass by truth. Having heard the gossip about the untidy house of Wilde's parents in Dublin, and about Sir William Wilde's dirty fingernails, Yeats was unprepared for what he found in Tite Street. The drawing room and dining room were done in white, the walls, furniture, and carpets too. The exception was the red lampshade suspended from the ceiling, which cowled a terra-cotta statue on a diamond-shaped red cloth in the middle of the white table. Yeats felt embarrassed by this elegance, especially when Wilde visibly started at his yellow shoes – a botched attempt at the vogue of undyed leather. Yeats's effort to tell Cyril Wilde a story about a giant frightened the child to tears and earned a reproachful look from the father, whose own stories of giants dwelt upon amiability rather than monstrosity. Flustered by his gaucheries, Yeats was not entirely at a disadvantage. He knew himself to be a better poet than Wilde. Something of this feeling must have been conveyed to Wilde at the Christmas dinner, for he converted the muted disparagement into articulate victory by saying, 'We Irish are too poetical to be poets; we are a nation of brilliant failures, but we are the greatest talkers since the Greeks.'*

After dinner Wilde brought out the proofs of 'The Decay of Lying,' which James Knowles was to publish the next month in the *Nineteenth Century*. It could hardly have found a more willing listener. Yeats did not share the fashionable aversion to critical theory, but until this time his literary ideas had been fostered by occultism and nationalism. He needed an aesthetic which would take into account the intense speculation about the nature and function of art that had been going on in Europe since the pronouncements of the early romantic poets. In the dialogue Wilde summed up the disdain for life and nature of writers from Gautier to Mallarmé, the disdain for common morality of Poe and Baudelaire, the

---

* He had said in a review that women are too poetical to be poets, a point also made by George Eliot's Will Ladislaw in *Middlemarch*.

284

disdain for content of Verlaine and Whistler. Such views were counterposed by Wilde against conventional theories of sincerity and verisimilitude. Through the dialogue form, which Yeats followed him in using, he sharpened the central paradox – that art creates life – with all its dialectical possibilities.

'The Decay of Lying' began as a mockery of the current talk of Neronian decadence. Wilde spoke of a club called 'The Tired Hedonists' and explained, 'We are supposed to wear faded roses in our buttonholes when we meet, and to have a sort of cult for Domitian.' To the suggestion that the members must be bored with each other, he agreed: 'We are. That is one of the objects of the club.' So Wilde smiled decadence away. Another target was Zola's essay published nine years before, *Le Roman expérimental* (1880), which minimized imagination, and made the artistic labyrinth into a laboratory. The real decadence, Wilde said, was this trespass of life into art.

The approach he proposed was less salvationist than that of Matthew Arnold, whose recent death appeared to make room for a new aesthetic. Wilde praised art's rejection of sincerity and accuracy in favor of lies and masks. He largely avoided the word imagination, grown stale and innocuous, though he is of course upholding imagination against reason and observation. Imagination was also a word that sounded too natural and involuntary for Wilde. Lying is better because it is no outpouring of the self, but a conscious effort to mislead. It also sounds sinful and willful. 'All fine imaginative work,' he declares, 'is self-conscious and deliberate. A great poet sings because he chooses to sing,' but 'if one tells the truth, one is sure, sooner or later, to be found out!' Wilde celebrates art unsentimentally in the name of Ananias, not of Ariel.

He identified two basic energies in art, both subversive. One asserts a magnificent isolation from experience, an unreality, a sterility. Art is a kind of trick played on nature and God, an illicit creation by man. 'All art is entirely useless,' said Wilde, like Gautier and Whistler before him. 'Art never expresses anything but itself.' 'Nothing that actually occurs is of the smallest importance.' Form determines content, not content form. Wilde turned Taine upon his head: the age does not shape art, but it is art which gives the age its character. So far from responding to questions posed by the epoch, art offers answers before questions have been asked. 'It is the ages that are her symbols.'* Yeats was attentive, since his historical chapter in *A Vision* is an illustration of the thesis.

* Other epigrams of Wilde in a notebook are related:

  Life is the only thing that is never real.
  Life is a dream that prevents one from sleeping.
  The impossible in art is anything that has happened in real life.
  The improbable in art is anything that has happened too often in real life.
  By the artificial separation of soul and body men have invented a Realism that is vulgar, an Idealism that is void.[26]

The second energy of art is its insemination of images. Life, straggling after art, seizes upon forms in art to express itself. Life imitates art. Aristotle like Taine is stood on his head. 'Think of what we owe to the imitation of Christ, of what we owe to the imitation of Caesar.' No one had so clearly invoked the antinomies for Yeats as Wilde did. He would follow Wilde's lead, though he would use St Francis and Cesare Borgia.[27] In one of his most splendid passages, Wilde said, 'This unfortunate aphorism about Art holding the mirror up to Nature is deliberately said by Hamlet in order to convince the bystanders of his absolute insanity in all art-matters.' If art is a mirror, we look in it to see a mask. (Herod would agree.) Actually 'life is the mirror, and art the reality.' Corot's paintings created the fogs they were thought to depict, an idea which Proust echoed when he said women began to look like Renoir's images of them. Wilde said, 'the whole of Japan is a pure invention' of its artists. 'There is no such country, there are no such people.' 'The nineteenth century, as we know it, is largely an invention of Balzac . . . One of the greatest tragedies of my life is the death of Lucien de Rubempré.' *Hamlet* has had its effect upon two centuries. 'The world has grown sad because a puppet was once melancholy.' (Yeats cavilled at Wilde's substitution of 'melancholy' for 'sad,' and did not accept his explanation that the sentence needed a full sound at the close; but Wilde was justified in using 'melancholy' as an Elizabethan clinical term.) As for sculpture, 'The Greeks . . . set in the bride's chamber the statue of Hermes or Apollo, that she might bear children as lovely as the work of art she looked at in her rapture or her pain.* They knew that Life gains from Art not merely spirituality . . . but that she can form herself on the very lines and colours of art, and can produce the dignity of Pheidias as well as the grace of Praxiteles.'

The indifferent conferring of forms upon life by art slips into the idea that art may infect life rather than isolate it. Wilde would have said that both could happen. In 'The Decay of Lying' he speaks of 'silly boys who, after reading the adventures of Jack Sheppard or Dick Turpin, pillage the stalls of unfortunate applewomen, break into sweetshops at night, and alarm old gentlemen who are returning from the city by leaping out on them in suburban lanes, with black masks and unloaded revolvers.' Art may charge its audience with criminal impulses. Like Whitman, Wilde could say, 'Nor will my poems do good only, they will do just as much evil, perhaps more.' Whitman, Wilde, and Yeats all envisaged going beyond good and evil, at least in their conventional guises. With this idea of the artist as a sacred malefactor, the opposite of Wilde's idea of the artist as

---

* So it is said in Yeats's *The King's Threshold,*

> But why were you born crooked?
> What bad poet did your mother listen to
> That you were born so crooked?

isolato, he brought his theories full circle. The function of art is to make a raid on predictability.

The subversiveness of Wilde's views is matched by the grace of their expression. In the dialogue two characters talk to entertain and persuade each other, the author keeping a little apart from both sides, even that which he obviously favors. The delight in debate is greater than the desire for conviction. Wilde went further than Pater, who had dared only to hint at the overthrow of an old world by new art. Pater did not speak of art's indifference to life, since for him life was composed of feelings and art provided the most intense of them. Wilde's infusion of irony into aesthetics was adroit; he found a way of saying that art should please and instruct without making it obsequious or didactic. Yeats spoke of 'our more profound Pre-Raphaelitism,' but it was Wilde's more profound post-aestheticism which set him going. Still, he was not entirely dazzled. He thought Wilde by nature 'a man of action,' and was surprised to learn that he had turned down a safe seat in Parliament. As a writer, Wilde seemed to Yeats 'unfinished,' a man who 'by sheer vehemence of nature, all but saw the Grail.'[28]

Wilde's form of greatness was different from Yeats's. But with 'The Decay of Lying' he gave his theories a voice. His paradoxes danced, his wit gleamed. His language resounded with self-mockery, amusement, and extravagance. 'The Decay of Lying' became the *locus classicus* for the expression of the converging aesthetic ideas of writers everywhere. Art was not to be put down by politics, economics, ethics, or religion. Its pride and power could no longer be challenged as frivolous or futile. Degeneration was regeneration. By cunning and eloquence Wilde restored art to the power that the romantic poets had claimed for it, able once again to legislate for the world.

CHAPTER XII

The Age of Dorian

Aesthetics are higher than ethics. They belong to a more spiritual sphere. To discern the beauty of a thing is the finest point to which we can arrive. Even a colour-sense is more important, in the development of the individual, than a sense of right and wrong.

The New Aestheticism

The Nineties began in 1889 and ended in 1895. At least the Wildean Nineties did so, and without Wilde the decade could not have found its character. These were the years in which aestheticism was revised and perfected. During the Eighties Wilde's extremist sponsorship had helped to discredit it and provoked extravagant scorn. Now he conferred a new complexity upon the movement. Without surrendering the contempt for morality, or for nature, that had alarmed and annoyed his critics, Wilde now allowed for 'a higher ethics' in which artistic freedom and full expression of personality were possible, along with a curious brand of individualistic sympathy or narcissistic socialism. He also made it clear that nature might mirror, through art, what Shelley called 'the gigantic shadows which futurity casts upon the present.' To these he added another feature of aestheticism, the invasion of forbidden areas of thought and behavior. Decorum became merely a formal attribute of works of art, not a question of morality.

Aestheticism in its new guise modified the relationship between reader and writer. If matter once the exclusive preserve of pornography could be broached, then the reader's calm and sense of unthreatened distance were violable. Many young men and women learned of the existence of uncelebrated forms of love through the hints in *The Picture of Dorian Gray*. (Unofficially Wilde took note of what he officially denied, and told young Graham Robertson, the artist, 'Graham, the book was not written for you, and I hope you will not read it.') People also learned from Wilde how to shape a sentence and live in style. In the Eighties aestheticism suffered for lack of example: *Dorian Gray* filled the need. With its irreverent maxims, its catch phrases, its conversational gambits, its insouciance and contrariness, it announced the age of Dorian.

In the Eighties aestheticism had been less a movement than an expostulation with the lack of one. Yet its influence, and the influence of the movement of which it was a part – that propaganda for art and artist against 'factification' and 'getting-on' – grew stronger. The claims of action over art were challenged by the idea that artistic creation, related to that contemplative life celebrated by Plato, was the highest form of action. Wilde summed up ideas that were only implicit in England, but expressed in the poems of Mallarmé and Verlaine, and in the novels of Flaubert and D'Annunzio. These writers propounded their positions more carefully than Wilde, but he vied with them in one respect: he was spectacular always.

He was the more spectacular because his views, which agitated among the roots of literature and life, were presented with nonchalance. The use of dialogue lent undogmatic informality to his expression. He said, 'I can invent an imaginary antagonist and convert him when I choose by some absurdly sophistical argument.'[1] Even when he relinquished that form, as in 'The Soul of Man under Socialism,' he seemed to allow for debate with his position. It was as essential to disturb complacencies as to convince, or possibly more. In a diary for 21 July 1890 Katharine Bradley (of the 'Michael Field' collaboration) recorded how Wilde affirmed his role of lounge lizard:

> We agreed – the whole problem of life turns on pleasure – Pater shows that the hedonist – the perfected hedonist – is the saint. 'One is not always happy when one is good; but one is always good when one is happy.' He is writing two articles at present in the *Nineteenth Century* on the *Art of Doing Nothing*. He is at his best when he is lying on a sofa thinking. He does not want to do anything; overcome by the '*maladie du style*' – the effort to bring in delicate cadences to express exactly what he wants to express – he is prostrate. But to think, to contemplate . . .[2]

Wilde was referring to his articles on 'The True Function and Value of Criticism: with Some Remarks on the Importance of Doing Nothing: A Dialogue,' published in the *Nineteenth Century* in July and September 1890. In *Dorian Gray*, first published in Lippincott's on 20 June 1890, Lord Henry Wotton speaks 'languidly' three times and 'languorously' once. He gave a new sanction to these words, as Verlaine had given it to 'langueur' in French seven years before. Wilde was not indolent: he read voraciously, he devised and tried out conversational gambits, and touched them up in accordance with the shock, amusement, acquiescence, or delight that they aroused. He attributed the same interest in speech to the Greeks: 'Their test was always the spoken word in its musical and metrical relations. The voice was the medium, and the ear the critic.' He radiated, in Katharine Bradley's words, '*bien être*' with his 'mossy voice.' Most of his writing, Pater noted half in dispraise, had the air of 'an excellent talker.'[3] Yet in 1891, his *annus mirabilis*, he published four books (two volumes of stories, one of critical essays, and a novel), a long political essay ('The Soul of Man under Socialism') and wrote his first successful play, *Lady Windermere's Fan*, as well as most of *Salome*. Languor was the mask of industry.

The group of young men who followed Wilde swelled with his success. He had only to hear of a young poet to tender compliments and hospitality; he treated such literary aspirants as kindly as Mallarmé – a comparable *chef de cénacle*. New ones were constantly added. Wilde and Constance happened to be at Edward Burne-Jones's house on 12 July 1891, when the eighteen-year-old Aubrey Beardsley arrived unannounced, with his face 'like a silver hatchet' under his chestnut hair.[4] Burne-Jones, usually noncommittal when shown work by young artists, offered Beardsley every encouragement. The Wildes took Beardsley and his sister Mabel home in their carriage and became friends. It was perhaps under Wilde's influence that Beardsley's style became more satirical and sinister. He would say later that he had created Beardsley, and perhaps he had.

His principal young man until well into 1892 was one who arrived in Wilde's circle like a new star – John Gray. Born on 2 March 1866, the son of a carpenter, Gray longed to join the world of cultivated people. Forced to leave school at thirteen and become a metal-turner, he studied languages, music, and painting on the side. At sixteen he passed a civil service examination and landed a clerkship first in the Post Office, and six years later in the Library of the Foreign Office. Just when he and Wilde met is uncertain, because both of them said it was later than it was. But by 1889 the association had begun.

In August of that year Ricketts and Shannon, with whom Gray was on close terms, included two pieces by him in the first number of their magazine, the *Dial*. One was an article on the Goncourt brothers, the other a fairy tale in Wilde's manner entitled 'The Great Worm.' On receiving a copy Wilde promptly came to No 1, The Vale, to thank them for it. 'It is quite delightful,' he told them, 'but do not bring out a second number, all perfect things should be unique.' The subject of his young imitator with the passion for French literature must have come up, and Ricketts and Shannon could not have failed to describe their young, fair, and beautiful contributor. The writer Frank Liebich also attended a dinner party in 1889 at which Wilde and Gray were present.[5]

To give the hero of his novel the name of Gray was a form of courtship. Wilde probably named his hero not to point to a model, but to flatter Gray by identifying him with Dorian. Gray took the hint, and in letters to Wilde signed himself 'Dorian.' Their intimacy was common talk, for after a meeting of the Rhymers' Club about 1 February 1891, where Gray read and Wilde turned up to listen, Lionel Johnson and Ernest Dowson both alluded to it. Johnson wrote in a letter of 5 February 1891, 'I have made great friends with the original of Dorian: one John Gray, a youth in the Temple, aged thirty [actually twenty-five], with the face of fifteen.' Dowson wrote on 2 February that '"Dorian" Gray [read] some very beautiful and obscure versicles in the latest manner of French Symbolism.'[6] The next month Wilde announced that he was going to write an article entitled 'A New Poet' for the *Fortnightly Review*, and was only waiting for Gray to produce enough poems to be so heralded.

Wilde and Gray were assumed to be lovers, and there seems no reason to doubt it. Wilde probably wrote to Gray the two sentences which Dorian recalls having received from someone, 'The world is changed because you are made of ivory and gold. The curves of your lips rewrite history.' For a time Gray was overwhelmed – Bernard Shaw observed that he was 'one of the more abject of Wilde's disciples.'[7] But Wilde's attention was not so concentrated.

His special fondness was for students of his university. He traveled to Oxford in mid-February 1890, primarily because the Oxford University Dramatic Society had promised to follow his suggestions for their production of Browning's *Strafford*. While there he called on Pater and heard, perhaps from him, about a new poet at New College, Lionel Johnson. Wilde went to New College at noon to visit Johnson, only to be told that he was still in bed. He sent in a note 'plaintively' asking him to get up and receive him. Johnson, who was reading T. H. Green, read no more that day. He wrote to a friend, 'I found him as delightful as Green is not. He discourses, with infinite flippancy, of everyone: lauded the *Dial* [of Ricketts and Shannon]: laughed at Pater: and consumed all my cigarettes. I am in love with him.'[8] Wilde promised to come back, but was prevented by theatre business; he sent a letter from London addressed to 'Dear Mr Johnson,' praising his poems, and asking to know their author better.

Another New College friend was the half-demented poet John Barlas, who threatened to blow up the Houses of Parliament. When he was arrested in 1891, Wilde went with another friend of Barlas to the Westminster Police Court to offer himself as a surety for Barlas's good behavior. On the way, he learned from his companion that Barlas regarded himself as a reincarnated Biblical figure, and imagined that people were showing their reverence by crossing their hands in passing. Wilde commented with great sincerity, 'My dear fellow, when I think of the harm the Bible has done, I am quite ashamed of it.'[9] They were able to persuade the judge to accept their guarantees.

A more total convert to Wilde than Johnson or Barlas was Max Beerbohm, who met him first in 1888, while still at school at Charterhouse, and became a friend in the early 1890s when his brother, Herbert Beerbohm Tree, produced a Wilde play. Beerbohm was quick and clever: Wilde taught him to be languid and preposterous. Beerbohm referred to

291

Wilde as 'the Divinity'; Wilde said that Beerbohm had 'the gift of perpetual old age.' If Wilde celebrated the mask, Beerbohm in his first essays would celebrate *maquillage*; if Wilde wrote *Dorian Gray* about a man and his portrait, Beerbohm would write *The Happy Hypocrite* about a man and his mask. To some extent the disciple went beyond the master; Wilde complained to Ada Leverson, 'He plays with words as one plays with what one loves. When you are alone with him, Sphinx, does he take off his face and reveal his mask?'[10] The exquisite triviality of *Zuleika Dobson* tried to match *The Importance of Being Earnest*. Its discussion of peacocks and presents came straight from *Salome*. Beerbohm admired, learned, and resisted; aware that Wilde was homosexual, and anxious not to follow him in that direction, he drew back from intimacy. He was to caricature Wilde savagely; this was ungrateful, but it was a form of ingratitude, and of intimacy, into which other followers of Wilde lapsed.

The ideas and themes he scattered were sometimes reaped by his young admirers. The novelist W. B. Maxwell, while a boy, had heard many stories from Wilde, and wrote one of them down and published it. He confessed to Wilde, whose face clouded, then cleared as he mixed approval with reproach, 'Stealing my story was the act of a gentleman, but not telling me you had stolen it was to ignore the claims of friendship.' Then he suddenly became serious, 'You mustn't take a story that I told you of a man and a picture. No, absolutely, I want that for myself. I fully mean to write it, and I should be terribly upset if I were forestalled.'[11] This first mention of *The Picture of Dorian Gray* antedated by several years, Maxwell says, the actual composition.

Painting Dorian's Portrait

'Harry,' said Basil Hallward, looking him straight in the face, 'every portrait that is painted with feeling is a portrait of the artist, not of the sitter.'

For Wilde aestheticism was not a creed but a problem. Exploring its ramifications provided him with his subject, and he responded to it with a mixture of serious espousal and mockery – an attitude that Beerbohm found it fruitful to copy. Gautier had preached an icy aestheticism – Wilde did not subscribe, but sometimes enjoyed pretending that he did. The slogan of art for art's sake he had long since disavowed. But he saw his story of a man and his portrait as containing most of the ingredients that he wanted to exploit. 'To become a work of art is the object of living,' he wrote.[12] Dorian was one of two portraits he would write of a man in decay, the other being the professed self-portrait in *De Profundis*. Wilde's novel connects somewhat with other narratives. In Henry James's *The Tragic Muse*, published in 1890, the aesthete, Gabriel Nash, bears traces of

Wilde, including the aesthetic cosmopolitanism which James found so annoying in 1882. When Nick Dormer asks Nash, 'Don't we both live in London, after all, and in the Nineteenth Century?' Nash replies, 'Ah, my dear Dormer, excuse me. I don't live in the Nineteenth Century. *Jamais de la vie!*' 'Nor in London either?' 'Yes – when I'm not in Samarcand.' Nash sits for a portrait, but disappears: no one knows where he has gone, and his unfinished image on the canvas fades away as impalpably as the original. James's theme was that aestheticism, being indifferent to concrete detail, could confer upon its followers only an illusory existence. But if James was hard on aestheticism, Wilde would be hard on it too, at least in his novel.

Wilde liked telling stories about portraits. Charles Ricketts remembered someone speaking to Wilde of the excellence of Holbein's portrait of Anne of Cleves. Her ugliness had overwhelmed Henry VIII. 'You believe she was really ugly?' said Wilde. 'No, my dear boy, she was exquisite as we see her in the Louvre. But in the escort, sent to bring her to England, travelled also a beautiful young nobleman of whom she became passionately enamoured, and on the ship they became lovers. What could be done? Discovery meant death. So she stained her face, and put uncouth clothing upon her body, till she seemed the monster Henry thought her. Now, do you know what happened? Years passed, and one day, when the king went hawking, he heard a woman singing in an orchard close, and rising in his stirrups to see who, with lovely voice, had entranced him, he beheld Anne of Cleves, young and beautiful, singing in the arms of her lover.'[13]

Among the many sources that have been offered for *The Picture of Dorian Gray* are Balzac's *La Peau de chagrin*, Stevenson's *Dr Jekyll and Mr Hyde*, Goethe's *Faust*, Meinhold's *Sidonia*. The list could be multiplied indefinitely. As Yeats says, 'Works of art beget works of art.' No specific work is exactly comparable. Wilde had hit upon a myth for aestheticism, the myth of the vindictive image, an art that turns upon its original as son against father or man against God. He began with a familiar theme: 'I first conceived the idea of a young man selling his soul in exchange for eternal youth – an idea that is old in the history of literature, but to which I have given new form,' he said in a letter to an editor about the book. The new form came from localizing this theme in the contemporary controversy of art versus life. That the story was as old as Salome's did not distress him. He wanted to make Dorian a figure to vie with Marius and Des Esseintes, not to mention Balzac's Lucien de Rubempré – and succeeded.

There was a long brooding before *Dorian Gray* came into being. Wilde had been much concerned with images. He had painted self-portrait after self-portrait: at Trinity College he experimented with a beard, then shaved it off; he let his hair grow long at Oxford and had it waved, then in Paris had it cut and curled Roman-style, then let it grow long again. His clothing also passed through transformations: dandiacal in London, it became *outré* in America, elaborately decorous afterwards. No wonder he spoke often about poses and masks. 'The first duty in life is to assume a pose,' he said, 'what the second duty is no one yet has found out.' As Yeats would insist after him, the imaginative creation of oneself goes on almost from birth. He was moved by the attempt of Des Esseintes in *A Rebours* to construct an artistic world in which to live artistically, and he spoke approvingly in 'Pen, Pencil and Poison' of life as art. He disagreed with those who called him artificial. He thought of the self as having multiple possibilities, and of his life as manifesting each of these in turn.

Portraits, and mirrors, were therefore subjects for his dialectic. Mirrors may be naturalistic, as in 'The Birthday of the Infanta,' where the dwarf dies at the sight of his image, or in Dorian's favorite book, in which the hero has 'a grotesque dread of mirrors and polished steel surfaces and still water' because they will disclose his fading beauty. But they may also be symbolic. In Wilde's fable Narcissus looks at his image in the water, but does not know that the water sees only its own image in his eyes. In 'The Decay of Lying,' instead of art mirroring nature, nature mirrors art. The preface to *Dorian Gray* declares, 'It is the spectator, and not Life, that art really mirrors,' yet in the novel the portrait ceases to mirror Dorian's external beauty and mirrors only his internal ugliness.

He also had in mind his controversy with Whistler, when he had argued, in his 1885 review of 'Mr Whistler's Ten o'Clock,' that the supreme artist was the poet (not as Whistler maintained the painter), because the poet could make use of all experience rather than a part. He knew Lessing's theory that painting was spatial and literature temporal, and 'The Critic as Artist,' written at the same time as *Dorian Gray*, insists that the time world is superior, since it involves a psychic response to one's own history:

> The statue is concentrated in one moment of perfection. The image stained upon the canvas possesses no spiritual element of growth or change. If they know nothing of death, it is because they know little of life, for the secrets of life belong to those, and those only, whom the sequence of time affects, and who possess not merely the present but the future, and can rise or fall from a past of glory or of shame. Movement, that problem of the visible arts, can be truly realised by Literature alone.

For his novel he dreamed of transcending these generic limits. It had to be written in words, but with the words he could describe a painting with the attributes Lessing had denied to pictorial art: once the portrait had transfigured its object – the sitter – by concentrating him in one moment of perfection, it would disfigure its achievement as though it would claim time rather than space. That literature and painting could not exchange their roles was the idea which *Dorian Gray* would alter; in the end each art would revert to its norm, but literature would show itself capable of doing what painting could not do, exist temporally rather than eternally, and yet enshrine a portrait of its beautiful and monstrous hero. Though he had removed all traces of Whistler from the book, the novel carries on their old dispute about the relative merits of their two arts. Wilde wins by bringing together, as Whistler could not, the exalted moment and its disintegration.

This concern with time reflected Wilde's sense of his own changes. Now that he was firmly homosexual, he wondered if he had always been so. Dorian moves from innocence to guilt. Wilde did not feel particularly guilty, but he could wonder if he had ever been innocent. Had his youthful love life been only a pretense? Such questions led him to the two Dorians.

So many people asked about the originals of the characters that Wilde amused himself by giving conflicting answers. Hesketh Pearson reports one, that Basil Hallward was so named because in 1884 Wilde sat for the painter Basil Ward. Having finished the picture, Ward remarked, 'How delightful it would be if you could remain exactly as you are, while the portrait aged and withered in your stead.'[14] The story would be more convincing if there was any evidence that a Basil Ward had painted Wilde, and if Wilde had not spread a second explanation. He was obviously the source for a story that appeared in the *St James's Gazette* of 24 September 1891: the Canadian artist Frances Richards, whom Wilde had met in Canada in 1882, painted his portrait in 1887. It prompted Wilde to say, 'What a tragic thing it is. This portrait will never grow older, and I shall. If it was only the other way.' Still another version was recorded by Ernest Dowson, who heard Wilde say at Herbert Horne's house on 9 October 1890 that the original of Basil Hallward was Charles Ricketts. This seems likely, at least for the homosexual tastes of Basil Hallward, which were more distinct in the magazine version than in the book. But the novel's theme, the relation of passion to art, goes back to Charmides' fevered night with Athena's bronze nakedness in Wilde's poem. Charmides' violation of art by life was a sacrilege like Dorian's attempt to substitute one for the other.

That Wilde wrote the book down instead of continuing to tell it to young men like Maxwell was partly owing to J. M. Stoddart, the Philadelphia publisher with whom seven years before Wilde had called on Walt Whitman, and who had been persuaded to publish Rennell Rodd's *Rose Leaf and Apple Leaf.* One of his enterprises was *Lippincott's Monthly Magazine*, and in an attempt to promote it Stoddart came to London about September 1889. He thought some short novels were needed, and so had two of his best prospects, Arthur Conan Doyle and Oscar Wilde, with an Irish Member of Parliament, T. P. Gill, to dinner. Doyle left an account of the talk. There was some reference to Rodd's or somebody else's defection, which prompted Wilde to remark, as he would in 'The Soul of Man under Socialism,' 'Anyone can sympathise with the sufferings of a friend, but it requires a very fine nature – it requires, in fact, the nature of a true Individualist to sympathise with a friend's success.' He illustrated the maxim with an anecdote:

The devil was once crossing the Libyan desert, and he came upon a spot where a number of small fiends were tormenting a holy hermit. The sainted man easily shook off their evil suggestions. The devil watched their failure and then he stepped forward to give them a lesson. 'What you do is too crude . . . Permit me for one moment.' With that he whispered to the holy man, 'Your brother has just been made Bishop of Alexandria.' A scowl of malignant jealousy at once clouded the serene face of the hermit. 'That,' said the devil to his imps, 'is the sort of thing which I should recommend.'

The conversation turned to wars of the future, and Doyle remembered Wilde's saying with 'upraised hand and precise face,' his expression conjuring up a grotesque scene, 'A chemist on each side will approach the frontier with a bottle.' Stoddart brought the subject back to literature. Wilde had read Doyle's *Micah Clarke*, and praised it, to the author's pleasure. Doyle offered Stoddart his second Sherlock Holmes story, 'The Sign of Four,' the first having had the aesthetic title, 'A Study in Scarlet.' Wilde, possibly in response to Doyle's description of a string of fearful murders, recounted his own story of Dorian's murder of Hallward and himself, equally beyond ordinary detection. Stoddart closed with both writers immediately, and asked Wilde to send him the story by October.[15] Wilde put him off until November, and does not seem to have delivered it until the next spring. In the meantime Stoddart asked for 100,000 words, but Wilde replied by cable, 'There are not 100,000 beautiful words in the English language.'

The Picture of Dorian Gray was his longest prose narrative, and gave him much trouble. 'I am afraid it is rather like my own life – all conversation and no action,' he wrote early in 1890 to a writer friend, Beatrice Allhusen. 'I can't describe action: my people sit in chairs and chatter.' He was as careful as he could be with the events he did narrate, such as the disposal of Hallward's body. (A friendly surgeon informed him how this could be done by chemical means.)[16] Other difficulties also gave way, and the novel was published on 20 June 1890, as pp 3–100 of the July issue of *Lippincott's Monthly Magazine*. After this date Victorian literature had a different look.

Dorian Repudiated

> *Soul and body, body and soul – how mysterious they are! There is animalism in the soul, and the body has its moments of spirituality. The senses can refine, and the intellect can degrade.*

Both in its magazine form, and in its form as a separate novel, *Dorian Gray* has faults. Parts of it are wooden, padded, self-indulgent. No one could mistake it for a workmanlike job: our hacks can do that for us. But its continual fascination teaches us to judge it by new standards. Wilde made it elegantly casual, as if writing a novel were a diversion rather than 'a painful duty' (as he characterized Henry James's manner). The under-lying legend, of trying to elicit more from life than life can give, arouses deep and criminal yearnings. These contrast with the polish of English civilization at its verbal peak, and create a tension beyond what the plot appears to hold. Wilde put into the book a negative version of what he had been brooding about for fourteen years and, under a veil, what he had been doing sexually for four. He could have taken a positive view of reconsidered aestheticism, as he would in 'The Critic as Artist,' and 'The Soul of Man under Socialism,' as he had already done in 'The Decay of Lying.' Instead, *Dorian Gray* is the aesthetic novel *par excellence*, not in espousing the doctrine, but in exhibiting its dangers. Pater's refurbishing of aestheticism in the late 1860s and early 1870s had been followed by a series of attacks upon it: by James in *Roderick Hudson*, 1876; by Mallock in *The New Republic*, 1877; by Gilbert and Sullivan in *Patience*, 1881; and by *Punch* and many others. In 1890 it would have been old hat for Wilde to offer an unequivocal defense. What he did instead was to write the tragedy of aestheticism. It was also premonitory of his own tragedy, for Dorian has like Wilde experimented with two forms of sexuality, love of women and of men. Through his hero Wilde was able to open a window into his own recent experience. The life of mere sensation is uncovered as anarchic and self-destructive. Dorian Gray is a test case. He fails. Life cannot be lived on such terms. Self-indulgence leads him to vandalize his own portrait, but this act is a reversal of what he intends and he discloses his better self, though only in death. Wilde's hero has pushed through to the point where extremes meet. By unintentional suicide, Dorian becomes aestheticism's first martyr. The text: Drift beautifully on the surface, and you will die unbeautifully in the depths. In response to critical abuse, Wilde added the preface, which flaunted the aestheticism that the book would indict. *Dorian Gray* is reflexive in the most cunning way, like its central image.

Dorian progresses, or regresses, to art and back to life. Everything in the book has an aesthetic and clandestine quotient, in terms of which it can eventually be measured. The portrait of Dorian is executed by Basil Hallward just at the moment when Lord Henry is fishing for Dorian's soul. Although Wilde states in the book's preface, 'To reveal art and conceal the artist is art's aim,' Hallward fears that the portrait is too revealing of his love for Dorian, as Dorian later fears that it is too revealing of himself. Wilde the preface-writer and Wilde the novelist deconstruct each other. Dorian offers a Faustian pact (with no visible devil) that he will exchange places with his portrait, to preserve himself as a work of art.

But he is not to achieve timelessness easily. His role of invulnerable and detached profligate is challenged by love. His attachment to Sibyl Vane is an experiment in the aesthetic laboratory. The affair ends as badly as Faust's with Gretchen, but Sibyl Vane differs from Gretchen in being an actress. She plays Shakespearean heroines, so Dorian is able to aestheticize her in his imagination. 'I have been right,' he congratulates himself, 'to take my love out of poetry and to find my wife in Shakespeare's plays.' Put to the test, however, Sibyl is no mere performer; her fatal weakness in his eyes is that she values life above art. She loses her capacity to act because, instead of preferring shadows to reality as she once did, she is drawn by love to prefer reality. She voices the heresy that 'all art is but a reflection' of that reality, and Dorian excommunicates her with the cruel words, 'Without your art you are nothing.' Like Faust's Gretchen, she poisons herself in despair. And even her death is rendered aesthetic, first by Lord Henry and then by Dorian. Lord Henry finds that she has played out her part, 'a strange lurid fragment from some Jacobean tragedy,' and that 'The girl never really lived, and so she has never really died.' Dorian agrees with the same glibness, 'She passed again into the sphere of art.' Only her brother, and the reader, are left to mourn, and to judge. Sibyl is the opposite of Dorian. She gives up the pretense of art so as to live entirely artlessly in this world, only to commit suicide. Dorian tries to give up the causality of life and to live in the deathless (and lifeless) world of art, only to commit suicide too.

Dorian commits the primal sin against love, and it leads to his second crime. Basil Hallward discovers the secret of the portrait, and urges him to accept the consequences. For this insistence upon the moral causality of life, Basil too has to die. Dorian manages the murder, and the disposal of the body, as if De Quincey were right about murder being one of the fine arts. After the murder he sleeps insouciantly; next morning he chooses his tie and rings with special care, and reads Gautier's *Emaux et Camées*, finding in its chiselled quatrains some of the reassuring impersonality that Pound and Eliot were to derive from the same book during the First World War. The friend who helps to dispose of the body commits suicide like Sibyl. What few twinges Dorian feels he obliterates in an opium den.

The first chapters deal with Dorian's infection by Lord Henry, the later ones with his poisoning by a book. Wilde does not name the book, but at his trial he conceded that it was, or almost was, Huysmans's *A Rebours*. Of course he also had in mind a book which preceded Huysmans's, Pater's *Studies in the History of the Renaissance*. In the first draft he gave the mysterious book a name, *Le Secret de Raoul* by Catulle Sarrazin. This author was a blend of Catulle Mendès, whom he had known for some years, and Gabriel Sarrazin, whom he met in September 1888, and the name of Raoul came from Rachilde's *Monsieur Vénus*. To a correspondent he wrote that he had played 'a fantastic variation' upon *A Rebours*, and some day must write it down. The references in *Dorian Gray* to specific chapters of the unnamed book are deliberately inaccurate. Dorian is said to relish especially the seventh chapter in which the hero fancies himself as Tiberius, Caligula, Domitian, and Elagabalus, and the eighth and ninth chapters in which Renaissance crimes are described. Huysmans's book has none of these: Des Esseintes shows no interest in imperial power, and Wilde borrowed the Renaissance scenes not from Huysmans but from his friend John Addington Symonds' *Renaissance in Italy*.[17] In fact, the mythical book which so affects Dorian, the pseudo-*A Rebours*, reads as if it had been plagiarized from Wilde. (He told a correspondent that he must some day write it.) The hero is said to be alarmed 'by the sudden decay of a beauty that had once, apparently, been so remarkable.' Huysmans never describes Des Esseintes as beautiful, nor as concerned about no longer being so. Dorian says the hero has a dread of mirrors: Des Esseintes has none, though he does read a passage in Mallarmé's 'Hérodiade' where this dread is expressed by her. The more genuine points of comparison are the cultivation of artificial pleasures and the alternations of exaltation and abasement. Though Wilde borrowed the idea for artificial sensation-seeking from Huysmans, he gives Dorian a more specialized interest in jewelry, for which, it appears, no French source was required. He borrowed all the details from South Kensington Museum pamphlets on musical instruments, precious stones, embroidery and lace, and textile fabrics.[18]

When Dorian tells Lord Henry that the pseudo-*A Rebours* has corrupted him, his friend denies that this could happen. 'As for being poisoned by a book, there is no such thing as that. Art has no influence upon action. It annihilates the desire to act. It is superbly sterile. The books that the world calls immoral are books that show the world its own shame. That is all.' But a book has completed for Dorian what Lord Henry began. We are not allowed to accept Wotton's judgment, for it has already been made clear that he himself, when he was sixteen, had been overwhelmed by a book. His book is also left unnamed, but its identity can be established from his talk. Lord Henry is forever quoting, or misquoting, without acknowledgment, from Pater's *Studies in the History of the Renaissance*. Plagiarism is the worst of his crimes. He brazenly takes over the best known passages. Pater had urged that we 'be present always at the focus where the greatest number of vital forces unite in their purest energy,' and Lord Henry echoes him (though omitting the attribute of 'purest') when he says, 'To realise one's nature to perfection – that is what each of us is here for.' Pater says we must not allow 'theory or idea or system' to oblige us to the 'sacrifice of any part of this experience.' Lord Henry goes further, 'We are punished for our refusals. Every impulse that we strive to strangle broods in the mind, and poisons us. The body sins once, and has done with its sin, for action is a mode of purification . . . The only way to get rid of a temptation is to yield to it. Resist it, and your soul grows sick.' Wilde was quite capable of taking this position himself, and in fact did so to André Gide; but coming from Lord Henry it is only a seducer's version of the perils of repression. In the same way, Pater's promise of a new hedonism attainable through art, which promises 'frankly to give nothing but the highest quality to your moments as they pass, and simply for those moments' sake,' is like Dorian's new movement beyond asceticism and profligacy that will 'teach man to concentrate himself upon the moments of life that is itself but a moment.' Pater reviewed the book at Wilde's request, and objected that Dorian's and Lord Henry's hedonism left no place for the higher pleasures of generosity and renunciation.

Dorian turns this argument around to justify himself:

> There had been mad wilful rejections, monstrous forms of self-torture and self-denial, whose origin was fear, and whose result was a degradation infinitely more terrible than that fancied degradation from which, in their ignorance, they had sought to escape. Nature, in her wonderful irony, driving out the anchorite to feed with the wild animals of the desert and giving to the hermit the beasts of the field as his companions.

In 'The Critic as Artist' Wilde returns to the idea, with approval:

> Self-denial is simply a method by which man arrests his progress, and self-sacrifice a survival of the mutilation of the savage, part of that old worship of pain which is so terrible a factor in the history of the world, and which even now makes its victims day by day, and has its altars in the land.

Through carelessness, impatience, or whim, Wilde sometimes forgot that his characters should always carry aestheticism to excess, and allowed them to articulate his own sentiments. But apart from these, he kept to his original plan, that Lord Henry should separate himself from life by being unwilling to recognize its obligations. Wotton denies the soul, denies suffering, thinks of art as a malady and love as an illusion. He is wrong in supposing that books cannot influence conduct, when they have influenced his own; he is wrong in praising Dorian's life as a work of art when it has been a failure. Dorian quotes with approval one of Wotton's misguided statements, 'To become the spectator of one's own life, as Harry says, is to "escape the sufferings of life."' In defending the book Wilde explained, 'Lord Henry Wotton seeks to be merely the spectator of life. He finds that those who reject the battle are more deeply wounded than those who take part in it.' The cultivation of art apart from life is to build a fire that cannot burn. The artist cannot be all ice, chiselling in marble, as Gautier prescribed. Yet as Des Esseintes says in a passage often overlooked, aestheticism is fundamentally an aspiration towards an ideal, towards an unknown universe, towards a beatitude, as desirable as that promised by the Scriptures.[19]

Dorian Gray, besides being about aestheticism, is also one of the first attempts to bring homosexuality into the English novel. Its appropriately covert presentation of this censored subject gave the book notoriety and originality. As Wilde had written in 'The Soul of Man under Socialism,' 'Any attempt to extend the subject-matter of art is extremely distasteful to the public; and yet the vitality and progress of art depend in a large measure on the continual extension of the subject-matter.' Not that all Wilde's principals are homosexuals, but they are scarcely anything else. Lord Henry is feebly married; rather to his satisfaction, his wife leaves him. He takes a cottage in Algiers (often a vacation spot for English homosexuals) for himself and Dorian, and his attempt to inseminate his friend spiritually is at least ambiguous. Dorian ruins men and women alike, as if his love in either mode was genuine only to the extent that it is tainted. As in *A Rebours*, both forms of love are rendered as corrupt. Hallward is murdered by the man he excessively loves. Dorian's face has in fact been for Hallward's art 'the counterpart of Antinous' in Greek sculpture. Not surprisingly, Hallward has painted Dorian 'crowned with heavy lotus-blossoms ... on the prow of Adrian's barge.' Dorian is perfectly aware of what love he has inspired in Basil: 'It was such love as Michael Angelo had known, and Montaigne, and Winckelmann, and Shakespeare himself.' Like Proust, Wilde made use of the theme of homosexuality, but only in terms of unhappiness. Dorian's propensities are made clear: he shares with Wilde the delight in dressing up, often as a king's favorite such as Anne de Joyeuse, admiral of France – a darling for Henry III as Gaveston was for Edward II; and he likes to look at the portrait of his ancestor Philip Herbert, who was 'caressed by the court [or, as the *Lippincott's* version said, by James I] for his handsome face.' There is something dubious in his identification of himself with Elagabalas, who had 'painted his face with colours, and plied the distaff among the women, and brought the Moon from Carthage, and given her in mystic marriage to the Sun.' Dorian's spiritual ancestry is strong in him. No wonder that Wilde's friend, the novelist Ouida, to whom he sent a copy, said that she *did* understand it.

Wilde saw the three characters as refractions of his own image. He explained to a correspondent, 'Basil Hallward is what I think I am: Lord Henry what the world thinks me: Dorian is what I would like to be in other ages, perhaps.' At moments Dorian's history conforms closely to Wilde's: he has been rumoured to be 'about to join the Catholic communion,' and has sampled mysticism as Wilde sampled Masonry. Dorian has narrowly missed being blackballed at a West End club; Wilde had suffered being removed from the list of prospective members of the Savile. Wilde gives a clue to himself and his work when he says that Dorian 'would often adopt certain modes of thought that he knew to be really alien to his nature, abandon himself to their subtle influences, and then, having as it were caught their colour and satisfied his intellectual curiosity, leave them with that curious indifference that is not incompatible with a real ardour of temperament, and that, indeed, according to certain modern psychologists, is often a condition of it.' Four years earlier he had written to Harry

Marillier about his own 'curious mixture of ardour and indifference.' Lord Henry echoes Pater's early ascendancy over Wilde, though some of his pronouncements on the arts, on women, and on America are Wilde's own. But he is the spokesman for an aestheticism gone extreme and insensitive. Hallward's good-heartedness and delight in young men, and his image-making power, are close to Wilde too. But Wilde is larger than his three characters together: they represent distortions or narrowing of his personality, none of them reproducing his generosity of spirit or his sense of fun or his full creativeness.

The publication of *Dorian Gray*, though it had taken place only in a magazine, brought Wilde all the attention he could desire. It brought his wife more than she wanted, and she said, 'Since Oscar wrote *Dorian Gray*, no one will speak to us.' His mother was rapturous: 'It is the most wonderful piece of writing in all the fiction of the day . . . I nearly fainted at the last scene.'[20] One effect can be measured by Wilde's invitation to the Crabbet Club on 4 July 1891. George Curzon had agreed to play devil's advocate and oppose Wilde for membership. Wilfrid Scawen Blunt wrote,

> He had been at Oxford with Wilde and knew all his little weaknesses and did not spare him, playing with astonishing audacity and skill upon his reputation for sodomy and his treatment of the subject in *Dorian Gray*. Poor Oscar sat helplessly smiling, a fat mass, in his chair . . . (He was sitting on my left and when he rose to reply I felt sorry for him – it seemed hardly fair). But he pulled himself together as he went on and gradually warmed into an amusing and excellent speech – What is really memorable about it all is that, when two years later he was arraigned in a real Court of Justice, Oscar's line of defence was precisely the same as that made in his impromptu speech that evening at Crabbet.

Wilde was not content only to defend himself. He told Frank Harris that he had commented on Curzon's mediocrity, his desperately hard work in pursuing a second-class degree and then a second-class career.[21] But he never went back to the Crabbet Club.

The book repelled several of the reviewers, and Wilde bravely wrote long and persuasive letters in reply. His letters to editors are as good as any exercises in the form. The principal charges against him were that the novel was tedious and dull, that its characters were 'puppies,' that it was merely self-advertisement, and that it was immoral. As for tedium, Wilde contended that, on the contrary, 'it is far too crowded with sensational incident, and far too paradoxical in style . . . I feel that from a standpoint of art these are two defects in the book. But tedious and dull the book is not.' As for puppies, he replied, 'They *are* puppies. Does he [the reviewer] think that literature went to the dogs when Thackeray wrote about puppydom?' As for self-advertisement, Wilde wrote,

I think I may say without vanity – though I do not wish to appear to run vanity down – that of all men in England I am the one who requires least advertisement. I am tired to death of being advertised – I feel no thrill when I see my name in a paper . . . I wrote this book entirely for my own pleasure . . . Whether it becomes popular or not is a matter of absolute indifference to me.

To the charge of immorality, he retorted, as Coleridge did with 'The Ancient Mariner,' that *Dorian Gray* was too moral. He summed up the message: 'all excess as well as all renunciation, brings its own punishment.' The difficulty is that the book contains no renunciant, and while Dorian Gray does say that anchorites and hermits are as bestial as sybarites, the point cannot be regarded as fictionally demonstrated. Wilde was on safer ground when he said, 'in his attempt to kill conscience Dorian Gray kills himself,' a moral for which he claimed an 'ethical beauty.' The moral for aestheticism is that those who would be spectators only discover they are more spied upon than spying, and that to seek to become an aesthetic object, outside of time, is to die. In a letter to the editor of what he termed 'a paper called the *Daily Chronicle,*' Wilde wrote 'My story is an essay on decorative art. It reacts against the crude brutality of plain realism. It is poisonous if you like, but you cannot deny that it is also perfect, and perfection is what we artists aim at.' He concluded his correspondence with the *St James's Gazette* by saying, 'As you assailed me first, I have a right to the last word. Let the last word be the present letter, and leave my book, I beg you, to the immortality that it deserves.'[22]

Following this acerbic exchange he went to see the editor of the *St James's Gazette*, Sidney Low, whom he had known at Oxford. Low summoned his assistant, a man named Samuel Henry Jeyes, who had written the review under the title 'A Study in Puppydom.' Wilde contended that no conclusions of a personal nature should be drawn from any theory of art. Jeyes replied belligerently, 'What is the use of writing of, and hinting at, things that you do not mean?' Wilde replied, 'I mean every word I have said, and everything at which I have hinted in *Dorian Gray.*' 'Then,' said Jeyes, 'all I can say is that if you do mean them you are very likely to find yourself at Bow Street one of these days.'* Wilde called on Low three days later at the Whitefriars Club and had a long talk with him about *Dorian Gray*, after which the tone of the *St James's Gazette* became more moderate.[23]

As a result of the initial response, Wilde composed a series of aphorisms, originally under the title, 'Dogmas for the Use of the Aged.'[24] There were two that caught the eye of James Joyce, and went in modified form

---

* In 1895, when Wilde was convicted, Jeyes editorialized (on 27 May) that the *St James's Gazette* had been right to say that *Dorian Gray* was a matter for the police, not the critic.

into his *Ulysses*: 'The nineteenth century dislike of Realism is the rage of Caliban seeing his own face in a glass. The nineteenth century dislike of Romanticism is the rage of Caliban not seeing his own face in a glass.' Some of them are answers to the critics: 'Those who find ugly meanings in beautiful things are corrupt without being charming. That is a fault.' 'There is no such thing as a moral or an immoral book. Books are well written or badly written. That is all.' (But Dorian is corrupted by a book.) 'Vice and virtue are to the artist materials for an art.' 'Diversity of opinion about a work of art shows that the work is new, complex, and vital.' To prevent the book's being treated as immoral, Wilde excluded morality from its province, although it exposed the follies of a false and excessive aestheticism.

Wilde took his 'Preface,' as he called it, to Frank Harris at the *Fortnightly Review*. Harris tried to persuade him that some aphorisms should be dropped as too weak. Wilde listened attentively, but the next day said those that Harris had singled out as weakest were the strongest, and he wanted them all to be published. Harris agreed, and the Preface appeared in March 1891. The stage was now set for the novel's publication in book form a month later. Wilde wrote to Ada Leverson, 'It is quite tragic for me to think how completely *Dorian Gray* has been understood on all sides.' He added some chapters and took out – at Pater's urging – an explicitly homosexual sentence about Hallward's affection for Dorian. His friend Coulson Kernahan urged him to remove the remark, 'The only way to resist temptation is to yield to it.' Wilde declined, saying, 'it is merely Luther's *Pecca Fortiter* [Sin Boldly] put dramatically into the lips of a character.'[25] After touching it up here and there, he asked Macmillan to publish it. They declined, on the ground that it contained unpleasant elements. A small firm, Ward, Lock & Co, agreed to bring it out. Wilde was about to dart off for Paris, but before leaving asked Kernahan to go over the proofs and check the usage of 'shall' and 'will' about which 'as an Irishman' he was always hazy. Then a telegram from Paris arrived: 'Stop all proofs. Wilde.' He arrived by cab with a last-minute correction. He had given a picture-framer in the book the name Ashton. It would not do. 'Ashton is a gentleman's name. And I've given it to a tradesman. It must be changed to Hubbard. Hubbard particularly smells of the tradesman.'[26] Hubbard it became.*

---

* In Paris on 11 March 1891, Wilde went with Sherard and Carlos Blacker to call on Zola. 'I consider it a great honor to receive your visit,' Zola said. He discussed his novel *La Guerre*, and said he must go down to Sedan to visit the battlefield. But before that he must go through heaps of documents about the battle. 'You believe absolutely in the value of documents for novel-writing then?' asked Wilde. 'Oh, absolutely. There is no good novel which is not based on documents.' 'It's what I was saying last night at Daudet's,' said Wilde. 'In writing my *Dorian Gray* I studied long lists of jewelry. The other day I spent hours over a catalogue published by a firm of horticulturists, to learn the names of various kinds of flowers and their technical

Dorian Gray was published as a book in April 1891. Almost at once W. H. Smith refused to carry it, on the grounds that it was 'filthy.' But the *Athenaeum* and the *Theatre* treated it with respect. Pater, who had – according to Frank Harris – refused to write an appreciation of the earlier version for the *Fortnightly Review* on the grounds that it was 'too dangerous,' wrote a notice for the *Bookman*. Pater, being now what D. S. MacColl terms 'a saint of sensation,' insisted that Lord Henry Wotton, who speaks so many of Pater's sentences, was not a true Cyrenaic or Epicurean. But otherwise he was delighted with the book.[28]

The effect of *Dorian Gray* was prodigious. No novel had commanded so much attention for years, or awakened sentiments so contradictory in its readers. Wilde's circle of young men were delighted. Max Beerbohm wrote his 'Ballade de la Vie Joyeuse' about it, and Lionel Johnson, who had also received a copy from the author, wrote an effusive and witty Latin poem:

In Honorem Doriani Creatorisque Eius

Benedictus sis, Oscare!
Qui me libro hoc dignare
    Propter amicitias:
Modo modulans Romano
Laudes dignas Doriano,
    Ago tibi gratias.

Juventutis hic formosa
Floret inter rosas rosa,
    Subito dum venit mors:
Ecce Homo! ecce Deus!
Si sic modo esset meus
Genius misericors!

Amat avidus amores
Miros, miros carpit flores
    Saevus pulchritudine:
Quanto anima nigrescit,
Tanto facies splendiescit,
Mendax, sed quam splendide!

---

descriptions. You cannot draw a novel from your brain as a spider draws its web out of its belly.'

But with Max Beerbohm he was more candid: 'Do you know, whenever that man writes a book he always takes his subjects directly from life. If he is going to write about dreadful people in hovels he goes and lives in a hovel himself for months in case he shouldn't be accurate. It is strange. Take me for example. I have conceived the idea for the most exquisite tale that was ever written. The period is the eighteenth century. It would require a morning's reading at the British Museum. Therefore,' he sighed, 'it will never be written.'[27]

Hic sunt poma Sodomorum;
Hic sunt corda vitiorum;
   Et peccata dulcia.
In excelsis et infernis,
Tibi sit, qui tanta cernis,
   Gloriarum gloria.

Lionellus Poeta.*

All this is Latin for a thousand thanks[29]

Among Johnson's friends was a young cousin from Winchester College who was now up at Magdalen. Johnson lent him his copy of *The Picture of Dorian Gray*, and he was soon 'passionately absorbed' in it. He read it nine times over or as he said to A. J. A. Symons, 'fourteen times running.' At the first opportunity, which must have been in late June, he went with Johnson to meet Wilde in Tite Street.[30] This was the first meeting of Oscar Wilde and Lord Alfred Douglas. The youngest son of the Marquess of Queensberry had a pale alabaster face and blond hair – he was even better looking than John Gray, and even less talented. He was slight of build, by his own reckoning five feet nine though Wilde regarded him as short. His friends – and he never lacked friends – thought him charming. In temperament he was totally spoiled, reckless, insolent and, when thwarted, fiercely vindictive. Wilde could see only his beauty, delighted in his praise of *Dorian Gray*, and gave him a deluxe copy. On hearing that Douglas was reading Greats, he offered to coach him.[31]

Six years later Henry Davray (one of Wilde's translators) helped a drunken Lionel Johnson home. Wilde and Douglas were on their minds. Johnson looked tipsily at the framed portraits of the two on his wall, and moaned, 'Mon Dieu! Mon Dieu!'[32]

---

*   'In Honour of Dorian and His Creator

'Bless you, Oscar, for honouring me with this book for friendship's sake. Casting in the Roman tongue praises that befit Dorian, I thank you.

This lovely rose of youth blossoms among roses, until death comes abruptly. Behold the man! Behold the God! If only my soul could take his part.

He avidly loves strange loves and, fierce with beauty, he plucks strange flowers. The more sinister his spirit, the more radiant his face, lying – but how splendidly!

Here are apples of Sodom, here are the very hearts of vices, and tender sins. In heaven and hell be glory of glories to you who perceive so much.

Lionel the Poet.'

Wilde as Criminologist

*If we lived long enough to see the results of our actions it may
be that those who call themselves good would be sickened
with a dull remorse, and those whom the world calls evil
stirred by a noble joy.*

But for the moment Wilde had other concerns. If *Dorian Gray* presented
aestheticism in an almost negative way, his essays, 'The Critic as Artist'
and 'The Soul of Man under Socialism,' gave it affirmation. The first was
published in July and September 1890 in the *Nineteenth Century*, and
retouched for the volume *Intentions* (1891); the second in the *Fortnightly
Review* in February 1891. To a considerable extent the first essay was a
resolution of the conflict with Whistler. That difficult man had raised a
fuss early in 1890, on the by now well worn theme of Wilde's putative
borrowings from him. The immediate cause was that Herbert Vivian, a
young acquaintance of both men, had begun to publish a series of
Reminiscences in the *Sun*. In the first, on 17 November 1889, he recounted
how after lecturing to the art students in 1883, Wilde was asked by
Whistler what he had said, and had to suffer the bow of acknowledged
ownership as each idea was enumerated. Vivian had also noticed that in
'The Decay of Lying' Wilde had thoughtlessly used Whistler's joke,
which went back to his letter to the *World* of 17 November 1888, that
'Oscar has the courage of the opinion of . . . others.' He had borrowed his
own scalp, Whistler chortled. Wilde was extremely annoyed at Vivian, as
well as at Whistler. He curtly refused Vivian's request for his promised
introduction to the *Reminiscences* in a book, and forbade him to use any
private letters or conversation. He replied with acerbity to Whistler's
charge, though not until 9 January 1890, when his letter to *Truth* began: 'It
is a trouble for any gentleman to have to notice the lucubrations of so
ill-bred and ignorant a person as Mr Whistler, but your publication of his
insolent letter has left me no option in the matter.' The joke which
Whistler said had been stolen was too old for even Whistler to claim it.
This defense was weak. Wilde was on solider ground in declaring that
Whistler was ignorant of the history of criticism. The week after, on 16
January, Whistler replied that Wilde was now 'his own "gentleman."' 'In
all humility, therefore, I admit that the outcome of my "silly vanity and
incompetent mediocrity" must be the incarnation – Oscar Wilde.' Wilde's
more adroit reply was reserved for 'The Critic as Artist,' where he said,

> such accusations proceed either from the thin colourless lips of impotence,
> or from the grotesque mouths of those who, possessing nothing of their
> own, fancy that they can gain a reputation for wealth by crying out that they
> have been robbed.

The whole essay was Wilde's declaration of freedom from Whistler's theories. Gautier had said in his preface to *Mademoiselle de Maupin*, 'There was no art criticism under Julius II,' and Whistler had embraced this view without acknowledgment. Wilde has Ernest, the straight man in his dialogue, say, 'In the best days of art there were no art critics,' to have Gilbert reply, 'I seem to have heard that observation before, Ernest. It has all the vitality of error and all the tediousness of an old friend. On the contrary,' he proceeds, echoing Symonds and Pater, 'the Greeks were a nation of art critics.' He repudiates the romantic idea of art as a spontaneous overflow of powerful feelings, and insists that it is a highly self-conscious process. 'All bad poetry comes from genuine feeling,' he says, as Auden would say after him. 'The great poet sings because he chooses to sing,' and sings not in his own person but in one he has assumed: 'Man is least himself when he talks in his own person. Give him a mask and he will tell you the truth.' Most of Yeats's speculations about the mask derive encouragement from this essay. Wilde finds that what keeps creation from being repetitive is the critical faculty, which generates fresh forms.

Just what criticism is, Wilde explained by direct and oblique references to his Oxford predecessors. Matthew Arnold as the Oxford Professor of Poetry had lectured in 1864 on 'The Function of Criticism at the Present Time,' a title which Wilde had echoed in his original title for 'The Critic as Artist,' which was 'The True Function and Value of Criticism.' Arnold memorably declared that 'the aim of criticism is to see the object in itself as it really is.' The definition went with his demand for 'disinterested curiosity' from the critic. Its effect was to put the critic on his knees before the work he was discussing. Not everyone enjoyed this position. Nine years later Pater wrote his preface to the *Renaissance*. Pretending to agree with Arnold's definition of the aim of criticism, he quoted it and added, 'the first step towards seeing one's object as it really is, is to know one's impression as it really is, to discriminate it, to realise it distinctly.' Pater's corollary subtly altered the original proposition, shifting the center of attention from the rock of the object to the rivulets of the perception. It made the critic's own work more important as well as more subjective. If observation is still the word, the critic looks in on himself as often as out to the object.

Wilde outdid Pater. He proposed in 'The Critic as Artist' that the aim of criticism is to see the object as it really is not. This aim might seem to justify the highly personal criticism of individual works which Arnold and Pater wrote, and Wilde uses them as examples. But his contention goes beyond their practise. He wants to free critics from subordination, to grant them a larger share in the production of literature. While he does not forbid them to explain a book, they might prefer – he says – to deepen its mystery. (The suggestion is amusing but dated: who could deepen the mystery of *Finnegans Wake*?) At any rate, the critic's context would be different from that of the artist whom he was judging. For just as the artist claimed independence of experience (Picasso tells us that art is 'what nature is not') so the critic claims independence of the books he is writing about. 'The highest criticism,' according to Wilde, 'is the record of one's own soul.' The critic must have all literature in his mind and not see particular works in isolation. So he, and we, 'shall be able to realise, not merely our own lives, but the collective spirit of the race, and so to make ourselves absolutely modern in the true meaning of the word modernity. To realise the nineteenth century, one must realise every century that has preceded it and that has contributed to its making.'

Wilde's essay moves smoothly from classical examples – Homer, Plato and Aristotle – to Dante. He demonstrated the power of the modern critic to control both Greek and medieval dispensations. He also extends the innovative function of the critic by comparing it with that of the criminal. Transvaluating language in the way of Nietzsche and Genet, Wilde finds that critics grow 'less and less interested in actual life, and will seek to gain their impressions almost entirely from what art has touched.' Life is a failure, incapable of repeating the same emotion, and bringing us to action when beauty lies rather in contemplation. As Joyce followed him in saying, sensual or didactic art urges us to action – pornography and puritanism interfere with the aesthetic response. 'Aesthetics are higher than ethics. They belong to a more spiritual sphere.' Art and criticism are dangerous, because they open the mind to new possibilities .

These sentiments particularly impressed one reader, the influential editor of the *Fortnightly Review*, Frank Harris. He wrote to Wilde that 'Plato might have been proud to sign pages 128–9,' those dealing with sin and virtue. 'I've done you wrong in my thoughts these many years, of course, ignorantly, but now, at last, I'll try to atone. You're certain, I think, to be a *chef-de-file* (if I may use Balzac's coinage without offence) of the generation now growing to manhood in England.'[33] From now on Harris was an important friend and advocate. One day he would write his biography of Wilde, which suffered from Harris's deficiencies as a listener, and was based on improvisation rather than memory. But he published 'Pen, Pencil and Poison' in his review, as well as the more subversive essay, 'The Soul of Man under Socialism.'

The second of these broadens and sharpens the argument in 'The Critic as Artist,' and where that essay dwells upon past and present, 'The Soul of Man under Socialism' dwells upon the future. Wilde saw that his reconsideration of aestheticism must deal with social and political ideas in a more concerted fashion than in the earlier days when he had discussed the beautification of life. A lecture by Bernard Shaw probably stimulated him, though socialism meant something quite different to Wilde. He annoyed his friend Walter Sichel by arguing for socialism on the grounds that it was so 'beautiful' to do as one likes. (Engels surprisingly agreed

with Stirner about the importance of egoism, as Lukács points out.[34])
Wilde's essay has been translated into many languages. It is based on the
paradox that we must not waste energy in sympathizing with those who
suffer needlessly, and that only socialism can free us to cultivate our
personalities. Charity is no use – the poor are right to be contemptuous of
it, and right to steal rather than to take alms. To demand thrift of the poor
is insulting, like telling a starving man to diet. To speak of the dignity of
manual labour is wrong when everyone knows that manual labor is
degrading.

As for the type of socialism, Wilde is opposed to authoritarianism, for
that would mean the enslavement of the whole society instead of the part
that is at present enslaved. He foresees with approval the annihilation of
property, family life, marriage, and jealousy. His model for the artist is
Christ, in the style of Blake and D. H. Lawrence, a Christ who teaches the
importance of being oneself. Art is a disturbing force. Like criticism, it
prevents mere repetition; people must not live each other's lives over and
over again. For the artist the best government is none at all, and here
Wilde seems to be advocating anarchism rather than socialism. 'I am
something of an anarchist,' he told an interviewer in 1894.

'There are three kinds of despots,' he says in a passage that impressed
James Joyce. 'There is the despot who tyrannises over the body. There is
the despot who tyrannises over the soul. There is the despot who
tyrannises over the soul and body alike. The first is called the Prince. The
second is called the Pope. The third is called the People.' In *Ulysses*
Stephen Dedalus remarks, 'I am the servant of two masters, an English
and an Italian . . . And a third . . . there is who wants me for odd jobs.'
They are, he explains, 'the Imperial British State . . . and the holy Roman
catholic and apostolic church,' and his compatriots, the Irish. He too
would like to be rid of the three despotisms. Christ serves as Wilde's
example because he protests against them. But Christ has one limitation:
he dwells upon pain. The ultimate purpose shared by life and art is joy.
Such joy is to be found in the new hellenism, in which the best of Greek
culture and Christian culture can be synthesized.

Wilde is determined to find a justification for sin. Like criticism, like
art, 'What is termed Sin is an essential element of progress.' Without it,
the world would grow old and colorless. 'By its curiosity [Arnold's word
with Wilde's meaning] Sin increases the experience of the race. Through
its intensified individualism it saves us from monotony of type. In its
rejection of the current notions about morality, it is one with the highest
ethics.' Sin is more useful to society than martyrdom, since it is self-
expressive not self-repressive. The goal is the liberation of personality.
When the day of true culture comes, sin will be impossible because the
soul will transform 'into elements of richer experience, or a finer suscepti-
bility, or a newer mode of thought, acts or passions that with the common
would be commonplace, or with the uneducated ignoble, or with the

shameful vile. Is this dangerous? Yes; it is dangerous – all ideas, as I told you, are so.'

With these essays Wilde clarified the meaning of *Dorian Gray*. Dorian was right to seek escape from the repetitious daily round, wrong in expressing only parts – the ungenerous parts – of his nature. Wilde balances here two ideas from his dialogues which look contradictory: one is that art is disengaged from life, the other that it is deeply incriminated with it. That art is sterile, and that art is infectious, are attitudes not beyond reconciliation. Wilde never formulated their union, but he implied something like this: by its creation of beauty art reproaches the world, calling attention to the world's faults by disregarding them, so the sterility of art is an affront or a parable. Art may also outrage the world by flouting its laws or by indulgently positing their violation. Or art may seduce the world by making it follow an example which seems bad but is really salutary. In these ways the artist moves the world towards self-recognition, with at least a tinge of self-redemption, as he compels himself toward the same end.

By exposing the defects of orthodox aestheticism in *Dorian Gray*, and the virtues of reconsidered aestheticism in 'The Critic as Artist' and 'The Soul of Man under Socialism,' Wilde presented the case as fully as he could. However gracefully he expresses himself, there is no doubt that he attacks Victorian assumptions about society. Because that society was beginning to disintegrate did not make it more amenable to what Wilde was proposing; if anything, less so. He asked it to tolerate aberrations from the norm, such as homosexuality, to give up its hypocrisy both by recognizing social facts and by acknowledging that its principles were based upon hatred rather than love, leading to privation of personality as of art. Art is the truest individualism the world has known. The threat of Bow Street that Jeyes had made in the *St James's Gazette* office was not idle, but Wilde meant what he said, and thought that not to take risks was not to live. Like Jean Genet after him, he proposed an analogy between the criminal and the artist, though for him the artist, not needing to act, occupies a superior place.* Rebelliousness and extravagance are needed if society's molds are to be broken, as broken they must be. Art is by nature dissident.

---

* Wilde's reaction to the theft of his family's silver in this year is unrecorded.[35]

Lady of the Lake

*The characters in these plays talk on the stage exactly as they
would talk off it; they have neither aspirations nor aspirates;
they are taken directly from life and reproduce its vulgarity
down to the smallest detail; they present the gait, manner,
costume, and accent of real people; they would pass unnoticed in a third-class railway carriage. And yet how
wearisome the plays are!*

Ever since the failure of *Vera* in 1883 Wilde had been reduced from
playwright to playgoer. He was always at first nights, and theatrical parties,
and had achieved an easy ascendancy as someone to advise about
productions or comment on performance. An example of his interest and
influence was the help he gave in 1888 to Elizabeth Robins. She was a
young American actress who aspired to success on the London stage.
Wilde met her at a reception at Lady Seton's house, and took an interest in
her as an American. She reminded him that during his American tour he
had met her cousin, a St Louis philanthropist. Wilde, who had met so
many people, responded by commenting on 'those stretches of wilderness' in the United States, to which he contrasted its cities, such as
Boston, which he called 'an invention,' as opposed to London, which was
'a growth.' 'The townbred man is the civilised being,' he assured her. His
practical advice was that she should give a matinée performance, and he
promised to speak to Beerbohm Tree about her. He introduced her to his
mother, whose comment, 'You have a dramatic face,' was also encouraging.

Thanks to Wilde's intervention, Tree offered her a part in a play called
Adrienne. She suggested *Man and Wife* instead, an adaptation of Wilkie
Collins's *The Woman in White.* Tree did not reply to this counter-
proposal. Wilde wrote to her, 'You must play *Adrienne* with Tree. *Man and
Wife* won't do, the English public finds it tedious. I will see Tree about
Adrienne.'[36] Tree dragged his feet, and Elizabeth Robins was approached
by another producer, Sir Marvyn Owen, to replace an American actress,
Eleanor Calhoun, in a play called *A Fair Bigamist* by U. Burford. She was
delighted, and, on meeting Wilde on the street, told him the good news.
Wilde was anything but pleased. He described Owen as 'a penniless
adventurer,' and found her part vulgar and useless for a début. She must
sign nothing and consult George Lewis, the solicitor, before making any
agreements: 'Oh, he knows all about us – and forgives us all.' He arranged
a meeting with Tree between the acts of *Captain Swift*, in which Tree was
starring, and Miss Robins·was so 'smitten' with Tree that she put off her
return to America on a ship that was leaving the next day. Wilde's
advocacy, and Tree's eventual compliance, enabled her to get a small part,
though Wilde warned her, 'Absurd you should be cast for a part quite out

of your line. The wonder – the *danger* is, you do it so well.' Fortunately, she took a trip to Norway, was captivated by Ibsen, and was instrumental in arranging for a series of English productions of his plays in which she took the leading roles. She always regarded Wilde as her benevolent pilot through theatrical shoals.

Wilde edged back towards playwriting with the dialogues in 1889 and 1891. In 1889 he had an unexpected and unsought piece of luck. Lawrence Barrett, a well known American actor, wrote to him about *The Duchess of Padua*. Barrett had read it in New York years before and liked it; he thought he might stage it successfully, and asked Wilde to meet him in July at a place on the Rhine called Kreuznach. Wilde responded at once:

July 1889

My dear Mr Barrett, I am very proud and pleased to learn that you have not forgotten the Duchess of Padua. I should be very glad to make any alterations in it you can suggest, and indeed I have no doubt that the play could be vastly improved.

I could go to Kreuznach the end of this month for five or six days, but would it be impossible to arrange the alterations by correspondence? I do not know what the expense of the journey is, and have not much money to spare. Your kind offer to be your guest I accept with great pleasure.

It is right to tell you that before I received your letter Miss Calhoun had approached me on the subject of the play. But nothing is settled, as she has, as yet, made me no offer. Personally I would sooner that my work should be presented to the public by an artist of your experience and knowledge. I know how very perfect all your productions are, and what unity of effect you have been able to present by means of right balance and artistic tact. 'Francesca da Rimini,' which I saw in New York, always remains in my memory as one of the best modern productions of our stage.

OSCAR WILDE[37]

Barrett evidently defrayed his expenses; and Wilde wrote to Robert Ross, 'I thought it would be a superb opportunity for forgetting the language.' They agreed on some changes, and now or later Barrett told Wilde that the play would have more success if given a new title, *Guido Ferranti*, and staged anonymously. The shadow of *Vera* might otherwise hang over it. Wilde agreed. It was the first of two occasions when his name would be left off the billboards.

Barrett did not get round to producing *Guido Ferranti* until January of 1891, that year so triumphant for Wilde. The newspapers, as if their old venom had been drained by lapse of time and Barrett's reputation, let Wilde off lightly this time. The *New York Herald* and *New York Times* reviewers treated it respectfully. The *New York Tribune* reviewer, William Winter, commented on 27 January 1891:

In the Broadway Theatre last night, in the presence of a numerous, eagerly attentive, and often kindly responsive audience, Lawrence Barrett, whose enterprise is incessant and whose noble ambition never tires, produced another new piece, under the name of *Guido Ferranti* . . . The new play is deftly constructed in five short acts, and is written in a strain of blank verse that is always melodious, often eloquent, and sometimes freighted with fanciful figures of rare beauty. It is less a tragedy, however, than a melodrama . . . The radical defect of the work is insincerity. No one in it is natural. The chief part is the woman – Beatrice, Duchess of Padua; and Beatrice is practically insane . . . she . . . stabs and murders her objectionable husband, in order that she may remove all obstacles to the gratification of her passion . . .

The authorship of *Guido Ferranti* has not been disclosed. There need not have been any hesitation about it – for he is a practised writer and a good one. We recognize in this work a play that we had the pleasure of reading several years ago, in manuscript. It was then called *The Duchess of Padua.* The author of it is Oscar Wilde.

After the first night the advertisements read, 'Oscar Wilde's Love Tragedy.' Barrett stopped the performances after three weeks, possibly because of ill health (he died in March), but Wilde was pleased by the run, and hoped to have the play put on in London. He reminded Henry Irving that he already had a copy, and urged him to produce it. Irving refused. Then George Alexander, late in 1890, took over the St James's Theatre with the intention of producing plays by English rather than continental or Scandinavian writers. He approached Wilde for a play, and was offered *The Duchess of Padua.* Although he liked it, he decided the scenery would cost too much, and asked Wilde to write on a modern subject. In February he offered him fifty pounds (not a hundred as he afterwards said) in advance, on a play to be submitted by 1 January 1891, and Wilde accepted. But as the months passed and Alexander importuned in vain, Wilde offered to return the advance. Alexander shrewdly declined.

In the summer of 1891 Wilde suddenly saw how he might write the play. He said to Frank Harris, 'I wonder can I do it in a week, or will it take three? It ought not to take long to beat the Pineros and the Joneses.'[38] (Pinero was well known to take, like Ibsen, a year on each play, affording producers a much desired respite.) Wilde went to the Lake Country to stay with a friend, and on the way back stopped in a hotel where Ross joined him. He returned saying he had borrowed the name of the principal part from the longest lake. (Actually he had used Lady Windermere in 'Lord Arthur Savile's Crime' several years before.) On his trip he had passed through Selby, to which the Windermeres are going at the end of the play.[39] He finished the play in October, and asked Alexander when he might read it to him. An appointment was made, and Wilde was late because at the last moment he was summoned to help John Barlas, who had been arrested. In the flurry of departure, the script fell to the ground, curled up. He was glad to see that it had not fallen flat, and remembered it afterwards as a good omen.[40]

The play he now read aloud avoided the method of Ibsen, which Shaw was to expound in *The Quintessence of Ibsenism* the same year. Wilde did not underrate his Norwegian rival; he allowed that *Hedda Gabler* was Greek in its power to generate pity and terror. But his own goal, he saw, was to make dialogue as brilliant as possible, while Ibsen confined his characters to ordinary words in ordinary life. Ibsen, said Wilde, was analytic; his own method he called dramatic. One probed a situation to uncover an infection; the other relied on verbal ricochet, to express 'a conflict between our artistic sympathies and our moral judgment.'[41] For Wilde, unlike Ibsen, the setting had to be in the leisure class, people with time, money, and education, proficient in conversation. The taut opening scene of *Lady Windermere's Fan* foreshadowed later events, but its more original contribution was to counterpose two language systems, one of platitude, the other of epigram. 'Believe me,' says Lady Windermere, 'you are better than most other men, and I sometimes think you pretend to be worse,' to which Lord Darlington, instead of disclaiming such an intention, replies, 'We all have our little vanities.' His remark embraces the fascination of wickedness, which he reverses in another speech: 'As a wicked man, I am a complete failure. Why, there are lots of people who say I have never really done anything wrong in the whole course of my life. Of course they only say it behind my back.' Here he turns non-wickedness – or goodness – into a fault. Such remarks disturb conventional morality by proposing its absurdity, as the play does on a larger scale.

When he had finished reading the play to Alexander, Wilde asked, 'Did you like it?' 'Like it is not the word, it is simply wonderful.' 'What will you give me for it?' 'A thousand pounds,' said Alexander. 'A thousand pounds! I have so much confidence in your excellent judgement, my dear Alec, that I cannot but refuse your generous offer – I will take a percentage.'[42] As a result, he made £7,000 in the first year.

Shortly after the agreement was signed for a production early in 1892, Wilde was asked by William Heinemann to write the introduction for two plays of Maeterlinck in English translation. He came to lunch, to discuss the matter, on 16 October 1891. Heinemann was astonished at his guest's wearing deep mourning and melancholy looks. On being pressed about his bereavement, Wilde replied, 'This day happens to be my birthday, and I am mourning (as I shall henceforth do on each of my anniversaries) the flight of one year of my youth into nothingness, the growing blight upon my summer.'[43] (He was thirty-seven.) It was a costume that he would assign, with the same mock-seriousness, to John Worthing in *The Importance of Being Earnest*. As for introducing Maeterlinck, he must wait for inspiration. It never came. As a successful playwright, Wilde no longer needed this kind of work.

CHAPTER XIII

Hellenizing Paris

Only the great masters of style ever succeed in being obscure.

Mallarmé

London at his feet, though unwillingly so, Wilde turned his attention to France. He was in a triumphant mood. Success, said André Gide, seemed to run ahead of him and he had only to collect it.[1] Wilde had been gradually enlarging his acquaintance in Paris, but he could now celebrate his transformation from conversationalist to author. Most of the writers he had come to know in the Eighties were *décadents*, but he had signalled the passing of this movement in 'The Decay of Lying,' not only in its title, but in the allusion to 'a sort of cult for Domitian.' In England decadence had always been tinged with self-mockery. By 1890 symbolism, not decadence, had the cry, as Wilde acknowledged in the Preface to *Dorian Gray*, 'All art is at once surface and symbol. Those who go beneath the surface do so at their peril. Those who read the symbol do so at their peril.' These aphorisms were a bow to Stéphane Mallarmé, whom he had visited in February 1891, when he was writing the Preface.

Mallarmé was a new phenomenon for Wilde. His eloquence, depending upon uncommon vocabulary and syntax, and a refusal to grandstand for an audience, was quite unlike the manner of great talkers. His *mardis* were famous, and his disciples came to listen to him rather than talk themselves. Wilde was prepared to perform the same sacrifice, though with all his attentiveness to the 'maître' he made his mark. He went to his first *mardi* on 24 February, and the conversation must have lit upon Poe, for whom he and Mallarmé shared an admiration. Mallarmé presented Wilde with 'Le Corbeau,' his translation of Poe's 'The Raven,' which he had re-published a year before. Next day Wilde thanked him for it:

Mercredi   Hôtel de L'Athénée

Cher Maître, Comment dois-je vous remercier pour la gracieuse façon avec laquelle vous m'avez présenté la magnifique symphonie en prose que vous a inspiré [sic] les mélodies du génie du grand poète celtique, Edgar

Allan Poe. En Angleterre nous avons de la prose et de la poésie, mais la prose française et la poésie dans les mains d'un maître tel que vous deviennent une et la même chose.

Le privilège de connaître l'auteur de *L'Après-midi d'un Faune* est on ne peut plus flatteur, mais de trouver en lui l'accueil que vous m'avez montré est en vérité inoubliable.

Ainsi, cher maître, veuillez agréer l'assurance de ma haute et très parfaite considération

OSCAR WILDE*[2]

He attended a second *mardi* the following week, and the disciples took account of Mallarmé's tacit endorsement.

The situation was a little touchy because Mallarmé was on close terms with Whistler, whom he had met years before in Manet's studio. He had the greatest regard for him, and addressed a prose poem to him as the type of the artist. Wilde trusted to Mallarmé's intelligence, and his own, to overcome the difficulty, and was not disappointed. He was made to feel that he was welcome at Mallarmé's every time he visited Paris, and so when he returned at the end of October 1891 he announced that he would be coming on 3 November. He enclosed a copy of *The Picture of Dorian Gray* with homage to Mallarmé's 'noble and severe art.' This happened to be a time when Whistler was also in Paris, supervising some color lithographs, and trying to speed up the sale of his portrait of his mother to the French government. He was determined not to meet Wilde. They had not spoken for years. Still, if he left the field to his rival, he would do so with as bad grace as he could muster. On Monday, 2 November, Whistler wrote to Mallarmé with his usual disregard of spelling and accents:

Mon cher ami – Le travail est fini – ainsi je pars – Vous m'avez rendu ma visite bien charmante – comme c'est bien de votre habitude – C'est donc un peu ingrat de ma part de ne pas rester pour dénoncer Oscar devant vos disciples demain soir! –

C'est un service que je vous dois – je le sais bien – et cela aurait peut être même ajouté à l'agrément de votre Soirée! –

---

* 'Dear Master, How can I thank you for the gracious way in which you presented me with the magnificent symphony in prose which the melodies of the great celtic poet Edgar Allan Poe have inspired in you. In England we have prose and we have poetry, but French prose and poetry become in the hands of such a master as you one and the same thing.

The privilege of acquaintance with the author of *L'Après-midi d'un faune* is more flattering than I can say, but to receive from him the welcome that you have accorded me is really unforgettable.

Yours faithfully,
OSCAR WILDE'

Les Mardis de Mallarmé sont maintenant historiques – exclusifs – et
réservés aux artistes *honêtes* – L'entrée est un privilège – et une preuve de
valeur – Une distinction dont nous sommes fier – Et la Porte du Maître ne
doit pas être enfoncée par tout farceurs qui traverse[nt] la Manche pour
plus tard s'imposer en détaillant, à bon marché les belles fleurs de
conversation et les graves verits que pratique Notre Poete en bel humeur! –
Adieu . . .*

This was not enough. The following evening a telegram from Whistler
arrived a few minutes before Wilde. It said – with an allusion to Wilde's
Preface to *Dorian Gray* and its propositions, to which latter Whistler laid
claim:

> PREFACE PROPOSITIONS PREVENIR DISCIPLES
> PRECAUTION FAMALIARITE [sic] FATALE SERRER LES
> PERLES BONNE SOIREE
> WHISTLER†[3]

Mallarmé knew that Whistler was overwrought about the visit, and made a
point of smoothing him down, assuring him that the soirée had been dull
without him – '*le personnage même de l'artiste*' – although the telegram had
amused the company. The disciples had seen Whistler's portrait at a Paris
gallery, and when once Mallarmé had 'thrown Whistler's name aloft, they
spread themselves in admiration, which Wilde echoed; and such were the
highlights of this *mardi*. The telegram, placed on a table at the side, had to
amuse itself.'

Whistler returned to the charge. He alerted Mallarmé to Wilde's telling
the newspapers that he basked in the Master's admiration and frequented
the cafés with the disciples. Mallarmé replied that there was a to-do about
Wilde, but that he had not seen him again, having been obliged to decline
two dinner invitations from disciples when Wilde was also to be a guest.
Whistler interpreted this letter to mean that Mallarmé had been slighted:

* 'My dear friend – my tasks are done – so I am leaving – You have made my visit
very pleasant – as you always do. So it's a bit ungrateful of me not to stay and
denounce Oscar Wilde in front of your disciples tomorrow evening!
  It's a service I owe you – I'm well aware of that – and it would even have
contributed to the conviviality of your evening!
  Mallarmé's *mardis* are now historical – exclusive and reserved for artists who
are *honest* – Entry to them is a privilege and a proof of worth – a distinction that
makes us proud. And the Master's Door should not be crashed by any jokester
who crosses the Channel so as to gain respect later by retailing on the cheap the
conversational blooms and the weighty truths Our Poet offers in such good
temper! Farewell.'

† 'PREFACE PROPOSITIONS FOREWARN DISCIPLES
PRECAUTION FAMILIARITY FATAL HIDE THE
PEARLS HAVE A GOOD EVENING
WHISTLER'

No O.W. –! comment toujours! Il pousse donc l'ingratitude jusqu'à l'indécence? – Et toutes ses anciennes rengainnes – il ose les offrir à Paris comme du neuf! – les histoires du Tourne-Soleil – ses promenades au lis – ses culottes – ses plastrons rose – que sais-je! – et puis l''Art' par ici – l''Art' par là – C'est vraiment obscène – et cela finira mal – Enfin nous verrons – et vous me le raconterez –*

Whistler had become manic on the subject of Wilde. He met Huysmans and Jules Bois at the Louvre and, to prove how jealous Wilde was of him, said, 'Since the Luxembourg has taken one of my paintings, Wilde has deposited one of his books there.' Bois and Huysmans concluded that the jealousy was on Whistler's side.[4]

Mallarmé did not accept Whistler's animus. He was impressed by *The Picture of Dorian Gray*, which Wilde gave him. He could scarcely have failed to notice it as a central document in symbolism. It shared the preoccupation of Mallarmé's verse with the way that the borders of life and art, the real and the unreal, shift under the pressure of the imagination. The transformation from a flower to the 'Flower absent from all bouquets,' from the man to the simulacrum, was consonant with the master's ideas. Mallarmé conveyed as much in elliptical but admiring phrases:

J'achève le livre, un des seuls qui puissent émouvoir, vu que d'une rêverie essentielle et des parfums d'âme les plus étranges s'est fait son orage. Redevenir poignant à travers l'inouï raffinement d'intellect, et humain, en une pareille perverse atmosphère de beauté, est un miracle que vous accomplissez et selon quel emploi de tous les arts de l'écrivain!

'It was the portrait that had done everything.' Ce portrait en pied, inquiétant, d'un Dorian Gray, hantera, mais écrit, étant devenu livre lui-même.

STÉPHANE MALLARMÉ†[5]

---

*   'No O.W – ! just like him! He pushes ingratitude to the point of indecency then? – And all the old chestnuts – he dares offer them in Paris like new ones! – the tales of the sunflower – his walks with the lily – his kneebreeches – his rose-colored stiff shirts – and all that! – and then 'Art' here – 'Art' there – It's really obscene – and will come to a bad end – As we shall see – and you will tell me how it happens –'

†   'I am finishing the book, one of the few that can take hold of the reader, since from an inner revery and the strangest perfumes of the soul it stirs up a storm. To make it poignant again, amid the outrageous refinements of intellect, and human as well, in so perverse an atmosphere of beauty, is a miracle that you bring about, and necessarily by all the writer's arts!

"It was the portrait that had done everything." This full-length disquieting portrait of a Dorian Gray will haunt, but by virtue of being written, has itself become a book.

STÉPHANE MALLARMÉ'

Both Mallarmé and Wilde saw literature as the supreme art, and one that could transform a painting into words, a life into an artifice.

Wilde had in mind a challenge to the master more profound than *Dorian Gray*. One of Mallarmé's central works, 'Hérodiade,' was still unfinished after many years, the best known unfinished poem since 'Kubla Khan.' Wilde determined to use the same subject, the beheading of John the Baptist at the instigation of Herodias. Whether or not he intended to compete directly, he did so, and Mallarmé, in his futile effort to complete 'Hérodiade,' had to take note of Wilde's efforts, and said he would retain the name of Herodias to differentiate it from that other (*Salome*) 'which I shall call modern.' Years later (after his release from prison) Wilde was asked by a journalist in Dieppe for his opinion of Mallarmé. He replied, 'Mallarmé is a poet, a true poet. But I prefer him when he writes in French, because in that language he is incomprehensible, while in English, unfortunately, he is not. Incomprehensibility is a gift, not everyone has it.'[6] He obviously felt on equal terms with the great master.

Wilde is not known to have attended any more *mardis*, and perhaps he experienced some embarrassment, as if his treatment of Salome was in some way a trespass. Whistler's reaction is unrecorded, but can be imagined. Robert Ross says that once when Wilde complained that a well-known novel had been borrowed from an idea of his, Ross replied that Wilde was himself 'a fearless literary thief.' 'My dear Robbie,' Wilde drawled in answer, 'when I see a monstrous tulip with *four* petals in someone else's garden, I am impelled to grow a monstrous tulip with *five* wonderful petals, but that is no reason why someone should grow a tulip with only *three* petals.'[7]

His interest in the legend of Salome antedated his meetings with Mallarmé, even if Mallarmé quickened it. Salome, having danced before the imaginations of European painters and sculptors for a thousand years, in the nineteenth century turned her beguilements to literature. Among those who made artistic overtures to her were Heine, Flaubert, Huysmans, and Laforgue. Jaded by exaltations of nature and humanism, they inspected with relief a Biblical image of the unnatural. They daringly reconstituted the Salome of the Bible. As there are many Iseults, many Marys, so there were many Salomes, without monotony.

W. S. Blunt's diary confirms that Wilde had the idea before he went to France. Some time after his arrival in Paris he had breakfast with Curzon and Blunt, and told them he was writing a play in French, for which he would be made an Academician. They promised to attend the first night, Curzon as Prime Minister.[8] Certainly *Salome* was consonant with Wilde's theory of tragedy, which he expressed to a correspondent in 1894:

Dear Sir,

Whether a comedy should deal with modern life, whether its subject should be society or middle class existence, these are questions purely to the artist's own choice. Personally I like comedy to be intensely modern, and like my tragedy to walk in purple and to be remote: but these are whims merely.

As for 'success' on the stage, the public is a monster of strange appetites: it swallows, so it seems to me, honeycake and hellebore, with avidity: but there are many publics – and the artist belongs to none of them: if he is admired it is, a little, by chance.

Yours sincerely,
OSCAR WILDE

The principal engenderer of the story was an account in the fifth chapter of Huysmans's *A Rebours* of two paintings of Salome by Gustave Moreau, and in the fourteenth chapter of the same book a quotation from Mallarmé's 'Hérodiade.' In one painting the aged Herod is being stirred by Salome's lascivious but indifferent dance; in the other Salome is being presented with the Baptist's head giving forth rays on a charger. Huysmans attributes to Salome the mythopoeic force that Pater attributes to the Mona Lisa, and mentions that writers have never succeeded in rendering her adequately. Only Moreau has conveyed that she is not just a dancing girl, but 'the symbolic incarnation of undying lust, the goddess of immortal Hysteria, the accursed beauty exalted above all other beauties by the catalepsy that hardens her flesh and steels her muscles, the monstrous Beast, indifferent, irresponsible, insensible, poisoning, like the Helen of ancient myth, everything that she touches.' Yet this is not the whole story, for in the second painting, a water-color, Moreau showed her horror at the sight of the bodiless head.

Wilde did not perhaps need much more impulsion, but he received some from an American named J. C. Heywood, whose *Salome* he reviewed in the *Pall Mall Gazette* on 15 February 1888. Heywood had written his dramatic poem in the 1860s, and in 1888 it was reprinted by the London publisher Kegan Paul. He had profited from Heine's retelling of the story in *Atta Troll*, Heine having portrayed a procession in which a phantom Herodias, mounted on a horse, kisses the prophet's head. Heywood's contribution was to make her do this before she has turned into a ghost, while still alive. This detail is not in the other sources. Wilde saw, as Heywood did not, that kissing the head might constitute the climax. In 1890 he announced he would write about Salome. He had dinner at a Piccadilly restaurant with Edgar Saltus, and afterwards they visited Lord Francis Hope in his rooms across the street. The décor of the rooms was generally sober, an exception being an engraving of Herodias dancing on her hands, as she is pictured doing in Flaubert's 'Hérodias.' Wilde went up to the picture, and said, '*La bella donna della mia mente.*'

According to Mrs Saltus, Wilde said he would write about her, and Saltus, who planned to write about Mary Magdalene, replied, 'Do so. We will pursue the wantons together.' Saltus's book came out first, and Wilde praised it as 'so pessimistic, so poisonous, and so perfect.' (But he commented on another work of Saltus on Tristram, 'All that is related in the style of *A Painful Accident in New Jersey*.') Saltus returned the compliment when he read *Salome*, saying that the last line had made him shudder. 'It is only the shudder that counts,' Wilde answered.[9] He began to conceive of the play as posing a perverse passion, the desire of vice for virtue, pagan for Christian, living for dead (as in 'The Canterville Ghost'), and the abhorrence of vice by virtue, the extremity of renunciation.

Virgin Cruelty

IOKANAAN: *Back! Daughter of Babylon! Come not near the chosen of the Lord.*

This plethora of suggestion encouraged Wilde in his search for his own Salome, though he did not as yet know how to engender her. In Paris he began to formulate a work, talking with everyone except, presumably, Mallarmé about it. The Mallarmé entourage was drawn into the gestation of the subject; Marcel Schwob, Adolphe Retté, and Pierre Louÿs, were asked to correct various drafts. It suited Wilde to have a subject of such general interest.

A writer, Yvanhoe Rambosson, has described Wilde's state of mind at this time, November 1891. Rambosson and Wilde had lunched at the apartment of the translator Henry Davray. Afterwards they went to the Café d'Harcourt, where they were joined by Enrique Gomez Carrillo, a young Guatemalan diplomat and writer, who was with Paul Verlaine. Wilde did the talking while Verlaine drank his Pernod and seemed absorbed in it. Once in a while, however, he would mumble some street-arab comment in answer to one of Wilde's careful phrases. As in 1883 Wilde disliked Verlaine's appearance, and therefore devoted himself to Gomez Carrillo, an exuberant youth with a lively intelligence and a picturesque speech. Wilde spoke of his life, his travels, his love of existence and sensation, and he remarked, as he would also to Gide, 'I have put only my talent into my works. I have put all my genius into my life.' At this Verlaine became suddenly serious, and leaned over to say to Rambosson aside, 'This man is a true pagan. He possesses the insouciance which is half of happiness, for he does not know penitence.'[10]

This may have been Wilde's first meeting with Gomez Carrillo, who became a confidant. When they were alone, Wilde objected to Verlaine's unkempt appearance. 'The first duty of a man is to be beautiful, don't you think?' he asked. Gomez replied, 'The only beauties I know are women.'

Wilde would not have this: 'How can you say that? Women aren't beautiful at all. They are something else, I allow: magnificent, when dressed with taste and covered with jewels, but beautiful, no. Beauty reflects the soul.' He objected to Gomez's being so often in the company of a certain woman, and did not withdraw his objection when Gomez explained that he was in love with her. She, for her part, said that Wilde was a pederast, but Gomez liked him and was happy to spend time with him.

Wilde's knowledge of the iconography of Salome was immense. He complained that Rubens's Salome appeared to him to be 'an apoplectic Maritornes.' On the other hand, Leonardo's Salome was excessively incorporeal. Others, by Dürer, Ghirlandaio, van Thulden, were unsatisfactory because incomplete. The celebrated Salome of Regnault he considered to be a mere 'gypsy.' Only Moreau satisfied him, and he liked to quote Huysmans's description of the Moreau paintings. He was eager to visit the Prado to see how Stanzioni had painted her, and Titian, about whom he quoted Tintoretto's comment, 'This man paints with quivering flesh [*carne molida*].'

Wilde seemed to want to obsess himself with his idea, and every day he talked of Salome. The women in the streets seemed possible princesses of Israel to him. If he passed the rue de la Paix, he would examine the jewelry shops for proper adornment for her. One afternoon he asked, 'Don't you think she would be better naked? Yes, totally naked, but draped with heavy and ringing necklaces made of jewels of every colour, warm with the fervor of her amber flesh. I don't conceive of her as unconscious, serving as a mute instrument. No, her lips in Leonardo's painting disclose the cruelty of her soul. Her lust must needs be infinite, and her perversity without limits. Her pearls must expire on her flesh.' He began to imagine Sarah Bernhardt dancing naked before the Tetrarch, who in his mind had become a compound of three Herods – Herod Antipas (Matthew IV:14), Herod the Great (Matthew II:1), and Herod Agrippa I (Acts XII:19).[11]

Yet at times he veered round to make Salome chaste. She would dance before Herod out of divine inspiration, to accomplish the death of the impostor John, that enemy of Jehovah. 'Her body, tall and pale, undulates like a lily,' as this narrative went. 'There is nothing sensual in her beauty. The richest laces cover her svelte flesh . . . In her pupils gleam the flames of faith.' The image was suggested to him by a painting of Bernardo Luini. He had to endure another interpretation one night at dinner at the home of Stuart Merrill, the American poet who wrote in French, when the unprepossessing but self-assured Rémy de Gourmont broke into Wilde's fantasies about Salome by telling him, 'You have confused two Salomes. One was the daughter of Herod, but as Josephus attests, she had nothing to do with the dancer in the Bible.' Wilde listened to Gourmont's rebuke, but commented later to Gomez, who was also present, 'That poor Gourmont thinks he knows more than anybody else. What he told us was the truth of a professor at the Institute. I prefer the other truth, my own, which is that of the dream. Between two truths, the falser is the truer.'[12]

One evening, Wilde went to the house of Jean Lorrain, with Marcel Schwob, Anatole France, Henry Bauer, and Gomez Carrillo as fellow guests. He asked to see a bust of a decapitated woman he had heard about. As he examined the bloodstains painted on the neck above the place where the sword had cut, he cried, 'It is Salome's head, Salome who has had herself beheaded out of despair. It is John the Baptist's revenge.' The image stirred him to add, 'A Nubian gospel discovered by Boissière tells of a young philosopher to whom a Semitic dancer sends, as homage, the head of an apostle. The young man bows and says, smiling, "What I really want, beloved, is your head." She quails and goes off. The afternoon of the same day a slave presents the philosopher with his darling's head on a gold platter. And the philosopher asks, "Why are they bringing this bloody thing to me?" and goes on reading Plato. Doesn't it seem to you that this princess is Salome? Yes, and' (pointing to the bust) 'this marble is her head. With this execution John the Baptist had his revenge.' Lorrain was dubious: 'You are writing a singular poem,' he said. Since Lorrain wrote singularly himself, this was deferential.[13]

Another contributory image came to Wilde one day when he and Stuart Merrill went into the Moulin Rouge and saw a Rumanian acrobat dancing on her hands. Wilde hastily wrote something on his calling card and sent it to her, but to his disappointment she did not respond. He had wanted, he said, to make her an offer to dance the part of Salome in a play he was writing. 'I want her to dance on her hands, as in Flaubert's story.'[14]

But according to Gomez Carrillo, Wilde did not start with the idea of writing a play. He first wrote some pages in prose, then broke off and decided to write a poem. Only gradually did he realize that a play was in order. One night he told the Salome story to a group of young French writers, and returned to his lodgings in the boulevard des Capucines. A blank notebook lay on the table and it occurred to him that he might as well write down what he had been telling them. 'If the book had not been there I should never have dreamed of doing it,' he told O'Sullivan. After writing a long time, he looked at his watch and thought, 'I can't go on like this.' He went out to the Grand Café, then at the corner of the boulevard des Capucines and the rue Scribe. 'That fellow Rigo who ran away with the Princesse de Chimay, Clara Ward, was then the leader of the orchestra of Tziganes. I called him over to my table and said, "I am writing a play about a woman dancing with her bare feet in the blood of a man she has craved for and slain. I want you to play something in harmony with my thoughts." And Rigo played such wild and terrible music that those who were there stopped talking and looked at each other with blanched faces. Then I went back and finished *Salome*.'[15]

According to Robert Ross, he did not at first imagine its being put on the stage. Gradually, however, he began to cast it in his mind. The idea of Bernhardt acting in it perhaps encouraged him to write it in French, but he must also have dreamed of outrivalling Mallarmé in a drama which should be a '*Mystère*,' a revelation of a '*Passion de l'Homme*.' He complained of the docility of the Biblical Salome, who simply obeys Herodias, and once she receives the head conveys it to her mother. The inadequacy of this account, Wilde said, 'has made it necessary for the centuries to heap up dreams and visions at her feet so as to convert her into the cardinal flower of the perverse garden.' In all his talk about the play, he was loyal to one incident and never changed it: Salome, after dancing, demands John's head not to obey her mother, but out of unrequited love. The tetrarch, after battling with his conscience, grants her wish, and the head with its black eyes and red lips is handed to her on a silver charger. She receives it, takes hold of it with her hands, and exclaims, 'Ah, you did not want to let me kiss your lips? You can hardly hinder me now.' And she kisses it as she would bite a tasty fruit. As Gomez Carrillo says, Wilde's heroine was a woman who loves, suffers, hates. Faith does not concern her. That John is involved in a prohibited religion, or that he is faithful to official rites, does not touch her. What disturbs, tortures, agitates her are the black eyes and red lips of the man. 'Your flesh,' she says when she visits him in prison, 'your flesh is white like snow on the mountain.' That, and all the rest she speaks with such ardour, is replete with the immorality of the Song of Songs. (But the Songs of Songs describes a woman's beauty, not a man's.) 'I flee from what is moral as from what is impoverished,' said Wilde to Gomez; 'I have the same sickness as Des Esseintes.'[16]

In its earlier dramatic form, Wilde thought he would call the play, 'The Decapitation of Salome.' The title seems to have gone with a story he told Maeterlinck and Georgette Leblanc. It was of how Salome eventually became a saint. Herod, incensed at her kissing the decollated head, wanted to have her crushed, but at the pleas of Herodias contented himself with banishing her. She went off to the desert, where for years she lived on, maligned, solitary, clothed in animal skins, and subsisting on locusts and wild honey like the Prophet himself. When Jesus passed by, she recognized him whom the dead voice had heralded and she believed in him. But feeling unworthy of living in his shadow, she went off again, with the intention of carrying the Word. Having passed over rivers and seas, she encountered, after the fiery deserts, the deserts of snow. One day she was crossing a frozen lake near the Rhône when the ice broke under her feet. She fell into the water and the jagged ice cut into her flesh and decapitated her, though not before she managed to utter the names of Jesus and John. And those who later went by saw, on the silver plate of the re-formed ice, showing like the stamen of a flower with rubies, a severed head on which gleamed the crown of a golden nimbus.[17] Wilde's brain overflowed with such images.

To decapitate both would suit Wilde's apothegm about *Dorian Gray*, that 'all excess, as well as all renunciation, brings its own punishment.'

Christian Iokanaan and pagan Salome, one animated by piety and the other by sensuality, would both be brought low. Dorian Gray's dilemma, of abandon and horror, would find another example, this time without preternatural aid. But Wilde eventually gave up the decapitation of Salome, as too pat and repetitive.

The character of Salome evolved along with that of Herod. Herod's lust for Salome's body pales in comparison with Salome's lust for Iokanaan's bodiless head. Hers is a passion which drowns in its own excess. Sensation at this utmost bound is almost mystical. With all her savagery Salome has a virgin innocence. Like Huysmans's Des Esseintes, she is a *jusqu'au-boutiste*, willing her passion beyond human limits, beyond the grave even. Those who do this become exemplary; their value as illustrations mitigates their monstrousness. When death comes to Salome, it takes the measure of her boundless desire. She dies into a parable of self-consuming passion.

Wilde made the central character neither Salome nor Iokanaan, but Herod. Swayed by rival dispensations, Herod eventually detaches himself from both. One cancels out the other. Herod is strong in his tremblings, a leaf but a sinuous one, swept but not destroyed by successive waves of physical attraction and spiritual revulsion. By yielding to each in turn, Herod remains Herod, beyond both.

In the tenebrous happenings of *Salome* there are vestiges of the house of Atreus. A sense of doom pervades the play. Iokanaan is like Cassandra, and Salome has some traits of Clytemnaestra. Wilde had Aeschylus in mind as much as the Bible.

The Seduction of Paris

> *'I like hearing myself talk. It is one of my greatest pleasures. I often have long conversations all by myself, and I am so clever that sometimes I don't understand a single word of what I am saying.'*

On 19 December 1891 *L'Echo de Paris* said that Wilde was '*le "great event" des salons littéraires parisiennes*' of the season. The two months that he spent there were a continuous feast. Marcel Schwob, a young lion of the day, writer and journalist, was his principal guide, though Pierre Louÿs, another young lion, was also much in evidence. Schwob asked Wilde's permission to translate his story, 'The Selfish Giant,' into French in December, and on the 27th of the month the story was published in *L'Echo de Paris*. He dedicated his own story, 'Le Pays bleu,' to Wilde, in 1892, and Wilde dedicated 'The Sphinx' to him in the same year. Schwob was at that time secretary to Catulle Mendès, on *L'Echo de Paris*, and consoler of Mendès' wife, Marguérite Moreno, who was working for

Sarah Bernhardt. Schwob's mother had been the teacher of Miss Lip-
mann, who became Mme Arman de Caillavet and the official Egeria of
Anatole France. Through these associations Schwob could be and was
extremely helpful. Jean Lorrain, to whom Schwob introduced Wilde, says
Schwob was Wilde's pilot and *cornac* (elephant-keeper). Jules Renard said
that at Léon Daudet's Schwob seemed to confuse Wilde with
Shakespeare.[18]

After Wilde's visit Schwob wrote of him in his journal without rapture.
He described him as 'A big man, with a large pasty face, red cheeks, an
ironic eye, bad and protrusive teeth, a vicious childlike mouth with lips
soft with milk ready to suck some more. While he ate – and he ate little –
he never stopped smoking opium-tainted Egyptian cigarettes. A terrible
absinthe-drinker, through which he got his visions and desires.' Wilde
wore a long brown frockcoat, a peculiar waistcoat, and carried a walking
stick with a gold pommel. Once Schwob called for him, and Wilde, not
finding his stick, said, 'My goldheaded cane has disappeared. Last night I
was with the most terrible creatures, bandits, murderers, thieves – such
company as Villon kept. [He knew Schwob had just written about Villon.]
They stole my goldheaded cane. There was a youth with beautiful sad
eyes who had slain his mistress that morning because she was unfaithful. I
feel sure it was he who stole my goldheaded cane.' He concluded with
relish, 'My goldheaded cane is now between the hands that slew the frail
girl who had the grace of a spent rose-bush in the rain.' 'But Mr Wilde,'
said Schwob, 'there is your goldheaded cane in the corner.' 'Ah yes,' said
Wilde, much put out, 'So it is. There is my goldheaded cane. How clever
of you to find it.'[19]

Schwob entertained Wilde in his apartment at 2 rue de l'Université.
Léon Daudet sometimes met him there, and was attracted and repelled.
He thought Wilde's stories delicious, and his conversation fatiguing.
Words came tumbling out of his slack mouth, and he would roar with
laughter like a fat, gossipy woman. At their third meeting Wilde said to
him, sensing reservations, 'And what do you think of me, Monsieur Léon
Daudet?' Daudet referred to his complexity and possible guile. The next
day he received a letter from Wilde in which he declared himself to be 'the
simplest and most candid' of mortals, 'just like a tiny, tiny child.'[20]

The artist Jacques-Emile Blanche, long an admirer, introduced Wilde
to Proust at the house of Madame Arthur Baignères. Wilde was impressed by Proust's enthusiasm for English literature, especially for
Ruskin (whom he translated) and George Eliot, and accepted Proust's
invitation to dinner at the boulevard Haussmann. What happened,
according to two grandsons of Madame Baignères, was that 'On the
evening of the dinner Proust, who had been held up at Madame
Lemaire's, arrived very out of breath two minutes late. He asked the
servant, "Is the English gentleman here?" "Yes, sir, he arrived five
minutes ago; he had hardly entered the drawing room when he asked for

the bathroom, and he has not come out of it." Proust ran to the end of the passage. "Monsieur Wilde, are you ill?" "Ah, there you are, Monsieur Proust." Wilde appeared majestically. "No, I am not in the least ill. I thought I was to have the pleasure of dining with you alone, but they showed me into the drawing room. I looked at the drawing room and at the end of it were your parents, my courage failed me. Goodbye, dear Monsieur Proust, goodbye . . ."' Afterwards his parents told Proust that Wilde had looked about the drawing room and commented, 'How ugly your house is.'[21]

Stuart Merrill was helpful. It was he who gratified Wilde's desire to meet Jean Moréas, as Iannis Pappadimantopoulos called himself. Moréas, born in Athens but resident in Paris since 1870, arranged for Wilde to dine at the Côte d'Or with him and his followers. For once Wilde had to yield the floor, as Moréas expounded the theories of the Ecole Romane, to which he, Charles Maurras, Ernest Raynaud, Maurice Du Plessys, Raymond de la Tailhède, and others had rallied. They proposed to return to the classical traditions of earlier French poetry, in opposition to the Symbolistes. Moréas denounced the nineteenth-century poets: Hugo was vulgar, Baudelaire paradoxical, and so on. At dessert, according to Merrill, Wilde asked Moréas to recite some verses. 'I never recite,' replied Moréas, 'but if you would like it, our friend Raynaud will recite us something.' Raynaud stood up, and resting his redoubtable fists on the table announced, 'Sonnet to Jean Moréas.' His reading was applauded and once more Wilde pressed Moréas to recite. 'No, but our friend La Tailhède –' In his turn La Tailhède rose, and, his eyeglass fixed, launched in a clear voice: 'Ode to Jean Moréas.' Wilde grew visibly uneasy at the worship of Moréas, but out of courtesy tried again. 'Du Plessys, let us hear your latest verses,' commanded the master. Leaping up, Du Plessys trumpeted in vibrant tones: 'The Tomb of Jean Moréas.' At this, says Merrill, 'Oscar Wilde choked, conquered, routed, he who had silence about him in the salons of London, asked for his hat and coat and fled into the night.' He recovered later, and asked Moréas, Merrill, La Tailhède, Gomez Carrillo and others to dinner. This time he ruled the table with his stories. Moréas commented as he left, '*Cet anglais est emmerdant* [This Englishman is a shit].' When Moréas was mentioned afterward Wilde would say, '*Moréas, existe-il vraiment?*' Answered in the affirmative, he went on, '*Comme c'est curieux! J'ai toujours cru que Moréas est un mythe* [Moréas, does he really exist? . . . How strange! I've always thought that Moréas was a myth].'[22]

Ernest Raynaud claims that Merrill exaggerated what happened at that first meeting, as no doubt he did, but acknowledges that Wilde suddenly pleaded another engagement and left. Some time later, as he was coming out of his hotel, he met Raynaud on the boulevard des Capucines, and said to him solemnly: 'I approve of Moréas and his school for wanting to reestablish Greek harmony and to bring back to us the Dionysian state of mind. The world has such a thirst for joy. We are not yet released from the Syrian embrace and its cadaverous divinities. We are always plunged into the kingdom of shadows. While we wait for a new religion of light, let Olympus serve as shelter and refuge. We must let our instincts laugh and frolic in the sun like a troop of laughing children. I love life. It is so beautiful –' and here Wilde pointed to the scene around them, lit up by sunlight, 'Ah,' he went on, 'how all this outdoes the languishing beauty of the countryside. The solitude of the country stifles and crushes me . . . I am not really myself except in the midst of elegant crowds, in the exploits of capitals, at the heart of rich districts or amid the sumptuous ornamentation of palace-hotels, seated by all the desirable objects and with an army of servants, the warm caress of a plush carpet under my feet . . . I detest nature where man has not intervened with his artifice.' He went on in Nietzschean fashion to compare a diamond and a piece of charcoal to the poet and the ordinary man; a miracle of crystallization produced the diamond. Just as the diamond retained its properties at different temperatures, so the poet retains his rights in the face of ordinary laws and communal necessities. 'When Benvenuto Cellini crucified a living man to study the play of muscles in his death agony, a pope was right to grant him absolution. What is the death of a vague individual if it enables an immortal word to blossom and to create, in Keats's words, an eternal source of ecstasy?'[23]

Before this torrent Raynaud ventured to speak of Wilde's writings, but was stopped with a gesture: 'Oh let's drop that! I consider those things to be so unimportant. I do them to relax and to prove to myself, as your Baudelaire used to do with more genius, that I am not inferior to my contemporaries whom I hold in low esteem. My ambitions do not stop with composing poems. I want to make of my life itself a work of art. I know the price of a fine verse but also of a rose, of a vintage wine, of a colourful tie, of a delicate dish.'

They walked on past Le Napolitain, where Ernest La Jeunesse hailed them. Catulle Mendès was there, and invited them to join him. The subject of Wilde's paradoxes arose, and Wilde said to Mendès that paradoxes, though half-truths, were the best to be had, there being no absolute truths. He pointed out that the New Testament is full of paradoxes, though familiarity makes them less startling. 'What greater enormity could there be than "Blessed are the poor"?'[24] When Wilde asked his views of recent French verse, Mendès obliged with a harangue. He praised the Parnassiens and spoke of Armand Silvestre as the best poet. Silvestre's sixty thousand verses were a long struggle towards the purest ideal; his prose was good too, and neither coarse nor trivial. Wilde listened without a word, smiling almost imperceptibly, as Mendès spoke with oracular certainty, head thrown back, shaking his locks or adjusting his tie. Mendès made a full scale attack on the symbolists, and La Jeunesse's defense fueled his fire: 'the symbolists make us laugh. They've invented nothing. The symbol is as old as the world . . . Mallarmé is . . . a broken Baudelaire whose fragments have never come together.' He came down to the young poets whom Wilde had met: Henri de Régnier was all contained in Banville and Hugo. Paul Fort had a false simplicity and suffered from 'the Belgian aesthetic.' As for Vielé-Griffin, Mendès hoped he was missing something in this poet because, if there was no more in him than what he could see, there wasn't much. On the way out Raynaud warned Wilde that Mendès was probably responding to criticism by Vielé-Griffin of his work. Wilde said only, 'None the less, this devil of a man is terribly amusing.'[25]

Most of the time Wilde did not have to listen. A book given to him by Aristide Bruant on 8 December 1891 bears the inscription, 'Pour Oscar Wilde le joyeux fantaisiste anglais.'[26] Friends turned up from London, such as J. E. C. Bodley, who gave a party for Wilde and some French writers, then drove him out to the Bois de Boulogne with the intention of warning him not to repeat the scandal of *Dorian Gray*. Wilde insisted that the book struck a moral note, and had been misread; he said he had received commendatory letters from the Bishop of London and the Archbishop of Canterbury. Bodley was unconvinced but silenced. Another excursion was to the Château Rouge, a sort of dosshouse, to which Wilde went in company with Will Rothenstein, Sherard, and Stuart Merrill. Sherard added to their discomfort by threatening loudly that anyone who meddled with his friend Oscar Wilde would soon regret it. 'Robert,' said Wilde, 'you are defending us at the risk of our lives.'[27]

Wilde's brother-in-law, Otho Lloyd, and his wife had a house in the rue Vivienne. At a luncheon party, where Wilde was to be guest of honour, he arrived an hour late. He asked for the shutters to be closed and candles lighted, having his mother's dislike of sunlight for social occasions. The table cloth had also to be changed because the flowers on it, before he banished them too, were mauve, a color he superstitiously feared. He brusquely disregarded the names of the people to whom he was introduced. With the *hors d'oeuvres* he took over the conversation. His listeners were disappointed. He put on airs, he questioned people and did not listen to their answers, or indelicately forced them to speak: 'You have never seen an apparition? No. Oh really now, you, madame, yes, you, madame. Your eyes seem to have contemplated phantoms.' He attested that one night, in a bar, the tables were put in order and the floors swept not by the waiters but by the angels of the day's end. He told paradoxical stories, in a low voice, like secrets, and then gave a discourse about morgues in different capitals. The French had heard Villiers and Baudelaire try to shock in this way, and fashions had changed. Wilde realized that he had misjudged the occasion, and during the latter part of the meal was silent.

Over coffee, when people began to talk about a French vaudeville company touring Germany and England, he proposed almost diffidently that the prodigious theatrical sense in France explained most of its history.

French foreign policy, he said, was scenic: it searched for the fine attitude, the decorative words, the marked gesture, rather than practical success. And he unwound the history of France, from Charles X to the present day, in paradoxes. Renaud was amazed as Wilde deployed men, deeds, treaties, wars. He made them sparkle like jewels by the light of his words. A question led him to talk of Disraeli, and the salon of Lady Blessington, where Disraeli, though Jewish and obscure, stood up to the Count d'Orsay. He described and joked, with the generalizing power of a great historian and with the command of emotions of a great playwright and poet. In recounting Lady Blessington's love affairs he became lyrical, his voice resonated like a viol. If he had seemed pretentious, he went on to succeed by simplicity. Several of the guests wept, says Renaud, to think that words should achieve such splendor. And yet it was done so naturally, like ordinary conversation.[28]

So Wilde pervaded Paris. Stuart Merrill described him as 'gigantic, smooth-shaven and rosy, like a great priest of the moon in the time of Heliogabalus. At the Moulin Rouge the habitués took him for the prince of some fabulous realm of the North.' A blowsy woman, meeting him for the first time, said, '*Ne suis-je pas la femme la plus laide de Paris, Monsieur Wilde?*' '*Du monde, Madame,*' he replied.* As Merrill said, 'He could awaken the enthusiasm of Henri de Régnier on the one hand, and of Bibi la Purée on the other.' Not everyone took this view, but Wilde disregarded detractors. The only one he recognized was Edmond de Goncourt, who happened to publish in *L'Echo de Paris* on 17 December 1891 his journal entries of meetings with Wilde on 21 April and 5 May 1883. In the latter he referred to Wilde as 'this individual of doubtful sex, with a ham-actor's language, and tall stories.' In the former he said Wilde had talked of Swinburne as a flaunter of vice. Wilde ignored the attack on himself, and wrote to clarify what he had said of Swinburne. It was one of his most adroit letters:

[17 December 1891]   9 Boulevard des Capucines
Cher Monsieur de Goncourt,
     Quoique la base intellectuelle de mon esthétique soit la Philosophie de l'Irréalité, ou peut-être à cause de cela, je vous prie de me permettre une petite modification à vos notes sur la conversation où je vous ai parlé de notre cher et noble poète anglais M. Algernon Swinburne . . . Sans doute c'était de ma faute. On peut adorer une langue sans bien la parler, comme on peut aimer une femme sans la connaître. Français de sympathie, je suis

---

* 'Am I not the ugliest woman in Paris, Mr Wilde?' 'In the world, madam.' It was like his remark to Mrs T. P. O'Connor. Wilde had asked her if she were not jealous of her husband's flirtation with a young blonde. 'No,' she said, 'T. P. doesn't know a pretty woman when he sees one.' Harold Frederic, who was present, said, 'I beg leave to differ – what about yourself?' 'Oh, I was an accident.' 'Rather,' said Wilde, 'a catastrophe.'[29]

Irlandais de race, et les Anglais m'ont condamné à parler le langage de Shakespeare.

Vous avez dit que je représentais M. Swinburne comme un fanfaron du vice. Cela étonnerait beaucoup le poète, qui dans sa maison de campagne mène une vie bien austère, entièrement consacrée à l'art et à la littérature.

Voici ce que j'ai voulu dire ... Dans Shakespeare, et dans ses contemporains Webster et Ford, il y a des cris de nature. Dans l'oeuvre de Swinburne, on rencontre pour la première fois le cri de la chair tourmentée par le désir et le souvenir, la jouissance et le remords, la fécondité et la stérilité. Le public anglais, comme d'ordinaire hypocrite, prude et philistin, n'a pas su trouver l'art dans l'oeuvre d'art: il y a cherché l'homme. Comme il confond toujours l'homme avec ses créations, il pense que pour créer Hamlet il faut être un peu mélancolique, pour imaginer Lear absolument fou. Ainsi on a fait autour de M. Swinburne une légende d'ogre et de mangeur d'enfants. M. Swinburne, aristocrate de race et artiste de temperament, n'ai fait que rire de ces absurdités ...

J'espère que lorsque j'aurai l'honneur de vous rencontrer de nouveau, vous trouverez ma manière de m'exprimer en français moins obscure que le 21 avril 1883.*

Goncourt was shown the letter by Catulle Mendès, and it was then printed. In publishing the same passages from his journal in book form Goncourt omitted both the lines about Swinburne as flaunter of vice and of Wilde as doubtful-sexed. It was his compliment to a man whose letter proved him to be, whatever else, a genuine writer, and entitled to the

---

* 'Dear Monsieur de Goncourt: Although the intellectual basis of my aesthetic is the Philosophy of Unreality, or perhaps because of that, I ask you to permit me a small rectification of your notes on the conversation when I spoke to you about our dear and noble English poet M. Algernon Swinburne ... No doubt it was my fault. One can adore a language without speaking it well, as one can love a woman without understanding her. French by sympathy, I am Irish by race, and the English have condemned me to speak the language of Shakespeare.

You said that I represented M. Swinburne as a flaunter of vice. That would surprise the poet very much, since he lives an austere life in a country dwelling, consecrated entirely to art and literature.

Here is what I meant to say ... In Shakespeare, and in his contemporaries Webster and Ford, there are cries of nature ... In Swinburne's work, we meet for the first time the cry of flesh tormented by desire and memory, joy and remorse, fecundity and sterility. The English public, as usual hypocritical, prudish, and philistine, has not known how to find the art in the work of art: it has searched for the man in it. As it always confuses the man and his creations, it thinks that to create Hamlet you must be a little melancholy, to imagine Lear completely mad. So it has built around M. Swinburne a legend of an ogre and a devourer of children. M. Swinburne, an aristocrat by birth and an artist by temperament, has merely laughed at these absurdities ...

I hope that when I have the honour of meeting you again, you will find my way of expressing myself in French less obscure than on the 21 April 1883.'

courtesies of a fellow-craftsman. When, on Goncourt's death in 1896, the Académie Goncourt was founded, a French Academician, actuated by like feelings, proposed Wilde along with Tolstoy for membership.[30]

New Disciples

I choose my friends for their good looks, my acquaintances for their good characters, and my enemies for their good intellects.

The principal friendships Wilde made in Paris were with Schwob, Pierre Louÿs, and André Gide. Gide and Louÿs, both a little over twenty-one, were of almost opposite temperament, Gide furtive and self-aware, Louÿs outspoken and outrageous, given to cruel practical jokes of which Gide was for a time – until he broke off with Louÿs – the butt. The one attracted to men and the other to women, Gide and Louÿs both admired Wilde, who admired them. He inscribed *The House of Pomegranates* to Louÿs in gaudy terms:

> Au jeune homme qui adore la Beauté
> Au jeune homme que la Beauté adore
> Au jeune homme que j'adore*

They wrote a composite autograph, Wilde's part being a quotation from *Salome*,

> Il ne faut regarder ni les choses ni les personnes
> Il ne faut regarder que dans les miroirs. Car les
> miroirs ne nous montrent que les masques.†

Louÿs wrote earnestly, '*Il faut montrer la Beauté aux hommes.*'[31] By January 1892 Louÿs, preparing his book of poems, *Astarté*, for the printer, followed Wilde's method in *The House of Pomegranates* by dedicating each poem to a friend, one being Wilde himself; and he quoted Wilde's story, 'The Young King,' in an epigraph. His letters to Wilde begin, '*Cher Maître.*' He was won.

Gide and Wilde first met about 26 November 1891, by which time Wilde was thirty-seven and Gide just twenty-two. We know almost too well the schedule of their meetings, which occurred nearly every day,

---

* 'To the young man who adores Beauty / To the young man whom Beauty adores / To the young man I adore'

† 'One should not look either at things or people. One should look only in mirrors. Because mirrors only show us masks.'

lasting often for hours on end, during three weeks. The second was at the poet Heredia's, a day or two later. (Louÿs was to marry Heredia's youngest daughter.) Then Louÿs, at Gide's request, arranged a small dinner for Wilde at the Café d'Harcourt, Place de la Sorbonne, on the 28th, probably with Stuart Merrill making a fourth. Perhaps at Wilde's counter-invitation, Gide met him again at five o'clock the next day; and the two men dined with Stuart Merrill on 2 December, with Marcel Schwob at Aristide Bruant's on the 3rd. These were presumably some of the three-hour dinners at which, according to Gide in a letter to Paul Valéry of December 1891, Wilde talked so well he seemed to be Baudelaire or Villiers (a comparison he was more indulgent towards than Renaud had been). On the 6th they were at the house of Princess Ouroussoff, who claimed – in the midst of one of Wilde's verbal flights – to see a halo round his head. Gide also said, '*il rayonnait* [he emitted rays].' To follow out this social calendar, there was dinner for Gide and Wilde at Schwob's on the 7th, at Bruant's again on the 8th. Gide's daybook records (says Jean Delay) the single name WILDE in large letters for the 11th and 12th; on the 13th Princess Ouroussoff entertained them both again for dinner, along with Henri de Régnier; and on the 15th Gide and Schwob met Wilde once more, after which Gide went to the country to visit relations, and Wilde, a few days later, went back to London. For Wilde this social round was almost routine, but for Gide it was a complete change; ordinarily he did not frequent either the Café d'Harcourt or Aristide Bruant's and did not meet so many people in a year.

In these early days of their friendship, Gide was overwhelmed by Wilde. Stuart Merrill remembered that when Wilde told his stories, Gide stared distractedly into his plate. The bearded Jules Renard, who found the cleanshaven faces of both Gide and Wilde offensive (he emphasizes in separate descriptions that each was *imberbe*), met Gide at Schwob's on 23rd December just after Wilde had left Paris. He too thought the young Gide was in love with Wilde.[32] As for Wilde, he liked Gide, but apparently preferred the company of Louÿs and of Schwob, whose help he solicited – along with Retté's – for *Salome*. (He dedicated the play to Louÿs.) Though his feelings may not have been reciprocated, some process occurred which was vital to Gide though he never specified exactly what had happened. He did give enough particulars to suggest the nature of a typical Wilde friendship.

The relation between them was probably much like that between Dorian and Lord Henry Wotton. 'To project one's soul into some gracious form, and let it tarry there for a moment; to hear one's own intellectual view echoed back with all the added music of passion and youth; to convey one's temperament into another as though it were a subtle fluid or a strange perfume; there was a real joy in that.' Gide chose to feel that Wilde spiritually seduced him. Until that time Gide had gone through life in a dream, like a sleepwalker. Now he suddenly woke up to find himself on a sloping roof. It was well to have a companion to blame or to thank. He did not need to have been a student of Goethe, though he was, to rejoice at finding somebody to play Mephisto to his Faust or Faust to his Gretchen.

The stages in the seduction are marked in Gide's correspondence and journal. At first he was dazzled: in a letter of 28 November 1891, to Paul Valéry, he describes meeting '*l'esthète Oscar Wilde*' along with others, and then comments, '*O, admirable, admirable, celui-là.*' But the tone quickly changes as he finds himself imperilled. A week later he represents Wilde as besieging him, and tells Valéry (4 December), '*Wilde s'ingénie pieusement à tuer ce qui me restait d'âme, parce qu'il dit que pour connaître une essence, il faut la supprimer: il veut que je regrette mon âme. L'effort pour la détruire est la mesure de toute chose. Toute chose ne se constitue que de son vide . . . etc.*'*

This idea was good enough for Gide to restate it five years later in *Les Nourritures terrestres*, where he declares, 'on certain evenings I was mad enough almost to believe in my soul, I felt it so near escaping from my body.' He adds scrupulously, 'Ménalque [Wilde] said this too.' And in 1924 (24 August), in his journal for *Les Faux-monnayeurs*, he writes 'We name things only when we are breaking with them' and then adds that this 'formula . . . may well presage a new departure.'[33] The idea that the devil should circulate in the book incognito, his reality growing stronger the less the other characters believe in him, is a corollary to Wilde's theorem. Beyond the evocation of a stagey devil, Gide's remarks reflect his eagerness to abandon the idea of self which should be sequential and predictable, and to accept fits and starts as his natural medium.

When Wilde had left Paris in 1891, Gide almost ceased to write letters – a sure sign of turmoil in this relentless correspondent. After an interval he communicated with Valéry, 'Forgive my being silent: since Wilde I only exist a little.' He was conscious of something gone out of his existence, out of his innocence. This feeling of being 'devirginated,' and rather too easily, persisted and stirred in him some resentment. (Wilde too was fatigued by the speed of Gide's spiritual submission.) Gide begins his diary of 1 January 1892, two weeks after his last encounter with Wilde, with a solemn verdict: 'Wilde, I believe, did me nothing but harm. In his company I lost the habit of thinking. I had more varied emotions, but had forgotten how to bring order into them.' He plunged with relief into his readings in philosophy. The damage was not permanent. Paul Valéry had anticipated as much by joking about Wilde, even when Gide was enrap-

---

* 'Wilde contrives piously to kill what was left to me of soul, because he says that to know an essence, one must suppress it; he wants me to miss my soul. The effort to destroy a thing takes its measure. Everything constitutes itself only by being rendered void . . . etc.'

As Lord Illingworth says, 'Thought is by its nature destructive. Nothing survives being thought of.'

tured, as a 'symbolic mouth *à la* Redon which swallows a mouthful and mechanically transforms it at once into a satanic aphorism.'

Gide never said explicitly what evangel Wilde had imparted to him, but in the character Ménalque, who appears in both *Les Nourritures terrestres* and *L'Immoraliste*, there is a bow to Wilde, though an ironic one, especially in the later book. The narrator feels for Ménalque more than friendship, but less than love. Ménalque is a man who no longer lives under the old dispensation. He is not dissolute, but unconstrained. Gide represents him as much older – each time Gide met Wilde afterwards he noted how terribly he had aged since their last encounter. In the section about Ménalque published in the review *L'Ermitage* before the rest of *Les Nourritures terrestres*, Ménalque was approximately Wilde's age; in the later version Gide heaped on another decade, perhaps to qualify the allusion. Ménalque is a grandfather then, but a newborn one, an elderly apostle of youthful sensation. If Wilde recognized this unsmiling portrait of himself, he gave no hint. Wilde's main influence on the book came from his faith in himself as bearer of a new gospel to be transmitted above all to the young. Gide took over this role for his own; it is he who tutors Nathanaël, while Ménalque is relegated to the lesser part of precursor.

Besides this fictional transformation of Wilde, Gide wrote about him nonfictionally many times. His finest tribute may however be not what he published, distinguished though that is, but his removal from his journal of those pages dealing with the first three weeks of their friendship. The main document about the psychic possession of Gide by Wilde is an absent one – a truly symbolist piece of evidence, like Mallarmé's *'l'Absente de tous bouquets.'* We know it, as Wilde said we might know the soul, by its having been eliminated.

One can speculate about Wilde's message to Gide, and its disturbing effect. Much that the two men have in common derives from their equal saturation in a literary movement which sought, by imbedding symbol within symbol and perspective within perspective, to reach 'the mind's native land,' as Mallarmé called it. Yet speculation about the missing pages is possible and need not be too risky, since we have Gide's essays on Wilde which, for all their evasions, are highly informative. We have one remark from their conversation which Wilde recorded. And there are, of course, their writings. No doubt much that passed between them was unspoken, a matter of assumptions, smiles, calculated disdain or indifference, exclusion. The subject of homosexuality, for example, was not mentioned – so Gide says – although it must have been at least behind the scenes like the Devil in *Les Faux-monnayeurs*.

Wilde had his parables to impart. One had to do with Narcissus, about whom Gide had just published a book. According to Wilde,

When Narcissus died, the flowers of the field were desolate and asked the river for some drops of water to weep for him. 'Oh!' answered the river, 'if all my drops of water were tears, I should not have enough to weep for Narcissus myself. I love him.' 'Oh!' replied the flowers of the field, 'how could you not have loved Narcissus? He was beautiful.' 'Was he beautiful?' said the river. 'And who should know better than you? Each day, leaning over your bank, he beheld his beauty in your waters.' 'If I loved him,' replied the river, 'it was because, when he leaned over my waters, I saw the reflection of my waters in his eyes.'[34]

The name of this story, said Wilde, was 'The Disciple.' The point was that there are no disciples – a lesson to one of Mallarmé's disciples from a rival master. People are suns, not moons.

Wilde's conquest of Gide was partly by parable. But he had precepts as well. He soon realized that Gide was of Huguenot ancestry, and would complain later to Alfred Douglas that Gide was a French Protestant, 'the worst kind, except of course for the Irish Protestant.' But Irish Protestantism, at least in Dublin, had spent its force. Wilde thought Gide dominated by inhibitions that originated in his religious training. He complained that Gide's lips were too straight, the lips 'of someone who has never lied. I must teach you to lie, so your lips will be beautiful and curved like those on an antique mask.' Wilde presumably broached the subject of religion to Gide in 1891, as he had broached it to Bernard Berenson a year before, by saying, 'Tell me at once. Are you living with the Twenty Commandments?' In *Les Nourritures terrestres* Gide begins one section with the question, 'God's commandments, are there ten of you or twenty?' Wilde had made the same kind of joke at Oxford about the 'Forty-Nine Articles.' He probably said to Gide, as to another young man, 'Creation began when you were born. It will end on the day you die.'[35] Nothing could have so completely pervaded Gide's consciousness as the disclosure that the Biblical terrain, on which he and his ancestors had trod so confidently, was mined.

If, as is likely, Wilde knew about Gide's domination by his pious mother (Louÿs would have hardly kept quiet about such things), he may have quoted, as he did in 'The Soul of Man under Socialism,' Christ's question, 'Who is my mother?' Gide, in his developing filial revolt, used a comparable quotation, 'Woman, what have I to do with thee?' More to the point, Wilde approached Gide at a party at Heredia's and asked, 'Would you like me to tell you a secret? . . . but promise me not to tell it to anyone . . . Do you know why Christ did not love his mother?' He paused. 'It's because she was a virgin!'[36]* To Gide, himself a virgin and obliged to

---

* Wilde had a moral tale about Androcles, who he said was one of the best dentists of his age. In the desert he found a lion who had broken his teeth in trying to eat someone. Androcles was moved to construct a new set of gold teeth for the lion, which fitted him perfectly. Some years later Androcles, being a Christian, was exhibited in the Roman circus before being thrown to the wild beasts. A lion came out of a gilded cage and went for him, his mouth gaping wide. But Androcles recognized his

remain one for another year, the idea that purity might be monstrous must have been agitating. Up to now under his mother's thumb, he began to behave towards her with calculated ferocity, hinting, with less and less disguise, at the homosexuality which he knew she would abhor.

In the first essay he wrote after Wilde's death, Gide declares that Wilde posed pagan naturalism against Christian miracles so as to put Christianity out of countenance. He did do this at times, as when he said to Yeats, 'I have been inventing a new Christian heresy. It seemed that Christ recovered after the Crucifixion, and escaping from the tomb lived on for many years, the one man upon earth who knew the falsehood of Christianity. Once St Paul visited his town and he alone in the carpenters' quarter did not go to hear him preach. Henceforth the other carpenters noticed that, for some unknown reason, he kept his hands covered.'[38]

Other examples, which Gide gives, do not so much discountenance Christianity as suggest its joylessness, while adding a further meaning to the original. It is a fifth gospel, the gospel according to Saint Thomas, as Wilde says of Renan's life of Jesus. In Wilde's version of the raising of Lazarus, Christ comes upon a young man weeping and asks why. The man replies, 'Lord, I was dead and you raised me up. What else should I do but weep?' In another version, told at this time to Jean Lorrain, the resurrected Lazarus bitterly reproaches Christ for lying, 'There is nothing in death, and he who is dead is dead indeed.' Jesus puts his finger on his lips, 'I know it, but don't tell them.'[39] This is not pagan naturalism, but the novelist amending, as Yeats would say, 'what was told awry / By some peasant gospeller.' Gide forgets he is borrowing from Wilde when, in his autobiography, he speaks of 'that kind of abominable anguish that Lazarus must have felt after his escape from the tomb.'* His own play about King Saul, which was the first of his works to interest Wilde, was a similar extension of Biblical narrative, depicting Saul in love with David. Gide understandably preferred not to think of Wilde's method as being as close to his own as it was. Once he had received the impetus, he had no need for tutelage, and could vie with Wilde in rewriting both Testaments.

But Wilde had something else to inculcate, something even more useful to Gide, a way of bridging the divide between art and life – a problem in

---

handiwork, and the lion recognized the dentist, and began to lick his feet. Then he thought, 'How can I show my gratitude to this man who saved my life? I must give him enormous publicity.' So saying, he gathered himself, and, to demonstrate to all the excellence of the set of false teeth, in a few mouthfuls he ate him up.[37]

* Gide had another Wilde fable, which he did not much like and therefore recalled only for its ending. The ghosts of two saints, one a woman and one a man, converse from opposite sides of the river Nile. At the end of their dialogue, the man, who has been describing his life of renunciation and sacrifice, concludes: 'And this body, to which I refused all its natural joys, this body that I mortified, that whips have lashed, that torturers have burned and broken, this wretched body that I've always treated as an enemy – after my death, do you know what they did? They embalmed it!'[40]

Gide's *Le Traité du Narcisse*. According to this theory the artist makes models of experience which people rush to try out. As his supreme artist Wilde ingeniously named Christ. For Christ urged others to live artistically, and lived artistically himself. 'His entire life is the most wonderful of poems,' Wilde said. 'He is just like a work of art himself.' Gide's journal contains a note written a month after he had come to know Wilde, 'A man's life is his image.'[41] In Wilde's work this is an old theme, in Gide's a new one.

That Wilde did talk in this vein to Gide is also confirmed by *De Profundis*, where Wilde remarks, 'I remember saying once to André Gide, as we sat together in some Paris café, that while Metaphysics had but little real interest for me, and Morality absolutely none, there was nothing that either Plato or Christ had said that could not be transferred immediately into the sphere of Art, and there find its complete fulfillment. It was a generalisation as profound as it was novel.' For Gide, a young man bent upon the exculpation of his instincts yet addicted to Biblical quotation, this idea was like an explosive device. In 1893 he writes in his journal, 'Christ's saying is just as true in art: Whosoever will save his life (his personality) shall lose it.'[42] He proceeded with this translation of Christianity to a higher level, and even projected a book to be entitled, *Christianisme contre le Christ*. Wilde also, if he had lived, might well have taken over Christianity as he took over socialism; to one of his friends he projected a book that would rescue his religion from its adherents and be, as he said, 'the Epic of the Cross, the Iliad of Christianity.'[43]

To some extent he carried out this plan, first in 'The Soul of Man under Socialism,' and later in his *De Profundis* letter. In the first, Wilde insisted that Christ taught the importance of the individual, and, a Pater before the fact, urged total self-expression. ' "Know thyself!" was written over the portal of the antique world . . . the message of Christ to man was simply, "Be thyself." ' In *Les Nourritures terrestres* Gide similarly insists that 'Know thyself' is 'a maxim as pernicious as it is ugly,' a phrase which itself suggests Wilde's aesthetic-ethical blend. 'Whoever observes himself arrests his development.' The family and personal property, impediments to self-expression, must go. (Both men said this.) Gide was willing to be rid of his mother (as Wilde was not), and to spend his ample inheritance, as Wilde would have done if only he had had one. Wilde held that art was 'the most intense mode of individualism that the world has known,' so the better the artist the more perfect his imitation of Christ.[44] The artistic life is a guide to conduct. Gide was to complain in *Les Faux-monnayeurs* that symbolism offered an aesthetic but no ethic. Wilde brought the two together before Gide.

The relation of art to life was a subject Wilde brooded over. He had said in *Intentions* that life would repeat itself tediously were it not for the daemonic changes art forces upon it. Art would be repetitious too if the critical impulse did not impel the artist to new and subversive modes of thinking and feeling. Wilde is willing to see this idea through; and he finds in art the impulse to destroy along with the impulse to create. Unlike Yeats, who says that works of art beget works of art, Wilde believes that works of art murder works of art. He put this idea to Gide in one of his best parables, which Ricketts says was invented in 1889.

> There was a man who could think only in bronze. And one day this man had an idea, the idea of joy, of the joy which dwells in the moment. And he felt that he had to tell it. But in all the world, not a single piece of bronze was left; for men had used it all. And this man felt that he would go mad if he did not tell his idea. And he thought about a piece of bronze on the grave of his wife, of a statue he had made to ornament the tomb of his wife, the only woman he had loved; it was the statue of sadness, of the sadness which dwells in life. And the man felt that he would go mad if he did not tell his idea. So he took the statue of sadness, of the sadness which dwells in life; he smashed it, he melted it down, and he made of it the statue of joy, of the joy which dwells only in the moment.[45]

Each new work repudiates its predecessor, as its successor will repudiate it. Gide adopted this idea, too, as he declares in a letter to Francis Jammes of 6 August 1902: 'Each of my books is an immediate reaction against the preceding one. No one of them ever completely satisfies me, and I never dance on more than one foot at a time: the main thing is to dance well all the same; but with every book I change feet, as one is tired from having danced, and the other from having rested all that time.' He was fond of having his books murder each other, and proposed that Wilde's *De Profundis* was the opposite of *Intentions*, as if he recognized that Wilde had subjected himself to the same law. He must also have been aware that 'The Soul of Man under Socialism' is killed by *Salome* as certainly as *L'Immoraliste* – that hollow victory of the flesh – is killed by *La Porte étroite* – that hollow victory of the spirit.

For Wilde this oscillation is a cardinal principle; it can be observed at work within each book as well as between books. In *Dorian Gray*, Wilde writes that 'Nothing can cure the soul but the senses just as nothing can cure the senses but the soul.' (Gide writes likewise in *Les Nourritures terrestres*, 'I owed the health of my body only to the irremediable poisoning of my soul.') In *Salome* Wilde re-interprets the biblical legend and, in putting both Salome and Iokanaan to death, turns virtue into a kind of sin, a debauchery of the spirit not to be exalted over other forms of debauchery.

What Wilde provided for Gide, at a crucial moment in the latter's youth, was a way of extricating himself from an aestheticism which had not yet come to grips with love, religion, or life, and from a religion which offered safety only at the cost of being perpetually on guard. He did this not by rejecting aesthetics or ethics, but by turning sacred things inside out to make them secular, and secular things inside out to make them sacred. He showed souls becoming carnal and lusts becoming spiritual. He showed the aesthetic world not isolated from experience, but infused into it. This was the new hellenism of which he liked to speak. Gide developed it.

Wilde knew that his effect on the French had been extraordinary and unprecedented. Whistler tried to minimize it. He wrote from Paris that Wilde had 'left Paris precipitately – utterly collapsed – saddened and demoralized – knowing that the Gaff was blown, and that it would be hopeless ever to try it on again. Besides, my "Oscar, *le bourgeois malgré lui*," nearly finished him.'[46] In fact, Wilde returned home in late December well pleased with himself and with *Salome*, which he had nearly finished. There had been talk of putting it on in Paris, though nothing had come of it. But *Lady Windermere's Fan* was soon to be staged, and its success would set his literary course for the next four glorious years.

CHAPTER XIV

A Good Woman, and Others

'And what sort of lives do these people, who pose as being moral, lead themselves? My dear fellow, you forget that we are in the native land of the hypocrite.'

Success in Piccadilly

Wilde was back in London about 22 December 1891, in time to spend Christmas with his wife and sons. He called on his mother, now a little better off because of the Civil List grant he had obtained for her in 1890. There was news about Willie, whose last memorable act had been to get himself declared bankrupt on 31 August 1888. This time his prospects sounded more encouraging. During the summer of 1891 he had met Mrs Frank Leslie, a wealthy American widow and newspaper publisher. She was fifty-five, he was thirty-nine. Within a few days Willie proposed, but she left London in early August without committing herself. Oscar urged Willie to get a prenuptial settlement. Willie did not do so. But in September 1891 he pursued her to New York and had married her there on 4 October in the Church of the Strangers, 229 Mercer Street.

The new Mrs Wilde did not understand her husband's indolence or his drinking. It soon became clear that Willie was not planning to do even as much work as he had done in London. 'What New York needs,' he said, 'is a leisure class, and I am determined to introduce one.' He spent his time and his wife's money at the fashionable Lotos Club. Their sexual relations were unsatisfactory. 'He was of no use to me, either by day or night,' was his wife's verdict. Early in 1892 she came to London with him, and said to a friend, 'I'm taking Willie over, but I'll not bring Willie back.' She told Lady Wilde that she would not go on supporting him in idleness. 'I hear your marriage has broken up,' said Oscar when he and Willie met. 'No,' said Willie, 'it's broken down.' 'What's the difference?' 'She's up, I'm down.'[1] Willie went back to the *Daily Telegraph* to offer his services again, but was taken on only for occasional assignments.

Willie was difficult to help and beyond the reach of admonition. In the last days of December 1891 his industrious brother went to Torquay, and

342

stayed there until January finishing *Salome*. *Lady Windermere's Fan* also needed some last minute work before George Alexander produced it in February. For the moment Wilde called the play *A Good Woman*, to the annoyance of his mother, who assured him that the title would attract no one. Wilde probably had the final title in mind, but he remembered his American experience of having both *Vera* and *The Duchess of Padua* written about exhaustively before they could be produced. He also liked the ambiguity of 'good,' and when he published it as a book, the play was given the composite title: *Lady Windermere's Fan, A Play About a Good Woman*.

Writing about a good woman and a bad one at the same time illustrated his belief that in art contraries are equally true. But neither Lady Windermere nor Salome lived up to her advance billing. Salome is fatal to herself as well as to the young Syrian captain and to Iokanaan. Lady Windermere's pursuit of the good is tortuous, she is prepared to run off with a lover rather than admit an adventuress to her ball. Puritanism, as Wilde never tired of showing, produces its viciousness as much as debauchery. Thoughtless goodness is as self-destructive as evil, and becomes what it despises. In this play Wilde was continuing the dialectic of *Dorian Gray*, where the degradation of the anchorite's self-denial is 'infinitely more terrible than that degradation from which, in their ignorance, they had sought to escape.' It was also the dialectic of 'The Soul of Man under Socialism,' in which he warned that the world has to suffer more from its martyrs than its sinners. Of the two heroines, Salome might be defended, since she serves and expresses love, if perversely, while Lady Windermere represses it.

Lady Windermere's Fan is a more radical play than it appears. To dismiss it as about a fallen woman's rescue of her puritan daughter, who eventually becomes less puritan, is to ignore Wilde's critique of catch-phrases and conventional moral blame. Lady Windermere is tempted by her own morality to behave in a way alien to her character as well as to that morality; she has to be rescued by the maternal adventuress, who knows much more about goodness than her daughter ever will. On the other hand, Lord Darlington, who has been taken for a man about town, and who talks like Lord Henry Wotton, differs from Wotton in his possession of deep feelings. He seems to be parading Pater-like phrases about 'living one's own life, fully, entirely, completely,' instead of 'dragging out some false, shallow, degrading existence that the world in its hypocrisy demands.' But he means them. This hinting at Lord Windermere's putative infidelity is not really ungentlemanly. When the play was given in New York with Maurice Barrymore (the father of John, Ethel, and Lionel) in the role, Wilde complained that Barrymore had failed to see that 'Darlington is *not* a villain, but a man who really believes that Windermere is treating his wife badly, and wishes to save her. His appeal is not to the weakness, but to the strength of her character (Act II): in Act III his words show he really loves her.' It is because of her that he is leaving England for many years; he is a better man than Windermere.

Wilde is ingenious in his ending. He resolved not to admit the total recognition which was the staple of comedy. Three secrets are left at the end, undisclosed: Windermere will never know that his wife was at Darlington's rooms, on the verge of running away with him; Lady Windermere will never know that Mrs Erlynne is her mother; Lord Augustus will never recognize how Mrs Erlynne has hoodwinked him. *Lady Windermere's Fan* withholds the conventional ending of comedy, and concludes with collusive concealment instead of collective disclosure. Society profits from deception. Wilde also shelves the stereotype of the fallen woman: Mrs Erlynne is singularly impenitent. She gives way to an access of maternal feeling, which she has never felt, and abruptly sheds it. As Wilde explained, by the next day she feels '"This passion is too terrible. It wrecks my life. I don't want to know it again. It makes me suffer too much. Let me go away. I don't want to be a mother any more." And so the fourth act is to me the psychological act, the act that is newest, most true.'[2] It is this act which prompts him to claim for Mrs Erlynne that her character is 'as yet untouched by literature.' She follows that pattern which Wilde had discovered in himself, of venting a passion to exhaust it. Lady Windermere, blinded by puritanism, is obliged to see a different world. Both bear out Wilde's idea that emotions are finite, their limits defined only when exceeded. In this sense we kill the thing inside us that we love. Goodness turns out to be a subtler commodity than it has appeared.

In February 1892, *Lady Windermere's Fan* went into rehearsal. As with all his plays, Wilde attended every day and was full of suggestions and revisions as he observed the effect of his lines. He did not hesitate to tell Alexander his views, and they often disagreed. Two of his surviving letters to Alexander from the rehearsal period refer to discourtesy and friction. Wilde dictated the finest details of position and inflection. He wanted no word of the dialogue to be lost. At first he rejected Alexander's suggestion that the audience should be allowed to know at the end of Act II that Mrs Erlynne and Lady Windermere are mother and daughter. (After the first night he gave in on this point and rewrote the speeches.) The stress of rehearsal, and of quarreling with Alexander, made Wilde so ill that he said he would have to go away for a rest after the opening night. In fact, his malaise dissipated in euphoria.

The theatre was fully booked for the first performance on 20 February 1892. Wilde's old flames Florence Balcombe, now Stoker, and Lillie Langtry were there, and so was his wife. He got tickets for friends, though not nearly so many as he wished. One went to Pierre Louÿs, who came over from France, and one to Edward Shelley, a clerk at the Bodley Head whom Wilde was courting and would take to bed that night at the Albemarle Hotel. He sent one to the young artist Graham Robertson and asked him to participate in a little sub-plot. Robertson was to buy a green carnation at Goodyear's in the Royal Arcade – 'They grow them there,' said Wilde – and to wear it at the performance. Other friends, such as Robert Ross, were to be similarly adorned, and so was Ben Webster, who played Cecil Graham (a surname borrowed back from 'The Picture of Mr W. H.'). 'And what does it mean?' asked Robertson. Wilde replied, 'Nothing whatever, but that is just what nobody will guess.'[3] The suggestion of a mysterious confraternity enigmatically binding one of the players with some members of the audience, gave Wilde the delight he had found in Masonic signs. The green carnation was to take on some of the suggestiveness of lilies and sunflowers. With a hint of decadence, the painted flower blended art and nature.

But the audience was not composed only of accomplices. The *New York Times* acknowledged that it was 'the most brilliant audience that had gathered for years.' Frank Harris was there and brought with him a writer for *The Times*, Arthur Walter, in the hope that this paper would praise the play. Unfortunately Walter disliked it. So did Henry James to whom it was 'infantine . . . both in subject and form.'[4] Harris came down to the foyer at the interval and discovered that most of the critics were against it.* A big man named Joseph Knight, whose life of Rossetti Wilde had disparaged in the *Pall Mall Gazette*, was getting his own back. 'The humour is mechanical, unreal,' he said to Harris, who said nothing. 'What do you think of it?' 'That is for you critics to answer,' said Harris. 'I might say in Oscar's way, "Little promise and less performance,"' said Knight, laughing uproariously, 'That's the exact opposite of Oscar's way,' said Harris, 'it is the listeners who laugh at his humour.' 'Come now, really,' said Knight, 'you cannot think much of the play?' Harris at last allowed himself to be drawn: 'I have not seen the whole play. I was not at any of the rehearsals. But so far it is surely the best comedy in English, the most brilliant, is it not?' And, ignoring hoots of derision, he added, 'I can only compare it to the best of Congreve, and I think it's better.' Bernard Shaw also admired it, and on sending Wilde his own first play, *Widowers' Houses*, which was produced later the same year, hoped he would find it 'tolerably amusing, considering that it is a farcical comedy. Unfortunately,' he added with some deference, 'I have no power of producing beauty; my genius is the genius of intellect.'[6]

Most of the audience agreed with Harris and Shaw. By the second interval, Wilde was already feeling jubilant. He was standing drinks for his friends in the bar when he caught sight of Le Gallienne and his 'poem' (otherwise woman friend) to whom he had sent tickets with the words, 'Come, and bring your poem to sit beside you.' 'My dear Richard, where

---

* Wilde commented that the criticism displayed 'in its crudest form the extraordinary Boeotianism of a country that has produced some Athenians, and in which other Athenians have come to dwell.'[5]

have you been?' he asked. 'It seems as if we hadn't met for years. Now tell me what you have been doing? Ah I remember . . . Yes . . . You have pained me deeply, Richard.' 'I pained you! How?' 'You have brought out a new book since I saw you last.' 'Well, what of it?' 'You have treated me very badly in your book, Richard.' 'I treated you badly? You must be confusing my book with somebody else's. My last book was *The Religion of a Literary Man.* You must be dreaming, man. Why, I never so much as mentioned you in it.' 'Ah, Richard! that was just it!' In soberer mood he went on to ask what else Le Gallienne had been writing. 'On loving one's enemies,' said Le Gallienne. 'That's a great theme,' said Wilde. 'I should like to write on that, too. For do you know, all my life I have been looking for twelve men who didn't believe in me . . . and so far I have only found eleven.'[7]

After the final curtain the applause was long and hearty, and Wilde came forward from the wings in response to cries of 'Author!' He knew how he wished to look, and what he wanted to say. In his mauve-gloved hand was a cigarette ('out of nervousness,' according to Mrs Jopling), and in his buttonhole a green carnation.[8] The 'delightful and immortal speech' (as he himself described it in a letter to the *St James's Gazette*) was accentuated, according to Alexander, in this way: 'Ladies and gentlemen: I have enjoyed this evening *immensely.* The actors have given us a *charming* rendering of a *delightful* play, and your appreciation has been *most* intelligent. I congratulate you on the *great* success of your performance, which persuades me that you think *almost* as highly of the play as I do myself.'*

* Jean-Joseph Renaud said that Wilde began by saying, after taking a pull on his cigarette, 'Ladies and gentlemen, it's perhaps not very proper to smoke in front of you, but . . . it's not very proper to disturb me when I am smoking.'[9]

The *Boston Evening Transcript* for 10 March 1892 carried an article by Marie de Mensiaux in which she reported Wilde's speech in what appears to be a more accurate, if less spectacular, version than Alexander's. According to her, Wilde said:

'I believe it is the privilege of an author to allow his works to be reproduced by others while he himself remains silent. But as you seem to wish to hear me speak, I accept the honor you are kind enough to confer upon me. The more especially am I pleased to do this as your goodness gives me the opportunity of thanking all who have been instrumental in securing the success that has crowned this evening's entertainment. And to express my gratification at your so well appreciating the merits of the play. My acknowledgements are due in the first instance to Mr Alexander, who has placed my play upon the stage with the admirable completeness that has characterized all the productions at the St James's Theatre during the time it has been under his management. If I praise all I wish to praise in the interpretation of the piece, I would have to read to you the entire cast as it appears upon the programme. But I have to thank the company, not only for repeating the words I have set down for them to speak, but also for entering, as it were, into the atmosphere of the world I have endeavored to reproduce before you. I have to thank them, one and all, for the infinite care they have taken to fill in every detail, until my sketch has become a finished picture. I think that you have enjoyed the performance as much as I have, and I am pleased to believe that you like the piece almost as much as I do myself.'

The conservative critics, his old friend Clement Scott for one, found the cigarette even more outrageous than the egotism. Henry James wrote to Henrietta Reubell, his friend and Wilde's, that 'the unspeakable one had responded to curtain calls by appearing with a metallic blue carnation in his buttonhole and a cigarette in his fingers.' (The color was green-blue, verdigris.) Wilde's speech he considered inadequate. '*Ce monsieur* gives at last on one's nerves,' James confided. Robert Ross, in an interview with Wilde in the *St James's Gazette* of 18 January 1895, asked whether Wilde recognized that people found fault with his curtain speeches. Wilde replied, 'Yes, the old-fashioned idea was that the dramatist should appear and merely thank his kind friends for their patronage and presence. I am glad to say I have altered all that. The artist cannot be degraded into the servant of the public. While I have always recognised the cultural appreciation that actors and audience have shown for my work, I have equally recognised that humility is for the hypocrite, modesty for the incompetent. Assertion is at once the duty and privilege of the artist.'

The crowds came. The Prince of Wales approved. And Alexander noticed that the pit and galleries were as full as the stalls and boxes. 'My dear Alexander,' said Wilde, 'the answer is easy. Servants listen to conversations in drawing rooms and dining rooms. They hear people discussing my play, their curiosity is aroused, and so they fill your theatre. I can see they are servants by their perfect manners.' Lady Wilde wrote to her son on 24 February, 'You have had a brilliant success! and I am so happy.' The play ran from February until 29 July, toured the provinces, and was back on the boards on 31 October. It has held the stage since, just as *Dorian Gray* has kept its public, because it is better than it seems to be. A kind of poetical glamor pervades it, as Shaw noticed. The audience cannot bear to be inattentive. The characters and plot may be implausible, but the tension of conflicting impulses is expertly sustained, the wit pungent, and the central transvaluation of values, by which the bad woman appears in a good light, the good woman in a bad one, and society in the worst light of all, is cunning.

After the performances Wilde sometimes went to the Crown, a public house off Charing Cross Road, where Symons, Dowson, Beardsley, Beerbohm, Johnson, and their friends used to congregate, meeting in a little room away from the bar, drinking hot port until 12:30 and till later outside. There was much talk about his play. On 26 May Wilde spoke at a meeting of the Royal General Theatrical Fund, with his friend George Alexander in the chair. An alderman named Routledge had praised Wilde for calling a spade a spade and for lashing vice in *Lady Windermere's Fan*. Wilde disavowed both intentions. 'I would like to protest against the statement that I have ever called a spade a spade. The man who did so should be condemned to use one. I have also been accused of lashing vice, but I can assure you that nothing was further from my intentions. Those who have seen *Lady Windermere's Fan* will see that if there is one particular doctrine contained in it, it is that of sheer individualism. It is not for anyone to censure what anyone else does, and everyone should go his own way, to whatever place he chooses, in exactly the way that he chooses. It is said that literature should be considered an adjunct to the drama, but I am entirely at variance with every intelligent man to whom I have spoken on the subject. Whatever form of literature is created, the stage will be ready to embody it, and to give it a wonderful visible colour and presentation of life. But if we are to have a real drama in England, I feel quite sure it will only be on condition that we wean ourselves from the trammelling conventions which have always been a peril to the theatre. I do not think it makes the smallest difference what a play is if an actor has genius and power. Nor do I consider the British public to be of the slightest importance.'[10]

Discerning reviewers recognized Wilde's borrowings. One derived the play from *The School for Scandal* – a distant cousinship at best. A. B. Walkley, who wrote the best review in *The Speaker* (Cassell's publication tended to be kind to a former Cassell's editor), traced Lady Windermere to Dumas *fils*'s *Francillon*, where the heroine also believes in a single law of fidelity for husband and wife; the scene in which Mrs Erlynne braves a hostile drawing room echoes Act I of Dumas *fils*'s *L'Etrangère*; Mrs Erlynne's fear that her daughter will repeat her mistake recalls Jules Lemaître's *Revoltée*; the fan is like the bracelet in Scribe's *Adrienne Lecouvreur*. Others said it was from Sardou. Wilde's reply was in an interview with Gelett Burgess in the *Sketch* (9 January 1895). 'It does not occur in any of Sardou's plays, and it was not in my play until ten days before production. Nobody else's work gives me any suggestion.' Walkley allowed that Wilde improved as he borrowed. One unexpectedly captious review in the *Daily Telegraph* on 22 February 1892 was attributed to Willie Wilde. It said in part, 'Mr Oscar Wilde has spoken. He has publicly announced his complete satisfaction with his new and original play . . . The author peoples his play with male and female editions of himself . . . The play is a bad one, but it will succeed.' Willie Wilde, if he was indeed the author, grudged his brother's success. Soon after writing the review, he cajoled his wife into taking him back to New York.

Revolt of the Puppets

There are many advantages in puppets. They never argue. They have no crude views about art. They have no private lives.

Wilde's belittlement of the audience in his curtain speech offended many, and an article in the *Daily Telegraph* ten days earlier showed distaste for the actors too. It quoted him as saying, 'The long-accepted truth that the test of a play lies in the actable nature thereof is a ridiculous fallacy. The stage is only a frame furnished with a set of puppets. It is to the play no more than a picture-frame is to a painting, which frame has no bearing on the intrinsic merit of the art within.' Wilde wrote a reply, which the newspaper headed, 'The Poet and the Puppets,' to say that he had been misquoted: while he liked puppet theatres (even when the leading actress failed to acknowledge his bouquet), they did not suit the desire of the modern theatre for actuality. It was true that puppets did not impose their own personalities, as actors sometimes did. 'For anybody can act. Most people in England do nothing else. To be conventional is to be a comedian. To act a particular part, however, is a very different thing, and a very difficult thing as well.' On his honeymoon he had said that the actor was as important as the playwright. Now that he was a playwright, he no longer thought so.

The title given to Wilde's reply took the eye of Charles Brookfield, an actor and writer of burlesques, who was to play the role of a minor devil in Wilde's life. (The fact that Brookfield may have been Thackeray's illegitimate son made him particularly sensitive to immorality.) He proposed to Charles Hawtrey a travesty of Wilde's play, and Hawtrey assisted him with its composition, while Wilde's fellow-Dubliner Jimmy Glover wrote the music. They discovered from some biographical dictionary that Wilde's middle name was O'Flahertie, and began their piece, *The Poet and the Puppets*, with a song to the tune of 'St Patrick's Day,' which ran in part,

> They may bubble with jest at the way that I'm dressed,
> They may scoff at the length of my hair.
> They may say that I'm vain, overbearing, inane,
> And object to the flowers that I wear.
> They may laugh till they're ill, but the fact remains still,
> A fact I've proclaimed since a child,
> That it's taken, my dears, nearly two thousand years
> To make Oscar O'Flaherty – Wilde.

Someone leaked the song to Wilde. Having had to suffer parodies in the past, by Gilbert and others, he was furious at the prospect of fresh vulgarization. He appealed to E. F. S. Pigott, the licenser of plays, and it was specified that the authors must read the script to Wilde. He refused to allow them the use either of 'Oscar' or of 'Wilde,' but did not object to O'Flaherty, so the last line was altered to

> To make Neighbour O'Flaherty's child.

Having gained this point, he listened amiably to the rest, praising each page, 'Charming, my old friends!' 'Delightful!' 'It's exquisite!' Only as they reached the door did he add acid to his syrup: 'I felt, however, that I have been – well – Brookfield, what is the word? – what is the thing you call it in your delightfully epigrammatic Stage English? eh? Oh yes! delightfully spoofed.'[11]

'The Poet of the Lily' is seen at the beginning of the play to be devising a new triumph and summons a fairy. Having invented flowers, music, and fairies, he proposes to imagine a play and players. The fairy helpfully calls up Shakespeare, Ibsen, Sheridan, and others to furnish him with stage devices. They produce the play, and the poet drills his puppets in mimicry of various actors: Hawtrey, made up as Wilde, also played the actor Rutland Barrington, Brookfield took on the mannerisms of Beerbohm Tree in *Hamlet*, and Lottie Venne those of Mrs Tree as Ophelia. Wilde's epigrams were replaced by Joe Miller jokes. The discovery scene revealed not one but half a dozen Lady Teazles. The travesty, battening on *Lady Windermere's Fan* and its author, ran from 19 May to the end of July. Hawtrey lost a little money on the production, but did not begrudge it, because of Brookfield's 'brilliance.'

Overtures to *Salome*

The form of government that is most suitable to the artist is no government at all. Authority over him and his art is ridiculous.

The success of *Lady Windermere's Fan* made Wilde the most sought-after man in London. He had an entourage that included Ross, Robertson, Gray, the novelist Reggie Turner, and others, such as Edward Shelley. They were what he termed 'exquisite Aeolian harps that play in the breeze of my matchless talk.'[12] Among those regarding him with new eyes was Sarah Bernhardt, 'that serpent of old Nile' (as Wilde called her), who had taken a London theatre for a none too successful season in 1892. At a party at Henry Irving's she remarked to Wilde that he should write a play for her one day. 'I have already done so.' As soon as she read *Salome* she decided to play the title role, though, as she told an interviewer, Wilde had said the leading part was that of the moon. A copy of the fifth edition of his poems, published in May, was accordingly inscribed,

À Sarah Bernhardt, 'Comme la Princesse Salomé est belle ce soir.' Londres '92.[13]

Her comments were as gratifying as he could wish. According to Charles Ricketts, she said, *'Mais c'est héraldique; on dirait un fresque,'* and *'Le mot doit tomber comme une perle sur un disque de cristal, pas de mouvements rapides, des gestes stylisés* [But it's heraldic, you'd think it was a fresco . . . The word should fall like a pearl on a crystal disc, no rapid movements, with stylised gestures].' The play seemed like a rendering of the line in *Poems* (1881):

> The joy of passion, that dread mystery
> Which not to know, is not to live at all,
> And yet to know is to be held in death's most deadly thrall.

Its one defect for Sarah was that Herod, not Salome, was the central figure.[14]

Wilde persuaded Ricketts to do the stage design. Ricketts proposed 'a black floor – upon which Salome's white feet would show.' The idea was meant to captivate Wilde. 'The sky was to be a rich turquoise green cut by the perpendicular fall of strips of Japanese matting, forming an aerial tent above the terraces.'[15] Wilde suggested that the Jews should be in yellow, the Romans in purple, and John in white. They discussed Salome's costume endlessly. 'Should she be black like the night? silver, like the moon?' Wilde's suggestion was 'green like a curious and poisonous lizard.' Ricketts wanted the moonlight to fall on the ground, the source not being seen; Wilde insisted upon a 'strange dim pattern in the sky.' Graham Robertson was also called in, and suggested a violet sky. 'A violet sky,' said Wilde. 'Yes, I never thought of that. Certainly a violet sky and then, in place of an orchestra, braziers of perfume. Think – the scented clouds rising and partly veiling the stage from time to time – a new perfume for each emotion.' Robertson pointed out that the theatre could not be aired between each emotion. Sarah Bernhardt, who was paying, decided to borrow a set from Irving.

She also borrowed some Cleopatra costumes. Robertson designed 'a golden robe with long fringes of gold, sustained on the shoulders by bands of gilt and painted leather which also held in place a golden breastplate set with jewels. On her head was a triple crown of gold and jewels and the cloud of hair flowing from beneath it was powdered blue.' Wilde objected that it was Herodias whose hair was powdered blue, but the actress insisted, 'I *will* have blue hair.' Robertson asked if she would have a stand-in to do the dance. 'I'm going to dance myself,' she replied. 'How will you do the dance of the seven veils?' 'Never you mind,' said Sarah, smiling enigmatically.[16]

The rehearsals began in the second week in June and had been going on for about two weeks when it became clear that Pigott, the licenser of plays, was considering whether the play should be banned. There was an old law that forbade the depiction on the stage of Biblical characters, and since Pigott was straitlaced, prospects were bleak. As Wilde pointed out, Saint-Saëns's *Samson and Delilah* and Massenet's *Hérodias* were also prohibited. 'Racine's superb tragedy of *Athalie* cannot be performed on an English stage.' When Robert Ross interviewed Wilde for the *Pall Mall Budget*, Wilde threatened, 'If the Censor refuses *Salome*, I shall leave

England to settle in France where I shall take out letters of naturalization. I will not consent to call myself a citizen of a country that shows such narrowness in artistic judgement. I am not English. I am Irish which is quite another thing.' He was indignant that the Lord Chamberlain 'allows the personality of an artist to be presented in a caricature on the stage, and will not allow the work of that artist to be shown under very rare and beautiful conditions.'

On this occasion, too, he explained why he wrote the play in French. 'I have one instrument that I know I can command,' he said to Ross in the interview, 'and that is the English language. There was another instrument I had listened to all my life, and I wanted once to touch this new instrument to see whether I could make any beautiful thing out of it . . . Of course there are modes of expression that a French man of letters would not have used, but they give a certain relief or colour to the play. A great deal of the curious effect that Maeterlinck produces comes from the fact that he, a Flamand by race, writes in an alien language. The same is true of Rossetti who, though he wrote in English, was essentially Latin in temperament.' To a representative of *Le Gaulois* Wilde declared, 'To me there are only two languages in the world: French and Greek. Here people are essentially anti-artistic and narrowminded. Though I have English friends, I do not like the English in general. There is a great deal of hypocrisy in England which you in France very justly find fault with. The typical Briton is Tartuffe, seated in his shop behind the counter. There are numerous exceptions, but they only prove the rule.'[17]

Pigott stopped the play, to Wilde's great disappointment. Friends and enemies were not sympathetic. Max Beerbohm, who had not read the play, wrote to Reggie Turner,

> Isn't it killing also about Oscar's *Salome* being interdicted by the Lord Chamberlain? I have designed a great picture in which King Bull makes a great feast and when they have feasted the daughter of Mrs Grundy dances before them and pleases the King – insomuch that he promises her whatsoever she shall desire. After consultation with her mother she demands that 'they bring unto her by and by the head of Oscar the Poetast on a charger.' The picture – which will be called *The Modern Salome* – represents Lord Lathom [the Lord Chamberlain] holding the charger.

There was general merriment at the fact that Wilde, if he became a French citizen, would be subject to military service, and Partridge of *Punch* surpassed himself with a caricature of Wilde uniformed as a *poilu*. The *New York Times*, never friendly to Wilde, summarized on 3 July, 'All London is laughing at Oscar Wilde's threat to become a Frenchman.' And Whistler, not one to let off a downed opponent, said tersely, 'Oscar has scored another brilliant – exposure.'[18]

But Wilde's grievance was real, and he argued it well. It was absurd that painter and sculptor might depict what they liked, and only the poet be subject to censorship. Not that the musician escaped: 'What can be said of a body that forbids Massenet's *Hérodiade*, Gounod's *La Reine de Saba*, Rubinstein's *Judas Maccabaeus*, and allows [Sardou's] *Divorçons* to be played on any stage?'[19] Among established critics of the day, only William Archer and Bernard Shaw took Wilde's part, and the rest of them, along with actors like Henry Irving, endorsed the censorship in testimony before a commission of inquiry.

Wilde went ahead with plans to publish his play whether or not it could be staged. The title page was to name the Librairie de l'Art Indépendent in Paris along with Elkin Mathews & John Lane in London as joint publishers, though the printing was in Paris, and Mathews and Lane simply bought copies from Wilde. Correspondence with the printer indicates that Wilde made many corrections, chiefly excisions, in the first proofs. Stuart Merrill says that Wilde wished to be sure that his French was free of solecisms, but had no great confidence in the various young men whose advice he solicited. Merrill persuaded him that the tirades of the personages must not all begin with 'Enfin,' as they originally did, and all the 'enfins' were deleted. But when Wilde was reluctant to accept other suggestions, Merrill put him on to Adolphe Retté. Retté corrected some anglicisms, and made Wilde give up a few sentences in the excessively long list of precious stones spoken by Herod. Gradually Wilde lost confidence in Retté as well, and consulted Pierre Louÿs, who had seen the play at an earlier stage. Louÿs, who acted as middleman with the printer, proposed further emendations, most of which Wilde ignored, allowing only grammatical changes. Two final touches, of a minor kind, were put in by Marcel Schwob. Schwob's help and friendship were acknowledged by Wilde in the dedication to 'The Sphinx,' which was published in book form with Ricketts's illustrations in 1894. But nothing could compensate for Wilde's disappointment at not having his name linked with Bernhardt's.

If *Salome* could not be staged, it was defiantly published in February 1893. Wilde said he had had it bound in 'Tyrian purple' wrappers to go with Alfred Douglas's gilt hair. He liked to speak of the lettering as in 'fading' or 'tired' silver. 'That tragic daughter of passion,' Wilde wrote to a friend, 'appeared on Thursday last, and is now dancing for the head of the British public.'[20] He was generous with his copies. Presenting one to Charles Ricketts, he said, 'You do not know that since we last met I have become a famous French author.' A copy went to Shaw, whom Wilde playfully regarded as a fellow-member of the Celtic school for which in *Intentions* he had predicted a great future. Florence Stoker got a copy, and among literary men, Le Gallienne, Swinburne, Pater, and two critics who had written sympathetically of Wilde, Edmund Gosse and William Archer. (The unsympathetic Henry James bought a copy.) Wilde was particularly interested in the response of his French compeers, who took his book as seriously as he could wish, and perhaps, as Robert Ross suggested, more seriously than he had expected. The best was the letter from Mallarmé of March 1893:

> Mon cher Poète
> J'admire que tout étant exprimé par de perpétuels traits eblouissants, en votre *Salomé*, il se dégage, aussi, à chaque page, de l'indicible et le Songe.
> Ainsi les gemmes innombrables et exactes ne peuvent servir que d'accompagnement sur sa robe au geste surnaturel de cette jeune princesse, que définitivement vous évoquâtes
>
> Amitiés de
> STÉPHANE MALLARMÉ*[21]

Another laudatory letter came from Pierre Loti,

> Merci, monsieur, de m'avoir fait connaître votre *Salomé* – c'est beau et sombre comme un chapitre de L'Apocalypse – Je l'admire profondément.†

and one from Maurice Maeterlinck,

> Je vous prie de m'excuser, Monsieur, si les circonstances ne m'ont pas permis de vous remercier plus tôt au don de votre mystérieux, étrange et admirable *Salomé*. Je vous ai dit merci aujourd'hui en sortant, pour la troisième fois, de ce rêve dont je ne me suis pas encore expliqué la puissance. Croyez, Monsieur, à mon admiration très grande.‡
>
> M. MAETERLINCK

Charles Morice and Henri Barbusse praised it. Will Rothenstein could not help saying that the play reminded him of Flaubert's story 'Hérodias.' Wilde took the comment cheerfully: 'Remember, *dans la littérature il faut*

---

* 'My dear Poet
   I marvel that, while everything in your *Salome* is expressed in constant, dazzling strokes, there also arises, on each page, the unutterable and the Dream.
   So the innumerable and precise jewels can serve only as an accompaniment to the gown for the supernatural gesture of that young princess whom you definitively evoked

   Friendly greetings from
   STÉPHANE MALLARMÉ'

† 'Thank you, sir, for having introduced me to your *Salome* – it is fine and sombre like a chapter of the Apocalypse – I admire it deeply.'

‡ 'Pray excuse me, dear sir, if circumstances have not permitted me to thank you sooner for the gift of your mysterious, strange and admirable *Salome*. I expressed my thanks to you today as I emerged, for the third time, from this dream whose power I have not yet explained to myself. I assure you of my great admiration.'

tuer son père [in literature you must always kill your father].' When Mrs Bancroft, the actress, once said that a scene in one of his plays reminded her of a great scene in a play by Scribe, Wilde replied unblushingly, 'Taken bodily from it, dear lady. Why not? Nobody reads nowadays.' He took a similar tack with Max Beerbohm: 'Of course I plagiarise. It is the privilege of the appreciative man. I never read Flaubert's *Tentation de St Antoine* without signing my name at the end of it. *Que voulez-vous?* All the best Hundred Books bear my signature in this manner.'[22]

Wilde next decided to have John Lane, who was publishing *Lady Windermere's Fan,* bring out *Salome* in English. The question of who would illustrate it was important. There was Ricketts, whom he had commissioned to do the design for John Gray's *Silverpoints* as well as for the deluxe edition of *The Sphinx.* But in the *Studio* for April 1893 a drawing showing Salome holding the head of John the Baptist had caught Wilde's eye, as perhaps the artist, Beardsley, intended it should. Wilde engaged Beardsley to illustrate the book. The young man was strange, cruel, disobedient. He was making his way from a Japanese style towards an eighteenth-century English one. Wilde had expected a Byzantine style like Gustave Moreau's. Instead Beardsley combined jocular impressions of Wilde's face, as in the moon or in the face of Herod, with sinister, sensual overtones. He saw the play as hieratic absurdity. One drawing, of Herodias, had to be cancelled as indecent. The artist's reaction went into a quatrain:

> Because one figure was undressed
> This little drawing was suppressed.
> It was unkind. But never mind,
> Perhaps it was all for the best.

To Wilde's credit he saw that the drawings were 'quite wonderful,' and recognized the homicidal energy of Beardsley's work. But he lamented to Ricketts, 'My Herod is like the Herod of Gustave Moreau, wrapped in his jewels and sorrows. My Salome is a mystic, the sister of Salammbo, a Sainte Thérèse who worships the moon.' Her dance was more metaphysical than physical. He deprecated Beardsley's naughtiness and when Ricketts tried to defend the drawings, he silenced him by saying: 'No, no, my dear Ricketts, it is impossible that you should like them. You say you do to seem impartial. The true artist is incapable of impartiality; the men of the Renaissance destroyed Gothic buildings, just as the Gothic craftsmen had destroyed the masonry of the Normans.' Wilde did not however let Beardsley's sophistication escape unscathed. 'Yes, dear Aubrey is almost too Parisian,' he said, 'he cannot forget that he has been to Dieppe – once.'[23]

Importance of Mrs Arbuthnot

*Love can canonise people. The saints are those who have
been most loved.*

Wilde's illness had disappeared after *Lady Windermere's Fan*, but the
fiasco of *Salome* revived it. He had enjoyed hearing Sarah Bernhardt
speak his words, had looked forward to their public association, and had
been so cast down by the censorship that he thought he must take a rest
cure. On 3 July 1892 he went with Alfred Douglas to Bad Homburg.
There the doctors put him on a diet, forbade him to smoke, and generally
made him miserable. He met Douglas's grandparents, the Montgomerys,
but Alfred Montgomery did not care for him at all.[24] On his return,
however, Wilde rallied and started work on a new play. This one he had
promised to an old friend, Herbert Beerbohm Tree, who was manager of
the Haymarket Theatre as well as its chief actor. For the moment Wilde
called it 'Mrs Arbuthnot' to conceal the true title, *A Woman of No
Importance.* To get on with it during August and September he took a
farmhouse at a village called Felbrigg near Cromer in Norfolk – a place
where Alexander had been earlier in August – while Constance and his
children stayed at Babbacombe Cliff, near Torquay in Devon, a house
belonging to her kinswoman, Lady Mount-Temple. Edward Shelley was
invited to Felbrigg but declined.[25] Wilde invited Alfred Douglas, who
came and was ill, and Wilde may have used this as the pretext for not
rejoining his wife at Babbacombe. A letter from her dated 18 September
begins,

> Dearest Oscar, I am so sorry about Lord Alfred Douglas, and wish I was
> at Cromer to look after him. If you think I could do any good, do telegraph
> for me, because I can easily get over to you.

She was not sent for.

Douglas's presence did not prevent Wilde from finishing his play,
which Tree accepted on 14 October 1892. Wilde read an act of it at the
house of Lady (Walter) Palmer. His audience was moved to tears.
Preempting the usual accusations of influence, Wilde then informed
them, 'in his most impressive manner, "I took that situation from *The
Family Herald*."'[26] This play also reconstituted certain elements in *Lady
Windermere's Fan*. Again there is a dreadful secret, but as Wilde had
written to Alexander, it could be discovered much sooner than in the
original version of *Lady Windermere's Fan*. The secret, that Gerald
Arbuthnot is Lord Illingworth's illegitimate son, is made known early in
the second act. Mirroring Mrs Erlynne's visit to her long lost daughter,
here a father discovers his long lost son. The theme of the foundling in
Wilde's plays can be best thought of as a secret that stands for all secrets.

For Wilde, errant husband and brother to three illegitimate siblings of uncertain maternity, it had a subconscious meaning. We are not what we think we are or what other people think us, and our ties to them may be greater or less than we imagine.

Lord Illingworth is one of Wilde's verbal dandies, not the most attractive. Unlike Lord Darlington in *Lady Windermere's Fan*, Lord Illingworth has no deep feeling for anyone.*

A Woman of No Importance is the weakest of the plays Wilde wrote in the Nineties, but it does more than offer the stale theme of the Victorian fallen woman, and her defiance of her seducer. Lord Illingworth is a Lovelace, a dandy and aesthete whose scepticism is not always misguided. He utters some of Wilde's most critical epigrams, like 'The English gentleman galloping after the fox – the unspeakable in full pursuit of the inedible.' The play is essentially a woman's play (a point that Lytton Strachey understandably ignores), and the women's voices are sharply critical of male presuppositions. The women range from puritans to profligates. Some are unconsciously funny, such as Lady Hunstanton, unable to choose between alternatives: 'Lady Belton eloped with Lord Fethersall . . . Poor Lord Belton died three days afterwards of joy, or gout. I forget which.' Mrs Allonby is a conscious wit and a match for Lord Illingworth; when he remarks, 'The Book of Life begins with a man and a woman in a garden,' she retorts, 'It ends with Revelations.' She explains ingeniously

---

* Lytton Strachey went to see a revival of the play by Tree in 1907, and in a letter to Duncan Grant interpreted it in his own way:

It was rather amusing, as it was a complete mass of epigrams, with occasional whiffs of grotesque melodrama and drivelling sentiment. The queerest mixture! Mr Tree is a wicked Lord, staying in a country house, who has made up his mind to bugger one of the other guests – a handsome young man of twenty. The handsome young man is delighted; when his mother enters, sees his Lordship and recognises him as having copulated with her twenty years before, the result of which was – the handsome young man. She appeals to Lord Tree not to bugger his own son. He replies that that is an additional reason for doing it (oh! he's a *very* wicked Lord!). She then appeals to the handsome young man, who says, 'Dear me! What an abominable thing to do – to go and copulate without marrying! Oh no, I shall certainly pay no attention to anyone capable of doing *that*,' and then suddenly enters (from the garden) a young American millionairess, with whom (very properly) the handsome young man is in love. Enter his Lordship. Handsome Y.M.: 'You devil! You have insulted the purest creature on God's earth! I shall kill you!' But of course he doesn't, he contents himself with marrying the millionairess, while his mother takes up a pair of gloves, and slashes the Lord across the face. It seems an odd plot, doesn't it? But it required all my penetration to find out that this was the plot, as you may imagine. Epigrams engulf it like the sea. Most of them were thoroughly rotten, and nearly all were said quite cynically to the gallery. Poor old Tree sits down with his back to the audience to talk to a brilliant lady, and swings round in his seat every time he delivers an epigram. The audience was of course charmed.[27]

why women have a better time than men, 'There are far more things forbidden to us than are forbidden to them.' Through these women, and others such as the American Hester Worsley, Wilde presents society scathingly, as it radiates into innocence and guilt, conventionality and unconventionality, steadfastness and whim. Though Mrs Arbuthnot (like Sibyl Vane) is too singleminded for wit, she is the vehicle through which morality loses out, as it must in Wilde, to the 'Higher Ethics.'

Wilde's sense that the world wore a mask but took it off at intervals found many demonstrations. There was his affectionate brother Willie, for example, who managed to betray him far off in New York. After returning there with his wife in a partial reconciliation, Willie had soon reverted to the Lotos Club. When his wife declined to finance him, he took to sponging drinks. His favorite act was to parody Oscar's poems, no doubt hitting the mark with fraternal insight. He could strike aesthetic attitudes and speak in a 'potato-choked' voice near enough to Oscar's to amuse his cronies. From time to time he said, 'I'm going to buy a second-hand copy of Rochefoucauld's *Maxims*, and then I'll set up a play foundry in opposition to my brother Oscar.' After his wife divorced him on 10 June 1893, he lingered on at the Lotos Club, more and more of a nuisance. On 17 September 1893 his fellow members expelled him, nominally for non-payment of a $14 debt. They filled in a reporter for the *New York Times* on Willie's antics, and an article in that newspaper, on the day following his expulsion, gave a detailed account of his mockery of Oscar. The article reached London in October. Willie, back with his mother, insisted that it was all lies, but Oscar did not believe him.[28] He could now recall the negative review of *Lady Windermere's Fan* Willie had probably written in the *Daily Telegraph*. Willie was one more example of the treacherous friend and disciple, a staple character in Wilde's fable-spinning. They stopped speaking to each other.

Success Compounded

The originality I mean, which we ask from the artist is originality of treatment, not of subject. It is only the unimaginative who ever invent. The true artist is known by the use he makes of what he annexes, and he annexes everything.

At the end of March 1893 *A Woman of No Importance* was put into rehearsal by Tree. He had been impressed by the quality and the success of *Lady Windermere's Fan*, and had immediately asked Wilde to do a play for the Haymarket. At first Wilde refused. According to Hesketh Pearson, who knew Tree well, Wilde said, 'As Herod in my *Salome* you would be admirable. As a peer of the realm in my latest dramatic device, pray forgive me if I do not see you.' Tree pointed out that his portrayal of a duke in Henry Arthur Jones's *The Dancing Girl* had been widely praised. 'Ah! that's just it,' said Wilde. 'Before you can successfully impersonate the character I have in mind, you must forget that you ever played Hamlet; you must forget that you ever played Falstaff; above all, you must forget that you ever played a duke in a melodrama by Henry Arthur Jones.' 'I'll do my best.' 'I think you had better forget that you ever acted at all.' 'Why?' 'Because this witty aristocrat whom you wish to assume in my play is quite unlike anyone who has been seen on the stage before. He is like no one who has existed before.' The baffled Tree exclaimed, 'My God! He must be supernatural.' To which Wilde responded, 'He is certainly not natural. He is a figure of art. Indeed, if you can bear the truth, he is MYSELF.'[29]

But he gradually came round and accepted Tree's offer. When he read the play to Tree, Tree complimented him on the development of the plot. Such praise was unacceptable: 'Plots are tedious. Anyone can invent them. Life is full of them. Indeed one has to elbow one's way through them as they crowd across one's path.' And he said again, 'I took the plot of this play from the *Family Herald*, which took it – wisely, I feel – from my novel *The Picture of Dorian Gray*. People love a wicked aristocrat who seduces a virtuous maid, and they love a virtuous maiden for being seduced by a wicked aristocrat. I have given them what they like, so that they may learn to appreciate what I like to give them.'

At the rehearsals Wilde kept trying to make Tree less theatrical, probably because Lord Illingworth was already theatrical enough. Tree liked the part so well he began to play it outside the theatre. 'Ah,' said Wilde, 'every day Herbert becomes *de plus en plus oscarisé*. It is a wonderful case of nature imitating art.'[30] Another problem was that Fred Terry, who was to play the ingenuous Gerald Arbuthnot, was determined to make Gerald a man of the world. When Wilde objected, Terry replied, 'Oh well, you know, Mr Wilde, you can lead a horse to water, but you can't make him drink.' 'No, Terry. But you have a circus. In that circus is a ring. A horse enters the ring and approaches a trough of water. The ringmaster cracks his whip and says, "Drink!" and the horse drinks. That horse, Terry, is the actor.' 'So, Mr Wilde, you compare the stage to a circus.' 'Ah,' said Wilde, 'yours was the metaphor.' Terry remaining truculent, Wilde went to his flat to lunch with him. By chance Terry happened to say he loved Dickens, and Wilde talked with great enthusiasm about Dickens's characters. (He did not say what he thought, that Dickens failed with all his characters who were not caricatures.) Terry's hostility vanished, and he said, 'Well, Mr Wilde, it's been a very great pleasure for me to find another person who is fond of Dickens.' 'Oh, my dear boy, I've never read a word of his in my life,' said Wilde, belittling their newly formed bond.[31]

When asked later by Hesketh Pearson if he had produced the play with the help of Wilde, Tree said sourly, 'With the interference of Wilde.' Wilde had written in 1886 that Tree was 'the perfect Proteus of actors,' but now he lamented that Tree could not fail to be invariably Tree. At rehearsal he realized that certain scenes were flawed. He reluctantly removed Illingworth's long and inappropriate denunciation of puritanism to his son in Act II.

The play opened on 19 April 1893. Balfour, Chamberlain, and other dignitaries attended. The actors were heartily applauded, but when the author was called for there were boos, perhaps because of a line in the script (later removed) that said, 'England lies like a leper in purple.' Wilde, before the curtain, only said, 'Ladies and gentlemen, I regret to inform you that Mr Oscar Wilde is not in the house.' There was some disappointment at this new-found reticence. To make up, Beerbohm Tree then said, 'I am proud to have been associated with this work of art.' (Wilde would compliment him later: 'I have always regarded you as the best critic of my plays.' 'But I have never criticised your plays,' said Tree. 'That's why,' said Wilde.)[32] Max Beerbohm described the occasion to a correspondent, 'When little Oscar came on to make his bow there was a slight mingling of hoots and hisses, though he looked very sweet in a new white waistcoat and a large bunch of little lilies in his coat. The notices are better than I had expected: the piece is sure of a long, of a very long run, despite all that the critics may say' (here Beerbohm fell into an Oscarism) 'in its favour.'[33] The Prince of Wales attended on the second night, with the Duchess of Teck, noted for her hearty laugh. Both delighted in it, and the Prince enjoined Wilde, 'Do not alter a single line.' Wilde is reported to have replied, 'Sire, your wish is my command.' His pleasure in the exchange was confirmed by a subsequent comment, 'What a splendid country where princes understand poets.'[34]

That evening Wilde dined at Blanche Roosevelt's house. Before dinner the guests put their hands through a curtain so that the palmist Cheiro could read their palms without knowing who they were. When Wilde held out his hands, Cheiro found the markings on each so different from the other that he explained how in palmistry the left hand denotes hereditary tendencies and the right hand individual developments. The left hand in front of him, he said, promised a brilliant success, the right, impending ruin. 'The left hand is the hand of a king, but the right that of a king who will send himself into exile.' Wilde, a superstitious man (he had refused to join the sceptics of the Thirteen Club), asked 'At what date?' 'A few years from now, at about your fortieth year.' (He was then thirty-eight.) Without another word Wilde left the party.[35]

The word that triggered his response may have been 'king.' It was associated in his mind from Portora days with Aeschylus's *Agamemnon*. Wilde's sense of being lucky did not prevent his thinking of himself as unlucky, too. In *De Profundis* he repeatedly used the word 'doom' as opposed to mere 'destiny,' and he pointed to 'the note of Doom that like a purple thread runs through the gold cloth of *Dorian Gray*.' Wilde was too good a classicist not to piece together from the plays of Aeschylus and Euripides and the *Iliad*, the stages of doom for Agamemnon. Prosperous, he became blasé, the man who has everything, and later Wilde would invoke another rule and speak of 'my Neronian hours, rich, profligate, cynical, materialistic.'[36] With success 'I grew careless of the lives of others.' Deaf to prudent counsel, he was an apt candidate for Nemesis. 'By suffering they shall win understanding,' says the chorus in *Agamemnon*, quoting Zeus.

Still, Cheiro might be wrong. The success of *A Woman of No Importance* could lighten dark thoughts. The play brought in £100 a week to its author. Wilde's head hit the stars. He happened to meet Conan Doyle, and asked if he had seen the play. Doyle had not. Wilde said with a grave face, 'Ah, you must go. It is wonderful. It is genius.' Doyle, unused to such exaltation in a fellow author, thought him mad. Though the reviews had been mixed, and Henry James detested the play, there was a general awareness that Wilde had made a place for himself. *The Times*, which had been dour about *Lady Windermere's Fan*, swung over to Frank Harris's position: 'The play is fresh in ideas and execution and is written moreover with a literary polish too rare on the English stage.'[37] William Archer proved loyal: the play depended for its success not upon wit or paradox, he said, but upon the keenness of its author's intellect, the individuality of his point of view, the excellence of his verbal style, and the genuine dramatic quality of his inspiration. He praised in particular the scene between Lord Illingworth and Mrs Arbuthnot at the end of Act II as 'the most virile and intelligent piece of English play-writing of our day.' The unexpected use of virility as a criterion suggests that the more usual charge was aesthetic effeminacy.

CHAPTER XV

A Late Victorian Love Affair

*What a silly thing love is! It is not half as useful as logic, for
it does not prove anything and it is always telling one things
that are not going to happen, and making one believe things
that are not true.*

High Romance

Wilde wanted a consuming passion; he got it and was consumed by it.
Lord Alfred Douglas's account of their early months of acquaintance
differed from his. Douglas says that Wilde laid siege to him and after
about six months won him. Wilde's nature, however, was to court
everyone, so Douglas may have mistaken for wooing what was meant only
as benevolent flattery. Wilde denied that the initiative lay with him. He
said their acquaintance was slight until the spring of 1892, when Douglas
suddenly came or wrote to him for help. The reason was blackmail over an
indiscreet letter. Wilde went up to Oxford and stayed the weekend in
Douglas's rooms in the High Street. He resolved the crisis airily enough
by putting his friend and solicitor George Lewis on to it. Lewis, accustomed to saving his clients embarrassment, paid the blackmailer a
hundred pounds for the incriminating document.

The love affair began under the threat of blackmail and under this
threat it flourished. Up to now Wilde had been attracted most strongly to
John Gray, but that young man began to recede from his place in Wilde's
affections. The progress of the intimacy with Douglas can be gauged by
gifts of two books: The first, *The Picture of Dorian Gray*, Wilde gave to
Douglas soon after they met, and inscribed it discreetly,

Alfred Douglas from his friend who wrote this book.
July 91   Oscar

The second, his *Poems*, has a different inscription:

362

From Oscar
To the Gilt-mailed
Boy
at Oxford
in the heart
of June
Oscar Wilde[1]

This was June 1892, and by that month Wilde was captured. They spent much of the summer in each other's company. Robert Ross claimed no rights over Wilde, so could be confided in. A letter to Ross assumes his sympathy and confirms Wilde's passion:

> My dearest Bobbie, Bosie has insisted on stopping here for sandwiches. He is quite like a narcissus – so white and gold. I will come either Wednesday or Thursday night to your rooms. Send me a line. Bosie is so tired: he lies like a hyacinth on the sofa, and I worship him.
>
> You dear boy. Ever yours
> OSCAR

Douglas talked to his mother about his new friend. Lady Queensberry, at her wits' end about Bosie's academic difficulties at Oxford, decided to invite the Wildes to her house at Bracknell and consult them about her son. The visit, in October 1892, had all the embarrassment associated with meeting one's beloved's mother. Lady Queensberry always looked, according to Desmond MacCarthy, 'as though she had been struck, and was still quivering from the blow,' but never more than now. She appealed to Wilde for advice and help, and spoke frankly and warningly of Bosie's vanity and extravagant habits. Wilde, vain and spendthrift himself, was too enamored to do more than smile at these alleged defects. Notwithstanding her indirection, an admonitory element was still present enough for Wilde to give the name Lady Bracknell to the proper and proprietary mother in *The Importance of Being Earnest.* Her effort with Wilde failed, but within a month he was to discover what a spendthrift was. His letters to Douglas become declarations of heightened financial embarrassment and deepening love. The combination had its own allure as paired abandonments of control.

Even when Wilde became recriminatory later, he conceded that Douglas had the saving grace of being really in love with him. During this period, 'the young Domitian,' as he called him, began to write verse. Bosie sent him poems, the first dated November 1892, a month when Wilde first experienced the effects of Bosie's extravagance. It is likely that in this month they became firmly committed to each other. The first poem Douglas sent was entitled 'De Profundis,' a proleptic irony: its tenor is that he has a love but cannot say, because of its nature, who his love is. This was part of that mixed disclosure and concealment of homosexuality that *Dorian Gray* had popularized. It underlay Douglas's poem, 'The Two Loves,' written a bit later, which contained the famous line, 'I am the love that dare not speak its name.' In fact, Douglas spoke about it a good deal. If Wilde was bold, Douglas was bolder. He was understandably boastful about Wilde's love, and eager to lord it over other young men like John Gray who had once claimed it.

From November 1892 to December 1893, when a three-month respite began, Wilde's life was inseparable from that of Douglas. Until June 1893 Douglas was still at Magdalen, in his fourth and final year of Greats. He took over the editorship of an Oxford literary magazine called the *Spirit Lamp*, and remade it with the covert purpose of winning acceptance for homosexuality. To this end he printed contributions from Ross, Symonds, and Wilde, and included poems about Hylas and Corydon. In letters to his friend Kains Jackson he confided that Wilde had made considerable efforts for 'the new culture' and the 'cause.' 'If Bosie has really made Oxford homosexual,' wrote George Ives, a young supporter of the movement, in his diary on 15 November 1894, 'he has done something good and glorious.'[2]*

Aside from this covert propaganda, Douglas began to develop considerable faith in his poetic powers. Wilde lavished praise on him and on his 'lovely' sonnets. It was fine to bask in Wilde's sun, but he wished to be more than what Max Beerbohm called 'a very pretty reflection of Oscar.' And as he felt more and more entitled to the name of poet, he grew out of the role of student.

During this period Wilde came to realize that Douglas was not only beautiful but reckless and unmanageable. His temper was ferocious. Beerbohm, who liked him, said he was 'obviously mad (like all his family, I believe).' When not in a fury Douglas could be 'very charming' and 'nearly brilliant.'[3] He wanted to be loved, and he wanted to be treated as an intellectual equal. One way of confirming his power over his friend was by financial dependence. He had no need to importune Wilde, who was as excessive in generosity as in everything else, and it would have taken considerable restraint not to spend Wilde's money as freely as his own. He wrote later to Ross when Wilde was in prison, 15 July 1896, 'I remember very well the sweetness of asking Oscar for money. It was a sweet humiliation and exquisite pleasure to both of us.'[4] Being kept was part of the pleasure of being loved. Wilde's pleasure in the arrangement was

---

* At the Authors' Club on 30 June 1892 Wilde met Ives, whose Order of Chaeronaea was supposed to provide a secret power base for homosexuals. Wilde's first remark to Ives was 'Why are you here among the bald and the bearded?' He was sympathetic to Ives's Order, though there is no evidence that he ever joined it. He suggested to Ives that a pagan monastery might be established on some small island in the Mediterranean, where, as Ives wished, all loves might be free. Wilde was put in mind of the friendship of Byron and Shelley, which he said ended when Byron attempted to make love to Shelley, and Shelley broke off the relationship.

perhaps a little less exquisite. Granted that he liked being abused a little, he could have forgone being abused so much. But Douglas enjoyed demanding ever higher flights of loving-kindness. When in 1894 his father threatened to cut off his allowance, Douglas encouraged him, and threw himself upon Wilde's generosity. Since neither Wilde nor Douglas practiced or expected sexual fidelity, money was the stamp and seal of their love.

The Queensberrys

. . . the mad, bad line from which you are come.

Alfred Douglas is perhaps best understood in relation to his father, John Sholto Douglas, ninth Marquess of Queensberry. The impression that has been given of Queensberry is that he was a simple brute. In fact he was a complex one. Insofar as he was brutal, he practiced a rule-bound brutality. That was why at the age of twenty-four he had changed the nature of boxing by persuading England and America to agree to the Queensberry rules, and also by securing adoption of weight differences, so that boxers might be evenly matched. He had channeled together his belligerence and his litigiousness. He made himself known as a fulminator against Christianity, and was always raging publicly and indecorously against someone else's creed. He fancied himself as an aristocratic rebel, socially ostracized because of his iconoclasm.

Besides being a good boxer and an excellent hunter, Queensberry was a poet of sorts. In the *Spirit Lamp* Douglas printed one of his father's poems, 'Lines Suggested by Fred Leslie's Death 3 Feb. 1893,' lines perhaps suggested also by a poem of Christina Rossetti. 'When I am dead, cremate me,' was its resonant opening. In 1880 Queensberry published in pamphlet form his most ambitious poem, *The Spirit of the Matterhorn*. (His brother, Lord Francis Douglas, had died climbing that mountain.) In it he expressed certain views which he thought might placate the Scottish nobility. The Scottish lords had just then voted not to re-elect him as one of their representatives to the British House of Lords (something he and his ancestors considered their due because of their ancient title), on the grounds that he had publicly denied the existence of God. This rebuff wounded Queensberry deeply. He explained in a preface to his poem that he did not deny the existence of God, but preferred to call him the Inscrutable. His poem was mostly a versification of a theory that the soul is not distinct from the body, but is a result of the body itself. Consequently, one must choose one's mate carefully so that the descent will be as eugenic as possible, since we reproduce not only our children's bodies but their souls. 'Go, tell mankind, see that thy blood be pure.' The Godfearing Scottish lords were not mollified.

A glimpse of his character is afforded by his attempt to break up a performance of Tennyson's *The May Queen* in December 1885 on the grounds that an atheist was badly treated in it. A weekly, the *Bat*, editorialized, 'The more the Marquess of Queensberry orates to his own class the less effect he seems to create. His celebrated speech on his brother peer's play only succeeded in obtaining for him ejection from the theatre.' The next issue contained Queensberry's reply:

> Sir, – I thank you for your advertisement in your scurrilous journal – Conservative, I presume. You say I was ejected from a certain theatre. So I was. Also another advertisement. I believe the play was taken off three weeks afterwards ... Thanking you for further advertisement, yours faithfully,
>
> QUEENSBERRY[5]

It was clear that this man would prove a formidable antagonist, eager for public gestures, as arrogantly indifferent as Wilde to what the world thought of him, and much less vulnerable. On 22 January 1887 his wife won a divorce from him on the grounds of his adultery with Mabel Gilroy of 217 Hampstead Road, Camden Town. Though he had made a poor husband to his first wife, to whom he was not at all suited, he had paid for his children's needs and pleasures and taken a considerable, if tactless, interest in their welfare. He was delighted when Alfred, his third son, went up to Oxford, and distressed when his career there showed signs of coming to nothing. His rage was, however, still to come.

Rough Trade

*I don't regret for a single moment having lived for pleasure. I
did it to the full, as one should do anything that one does ...
I lived on honeycomb.*

The relationship of Wilde and Douglas was intense and romantic, but they pursued more transient attachments. Douglas was fascinated by young men who for a few pounds and a good dinner would prostitute themselves. He introduced Wilde to this world, and there was a kind of competition between them. With this encouragement, Wilde stepped up the pace of his casual affairs in the autumn of 1892. Through Maurice Schwabe, a nephew of the Solicitor-General, whom Douglas brought into his circle, he met Alfred Taylor, the errant son of a cocoa manufacturer, and once a public school boy at Marlborough. Taylor in turn introduced him to a series of boys, the first important one being Sidney Mavor, later a Church of England priest. In October 1892 Wilde invited Taylor, Mavor, Douglas, and Schwabe to dinner at Kettner's. He continued to see Mavor for the next year and a half. Schwabe also introduced Wilde to Freddy Atkins in October 1892; Atkins, not yet eighteen, was already an accomplished blackmailer. Wilde lavished money and cigarette cases and other gifts upon these boys, and cultivated a reputation for generosity and goodwill of which they took shameless advantage. This was the 'feasting with panthers' of which he spoke later.

During 1893 he established a practice of staying at hotels, ostensibly so he could work, actually so he could play as well. From 1 to 17 January he was at the Albemarle Hotel, but his behavior was sufficiently dubious for the proprietor to welcome his departure. Several young men paid him visits. He was pursuing his affair with Edward Shelley. It had begun early in 1892 when, having seen Shelley in John Lane's office, Wilde invited him to dinner. Shelley was extremely nervous about the relationship, and in March 1893 wrote to Wilde that he wanted to break off. Wilde made no objection, and offered him £100 if he wished to return to his studies. Shelley refused, but continued to count on Wilde for help in emergencies over the next two years.[6] Meanwhile, in February 1893, Douglas passed on to Wilde a boy he had met, a seventeen-year-old named Alfred Wood. Wilde received him by pre-arrangement at the Café Royal, gave him a drink, dined him in a private room at the Florence in Rupert Street, and took him off to Tite Street to make love. (The house was empty at the time.) They continued to meet. Douglas went on seeing Wood, and gave him some cast-off clothes, carelessly failing to notice that there were letters from Wilde in the pockets. Wood decided to exploit this find to get money for a trip to America, and in April he sent a copy of one letter* to Beerbohm Tree, then rehearsing *A Woman of No Importance*, and waited for Wilde outside the stage door. Wilde, alerted by Tree, refused to give Wood anything, saying that if Wood could – as he pretended – get £60 for one of the letters, he should take advantage of this price, unusual for a prose piece of this length. Wood and two confederates eventually decided to give the letters to Wilde, except for the Hyacinth letter, and Wilde obligingly gave him £25 then and £5 a day later. After this transaction Wood went to America for a year.

At this period Wilde and Douglas had met through Taylor a boy named Charles Parker, and various other hangers-on. While the meetings were

---

* Presumably this was the one sent by Wilde from Babbacombe Cliff in January 1893:

My Own Boy, Your sonnet is quite lovely, and it is a marvel that those red rose-leaf lips of yours should have been made no less for music of song than for madness of kisses. Your slim gilt soul walks between passion and poetry. I know Hyacinthus, whom Apollo loved so madly, was you in Greek days.

Why are you alone in London, and when do you go to Salisbury? Do go there to cool your hands in the grey twilight of Gothic things, and come here whenever you like. It is a lovely place – it only lacks you; but go to Salisbury first. Always, with undying love, yours   OSCAR not numerous, the detailed accounts of them later to emerge tend to ignore that they occurred over a period of years. With Sidney Mavor, Wilde went off to Paris in February 1893, wishing to be there for the publication of *Salome,* and put him up in a suite at one of the best hotels. What seems to characterize all Wilde's affairs is that he got to know the boys as individuals, treated them handsomely, allowed them to refuse his attentions without becoming rancorous, and did not corrupt them. They were already prostitutes. The excitement of doing something considered wrong, and the professional avarice of the blackmailing, extortionate, faithless boys may have been as important for Wilde as sexual gratification.

From late 1892 Wilde saw his life divide more emphatically between a clandestine, illegal aspect, and an overt, declarable side. The more he consorted with rough but ready boys, in deliberate self-abandonment, the more he cultivated a public image of disinterestedness and self-possession. (Douglas had his place in both lives.) If he had sought ways to imperil himself, Wilde could hardly have found better ones. English society tolerated homosexuality only so long as one was not caught at it. His chances of being caught were enormously increased as he combined casual associations with his more idealized ones with Ross, then Gray, and then Douglas. Wilde believed in his star: he even had a star painted on the ceiling of his bedroom in Tite Street. But he was always bringing himself to the brink.

John Gray and Raffalovich

How agitated little André was last night.

The constant presence of Douglas in Wilde's activities was irritating to other friends of Wilde. Robbie Ross was indulgent, feeling assured of his own place in the troop. The case of John Gray was harder. Wilde liked Gray's verse, and thought he had achieved 'a perfected mode of expression.' Accordingly he had agreed with John Lane on 17 June 1892 to defray all the publishing expenses of Gray's first book, *Silverpoints.*[7] During the early months of 1892 Gray was Wilde's constant companion, Alfred Douglas's turn being still to come. Wilde helped Gray to become a member of the Playgoers' Club, and suggested him as a speaker. On 8 February 1892, with Wilde in the chair, Gray took the position that art was manipulative and dandyistic, and the artist a pariah. Afterwards Wilde praised him 'for being misunderstood, a distinction that I myself share,' and denied that Gray's surname had suggested Dorian's. About 13 June Pierre Louÿs arrived in London with a woman friend; Wilde at once invited the two to dinner, and had John Gray, already known to Louÿs, there to meet them. The three men saw each other regularly until on 3 July

1892 Wilde went with Douglas for his rest cure to Bad Homburg, where Louÿs would visit him later. From Bad Homburg Wilde sent the *Silverpoints* contract to Lane.

Although Louÿs was heterosexual, he naïvely enjoyed the entrée to this homosexual clique. He would tell André Gide of their exquisite manners: instead of offering a cigarette directly, Wilde and his friends would light one first, take a puff, and then offer it. He heard with approval how two of them (Alfred Taylor and Charles Mason) had celebrated 'a real marriage' with an exchange of rings and a ceremony. 'They know how to envelop everything in poetry,' he told Gide approvingly.[8] The poetry must indeed have helped, but he was soon to be alerted by Gray to less felicitous aspects. Late in 1892 Gray informed Louÿs that he was thinking of committing suicide: Douglas's ascendancy over Wilde was preemptive and Gray felt jilted.

It was at this time that André Raffalovich, who had admired Gray without knowing him, intervened. Out of jealousy he had published an article attacking both Gray and Wilde for their literary styles. But when Arthur Symons introduced him to Gray in November 1892, he repented and fell in love. Pressing his suit, he denounced Wilde's intimacy with Douglas as vain and debauched. His sumptuous dinner parties, with which he had made a mark in London, now had Gray as a constant guest. Wilde was amused and contemptuous: Raffalovich was 'the man who sent the New Helen [Lillie Langtry] in to dinner with Cardinal Vaughan,' he said. 'André came to London to start a salon, and has only succeeded in opening a saloon.' Pursuing the joke, on his own last appearance at Raffalovich's he said to the butler on arrival, 'A table for six.' Wilde was irked enough to deride his rival's features: 'as ugly as Raffalovich,' he said. He would not sit next to him in the hairdressing establishment in Bond Street which they both patronized.[9]

Gradually Gray has won over. His last tribute to Wilde was an inscription in his translation of Paul Bourget's *A Saint and Others* in October 1892, 'To My Beloved Master, My dear Friend, Homage.' Soon after Raffalovich brought him out of modest lodgings in the Temple and installed him at 43 Park Lane, minutes away from his own house in South Audley Street. On 4 January 1893 Gray, no doubt at his friend's urging, had John Lane draw up a new contract for *Silverpoints* which left Wilde out except as a recipient of free copies. Ostensibly Lane agreed to pay all the costs of publication – a highly disadvantageous concession – so Raffalovich was presumably behind the scenes, guaranteeing him against loss. *Silverpoints* was published during the week of 4 March 1893. The response was disappointing, for the most part. Le Gallienne reproved Gray for modish decadence in March; Theodore Wratislaw was more severe in November, writing in the *Artist and Journal of Home Culture* (a homosexual journal), that Gray was 'an artist with a promising future behind him.'

The most amusing response was from Wilde's lately acquired friend, Ada Leverson, whom he called the Sphinx. Mrs Leverson, a witty woman and later a successful novelist, surveyed 'the tiniest rivulet of text meandering through the very largest meadow of margin,' and suggested that the next step was for Wilde to publish a book *all* margins, full of beautiful unwritten thoughts. The volume should be bound in some Nile-green skin powdered with gilt nenuphars and smoothed with hard ivory, decorated with gold by Ricketts (if not Shannon) and printed on Japanese paper. Wilde approved. 'It shall be dedicated to you and the unwritten text illustrated by Aubrey Beardsley. There must be five hundred signed copies for particular friends, six for the general public, and one for America.'[10]

By March 1893 Gray had broken with Wilde and told Louÿs he had done so. Louÿs, conscious of many favors and much hospitality, was slow to follow. Through Wilde he had met not only Marion Terry, who was playing Mrs Erlynne in *Lady Windermere's Fan*, but Bernhardt herself – an encounter which inspired him to write the first version of his *Aphrodite*. Then on 22 February 1893 he received a copy of *Salome* and found that the book was officially dedicated *À mon ami Pierre Louÿs*. He sent Wilde a facetious telegram, which Wilde returned to him, 'Is the enclosed really all that you have to say to me in return for my choosing you out of all my friends to whom to dedicate *Salome*? I cannot tell you how hurt I am . . . It is new to me to think that friendship is more brittle than love is.' Louÿs made peace by sending him a sonnet entitled 'Salomé,' which began:

> A travers le brouillard lumineux des sept voiles
> La courbe de son corps se cambre vers la lune,
> Elle se touche avec sa chevelure brune
> Et ses doigts caressants où luisent des étoiles.*

Wilde then invited him to the first performance of *A Woman of No Importance* on 19 April. On this trip Louÿs began to see what Gray had found so hard to bear. He wrote to his brother Georges that the crowd he was with had begun to embarrass him, and on 22 April he added, 'Oscar Wilde has been charming on my behalf, I have lunched with him almost every day. But I should have been glad if he had provided different company.'[11] The ubiquity of Douglas was oppressive.

Wilde and Douglas told Louÿs that they were worried about the possibility of blackmail over the Hyacinth letter which Wilde had written to Douglas, still in the hands of Alfred Wood. So that it might be given the status of a work of art, Louÿs obligingly prepared a version of it in French,

---

* 'Through the luminous mist of the seven veils / The curve of her body arches towards the moon, / She brushes herself with her dark hair / And her caressing and starlit fingers.'

Wilde, about 1891 (*Courtesy of the William Andrews Clark Library*)

Lord Alfred Douglas
(centre rear)
with schoolmates at
Winchester College,
about 1890

Wilde and Douglas at
Felbrigg, near Cromer
in Norfolk, about
September 1892

Wilde and Douglas in Oxford, about 1893 (*Library of Congress, Kaufmann Collection*)

Lord Alfred Douglas

Wilde, about 1894
(*Courtesy of the William
Andrews Clark Library*)

"A Dream of Decadence on the Cherwell":
Wilde and Douglas caricatured
in *The New Rattle,* Oxford, May 1893

The Marquess of Queensberry, as shown in *The Cycling World Illustrated*, 1896

Robert H. Sherard

Frank Harris, photographed
by A. L. Coburn (*Courtesy of
the International Museum
of Photography at George
Eastman House*)

Aubrey Beardsley, by William
Rothenstein (*Courtesy of
Sotheby's, London*)

André Gide, 1891

Caricature of Wilde in a top hat,
by Whistler (*Courtesy of the
Hunterian Art Gallery; University
of Glasgow, Birnie Philip Bequest;
and Weidenfeld Archives*)

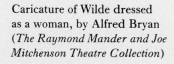

Caricature of Wilde dressed
as a woman, by Alfred Bryan
(*The Raymond Mander and Joe
Mitchenson Theatre Collection*)

Wilde in costume as Salome (*Collection Guillot de Saix, H. Roger Viollet, Paris*)

and the result was published in the *Spirit Lamp*, Douglas's Oxford magazine, on 4 May 1893, with an allusion to Wilde's play, as 'Sonnet. A letter written in prose poetry by M. Oscar Wilde to a friend, and translated into rhymed poetry by a poet of no importance.'*

By now Louÿs observed Wilde and his clique at close quarters. He was present one morning in the Savoy Hotel room which Wilde and Douglas were sharing, where there was one double bed and two pillows.† While they were talking, Constance Wilde arrived, because she saw so little of her husband, to bring him his post. When she besought him to come home, he pretended he had been away so long he had forgotten the number of his house, and Constance smiled through her tears.[13] This was the occasion when Wilde said aside in explanation to Louÿs, 'I've made three marriages in my life, one with a woman and two with men!'[14] Presumably the two men were Douglas, for certain, and either Ross or Gray. Louÿs was upset: he had not considered the wife. For his part, Wilde was frank about it. He related to Mme Melba how he had been telling his sons stories the night before about little boys who were naughty and made their mothers cry, and what dreadful things would happen to them unless they became better. 'Do you know what one of them answered? He asked me what punishment would be reserved for naughty papas, who did not come home till the early morning, and made mother cry far more.' The punishment for that would be severe indeed.

Louÿs returned to Paris, disgusted at what he had seen. He told Henri de Régnier that Wilde was now confessedly a pederast, and had aban-

---

*

Hyacinthe! Ô mon coeur! jeune dieu doux et blond!
Tes yeux sont la lumière de la mer! ta bouche,
Le sang rouge du soir où mon soleil se couche . . .
Je t'aime, enfant câlin, cher aux bras d'Apollon.

Tu chantais, et ma lyre est moins douce, le long
Des rameaux suspendus que la brise effarouche,
A frémir, que ta voix à chanter, quand je touche
Tes cheveux couronnés d'acanthe et de houblon.

Mais tu pars! tu me fuis pour les Portes d'Hercule;
Va! rafraîchis tes mains dans le clair crépuscule
Des choses où descend l'âme antique. Et reviens,

Hyacinthe adoré! hyacinthe! hyacinthe!
Car je veux voir toujours dans les bois syriens
Ton beau corps étendu sur la rose et l'absinthe.

Louÿs was evidently schooling himself to write his own *Chansons de Bilitis*.

† Max Beerbohm wrote to Ross in 1893: 'Poor Oscar! I saw him the other day, from a cab walking with Bosie and some other members of the Extreme Left. He looked like one whose soul has swooned in sin and revived vulgar. How fearful it is for a poet to go to bed and find himself infamous.'[12]

doned his wife and children for Douglas. Régnier passed on the details to Edmond de Goncourt, who entered them gloatingly in his journal for 30 April. But Louÿs had spoken not out of an urge to impart scandal, but out of a real dismay. He decided to urge Wilde to change his ways. An opportunity came in late May 1893, when Wilde stayed for a few days at the Hôtel des Deux-Mondes in the avenue de l'Opéra. Louÿs visited him, probably on the 23rd, and remonstrated with him about his relationship with Douglas and his mistreatment of wife and children. Wilde declined to offer any excuse or modify his conduct. Louÿs, he said, had no right to sit in judgment over him. In that case, Louÿs responded, he had no alternative but to break off relations. Wilde now gazed at him sadly and said, 'Goodbye, Pierre Louÿs. I had hoped for a friend; from now on I will have only lovers.'

But he gave an indignant account of the interview to Léon Daudet, and Louÿs, being duly informed by the unsympathetic Daudet, wrote to Wilde on 25 May 1893 a stinging letter: 'With regard to yourself, I have nothing to add to what I said to you the other day, except that I am astonished at your insistence and at the way you noise about an incident which I did not expect you to abuse.'[15] At Wilde's request Marcel Schwob tried to make peace, saying that Daudet had misrepresented what Wilde had said. It was to no avail. A few days later Louÿs notified John Gray: 'You know that I have broken with Wilde and that I cannot meet him anywhere.' Wilde's rift with Gray and Louÿs, lover and friend, Englishman and Frenchman, was a foretaste of worse to come. In his last years he would think back with regret of how he had lost their friendship because of Douglas. But for the moment he embraced danger as if it were a Ganymede.

Like a figure in Greek tragedy, Wilde had allowed his success to make him overweening. The behavior of his companions ostentatiously reinforced the childlike self-flattery in which he indulged. A letter from Beerbohm to Turner, written three days after the last performance of *A Woman of No Importance* on 16 August 1893, marks a distinct stage. Wilde came to the theatre with Douglas, Ross, and Beardsley. 'The last of these had forgotten to put vine-leaves in his hair, but the other three wore rich clusters – especially poor Robbie [who was getting bald]. Nor have I ever seen Oscar so fatuous: he called Mrs Beere "Juno-like" and [Henry] Kemble "Olympian quite" and waved his cigarette round and round his head. Of course I would rather see Oscar free than sober, but still, suddenly meeting him . . . I felt quite repelled.' That Wilde was not so arrogant as he pretended did not mitigate the unpleasantness of his effect on people.

Meanwhile Douglas was making a last attempt to catch up on his studies. In March 1893, he was being tutored at Oxford by a young scholar named Campbell Dodgson. Perhaps realizing that the game was up, he sent a long telegram to Wilde, and packed himself and tutor off to Babbacombe Cliff. Dodgson did his best to continue the instruction and camouflage Douglas's truancy, though he could appreciate Wilde's view that Babbacombe was 'combining the advantages of a public school with those of a lunatic asylum.' Wilde set out the school rules:

BABBACOMBE SCHOOL

Headmaster – Mr Oscar Wilde
Second Master – Mr Campbell Dodgson
Boys – Lord Alfred Douglas

Rules.

> Tea for masters and boys at 9.30 a.m.
> Breakfast at 10.30
> Work 11.30–12.30

At 12.30. Sherry and biscuits for headmasters and boys (the second master objects to this).

12.40–1.30. Work.

1.30. Lunch

2.30–4.30. Compulsory hide-and-seek for headmaster.

5. Tea for headmaster and second master, brandy and sodas (not to exceed seven) for boys.

6–7. Work.

7.30. Dinner, with compulsory champagne.

8.30–12. Ecarté, limited to five-guinea points.

12–1.30. Compulsory reading in bed. Any boy found disobeying this rule will be immediately woken up.

At the conclusion of the term the headmaster will be presented with a silver inkstand, the second master with a pencil-case, as a token of esteem, by the boys.

It was not in Douglas's nature to stay calm for long, and after a few days he flared up. His vituperation in these moods was more than Wilde could bear, and when Douglas went off in a tantrum to Bristol the next morning, Wilde welcomed the idea that their friendship might be at an end. Dodgson, no less flustered, remarked that Douglas was known at Magdalen as someone who at times was not responsible for what he said or did. But by the time he reached Bristol Douglas thought better of his outburst, and begged forgiveness. Wilde gave in, and Douglas returned to go back to London with him. On the way he asked Wilde to take rooms for them both at the Savoy, which Wilde did. It was here that Louÿs saw the tearful Constance. Douglas would never consent to go in by the side entrance of the hotel, but insisted on the front door so that everyone could see Oscar Wilde and his boy.[16] 'That was indeed a visit fatal to me,' Wilde would eventually recognize.

Oxford Revisited

*'Lord Henry, I am not at all surprised that the world says
that you are extremely wicked.'
'But what world says that?' asked Lord Henry, elevating
his eyebrows. 'It can only be the next world. This world and I
are on excellent terms.'*

In May of 1893 Wilde came, caped in glory, to Oxford, where he paid a
long visit to Douglas. During Eights Week there was a sudden attack in a
fly-by-night publication, the *Ephemeral*, edited by a young Oxford rugby
player named Alfred Hamilton Grant (later an important government
official in India) and an equally athletic friend, Arthur Cunliffe. Though
they were friendly with Douglas, who had shown some prowess as a
runner, they editorialized against his *Spirit Lamp* in their first issue of 18
May, suggested in a squib about Wilde that 'His face is his misfortune,'
and had a long article about a playwright called 'Ossian Savage': it began,
with tabloid sensationalism, 'Ossian Savage, a man of a coarse habit of
body and of coarser habits of mind, was enjoying the cool summer
morning in his own way in Piccadilly.' Douglas rose to the bait, denounc-
ing the phrase about Wilde's mind and body; they weaseled out of the
charge, made friends again, and kept up the game long enough to sell a
lot of copies. After Eights Week Douglas suggested that Grant should
meet the victim of the attack, and Grant agreed.

A dinner party was arranged in Douglas's rooms. Most of the guests
were not of Grant's athletic sort, being overdressed and effeminate. Wilde
was gracious and made no allusion to the *Ephemeral*: 'I hear that you are
called Gragger,' he said. 'But this is dreadful. It must not go on. We must
find a new name for you, something beautiful and worthy and Scotch.'
Grant disliked the way the young men and Wilde passed round gold-
tipped cigarettes between each course, and at the end of the meal he
ostentatiously took out a cigar. Douglas leaned over to caution him that
this might give offense to Wilde, who however said only, 'How too terrible
of you! But we shall call it a nutbrown cigarette – and you shall smoke it.'
Grant found all this too exclamatory, and was beginning to regret he had
come when someone said, 'Oscar, do tell us a story.' 'And what, my dear
boy, am I to tell you a story about?' A chorus of voices said, 'Early Church.'
Wilde shot out his great cuffs, and offered, as well as Grant could
remember, this tale of Christian fidelity:

In the days when Christianity was making its first struggles in the great
city of Rome, some of the idle rich began to be interested in this strange
new creed, with its odd inhibitions and its reversal of all normal human
impulses. Among those who saw the true beauty of the teaching was a
young girl, a patrician of a great House, by name Lydia. Daily she went to

the mean quarters where this earnest little community dwelt and met, and daily she became more and more drawn to their beliefs, until at last she accepted the Baptism of Christ and joined their ranks. All this time, however, she had an admirer, also, of course, a patrician, named Metellus, who loved her dearly. She told him from day to day of her spiritual leanings and of her communion with the Christians, and every day Metellus did all he could to dissuade her from what seemed to him social and religious shipwreck. He begged her to leave her mad quest and to marry him – but she refused and said she could never marry him unless he too became a Christian.

Goaded by his great love, Metellus consented to go with her to the Christians' meetings and to hear what they had to say. Truth to tell, he was but little moved by their discourses, and the whole thing seemed to him very foolish and unnecessary. But the flame of his love burnt fiercely, and seeing no other way of winning his Lydia, he affected complete conversion, and he too became a Christian. For a little while they were happy, very happy; but before long the attention of a ruthless Emperor was drawn to the activities of the Christians. False and cruel charges were brought against them and the persecution began. Many were seized and hurled into prison, and amongst them Lydia and Metellus, whose offence was the greater in that they were of patrician rank. Then Lydia in the solitude of her cell began to regret what she had done.

'Perhaps, after all,' she said to herself, 'the whole story of Christ is false and His teaching an error. The old gods were easy and comfortable. Why, oh why! have I been so foolish?'

And Metellus in *his* cell thought: 'Well, I was afraid that no good would come of this. I knew from the first that it was all wild talk with no practical purpose, that could not lead to anything but trouble.'

And the day came when they were each told that unless they would publicly renounce the Christian faith with contumely, they would be thrown to the wild beasts in the Great Circus before the Roman people. Terror and anguish filled their hearts – but Lydia said to herself: 'What have I done? I have brought myself and my dear, dear Metellus to this plight. If I now renounce Christ, he, who believes so fervently, will die despising me. That I could not bear.'

And Metellus said to himself: 'What a grievous business is this! I care not one straw for Christ or His doctrine and never did. But if I now renounce Him, Lydia, whose belief is as a rock, and who believes that I too believe as she does, will think me a common coward and will die despising me. That I could not bear.'

And so when the appointed day came, in their turn Lydia and Metellus were thrown to the wild beasts in the Circus – and thus they both died for a Faith in which they did not believe.

There were almost nightly dinners given in Wilde's honor by members of his coterie. It was like his old days in Oxford, but grander. One dinner was held on a Sunday night in a house in St Giles', where the first floor opened out to a balcony. The night was sultry and after dinner several guests, including Wilde, sat on the balcony. Some of the passing townsmen recognized Wilde, and one cried out, 'Why, there's Hoscar – let's 'ave a speech, Hauthor, Hauthor, Hoscar, Hoscar.' Disconcerted, Wilde went indoors. But Grant, who was again present, felt that more should be done, and summoned another athletic guest, 'We must read the Riot Act, then constitute ourselves into the Military, and charge and disperse this unlawful assembly.' The crowd did not stand up to them and left. Wilde welcomed his defenders with outstretched arms, 'Hail! You are magnificent. You are giants, giants with souls!' Grant proposed that as a reward Wilde should tell another story of the Early Church. After some reluctance, he began:

A little while ago I was browsing in the library of a country house. I happened to pick out a musty, calf-bound volume of ancient European history and, opening it at random, my eye caught the sentence, 'In that year died Pope John the Twenty-Second a shameful death.' This intrigued me. What was the manner of this shameful death? I tried to find illumination in that library, but without success. So I decided to discover the truth in the only way in which truth can with certainty be discovered – by evolving it from one's inner consciousness. Suddenly in the silence of the night the naked truth was delivered to me. It was this.

The aged Pope, who had for long been little more than a living corpse, passed away. During his long sickness, intrigue had been busy and the College of Cardinals was torn by bitter faction. After days of hot dispute, the College at length decided to compromise by appointing a complete nonentity who should be neutral. They bethought them of the young priest of a little church lying a few miles away in the Campagna. . . . Summoned to the Vatican, this young man was, with all the strange attendant ceremonies, duly elected Pope under the name of John the Twenty-Second.

In those days the Pope lived no secluded life within the walls of the Vatican, but mixed freely in the society of Rome. . . . It was little wonder that before long Pope John, daily meeting the most beautiful women of the capital, should fall in love. The lady of his affections was the young wife of an elderly noble of a great house. First they loved with the love that dies – the love of the soul for the soul; and then they loved with the love that never dies – the love of the body for the body. But in Rome itself, their opportunities were few.

They resolved, therefore, to meet in some secluded spot far from the city. The lady's husband owned a little villa with a beautiful orchard some miles out in the Campagna. . . . They agreed on a day and hour. Early on the day appointed Pope John arrayed himself in the gay fête-day dress of a Roman noble – and mounting his horse rode with exulting heart into the Campagna. When he had gone a few miles he suddenly saw in the distance the little church of which he had been such a little while ago the humble, unknown priest.

Drawn by an irresistible feeling, . . . he approached the little church and tethered his horse; and then a strange fancy took him, to don the priest's vestments and to sit in the confessional as he had so often done before. The church was open and empty, so putting on the vestments, he sat down beside the *grille*. Of a sudden the door opened and a man hurried in, with face half-masked, evidently in much perturbation of mind.

'Father,' he said in a broken voice, 'I have a question to ask of you. Is there any sin so great that Christ Himself could not absolve me from it?'

'Nay, my son, there is no such sin. But what grievous sin have you committed that you ask me this?'

'I have committed no sin,' said the man, 'but I am about to commit a sin so deadly that I do not think even Christ Himself could absolve me. I am about to kill the Vicar of Christ upon Earth, Pope John the Twenty-Second.'

'Even from this sin could Christ absolve you,' said Pope John.

The man rose and hurried from the church, and Pope John took off the priest's vestments, mounted his horse and rode on towards the orchard where his love awaited him. There on the sunlit green turf in a clearing between the trees stood his lady. With a little cry she ran towards him and threw herself into his arms. As they stood in that first long embrace, suddenly a figure sprang from the twilight of the trees and drove a dagger hilt-high into the back of Pope John. With a groan he fell to the ground – a dying man. Then with a supreme effort he raised his hand and, looking at his assailant, said in the last words of the Absolution:

'*Quod ego possum et tu eges, absolve te.*' And so died Pope John the Twenty-Second a shameful death.[17]

Star-crossed ambition and star-crossed love conveyed Wilde's anxiety about the realized ambition and fulfilled love he was experiencing. So a sceptic's history of popes and saints gradually took form.

The Greats examinations took place in June 1893; Douglas did not show up for them. Magdalen College expressed its disfavor. Douglas rushed to remove his name from the college books, and wrote indignantly to the President that some day this would be the greatest disgrace for Magdalen. Wilde congratulated him on having followed Swinburne's example by deciding to remain a permanent undergraduate.

The late spring and summer of 1893 were devoted to pleasure. Douglas had taken a fancy to a house at Goring-on-Thames, which Wilde called 'a most unhealthy and delightful place.' He persuaded Wilde to rent it and to engage a college scout of his named Grainger to work there. Wilde also had visits from his family, especially Cyril. Other visitors dropped in, one of them the young poet, Theodore Wratislaw, who had reviewed Gray's *Silverpoints* so unfavorably; though they scarcely knew each other, he came at Wilde's invitation at the end of August. Having stored his summer clothes, he appeared clad in a tail coat and a new straw hat, to the obvious irritation of Wilde, who was dressed all in white. After tea they went for a walk in the woods. At one point the path opened up for a short space, then wound its way around a blind corner to the right. Wilde suddenly stood still. 'There!' he exclaimed, 'that is as far as I ever wish to see in life. Let me be satisfied with what I can see. I do not want to know what lies beyond the turning a few paces ahead.' Uneasiness, rather than aesthetic contentment, was apparent.

They dined alone: Wratislaw had the nerve to suggest that Wilde's dialogue was too elaborate, and that Pinero's or Jones's was better adapted to the stage. For answer, Wilde put some plays of his two rivals in Wratislaw's hands and said, 'Read these.' Wratislaw was surprised to discover how commonplace their dialogue was, and told Wilde so the next morning. Wilde said nothing except that he had expected this response. At breakfast Cyril Wilde appeared, a beautiful child with golden curls. Afterwards Wilde took them sculling on the river. He was wearing a pale blue shirt with a pale pink silk tie, colors which the next day he would reverse. He used a white lilac perfume. In the boat Wratislaw thoughtlessly made a slighting remark about Home Rule for Ireland, and little Cyril flashed with anger as he asked, 'Are you not a Home Ruler?' Wilde turned the debate aside by saying, 'My own idea is that Ireland should rule England.' Another subject was the most recent volume of Richard Le Gallienne, and particularly a poem called 'The Decadent Poet to his Soul.' Wilde wondered who in the world Le Gallienne might have had in mind, and was taken aback when Wratislaw said it must be Wilde himself. He recovered to say, 'Well, it has always seemed to me that the finest feature of a fine nature is treachery.' To a sensitive nature, he explained, the burden of gratitude must be overwhelming, so it was a sign of the fineness of the debtor's character that he should find it necessary to betray his benefactor.[18]

As Wratislaw was leaving, another guest arrived, whom Wilde addressed as Harry (presumably this was Harry Marillier). In between these hospitable gestures Wilde wrote the first act of his new play, *An Ideal Husband*, in the house at Goring in early June. *A Woman of No Importance* had been all talk and no action in its first act, but *An Ideal Husband* advanced the plot much more rapidly. Then Douglas appeared with some Oxford friends. The moment the friends left, Douglas, in a fit of rage, denounced Wilde. It was a bright morning, and the two men were standing, as Wilde was to remember, on the level croquet ground with the lawn all round. When Douglas paused, Wilde said to him as calmly as he could that they must part. 'We are spoiling each other's lives. You are absolutely ruining mine and evidently I am not making you really happy. An irrevocable parting, a complete separation is the one wise philosophic thing to do.' Douglas stayed for luncheon, then went off, leaving with the butler one of those scorching letters that had become a recurrent event in their relationship. Yet again there was an about-face: in three days

Douglas was begging Wilde in telegrams from London to let him return. Wilde could never resist penitence.[19]

Crisis and Flight

Always! That is a dreadful word. It makes me shudder when I hear it. Women are so fond of using it. They spoil every romance by trying to make it last for ever. It is a meaningless word too. The only difference between a caprice and a lifelong passion is that the caprice lasts a little longer.

The worst quarrel of a quarrelsome year was still to come. Wilde's summer had been largely wasted, though he at least had projects. Douglas appeared to have none. Oxford was closed to him. Perhaps with the aim of giving him something to do, and also because he liked Douglas's appreciation of *Salome* in the *Spirit Lamp* for May 1893, Wilde proposed that Douglas should translate the play for the English edition. Since Douglas had no book bearing his name, the prospect of sharing a title page with Wilde was eagerly accepted.

The commission was a mistake. Wilde had not reckoned with his beloved's inadequate French. When Douglas proudly brought the translation to him at the end of August, Wilde found it unacceptable. For instance, '*On ne doit regarder que dans les miroirs*' had been translated as, 'One must not look at mirrors' instead of 'One should look only in mirrors.' Furious at having his ignorance pointed out, Douglas quickly retorted that if there were faults, they were in the original rather than the translation. The usual violent letters to Wilde followed. He had begun to preen himself as an author, and Wilde's shift from praise to blame was intolerable. Douglas said in one letter that he had 'no intellectual obligation of any kind' to Wilde; Wilde had not claimed such obligation, but it existed all the same, for Douglas, notwithstanding his failure to understand Wilde's play, had framed his literary life on Wilde's model, adopted his stances, his views, his patter. Wilde saw a chance, with this letter, to end 'the fatal friendship that had sprung up between us,' and to end it 'without bitterness.' He seems to have contemplated sending back Douglas's manuscript to him and assuring him that no obligation existed.

But when the danger of losing Wilde became real, Douglas wilted. He asked someone, almost certainly Robbie Ross, to intercede, and Ross pointed out to Wilde that to return the manuscript like a schoolboy's exercises would scar Douglas's life. Douglas did not know much French, and Wilde should not have expected so much from him. He also assured Wilde that, whatever Douglas said or did, he was utterly devoted to his lover. Wilde had no desire to be the first to check or discourage Douglas's beginnings in literature, as he said long afterwards, and had the less right to do so since he had encouraged them. 'So I took the translation and you back.'[20]

He evidently came to this decision at Dinard, where he had gone at the end of August to recover from twelve weeks of Douglas. 'I required rest and freedom from the terrible strain of your companionship,' he wrote in *De Profundis.* By 9 September he sent a conciliatory letter to Douglas in which he mentioned with deliberate casualness that Douglas would soon be receiving proofs. He did not give up his criticisms, however, and insisted on many changes. Douglas reasserted himself, and refused to make them. On 30 September he wrote to the publisher, John Lane,

Dear Lane,

Oscar and I have found it impossible to agree about the translation of certain passages, phrases and words in *Salome*, and consequently as I cannot consent to have my work altered and edited, and thus to become a mere machine for doing the rough work of translation, I have decided to relinquish the affair altogether.

You and Oscar can therefore arrange between you as to who the translator is to be. My private opinion is that unless Oscar translates it himself, he will not be satisfied.

Yours very truly
ALFRED DOUGLAS

The matter did not end there. In October or November Beardsley read the translation and said it would not do; he offered to make one of his own. Wilde, fortunately for Douglas, did not like this either. There ensued an acrimonious fourway controversy among Lane, Wilde, Douglas, and Beardsley. Lane said that Douglas had shown disrespect for Wilde, but backed down when Douglas accused him of stirring up trouble between them. Beardsley declared that it would be dishonest to put Douglas's name on the title page, when the translation had been so much altered by Wilde. Wilde then offered the wisdom of Solomon: he proposed to Douglas that the title page should bear only his own name, but that a dedication should be made to Douglas as translator. Beardsley stayed out of this controversy, and wrote to Ross in November,

I suppose you've heard all about the *Salome* row. I can tell you I had a warm time of it between Lane and Oscar and Co. For one week the numbers of telegraph and messenger boys who came to the door was simply scandalous. I really don't quite know how matters really stand now. Anyhow Bosie's name is not to turn up on the Title. The book will be out soon after Xmas. I have withdrawn three of the illustrations and supplied their places with three new ones (simply beautiful and quite irrelevant).[21]

Douglas sent Lane a letter explaining that the new arrangement was more honorific than the old:

In the meanwhile let me assure you that nothing would have induced me to sanction the publication of *Salome* without my name on the title-page (and the matter was left entirely in my hands by Mr Wilde), if I had not been persuaded that the dedication which is to be made to me is of infinitely greater artistic & literary value, than the appearance of my name on the title-page. It was only a few days ago that I fully realised that the difference between the dedication of *Salome* to me by the author and the appearance of my name on the title-page is the difference between a tribute of admiration from an artist and a receipt from a tradesman.[22]

He thrived on quarrels, but the others did not. He had an inexhaustible stock of combative energy, but when this had run its course, he was as shiftless as he had been before mistranslating *Salome*. His father was furious over his failure to take his degree, and having no one else to blame, blamed Wilde. Queensberry had other problems as well. His oldest son, Drumlanrig, was private secretary to Lord Rosebery, then Foreign Minister under Gladstone but to be Prime Minister the next year (1894). Queensberry had begun to see homosexuals everywhere, and suspected that Rosebery was influencing Drumlanrig in this direction. Quick to go on the rampage, and hearing that Rosebery was at Bad Homburg, Queensberry followed him there in August 1893 with a dogwhip. The Prince of Wales intervened, and the police asked the Marquess to leave. The next month, on 11 September, Queensberry's second son Percy married the daughter of a Cornish clergyman, an alliance opposed by the atheist Queensberry because he considered the family both too paltry and too pious. To the author of *The Spirit of the Matterhorn* the prospective descendants of such a match could hardly have been less promising. His personal life was also agitating. On 1 November 1893 Queensberry married for the second time. His wife was Ethel Weedon, a young woman of a respectable Eastbourne family, none of whom came to the wedding. She left him immediately, and started proceedings for annulment, alleging 'malformation of the parts of generation' as well as 'frigidity and impotency.' To be called impotent seven years after having been judicially declared adulterous, and after having begotten four children, was a heavy load for this active man of fifty. He contested the suit, claimed the marriage had been consummated, and hired George Lewis to defend him.

Queensberry repeatedly demanded that Douglas stop seeing Wilde. On 8 November 1893, Wilde wrote a long letter to Lady Queensberry about Douglas's disturbed state, which suggests some trepidation in the writer too:

16 Tite Street

Dear Lady Queensberry, You have on more than one occasion consulted me about Bosie. Let me write to you now about him.

Bosie seems to me to be in a very bad state of health. He is sleepless, nervous, and rather hysterical. He seems to me quite altered.

He is doing nothing in town. He translated my French play last August. Since then he has really done nothing intellectual. He seems to me to have lost, for the moment only I trust, his interest even in literature. He does absolutely nothing, and is quite astray in life, and may, unless you or Drumlanrig do something, come to grief of some kind. His life seems to me aimless, unhappy and absurd.

All this is a great grief and disappointment to me, but he is very young, and terribly young in temperament. Why not try and make arrangements of some kind for him to go abroad for four or five months, to the Cromers in Egypt if that could be managed, where he would have new surroundings, proper friends, and a different atmosphere? I think that if he stays in London he will not come to any good, and may spoil his young life irretrievably, quite irretrievably. Of course it will cost money no doubt, but here is the life of one of your sons – a life that should be brilliant and distinguished and charming – going quite astray, being quite ruined.

I like to think myself his greatest friend – he, at any rate, makes me think so – so I write to you quite frankly to ask you to send him abroad to better surroundings. It would save him, I feel sure. At present his life seems to be tragic and pathetic in its foolish aimlessness.

You will not, I know, let him know *anything about my letter.* I can rely on you, I feel sure. Sincerely yours   OSCAR WILDE

In spite of the request for secrecy, Wilde's *De Profundis* makes clear that the idea of Douglas's going to Lord Cromer in Cairo was a stratagem they had hit upon together. Douglas had reason enough to leave the country. There had been a scandal in which he was involved. A letter from Beerbohm to Turner offers a mystifying account:

Robbie Ross has returned to this country for a few days and of him there have been very great and intimate scandals and almost, if not quite, warrants: slowly he is recovering but has to remain at Davos during his convalescence for fear of a social relapse. I must not disclose anything (nor must you) but I may tell you that a schoolboy with wonderful eyes, Bosie, Bobbie, a furious father, George Lewis, a headmaster (who is now blackmailing Bobbie), St John Wontner [a police solicitor], Calais, Dover, Oscar Browning, Oscar, Dover, Calais, and returned cigarette-cases were some of the ingredients of the dreadful episode . . . The *garçon entretenu*, the schoolboy Helen 'for whom those horned ships were launched, those beautiful mailed men laid low,' was the same as him of whom I told you that he had been stolen from Bobbie by Bosie and kept at the Albemarle Hotel: how well I remember passing this place one night with Bobbie and his looking up sadly at the lighted windows and wondering to me behind which of the red curtains lay the desire of his soul.[23]

This highspirited jumble has to be supplemented by a letter from Oscar Browning to Frank Harris. Browning's brother-in-law, the Reverend Biscale Hale Wortham, kept a boys' school, St Laurence, in Bruges. Robert Ross went to visit the Worthams during the holidays. A sixteen-year-old boy named Philip Danney, son of an army colonel, was staying there, and Ross, who had known the boy since he was fourteen, invited him to visit him in London.

While Danney was staying with him, Ross mentioned the fact casually in a letter to Douglas, then at Goring with Wilde. Douglas responded by rushing to London and bringing the boy back to Goring. 'On Saturday,' says Browning, 'the boy slept with Douglas, on Sunday he slept with Oscar. On Monday he returned to London and slept with a woman at Douglas's expense. On Tuesday he returned to Bruges three days late. His master inquired into the facts and told them to me as I have related them.' Colonel Danney, an officer in the Guards, got wind of the matter, and the police solicitors were consulted. Ross and Douglas had to hotfoot it to Bruges on 15 October 1893 and meet with Wortham. Ross gave back Danney's letters. Wilde's name was kept out of it. 'It is an absolute fabrication,' said Ross. Colonel Danney, according to Browning, 'wished to prosecute the offenders, but the lawyer said, "They will doubtless get two years but your son will get six months."' So the father, unlike Queensberry after him, decided to let the matter drop. Ross's relations heard of the affair, and called him – as he later admitted in open court – 'the disgrace of the family, a social outcast, a son and brother unfit for society of any kind.' It was decided that he should leave the country, and he went to Davos partly for reasons of health but mostly as Beerbohm said to avoid 'a social relapse.'[24]* He ventured back to London in the first days of the next year, but life could never be so free and easy again. The tiger had flexed its paws; Wilde would not be warned.

Lady Queensberry was kept in the dark. She decided to follow Wilde's advice to send her son to Cairo, and arranged matters with the Cromers. Douglas prepared for departure. He had his own tremors, even if Ross was bearing the brunt. Wilde had begun to look forward to his absence, and Douglas may have detected this, for he fell into another fit of fury and Wilde escaped to Paris, leaving a false address. Telegrams and letters trailed after him, but this time he disregarded them. Douglas had a trump card to play: he threatened that he would not go to Egypt at all unless Wilde agreed to a reconciliation. Wilde knew how much Lady Queensberry had banked on the change of scene, and felt that since he had proposed it he must not allow Douglas to give it up. He made peace. Douglas went off to Cairo, once more confident of Wilde's love, though this was by no means unreservedly renewed.[26]

---

* At Davos he gave a talk before the English Literary Society on 'The Didactic in Art and Literature', in which he said, 'I do not think that Plato's morals or those of any Greek writer would withstand the British crucible.'[25]

Not all Wilde's time went into these anxieties. The opera singer Emma Calvé tells how, late in 1893, Wilde came up to the hostess at a large party and said he had with him a French poet who had been in prison, and asked her permission to bring him in. She agreed. It proved to be Paul Verlaine, unkempt as ever, but this time in favor with Wilde. At Wilde's urging Verlaine read a poem about his prison experience; his words cut through hypocrisy and evasion to touch the hearts of the respectable company. Wilde, on his way to becoming another of society's victims, joined proudly in the applause.[27]

CHAPTER XVI

Sailing into the Wind

HEROD: *And I hear in the air something that is like the beating of wings, like the beating of vast wings. Do you not hear it?*

'Falling Towers . . .'

A letter of Wilde to Douglas, written in the summer of 1894, tells of having been to sit with the aging Lady Wilde. 'Death and Love seem to walk on either hand as I go through life: they are the only things I think of, their wings shadow me.' Lady Wilde, now seventy-four, was in great distress at the rupture of relations between her two sons. In January of this year Willie married for the second time, his bride a pleasant woman named Lily Lees. Oscar was conspicuously absent. On 29 March Lady Wilde wrote to him, 'I am truly sorry to find that you and Willie meet as enemies. Is this to go on to my death? Not a cheering prospect for me, to have my two sons at enmity, and unable to meet at my deathbed. I think, to please me, you might write the 8 words I asked – "I forget the enmity. Let us be friends. Signed Oscar." *8 words!* Can you do it to oblige me? There need be no intimacy between you but at least *social civility*.'[1] Her pleas were unavailing, except to make Wilde take stock of himself and recognize, not for the first time, how solemn a vision underlay the insouciance he affected.

These dark thoughts perhaps prompted him in April to get out his old scenario for *The Cardinal of Avignon*, in the hope that the American tragic actor, Richard Mansfield, might play in it. In this sketch, which he had written in the flush of his first American fame in 1882, Wilde had planned to include a Masque of Death. The plot reads like something from Jacobean drama. The Cardinal – about to be elected Pope – has a passion for his ward, whom he alone knows to be his daughter. But she is in love with a young man, who, as only the Cardinal is aware, is her brother. Out of jealousy, not morality, the Cardinal informs the brother of his true relationship with the girl (though not with himself), and makes him tell her that he no longer loves her. When the Cardinal is elected Pope, he has

385

a change of heart, and tells the young man he will permit the marriage. But the girl is brought in on a bier: she has killed herself. The young man is about to commit the sin of killing the Pope, and is not swayed by the Pope's telling him, 'I am your father.' But when the Pope says, 'I too loved her,' his son flings open the doors of the palace and tells the soldiers, 'His Holiness the Pope rides to Rome tonight.' He throws himself on the bier and kills himself as his sister has done. The plot was Wilde's emulation of another neo-Jacobean drama, Shelley's *The Cenci*,* but differs in its lack of interest in the subject of incest. The tragedy is one of thwarted love, and the family relationships of lovers and rival do not seem to matter. Mansfield was interested, but the play got no further.

A masque of death weaves in and out of Wilde's life during these months. His public life was smooth and confident. He would lunch with the Asquiths, and W. S. Blunt describes such an occasion on 17 July 1894 when Wilde outshone a brilliant company, perversely crossing swords with each person in turn, and making special fun of Asquith, who would soon, as Home Secretary, be prosecuting him. This may have been the occasion when Asquith complained of a Wilde mannerism, 'The man who uses italics is like the man who raises his voice in conversation and talks loudly in order to make himself heard.' Wilde's rejoinder was, 'How delightful of you, Mr Asquith, to have noticed that! The brilliant phrase, like good wine, needs no bush. But just as the orator marks his good things by a dramatic pause, or by raising and lowering his voice, or by gesture, so the writer marks his epigrams with italics, setting the little gem, so to speak, like a jeweller – an excusable love of one's art, not all mere vanity, I like to think –.'[2] On the other hand, imputations of scandal involving Wilde and Douglas were so commonplace in London – that metropolitan small town – that the Marquess of Queensberry needed no private detectives to learn of them.

Wilde's difficulties were multiplied because, as was well known, the Criminal Law Amendment Act of 1885† which for the first time prohibited indecent relations between consenting adult males, had seen in the age of the blackmailer. Given Douglas's carelessness with letters received, and his own recklessness in writing them, Wilde could never be free of harassment on this score. The harshest persecution he suffered, however, came not from greedy boys or an indignant father, but from

* It may have been in his mind as he told the 'Early Church' story of Pope John XXII to Grant and others at Oxford in 1893.

† The amendment reads, 'Any male person who, in public or private, commits, or is a party to the commission of, or procures or attempts to procure the commission by any male person of, any act of gross indecency with another male person, shall be guilty of a misdemeanour, and, being convicted thereof, shall be liable, at the discretion of the Court, to be imprisoned for any term not exceeding two years with or without hard labour.' When it was pointed out to Queen Victoria that women were not mentioned, she is reported to have said, 'No woman would do that.'

Alfred Douglas. Douglas liked to live on a knife edge, and to have company there. He challenged Wilde into expenditures hitherto undreamed of, in a half-conscious effort to bog his friend down in debt-ridden emotions and emotion-ridden debts. If he wanted proof of his hold over Wilde, and no proof was ever enough, he had it every day in lavish meals and presents.

It says much for Wilde's seriousness as an artist that under such pressure he worked at his best. His art was his anodyne for the malice of his enemies and the profligacy that Douglas was making obligatory. Wilde explained this in a letter of condolence he wrote to his sometime friend Henley, in which he urged work as the only consolation for the convergence of love and death that life offers. 'That is what remains for natures like ours,' he declares. 'Work never seems to me a reality, but a way of getting rid of reality.'[3] The fifteen months from December 1893 to the beginning of his legal proceedings against Queensberry, with presages of coming disaster thick around him, were as productive as the beginning of the 1890s when all his powers seemed to find expression.

Douglas Away

The centaurs have hidden in the rivers, and the sirens have
left the rivers and lie under the leaves of the forest.

Wilde wrote most of four plays and planned a fifth. With Douglas out of the way in Egypt for three months, he was able to finish the last three acts of *An Ideal Husband*. He said to Ricketts, 'It was written for ridiculous puppets to play, and the critics will say, "Ah, here is Oscar unlike himself!—" though in reality I became engrossed in writing it, and it contains a great deal of the real Oscar.'[4] He was right. The play joined his two previous comedies in demonstrating the universal incapacity to come up to the ideal. The offense of Sir Robert Chiltern is the most serious in the three plays, since eighteen years before, at twenty-two, he has sold a state secret and with the money established his wealth and political position. Beside his, Mrs Erlynne's and Mrs Arbuthnot's offenses in earlier years are only indiscretions. The parallels are rather with Dorian Gray's murder of Hallward and Arthur Savile's of the cheiromancer, one treated seriously, the other frivolously. Wilde must have had in mind how he, at about the same age as Chiltern – and also eighteen years before – contracted syphilis at Oxford. Like murder, disease will out.

With this theme of youthful wrongdoing which was ineradicable in his work, Wilde built up the play by devising characters who, though they resemble those in his other plays, behave quite differently. Mrs Cheveley is an adventuress, like Mrs Erlynne in *Lady Windermere's Fan*, but instead

387

of sacrificing herself for her daughter, she wants to sacrifice Chiltern to her own ends. The cleverest character in *A Woman of No Importance* is Lord Illingworth, a dandy; in *An Ideal Husband* Lord Goring is equally clever, and equally a dandy, but he behaves well while Illingworth behaves villainously. Wit is no criterion of decency. Lady Chiltern, like Lady Windermere, is a puritan, whose puritanism must be made to vanish in the air in a scene of forgiveness and love. Even ideal husbands are, like other people, a bit criminal. The comic spirit, Wilde told Arthur Roberts, is a necessity in life, as a purge to all human vanity.[5]

The play's charm derives not from the exposure of hypocrisy, but from the gradual expansion of tenderness. Goring and Chiltern's daughter Mabel are witty and loving, and the affectionate relations of Goring and his father are an object lesson to the Queensberrys. The Chilterns too rediscover their bond. The kindness of the playwright is more evident here than in the other plays.

During these months Wilde wrote also *A Florentine Tragedy* and most of *La Sainte Courtisane*. As usual, he counterposed two forms of love, one moving to reconciliation and the other to antipathy. *La Sainte Courtisane* was an attempt to dramatize and perhaps improve upon Anatole France's *Thaïs*: an anchorite converts a courtesan to Christianity, in the process is himself converted to paganism, then rejected by his convert. (This too was like an 'Early Church' story of Wilde's.) He had a fresher plot in *A Florentine Tragedy*, which he wrote in blank verse, a blank verse more mature and subtle than in *The Duchess of Padua*. This play seems virtually finished. A Jewish cloth merchant finds a nobleman visiting his wife in his shop, and pretends to think it is a business visit. There is a good deal of verbal sparring before he forces the nobleman into a duel and kills him. The ending surprises: his wife expresses neither grief for her lover, nor revulsion from her husband. She asks, 'Why did you not tell me you were so strong?' and he replies, 'Why did you not tell me you were beautiful?' Wilde seems to have intended a trio of short plays, variations on love's cross-purposes, but could not finish them. He blamed their incompleteness on the return of Douglas.

Yet his productive period was stalled, not stopped. On the morning of 1 August he invented a plot which he immediately sent off to George Alexander. This one was also a reversal, of *Lady Windermere's Fan*. It was as if Wilde were trying to illustrate his aphorism that 'A truth in art is one whose contrary is equally true.' In this play, instead of the wife staying with her husband, as in his earlier play, she runs off with her lover. The play diverges from its antitype even further, as the husband begs his wife's lover to beg her to return. The lover self-sacrificially promises, but she refuses. 'All this self-sacrifice is wrong,' she insists, 'we are meant to live. That is the meaning of life.' She and the lover go off, but the husband eventually challenges the lover to a duel. In a final interview, the husband learns to his discomfiture that his wife hopes for his death, and that she is pregnant by the lover. He goes out, shots are heard, the lover complains that the husband has not turned up for the duel, then learns that he has killed himself. Wilde explained to Alexander that the play was to present 'the sheer passion of love,' with 'No morbid self-sacrifice. No renunciation.' It was a theme that he felt increasingly to be his own. But the husband does practice self-sacrifice and renunciation, as Wilde was to do in ways he did not expect. The plot of *The Cardinal of Avignon* failed to disapprove of incest, and this play failed to disapprove of adultery.[6] Alexander's response to the new plot is not recorded, but in August and September 1894 Wilde turned to writing his last and greatest play, *The Importance of Being Earnest.*

With all his literary and amorous preoccupations, he continued to be the same generous man he had always been. Nelly Sickert tells how when her father Oswald Sickert died, Wilde came to call on her mother. Mrs Sickert had shut herself up in dumb despair. Nelly told Wilde he would not be received, but he insisted. The widow as stubbornly refused. When Nelly relayed this message, Wilde said, 'But she must see me. She must. Tell her I will stay here till she does.' Back she went to be met by another refusal, her mother wringing her hands and saying, 'I can't. Send him away.' But she got up and went crying into the room where he was waiting. Nelly saw Wilde take both her hands and draw her to a chair, and then left. 'He stayed a long time, and before he went I heard my mother laughing . . . She was transformed. He had made her talk, had asked questions about my father's last illness, and allowed her to unburden . . . those torturing memories. Gradually he had talked of my father, of his music, of the possibilities of a memorial exhibition of his pictures. Then, she didn't know how, he had begun to tell her all sorts of things, which he contrived to make interesting and amusing. "And then I laughed," she said. "I thought I should never laugh again."'[7]

A letter of 28 April 1891 from some unknown person thanks Wilde for saving the family home. Edgar Saltus tells how he and Wilde were accosted in Chelsea on a cold night by a man who opened his jacket to show he had nothing on underneath. Saltus gave the man a gold coin but Wilde took off his overcoat and put it round him. Another such witness is Gertrude Pearce, who for about a year and a half was tutor to Vyvyan Wilde. In the summer of 1893 she accompanied the family to Goring and returned with them to London, remaining in their employ well into the following year. Wilde offered every kind of assistance to her. She wrote down in 1906 what she remembered of those days:

We all spent a very lovely time at 'The Cottage', Goring on Thames, where he wrote his play *The Ideal Husband* in which I believe I was one of the women mentioned, Gertrude [Chisholm]. It was an ideal country place, lovely gardens, and meadows which led on to the towing path to the river, of course there were all kinds of boats for our use, punts, skiffs, canoes, and to show how generous Oscar Wilde was, he told me if ever I went to the boat house and found the particular boat I wanted was out, to be sure to go to Saunders boat house and get what I wanted and put it down to his account.

We absolutely lived in the most luxurious style, there were 8 servants and everything done on a lavish scale. The servants I believe used to drink champagne in the kitchen, he told me how amusing it had been to him as *he* engaged all the servants and paid them very high wages. I spent one Christmas with them and Mr Wilde was as happy as a boy, doling out the Christmas pudding, pulling crackers and I have even now a small china doll he gave me from the pudding. I very much regret I destroyed all his photographs and I could have had the manuscript of the play I was mentioned in, or any play if I had wanted it.

I can also remember the time when things were not so prosperous (after our return from Goring) [October 1893] and the butcher even refusing to send a joint until the account was settled, Oscar himself driving round in a hansom and settling up, after which we were of course allowed to have a dinner. It may also sound strange when I tell you I once went to a well known shop to hire a few knives but as I had no money with me to pay at the time, they also refused and I very ignominiously had to return home to fetch the money . . .

Did I ever tell you that, when they decided to send my charge [Vyvyan] to school, they asked me to live with them, . . . knowing my parents were dead, even offering to send me to college to take up any particular subject I wished to, when I very stupidly refused this more than kind offer they then said knowing how independent I was would I live there and take a daily engagement so that they would have me with them. This too I regret to say I refused.[8]

Wilde's high spirits at Christmastime of 1893 reflected his temporary detachment from Douglas. For the time he was wonderfully disencumbered. He could write, he could talk to his friends, he could enjoy himself without the competitive strain which Douglas introduced into the pursuit of young men. As the weeks passed Wilde strengthened his resolve to have nothing more to do with his lover. Resolutions were all very well, but Douglas had his own sensitivity, and knew that the reconciliation he had extorted from Wilde before he left – by the threat of not leaving – was only a perfunctory one. Wilde still dominated his existence. On the eve of departure he had a long talk with his mother, who was explicit in her insistence that he should break off with Wilde. She told him she would almost like to murder Wilde for what he had done to him. Even Bosie, she said, had never pretended that Wilde was a good man.

Douglas reacted to the word 'good' with all an aesthete's verbosity. In a letter he sent from Cairo on 10 December 1893 he said that he did not speak of anybody as good, and did not regard the word as applicable to individuals. He indiscreetly quoted Wilde's remark in his Preface to

Dorian Gray, 'There is no such thing as a moral or immoral book, a book is well written or badly written, that is all.' What he claimed for Wilde was not goodness but character and distinction. Then, as if realizing that the arguments had not been very convincing so far, he added that Wilde had taught him how one could be good and splendid too, and had even inculcated a kind of religion. Douglas, once like his father a scoffer, now recognized that religion had a value and that Biblical stories had meanings. As for Wilde's effect on him, 'Why, I tell you I don't believe I had a soul before I met him.' Wilde had persuaded him to give up gambling and betting and going to race-meetings, because they were unworthy of him. (This renunciation proved temporary.) Their relationship was that of the philosopher and the disciple, like that of Shakespeare and Mr W.H., or of Socrates and Plato, and much nobler than that of Socrates and Alcibiades.

Lady Queensberry was not moved. She responded, 'If Mr Wilde has acted as I am convinced he has the part of a Lord Henry Wotton to you I could never feel differently towards him than I do, as the murderer of your soul.' She too had been obliged to read *Dorian Gray*, and must also have read the poem by Bosie's cousin, Lionel Johnson, which was entitled 'To the Destroyer of a Soul,' addressed secretly to Wilde.* It was from Wilde, she said, that her son had learned his 'eccentricities and peculiar views of morality.' No, said Douglas, he had come to these views two years before he met Wilde. He took the occasion to lecture her about *Dorian Gray*: Wilde was in no sense like Lord Henry Wotton, who had none of Oscar's 'sunny nature, his buoyant "joie de vivre," his quick wit and splendid sense of humour, and his loyal kind and forgiving nature which make him altogether more like a grown up boy than the sort of cynical subtle and morbid creature which you want to make him out.' Neither mother nor son showed signs of yielding; Lady Queensberry did not slacken her efforts to keep her son abroad.

Douglas also received in Cairo a series of letters from his father, to much the same effect as his mother's. Queensberry interpolated into his complaints about Bosie's life lamentations about the misery and loneliness of his own. Douglas read both without sympathy, and answered with growing impertinence. What he wanted was a letter from Wilde, but none came. Those that he wrote to Wilde were read and torn up. But Douglas knew Wilde and his own power, and had pleasant diversions in Egypt.[10] If Lord Cromer had no post to offer him, he and Lady Cromer were hospitable. There was the good fortune, perhaps not wholly accidental, that a number of Douglas's friends had come to Egypt at the same time, and were going up the Nile. He joined them. He could hardly have hoped

---

* Wilde's only comment on the diminutive Johnson was, according to George Santayana, 'Every morning at 11 o'clock you can see him come out very drunk from the Café Royal and hail the first passing perambulator.'[9]

for better company outside of London than Robert Hichens and E. F. Benson, both novelists, and Reggie Turner and his half-brother, Frank Lawson. Lawson had a stronger claim on the family wealth than Reggie, who was illegitimate, but was generous with his brother. He had taken a gilded barge moored in the Nile, which Douglas visited often.

Turner had met Max Beerbohm at Oxford, and they had formed a close and unending friendship. His father, one of the Lawsons who owned the *Daily Chronicle*, was Jewish, and Turner seems always to have been considered so too, though his mother was probably not. He was an easy and frequent subject for Max's caricature, being large-nosed and small-headed, with eyelids that blinked accidentally as well as deliberately. He was also excellent company, given to mimicry of sermons and the repartee that Wilde favored.* Beerbohm thought he detected latent tendencies in Turner towards heterosexuality, which he was eager to encourage, and warned off Ross from proselytizing for homosexuality. But such efforts were ineffective. Wilde would christen Turner 'the boy-snatcher of Clement's Inn.'

Hichens, Benson, Lawson and Turner all knew *Dorian Gray* almost by heart and vied with each other in quoting bits of it now, as they floated up the Nile to Luxor. Whether letters arrived from Wilde or not, he could not help being an unseen companion on their trip, constantly invoked in quotation and anecdote. Hichens listened attentively, and made notes for *The Green Carnation*, in which Wilde occupied literally, as Mr Amarinth, the place he had occupied only in their talk on their voyage.

When Wilde continued to leave Douglas's letters unanswered, the young man resorted to desperate stratagems. He used his wiles to cajole his mother herself, unwilling as she was, to urge Wilde to write to him. Wilde was astonished to receive a letter from her enclosing Bosie's address in Athens, where he had gone on the invitation of Benson, who was doing some archaeological work. He still did not write to Bosie, but he did urge Lady Queensberry to keep her son away from England at all costs. In fact the Cromers had arranged for Douglas to go to Constantinople as honorary attaché to Lord Currie, the British Ambassador. But his mother's plans went awry because Douglas seems to have taken the appointment very lightly, and not only visited Athens but determined to see Wilde again in Paris before he went among the Turks. Because of the delay or because of his association with Wilde, Currie, tipped off perhaps by his aide Rennell Rodd, denied him the post.

---

* At the end of the century Turner began to write novels, feeble in their kind, about people of uncertain parentage who marry surprisingly well. Though Beerbohm loyally praised each book as he received it, they were dismally amateurish and gave only the most faded sense of Turner's pungent wit. He lived on, as Wilde had once predicted, to become the most entertaining member of the English set in Florence, and Beerbohm would celebrate him in an essay as Comus, ugly and talented.

Whether Douglas knew he had lost it before he departed for Paris in the hope of an assignation with Wilde is unclear. (His *Autobiography* is never reliable.)

In any case, Douglas played his last card, an unexpected trump, by writing to ask Constance Wilde to intercede for him. (It was the same procedure he had used in soliciting the help of Robert Ross to make peace between him and Wilde over the translation of *Salome*.) Though Mrs Wilde was like Ross a rival for Wilde's affections, she also could not resist Bosie's appeal. She did not want her husband to be unkind. Subjected to this incongruous pressure from his wife to make up with his lover, Wilde continued to dig in his heels. He sent Douglas a telegram in March 1894, 'Time heals every wound but for many months to come I will neither write to you nor see you.' This challenge fired Douglas's blood. He was off to Paris at once, a journey of six days and nights, his only stops en route being to send Wilde telegrams. When he reached his Paris hotel, there was only a letter saying Wilde would not come. Douglas sent off a telegram of ten or eleven pages (he denied it later), saying he had travelled arduously across Europe only in the hope of a meeting, and would not be responsible for his actions if Wilde continued to refuse him. Wilde was well aware that in the annals of the Queensberrys there had been an uncle of Douglas who committed suicide in 1891, and a grandfather who had probably done the same some years earlier. Against such blackmail he could not stand out. It brought him to Paris, and over dinner at Voisin's and supper at Paillard's Wilde allowed himself to be vanquished by beauty, tears, contrition, and caresses.[11] Although he did not know it, this was a last chance to break free. Losing it, he saw his life move – almost independently of him – towards climax.

Douglas Returned

Children begin by loving their parents. After a time they judge them. Rarely, if ever, do they forgive them.

On their second day back in London, 1 April 1894, Wilde and Douglas were lunching at the Café Royal when the Marquess of Queensberry caught sight of them. He regarded their lunching together as an open defiance of him, a sign that his son had lapsed back into the old vile habits. They invited him to their table, however, and he was momentarily overborne by Wilde's charm. 'I don't wonder you are so fond of him,' he said to Douglas, 'he is a wonderful man.' Then, returning home, he had second thoughts. Taking his paternal duties seriously, he wrote a long letter to his son the same afternoon:

1 April 1894

Alfred, – It is extremely painful for me to have to write to you in the strain I must, but please understand that I decline to receive any answers from you in writing in return. After your recent hysterical impertinent ones I refuse to be annoyed with such, and I decline to read any more letters. If you have anything to say do come here and say it in person. Firstly, am I to understand that, having left Oxford as you did, with discredit to yourself, the reasons of which were fully explained to me by your tutor, you now intend to loaf and loll about and do nothing? All the time you were wasting at Oxford I was put off with an assurance that you were eventually to go into the Civil Service or to the Foreign Office, and then I was put off with an assurance that you were going to the Bar. It appears to me that you intend to do nothing. I utterly decline, however, to just supply you with sufficient funds to enable you to loaf about. You are preparing a wretched future for yourself, and it would be most cruel and wrong for me to encourage you in this. Secondly, I come to the more painful part of this letter – your intimacy with this man Wilde. It must either cease or I will disown you and stop all money supplies. I am not going to try and analyse this intimacy, and I make no charge; but to my mind to pose as a thing is as bad as to be it. With my own eyes I saw you both in the most loathsome and disgusting relationship as expressed by your manner and expression. Never in my experience have I ever seen such a sight as that in your horrible features. No wonder people are talking as they are. Also I now hear on good authority, but this may be false, that his wife is petitioning to divorce him for sodomy and other crimes. Is this true, or do you not know of it? If I thought the actual thing was true, and it became public property, I should be quite justified in shooting him at sight. These christian English cowards and men, as they call themselves, want waking up.

        Your disgusted so-called father,

QUEENSBERRY

Douglas's reaction to even mild criticism was ferocious. He had mentioned in a letter to his mother how once, when he had replied to some of her recriminations by a savage letter, he showed it to Wilde, who had torn it up with the words, 'After all, nobody has a right to be unkind to his mother.' But he did not give Wilde a chance to see the telegram which he sent off to his father on 2 April: 'WHAT A FUNNY LITTLE MAN YOU ARE.'[12] Queensberry was in fact an inch shorter than Douglas, being five feet eight inches. He matched his son in *amour propre* and ferocity. When Wilde heard about the telegram, he was dismayed. As he said later, but probably forbore to say at the time, 'it was a telegram of which the commonest street-boy would have been ashamed.'[13] Bosie could not stop doing things Wilde thought unworthy of him. Queensberry's reply on 3 April was vehement, but even in his rage he somewhat mollified his threat to cut Bosie off entirely. Still, it was hardly a letter to bring about better relations:

You impertinent young jackanapes. I request that you will not send such messages to me by telegraph. If you send me any more such telegrams, or come with any impertinence, I will give you the thrashing you deserve. Your only excuse is that you must be crazy. I hear from a man at Oxford that you were thought crazy there, and that accounts for a good deal that has happened. If I catch you again with that man I will make a public scandal in a way you little dream of; it is already a suppressed one. I prefer an open one, and at any rate I shall not be blamed for allowing such a state of things to go on. Unless this acquaintance ceases I shall carry out my threat and stop all supplies, and if you are not going to make any attempt to do something I shall certainly cut you down to a mere pittance, so you know what to expect.[14]

It was perhaps now that Wilde protested that he could not be a catspaw between father and son.[15] Douglas insisted that he had nothing to do with the quarrel, but seems to have thought it advisable nonetheless to take a month's trip to Florence, arranging for Wilde to follow him there, but surreptitiously. Wilde left for Paris on 27 April and stayed till 6 May before going on to Florence. His attempt to keep his presence in Florence a secret was perhaps doomed to fail, since his height and dress and theatrical nature made him conspicuous wherever he went.* One person known to have recognized them was André Gide, who met them in a café, and felt at first unwelcome. He was queasy about being seen with them. The relationship of Wilde and Douglas was notorious, and, in letters to Paul Valéry, Gide at first did not mention the encounter at all, and only after some weeks allowed that he had run into Wilde, accompanied by '*un autre poète d'une génération plus nouvelle*,' as if Douglas's name would give too much away. If Wilde was disconcerted, he recovered quickly; he offered Gide two drinks, four stories, and their flat, which they had hired for a month but used only for two weeks. Gide agreed, then decided to leave it for a *pensione*.[17]

Wilde had probably run out of money, and had to return early in June to London, probably to borrow. He had also decided to consult a solicitor, and did so in late May. Unfortunately, as he probably heard, George Lewis's services had been pre-empted by Queensberry, so he accepted a suggestion that came from Robert Ross and went to see another solicitor named C. O. Humphreys, a choice that turned out to be a bad one, since homosexuality was quite outside Humphreys' field of knowledge. What advice Wilde got from Humphreys on this occasion is unrecorded, but for the moment he did not try to bind the Marquess over to keep the peace. As for the Marquess, he had seen and heard enough, and made an

---

* Wilde seems to have gone alone, at the invitation of Mary Smith Costelloe, to visit the brother of the novelist Vernon Lee on 19 May: 'It was a great success. Oscar talked like an angel, and they all fell in love with him, even Vernon Lee, who had hated him almost as much as he had hated her. He, for his part, was charmed with her.'[16]

unannounced visit to Wilde in Tite Street on 30 June. The confrontation was described twice by Wilde, and once by Queensberry, who said in a letter that Wilde had shown him the white feather. The version Wilde gave was quite different. He said he denied all charges and made Queensberry leave the house. This was not quite the whole story. In *De Profundis* Wilde described the scene with more anguish: 'in my library at Tite Street, waving his small hands in the air in epileptic fury, your father, with his bully, or his friend, between us, had stood uttering every foul word his foul mind could think of, and screaming the loathsome threats he afterwards with such cunning carried out.'

Wilde evidently more or less outfaced the Marquess on this occasion, though it does not seem possible that he, as he later said, 'drove him out'; he quailed at the thought of such a scene being played in public. Chance appears to have protected him, for, as he said in *De Profundis*, 'He [went] from restaurant to restaurant looking for me, in order to insult me before the whole world, and in such a manner that if I retaliated I would be ruined, and if I did not retaliate I would be ruined also.' Douglas continued to taunt his father, claiming to be altogether unmoved by the threats which had obviously shaken Wilde. He wrote in early June 1894:

As you return my letters unopened I am obliged to write on a postcard. I write to inform you that I treat your absurd threats with absolute indifference. Ever since your exhibition at O.W.'s house, I have made a point of appearing with him at many public restaurants such as The Berkeley, Willis's Rooms, the Café Royal, etc., and I shall continue to go to any of these places whenever I choose and with whom I choose. I am of age and my own master. You have disowned me at least a dozen times, and have meanly deprived me of money. You have therefore no right over me, either legal or moral. If O.W. was to prosecute you in the Central Criminal Court for libel, you would get seven years' penal servitude for your outrageous libels. Much as I detest you, I am anxious to avoid this for the sake of the family; but if you try to assault me, I shall defend myself with a loaded revolver, which I always carry; and if I shoot you or he shoots you, we shall be completely justified, as we shall be acting in self-defence against a violent and dangerous rough, and I think if you were dead not many people would miss you. A.D.[18]

The 'ridiculous pistol' that Douglas carried went off in The Berkeley later, according to Wilde, and created further scandal. There was no doubt that Frank Harris was right in warning Wilde about this time that he was putting himself between the bark and the tree.[19] He had become the instrument of Douglas's ancient battle with his father. The dangerous quarrel somehow exhilarated Douglas. In cruel summary Wilde said later, 'The prospect of a battle in which you would be safe delighted you. I never remember you in higher spirits than you were for the rest of that season.

Your only disappointment seemed to be that nothing actually happened, and that no further meeting or fracas had taken place between us.' Although it has often been said that Wilde aspired to misfortune, he had no such conscious aim. As for Douglas, he demanded misfortune as the final token of Wilde's love.

Wilde's increasing anxiety is plain. At the beginning of July he approached George Lewis (now Sir George), perhaps within a few days of Queensberry's visit to Tite Street. Lewis's answer was polite but distant, considering how long and intimately Wilde had known him and his family.

7 July 1894

Dear Mr Wilde,
  I am in receipt of your note. The information that you have received that I am acting for Lord Queensberry is perfectly correct, and under these circumstances you will see at once that it is impossible for me to offer any opinion about any proceedings you intend to take against him.
  Although I cannot act against him, I should not act against you.
  Believe me

Yours faithfully
GEORGE M. LEWIS

Wilde now went again to Humphreys, who wrote to Queensberry asking him to retract his libels or risk litigation. The Marquess replied that he had nothing to retract, having made no direct accusation against Wilde, but that he wanted the association with his son to end. There the matter was allowed to rest for the moment.

Fortunately it was almost midsummer, and time for all concerned to leave London. Wilde had not deserted literature completely. During the summer he published *The Sphinx* with Lane and Mathews, with Ricketts's elaborate cover. The edition was limited to 250 copies. 'My first idea,' said Wilde, 'was to print only three copies: one for myself, one for the British Museum, and one for Heaven. I had some doubts about the British Museum.' He took care that the press got some, and the reviews were mostly favorable. From August to October Wilde was with his family in Worthing, determined to write *The Importance of Being Earnest*, on which he had already been paid an advance. There were many interruptions. The house at Worthing was small, the Wilde children were there with Constance and a Swiss governess. Douglas's brother Percy visited for a time, as did Douglas himself. He wrote to Robert Ross afterwards, 'I had great fun, though the last few days the strain of being a bone of contention between Oscar and Mrs Oscar began to make itself felt.'[20] As Wilde wrote to Douglas in *De Profundis*, 'Our friendship had always been a source of distress to her, not merely because she had never liked you personally, but because she saw how your continued friendship altered me, and not for the better.'

Anguishing Capers

*One should never take sides in anything. Taking sides is the
beginning of sincerity and earnestness follows shortly afterwards, and the human being becomes a bore.*

None of Wilde's plays cost him less effort than the best of them. *The
Importance of Being Earnest* flowed from his pen. According to Ricketts, the
plot was originally more complicated, involving double identity and placed
in the time of Sheridan. He changed his mind, and said later, 'There is no
use adding "place" and "time" to the scenario, as the unities are not in the
scheme. In art I am Platonic, not Aristotelian, tho' I wear my Plato with a
difference.'[21] It gathered together various themes that Wilde had been
developing since 1889. The title went back to the subtitle of his dialogue,
'The Critic as Artist,' which was, 'With Some Remarks on the Importance
of Doing Absolutely Nothing.' The assumed languor of Algernon and
Jack was the well-established posture of aestheticism since Schlegel's
Lucinde, where it is said, with a touch of Wilde's self-mockery, 'Laziness is
the one divine fragment of a godlike existence left to man from Paradise.'

In 'The Soul of Man under Socialism,' Wilde had repudiated marriage,
the family, and private property; in his play he repudiated them by
pretending they are ineradicable, urging their enforcement with a mad
insistence which shows how preposterous they are. In certain essays
Wilde made art into a kind of new ethics, replacing worn-out conventions
with new generosity, freedom, and individuality. This view of art as social
instrument co-existed with its own cancellation. *Salome* dwelt upon incest
and necrophilia, and displayed them as self-defeated, punished by execution and remorse. But with the critical intellect he could dissolve notions
of sin and guilt. He does so in *The Importance of Being Earnest*, all
insouciance where *Salome* is all incrimination. The philosophy of the last
play, he told Robert Ross, is 'That we should treat all trivial things very
seriously, and all the serious things of life with sincere and studied
triviality.'[22] In *The Importance* sins accursed in *Salome* and unnamable in
Dorian Gray are transposed into a different key and appear as Algernon's
inordinate and selfish craving for – cucumber sandwiches. The substitution of mild gluttony for fearsome lechery renders all vice innocuous.
There *is* a wicked brother, but he is just our old friend Algernon. The
double life which is so serious a matter for Dorian or for the *Ideal Husband*,
becomes Bunburying – playing Jack in the country and Ernest in town,
and only to avoid boring engagements. In the earlier, four-act version of
the play, Wilde even parodied punishment, by having a solicitor come to
take Algernon to Holloway Prison (as Wilde himself was soon to be taken)
not for homosexuality, but for running up food bills at the Savoy. 'I am not
going to be imprisoned in the suburbs for dining in the West End. It is
ridiculous,' Algernon replies. Elsewhere, the notion of expiation is

mocked; as Cecily observes, 'They have been eating muffins. That looks like repentance.' The theme of regeneration, not to mention religious zeal, is parodied in the efforts of Ernest and Jack to be rebaptized. (In the earlier version, when Prism too is about to be baptized, someone comments, 'To be born again would be of considerable advantage to her.') The ceremonial unmasking at the play's end, which had meant death for Dorian Gray, leaves everyone barefaced for a new puppet show, matrimony. Yet amusing as the surface is, the comic energy springs from the realities that are mocked.*

The Importance of Being Earnest constructs its wonderful parapet over the abyss of the author's disquietude and apprehension. By a desperate stratagem Wilde keeps the melancholy of the world at a distance. Deception is everywhere, cancelled by spontaneity and humor. Erotic passions compete with family ambition, innocence longs for experience, and experience for innocence. Tears are taboo. Wilde masked his cares with the play's insouciance, by a miracle of control. A friend said it should be like a piece of mosaic. 'No,' said Wilde, 'it must go like a pistol shot.'[24]

Kind Friends

Anybody can sympathise with the sufferings of a friend, but it requires a very fine nature to sympathise with a friend's success.

Beerbohm's life often converged with Wilde's at this time. He rejoiced in *Dorian Gray* as a mock-sacred book, to be set for examinations; during 'Hedony [from hedonist] Term 1894' he drew up a model for these, with such questions as: 'Is there any internal evidence to show that the custom of cigarette-smoking obtained in the period with which the story deals?' Another of his procedures was less innocent. He had become friendly with Robert Hichens, and early in the summer of 1894 Hichens showed him the manuscript of *The Green Carnation*. Neither he nor Hichens

---

* Many of the play's details had a real origin. In the original version, the solicitor who comes to take Algernon to Holloway Prison is from the firm Parker and Grigsby. Parker's name came from the Parker brothers, two of Wilde's young men, while Grigsby harked back to a character in du Maurier's aesthetic caricatures in *Punch*. Another such element was the naming of the two butlers: one was to be Lane and the other Mathews, to immortalize Wilde's displeasure with those publishers. (He expressed it also when asked what Beardsley's drawing for the cover of the *Yellow Book* was like: 'Oh, you can imagine the sort of thing. A terrible naked harlot smiling through a mask – and with ELKIN MATHEWS written on one breast and JOHN LANE on the other.'[23]) But he magnanimously changed Mathews to Merriman.

understood how dangerous the book would be for Wilde, but Beerbohm could not have been totally unaware of the risks, for in a letter to Turner of 12 August 1894 he pretends there has been a brush with the law: 'Oscar has at length been arrested for certain kinds of crime. He was taken in the Café Royal (lower room). Bosie escaped, being an excellent runner, but Oscar was less nimble.' These fancies were uncomfortably close to life: Beerbohm may have awaited with unconscious excitement the removal of the master from the London scene. At any rate, he wrote still more cruelly in April–May 1895 to Mrs Leverson, 'I look forward eagerly to the first act of Oscar's new Tragedy. But surely the title *Douglas* must have been used before.'

The Green Carnation was published in September 1894. It pretended to be a parody, but was more like a documentary. Its fictional veneer is thin and there could be no doubt of the identities of Lord Reggie and Mr Amarinth. The moral of the book – and like *Dorian Gray* it has too much moral – is Lord Reggie's slavish imitation of Amarinth's conversational leads. In the process he ceases to be himself or anyone at all. The book bore out the Queensberry version of the relationship. (Douglas's life-time work was to consist of telling and retelling his life with Wilde.) What Hichens saw, not unlike what Queensberry saw, was that Wilde was taking Bosie over, swallowing him up as in some of Beerbohm's caricatures.

The book's main burden of imitation was in the stance taken towards experience. Solemnity was something for other people, triviality was its antidote. Wilde said later that he had made literature out of brilliant triviality, but it was triviality of a special kind, subversive of established modes. Such a remark as 'I can resist anything but temptation' is as destructive of hypocrisy as St Augustine's recollection of his youthful prayer, 'Make me a good man, but not yet.' But the pointedness of such remarks might quickly be lost in impercipient wordplay. Hichens appears for example to be reproducing Douglas's actual remark – or a comparable one – about having laughed at a relative's funeral, when Lord Reggie says 'I forced my grief beyond tears, and then my relations said that I was heartless!' Or he says 'We always return to our first hates.' It is all a languid patina spread over appetites which are energetic enough, as Hichens demonstrates by showing Lord Reggie chasing a boy.

At first Wilde and Douglas were amused. (Queensberry, who read it, was not.) 'Hichens I did not think capable of anything so clever,' Wilde wrote to Ada Leverson, perhaps suspecting Beerbohm's assistance. 'The doubting disciple [Hichens] who has written the false gospel is one who has merely talent unrelieved by any flashes of physical beauty.'[25] He telegraphed Hichens that the secret was out, and Douglas sent another comically warning Hichens to flee the vengeance to come. What added to the irritation which Wilde began to feel over the book was the rumor that

he himself had written it. He felt it necessary to write to the editor of the
Pall Mall Gazette on 1 October:

> Sir, Kindly allow me to contradict, in the most emphatic manner, the
> suggestion, made in your issue of Thursday last, and since then copied into
> many other newspapers, that I am the author of *The Green Carnation*.
>   I invented that magnificent flower. But with the middle-class and
> mediocre book that usurps its strangely beautiful name I have, I need
> hardly say, nothing whatsoever to do. The flower is a work of art. The book
> is not.

The book made its small but noticeable contribution to the growing
disfavor Wilde was encountering. That it was written by a homosexual
added savor and the hint of authenticity. Wilde received as little consideration from Hichens as from Raffalovich, for that matter, although they
shared his proclivities. Hichens parodied the green carnation, Raffalovich
wrote a sonnet against it.

One other major change took place in the summer of 1894. Constance
Wilde, like her husband, had long been friendly with the manager of
Hatchard's bookstore, Arthur L. Humphreys. They talked of making a
small volume of Wilde's aphorisms, chosen by Constance (though Wilde
would thoroughly revise it).* A separate publication of 'The Soul of Man
under Socialism' was also arranged. But in 1894 Constance Wilde wrote
Humphreys two letters which suggest that she had taken on a more than
editorial role. The first, dated 1 June, testifies to an intense admiration for
Humphreys such as she had once owned for her husband. 'I stepped past
the limits perhaps of good taste in the wish to be your friend and to have
you for my friend.' She had spoken openly about her unhappy childhood
and felt apologetic in retrospect. Humphreys in return had spoken of his
marriage; she calls him 'an ideal husband,' a phrase that took on a special
meaning in her husband's play. The second letter is dated more than two
months later, 11 August 1894, and has a different tone. The first began,
'Dear Mr Humphreys,' the second, 'My darling Arthur.' She thanks him
for having made her so happy that day and for giving her his love. She is
pleased that he is so kind to both her children and to Oscar.[26] Constance
was clearly in love. She may have had a brief affair with Humphreys, but
she was away for much of the time in late summer and autumn, and early
the next year she spoke of having an operation on her back, made
necessary by a fall on the stairs at Tite Street. Her pleasure in the
attachment could only have been brief.

---

* A contract was signed on 14 August by Humphreys and Wilde, with Douglas as
witness. The book, *Oscariana*, was privately printed in January 1895, but not
published until 1910.

Queensberry *Furens*

Put out the torches. Hide the moon!
Hide the stars!

During the summer Queensberry was off in the wings, but he was prepared to upstage Wilde with even grander gestures of paternal love. *The Green Carnation* had upset him in September, and then two things happened in October to drive him frantic. One was at least expected, the final decree of nullity of his second marriage on 20 October 1894. The other was not: the death two days earlier of his eldest son, Drumlanrig, heir to the title, and the only one of his four sons for whom, in spite of quarrels, he had any respect. The newspapers reported a shooting accident, but suicide was generally suspected. Drumlanrig may have been afraid of blackmail over his relations with Lord Rosebery, of which his father had long been suspicious, and (unlike his brother) feared he would bring down the Foreign Minister as well as himself. Queensberry, writing to his first wife's father, Alfred Montgomery, was full of new suspicions:

November 1st 1894

Queensberry Estate Office

Comloncon Castle,
Ruthwell, N. B.

Sir

Now that the first flush of this catastrophe and grief is passed, I write to tell you that it is a *judgement* on the whole *lot of you.* Montgomerys, The Snob Queers like Roseberry & certainly Christian hypocrite Gladstone the whole lot *of you* / Set my son up against me indeed and make bad blood *between* us, may it devil on your own heads that he has gone to his *rest* and the quarrel not made up between him and myself. It's a gruesome message: If you and his Mother did not set up this business with that cur and Jew friend [?] *Liar* Rosebery as I always thought –

At any rate she [Lady Queensberry] acquiesced in it, which is just *as bad.* What fools you all look, trying to ride me out of the course and trim *the sails* and the poor Boy comes to this untimely end. I smell a Tragedy behind all this and have already *got Wind* of a more *startling one.* If it was what I am led *to believe*, I of all people could and would have helped him, had he come to me with a confidence, but that was all stopped by you people – we had not met or spoken frankly for more than a year and a half. I am on the right track to find out what happened. *Cherchez la femme*, when these things happen. I have already heard something that quite accounts *for it all*

QUEENSBERRY[27]

The conviction that one son had died in a homosexual scandal resolved Queensberry to make sure that a second did not die the same way. He was not certain how best to get at Wilde, but settled on a public demonstration at the first performance of *The Importance of Being Earnest*, scheduled provocatively enough for 14 February 1895.

Wilde again felt the discomfort of loving Bosie. Not only had he become an easy target for satire, but he was subjected to Bosie's caprices. Douglas had disliked the house in Worthing, and got Wilde to take him in October to the Grand Hotel at Brighton. In Brighton he caught influenza and had to be put to bed. All Wilde's solicitude was aroused, and he performed the functions of friend, reader, and nurse with the greatest patience. After four or five days Douglas recovered, and they moved into lodgings so Wilde could write some parts of his play. Then it was Wilde's turn to fall ill. Bosie had no intention of playing the nurse's part. Wilde was left unattended, could not get up even for water, and was subjected in the middle of the night to one of Douglas's more fiendish displays of temper. In the morning he repeated the scene, so threateningly that Wilde felt in physical danger and dragged himself down the stairs so that he could call for help if necessary. Douglas packed his bags and left for the Grand Hotel. On 16 October 1894, Wilde's fortieth birthday, a letter came from Douglas gloating over having charged all his hotel expenses to Wilde, and congratulating him on having had the prudence to go downstairs: 'It was an ugly moment for you, uglier than you imagine.' The letter concluded, 'When you are not on your pedestal you are not interesting. The next time you are ill I will go away at once.' These sentences Wilde was never able to forget.[28]

He was well enough to return to London on Friday, 19 October, and intended to ask Sir George Lewis to inform Queensberry that he would never under any circumstances see Douglas again. But as he looked at the morning paper before taking the train from Brighton, he saw the announcement of Drumlanrig's death. With one of those whirlarounds so valuable in his work, and so destructive in his life, he suddenly felt for Douglas nothing but 'infinite pity,' and telegraphed him to say so. The old dance began again.

There was another imprudence late in 1894. The attempt to win acquiescence at Oxford for homosexuality, begun by Douglas in the *Spirit Lamp*, was continued in a new magazine started by an undergraduate named Jack Bloxam. (His last name is used in *The Importance of Being Earnest*.) Being acquainted with George Ives, he went to London to talk over the idea with him. Ives proposed calling it the *Chameleon*, envisaging protective coloration. Bloxam was introduced to Wilde in Ives's room, E4 Albany. (Albany also appears in *The Importance*.) Wilde found him an 'undergraduate of strange beauty,' and promised him 'Phrases and Philosophies for the Use of the Young,' a collection of epigrams that began with 'The first duty in life is to be as artificial as possible. What the second duty is no one has as yet discovered.' Bloxam showed Wilde and Ives his story, 'The Priest and the Acolyte,' in which a priest, caught with a boy, poisons the wine in the chalice before administering the sacrament to his young communicant and himself. Wilde amused Ada Leverson by commenting only, 'The story is, to my ears, too direct: there is no nuance: it profanes a little by revelation: God and other artists are always a little obscure. Still, it has interesting qualities, and is at moments poisonous: which is something.'[29]

Ives, on the other hand, took alarm. He was still recovering from the one daring action of his life – an article in the October 1894 *Humanitarian* taking issue with Grant Allen's condemnation of homosexuality in the March *Fortnightly*. On that occasion Wilde had urged against publication 'at the outset of your career.' But now Wilde was encouraging Bloxam to publish 'The Priest and the Acolyte,' which Ives thought degraded homosexual love when it ought to have ennobled it. To his protests Wilde replied, 'You set off a bomb, and object to a cracker.'[30] But Ives was right. The *Chameleon*, which appeared only once, in December 1894, attracted adverse comment in *To-Day* on 29 December from Jerome K. Jerome, whose novel *Three Men in a Boat* Wilde had once described as 'funny without being vulgar.' *To-Day* recommended police action. More important, the *Chameleon* fell into the hands of Queensberry, who assumed that the unsigned story was by Wilde, and was still more inflamed.

In late December *An Ideal Husband* went into rehearsal, and Wilde insisted upon the cast's meeting even on Christmas day. This was too much for Charles Brookfield, who, not wanting to learn many of Wilde's lines, had consented to take the smallest part in the play, that of Lord Goring's servant, and felt particularly abused to have to give up his holiday to it. 'Don't you keep Christmas, Oscar?' he asked. 'No, Brookfield,' replied Wilde, 'the only festival of the Church I keep is Septuagesima. Do you keep Septuagesima, Brookfield?' 'Not since I was a boy.' 'Ah, be a boy again,' said Wilde.[31]

The play opened on 3 January 1895 to an audience that included the Prince of Wales, Balfour, Chamberlain, and many government ministers. Their applause called for the author, but Tree said Wilde had left the theatre. Afterwards Wilde, Beerbohm, Tree, and Douglas had dinner at the Albemarle Club.

Among the reviews Bernard Shaw's in the *Saturday Review* was the most discerning. He remarked, 'I am the only person in London who cannot sit down and write an Oscar Wilde play at will.' He particularly welcomed what he called 'the modern note' in 'Sir Robert Chiltern's assertion of the individuality and courage of his wrongdoing as against the mechanical idealism of his stupidly good wife, and in his bitter criticism of a love that is only the reward of merit.' He would deal with the same theme himself in *Major Barbara*.

Full of this success, Wilde wanted to help in George Alexander's rehearsals of *The Importance*, and begged Douglas to let him stay in London, 'but,' as Wilde wrote drily to Ada Leverson, 'so beautiful is his nature that he declined at once.'* Instead Wilde took a trip he had long had in mind, and which had been promised him by a London clairvoyante. On 17 January 1895 he and Douglas went off to Algeria, as the *Theatre* (1 March) reported; Wilde stayed in Algiers and Blidah until 3 February. A letter to Ross says, 'The beggars here have profiles, so the problem of poverty is easily solved.'[33] They sampled also the delights of hashish.

A partial record of the visit is in André Gide's autobiography, *Si le grain ne meurt* . . . Gide arrived in Blidah, a town thirty miles from Algiers much frequented by Englishmen in search of boys. He was about to sign the register when to his consternation he saw the names of Wilde and Douglas already on it. The memory of their uncomfortable meeting in Florence was only seven months old, and to be at the same hotel seemed to him too compromising. His own homosexual life had begun, but surreptitiously. He took his bags and started to go back to the station, only to decide that he was behaving ridiculously. He went back, registered, and soon after met with Wilde and Douglas.

When Gide expressed astonishment at Wilde's being there, Wilde said, 'I am running away from art. I want to worship only the sun. Have you noticed how the sun despises all thought, makes it retreat, take refuge in the shadows. Once thought lived in Egypt; the sun conquered Egypt. It lived for long in Greece; the sun conquered Greece. Then Italy, and then France. Today all thought is pushed back to Norway and Russia, where the sun never comes. The sun is jealous of art.' They spent the evening together, after which Wilde and Gide both returned to Algiers while Douglas, having once more quarreled fiercely with Wilde, took a boy off to Biskra for some weeks. In Algiers Wilde remarked 'I have a duty to myself to amuse myself frightfully.' Then he added, 'Not happiness. Above all not happiness. Pleasure! You must always aim at the most tragic.' He bore Gide off to a café, where the young man was captivated by an Arab boy playing the flute. Outside Wilde asked him, 'Dear, *vous voulez le petit musicien?*' Gide, 'in the most choked of voices,' said yes. Wilde burst into what Gide called 'satanic laughter' and made the arrangements. Gide felt he knew now what was normal for him.

They had several days in Algiers together. Wilde as he went through the streets was followed by a band of petty thieves. He talked with each, observed them with joy, and scattered money among them. 'I hope I have thoroughly demoralised this city,' he said. He confided that Queensberry was tormenting him. Gide warned him, 'But if you go back, what will happen? Do you realise the risk?' 'That one can never know. My friends advise me to be prudent. Prudent! How could I be that? It would mean

---

* In January 1895 Alexander was in difficulties with James's *Guy Domville*, and Wilde asked Charles Wyndham, with whom he had contracted for the production, to let Alexander have *The Importance* so he could realize on it at once. Wyndham had a success on at the time, so consented, but as soon as he did, his own play failed.[32]

going backward. I must go as far as possible. I cannot go any further. Something must happen ... something else ...' He had what Henry James calls 'the imagination of disaster.' Nothing less than total ruin would do. He left next day and stopped in Paris en route. There he called on Degas and said cheerily, 'You know how well known you are in England?' To which Degas replied, 'Fortunately less so than you.' He repeated to Wilde a comment he had made on the opening of a Liberty's shop in Paris, 'So much taste will lead to prison.'[34] Both remarks were ominous.

There were still a few more rehearsals for *The Importance of Being Earnest, A Trivial Comedy for Serious People.* By this time Alexander had persuaded Wilde to drop one of the four acts, in which Algernon is almost arrested for debt. Wilde came to a rehearsal and said, 'Yes, it is quite a good play. I remember I wrote one very like it myself, but it was even more brilliant than this.'[35] As the opening drew closer, Wilde heard by chance from a mutual acquaintance that Queensberry was planning a demonstration on the first night, and alerted Alexander, who cancelled Queensberry's ticket, and arranged for policemen to be present. The night of St Valentine's Day happened to be freezing cold. Wilde arrived, dressed, as Ada Leverson said, with 'florid sobriety,' green carnation and all. Everyone was there, except the Marquess of Queensberry and Douglas, still in Algiers. Everyone liked the play except Shaw, who thought it all froth and no pith. Thank God for froth.* The *New York Times*, not given to praising Wilde, announced next day, 'Oscar Wilde may be said to have at last, and by a single stroke, put his enemies under his feet.'

All his enemies except one. In concealed desperation and panic, Wilde set the stage for the next act, in which evil would masquerade as fatherly feeling and social orderliness, and good make do with the humiliating guise of the criminal. Wilde had always held that the true 'beasts' were not those who expressed their desires, but those who tried to suppress other people's. The society whose hypocrisies he had anatomized now turned them against him. Victorianism was ready to pounce.

---

* A list of names in the military directory at the end of the play includes one Maxbohm, a private joke with Beerbohm. Max proclaimed the play a masterpiece. In his copy, inscribed to him by Wilde, he had a note next to the beginning of Act I: 'What an admirable opening! You are instantly held – and prepared. *Cf. Hamlet!* – and plays by born men of the theatre.' The Prism scene in the last act he thought 'one of the funniest scenes ever written.' His copy contained two restorations based upon his memory of the first performance, which Wilde had forgotten: at the end of Act I, Jack says, 'Oh, that's nonsense, Algy, you never talk anything but nonsense,' to which Algernon replies, 'Nobody ever does.' Beerbohm says the speech should go on, 'And besides, I *love* nonsense.' He also corrected Miss Prism's words to Cecily in Act II: 'The chapter on the Fall of the Rupee you may omit. It is somewhat too sensational. Even these metallic problems have their melodramatic side.' Beerbohm preferred to this last sentence what he remembered from the original, 'It is somewhat too unconventional for a young girl.'[36]

DISGRACE

CHAPTER XVII

'I Am the Prosecutor in This Case'

It often happens that the real tragedies of life occur in such an inarticulate manner that they hurt one by their crude violence, their absolute incoherence, their absurd want of meaning, their entire lack of style.

Mounting Pressure

'All trials are trials for one's life,' Wilde would declare after his trials were over and his destruction by them was complete.[1] Still, it was a paradox after his own manner that the first trial should not be his own but the one he forced upon Queensberry, whose life was in no such jeopardy. John Sholto Douglas, the ninth Marquess, was a very rich man. He could have lost a dozen libel cases without flinching, and no doubt would have persisted in hounding Wilde whatever happened in court. This was so plain that Wilde's litigiousness gave proof of a distraught mind rather than an indignant one. The trial ended the two years of provocation. From Queensberry's point of view, of course, he was the victim not the aggressor. Wilde and Douglas had tauntingly continued to appear with each other in spite of his repeated threats to go to Scotland Yard. From Wilde's point of view, it was intolerable that a boor and bully should dictate his conduct. Moreover, his life with Douglas, including the publicity of their romantic passion, reflected his intention to oblige a hypocritical age to take him as he was.

Verbal abuse was something to which Wilde was accustomed, and few of the attacks he had suffered during his forty years had drawn blood. He had weathered the mockery of the American and British press over his aesthetic renaissance. Once Whistler had accused him of the purely literary crime of plagiarism, but he had outlived the charge and vindicated himself as an original genius. Much of the gossip about his homosexual tendencies had disappeared with his marriage, but, courting disfavor as he was prone to do, he had roused more gossip by *The Picture of Dorian Gray* and 'The Portrait of Mr W.H.' Even Lillie Langtry talked against him at this time. There had been literary attacks upon him in 1881, from *The*

409

Colonel and *Patience*; 1892, from *The Poet and the Puppets*; and 1894, from *The Green Carnation*. If he was accused of being precious, plumed and effeminate, he had checked his accusers by intellect and grace. After all, even Queensberry had submitted for an hour or two to his charm.

Wilde seems to have overlooked his vulnerability. He was confident of the devotion of his many friends in the political and literary world. With some of them he did not trouble to be circumspect. So he said to the actress Aimée Lowther, 'Aimée, if you were only a boy I could adore you.' Ellen Terry said innocently, 'Oscar, you really didn't mean it?' An embarrassed silence fell, and Henry Irving had to explain to her later.[2] His attitude to sexual transactions was the conventional one of his class. He did not think of his behavior with boys as of any consequence. Except for Shelley, they were prostitutes, to be bought or sold. The boys knew Wilde had treated them well, but tried to make him treat them better still. As for Douglas, Wilde had a right to feel virtuous rather than not. Having long since given up sexual relations with him, he might think of their attachment as an approximation of the Greek ideal. Wilde had made some effort to check Douglas's excesses, and had rescued him from a number of scrapes. If anyone had ruined Bosie, in Wilde's view, it was his parents. Queensberry had treated Bosie even in infancy with contempt for his physical weakness, and Lady Queensberry, in reaction to the paternal bullying, had spoiled him. Queensberry was unruly though he loved rules.

That Wilde anticipated the result of his actions is unlikely, though his sense of doom had been present since childhood. He believed in his unlucky star as much as in his lucky one. The exfoliation of his nature licensed recklessness and promoted foreboding. His first success, 'Ravenna,' had described a city fallen from greatness. That he might lose 'a soul's inheritance' is foreshadowed in his prefatory poem, 'Hélas!' Tragic themes had come to him earlier than comic ones. For a man who condemned sacrifice, his plays were full of it. Vera dies to save the Czar, Guido attempts to die to save the Duchess only to have her die as well. Mrs Erlynne sacrifices herself for her daughter as Mrs Arbuthnot has sacrificed herself for her son. The Happy Prince sacrifices himself to help the poor: sacrifice is close to suicide. In *Dorian Gray* both the hero and Sibyl Vane kill themselves, though Dorian does it with more ambiguity. Wilde needed less Greek than he had to know that overreaching would attract Nemesis.

His prosecution of Queensberry for criminal libel was the end not the beginning of a long series of legal maneuvers. He had consulted Humphreys about a prosecution in May 1894 and again in July. Queensberry had also taken advice. In the summer of 1894 some passionate letters of Wilde to his son fell into his hands, in particular the Hyacinth letter (either the original or a copy), and a letter of March 1893 which said, 'You are the divine thing I want, the thing of grace and beauty.' Wilde had bought back others, but not these. Queensberry's solicitor advised that the letters alone would not sustain a charge of sodomy against Wilde, so he had adopted the allegation that Wilde was a posing sodomite, which did not necessarily entail commission of the offense. His plea of privilege as a father could be invoked. If Queensberry was not a father in feeling, he was one in fact, and fully exploited this role. His blood was up and he was determined to make Wilde pay for what he appeared to be doing. He would protect his son from similar charges by his influence with the authorities. Queensberry's memories of the death of his son and heir, and of the nullification of his marriage, were still fresh. By bringing down an established reputation like Wilde's he could remake his own, as Prince Hal said he would do by conquering Hotspur.

Wilde and Douglas talked over the situation during the weeks that followed their separate returns from Algiers. Up to now they had told the other members of the family, including Bosie's brother Percy (Lord Douglas of Hawick), now the eldest son, that Queensberry was a victim of delusions. Wilde urged Douglas to tell his brother the truth, but Douglas, though reckless, was not brave, and refused. He proposed to go on just as in the past. By now Wilde was living entirely away from home. On 28 January Constance had to approach Ross to ask Wilde for some money for her when he came home from Algiers, as she was going to Torquay for a month. On 12 March she still did not know her husband's address. Three days later she thanked Ross for sending it. The reason for her ignorance of his whereabouts was that he was avoiding her.

During this time he took rooms at the Avondale Hotel in Piccadilly. Douglas came to stay with him, and ran up a lavish bill at once. Wilde was distinctly uneasy. Queensberry had been denied entrance to the opening night of *The Importance of Being Earnest*, and forced to content himself with leaving a bouquet of vegetables at the stage door instead of making the public denunciation which he had planned. Humphreys, consulted again, wrote on 28 February that he could do nothing because neither Alexander nor his staff would give evidence. When Douglas proposed to keep a young man in the hotel at Wilde's expense, Wilde refused. Douglas left the Avondale in a pet, and moved to another hotel with the friend. There followed a series of letters accusing Wilde of cowardice.

The Booby Trap

In your war of hate with your father I was at once shield and weapon to each of you.

The first of the letters came on Thursday morning, 28 February 1895, before Wilde set out for the Albemarle Club, not far from his hotel. The club was to prove no refuge from the father any more than the hotel had proved a refuge from the son. The hall porter, Sidney Wright, immediately handed him the card left by the Marquess of Queensberry ten days before. Wright had not deciphered the words – no one was to do so accurately – but he understood that an insult was intended, and had written on the back the details of its receipt, 4.30 on 18 February. Wilde probably made out the words as 'To Oscar Wilde, ponce and Somdomite.' He did not smile at Queensberry's aristocratic misspelling, but took it as a written and public repetition of the charge Queensberry had made in Tite Street. What Queensberry actually wrote was 'To Oscar Wilde posing Somdomite,' but in court he said that the words were 'posing as a Somdomite,' an easier accusation to defend.[3] What he had wanted, from leaving the card, was an interview. Wilde was goaded beyond that.

For Wilde the significance of the card was that Queensberry, having failed to invade his theatre, was invading his club. There was no hope of confining the matter to private correspondence, or to the knowledge of a small circle. Understandably Wilde felt sorry for himself, on receiving from the father a message as vitriolic as that he had received an hour earlier from the son. 'I felt I stood between Caliban and Sporus,' he wrote to Alfred Douglas later.[4] He went back to the hotel with the idea of bolting to Paris, as he had once before. But the manager, hearing of his intention, said that he must first pay his bill, and that until he did his luggage would be impounded. Wilde did not have the money, and felt trapped.

He was more vexed than despairing. Queensberry must be stopped from making these wanton attacks. He wrote to Douglas asking him to call early on Friday morning, but to Robert Ross he wrote more fully:

> Dearest Bobbie, Since I saw you something has happened. Bosie's father has left a card at my club with hideous words on it. I don't see anything now but a criminal prosecution. My whole life seems ruined by this man. The tower of ivory is assailed by the foul thing. On the sand is my life spilt. I don't know what to do. If you could come here at 11.30 please do so tonight. I mar your life by trespassing ever on your love and kindness. I have asked Bosie to come tomorrow.
>
> Ever yours
> OSCAR[5]

He wrote to George Lewis to ask his advice, but Lewis reminded him that he had already been engaged by Queensberry. Afterwards Lewis was to say that, if he had been free to advise Wilde, he would have told him to tear up Queensberry's card and forget about it.

When Ross came round that night, he urged Wilde to take no action, but when Wilde persisted suggested he consult Humphreys again. Wilde agreed, and in the morning took Douglas with him to the solicitor's chambers. Douglas was triumphant: his father had put down his charge in writing, and could now be prosecuted. Before his friend's eagerness

Wilde began to have doubts, but there was no resisting Douglas's fierceness. 'It is what we fear that happens to us,' he said. Humphreys displayed a combination of opportunism and naïveté. He scented a spectacular case, saw a celebrity eager to take on another celebrity in court, and urged prosecution. He cannot easily be absolved of blame, since he must have known that Ross, who had sent Wilde to him, was homosexual, and he had the evidence of great intimacy between Douglas and Wilde before him. He chose to suspect nothing, though he asked the routine questions and received decorous answers. As Wilde afterwards remarked, 'What is loathsome to me is the memory of interminable visits paid by me to the solicitor Humphreys in your company, when in the ghastly glare of a bleak room you and I would sit with serious faces telling serious lies to a bald man, till I really groaned and yawned with *ennui*.' Later he would dismiss Humphreys as one 'who would bluster, and threaten, and lie,' but the lying was not all on Humphreys' side. Ross offered to tell the truth to Humphreys and Lord Douglas of Hawick, who was sympathetic: Wilde and Douglas absolutely refused.[6] On the assumption of his client's innocence, Humphreys announced that a prosecution of Queensberry was bound to succeed. He was a hopeful man. By this time Wilde had lost his initial impetus, and played a last card which he expected to be decisive: he had no money. Bosie, determined to keep him up to the mark, announced that his brother Lord Douglas and Lady Queensberry would be delighted to pay costs. Goaded by the whole Queensberry clan, Wilde had no opportunity to withdraw. Humphreys and Douglas escorted him, a white flower in his buttonhole, to a four-wheeler, which took them to Marlborough Street police station on 1 March. He swore out a warrant for the arrest of Queensberry, which took place shortly afterwards. The Marquess was brought to Marlborough police court on the charge of publishing a libel against Wilde.

To some extent Wilde was the prey of his own consciousness as well as of Queensberry father and son. His inclination to betray himself, such as he attributed to mankind in general in 'Humanitad,' was not thorough-going. He thought of self-betrayal as proceeding in surges, after which there would be recoveries. The role of victim – Sebastian or Marsyas – was only one among several, including the dandy and the apostle of joy, through which he could see himself passing. In his flirtation with Catholicism, he spoke of going to see Newman 'to burn my fingers a little more.' He half invited obloquy, half lost his nerve in the process, meaning or almost meaning to pull back at the last. But the age in which he lived was unexpectedly eager (like most ages), and the right to choose left him before he had time to exercise it. So he emulated his father's disgrace – also over the implications of a libel suit, exceeded it even, and fulfilled his own half wish to kill the success he loved. It would be wrong to assume that this urge to destroy the beloved object, himself or another, came to him after his fall. In *The Ballad of Reading Gaol* the act of killing what we

413

love is made largely deliberate, as it is also in *Salome*, but in other works Wilde, like Lord Arthur Savile, blamed fate not will. We are by nature our own enemies, 'the lips betraying and the lips betrayed.' We seek the events that unconsciously befit us, which consciously we fear. Flaunting and fleeing, Wilde could not embrace a single course of action.

The Libel Suit

Blindly I staggered as an ox into the shambles.

The proceedings were launched. Humphreys appeared for Wilde, and Sir George Lewis made his first and only appearance for Queensberry, saying that the Marquess would plead justification. Wilde was asked, 'Are you a dramatist and an author?' He replied airily, 'I believe I am well known in that capacity.' 'Only answer the questions, please,' the magistrate admonished him. It was an untoward beginning. Queensberry, questioned by the magistrate as to whether he had anything to say, replied, 'I have simply, your worship, to say this. I wrote that card simply with the intention of bringing matters to a head, having been unable to meet Mr Wilde otherwise, and to save my son, and I abide by what I wrote.' On this he was committed for trial.

The case was adjourned for eight days. On 7 March Wilde, accompanied by his wife and Douglas, attended *The Importance of Being Earnest*. Mrs Wilde had tears in her eyes.[7]* At the hearing on 9 March, Lewis having kept his word and withdrawn from the case out of friendship for Wilde, a barrister appeared instead. This was Edward Carson, a fellow-student of Wilde's from Trinity College, Dublin, and a man of great forensic power.† Carson had been admitted to the English bar only a year before, but was beginning to be known. When Wilde learned that it would be Carson against him, he said at first, according to Carson's biographer, 'I'm going to be cross-examined by old Ned Carson,' as if he now had nothing to fear. But Travers Humphreys, who was C. O. Humphreys' son, remembered Wilde saying to him, 'No doubt he will perform his task with the added bitterness of an old friend.'[10] It was like Isaac Butt with Jane Wilde in the Mary Travers case years before. There is nothing like the courtroom to obliterate fellow-feeling.

* A letter from Constance Wilde to Marie Belloc Lowndes was written during this period: 'We should both be so pleased to come and meet your friend – Oscar sends his love – but as you may have seen in the papers we are very worried just now, and I do not find we can go out at present.'[8]

† Reggie Turner, himself a young barrister, advised Wilde to get Clarke and Carson to represent him as leaders, and Gill and Matthews as juniors. Carson and Gill being already retained by Queensberry, Wilde got Matthews, Clarke, and Travers Humphreys.[9]

Carson, to give him his due, had not entered the case at once. Queensberry's new solicitor, Charles Russell, invited him to accept the brief, but for a while Carson protested that Wilde was a fellow-Irishman from the same university. He had, however, offered another reason when one was enough, the second being that the case against Wilde was too weak. Russell took the hint and set himself to strengthen the case, meanwhile not approaching any other barrister. Help came from an unexpected quarter. Charles Brookfield and Charles Hawtrey, both of whom had profited from Wilde's career by acting in his plays and by writing their parody, *The Poet and the Puppets*, furnished information about his young friends. At the same time private detectives were looking about London, and one, a man named Littlejohn, happened to visit a shop in the West End which the police had under observation. A woman prostitute, asked how business was, said it was very bad because of competition for male clients from boys under the influence of Oscar Wilde. The detective asked eagerly for further information, and was told, 'All you have to do is break into the top flat at 13 Little College Street, and you will find all the evidence you require.' He went there, and pushed past the caretaker, an old woman, who tried to prevent his entry. He had come to the lodgings of Alfred Taylor. In the flat was a kind of post-box, containing the names and addresses of boys with whom Wilde consorted. On this information, he found William Allen and Robert Clibborn, who were hiding in Broadstairs, and soon Wood, Walter Grainger, Alfonso Harold Conway, and others. According to George Ives, these young men were sequestered in a house and terrified into giving evidence against Wilde.[11]

With this new information, and some other leads as well, Russell returned to Carson to ask him to take the brief. Carson deliberated: the details were revolting and abundant enough, and he could see himself triumphant. College loyalty faded before Protestant morality. As a final step he consulted Lord Hailsbury, the previous Lord Chancellor, who urged him to take the case. Finally he agreed. Wilde and Douglas were fairly confident, having no inkling of the new evidence that had been turned up. Douglas was even able to persuade Wilde to take him to Monte Carlo, where, though he said Wilde had cured him of gambling, he gave himself up to the gaming tables, while Wilde sat alone and disquieted. They were away from 13 March for a week or more. An article in the *Observer* said that they were expelled from their hotel in Monte Carlo at the request of other guests.[12] On their return they discussed the case with Humphreys, who advised them to find a reputable witness who would testify that *Dorian Gray* was not an immoral book. Wilde thereupon went, probably on Saturday 23 March, to see Frank Harris. Harris proved himself a true friend: he would give the evidence Wilde wanted. But he asked Wilde about the case, and Wilde explained that Queensberry would not only bring up his formal literary works, but also had got hold of some letters from Wilde to Douglas, in spite of Wilde's effort to pay blackmail and get them back. Harris needed to hear no more. He advised Wilde that the case was sure to go against him even if he were in the right. No jury would convict a father for protecting his son, and the letters would show that Douglas needed protecting. 'You are sure to lose it,' he warned, 'you haven't a dog's chance, and the English despise the beaten – *vae victis!* Don't commit suicide.' His words frightened Wilde enough to make him agree to meet Harris for a further talk on Sunday night. During the day Harris sampled the opinion of various people, including someone in the office of the Director of Public Prosecutions. The sentiment against Wilde was overwhelming: Queensberry's charges were generally regarded as true. The letters to Douglas and the fact that Wilde had paid blackmail would count heavily. Harris urged that Wilde, as a leading man of letters, had not the right to set the clock back fifty years by rousing full enforcement of the law.

It was agreed to meet again next day at the Café Royal, where Harris had already arranged to have lunch with contributors to the *Saturday Review*, including Bernard Shaw. Wilde asked if he might bring Douglas along, and Harris offered no objection. When he came, however, he was alone. Shaw and Harris were still sitting over their lunch. Shaw offered to leave, but Wilde told him to stay. Wilde asked Harris to testify to the high artistic character of *Dorian Gray*. Harris put the request aside as irrelevant. Instead of answering he now gave an accurate prediction of what was to come. If Wilde would not drop the case, he would certainly lose it. If he dropped it, he could go at once to Paris, and he must take his wife with him. There could be no staying on in London, since Queensberry would not relent. From Paris he could write to *The Times* in his best style, saying he despaired of receiving justice because Queensberry was pretending to be the good father. After Harris had finished, Shaw registered agreement, and Wilde was swaying that way. Just then Douglas came up to their table. He listened with mounting impatience as Harris reiterated his arguments, and then, as Harris described it, 'cried with his little white venomous, distorted face, "Such advice shows you are no friend of Oscar's."' 'What do you mean?' asked Harris, but Douglas had already turned on his heel to leave the restaurant. To Harris's astonishment, this exit overcame Wilde. He too rose: 'It is not friendly of you Frank, it really is not friendly,' he said. 'Don't be absurd,' cried Harris, but Wilde said, with forced anger, 'No, it is not friendly.' Leonine Wilde sheepishly followed Douglas out.[13]

Wilde had prepared himself to defend his writings, including the letters to Douglas. There was, however, one more legal step. English law requires that the defendant in a libel action must enter his Plea of Justification, with particulars, before the trial begins. This was done by Queensberry on 30 March. Humphreys brought Wilde and Douglas to see it on the 1st or 2nd of April, and they could only find it appalling. In fifteen separate counts, it accused Wilde of soliciting more than twelve boys, of whom ten were named, to commit sodomy:

1. Edward Shelley, between February and May 1892.
2. Sidney Mavor, in October 1892. (Mavor testified that Wilde had done nothing wrong.)
3. Freddie Atkins, on 20 November 1892, in Paris. (His evidence was thrown out.)
4. Maurice Schwabe, on 22 November 1892. (Did not testify.)
5. Certain (unnamed) young men, between 25 January and 5 February 1892, in Paris.
6. Alfred Wood, in January 1893.
7. A certain young man, about 7 March 1893, in the Savoy Hotel.
8. Another young man, on or about 20 March 1893, in the Savoy Hotel.
9. Charles Parker, in March and April 1893.
10. Ernest Scarfe, between October 1893 and April 1894. (Did not testify.)
11. Herbert Tankard, in March 1893 at Savoy Hotel. (Did not testify.)
12. Walter Grainger, in June 1893 in Oxford and in June, July and August at Goring.
13. Alfonso Harold Conway, in August–September 1894 at Worthing and about 27 September in Brighton.

The last two counts spoke of the immorality of *Dorian Gray* and of the maxims Wilde had published in the *Chameleon* in December 1894. These two counts were the ones with which Carson chose to begin.

Although Frank Harris, and other friends, urged Wilde to drop the case, Wilde was constantly being urged by Douglas not to play the coward. 'I can't, I can't,' he told Harris, 'you only distress me by predicting disaster.' Toulouse-Lautrec, in London at the time, found Wilde still outwardly confident and contemptuous of the British public. The strain showed, however, in his tirades and complaints.[14] (He refused to sit for a drawing.) That he accepted the idea of being a martyr may be true, but must be reconciled with his obvious preference for not being one. He was rushed along, by solicitor, lover, barrister, into a situation from which there could be no retreat except voluntary exile, something he detested. Confronted by this choice, better to suffer in Athens than glory in Thebes. If nothing else, he would put on a good show.

The trial opened on 3 April 1895 at the Old Bailey, before Mr Justice R. Henn Collins. There was the sense that a great legal battle was to be fought, and a crowd watched the arrival of the principals. Wilde drove to court in a brougham with two horses and liveried servants. He entered, without smiles. The Marquess of Queensberry, sporting a Cambridge-blue hunting stock instead of a collar and tie, was already in court. Collins arrived ten minutes late, and the trial began. Sir Edward Clarke made the opening speech for the prosecution. He had, as Harris noted, the bleak face and severe side whiskers that went with a nonconformist parson of some time back, but his manner was 'quiet and conversational.' It was not a good performance. Most of it had been composed before he saw the Plea of Justification, and he merely inserted a reference to that at the beginning of his speech. It was no longer simply a matter of injured reputation:

> By the plea which the defendant has brought before the Court a much graver issue has been raised. The defendant has said that the statement is true and that it is for the public benefit that the statement was made, and he has given particulars in the plea of matters which he has alleged show that the statement is true in regard to Mr Oscar Wilde. The plea has not been read to you, gentlemen. There is no allegation in the plea that Mr Oscar Wilde has been guilty of the offence of which I have spoken, but there is a series of accusations in it mentioning the names of persons, and it is said with regard to these persons that Mr Wilde solicited them to commit with him the grave offence, and that he has been guilty with each and all of them of indecent practices. It is for those who have taken the responsibility of putting into the plea those serious allegations to satisfy you, gentlemen, if they can, by credible witnesses, or evidence which they think worthy of consideration and entitled to belief, that these allegations are true. I can understand how it is that these statements have been put in the form in which they are found, for these people, who may be called upon to sustain these charges, are people who will necessarily have to admit in cross-examination that they themselves have been guilty of the gravest offences.

The rest was a defence of Wilde's letters to Douglas, which Clarke determined to quote before Carson had a chance to do so, and of his epigrams in the *Chameleon* and his novel *Dorian Gray*. (There was a certain naïveté on Clarke's part in not realizing that he would be dealing with worse stains than those made by ink.) It was an attempt to show that Wilde was orotund but not vicious, that his verbal flowers were not weeds. But the main interest attached to Wilde's testimony.

When he took the stand, he said, 'I am the prosecutor in this case,' though it was already clear that by this time matters had been turned round. 'I am thirty-nine years of age,' he said. Carson, a forty-one-year-old Trinity classmate, took note of this computation. The account Wilde now gave of his blackmail by Wood, Allen, and Clibborn was as adroit as it could have been:

Wilde: . . . From November 3rd, 1892, till March, 1894, I did not see the defendant, but in 1893 I heard that some letters which I had addressed to Lord Alfred Douglas had come into the hands of certain persons.

Clarke: Did anyone say that he had found letters of yours?

Wilde: Yes. A man named Wood saw me at the rooms of Mr Alfred Taylor and told me that he had found some letters in a suit of clothes which Lord Alfred Douglas had been good enough to give him . . .

Clarke: What happened?

Wilde: When he entered the room, he said, 'I suppose you will think very badly of me.' I replied, 'I hear that you have letters of mine to Lord Alfred Douglas which you certainly ought to have given back.' He handed me three or four letters, and said they had been stolen from him 'the day before yesterday' by a man named Allen, and that he (Wood) had had to employ a detective to get them back. I read the letters, and said that I did not think them of any importance. He said, 'I am very much afraid of staying in London, as this man and other men are threatening me. I want money to go to America.' I asked what better opening as a clerk he could have in America than in England, and he replied that he was anxious to get out of London in order to escape from the man who had taken the letters from him. He made a very strong appeal to me. He said that he could find nothing to do in London. I paid him £15. The letters remained in my hand all the time.

Clarke: Did some man shortly afterwards come with another letter?

Wilde: A man called and told me that the letter, a copy of which had been sent to Mr Beerbohm Tree, was not in his possession. His name was Allen.

Clarke: What happened at that interview?

Wilde: I felt that this was the man who wanted money from me. I said, 'I suppose you have come about my beautiful letter to Lord Alfred Douglas. If you had not been so foolish as to send a copy of it to Mr Beerbohm Tree, I would gladly have paid you a very large sum of money for the letter, as I consider it to be a work of art.' He said, 'A very curious construction can be put on that letter.' I said in reply, 'Art is rarely intelligible to the criminal classes.' He said, 'A man has offered me £60 for it.' I said to him, 'If you take my advice you will go to that man and sell my letter to him for £60. I myself have never received so large a sum for any prose work of that length; but I am glad to find that there is someone in England who considers a letter of mine worth £60.' He was somewhat taken aback by my manner, perhaps, and said, 'The man is out of town.' I replied, 'He is sure to come back,' and I advised him to get the £60. He then changed his manner a little, saying that he had not a single penny, and that he had been on many occasions trying to find me. I said that I could not guarantee his cab expenses, but that I would gladly give him half a sovereign. He took the money and went away.

Clarke: Was anything said about a sonnet?

Wilde: Yes, I said, 'The letter, which is a prose poem, will shortly be published in sonnet form in a delightful magazine, and I will send you a copy of it.'

Clarke: As a matter of fact, the letter was the basis of a French poem that was published in the *Spirit Lamp*?

Wilde: Yes.

Clarke: It is signed 'Pierre Louÿs.' Is that the *nom de plume* of a friend of yours?

Wilde: Yes, a young French poet of great distinction, a friend of mine who has lived in England.

Clarke: Did Allen then go away?

Wilde: Yes, and in about five minutes Clibborn came to the house. I went out to him and said, 'I cannot bother any more about this matter.' He produced the letter out of his pocket, saying, 'Allen has asked me to give it back to you.' I did not take it immediately, but asked: 'Why does Allen give me back this letter?' He said, 'Well, he says that you were kind to him, and that there is no use trying to "rent" you as you only laugh at us.' I took the letter and said, 'I will accept it back, and you can thank Allen from me for all the anxiety he has shown about it.' I looked at the letter, and saw that it was extremely soiled. I said to him, 'I think it is quite unpardonable that better care was not taken of this original manuscript of mine' (Laughter). He said he was very sorry, but it had been in so many hands. I gave him half a sovereign for his trouble, and then said, 'I am afraid you are leading a wonderfully wicked life.' He said, 'There is good and bad in every one of us.' I told him he was a born philosopher, and he then left.

Although Wilde had obviously paid at least £15 blackmail, the episode was too funny to take seriously. In his more heroic mode, Wilde then described the meeting with Lord Queensberry:

Wilde: . . . At the end of June, 1894, there was an interview between Lord Queensberry and myself in my house. He called upon me, not by appointment, about four o'clock in the afternoon, accompanied by a gentleman with whom I was not acquainted. The interview took place in my library. Lord Queensberry was standing by the window. I walked over to the fireplace, and he said to me, 'Sit down.' I said to him, 'I do not allow anyone to talk like that to me in my house or anywhere else. I suppose you have come to apologise for the statements you made about my wife and myself in letters you wrote to your son. I should have the right any day I chose to prosecute you for writing such a letter.' He said, 'The letter was privileged, as it was written to my son.' I said, 'How dare you say such things to me about your son and me?' He said, 'You were both kicked out of the Savoy Hotel at a moment's notice for your disgusting conduct.' I said, 'That is a lie.' He said, 'You have taken furnished rooms for him in Piccadilly.' I said, 'Somebody has been telling you an absurd set of lies about your son and me. I have not done anything of the kind.' He said, 'I hear you were thoroughly well blackmailed for a disgusting letter you wrote to my son.' I said, 'The letter was a beautiful letter, and I never write except for publication.' Then I asked: 'Lord Queensberry, do you seriously accuse your son and me of improper conduct?' He said, 'I do not say that you are it, but you look it' (Laughter).

Mr Justice Collins: I shall have the court cleared if I hear the slightest disturbance again.

Wilde: (continuing Lord Queensberry's remarks) 'But you look it, and you pose at it, which is just as bad. If I catch you and my son together again in any public restaurant I will thrash you.' I said, 'I do not know what Queensberry rules are, but the Oscar Wilde rule is to shoot at sight.' I then told Lord Queensberry to leave my house. He said he would not do so. I told him that I would have him put out by the police. He said, 'It is a disgusting scandal.' I said, 'If it be so, you are the author of the scandal, and no one else.' I then went into the hall and pointed him out to my servant. I said, 'This is the Marquess of Queensberry, the most infamous brute in London. You are never to allow him to enter my house again.'

The Cross-Examination

The sins of another were being placed to my account.

Carson rose to cross-examine. His performance has been very much praised. Professionals are impressed by proficiency, and unperturbed by disloyalty. Carson had so much evidence, and of such a kind, that he only needed to be persistent, not clever. Even if he failed to worst Wilde on literary matters, he would impugn the witness's reliability and prepare for unliterary accusations. He began well by forcing Wilde to admit that he was neither thirty-eight years of age, as Sir Edward Clarke had said, nor thirty-nine, as he had said himself, but forty. The purpose of this was not just to catch Wilde out, but also to emphasize the disparity in age between him and Alfred Douglas, who was twenty-four. Carson took up the subject of the *Chameleon*, his questions being intended to suggest that the magazine was a homosexual one. It contained Douglas's poem, 'Two Loves,' one heterosexual and one homosexual. 'Did you think that made any improper suggestion?' 'None whatever,' Wilde replied, and called it a beautiful poem. Carson went on to the story, 'The Priest and the Acolyte,' and presumed that Wilde had sanctioned the story and approved of its contents. Wilde denied both allegations.

As the cross-examination proceeded, it became clear that Wilde was retorting cavalierly to Carson's questions. Instead of expounding his theory of art as an enhancement and expansion of life, he presented himself as amoral artist and scorned the moral mob. Early in the prosecution case, as Ralph Hodgson recalled, Carson read a passage from *Dorian Gray*, and demanded, 'Did you write that?' Wilde said he had the honor to be the author. Carson laid down the book with a sneer and turned over some papers. Wilde was lost in thought. Presently Carson read aloud a piece of verse from one of Wilde's articles, 'And I suppose you wrote that also, Mr Wilde?' Wilde waited till you could hear a pin drop and then said, very quietly, 'Ah no, Mr Carson, Shakespeare wrote that.' Carson went scarlet. He turned pages again and read another piece of verse and said, 'And I suppose Shakespeare wrote that also, Mr Wilde?' 'Not as you read it, Mr Carson,' Oscar said. The judge said he would clear the court if there was more noise. Wilde deliberately turned his back, folded his arms, and looked far away through the ceiling in rapt concentration. It was effectively done. Carson thundered at him to conduct himself properly: and he appealed to the judge, 'M'lud, M'lud.' Wilde stared deeper into the void for a full minute. Suddenly he swung round as if he heard Carson for the first time and said, assuming a most apologetic tone, 'I beg your pardon, Mr Carson; I do beg your pardon.'[15] When Carson suggested that *Dorian Gray* was perverted, Wilde replied, 'That could only be to brutes and illiterates. The views of Philistines on art are incalculably stupid.' This élitism could scarcely have favored his cause, and Carson drove it home:

Carson: The affection and love of the artist of Dorian Gray might lead an ordinary individual to believe that it might have a certain tendency?

Wilde: I have no knowledge of the views of ordinary individuals.

Carson: Have you ever adored a young man madly?

Wilde: No, not madly. I prefer love – that is a higher form.

Carson: Never mind about that. Let us keep down to the level we are at now.

Wilde: I have never given adoration to anybody except myself. (Loud laughter)

Carson: I suppose you think that a very smart thing?

Wilde: Not at all.

Carson: Then you have never had that feeling?

Wilde: No. The whole idea was borrowed from Shakespeare, I regret to say – yes, from Shakespeare's sonnets.

Carson: I believe you have written an article to show that Shakespeare's sonnets were suggestive of unnatural vice.

Wilde: On the contrary I have written an article to show that they are not. I objected to such a perversion being put upon Shakespeare.

Carson was not capable of cornering Wilde through literary criticism. At last he began on the young men. Wilde had said in direct examination that he denied all the charges in the Plea of Justification which had to do with sodomy. But the mustering of a considerable list by Carson, the multifarious details, the constant (as it wrongly seemed) association with homeless and shiftless boys, as Carson persisted in calling them, had its effect. The defense had done its work well, and Carson had instance after instance to adduce. There were Wood, Allen, and Clibborn to begin with, whose association with Wilde had not been limited to blackmailing him. Wilde liked to talk of the pleasure of feasting with panthers, but these panthers had all been defanged by Queensberry's men, and were ready to say anything to stay free. If they often mixed up what they had done with Wilde with what they had done with Douglas, so much the better.

As Carson began to sink his teeth into Wilde, Clarke realized he must do something. Up to now he had withheld Queensberry's letters to his son and ex-wife, but he now read them out as evidence. They proved that Queensberry was beside himelf, but they also reasserted the wholesome fatherliness of his motives. On 1 April 1894 Queensberry had admonished his son for doing nothing, and for being intimate with Wilde. In the second letter, in answer to Douglas's telegram 'What a funny little man you are,' Queensberry threatened to thrash Douglas, and to create a public scandal if he caught him again with Wilde. On 6 July he wrote his father-in-law, Alfred Montgomery, complaining of his ex-wife's support of Alfred Douglas. 'Your daughter must be mad by the way she is behaving . . . I am now fully convinced that the Rosebery-Gladstone-Royal insult that came to me through my other son, that she worked that . . .' On 21 August 1894, in reply to a vicious postcard from his son, he said in part, 'You reptile. You are no son of mine and I never thought you were.' And on 28 August he wrote to 'You miserable creature . . . If you are my son, it is only confirming proof to me, if I needed any, how right I was to face every horror and misery I have done rather than run the risk of bringing more creatures into the world like yourself, and that was the entire and only reason of my breaking with your mother as a wife, so intensely was I dissatisfied with her as the mother of you children, and particularly yourself, whom, when quite a baby I cried over you the bitterest tears a man ever shed, that I had brought such a creature into the world, and unwittingly committed such a crime. If you are not my son, and in the Christian country with these hypocrites 'tis a wise father who knows his own child, and no wonder on the principles they intermarry on . . . You must be demented; there is madness on your mother's side.'

The effect of these letters was not what Clarke intended. According to Marjoribanks, who must have got it from Carson, the introduction of the names of Rosebery and Gladstone, which at once appeared in the continental press, made it inevitable that Wilde should be tried when the Queensberry case was over, in case it looked as if these men had favored him out of a need to protect themselves.[16]

In any case the letters did not stop the merciless march of Carson through Wilde's liaisons. There were Charley Parker and his brother, one a valet, the other a groom, whom Wilde had met through Taylor. Asked if he knew their occupations, Wilde replied, 'I did not know it, but if I had I should not have cared. I didn't care twopence what they were. I liked them. I have a passion to civilise the community.' This was the opposite of his condemnation of the general reading public, and Carson was quick to fasten upon 'the valet and the groom' as strange companions for an artist. Then there was Fred Atkins, whom Wilde had taken with him to Paris. There was Ernest Scarfe, whom he had met through Taylor. There was Sidney Mavor, who stayed at the Albemarle Hotel with Wilde one night. Carson came at last to Walter Grainger, a servant at a house in the High Street, Oxford, where Douglas had rooms. 'Did you ever kiss him?' 'Oh, dear no. He was a peculiarly plain boy. He was, unfortunately, extremely ugly. I pitied him for it.'

Carson: Was that the reason why you did not kiss him?

Wilde: Oh, Mr Carson, you are pertinently insolent.*

Carson: Why, sir, did you mention that this boy was extremely ugly?

Wilde: For this reason. If I were asked why I did not kiss a door-mat, I should say because I do not like to kiss door-mats. I do not know why I mentioned that he was ugly, except that I was stung by the insolent question you put to me and the way you have insulted me through this hearing. Am I to be cross-examined because I do not like it?

Carson persisted, and at last Wilde answered, 'You sting me and insult me and try to unnerve me; and at times one says things flippantly when one ought to speak more seriously. I admit it.' Carson went on to the Savoy, and asked whether an incident involving buggery had occurred. Wilde denied it absolutely. Carson returned to Atkins and Charley Parker, and took up various presents made to them and other boys. He then turned to Edward Shelley. Wilde denied any wrongdoing, and in rebuttal Clarke read letters written by Shelley asking Wilde for help and expressing admiration for his writings. Carson then ended with some questions about Conway and Wood. The exchange of letters between Humphreys and Queensberry in 1894 was read, and Carson also made clear that the 'exalted personages' – that is, Rosebery, Gladstone, and the Queen, were not mentioned in relation to the question of Wilde's sodomy. It was then time for Carson's opening speech. He said that Queensberry had been animated from the beginning to end 'by one hope alone – that of saving his son.' Wilde, on the other hand, was consorting with 'some of the most immoral characters in London,' such as Taylor, 'a most notorious character – as the police will tell the court.' He vividly contrasted Wilde's

* Probably a court reporter's error for 'You are impertinent and insolent.'

artistic élitism with his democratic taste for common boys. On the literary works of Wilde alone, Queensberry's charge would have been justified. But there was also his payment of blackmail to Wood, who was no longer out of the country, but was here and would testify. Carson did not allege any misconduct between Wilde and Douglas. 'God forbid! But everything shows that the young man was in a dangerous position in that he acquiesced in the domination of Mr Wilde, a man of great ability and attainments.' (Queensberry had succeeded in protecting his son.) He was now going to bring forward the young men, who would testify to 'shocking acts' with Wilde. Conway, for example, would testify to Wilde's having dressed him up in good clothes, so as to make him appear a fit companion.[17]

At this point Sir Edward Clarke plucked Carson by the gown and with the judge's permission went aside to confer with him. There had been a discussion that morning with Wilde, who was not in court. His solicitor Matthews said that he and Clarke would keep the trial going if Wilde wished so he would have time to get to France. The defense would be allowed to call its witnesses, as a delaying tactic. Otherwise Clarke would have to abandon the prosecution at once. 'I'll stay,' said Wilde. Clarke hoped that Carson would accept a verdict of not guilty, '"not guilty" having reference to the word "posing,"' and to *Dorian Gray* and the epigrams in the *Chameleon*. Nothing would then be conceded about Wilde's acts of sodomy as itemized in the Plea of Justification. Wilde agreed, but in the event Carson insisted, and Clarke had to consent, that the whole plea must be allowed, that is, Queensberry was justified in calling Wilde a sodomite in the public interest. The judge instructed the jury so to rule. Queensberry was applauded, and Mr Justice Collins, as Frank Harris noted, made no attempt to stop the cheering, but simply folded up his papers and left. He sent a message to Carson,

> Dear Carson
>   I never heard a more powerful speech nor a more searching crossXam. I congratulate you on having escaped the rest of the filth.
>
> > Yrs ever
> > R. HENN COLLINS

What made Carson unmade Wilde.

CHAPTER XVIII

Doom Deferred

GUIDO: *Guilty? – Let those*
Who know not what a thing temptation is,
Let those who have not walked as we have done,
In the red fire of passion, those whose lives
Are dull and colourless, in a word let those,
If any such there be, who have not loved,
Cast stones against you.

On Fortune's Wheel

The quarry was about to fall. If Queensberry had not brought Wilde down, someone else might well have done so. The easy and half acknowledged indulgence which he practiced with Alfred Douglas's ardent complicity involved a succession of young men, many of them Douglas's castoffs, any one of whom might have toppled Wilde. It was, as Henri de Régnier said, 'a chronological error.' If he had lived in the days of the Greeks, no one would have minded. That summer of 1893, when Douglas, having gone down from Oxford without a degree, joined Wilde at Goring, may stand for many instances of their common imprudence.

In *De Profundis* Wilde brings up the subject of Goring, so as to upbraid Douglas for making him spend the staggering sum of £1,340 in less than a summer. But he says nothing of their riskier joint enterprise, the Philip Danney case. Of it Oscar Browning commented, disingenuously, 'This was the first time I ever heard Oscar was given to those proceedings.'[1]

Wilde had to pick his way among blackmailing boys and furious fathers. He ran a risk with the father of Edward Shelley, John Lane's office employee, who was as indignant as Queensberry, and with the father of a public school boy, Sidney Mavor, just as earlier he had roused the indignation of Frank Miles's father. He was circling nearer to some kind of legal confrontation. Only self-assurance, and the thoughtless flurry of his activities, made him trust to his luck.

Still, the furious fathers mostly stayed in the background, while the blackmailing boys were always about, ready to sell themselves or Wilde.

426

The £35 (probably not £15) he had given to Wood in 1893, in the hope that the young man would go to America and stay there, was not likely to be enough. From America Wood had ominously written, 'Tell Oscar he can send me a draft for an Easter egg.' The gang – for Wood, Allen, Clibborn and others constituted a gang – had obviously marked Wilde for prolonged milking. It was as tricky a game for them as for him, since there were heavier penalties for blackmail than for indecency. Their running such risks fascinated Wilde. Clibborn and Allen, in particular, he admired for waging 'an infamous war against life.' Clibborn liked to tell Wilde of his adventures, and one, with Lord Euston – prominent in the Cleveland Street scandal – required such avaricious tenacity on Clibborn's part as to entitle him, Wilde said, to the Victoria Cross.

Clibborn continued to confide in Wilde as the trial drew near. One day he was telling him, as George Ives recounts, 'the plots that were being planned by threats and money and all kind of means, to bring about his [Wilde's] ruin.' Wilde paid little heed, but suddenly looked up and asked a question that had evidently been long in his mind: 'Bob, what I want to know is, did you ever *love* any boy for his own sake?' Clibborn replied, 'No, Oscar, I can't say I ever did!'[2] For Ives this was an instance of Wilde's mystical search for the truth of things even on the verge of his own collapse. His curiosity was less mystical when he suggested bringing together 'the panther,' as he often called Clibborn, with Ives, who prided himself on being a 'cold disciplined Hellenist,' to see what would happen. But that meeting never took place.

It must be said for Wilde that the risk was impossible to estimate. Society put up with a great deal that was illegal, and sometimes did so knowingly. Countenancing illegality did not amount to sanctioning it, however, and the atmosphere could change at any time. Wilde was dimly aware from the beginning that his genius gave him only a limited immunity. But the way of life which Alfred Douglas had opened up was necessarily reckless. There was something fascinating in being the rival, the accomplice, and the object of each other's love. Shared indiscretion cemented them romantically together. Prudence would have been a form of betrayal.

Events had taken him beyond erotic fantasy and indulgence. After Queensberry's exoneration Wilde was indecisive when others were decisive. Clarke's concession that Wilde's being called a sodomite was in the public interest made prosecution almost certain. To be quite sure, Charles Russell, within minutes of Queensberry's acquittal, addressed a letter to Hamilton Cuffe, Director of Prosecutions,

Dear Sir,
    In order that there may be no miscarriage of justice I think it my duty at once to send you a copy of all our witnesses' statements together with a copy of the shorthand notes of the trial.

Queensberry, for his part, informed Wilde, 'I will not prevent your flight, but if you take my son with you, I will shoot you like a dog.' He added, to the French press, 'But I don't think he'll be allowed to go. This case has cost me 30,000 francs, but I don't regret anything, since I know all I have done is for the good of my sons, the honour of my family, and the public benefit.'[3] He said later he had been misquoted; he had said that he would shoot Wilde like a dog, if he had a mind to do so and if it seemed worthwhile. It was probably Queensberry's detectives, rather than Scotland Yard's, who were instructed to stay on Wilde's trail.

That trail led Wilde first to his solicitor Humphreys, then to Sir George Lewis, who threw up his hands and said, 'What is the good of coming to me now?' Then to the Holborn Viaduct Hotel. Douglas, his brother Percy, and Robert Ross accompanied Wilde, and in the hotel he wrote a letter to the editor of the *Evening News*:

It would have been impossible for me to have proved my case without putting Lord Alfred Douglas in the witness-box against his father. Lord Alfred Douglas was extremely anxious to go into the box, but I would not let him do so. Rather than put him in so painful a position I determined to retire from the case, and to bear on my own shoulders whatever ignominy and shame might result from my prosecuting Lord Queensberry.

OSCAR WILDE[4]

The letter reads as if Wilde thought the matter might end there. After lunch he gave Ross a cheque to cash for £200 and went on to the Cadogan Hotel, where he was joined by Reggie Turner. Douglas had been staying there for five weeks. Ross and Turner urged Wilde to take a train for Dover and a boat for France, but he seemed incapable of decision. He said 'The train is gone. It is too late.' In fact he still had a chance, but seemed disinclined to take it. Douglas was off trying to see his cousin, the M. P. George Wyndham, and stir up influential friends. Wilde asked Ross to see Constance Wilde and inform her what had happened. She wept and said, 'I hope Oscar is going away abroad.' George Wyndham arrived at four o'clock and asked to see Wilde, but Wilde, fearing recriminations, had Ross talk with him. Wyndham began to scold Ross for allowing Wilde and Douglas to be together, but Ross disarmed him by saying that he and all Wilde's friends had been trying to separate them for years. Wyndham changed his tack and asked Ross to persuade Wilde to leave the country at once. They were still talking when Douglas rushed in, and took Wyndham off to see someone who might help.

At five o'clock a sympathetic reporter from the *Star* arrived and told Ross that the warrant for Wilde's arrest had been issued. In fact, Charles Russell had busily gone round to see Sir John Bridge at Bow Street in the early afternoon and persuaded him that Wilde should be arrested. Ross told Wilde, who 'went very grey in the face.' Up to now he had not let Ross give him the money from the bank, but he now asked for it, and Ross thought he must have decided upon flight. Instead Wilde settled down in his chair and said, 'I shall stay and do my sentence whatever it is.'

A half-packed suitcase lay on the bed, emblem of contradictory impulses. He was tired of action. Like Hamlet, as he understood that hero, he wished to distance himself from his plight, to be the spectator of his own tragedy. His stubbornness, his courage, and his gallantry also kept him there. He had always met adversity head on, to face hostile journalists, moralistic reviewers, and canting, ranting fathers. A man so concerned with his image disdained to think of himself as a fugitive, skulking in dark corners instead of lording it in the limelight. He preferred to be a great figure, doomed by fate and the unjust laws of a foreign country. Suffering was more becoming than embarrassment. Writers, after all, had been prisoners before him. Cunninghame Graham and Blunt came to mind. His mind would survive, superior to any indignities his inferiors could heap upon him. If he was to be immolated, so must be his age. Reveal him as pederast, reveal his society as hypocrite. So he waited, defiant. At ten past six came the expected knock at the door. A waiter entered, followed by two detectives. They said, 'We have a warrant here, Mr Wilde, for your arrest on a charge of committing indecent acts.' Wilde asked if he would be given bail and the detectives were doubtful. As he rose and groped unsteadily for his overcoat and for a book with a yellow cover, it was suddenly evident that he had been drinking heavily. He asked Ross to get him a change of clothes and bring it to him. 'Where shall I be taken?' he asked. 'To Bow Street,' was the reply. The cab drove off, and the Wilde epoch came to an end.

Despair and Its Anodynes

Every great love has its tragedy, and now ours has too.

Ross went as directed to Tite Street. Mrs Wilde had locked the bedroom door and library and gone out. Wilde's servant, Arthur, was there, and helped Ross to break into the bedroom and pack a bag. At Bow Street he was refused admission, either to see Wilde or to leave the clothing. He realized that Wilde's papers were in danger from Queensberry's men or the police, and hurried back to Tite Street. Again with Arthur's help, he broke open the library door, and removed some of Wilde's letters and manuscripts. He noted grimly that the two most recent writings, *A Florentine Tragedy* and an enlarged version of 'The Portrait of Mr W.H.,' which had been returned to Wilde a few days before, were not to be found. (Both survived.) After all this, Ross drove to his mother's house and collapsed.

Ross was named in the newspapers as having been with Wilde at the time of the arrest and had to resign from some of his clubs. Mrs Ross was understandably alarmed for her son and insisted that he go abroad. He demurred on the grounds that he would be abandoning his friend, and she offered £500 to help in Wilde's defense if he would leave at once. He allowed himself to be persuaded, and took himself off to the Terminus Hotel at Calais and a week later to Rouen. Reggie Turner and Maurice Schwabe also decamped. Henry Harland wrote to Edmund Gosse that six hundred gentlemen had crossed from Dover to Calais on a night when normally only sixty would have done so.[5] Douglas, however, elected to stay on, though he appeared to be in greater danger than the others. In fact, his father had evidently resolved to protect him, probably by having Russell arrange matters with the Director of Prosecutions. Robert Sherard and Ada and Ernest Leverson were the other friends of Wilde who remained conspicuously loyal and helpful. But dozens fell away.

Wilde left a message for Douglas that he would be at Bow Street Police Station that night, and asked him to try to get his brother Percy, and George Alexander and Lewis Waller (from the theatres where Wilde's plays were running), to attend next morning to give bail. Only Percy was willing. Wilde also asked Douglas to secure Humphreys' services for the hearings. Douglas went round to Bow Street in the evening in the hope of seeing Wilde, but like Ross he was refused. He resolved, however, to see him every day. For his part, Wilde ate a bit of cold chicken, drank some coffee, was refused permission to smoke, and spent a wretched night.

'With what a crash this fell!' Wilde wrote to the Leversons on 9 April. It was like the history of Timon of Athens, or of Wilde's old admiration, *Agamemnon*, yet meaner. Wilde's name was removed from the hoardings of the two theatres where *An Ideal Husband* and *The Importance of Being Earnest* were playing to large audiences, and soon, with public feeling running high, the plays were taken off. The same thing happened in New York, and the actress Rose Coghlan, who was about to take *A Woman of No Importance* on tour in the United States, cancelled it. Not only did Wilde's friends in England drop away; so did most of his friends in France. On 13 April 1895 Jules Huret, in his '*Petite chronique des lettres*' in *Le Figaro littéraire*, named three French writers as Wilde's intimates: Catulle Mendès, Marcel Schwob, and Jean Lorrain. A furore resulted. Schwob sent his seconds to meet Huret's seconds, and was angry when they accepted Huret's explanation. Lorrain had Huret publish a letter from him denying intimacy, and forgot having dedicated his story, 'Lanterne magique,' to Wilde in *L'Echo de Paris* of 14 December 1891. Catulle Mendès was not so easily fobbed off. He and Huret had a duel with épées in the 'premières feuilles' of the forest of St Germain, on 17 April at 3 p.m. Blood was shed, but as a commentator remarked, in droplets only.[6] Colette's husband, Willy, registered his amusement in *L'Echo de Paris* for 17 April at Wilde's behavior and England's embarrassment over it; but on 20 April Henry Bauer mocked Willy for pretending that homosexuality was only an English vice. 'I will not disavow now having known and visited him,' he said. Wilde's heteroclite tastes were not his affair. Nor had Wilde done any harm: 'Young Douglas was old enough to go out without his governess, and without his father's permission.' Octave Mirbeau also wrote sympathetically of Wilde in an article, *'A Propos du "Hard Labour."'*[7] As for Sarah Bernhardt, when Sherard asked her to buy the rights to *Salome* for $1,500 to $2,000 to cover court costs, she expressed sympathy, dithered, and did nothing.

If Wilde hoped that the hearings that began on 6 April would soon be over, he was mistaken. They dragged on and on, with intervals of several days between each. Meanwhile he was in Bow Street in physical pain, never saying a word to the other prisoners, making subdued groans as he changed his standing position from time to time.[8] He was then transferred to Holloway Prison except when recalled for another hearing. He hoped for bail, and the magistrate had it in his power to grant it. But Sir John Bridge was revolted by the crime of sodomy. As the French newspapers commented with some bewilderment, in England sodomy ranked only one step below murder. Though Humphreys pointed out that Wilde could have run away if he had wanted to, Bridge insisted that the gravity of the charge made bail unthinkable.*

Wilde's second hearing took place on 11 April, the third on 18 April. The Grand Jury found true bills against Wilde and Alfred Taylor, whose case was linked with Wilde's very much against Wilde's interest, on 23 April. The charges were indecency and sodomy. Meanwhile various incidents added to the tensions. On 11 April a stationer tried to sell photographs of Wilde; the resulting fracas made the police intervene and stop the sale. On 24 April, a bankruptcy sale of Wilde's effects was forced by Queensberry, who demanded payment of his £600 costs, and by other creditors who followed his lead. Douglas had promised that his family would pay the costs of the trial; they did not. Wilde was rendered miserable by the sale not only of his manuscripts and his own books, but of presentation volumes from Hugo, Whitman, Swinburne, Mallarmé, Morris, and Verlaine, his Burne-Jones and Whistler drawings, paintings by Monticelli and Simeon Solomon, expensive china, Thomas Carlyle's writing desk and a hundred other things. A few were bought by friends. There was still not enough money to pay off the debts, so the estate remained in receivership until Ross eventually rescued it, long after Wilde's death.

At the dismal proceedings Wilde was represented by young Travers Humphreys and later by Sir Edward Clarke, who offered to represent him without fee. The prosecutor was Charles Gill, like Carson a Trinity

---

* By coincidence, it was just at this time that Countess Russell was suing her husband for divorce on the grounds of his homosexuality, supposedly with the advice of Sir Edward Clarke, so that the two cases appeared to reinforce each other. (She lost her suit, however.)

College, Dublin man, and equally prejudiced against Wilde. There was some effort by the prosecution to persuade Taylor to turn state's evidence and so get off, but, perhaps because Wilde had talked to him before the trial, Taylor refused to betray his friend in any way. A long array of witnesses was produced, headed by the infamous Parker brothers, who claimed they had been recruited by Taylor to minister to Wilde's wishes.* At first Charles Parker pretended to be nineteen; under cross-examination he proved to be twenty-one. In fact, none of the young men was under the statutory age of seventeen. There was testimony from Taylor's fellow-tenants and landladies about his peculiarly curtained and perfumed rooms, and the young men who came to tea there. Alfred Wood the blackmailer was there to testify about receiving £35 from Wilde in exchange for the letters Wilde had sent to Douglas, who had failed to remove them from his clothes before giving them to Wood. Sidney (better known as Jenny) Mavor had been threatened into testifying, but Douglas managed to collar him before his appearance and to remind him that he was a public school boy with a a sense of honor, counselling him to deny having anything to do with Wilde. So this young man, asked what had happened the time he spent a night in Wilde's bed, replied, 'Nothing.'

The Savoy Hotel was represented by its 'professor of massage,' Antonio Migge, who testified to having seen a young man sleeping in Wilde's bed while Wilde was dressing. The chambermaid Jane Cotter also claimed to have seen a boy there. A former housekeeper at the hotel, Mrs Perkins, testified that there had been fecal stains on the bedsheets. As for Taylor, there was testimony that he had gone through a form of marriage, dressed as a woman. The more Sir John Bridge heard of this testimony, the more he bristled, and when asked again for bail he said that 'no worse crime than this' existed, and bail could not be allowed. After the Grand Jury presented its charge, Wilde's lawyers asked that the case be postponed until the May Sessions, to give the defense time to prepare and to allow public opinion to die down. The prosecutor, Gill, objected, and Mr Justice Charles, who was to hear the case, agreed to an immediate trial, beginning on 26 April, promising it would be a fair one.

Douglas on 19 April sent a letter to the *Star*, complaining that Wilde was being judged before his trial, not at it. What was only too clear about this and subsequent letters from him to the press was that he was thinking more about himself than about his friend, and Wilde in *De Profundis* was severe on the subject: 'they [the letters] were simply to say that you hated your father. Nobody cared if you did or not.'[9]

No doubt such thoughts glanced off his mind at the time. Mostly he was conscious only of Douglas's love for him, and his for Douglas. The almost

---

* Among them, Robert Clibborn was sentenced on 11 March 1898 to seven years for blackmailing, and William Allen in September 1897 to eighteen months for receiving stolen property.

daily visits meant a great deal. They were limited to about fifteen minutes, and there was so much noise that Wilde, who was rather deaf in one ear, could hardly hear. Wilde informed the Leversons on 9 April, 'I write to you from prison, where your kind words have reached me and given me comfort, though they have made me cry, in my loneliness. Not that I am really alone. A slim thing, goldhaired like an angel, stands always at my side. His presence overshadows me. He moves in the gloom like a white flower . . . I thought but to defend him from his father: I thought of nothing else, and now –.' To Ross and his close friend More Adey (translator of Ibsen's *Brand* and an art expert), both at Calais, he wrote on 9 April, 'Bosie is so wonderful. I think of nothing else. I saw him yesterday.' To Ada Leverson he wrote on 17 April, 'As for me, the wings of great love encompass me: holy ground.' As his trial approached, he wrote to her, 'I care less when I think that he is thinking of me. I think of nothing else.' In the meantime he sent Douglas a number of passionate letters.

But Sir Edward Clarke felt that Douglas's presence at the trial would be prejudicial to Wilde's interests, as stirring up recollections of the supposed corruption of the young man by him. Douglas would not go without Wilde's express request, and insisted upon having it in writing. At the last meeting, Douglas recalled, Wilde 'kissed the end of my finger through an iron grating at Newgate, and he begged me to let nothing in the world alter my attitude and my conduct towards him.' The young man joined Ross and Turner at the Hôtel Terminus in Calais, then went on to Rouen and Paris. He told the press that he had gone because of his mother's illness in Italy, but this pretext was quickly exploded. To a reporter for *Le Journal*, on 25 May 1895, he said that there had been danger of his being called as a witness, presumably by the prosecution, which he did not want. But in his *Autobiography*, Douglas said that on the third day of the trial he telegraphed certain information to Sir Edward Clarke, though it was prejudicial to himself, and again offered to give evidence. Presumably he took responsibility for the incidents of buggery, since Wilde did not practice this.[10] The solicitors replied that his telegram was very improper, and that he should not make Clarke's task more difficult than it was already. Wilde wrote to him on the last day of the trial, 29 April:

My dearest boy, This is to assure you of my immortal, my eternal love for you. Tomorrow all will be over. If prison and dishonour be my destiny, think that my love for you and this idea, this still more divine belief, that you love me in return will sustain me in my unhappiness and will make me capable, I hope, of bearing my grief most patiently. Since the hope, nay rather the certainty, of meeting you again in some world is the goal and the encouragement of my present life, ah! I must continue to live in this world because of that . . . If one day, at Corfu or in some enchanted isle, there were a little house where we could live together, oh! life would be sweeter than it has ever been. Your love has broad wings and is strong, your love comes to me through my prison bars and comforts me, your love is the light of all my hours. Those who know not what love is will write, I know, if fate is against us, that I have had a bad influence upon your life. If they do that, you shall write, you shall say in your turn, that it is not so. Our love was always beautiful and noble, and if I have been the butt of a terrible tragedy, it is because the nature of that love has not been understood. In your letter this morning you say something which gives me courage. I must remember it. You write that it is my duty to you and to myself to live in spite of everything. I think that is true. I shall try and I shall do it . . . I stretch out my hands towards you, Oh! may I live to touch your hair and your hands.

Wilde's First Trial

The form of government that is most suitable to the artist is no government at all.

The trial, which opened on 26 April 1895, went over the same ground as the Queensberry trial and the three hearings at Bow Street, and perhaps never in the Nineties was so much unsavory evidence given so much publicity. The prosecutor insisted upon a speedy trial, in which the cases of Taylor and Wilde would be joined because Taylor had procured young men to commit acts of indecency with Wilde. So some charges related to conspiracy. Mr Justice Sir Arthur Charles agreed, over Clarke's protest, but eventually the conspiracy charges were dropped voluntarily by the prosecution, and the judge then said he had never felt that they were properly joined to the other charges. Taylor, a bad witness (as Beerbohm says), and badly represented by J. T. Grein, was simply an additional weight on Wilde's head.[11] In other respects the case was conducted by the Treasury with considerable hypocrisy. Not only was homosexuality common in the English public schools which most of the legal personages present had attended. Also there had evidently been an agreement between Gill and Charles Russell, Queensberry's solicitor, that Douglas's name would be kept out of the case as far as possible in return for Queensberry's detailed evidence against Wilde. Who it was who introduced Atkins and Mavor to Wilde remained a mystery, though clearly a soluble one. As to why none of the important people whom George Wyndham approached saw fit to prevent the trial, there was a reluctance to interfere with the course of justice, and a lack of appetite to take on Queensberry as an adversary. There was also the old difficulty that Rosebery's name had been mentioned in one of Queensberry's letters. George Ives heard, nonetheless, that Rosebery had considered doing something to help Wilde until Balfour told him, 'If you do, you will lose the election.' (In the event, he lost the election anyway.) Everyone seemed to have a reason for leaning over backwards to avoid any suggestion of going easy on Wilde. As for Lockwood, the Solicitor-General, Carson is said to have suggested that he leave Wilde alone, as having suffered enough, but Lockwood said he had no alternative but to continue what Carson had initiated.

Wilde looked thin; his hair had been cut shorter than usual. He was, said the *New York Times*, 'careworn and anxious.'[12] His cross-examination had few surprises to offer. He admitted that he knew the boys who had testified, but not that he had had indecent relations with them. The serious addition to the charges had to do with one young man who was not a prostitute, Edward Shelley. His testimony, given with extreme discomfort, was somewhat vitiated by his admission that he had at times been out of his mind, and also by the fact that he had pursued Wilde's friendship and asked his help long after he had supposedly been corrupted by him.

In cross-examining Wilde, Gill tried to follow Carson's lead and besmirch him by association with the *Chameleon*, not so much with 'The Priest and the Acolyte' as with two homosexual poems by Douglas in it. 'What is the "Love that dare not speak its name"?' he asked. After all his lies, denials, and shifts, Wilde suddenly found a voice:

> The 'Love that dare not speak its name' in this century is such a great affection of an elder for a younger man as there was between David and Jonathan, such as Plato made the very basis of his philosophy, and such as you find in the sonnets of Michaelangelo and Shakespeare. It is that deep, spiritual affection that is as pure as it is perfect. It dictates and pervades great works of art like those of Shakespeare and Michaelangelo, and those two letters of mine, such as they are. It is in this century misunderstood, so much misunderstood that it may be described as the 'Love that dare not speak its name,' and on account of it I am placed where I am now. It is beautiful, it is fine, it is the noblest form of affection. There is nothing unnatural about it. It is intellectual, and it repeatedly exists between an elder and a younger man, when the elder man has intellect, and the younger man has all the joy, hope and glamour of life before him. That it should be so the world does not understand. The world mocks at it and sometimes puts one in the pillory for it.

This *cri de coeur* had its effect, though it could not, as the prosecutor noted, apply to the male prostitutes in the case, and Wilde himself said it could only happen once in a lifetime. For once Wilde spoke not wittily but well. As Max Beerbohm wrote to Reggie Turner after attending the trial, 'Oscar has been quite superb. His speech about the Love that dares not tell his name was simply wonderful and carried the whole court right away, quite a tremendous burst of applause. Here was this man, who had been for a month in prison and loaded with insults and crushed and buffeted, perfectly self-possessed, dominating the Old Bailey with his fine presence and musical voice. He has never had so great a triumph, I am sure, as when the gallery burst into applause – I am sure it affected the jury.'[13]

The rest of the cross-examination went less favorably. Wilde had again to defend his letters to Douglas. As for the evidence of the hotel servants, Wilde said, 'It is entirely untrue. Can I answer for what hotel servants say years after I have left the hotel?' He denied all Shelley's evidence of impropriety, as well as the Parkers', Atkins's, and Wood's.

Why did you take up with these youths? – I am a lover of youth. (Laughter)

You exalt youth as a sort of god? – I like to study the young in everything. There is something fascinating in youthfulness.

So you would prefer puppies to dogs and kittens to cats? – I think so. I should enjoy, for instance, the society of a beardless, briefless barrister quite as much as that of the most accomplished Q.C. (Laughter)

This time Sir Edward Clarke was better prepared. He persuasively denied that *Dorian Gray* or 'Phrases and Philosophies for the Use of the Young' was in any sense corrupting or corrupted. He pointed out that Wilde, instead of shrinking like a guilty man from public exposure, had sought publicity by prosecuting Lord Queensberry. As to the hotel evidence against Wilde, it was extraordinary that the prosecution had been able to find such a paucity of it, when Wilde had stayed in hotel after hotel for years. The evidence of the Parkers, of Wood, and of Atkins obviously superimposed on what was true much that was false, as the best lies do. Wilde was undoubtedly taken in by them, which was evidence of imprudence not crime. They were blackmailers whose evidence could not be trusted. Atkins had been proved on the stand to have perjured himself. 'I ask the jury,' Clarke said, 'to clear from this frightful imputation one of our most renowned and accomplished men of letters of today, and in clearing him, to clear society from a stain.' Grein then made a weak defense of Taylor. Gill, for the prosecution, insisted that the letters to Douglas 'breathe an unholy passion,' and that Wilde's admitted presents to these many boys were proof of his gratitude. As Ives commented in his journal, Wilde suffered because of his generosity, which was not confined to young men. Granted that some of the boys were not of the highest type, there was still the case of Shelley, whose testimony was not tainted by blackmail charges. Finally, Gill gave up the charges of conspiracy. The case now went to the judge.

Mr Justice Charles agreed to omit the conspiracy charges, and to direct a verdict of acquittal upon them. On the literary question he proved enlightened. He was inclined to agree with Clarke that Wilde was not culpable for having written *Dorian Gray* or for the *Chameleon* pieces which he had not written. As to the letters to Douglas, he was not inclined to accept Gill's statement that these proved anything. He acknowledged that

Shelley was unstable. He found the stories of the maids and other functionaries at the Savoy Hotel difficult to credit. As to the fecal stains, he pointed out that these might have an innocent explanation. The judge did not however reject the testimony of the witnesses about Wilde's and Taylor's behavior. He put four questions to the jury:

1) Do you think that Wilde committed indecent acts with Edward Shelley and Alfred Wood and with a person or persons unknown at the Savoy Hotel or with Charles Parker?

2) Did Taylor procure or attempt to procure the commission of these acts or of any of them?

3) Did Wilde and Taylor or either of them attempt to get Atkins to commit indecencies?

4) Did Taylor commit indecent acts with Charles Parker or with William Parker?

The jury was out from 1.35 to 5.15 p.m. They then reported that they could agree only on the question about Atkins, where their verdict was not guilty. One newspaper, *L'Echo de Paris* of 4 May, said that the vote to convict Wilde had been ten to two, as revealed by an indiscreet juror in a Pall Mall club, while Max Beerbohm heard that it was eleven to one, and Alfred Douglas agreed that only one juror voted for acquittal. Beerbohm reported to More Adey, 'Hoscar stood very upright when he was brought up to hear the verdict and looked most leonine and sphinx-like. I pitied poor little Alfred Taylor – nobody remembered his existence . . . Hoscar is thinner and in consequence finer to look at. Willie [Wilde] has been extracting fivers from Humphreys. It was horrible leaving the court day after day and having to pass through a knot of renters (the younger Parker wearing Her Majesty's uniform, another form of female attire) who were allowed to hang around after giving their evidence and to wink at likely persons.'[14]

Owing to the jury's failure to reach a verdict, a new trial was ordered. The judge again refused bail, but Clarke announced he would seek it from another judge in chambers. Clarke proposed that the next trial be postponed, but Gill said it would be the usual course to hold it in the next sessions, and the judge agreed. Many people urged that harm 'would be done to the public morals' if the case were renewed. T. M. Healy begged Lockwood not to put Wilde on trial again. Lockwood said, 'I would not but for the abominable rumours against Rosebery.'[15] So the long drawn-out farce went into its third and last act.

Between Trials

What are called criminals nowadays are not criminals at all.

Bereft of the company of his lover Douglas, and his friends Ross and Turner – all three fugitive in the Hôtel de la Poste in Rouen – and unsought by most of his other friends,* Wilde could feel the shades of the prison house drawing round him figuratively as well as literally. He had twenty-five days to go before his second trial ended. The first five were spent in Holloway Prison. There was now no reason to deny him bail, but Mr Justice Charles perhaps wished to indicate that he had no sympathy for pederasts, even those who might be innocent. Yet only a misdemeanor, not a felony, was involved, so bail could not long be refused. Two days later, on Monday 3 May, Charles Matthews applied again on Wilde's behalf, this time to Mr Baron Pollock in chambers, for bail until the new trial should begin. He proposed two sureties of £1,000 each.

On 4 May Pollock set bail at £5,000, of which £2,500 would be allowed to Wilde on his own recognizance. It took two days to round up sureties for the remaining £2,500. Frank Harris says he volunteered, but was ruled ineligible because he was not a householder. Bosie's brother Percy had no money in hand, but out of loyalty to Bosie scraped together half of what was required in defiance of his father. The other half was harder. It may have been Ernest Leverson who, being himself debarred by the terms of his business partnership from going bail for anyone, approached first Selwyn Image, who did not have the money, and then the Reverend Stewart Headlam, who did. Headlam – whom Wilde had privately dubbed 'the heresiarch' – was scarcely acquainted with him, having met him only twice, but he was a man of conviction, and strongly supported the view that Wilde was entitled not to be prejudged. Being a socialist and an unorthodox Christian, he knew that he would suffer notoriety for his kind of action, and worse, be thought to have sought it. His maid left his service, some of his friends defected, and an enemy accused him of wading in Gomorrah on his way to building Jerusalem. At least there would be no financial loss if Wilde jumped bail; so Leverson had promised, and Wilde gave his word not to flee. With Headlam's £1,225 and Percy Douglas's in hand, all impediments to bail were removed. The bail hearing at Bow Street Police Station on 7 May concluded with Wilde's release.

Where to go was not so easily decided. Two rooms had been engaged for him at the Midland Hotel at St Pancras, far from his usual haunts, but just as he was sitting down to a late dinner, the manager entered. 'You are

---

* Before the trial ended John Gray left the country and went to Berlin, where he was soon joined by Raffalovich. That sometime friend of Wilde published in the autumn of 1895 a 47-page pamphlet entitled, *L'Affaire Oscar Wilde*. It was a way of exculpating himself. Gray had a barrister named Francis Mathews attend the trial and hold a watching brief for him, but as it happened his name was not mentioned.

Oscar Wilde, I believe.' Wilde did not disavow it. 'You must leave the hotel at once.' Some of Queensberry's pugilistic roughnecks, egged on by the Marquess himself, had threatened the manager with reprisals for receiving Wilde, and they followed him as he drove across town to another hotel. There too, after a few minutes, the manager apologized, but said that some men had threatened to sack the hotel and raise the street against Wilde if he did not leave at once. By now it was near midnight. In the end Wilde had no alternative but to go to the house where his brother Willie was living with his second wife, Lily Lees, and Lady Wilde, 146 Oakley Street. It was not pleasant to have to plead with his brother, to whom he had not spoken for a year and a half, 'Willie, give me shelter or I shall die in the streets.' As Willie described the scene later, 'He came tapping with his beak against the window-pane, and fell down on my threshold like a wounded stag.'[16] For the moment magnanimity was in order.

Willie gave his brother a room with a small camp-bed in a corner between the fireplace and the wall, and here for some days Oscar was physically ill. His friends in France heard about it and asked Robert Sherard to go over and see him. Sherard did so. He found Wilde's face 'flushed and swollen.' 'Oh, why have you brought me no poison from Paris?' he asked alliteratively in a broken voice. Sherard offered to take him to the country to recover his health, but he did not want to move. Sherard managed to rouse him by proposing they read some Wordsworth; in one sonnet Wordsworth was caught out rhyming 'love' with 'shove,' and Wilde feigned outrage and said severely to the hapless descendant, 'Robert, what does this mean?'[17]

It soon became apparent that the family setting in Oakley Street would prove anything but easy. Willie was setting up as a moralist: 'At least my vices were decent,' he muttered in his cups. He told Oscar that he was defending him all over London, at which Oscar commented to a friend, 'My poor, dear brother, he would compromise a steam engine.' 'Willie makes such a merit of giving me shelter,' he told Harris, and confided that, as Beerbohm had said, his brother had sold old letters to Humphreys in what amounted to blackmail. For his part, Willie had his own rhythmical explanations of his brother's fall: 'It is his vanity that has brought all this disgrace upon him; they swung incense before him, they swung it before his heart.' Both Willie and Lady Wilde were determined that Oscar should stay and stand trial; Willie would assure visitors, 'Oscar is an Irish gentleman, and he will face the music.' As for Lady Wilde, she declaimed to Oscar in her grand manner, 'If you stay, even if you go to prison, you will always be my son. It will make no difference to my affection. But if you go, I will never speak to you again.' Wilde promised her that he would stay.[18]

But as he approached martyrdom his friends wished to deny him it. Percy, though one of his guarantors, declared, 'It will practically ruin me if I lose all that money at the present moment, but if there is a chance even of conviction, in God's name let him go.'[19] Sherard urged Wilde to leave, and Frank Harris brought matters to a head. Harris insisted upon taking Wilde out to lunch, against Willie's wishes, and proposed the Café Royal, scene of so many meals in the past. Oscar did not feel it would be seemly, so Harris brought him instead to a restaurant in Great Portland Street, where they had a private room. Harris wanted to stiffen Wilde's resistance. He proposed that Wilde should say he liked the company of young men because he liked writing about them. Wilde did not respond, and never adopted this tactic. Harris described the testimony as a pack of lies, and Wilde said that the testimony of the chambermaids at the Savoy Hotel was based on their mixing up his room with Douglas's. Harris offered to make a plan of the rooms and get the maids to admit their error, but Wilde did not want Douglas to be implicated. At any rate, he said, Shelley's testimony remained, and the judge had said that this was unimpugnable. Harris declared that Shelley was an accomplice, and therefore could not be believed without corroboration, of which there was none. At this Wilde broke out, and said, 'You talk with passion and conviction, as if I were innocent.' 'But you are innocent,' said Harris, 'aren't you?' 'No,' said Wilde. 'I thought you knew that all along.' Harris said, 'I did not believe it for a moment.' 'This will make a great difference to you?' asked Wilde, but Harris assured him it would not.[20]

He now developed his fallback plan, that Wilde should escape. A Jewish businessman of his acquaintance happened to mention owning a yacht, and Harris asked him if he would rent it for a month. The man was willing, and asked what Harris planned to do. On impulse Harris told him exactly what he wanted it for, and the yachtsman then said, 'In that case you can have it for nothing.' He too wanted Wilde to escape. Harris now made his proposal to Wilde. The yacht was at Erith, he said, and they could leave at once. Much scepticism has been shown about this yacht, yet both Yeats and Ada Leverson knew of the plan, and it seems to have been available even if it was not waiting at Erith with steam up, as Harris dramatically pictured it. Wilde however refused to go.[21]

It was while he was still in Oakley Street that the Leversons invited Wilde to dinner, and discovered how unhappy he was, living with his brother. They bravely invited him to stay with them, and he accepted. Before he arrived with his belongings, they called the servants together and offered them a month's wages if they wished to leave rather than be in the house with this notorious man. All chose to stay with 'poor Mr Wilde,' as one called him, and Mrs Leverson drove over to Oakley Street to fetch him, on about 18 May. The address was kept secret to ward Queensberry off. The Leversons' son was in the country, so Wilde was shown up to the nursery, which consisted of two large rooms and a bathroom. 'Shall I remove the toys?' she asked, but he replied, 'Please leave them.' So among the rocking horses and doll's houses he received his solicitors and friends, gathering the threads of destitution and disgrace. To avoid embarrassing his hosts he took his meals upstairs and did not come down until six o'clock. Then he appeared in dinner clothes, flower in buttonhole, and made a point of talking to Mrs Leverson about everything but his main concerns. His old hairdresser came to shave him and wave his hair every day.

Later Mrs Leverson would remember some of his conversation. He had romantic ideas about absinthe, and described its effect to her: 'After the first glass, you see things as you wish they were. After the second, you see things as they are not. Finally you see things as they really are, and that is the most horrible thing in the world.' 'How do you mean?' 'I mean disassociated. Take a top-hat! You think you see it as it really is. But you don't, because you associate it with other things and ideas. If you had never heard of one before, and suddenly saw it alone, you'd be frightened, or laugh. That is the effect absinthe has, and that is why it drives men mad.' He went on, 'Three nights I sat up all night drinking absinthe, and thinking that I was singularly clearheaded and sane. The waiter came in and began watering the sawdust. The most wonderful flowers, tulips, lilies, and roses sprang up and made a garden of the café. "Don't you see them?" I said to him. *"Mais, non, monsieur, il n'y a rien."'* There was no drug to make the world flower now. He turned to other subjects, especially books. Dickens was an old phobia, and it was to amuse her he made his classic remark, 'One must have a heart of stone to read the death of Little Nell without laughing.' Or he made up unChristian parables in the manner of *Lives of the Saints.* He liked one or another of these well enough to ask for something to write it down, but Mrs Leverson could not put her hand on anything. 'You have all the equipment of a writer, my dear Sphinx,' he said to her, 'except pens, ink and paper.'[22]

While Oscar Wilde was with the Leversons, Yeats came on 19 May to Oakley Street in search of him. Yeats's father had told him he owed it to Wilde to offer to testify for him, or do some service, and Yeats brought along a packet of letters he had collected from Irish men of letters, including George Russell, to encourage his friend. (Only Professor Edward Dowden refused.) He was met, however, by Willie, who said, 'Before I give him this, you must tell me what is in it. Are you telling him to run away? All his friends are telling him that, and we have made up our minds that he must go to prison if necessary.' Yeats replied, 'No, I certainly would not advise him to run away.' Which was true: to Yeats it seemed a great moment for Wilde to show his mettle.* He wrote to Dowden about his visit:

I went to try and see Wilde today and to tell him how much I sympathised with him in his trouble. He has left Oakley Street but they told me this much about his movements. A yacht and a very large sum of money was

* In a copy of *The Land of Heart's Desire* which he gave to John Quinn in 1904 he wrote of Wilde, 'He was an unfinished sketch of a great man, and showed great courage and manhood amid the collapse of his fortunes.'[23]

placed at his disposal and all settled for his flight but he refused to go. He says he will stand it out and face the worst and no matter how it turns out work on. He will not go down, they said, or drink, or take poison. I mentioned how I had found some of our Dublin literary men sympathetic to him and my words were received with most pathetic gentleness and I promised to tell them about his plans. I write to suggest that you either write direct to him, some sympathetic words, Morris has already written, or write some answer to this which I can get shown to him.[24]

Others were keener than Yeats and Willie to save him from prison, however it might spoil the drama. Constance Wilde came to see her husband at the Leversons' and spent two hours with him. She brought an earnest message from her lawyer, imploring him to go away before his next trial, which would undoubtedly be calamitous. She left in tears, and Ada Leverson saw on his face 'a look of immovable obstinacy.' Mrs Leverson herself had the temerity to send up a note asking him to do what his wife urged. There was no reply until he came down to dinner, when he handed her back her note, only remarking, 'That is not like you, Sphinx,' before he changed the subject.[25]

Wilde had made a decision, and intended to stick to it. Mrs Leverson thought him too involved in a fantasy of success to believe that anything bad could happen to him, but Wilde's life had offered no such cycle of triumphs as she supposed. There had been his broken engagement to Florence Balcombe, his removal from Frank Miles's house, the failure of his early plays, his troubled American lecture tour, years of not having enough money, and the chaotic affair with Douglas. As he was to declare later, his works had always had a telltale undercurrent of sorrow. And he knew what running away would be like, whether he did it in the boisterous company of Frank Harris or by himself. There would be no dignity in that. He might well be stopped, or if not stopped, he would have to slink about the Continent as a fugitive from British justice. As his trip to Florence had shown, slinking was not Wilde's style. Ostracism (a subject about which he had quarreled with Jebb years before) was not for him. What he wrote to Douglas just before the trial ended was what he felt all along: 'I decided that it was nobler and more beautiful to stay . . . I did not want to be called a coward or a deserter. A false name, a disguise, a hunted life, all that is not for me.' He chose to be convicted, knowing that people would wrongly say that he chose out of weakness or megalomania – yet neither obliged his choice. Could he really have preferred picking oakum to ruling a dinner table? He recognized that of the ignominious alternatives available to him, this was the least unheroic. (It was also the most modest.) Yeats was delighted when an old enemy of Wilde, perhaps Henley, met him in the street, and said with admiration of Wilde, 'He has made of infamy a new Thermopylae.' As for Yeats himself, he wrote later, 'I have never doubted, even for an instant, that he made the right decision, and that he owes to that decision half of his renown.'²⁶ He submitted to the society he had criticized, and so earned the right to criticize it further.

Heroics were not the daily fare at the Leversons' house. Wilde did not claim heroism, nor do any more than resist pleas that he run away, without giving any grounds in particular, least of all grandiloquent ones. As the day of the trial approached, he showed something like resignation. He told Sherard that he thought he could bear a year's imprisonment, but Sherard warned him that he might well get the maximum sentence of two years. Wilde fell back for comfort on his love of Douglas, and wrote him letters of the most fervent kind: 'Now, in anguish and pain, in grief and humiliation, I feel that my love for you, your love for me, are the two signs of my life, the divine sentiments which make all bitterness bearable.' Douglas had admitted his own blame (he would deny it later) but Wilde said 'Let destiny, Nemesis, or the unjust gods alone receive the blame for everything that has happened.' And again, 'My sweet rose, my delicate flower, my lily of lilies, it is perhaps in prison that I am going to test the power of love. I am going to see if I cannot make the bitter waters sweet by the intensity of the love I bear you.' These letters were of a different kind from those produced in court, which had been very nearly the formal literary productions that Wilde claimed. He was still prodigal of phrases: 'None of God's created beings, and you are the Morning Star to me, have been so wildly worshipped, so madly adored.' Beneath the purple alliteration was real feeling. Douglas wryly commented long afterwards in his *Autobiography*: 'The emotion of the great crisis fanned the waning fires of our devotion to each other.' He replied to Wilde with less eloquence, though with comparable emotion. He also wrote to his brother, begging him to make Wilde leave England while it was still possible. Percy replied that he hoped he would. In Paris Bosie took heart and wrote to Wilde, 'It seems too dreadful to be here without you, but I hope you will join me next week. Do keep up your spirits, my dearest darling. I continue to think of you day and night, and send you all my love. I am always your own loving and devoted boy BOSIE.'²⁷

Douglas's state of mind in this period was exceedingly disturbed. He sent a series of letters to the press, of varying degrees of indiscretion. On 19 April he had written to the *Star* to complain of Wilde's being prejudged, and of Sir John Bridge's obvious bias against him. But the principal part of the letter read:

I feel, therefore, that I am taking my life in my hands in daring to raise my voice against the chorus of the pack of those who are now hounding Mr Oscar Wilde to his ruin; the more so as I feel assured that the public has made up its mind to accept them as it has accepted everybody and everything connected with this case, at Mr Carson's valuation. I, of course, am the undutiful son who, in his arrogance and folly, has kicked against his kind and affectionate father, and who has further aggravated his offence by not running away and hiding his face after the discomfiture of his friend.

Wilde understandably felt even at the time, though he did not tell Douglas till later, that this was a commonplace production; it was worse, indeed, because Douglas saw himself as the center of interest. He followed this up five days later with a letter saying he had received thousands of letters in support of his stand for Wilde. By 25 May the French press had caught up with him and Georges Docquois published an interview with him on that date. Douglas had claimed that he left England (on the second day of Wilde's trial, according to Raffalovich) because of the illness of his mother in Italy, but the press had found out she was in fact well. He now admitted that he had left because Wilde's lawyers had warned him he might be called as a witness, which he did not want. He had arrived in Paris on 15 May, but dodged the press for eight days. Asked about his letter to *Le Temps*, he explained, 'You do not know what an absolutely abominable man the Marquess of Queensberry is . . . Until I was twelve, I saw him at most twenty times, and I didn't feel at all sure from the way he treated me that I was his son.' The reporter inquired delicately about his relationship with Wilde, but Douglas insisted it was extraterrestrial, a communion together in the symbol rather than something seedy ('*louche*'). He knew no joy greater than to dine with Wilde when the latter was in 'good form.' They had once been joined by a dilettantish pleasure, now they were joined by persecution. To another French journalist he wrote on 30 May that he knew a hundred overt homosexuals in the best English society.*

Lady Queensberry had some inkling of how Bosie was behaving, and she encouraged her son Percy to go to Rouen to see him at the end of May. She also consulted an old friend, the Reverend Sebastian Bowden, and asked him to find some trustworthy person to stay with Bosie and prevent

---

* He was beginning to speak out more boldly. He wrote to Henry Labouchere at *Truth*, on 12 June, to defend his departure before the first trial:

I stayed for three weeks after Mr Wilde's arrest, and visited him every day, and I did everything my mind could devise to help him, and I left on the day before his trial at his most urgent request, and at the equally urgent request of his legal advisers, who assured me that my presence in the country could only do him harm, and that if I were called as a witness I should infallibly destroy what small chance he had of acquittal. Mr Wilde's own counsel absolutely declined to call me as a witness, feeling the harm I might do him in cross-examination, so that had I been called as a witness at all, it would have only been under a subpoena from the prosecution. Now, sir, you must give the devil his due, and granting, for the sake of argument, that I am an exceptional young scoundrel, you have no right to call me a coward.

Truth commented that Douglas did have the courage of his opinions, 'but, these opinions being what they are, it is to be regretted that he is not afforded an opportunity to meditate on them in the seclusion of Pentonville.' Unfazed, Douglas answered

his behaving foolishly out of loyalty to the fallen Wilde. Bowden asked More Adey to do this; Adey replied that his first duty was to Robert Ross, but that he would deal with Douglas as soon as he had calmed Ross down. Ross's family meanwhile forbade his remaining with Douglas, and Douglas, as Adey informed Bowden, planned a trip to Florence to see Lord Henry Somerset, almost as scandalous a character as Wilde.

A New Thermopylae

How steep the stairs within kings' houses are.

Meanwhile Wilde was faced with the reality of his last trial. On its eve, 21 May, he serenely bade his friends farewell, and informed each of a little present from the few possessions left to him which would be a souvenir in case he did not return.[29] When he was going to his room he asked Ada Leverson to leave a sleeping draught for him on the mantelpiece, not that he would take it, but that its presence would have a magical effect. Next day, before leaving with More Adey to join Stewart Headlam, he said to her, 'If the worst comes to the worst, Sphinx, you'll write to me?' During the next six days he was met in the morning and escorted back at night by Headlam, sometimes by Percy Douglas as well. At the Old Bailey all the seats were taken, so Queensberry, wearing a white cravat and a flower, had to stand, listening attentively, small and ferocious. Sir Edward Clarke was determined to try to secure some advantage for Wilde, and moved that Wilde and Taylor should be tried separately. Sir Frank Lockwood as Solicitor-General opposed the motion, on the grounds that the cases were intertwined. But Mr Justice Sir Alfred Wills* ruled in Clarke's favor. Lockwood then proposed to take Taylor's case first, and Clarke again protested, for Taylor really had no defense at all, was well known to the

---

* Not of the Wills family from which Wilde derived one of his names.

---

privately (as he had told the French journalist) that he knew forty or fifty men in the best society, hundreds of undergraduates at Oxford, not to mention 'a slight sprinkling of dons,' who were homosexual. Lots of boys around Piccadilly lived on prostitution. He was sending a pamphlet by Krafft-Ebing, which he was now having translated, asking for the repeal of an Austrian law against homosexuals.[28] Finally, on 28 June, Douglas wrote from the Hôtel de la Poste, Rouen, to W. T. Stead, editor of the *Review of Reviews*. This time he dealt directly with homosexuality, pointed out that the laws were very different in France, that lesbianism was tolerated in England, that dealing with male prostitutes was no worse than dealing with female ones, and that his father practiced fornication and adultery, advocated free love, and maltreated both his first and second wives. Stead refused to publish this, and so did Labouchere. (This letter was produced against Douglas in his libel suit against Ransome, 18–23 April 1913.)

police, and certain to be convicted. Over Clarke's protest the judge agreed. He said that Taylor had been in prison for seven weeks already, without bail, and that his trial should be delayed no longer.

This decision, which seemed minor, was very much to Wilde's detriment. The testimony in the Taylor case would involve him as well, and if Taylor were convicted, Wilde could scarcely be acquitted by the same jury without evident injustice. The Taylor case was quickly heard and quickly decided. The prosecutor had decided to reduce the charge from sodomy to indecency, as being easier to prove, and to secure a conviction. Taylor was found guilty on two counts of indecency with the Parker brothers, but not guilty of procuring Wood for Wilde, since, as the judge pointed out, he had not introduced the two men to each other. One of the Parker brothers had been promised immunity by ex-Inspector Littlefield if he would turn state's evidence against Wilde, but he nobly refused. Mr Justice Wills deferred sentence. Queensberry sent a telegram to his son Percy's wife: 'To Lady Douglas – must congratulate on verdict. Cannot on Percy appearance. Looked like a dug-up corpse. Fear too much madness in kissing. Taylor guilty. Wilde's turn to-morrow. Queensberry.' He also, on the mistaken notion that Wilde was staying with Percy and her, went to their house that night, knocked on the door, and made a disturbance. To Percy's wife he sent an illustration from a popular weekly of an iguanodon, with a childish note, 'Perhaps an ancestor of Oscar Wilde.'[30] The following morning in Bond Street, in front of Scott's the hatters, Percy caught sight of his father and asked him if he were going to continue to annoy his wife with his communications. A street fight broke out, with Lord Douglas getting a black eye. They were both arrested and bound over next day on their own sureties of £500 to keep the peace for six months.*

In this atmosphere of near-hysteria, the second trial of Oscar Wilde was to take place. The press had been discussing Wilde for weeks, with condemnation general except for *Reynolds's News*, which had private information about the extraordinary zeal with which Wilde was being prosecuted. Most of the newspapers considered that Queensberry had rightly brought down the 'High Priest of the Decadents,' as the *National Observer* saw fit to label Wilde.

The trial had few surprises. It became clear that two of the most important witnesses, the brothers Parker, were being maintained at Chiswick under the care of a Crown detective. It did not become clear,

---

* The French press understandably mixed up Lord Alfred Douglas with Lord Douglas of Hawick, and the former indignantly fired off a telegram from Rouen to *Le Figaro* demanding an apology, and wishing that it had indeed been he who had struck Queensberry. He wrote the same day, 22 May, to *Le Temps* complaining of the mix-up, and asserting that the newspaper had mistakenly referred also to Lady Queensberry as 'the divorced wife' of the Marquess, when it was the Marquess who was the divorced husband.

though it was apparently true, that all the witnesses had been receiving £5 a week from the beginning of Wilde's prosecution of Queensberry until his conviction.[31] The star witness, Charles Parker, had received a new suit of clothes at Crown expense, ostensibly because he could not appear in court in a soldier's uniform. (He was to be cashiered.) This time the prosecution began not with him, however, but with Shelley, who made his usual blubbering denunciation of Wilde's sexual advances. This was again countered by the now familiar letters which he addressed to Wilde after the alleged offenses, asking for financial help. For a moment or two the case veered in Wilde's favor as the judge ruled that Shelley was, as Harris had claimed, an accomplice, and therefore not credible unless corroborated. This eliminated the prosecution's trump card, since Shelley alone of the important witnesses was neither male prostitute nor blackmailer. The next day Sir Frank Lockwood, once Wilde's friend, tried to persuade the judge to change his view, but the judge stood firm. Lockwood was heard to murmur outside, 'The old fool!' Testimony disclosed that the person who introduced Taylor to Wilde was Lockwood's nephew by marriage, Maurice Schwabe, a point upon which Lockwood was careful not to dilate.

Clarke did his best. He pointed out that, as anyone could see who had been at the other trials, Wilde was a broken man. It was inconceivable that he would have subjected himself to possible prosecution, by charging Queensberry with libel, if he had himself been so vulnerable. 'This trial seems to be operating as an act of indemnity for all the blackmailers in London,' he said, and it was obvious that the witnesses could better have been the accused rather than the accusers. They had nothing on Wilde, for otherwise they would have blackmailed him relentlessly. Charles Parker was an uncorroborated witness, and a peculiarly unstable one. The testimony of the chambermaids did not prove that Wilde had committed any improper acts. 'If on an examination of the evidence you, therefore, feel it your duty to say that the charges against the prisoner have not been proved, then I am sure that you will be glad that the brilliant promise which has been clouded by these accusations, and the bright reputation which was so nearly quenched in the torrent of prejudice which a few weeks ago was sweeping through the press, have been saved by your verdict from absolute ruin; and that it leaves him, a distinguished man of letters and a brilliant Irishman, to live among us a life of honour and repute, and to give in the maturity of his genius gifts to our literature, of which he has given only the promise in his early youth.'

The last day of the trial, 25 May, was the Queen's birthday. In the midst of patriotic fervor Lockwood made his final speech for the prosecution. He raked Wilde over; he dealt with the suspect letters to Douglas, the payment of blackmail to Wood, the relations with Taylor, Wood, Parker, Conway, which he insisted corroborated each other. If the evidence of the chambermaids was false, why had not Lord Alfred Douglas been called to deny it? As Wilde listened to 'Lockwood's appalling denunciation,' which sounded, he said later, 'like a thing out of Tacitus, like a passage in Dante, like one of Savonarola's indictments of the Popes at Rome,' he felt 'sickened with horror at what I heard. Suddenly it occurred to me, "*How splendid it would be, if I was saying all this about myself!*" I saw then at once that what is said of a man is nothing. The point is, who says it.' As he wrote to Ross later, 'the idea of "The Ballad of Reading Gaol" came to me while I was in the dock.'[32] He was not cowed, his imagination was secretly triumphing over the proceedings.

Then came the summing-up. Mr Justice Wills was too prosaic to accept the affectation of Wilde's letters to Douglas as anything but indecent, and he spoke of them in unpleasant terms as Mr Justice Charles had not. As he went on he became more vehement, as if the heinousness of the offense was being borne in upon him the more he talked of it. 'It is the worst case I have ever tried,' he declared. He agreed that the fecal stains on the Savoy sheets might have been due to diarrhoea, but did not encourage this supposition. He impressed upon the jury the importance of maintaining the highest moral tone. The jury retired at half past three, and returned at twenty-five minutes to six with a question about some minor evidence. Lockwood, conscious that the rejection of Shelley's testimony meant that only the testimony of accomplices was left, said to Clarke, 'You'll dine your man in Paris tomorrow.' But Clarke said, 'No, no, no.'[33] The jury retired again but returned a few minutes later to find the defendant guilty on all counts except that relating to Edward Shelley. Clarke asked the judge not to pass sentence until the next session, so as to consider a legal technicality. But the Solicitor-General opposed the motion, and the judge rejected it. He then turned to the prisoners:

Oscar Wilde and Alfred Taylor, the crime of which you have been convicted is so bad that one has to put stern restraint upon one's self to prevent one's self from describing, in language which I would rather not use, the sentiments which must rise to the breast of every man of honour who has heard the details of these two terrible trials. That the jury have arrived at a correct verdict in this case I cannot persuade myself to entertain the shadow of a doubt; and I hope, at all events that those who sometimes imagine that a judge is half-hearted in the cause of decency and morality because he takes care no prejudice shall enter into the case, may see that that is consistent at least with the common sense of indignation at the horrible charges brought home to both of you.

It is no use for me to address you. People who can do these things must be dead to all sense of shame, and one cannot hope to produce any effect upon them. It is the worst case I have ever tried. That you, Taylor, kept a kind of male brothel it is impossible to doubt. And that you, Wilde, have been the centre of a circle of extensive corruption of the most hideous kind among young men, it is equally impossible to doubt.

I shall, under such circumstances, be expected to pass the severest sentence that the law allows. In my judgement it is totally inadequate for such a case as this. The sentence of the Court is that each of you be imprisoned and kept to hard labour for two years.

A cry of 'Shame' was heard in the court. Wilde blanched and his discomposed face worked with pain. 'My God, my God!' he said. He struggled to speak, and may have managed to say (though witnesses differ), 'And I? May I say nothing, my lord?' But the judge merely waved his hand to the warders, who took hold of Wilde just as he swayed and seemed about to fall to the ground. Taylor followed him, indifferent, as if conscious of having no place in the drama. But he had shielded Wilde, as Wilde had shielded Douglas. (After serving his sentence Taylor emigrated to America and oblivion.)* Outside, Yeats said, the harlots danced on the pavement.[35] They were delighted to have this rival removed. Lord Queensberry, too, was triumphant, and that night he and Charles Brookfield and Charles Hawtrey held a victory dinner in celebration.†

* In the 1920s Douglas, staying at a Chicago hotel, rang the bell for the floor waiter. It was answered by Alfred Taylor.[34]

† Queensberry was said in a letter to the *Star* to have evinced sympathy for Wilde. The Marquess wrote to the editor to take it back:

Sir, – I must take exception to the word 'sympathy' that is placed in my mouth. I never used it. In my time I have helped to cut up and destroy sharks. I had no sympathy for them, but may have felt sorry, and wished to put them out of pain as far as possible.

What I did say was that as Mr Wilde now seemed to be on his beam ends and utterly done I did feel sorry for his awful position, and that supposing he was convicted of the loathsome charges brought against him that were I the authority that had to mete out to him his punishment, I would treat him with all possible consideration as a sexual pervert of an utterly diseased mind, and not as a sane criminal. If this is sympathy Mr Wilde has it from me to this extent.

Yours, &c.

24 April [1895]   QUEENSBERRY

CHAPTER XIX

Pentonville, Wandsworth, and Reading

The public is wonderfully tolerant. It forgives everything except genius.

Spring Days in Prison

The press lived up to Wilde's expectations by almost universally praising the verdict of the jury. His old acquaintance Clement Scott wrote in the *Daily Telegraph*, 'Open the windows! Let in the fresh air.' The *News of the World* on 26 May rejoiced that 'The aesthetic cult, in the nasty form, is over.' The *St James's Gazette* editorialized on 27 May that 'a dash of wholesome bigotry' was better than over-toleration. Only the *Daily Chronicle* and *Reynolds's News* offered any sympathy to the greatest dramatist of the age. *Reynolds's* in a leader of 20 May refused 'to gloat over the ruin of the unhappy man,' and pointed out that he had corrupted none of the young men. It complained of Lockwood's attitude, and of Queensberry's attendance at the trial, and suggested that the male strumpets who had given evidence should not go unpunished. As for Wilde's friends, few felt for him. Burne-Jones hoped that Wilde would shoot himself and was disappointed when he did not; but in a few months he relented and expressed sympathy. Yet Hall Caine said to Coulson Kernahan, 'It is the most awful tragedy in the whole history of literature.'[1]

What of Wilde? *Reynolds's News* on 9 June described what happened to him after the jury's verdict. He and Taylor were taken from court to Newgate prison, where the warrants authorizing their detention for two years were prepared. They were then brought in a prison van to Holloway. Here his belongings were taken from Wilde, and he was stripped to his shirt. An officer noted down a minute description of his appearance, distinctive marks, color of his eyes, hair, complexion, any scars. Some minutes later he was made to take a bath, on emerging from which he found a full suit of prison clothes ready for him, from the underlinen to the loose shoes and 'hideous' Scottish cap. The clothes were of the usual drab

450

color, with broad arrows all over them. As a concession to his importance, and because of his unusual height, the clothes were new, but no less
appalling for that. The rules were read to him, and he was marched to his
cell. Shortly afterwards he received his first prison meal, an allowance of
thin porridge (skilly) and a small brown loaf.

During the week of 9 June Wilde was moved to Pentonville, the prison
for convicted prisoners, as Holloway was for unconvicted ones. Here he
had a close medical examination. If declared fit, he was to take his first
month's exercise on the treadmill – six hours daily, making an ascent of
6,000 feet, twenty minutes on and five minutes rest. During this month,
also, he would sleep on a plank bed, a bare board raised a few inches above
the floor, supplied with sheets, two rugs, a coverlet, but no mattress. His
diet was to be: cocoa and bread for breakfast at 7.30; dinner at noon: one
day bacon and beans, another soup, another cold Australian meat, and
another brown flour suet pudding, with the last three repeated twice a
week, potatoes with every dinner; and tea at 5.30. After the first month he
would be put to some industrial employment, such as postbag-making,
tailoring, or picking oakum. He would exercise in the open air daily for an
hour, walking with the rest of his ward in Indian file, no talking being
allowed. Until three months of his sentence were over he could not
communicate with the outside; at that time he might write and receive one
letter, and be visited for twenty minutes by three friends, but separated
from them by wire blinds, and in the presence of a warder. The visit could
be repeated every three months. He could get off the plank bed only with a
certain number of marks awarded for work done. Every morning at 9 a.m.
and twice on Sundays, he had to attend chapel. He could be visited by the
chaplain, as often as he liked, and also daily by the governor or deputy-
governor. A government inspector would visit him once a month to hear
any complaint.

Reynolds's News noted that Wilde's health had been seriously affected
since his confinement, and that he would probably be transferred to the
infirmary. 'Already Wilde has grown much thinner, and since his conviction he has preserved, it is said, a settled melancholy and reticence. He has
had great difficulty in getting sleep, and from time to time he loudly
bemoans the bitterness of his fate.' There was no refuge in oblivion, only
pain.

Douglas Rampant

*behind my prison's blinded bars
I do possess what none can take away . . .*

Wilde's fictitious heroes generally manage to break the law without having
serious brushes with the police. Lord Arthur Savile escapes punishment

altogether, while Dorian Gray is obliged to punish himself. The only one of Wilde's protagonists who goes to jail is Guido Ferranti in *The Duchess of Padua*. Guido nobly assumes the guilt for having assassinated the duke, although he knows that the duchess has done the deed. Wilde had some feeling that he had allowed himself (in spite of his strictures on self-sacrifice) to be punished in place of Lord Alfred Douglas, and certainly he had taken the blame for several of Douglas's erotic encounters. There is also a resemblance to Guido Ferranti in Wilde's behavior after once being taken into custody. A passive resignation is all either would display. When the enamored duchess visits the imprisoned Guido, in disguise, and begs him to escape, he replies, 'Be sure I shall not stir.' Wilde showed the same resistance. He could not have failed to recall how one of his favorite heroes, Julien Sorel, also refuses to stir when he is imprisoned and his former mistress Madame de Renal begs him to escape.

Where both Guido and Julien differ from Wilde is that their beloveds too die for love. Douglas, scouting fictional decorum, lived on for fifty years. During the two years that Wilde was imprisoned, Douglas was a character searching for his tragic role and not finding it. There can be no doubt that he was greatly distressed. His mother and friends worried about him. He felt the need to make some public gesture on Wilde's behalf: it would have to be on the Continent, since he was warned by his mother's solicitor that his return to England during the next two years was inadvisable. He conceived of the term of his exile as comparable to Wilde's prison sentence. His father offered, if he would give up Wilde forever, to give him money to go to the South Sea Islands where 'you will find plenty of beautiful girls.'[2] Douglas's answer was to petition the Queen for clemency for Wilde on 25 June 1895; the Secretary of State said he was unable to advise Her Majesty to comply with this prayer.

At the same time Douglas still had a private life. His mother went through a complicated series of maneuvers to provide him with companionship. Lionel Johnson did not accept her offer to pay expenses if he would join Bosie. Ross's family forbade him to stay with Douglas.[3] But More Adey consented to go with him at Lady Queensberry's request. Other appointed companions were to follow. Douglas quickly resumed his former way of life with his accustomed recklessness. In Le Havre in late July, he rented a small yacht and hired a cabin boy. This boy brought another boy, and some adults joined them. There were reports of naked bathing and implications of other doings, so that the *Journal du Havre* published at the end of the month an editorial attack upon the young English lord who was corrupting the city's youth. Douglas responded with injured innocence in a letter to the editor:

For me who have suffered so much already, it would not matter a bit that a little provincial newspaper should accuse me of all imaginable crimes, but it is different for my little cabin boy, an innocent creature, and the good people who are his friends, whom you dismiss so carelessly.

Let us establish, sir, that I have rented a little yacht and that I have also employed a cabin boy and that I have made, with this cabin boy and a friend of his and several Havre fishermen who are accustomed to go with foreigners, several trips to the sea; is that any reason to insult and defame not merely me, but these other good people, your fellow countrymen?

For me it is already too clear that the world has the right to insult and attack me because I am the friend of Oscar Wilde.

There is my crime, not that I was his friend, but that I shall be until death (and even afterwards if God permit). Well, Sir, it is not part of my policy to moralize, to leave a friend in the lurch, to deny him even if that friend is in prison or in hell.

I may be wrong, but I still prefer to consult my own conscience rather than that of the *Journal du Havre*.

This was his farewell salute to Le Havre, for a day or two later he went off to Sorrento and Capri. Wilde is said to have commented 'Le prince du caprice est parti pour Capri.'[4]

It was Douglas's secret plan to write something more extended about the Wilde case. An Englishman, Dalhousie Young, came to see him in Le Havre, with an essay he had written in defense of Wilde. Douglas was also encouraged by a series of articles in the French press. On 3 June Henry Bauer had a leading article in *L'Echo de Paris* meditating on the barbarity of the sentence, the hypocrisy of London society, the brutishness of Queensberry, and the outrageousness of English law and judges. On 18 June 1895 Octave Mirbeau had a favorable piece in *Le Journal* (Paris). Paul Adam in *La Revue blanche* of 15 May 1895 argued that Greek love was less harmful than adultery. The most telling article was that of Hugues Rebell, a young poet and novelist, in the *Mercure de France* for August. This eloquent *'Défense d'Oscar Wilde'* denounced the conduct of the trial and rebuked the hypocritical and prudish court for its effrontery in mistreating a writer who was giving substance and character to English literature. Rebell called for Pentonville to take its place beside the Bastille: 'With what joy should I see Pentonville in flames! And not only on Wilde's behalf, but on behalf of all of us pagan artists and writers who are by rights honorary prisoners.' Douglas, on reading this at the beginning of August, urged More Adey to buy several copies for distribution. He also wrote to the Secretary of State on 30 July 1895 asking if it was true that journalists were allowed to observe Wilde in prison. In Sorrento he decided to write his own article and submit it to the same review. He said nothing about it in his letters, in case his friends should try to dissuade him.

Behind Bars

The prison system – a system so terrible that it hardens their hearts whose hearts it does not break, and brutalises those who have to carry it out no less than those who have to submit to it.

Meanwhile there was no fishing for boys or mackerel in Pentonville. (Sir Edward Clarke's demurrer about the prosecution's conduct in linking the cases of Wilde and Taylor came to nothing by 19 June.) Much nonsense has been written about prison, and some of it, in the days before he experienced it, was written by Wilde. The detachment with which he had once remarked, in a review of Wilfrid Blunt's poems, that prison had improved Blunt's style, was not something to be reminded of now. Nor was his admirable but shortsighted argument in 'The Soul of Man under Socialism': 'After all, even in prison a man can be quite free. His soul can be free. His personality can be untroubled. He can be at peace.' It was just such nonsense that the prison authorities found insupportable. They knew, if Wilde did not, that a man with a pain tearing at his bowels cannot be at peace. They were determined on a course which unwittingly confirmed a wiser remark from the same essay: 'As one reads history, not in the expurgated editions written for schoolboys and passmen, but in the original authorities of each time, one is absolutely sickened, not by the crimes that the wicked have committed, but by the punishment that the good have inflicted.' The chaplain minced in and asked, 'Mr Wilde, did you have morning prayers in your house?' 'I am sorry. I fear not.' 'You see where you are now,' said the chaplain.[5]

Wilde had first to suffer the grief of loss. A fellow convict whispered to him as they trod in enforced silence the prison yard, 'I am sorry for you: it is harder for the likes of you than it is for the likes of us.'[6] Such sympathy was scarce. Open contempt had replaced the mockery under which in the past he had learned not to smart, as infamy had replaced fame. It was as if he had never written any of those plays, dialogues, stories and poems. All his acts had been erased except those memorialized in the courtroom, encounters with male prostitutes in which Wilde, probably rare among their customers, had always behaved kindly and generously. The only things that survived from his earlier life were his love for Douglas and his sense of being loved by him, and these quickly came under challenge.

Besides the wormwood of obloquy, there was physical pain. Wilde's first month of imprisonment, at Pentonville, introduced him to treatment which outvied in harshness, as he said later, that meted out to animals. 'Three permanent punishments authorized by law,' he said, were '1. Hunger, 2. Insomnia, and 3. Disease.' As for insomnia, that was enforced by a plank bed on which Wilde had to sleep until his behavior showed him to be sufficiently cowed to be allotted a hard mattress. 'I shivered all night long,' he told Frank Harris. Sleeplessness became an ingrained habit. As for hunger and disease, they were related. Apart from soup – the one thing in the prison diet that Wilde could eat, and that an infrequent one – the staples were weak gruel, suet and water, measured out 'ounce by ounce.' Such food was revolting and insufficient. 'Every prisoner suffers day and night from hunger,' Wilde wrote later.[7] Given his unusual height and girth, he suffered more than most. As if hunger and nausea were not enough, the disease that came with them was diarrhoea. This successfully resisted the two or three daily doses of antidote brought by the prison warders.

Even diarrhoea might have been borne had it not been for the prison's sanitary arrangements. Because of the danger that the prisoners should communicate by tapping drain pipes, pipes and latrines had been removed. A small tin vessel which the prisoner could empty three times a day was substituted. The prison lavatories could be used only during the one hour of exercise allowed daily in the yard, and after five o'clock no prisoner could leave his cell for any reason. To use the tin vessel rather than suffer intolerable pain meant that the cell during the night became 'indescribable' as the slops ran over the floor. On three occasions, Wilde said later, he had seen warders become violently sick when they opened the cell in the morning and saw the condition to which the helpless prisoner had been forced to bring it during the night. According to Rebell, someone who had seen Wilde at Pentonville described him as '*humilié et anéanti*,' shattered by fatigue, malnutrition, and diarrhoea. His brother wrote to express his concern, and had an answer from the governor of Pentonville asserting that 'the convict was perfectly well and that every care was being taken of him.'[8] His weight was down from 190 to 168 pounds.

R. B. Haldane, who had known Wilde earlier and who as a member of a Home Office committee investigating prisons had access to any prison at any time, took it upon himself to be Wilde's first visitor, on 12 June 1895. (Margaret Brooke, the Ranee of Sarawak, an old friend of Wilde,* had urged Haldane to go.)[9] The chaplain was summoned first, and acknowledged that Wilde was depressed and would not listen to any spiritual comfort. 'I could be patient,' he told someone at the time, 'for patience is a virtue. It is not patience, it is apathy you want here, and apathy is a vice.'[10] Haldane entered Wilde's cell for a private interview. At first Wilde refused to speak a word. Then, Haldane recalled, 'I put my hand on his prison-dress-clad shoulder and said that I used to know him and that I had come to say something about himself. He had not fully used his great literary gift, and the reason was that he had lived a life of pleasure and had not made any great subject his own. Now misfortune might prove a blessing for his career, for he had got a great subject. I would try to get for him books and pen and ink, and in eighteen months [i.e., twenty-three] he would be free to produce.' Wilde burst into tears. He responded to

---

* He dedicated 'The Young King' to her.

Haldane's analysis of his career, for it was essentially the view he was to take of it himself in *De Profundis*. He made no effort to deny his guilt, said only that the temptation of such a life had been too great for him. He promised to try to do what Haldane proposed, and asked eagerly for books. Aside from the Bible, he had been allowed only *Pilgrim's Progress*, he said. One author he named was Flaubert, whose *La Tentation de Saint Antoine* had always accompanied him on his travels. But Haldane half jokingly reminded him that the dedication by Flaubert of his works to his advocate for having defended him against a charge of indecent publication made the granting of such a request unlikely. Wilde laughed for the first time, and cheered up a little. They decided on a decorous list which included:

> St Augustine, *De Civitate Dei* and *Confessiones*
> Pascal, *Provincial Letters* and *Pensées*
> Pater, *The Renaissance*
> Theodore Mommsen, *History of Rome* (5 vols.)
> Cardinal Newman, Essays on Miracles, *The Grammar of Assent*, *Apologia pro Vita Sua*, and *The Idea of a University*

There were fifteen volumes in all. The governor of Pentonville objected that books were contrary to the Prison Act of 1865, but the Secretary of State had agreed so they were delivered.[11] Pen and ink were still debarred for the prisoner. Haldane had promised him also that his wife and children would be looked after, and asked a friend of his, Lady Cowper, for help, which he afterwards said she had given. He also had Wilde transferred from Pentonville to Wandsworth on 4 July. His clothes were sent with him, but one waistcoat was missing. Wilde became furious, storming and raving until it was found. Then, pacified, he said to his warder, 'Pray pardon my ebullition of feeling.'[12] Taylor had meanwhile (according to the Home Office records) been transferred to Wormwood Scrubs. On 17 August 1895 Wilde's books were received from Pentonville and put into the Wandsworth library so they could be issued to him under the usual regulations. They would go with him on his subsequent changes of prison. Three years later, Haldane would receive anonymously in the post *The Ballad of Reading Gaol*, and would think of it as Wilde's fulfillment of his promise.

Another visitor who was exceptionally allowed entrance, it appears, was Otho Holland, Mrs Wilde's brother. He made clear to Wilde that Constance was being urged by her solicitor, J. S. Hargrove, to take divorce proceedings, and would certainly do so if he did not write to her at the first opportunity, which would be in September when his first three months had been served. Wilde said he wished at all costs to prevent the parting from wife and children which would follow a divorce. Holland so informed his sister, who had gone with her boys to Glion in Switzerland.

At the same time, she received a letter from Robert Sherard pleading for a reconciliation. Mrs Wilde needed little persuading: on 8 September she wrote to Wilde from Glion that she had decided to drop the divorce proceedings, and added comfortingly that his son Cyril never forgot him. The next day the hard-bitten Hargrove arrived, and she was afraid that he would disapprove; but he produced a letter from Wilde confessing his folly and promising amendment, which in her interests he had already read, and described as 'one of the most touching and pathetic letters that had ever come under his eye.' If she called off the divorce, he warned her, she would have to live on 'the other side of the world.'[13] Constance agreed and wrote a second letter to her husband, to say that there was forgiveness for him, and at the same time, on 13 September, wrote to the governor of Wandsworth asking permission to see Wilde in prison.

Love and Publicity

What letters? The letters I had written to you from Holloway Prison! The letters that should have been to you things sacred and secret beyond anything in the whole world.

Wilde's preoccupation with his family surprised and alarmed Bosie Douglas. He had written in August 1895 to the prison governor for permission to write to Wilde, but was refused because of the correspondence with Constance. Douglas took the rebuff badly, as he indicated to Ada Leverson.[14] But she, like the rest of Wilde's friends, was well aware that the love affair with Douglas had been the center of Wilde's downfall, so she did not feel much sympathy.

Meanwhile Robert Sherard, who lived near Wandsworth in south-west London, had arranged to be Wilde's next visitor. He had delighted the Wilde circle by challenging Queensberry to a duel on French soil following the trial, but Queensberry was for once prudently silent. 'Don't fight more than six duels a week!' Wilde had cautioned his friend.[15] Since Sherard's ticket of admission for 26 August allowed a second visitor, he asked George Ives and others to accompany him. All, as he afterwards said, pleaded conflicting engagements while expressing sympathy. So Sherard went alone.

He described his visit in detail. There was much unlocking and relocking of metal doors before he was ushered into a vaulted room divided by two rows of iron bars. Between the rows stood a warder watching the clock and making sure that no complaints of prison conditions were uttered by the convict to the visitor. Sherard found Wilde courageous and resigned, as he told a reporter when he emerged; but on reflection he amended this and said that Wilde was 'greatly depressed' and on the verge of tears. Probably both were true: Wilde, given any chance at all, had great powers of self-rescue. Still, there were unmistakable signs of what he had endured. Sherard noted that his hands, which clasped the bars, were disfigured, their nails broken and bleeding. His hair was unkempt, and a small straggly beard had been allowed to grow. Wilde's face was so thin that Sherard could scarcely recognize him.[16] They soon began to talk about books: Wilde's spirits had been lifted a little by his having received the books specified by Haldane and even a few more, including Pater's *Greek Studies*, *Appreciations* and *Imaginary Portraits*.

One piece of literary news proved disturbing. Sherard had learned from a friend on the *Mercure de France* that the review was about to publish an article on Wilde by Alfred Douglas, that quoted three love letters written by Wilde at the time of the trials. What alarmed Sherard was that the article would rupture the delicate negotiations with Constance Wilde for a reconciliation. He asked if it were really by Wilde's wish that his letters were being published. The subject raised bitter memories. Wilde remembered that the last letters from him which Douglas had made public had led to his imprisonment. If the blackmailing boys had not sold two letters to Queensberry, the Marquess's case against him would have lacked exhibits. Now his beloved Bosie proposed to offer his later letters, which were fervently and brazenly homosexual, to the gaze of an unsympathetic public in a foreign country, without even asking his consent. To Wilde those letters should have been 'sacred' and 'secret.'[17] Douglas had no right in common law to publish another man's letters, but what Wilde minded was the blatant lack of concern for the ignominy his children would suffer if their father were proved to have perjured himself on the stand. Constance would be outraged and hurt. Then too, the article would preclude any mitigation of sentence, something for which Wilde had not ceased to hope. Without hesitation Wilde asked Sherard to try by every means to stop the publication of Douglas's article.

It seems from this that he had already turned away from Douglas. On a plank bed he could hardly have failed to review the events of the last months and years, to see again the beautiful fierce face egging him on against Queensberry, calling him a coward if he considered desisting from the prosecution, battening on his precarious income and marring his calm with constant quarrels and reconciliations, detesting him when he was weakened by illness.

Sherard obeyed Wilde by writing at once to both Douglas and the *Mercure de France*. Douglas in his turn was shocked and disappointed. His article, of which he was proud, began by quoting the letter of Wilde from Holloway which began, 'This is to assure you of my immortal, my eternal love for you'; if others should write that their love was evil, Bosie would write that it was not so. Douglas took this remark of Wilde's as an assignment: 'I do not hope to gain any sympathy by lies, so I shall not pretend that the friendship between Mr Wilde and myself was an ordinary friendship nor simply an intellectual friendship, nor even that it was like the feeling which an older brother might have for his younger brother. No, I say now frankly (let my enemies interpret it as they will!) that our friendship was love, real love – love, it is true, completely pure but extremely passionate. Its origin was, in Mr Wilde, a purely physical admiration for beauty and grace (*my* beauty and *my* grace); it matters little whether they are real or whether they exist only in the imagination of my friend; what must be remarked is that it was a perfect love, more spiritual than sensual, a truly Platonic love, the love of an artist for a beautiful mind and a beautiful body.' The contradiction between 'purely physical' and 'more spiritual than sensual' left Plato in tatters. Douglas attested Wilde's fatherliness in attempting to prevent his addictions to racing, gambling, hunting, and vice; in fact, Wilde's injunctions had proved useless. Most of all, Wilde had turned him towards art, 'the art of living as well as the other arts . . .' Douglas explained how all this infuriated his father, and how Wilde had brought the suit for Bosie's sake. Then Queensberry, aided by a solicitor named Bernard Abrahams, had succeeded by the use of two or three thousand pounds in securing witnesses. Douglas next reviewed the trials, and accused judges and prosecutors of misusing their authority. He insisted that they had knuckled under to Queensberry's threats that members of the government would be implicated if Wilde was released. The family connection of Schwabe with the Solicitor-General was one that Wilde studiously refused to pursue, even though it would have been to his advantage. Mr Justice Wills was 'an old woman.' He then quoted two other letters from Wilde to him, as passionate as the first. 'Why reveal to the whole world the secret of my life? I have been advised not to do it, prudent friends have told me that I was committing a folly!' With Plato and Shakespeare invoked as his witnesses, he asked rhetorically why, even if Wilde were guilty of the offenses of which he had been accused, he should be 'punished for being a man who preferred the physical beauty of man to that of woman.'[18] And so on.

As a defense of Wilde this was futile; Hugues Rebell had done it much better than Douglas could possibly do. What it came to was a brag that it was Wilde's love for him that had brought him down, and a candid admission that this love was on both sides homosexual. When Sherard asked him to withdraw the article, Douglas at first agreed. Then he had second thoughts: in November 1895 he wrote to the governor of Wandsworth asking for permission to publish Wilde's letters in a French journal 'corresponding to' the *Fortnightly Review*. Wilde, through the governor, absolutely refused.[19] It would seem that Douglas had not yet officially withdrawn the article, for he received a letter from the editor of the *Mercure* saying that, in view of Sherard's representations, they wished to know Douglas's attitude. His reply of 28 September 1895 was written from Capri, where he had taken a villa after moving from Sorrento:

Dear Sir,
I was about to write to you when I received your letter. I am the nearest and dearest friend of Mr Oscar Wilde, and the injuries and insults, and

practical social ruin which I have endured entirely on account of my steadfast devotion to him are too well known to make it necessary to recall them. I consider that I am a better judge of what is best for Mr Wilde and more likely to undersand what his wishes would be, than Mr Sherard. I am convinced that the publication of my article would bring nothing but pity and sympathy to Mr Wilde, and that he himself would approve of it. In fact in writing the article I was really fulfilling a request of Mr Wilde's. Nevertheless after what has been said by Mr Sherard I will not undertake the responsibility of running the risk of doing what he, as a sincere friend of Mr Wilde's, thinks so fatal. I think Mr Sherard is quite wrong and I object both to his interference and to his manner of interfering, yet since he has found out prematurely my intentions of publishing the article, and objects to it in such terms, I would rather that the article should not be published . . . I was particularly anxious that nobody should know of my intention to write the article before it appeared, as I anticipated that many of Mr Wilde's friends would think it unwise, and I had written it, well knowing that it would cause me trouble and misunderstanding, because after careful consideration I considered it would be a service to my friend and would be for his good.

That Douglas remained of two minds about the matter, and did not really renounce the temptation of writing Oscar Wilde's confession for him, would become clear the following year. He brought the matter up again with the *Mercure*. He also wrote to Sherard complaining that his meddling in the matter had been 'exceedingly impertinent and in the worst possible taste.' When Sherard held firm, and mentioned the importance of Wilde's being reconciled to his wife, Douglas responded that if Sherard did anything to alienate Wilde from him, Douglas would shoot him 'like a dog.'[20] It was the same threat that Queensberry had made to Wilde. Dogs had little to hope for from the Queensberry family arsenal.

Though Wilde's enforced meditation on Bosie had already swung him round, as is indicated by the contrition he expressed to his wife, the *Mercure de France* episode provided evidence of Douglas's 'hideous rashness' and incapacity to enter imaginatively into anyone else's feelings. What Douglas called love was the opposite of wishing the beloved well. In *De Profundis* Wilde castigated such devotion repeatedly as 'shallow.' He had long tried to keep from recriminating, and to imagine that Douglas was suffering; but it appeared that his anguish had an element of self-seeking, that in fact the Wilde case had become simply a subject on which he might publish. In his bitterness Wilde imagined Douglas on Capri, busying himself, in the midst of his local pleasures, with the destruction of any scrap of Wilde's reputation still surviving. That the Queensberry family consisted not of two totally different beings, but of two very similar ones, both determined to expose him, one out of purported love and one out of evident hate, suddenly became clear. Wilde, as he picked oakum in Wandsworth, could wake in the night to look back on a senseless love.

From now on Douglas could do nothing right. He heard from Ross or Adey that Wilde was to suffer a further indignity of bankruptcy proceedings. There had been some talk of his brother Percy's paying Wilde's debts, which came to £3,591, Queensberry's costs being £677 of the total. Percy after having volunteered decided to think again. Douglas complained that Wilde's friends appeared to be unwilling to do anything, and in blaming them he found reason for releasing his own family from the promise they had made to Wilde long before. Douglas wrote privately to his mother that they need do nothing, and she replied, 'I told Black [her solicitor] of what you told me of the bankruptcy proceedings, he quite agreed you should all get out of it and said he would see to that.'[21] But Bosie kept in mind the fact that Wilde would be let out of prison for a few hours, and ascertained from his friends the name of the solicitor's clerk who would take Wilde's depositions. He prevailed upon this man to say to Wilde, 'Prince Fleur de Lys wishes to be remembered to you.' Wilde stared blankly at the clerk, who repeated the message and added, to be sure he was understood, 'The gentleman is abroad at present.' In former times Wilde had spoken of Douglas by this name, borrowed from a fatuous ballad Douglas had written about a prince and a peasant boy who, after changing clothes, are mistaken for each other. But on hearing it now, in those unspeakable surroundings, Wilde laughed aloud, as he wrote later, 'for the first and last time in my entire prison-life. In that laugh was the scorn of all the world.' He had occasion to contrast Douglas's absurd greeting with that of Robert Ross, who waited in the corridor of the Bankruptcy Court on 25 September so that when Wilde went by, handcuffed and with bowed head, he could 'gravely raise his hat to me.'[22]*

---

* On 21 October 1895 Ross wrote to Oscar Browning asking him to contribute to a sum being collected to annul the bankruptcy proceedings. If the sum collected should prove insufficient, the money was to be returned to the donors. But on 12 November he wrote that it had been decided to let the bankruptcy take effect, because new creditors had appeared and the amount collected was not enough. He went on:

'After the proceedings by special privilege the trustee [Arthur Clifton] and myself were allowed to see him in a private room for half an hour each. You may easily imagine how very painful this was for both of us. I have not seen him since the day he was arrested, as you know I was with him at the time. Mentally his condition is much better than I had dared to hope though his mind is considerably impaired. Physically he was much worse than anyone had led me to believe. Indeed I really should not have known him at all. This I know is an ordinary figure of speech, but it exactly described what I experienced. His clothes hung about him in loose folds and his hands are like those of a skeleton. The colour of his face is completely changed, but this cannot be altogether attributed to his slight beard. The latter only hides the appalling sunken cheeks. A friend who was in court would not believe it was Oscar when he first came in. I cannot understand how any human nation, the English being Protestant of course are not Christians, can keep him in this condition. He is still in the infirmary, but told me he wanted to leave as he hoped to die very soon. Indeed he only spoke calmly about death, every other subject caused him to break down.'[23]

Wilde's alienation from Douglas was violently expressed to Constance Wilde, who had obtained the special permission to see her husband which she had requested from Switzerland. The interview took place on 21 September 1895, in the same vaulted room that Sherard had used. Its effect upon her was beyond any expectation. As she wrote to Sherard next day,

> My dear Mr Sherard, It was indeed awful, more so than I had any conception it could be. I could not see him and I could not touch him, and I scarcely spoke . . . He has been mad the last three years, and he says that if he saw Lord A. he would kill him. So he had better keep away, and be satisfied with having marred a fine life. Few people can boast of so much.

In these painful circumstances, she promised Wilde that on his emergence from prison he might rejoin her and their sons. The news cheered him very much, as Sherard learned in a long interview, this time in a private room, two or three days later. Constance Wilde held to her decision: on 15 October she wrote to Hannah Whitall Smith from Neuchâtel that, while she was changing her name to Holland, she was withdrawing from divorce proceedings. 'My poor misguided husband, who is weak rather than wicked, repents most bitterly all his past madness and I cannot refuse to him the forgiveness that he has asked.'[24]

Unfortunately Wilde's state of health did not respond to her generosity. On 15 October the *Daily Chronicle* reported that he was in the infirmary; his brother's wife Lily visited him there on 22 October, and afterwards wrote, 'He is in the Infirmary as he is suffering from dysentery brought on I should say by great bodily weakness. He is hungry but cannot eat the food and at present is only allowed a little beef tea. Mentally he is very unhappy . . . He is very altered in *every* way.' Wilde told Sherard, who managed to see him again, that he would be dead before long. On 12 November he was well enough to attend the second and final stage of his bankruptcy hearing. His friends not having raised enough to meet all his debts, he was officially declared bankrupt and his affairs put in the hands of a receiver. The *Labour Leader* on 16 November commented sympathetically on his appearance: 'They have cut his hair in a shocking way and parted it down the side and he wears a short, scrubby, unkempt beard.'

A Change in Mood

All this took place in the early part of November of the year before last [1895]. A great river of life flows between you and a date so distant.

The popular revulsion against Wilde's 'crimes' had begun to be checked by compassion. His friends in London and Paris took advantage of the shift by circulating petitions for mitigation of sentence. The one drafted in London by More Adey at the beginning of December 1895 argued that Wilde, being a man of intelligence, had already suffered enough punishment. In Paris Stuart Merrill's petition was to the same effect. But both experienced difficulties: Adey secured the signatures of Frederick York Powell, Regius Professor of History at Oxford, and probably of Selwyn Image and Walter Crane. But W. Holman Hunt declined without a trace of Pre-Raphaelite nostalgia for his old defender:

> I must repeat my opinion that the law treated him with exceeding leniency, and state that further consideration of the facts convinces me that in justice to criminals belonging to other classes of society I should have to join in the cry for doing away with all personal responsibility for wickedness if I took any part in appealing . . . and while such a course might seem benevolent to malefactors, it would scarcely be so to the self-restrained and orderly members of society.

Henry James, asked by Merrill to sign, gave a prudent answer through Jonathan Sturges on 27 November: 'James says that the petition would not have the slightest effect on the *authorities* here who have the matter in charge, and in whose nostrils the very name of Zola and even of Bourget is a stench, and that the document would only exist as a manifesto of personal loyalty to Oscar by his friends, of whom he was never one.' Bourget may have signed, but Zola refused; Gide signed, but Sardou said, 'This muck is too vile for me to get mixed up in it.' Jules Renard, never friendly to Wilde, wrote in his journal. 'Je veux bien signer la pétition pour Oscar Wilde, à la condition qu'il prenne l'engagement d'honneur . . . de ne plus jamais écrire.'*[25] François Coppée agonized over the matter in a column of print before saying he would sign, but only as a member of the society for the prevention of cruelty to animals. 'A writer pig is still a pig,' he said. Discouraged by reluctance and refusal, neither Adey nor Merrill presented a petition. Later Frank Harris was to draw up another and confidently ask George Meredith to start it off, only to receive a direct refusal. Douglas, continuing to find his subject in his friend's cause, inscribed a sonnet to the French writers who had refused to sign Merrill's petition, and sent it to Merrill for publication in *La Plume*. Merrill did not use it.

The months following Wilde's bankruptcy had not been easy for Douglas. He came to perceive that Wilde did not love him any longer, and while he could put this down to treachery on the part of their mutual friends, he could not accept it. There were frantic letters to Sherard, to Ada Leverson, to Ross, to Adey. When some of Wilde's new detestation

---

* 'I shall be glad to sign the petition for Oscar Wilde, on condition that he give his word of honor . . . never again to use his pen.'

reached him through these filters, he responded on 30 November to Adey, from Capri where Ross was staying with him.

> I am not in prison but I think I suffer as much as Oscar and in fact more, just as I am sure that he would have suffered more if he had been free and I in prison. Please tell him that . . . Tell him I know that I have ruined his life, that everything is my fault, if that pleases him. I don't care. Doesn't he think that my life is just as much ruined as his and so much sooner?

He wished that he and Wilde were both dead. Adey responded that he had seen Wilde on 30 November, that there had been no general complaints against Douglas, only a specific one about a letter – presumably the one requesting permission to publish Wilde's love letters – sent by Douglas to the governor of Wandsworth, which Wilde had been told about but not allowed to see. He said that Wilde's revulsion from Douglas was 'a passing delirium of gaol moral fever,' which Douglas could overcome if only he had patience.[26] Good advice, but to the wrong man.

Transfer to Reading

A community is infinitely more brutalised by the habitual employment of punishment than it is by the occasional occurrence of crime.

Haldane, who had visited Wilde at Pentonville, came to see him in Wandsworth too. It was clear that things were not going well. The deputy chaplain on visiting him had smelled semen, and wrote on 11 September 1895 that Wilde had degenerated into masturbating* – a charge the authorities indignantly denied (attributing the smell to Jeyes's disin-

---

* The chaplain, W. D. Morrison, wrote:

When he first came down here from Pentonville he was in an excited flurried condition, and seemed as if he wished to face his punishment without flinching. But all this has passed away. As soon as the excitement aroused by the trial subsided and he had to encounter the daily routine of prison life his fortitude began to give way and rapidly collapsed altogether. He is now quite crushed and broken. This is unfortunate, as a prisoner who breaks down in one direction generally breaks down in several, and I fear from what I hear and see that perverse sexual practices are again getting the mastery over him. This is a common occurrence among prisoners of his class and is of course favoured by constant cellular isolation. The odour of his cell is now so bad that the officer in charge of him has to use carbolic acid in it every day . . . I need hardly tell you that he is a man of decidedly morbid disposition . . . In fact some of our most experienced officers openly say that they don't think he will be able to go through the two years . . . It seems to me that it would be prudent in case of trouble to have Wilde examined by a first class medical expert.[27]

fectant), and answered by sending the chaplain to another post. Wilde, deathly weak from dysentery and hunger but suspected by the prison doctor of malingering, had been forced to attend chapel. He had fainted there and fallen, and the fall had injured his right ear, in which the hearing was already impaired. The result of this accident and dysentery was that he remained for two months in the infirmary. He had also come short of being a model prisoner, his oakum pickings being very skimpy, his obedience to the prescribed silence among prisoners desultory. As he told Frank Harris, some of the warders at Wandsworth were brutes.[28] Haldane heard enough of this to conclude that Wilde would be better off at Reading prison, and he arranged for him to be transferred there. The move took place on 21 November, and proved to be the single most humiliating experience of Wilde's prison life. Handcuffed and in prison clothing, he had to wait on the platform at Clapham Junction from 2.00 to 2.30 on a rainy afternoon. A crowd formed, first laughing and then jeering at him. One man recognized that this was Oscar Wilde, and spat at him. 'For a year after that was done to me,' Wilde wrote in *De Profundis*, 'I wept every day at the same hour and for the same space of time.'

There was some stir at Reading about his arrival. At the time there were 170 inmates, thirteen of them female. The governor, Lieutenant-Colonel J. Isaacson, was flattered at Haldane's preference for Reading over Wandsworth. He addressed the staff: 'A certain prisoner is about to be transferred here, and you should be proud to think the Prison Commissioners have chosen Reading Gaol as the one most suitable for this man to serve the remainder of his sentence in.' He did not tell the prisoner's name, but any doubt of the identity of the man placed in cell C.3.3 was dispelled when Wilde was brought forward. One warder was assigned to cut his hair, which at Wandsworth had been allowed to grow out a little. 'Must it be cut?' asked Wilde, with tears in his eyes, 'you don't know what it means to me.' It was cut. 'The horror of prison-life,' Wilde wrote later to Leonard Smithers, 'is the contrast between the grotesqueness of one's aspect and the tragedy in one's soul.'[29]

That the new prisoner was unfit for any hard manual work was evident from the start. Wilde was assigned to work in the garden, and to act as 'schoolmaster's orderly.' This involved taking charge of the library and bringing books to other prisoners, but he did not perform even these light duties in the prescribed manner. He was allowed, by special favor, to spend time in his cell reading, but still not allowed to write. He thought of returning to the books he had loved at Oxford, and in January 1896 he requested and received Liddell and Scott's *Greek Lexicon*, the *Corpus Poetarum Latinorum*, Short's *Latin Dictionary*, Dante's *La Divina Commedia*, *Poetae Scenici Graeci*, and an Italian dictionary and grammar. But his attention wandered from the classical poets, and only Dante's *Inferno* fixed his mind.

His reputation as a writer proved to be more tenacious than he had imagined at Pentonville. Some of his books were republished, notably *The Soul of Man* (omitting the words *under Socialism*) by Arthur L. Humphreys at 187 Piccadilly (Hatchard's) on 30 May 1895. Then in October Ward, Lock published a six-shilling edition of *Dorian Gray*. Meanwhile in Paris the Théâtre Libre and the Théâtre de l'Oeuvre both wanted to stage *Salome*. The request of the former was sent back by Colonel Isaacson with a curt notation that the prisoner was not entitled to receive it. But Lugné-Poë produced it at the Théâtre de l'Oeuvre on 11 February 1896, and himself took the role of Herod. Ernest Dowson and Aubrey Beardsley attended, and Dowson wrote a long letter to Constance describing the enthusiasm of the audience for this 'triumphant performance.'[30] The production was reported in the English press, and Wilde said that it modified the attitude of the prison officials towards him.

But Isaacson found his distinguished inmate difficult. Wilde recipro-cated, describing the governor to Chris Healy; 'He had the eyes of a ferret, the body of an ape, and the soul of a rat.' To someone else he said, perhaps more mildly, that Isaacson was, like Sulla, 'a mulberry-coloured Dicta-tor.' The prisoner's infractions of the rules continued. Wilde gave an example to André Gide later. After he had been at Reading for six weeks, as he and the other prisoners were walking silently in single file during the exercise hour, he heard someone murmur, 'Oscar Wilde, I pity you because you must be suffering more than we are.' Wilde almost fainted at the human sound. Without turning, he said, 'No, my friend, we are all suffering equally.' That day, he told Gide, 'I no longer wished to kill myself.'[31] Though they were absolutely forbidden to talk, Wilde managed on subsequent days to find out the man's name and what he did. He had not yet learned, however, to talk without moving his lips, and their conversation was observed. One evening a warder called out, 'C.3.3 and C.4.8, step out of line! You're going to be brought up before the warden.'

The question Isaacson had to resolve was which of the two had spoken first, since the one who started the conversation would receive greater punishment. He called in C.4.8, and the man confessed to having spoken first. But when Wilde came in, out of pity for the other man, he made the same confession. Isaacson went redder than usual: 'But he says *he* started it! I can't understand . . . All right, if that's how things stand, I'm going to give both of you two weeks.' Wilde complained to Gide not that Isaacson was cruel, but that he had no imagination, as once he would have said that Isaacson was absurd. To someone else, he said that Isaacson could not eat his breakfast until he had punished someone.[32]

The smallest thing would be reported to the warden. One day the prison chaplain, Reverend M. T. Friend, was visiting Wilde, and the prisoner spoke sorrowfully of the 'thickly-muffled glass' in the cell window which allowed him no view of the sky. The chaplain, to comfort him, said 'Oh my friend, let me entreat you to desist from such thoughts and not let your mind dwell on the clouds, but on Him who is above the clouds, Him who –' 'Get out, you damned fool!' Wilde shouted, and pushed him towards the door.[33] This too reached the governor's ears. Yet some of the men assigned to watch the prisoners were less cruel. Since Wilde, like Wainewright (who refused to sweep his cell), was most inefficient at cleaning his cell, one of them was sweeping it when a spider darted across the floor. The warder stepped on it, only to see Wilde gazing at him with horror. 'It brings bad luck to kill a spider,' he said, 'I shall hear worse news than any I have yet heard.' He said later that he had heard the cry of the Banshee, and that he had had a vision of his mother. She was dressed for out-of-doors, and he asked her to take off her hat and cloak and sit down. She shook her head sadly and vanished.[34] The next day, 19 February 1896, he was summoned to talk to his wife in a private room. Constance herself had not been well but, notified by Willie of Lady Wilde's death, she had travelled from Italy to tell her husband the news that she knew would be excruciatingly painful to him. 'I knew it already,' he said, and told her of his vision.

Wilde felt a new burst of misery and remorse. His mother, he boasted to Douglas in *De Profundis*, ranked intellectually with Elizabeth Barrett Browning and historically with Madame Roland. Her last year of life had been wracked by illness and by her sorrow for 'dear Oscar.' She had never left her room and had seen almost no one. A notebook she kept has a bitter entry, 'Life is agony and hope, illusion and despair all commingled, but despair outlasts all.'[35] Willie Wilde said that Oscar had helped her even from prison, presumably with money. He had good reason to know, for there is evidence that he obliged her to give the money to him. That Oscar knew of this is suggested by a letter from Willie Wilde to More Adey on 4 February, the day of Lady Wilde's burial, in 1896: 'For many reasons he wd not wish to see me.'[36] On her deathbed she had asked if Oscar might not be brought to see her, but on being told this was impossible, she said, 'May the prison help him!' and turned to the wall. Her death occurred on 3 February 1896. She left a private letter requesting that no one come to the funeral, and was buried in Kensal Green Cemetery. (She had always wished to be thrown in the sea or buried near a rock on some wild coast, lest she lie next to some common tradesman.) Lily Wilde, Willie's wife, sadly sent all Oscar's things to More Adey because, as she acknowledged, 'I feel sure now his mother is dead he will not wish to hold any further communication with us.'[37]

The interview between husband and wife on 19 February offered nevertheless some consolation. She kissed him and comforted him. Wilde was touched at her taking so much trouble to tell him the grim news, and he wrote that she had been 'gentle and good to me here, when she came to see me.' They talked of their children, and he urged Constance not to spoil Cyril as Lady Queensberry had spoiled Alfred Douglas. 'I told her,' he wrote, 'that she should bring him up so that if he shed innocent blood he would come and tell her, that she might cleanse his hands for him first, and then teach him how by penance or expiation to cleanse his soul afterwards.'[38] They agreed that he should have an income of £200 a year after his release, and a third of his life interest in her marriage settlement if he survived her. He also suggested that if the responsibility of looking after the children should prove too heavy for her, she should appoint a guardian for them. Later he learned with satisfaction that her cousin Adrian Hope had been so designated.

Constance, shaken by the interview, wrote to her brother, 'They say he is quite well, but he is an absolute wreck compared with what he was.'[39] During her brief stay in London she paid a visit to Edward Burne-Jones and his wife. Burne-Jones had taken at first a severe view of Wilde's offenses, but her visit crystallized his growing sympathy. As he noted in his diary for 22 February 1896,

> When there was announced a lady by the name of Constance Holland, and lo! it was poor desolate heartbroken Constance Wilde. I was glad to see the poor waif, and so was Georgie [Georgiana, Lady Burne-Jones]. And she had a warm welcome – she had come across from near Bordighera to tell her husband of his mother's death – which had not been told him – the poor lady had died three weeks ago – and it took ten days to get leave to see him, and four days to come – but she saw him and told him of it. She says he was changed beyond recognition and they give him work to do in the garden and the work he likes best is to cover books with brown paper – for at least it is books to hold in his hand: but presently the keeper made a sign with his finger, and like a dog he obeyed, and left the room.

Constance told the Burne-Joneses that Vyvyan had already forgotten his father, but that Cyril continued to ask about him, and had learned from a newspaper that his father was in prison, 'he thinks for debt.' Vyvyan Holland remembered that Cyril knew more about the cause of imprisonment than his mother suspected.[40]

The small band of Wilde's constant friends continued to visit him. In February 1896 More Adey accompanied the faithful Sherard, but at the next three-monthly visit, in May, Sherard came with a welcome old friend, Robert Ross. Ross had apparently darted back to London for the bankruptcy hearings in November 1895, and then returned to the Continent. Since he had not seen Wilde for six months, the report he made of his interview, based on notes pencilled immediately after it, provides a summary of the effect of a year's imprisonment. He found Wilde to be much thinner, emaciated even, an effect made more apparent by the shaving off of his beard. His face, from working in the garden in the sun, had turned a dull brick color. His once thick hair was thinner, streaked with white and grey, and showed a bald patch on the crown. 'His eyes were terribly vacant,' said Ross, and 'he cried the whole time.'[41]

Wilde said that the doctor was 'very unkind to him.' He was constantly suspected of malingering. Nonetheless, he had spent only two days in the infirmary at Reading as compared with two months at Wandsworth. Though he did not mention the fact to Ross, he was still suffering from the fall he had taken in the chapel at Wandsworth. During the winter his ear ached and often bled a little, [42] and his hearing was further impaired. He told Ross of other difficulties, anaemia and gout. In the winter, reading by gas jets, he had had trouble with his eyes, but they were a little less painful now. It was easier to sleep at Reading than it had been at Wandsworth or Pentonville. But his main fear was of going mad, and he asked Ross whether his brain seemed all right to him.

Of his life in prison Wilde could not bring himself to speak, and Ross thought his relative silence not only uncharacteristic but ominous. He did say that he was forbidden to write anything except a quota of letters, but was allowed to read; he had read every book in the prison library several times. Ross asked him what books he would like, if permission could be secured for them, and Wilde asked for Chaucer, a prose translation of Dante, Pater's new book of which Ross had spoken (*Gaston de Latour*) and some large volume of Elizabethan dramatists. He was pleased to have messages from French and English friends, commented on them briefly, and asked that his thanks be conveyed. On leaving, Ross and Sherard encountered the forbidding Colonel Isaacson, and Ross steeled himself to speak to him about Wilde. At first Isaacson was haughty and impatient, but softened when Ross said Wilde's health was better at Reading than at Wandsworth. To Ross's vivid concern, Isaacson replied that he knew Wilde felt imprisonment more than other people, but thought that he was doing as well as could be expected. If he felt ill, he could see the doctor every day if he liked. The Home Office had sent books for him. His friends would be notified of any serious change in his condition. Ross felt that Wilde was not being singled out for maltreatment.

The most important information that Ross imparted to Wilde had to do with something outside the prison. This was that a book of poems by Alfred Douglas was about to appear in English under the imprint of the *Mercure de France*, with accompanying prose translations by Eugène Tardieu, the editor of *L'Echo de Paris*. The book was to be dedicated to Wilde. Wilde replied curtly, 'I would rather not hear about that *just now*.'[43] The next day (23 or 30 May 1896) he wrote to Ross a firm answer, in which he referred to Bosie distantly as 'Douglas':

You said that Douglas was going to dedicate a volume of poems to me. Will you write at once to him and say he must not do anything of the kind. I could not accept or allow such a dedication. The proposal is revolting and grotesque. Also, he has unfortunately in his possession a number of letters of mine. I wish him to at once hand all these without exception over to you; I will ask you to seal them up. In case I die here you will destroy them. In case I survive I will destroy them myself. They must not be in existence.

The thought that they are in his hands is horrible to me, and though my unfortunate children will never of course bear my name, still they know whose sons they are and I must try and shield them from the possibility of any further revolting disclosure or scandal.

Also, Douglas has some things I gave him: books and jewellery. I wish these to be also handed over to you – for me. Some of the jewellery I know has passed out of his possession under circumstances unnecessary to detail, but he has still some, such as the gold cigarette-case, pearl chain and enamelled locket I gave him last Christmas [1894]. I wish to be certain that he has in his possession nothing that I ever gave him. All these are to be sealed up and left with you. The idea that he is wearing or in possession of anything I gave him is peculiarly repugnant to me. I cannot of course get rid of the revolting memories of the two years I was unlucky enough to have him with me, or of the mode by which he thrust me into the abyss of ruin and disgrace to gratify his hatred of his father and other ignoble passions. But I will not have him in possession of my letters or gifts. Even if I get out of this loathsome place I know that there is nothing before me but a life of a pariah – of disgrace and penury and contempt – but at least I will have nothing to do with him nor allow him to come near me.

In writing to Douglas you had better quote my letter fully and frankly, so that he should have no loophole of escape. Indeed he cannot possibly refuse. He has ruined my life – that should content him.

Douglas was staggered when Ross transmitted Wilde's message: he wrote on 4 June,

My dear Bobbie – I have just got the terrible letter from Oscar. It has deprived me of all power of thought and expression. There is no need for me to tell you how terrible it is, for you must guess it. Tell him that my book, which was to have appeared in three or four days, and is practically ready, I will withdraw. I could not publish it if it were not dedicated to him. The idea that he will not have it dedicated to him stabs the book and kills it . . . With regard to the letters, I cannot give them up to anyone. Possession of these letters and the recollections they may give me, even if they can give me no hope, will perhaps prevent me from putting an end to a life which has now no *raison d'être*. If Oscar asks me to kill myself I will do so, and he shall have back the letters when I am dead . . . Morning and evening I have kissed them and prayed over them.

Ross must have replied that Wilde felt Douglas had sponged on him for years, and Douglas answered on 15 July, 'I had nothing to contribute and Oscar contributed everything. What difference does it make? Everything that I had and was going to have in the future was and always will be his.'[44]

The refusal was embarrassing for another reason. Douglas, after first giving up his article in the *Mercure de France*, had written a second one, also without consulting anybody. It was entitled, 'Introduction to my Poems, with some remarks on the Oscar Wilde case,' and had just been published in *La Revue blanche* on 1 June 1896. This time he omitted Wilde's letters, but the tenor was the same as in the earlier article: 'Today I am proud that I have been loved by a great poet who perhaps esteemed me because he recognized that, besides a beautiful body, I possessed a beautiful soul.' 'Oscar Wilde is now suffering for being a uranian, a Greek, a sexual man . . . I have already said that such men are the salt of the earth.' Twenty-five per cent of all great men are *sodomites*, he said. As for his father, Queensberry, he was as interesting as Nero or Tiberius or Jack the Ripper or Gilles de Retz. More directly than before, Douglas accused Rosebery, whose name had appeared somewhat equivocally in one of Queensberry's letters, of threatening Asquith with the loss of the next general election if Wilde was allowed to go free. The article concluded weakly with a swipe at André Raffalovich, who had followed Max Nordau's *Degeneration* (1895 edition) in exploiting the Wilde case, by rushing into print first with a pamphlet and then with a book, *Uranisme et unisexualité*. There he had not only condemned Wilde for rampant and catastrophic egoism, but Douglas, too, for being '*un jeune homme pâle et artificiel*.'[45] Douglas seemed to feel he was making a great riposte by proclaiming that Raffalovich was himself a sodomite, and that the rancor of the attack stemmed from Wilde's open contempt for its author. Douglas's article was incoherent enough to register his extreme agitation over the loss of Wilde's favour. He had to defend it the next month, because some French journalists demanded that he say exactly what kind of love he and Wilde had enjoyed, and charged him with swelling a scandal just to advertise his poems. Henry Bauer wrote that Douglas, having made life impossible for Wilde in England, was now making it impossible for him to live in France on his release. 'My friend's love for me was Platonic, that is to say, pure,' Douglas declared. As for advertising his book, he had by now learned of Wilde's refusal to allow the dedication, and, without mentioning that, could say tersely, 'My poems will not appear.' Like other decisions of Douglas, this one was susceptible to reconsideration, but Wilde's firm letter had at least the effect of slightly deferring publication. The volume appeared in 1896, without dedication.*

If Douglas was agitated, so was Wilde. He began in June to write his most anguished plea for release: 'The petition of the above-named prisoner humbly sheweth that he does not desire to attempt to palliate in any way the terrible offences of which he was rightly found guilty.' He acknowledged that he had been suffering from sexual madness, but hoped that this might be considered a disease for cure rather than a crime for

---

* Mallarmé, perhaps moved by the situation, thanked Douglas for a copy by saying, '*Une des rares fois que je me suis félicité de connaître l'anglais, c'est le jour où m'arrivèrent vos poèmes.*'[46]

punishment. He called attention to Nordau's analysis of his behaviour in this light in *Degeneration*. It was insanity, he said, of which he was particularly terrified; the insufficiency of books, the closing off of the world of ideas in 'this tomb for those who are not yet dead' had encouraged the most morbid and polluted thoughts. His mind could not bear any more, and the purpose of prison is not to destroy the reason. 'Though it may not seek to make men better, yet it does not desire to drive them mad.' As for his body, his abscessed ear had never been properly treated and his eyesight had become blurred from the gas jets, so that blindness and deafness were probably to be added to the certainty of insanity.

There are other apprehensions of danger that the limitation of space does not allow the petitioner to enter on: his chief danger is that of madness, his chief terror that of madness, and his prayer that his long imprisonment may be considered with its attendant ruin a sufficient punishment, that the imprisonment may be ended now, and not uselessly or vindictively prolonged till insanity has claimed soul as well as body as its prey, and brought it to the same degradation and the same shame.

OSCAR WILDE

Colonel Isaacson was duty-bound to transmit this letter, surely one of the most clear-headed predictions of impending insanity that could be written, but he attached a report by the prison surgeon, Mr O. C. Maurice, attesting that Wilde was in good health.[47]

An Execution

In Memoriam
C.T.W.

Five days after Wilde submitted this petition, an event occurred which focused his sufferings vicariously. A man of thirty, Charles Thomas Wooldridge, was hanged in Reading Gaol. He was a trooper in the Royal Horse Guards. The crime for which he had been promptly condemned to execution was the murder of his twenty-three-year-old wife Laura Ellen Wooldridge on 29 March. She had roused his jealousy; he had deliberately waited for her on the road near her house, between Windsor and the village of Clewer, and slit her throat three times over with a razor borrowed from a soldier friend for the purpose. Pleas on his behalf for a respite had been rejected by the Home Secretary because of the obvious premeditation of the crime. The scaffold at Reading Prison had been used only once since its installation for a double execution eighteen years before. Wilde saw the hangman crossing the yard with gardener's gloves and a little bag. At eight o'clock on the morning of 7 July the hangman Billington fastened Wooldridge's feet, adjusted the cap, and drew the bolt. Wooldridge died bravely, without a struggle or a cry.

The execution of a fellow prisoner brought together many of Wilde's thoughts. He could remember what he had told Constance of the importance of helping their sons, if they shed human blood, to penance and expiation. But he had also written long before in 'Humanitad' that in killing Christ men killed themselves:

And we were vain and ignorant nor knew
That when we stabbed thy heart it was our own real hearts we slew.

Wooldridge's crime was appalling, but so was his execution, and like Wilde's punishment, inhuman for a crime that was human. But he thought also of something else: in August of 1895 he had rejected Douglas's article celebrating their love, and then in May of 1896 he refused to accept Douglas's dedication of his poems, an insult he knew would wound to the marrow. The gesture grew out of the feeling that Douglas had destroyed his life, a feeling which – as he said in a letter – had first crystallized in his mind as he stood up in court to hear his sentence. The moral pressed upon him, though he would not write it down at once: Wooldridge as a real image, and Douglas and himself in parable, had all conformed to an unwritten law:

For each man kills the thing he loves.

There would come a time later when Douglas would ask Wilde what he meant by this line, and Wilde would reply, '*You* ought to know.'[48]

CHAPTER XX

Escape from Reading

I . . . wish we could talk over the many prisons of life –
prisons of stone, prisons of passion, prisons of intellect,
prisons of morality and the rest – all limitations, external or
internal, all prisons, really. All life is a limitation.

Isaacson to Nelson

That love has a murderous element was a home truth without comfort for
the victim of society's loveless sequestration. Wilde compared himself
again with Lucien de Rubempré and Julien Sorel, and said, 'Lucien
hanged himself, Julien was executed, and I died in prison.'[1] So long as
Colonel Isaacson had authority for Reading Gaol, Wilde was caught up in
a cycle of substantial punishments for small offenses such as not sweeping
his cell quite clean, or uttering a word or two to another prisoner. In
Isaacson the now antiquated prison 'system' had an efficient instrument:
he believed in the Prison Act of 1865, he had risen to the top echelon of
wardens within its terms, and he had no intention of relaxing discipline.

People not familiar with prisons had no idea what their procedures
were. That is perhaps the only excuse for Henry James, who wrote to Paul
Bourget that Wilde's sentence to hard labor was too severe, that isolation
would have been more just.[2] Wilde had no mercy from him. What made
James's finely shaded discrimination particularly repulsive was that Wilde
had experienced both hard labor and isolation. Fortunately, Wilde did not
have to rely upon the punitive theories of other novelists. As a veteran of
four prisons (counting Newgate), he had developed some wariness, and
the number of people of consequence concerned about him made at least
a few of the warders respect him. Even in prison his personality was
overwhelming. But there was also a change in attitude towards prisons on
the part of the public which had some effect upon administration.

During the Nineties, with Cesare Lombroso and others considering
problems of the criminal, prison reform became a center of attention. The
simple-minded theory behind the 1865 act, that 'hard labour, hard fare
and a hard bed' would deter criminals and make them law-abiding, had

lost its persuasiveness. Wilde's misfortune was to serve his sentence just before prison conditions were officially changed by the 1898 Prison Act. Already in 1895, however, when he began his term, a departmental committee under the chairmanship of H. J. Gladstone declared two years' hard labor to be an excessively severe sentence, and the 1898 law specifically abolished it. Gladstone's report said that prisoners should no longer be treated 'as a hopeless and worthless element of the community.' This shift in opinion had its effect even in Reading.

The case of Wilde was not easily forgotten in the wave of reform. His old sponsor, Haldane, continued to urge the Home Office to provide him with more books and with writing materials, but the Home Office did not want to be accused of preferential treatment. Still, there was a new chairman of the Prison Commission since 1895, Evelyn Ruggles-Brise, who had every intention of implementing the Gladstone proposals. He could not abolish the crank and the treadmill on his own, or put an end to the prohibition of speech among prisoners, but his influence counted in the Parliamentary debates that brought about these changes in 1898. Just what could be done at once was not too certain. In the summer of 1896 Wilde's friends were alarmed for his health, and they decided to ask for mitigation of his sentence on medical grounds. Frank Harris had been out of the country for some months, but it was thought that he could present the Wilde point of view most forcefully to the authorities. Harris accordingly asked for an interview with Ruggles-Brise in June, and urged upon him that Wilde was not likely to survive being in prison for two years. Ruggles-Brise asked Harris to visit Wilde and get particulars of his health, and on 13 June sent an order to Colonel Isaacson that Harris be granted an interview with Wilde out of the warder's earshot. At the same time he asked for a confidential report about Wilde's mental condition.

Isaacson responded to this challenge, and promptly sent the prison doctor's certification that Wilde was in good health. The two officials received Harris on 13 or 14 June 1896 unpleasantly; Isaacson told Harris he wished to knock the nonsense out of Wilde. The interview with Wilde took place in a bare room with two chairs and a table. Wilde struck Harris as looking much older, though on the other hand much thinner, a favorable sign to a lean man like Harris. After a warm greeting Harris asked Wilde to specify those aspects of prison life which might have a bearing on the reduction of his sentence. Wilde replied, according to Harris, 'The list of my grievances would be without end. The worst of it is I am perpetually being punished for nothing; this governor loves to punish, and he punishes by taking my books away from me.' His main fear was insanity: 'If you resist, they drive you crazy,' he said, in reference to the dark cell where he had probably more than once been placed and given bread and water. Physically, he spoke of his chronic ear pain since the fall at Wandsworth. Why did he not ask the doctor for help? asked Harris. No, he knew prison ways too well for that: no prisoner would summon the doctor or warder for a mere earache. But the interview concluded by his begging Harris not to divulge his complaints, since he would be punished for having made them.[3]

While Harris conveyed some of this to Ruggles-Brise, Wilde drew up and sent his own petition to the Home Office; Isaacson inevitably accompanied it with the prison doctor's report that Wilde's fears of insanity and physical complaints were groundless. But between them Harris and Wilde had stirred up the authorities. The Home Office dispatched a visiting committee of five men – Cobham, Thursby, Palmer, Hunter, and Hay – to Reading. It may have been on this occasion that Wilde was spied upon in the infirmary; as usual when he had a chance to talk, he enthralled the other patients and gave no sign of being unwell. On 10 July the committee reported that Wilde was in no danger of insanity, and that he had put on some of his lost weight. But Ruggles-Brise pursued the matter further; he had Dr Nicholson, who had examined Wilde at Wandsworth, make an independent examination, and Nicholson's report showed sufficient concern to justify the Home Office, on 25 July, in ordering more books and, at last, a sufficiency of writing materials, for Wilde. More to the point, Colonel Isaacson was transferred to Lewes Prison, and his successor, Major J. O. Nelson, proved to be a warden of a different stamp. One of Nelson's first acts was to go up to Wilde and say, 'The Home Office has allowed you some books. Perhaps you would like to read this one; I have just been reading it myself.' Wilde melted into tears. He was afterwards to praise Nelson as 'the most Christlike man I ever met.'[4]

Under Nelson's authority Wilde could learn to distinguish Reading from the Inferno. His imagination at last escaped beyond the walls. He cannot have had great hopes for remission of sentence – the nature of his offense, and the importance of the offender, precluded that – but he began to dream of a day when his name would no longer be the number of a cell. Three lists of his requested books have survived, and they show that he began to turn his mind from the lives of the saints and to accept the visible universe once more. A sense of the future became apparent as he studied Italian systematically, and not only for the purpose of reading Dante; also German, which he had known in boyhood but had largely forgotten, so that on his release from Reading it was reported that he had learned two languages in prison. Wilde probably foresaw that they would be of the greatest use to him on the Continent.

The first list was submitted quickly to Major Nelson, who passed it on to the Home Office on 28 July after marking the titles he considered inappropriate for the prison library. Wilde was still eager to give his reading a certain solemnity. The amended list was approved by the Home Office, with the proviso that the total net cost not exceed £10, which was the prison's allotment for the year. A second list of books (not in Wilde's hand) was submitted by Nelson on 3 December 1896 and approved on 10

December by the Home Office after More Adey had assumed responsibility for providing the books. This group is entirely secular. A third list, in Adey's hand, is dated March 1897.*

---

* The first list:
A Greek Testament
Milman's *History of the Jews* and *Latin Christianity*
Stanley's *Jewish Church*
Farrar's *St Paul*
Tennyson's Poems (complete in one volume)
Percy's *Reliques* (the collection of old ballads)
Christopher Marlowe's *Works*
Buckle's *History of Civilisation*
Carlyle's *Sartor Resartus* and *Life of Frederick the Great*
Froude's *Short Studies on Great Subjects*
A Prose translation of Dante's *Divine Comedy*
Keats's Poems
Chaucer's Poems
Spenser's Poems
Letters of R. Louis Stevenson (edited by Sidney Colvin)
Walter Pater's posthumous volume of essays
Renan's *Vie de Jésus* and *Les Apôtres* (the chaplain sees no objection to these if
   they are in the original French) ['In French' wrote Nelson in the margin]
[E. B.] Tylor's *Primitive Culture* [1871]
Ranke's *History of the Popes*
Critical and Historical Essays by Cardinal Newman
En Route [by J. K. Huysmans]. Translation from the French by C. Kegan Paul. I
   would of course prefer it in the French if it would be allowed. If not I would
   like to read it in the translation. It is a book on modern Christianity.
Lecky's *History of Rationalism*
Emerson's Essays (if possible in one volume)
Cheap edition of Dickens's Works. The Library here contains no example of
   any of Thackeray's or Dickens's novels. I feel sure that a complete set of
   their works would be as great a boon to many amongst the other prisoners as
   it would certainly be to myself. ['Cheap Edition of Dickens's Works,' wrote
   Nelson in the margin]

The second list:
   Gaston de Latour by Walter Pater, M. A. (Macmillan)
   Milman's *History of Latin Christianity*
   Wordsworth's Complete Works in one volume with preface by John Morley
      (Macmillan.   7/6)
   Matthew Arnold's Poems. One volume complete (Macmillan.   7/6)
   Dante and Other Essays by Dean Church (Macmillan.   5/-)
   Percy's *Reliques*
   Hallam's *Middle Ages (History of)*
   Dryden's Poems (1 vol, Macmillan.   3/6)
   Burns's Poems   ,,   ,,
   Morte d'Arthur   ,,   ,,

[footnote contd. overleaf]

By 1897 Wilde was reading new books rather than classical ones, bringing himself up to date. He regretted, since the later books were bought at the expense of his friends, that all were doomed to 'perpetual imprisonment.' Such was the Home Office ruling. They have since escaped, no one knows where. (One, a book by Pater, is in a private collection.)[5]

Froissart's *Chronicles* xx
Buckle's *History of Civilisation*
Marlowe's Plays
Chaucer's *Canterbury Tales* (edited by A. Pollard.   2 vols.   10/-)
Introduction to Dante by John Addington Symonds
Companion to Dante by A. J. Butler
Miscellaneous Essays by Walter Pater
An English Translation of Goethe's *Faust*

       Educational
Ollendorff's *German Method.*   5/6
Key to the same.   3/6F.   Norgate
Wilhelm Tell. Hamiltonian System.   5/-   44 Shaftesbury Ave.
German-English Dictionary   London, W
Faust by Goethe (in the original)
Key to Mariotti's *Italian Grammar.*   1/-
Guide to the Italian Language by A. Bioaggi[?].   5/-
Biaggi's[?] *Prosatori Italiani.*   5/-
Italian-English Dictionary

The third list, with the last title and final note in Wilde's hand:
A French Bible
German Grammar
German Conversation Book
French-Italian Conversation Book
Dante: *Vita Nuova*
    ,,   *Vita Nuova.* English Translation
Goldoni. *Commedie.*
Auguste Filon. *L'Art Dramatique en Angleterre* [18]
Journal de Goncourt. Latest volume
[François de] Preslense. *Vie du Cardinal Manning* [18]
°Huysmans. *En Route* [1895]
Letters of Dante Gabriel Rossetti [1895]
George Meredith. *Essay on Comedy* [1897]
    ,,   ,,   *Amazing Marriage* [1895]
Thomas Hardy. *The Well-Beloved.* [1897]
Harold Frederic. *Illumination* [1896]
Nineteenth Century for 1896
Robert Louis Stevenson. *Treasure Island.*
° This is the religious novel of which Mr Gladstone wrote in terms of such high commendation [Wilde's footnote].

Important as the books were, the writing materials were more impor-tant still. Under Colonel Isaacson Wilde had been allowed pen and ink only for the purpose of writing letters to solicitors or to the Home Office, or, in very limited quantities, to friends. What he wrote was then collected and inspected, and the writing materials removed. Because of Dr Nicholson's representations, under Major Nelson Wilde was allowed pen and ink all the time. What he wrote was still to be turned over each night to the warden, however, and not returned to the prisoner next day. At first he was given separate sheets to write on, then a manuscript book. Haldane had hoped he would write something about his imprisonment, but the Home Office obviously did not intend to allow a public exposure of the prison system to come out of Reading. Nor was it a situation congenial for writing a purely imaginative work, even if Wilde had had the stomach for it, since he could scarcely keep all the details of an entire play in mind.

Letter Writing

It is the most important letter of my life.

Wilde therefore devised a stratagem in which Major Nelson was to indulge him. He would write a letter to Alfred Douglas, as he was allowed to do by rule, but such a letter as would also offer an autobiographical account of his last five years. It would follow, like a parable, his progress from pleasure to pain and then, in the last months, to a change of heart and mastery of pain. Remorse, purgation, and hope would all play their parts, the old life and the *Vita nuova*. Major Nelson recognized that his prisoner might write something comparable to *Pilgrim's Progress*; he appears to have encouraged him, and also to have relaxed the rules by allowing Wilde to see when necessary parts he had completed on earlier days. Because of this concession, the letter is revised almost throughout, and some pages appear to have been totally rewritten and substituted for an earlier version.[6]

It took Wilde the better part of three months, from January to March 1897, to write the letter. He suggested it be entitled *In Carcere et Vinculis,* but Ross took another suggestion and entitled it instead *De Profundis.*[7] The fact that, when it was published posthumously, its true nature as a letter to Douglas was at first concealed by Ross out of concern for Douglas's feelings, led to misunderstanding of Wilde's intentions in it. *De Profundis* had its origin as an answer to Douglas's silence, and draws its force from its author's sense of being neglected. After Wilde had refused the dedication of his poems, Bosie made no further effort to communicate with him directly. Instead he asked More Adey and Robert Ross, with whom he kept closely in touch by letter, to intercede for him with Wilde. Adey responded in mid-September 1896 that Wilde was obdurate, and insisted on the return of his mementoes. This time it was Douglas's turn, on 20 September, to be firm and even minatory:

My dear More
Thanks for your letter. I am sorry to hear that Oscar continues to be so unreasonable and so ungrateful. But I have determined to regard anything he says now as non-existent. If he continues in the same strain after leaving prison it will be another matter, and it will perhaps become necessary for me to make my side of the question and my *indignation* heard more forcibly from my own lips in default of those of my friends. In the meantime I say nothing except that I utterly decline to entertain for a moment any proposition relating to the giving up to him of anything which belongs to me, and I prefer that you should tell him so quite frankly if you see him. Of my undying (I use the word in its real sense not that in which he so often used it to me) love and devotion to him he may rest assured whether he continues to deserve it or not, but it might almost be worth while to remind him that if he desires any special favour from me the best way to obtain it is not by insult and undeserved abuse of one who has done so much and suffered so much for his sake.
Give my love to Bobbie.   Yours ever

BOSIE

The contents of Douglas's letter were quickly transmitted to Wilde, who answered Adey on 25 September: 'From your silence I see he still refuses to return my presents and letters . . . It is horrible he should still have the power to wound me and find some curious joy in doing so . . . He is too evil.' With the same rapidity, Adey wrote to Douglas, who replied on 27 September, 'When he comes out of prison, if he chooses to say he does not want my friendship, and that he wants his letters back, he can do so with his own mouth.'[8]

Though Douglas was later to impute to Robert Ross the most treacherous betrayal of his interests during Wilde's imprisonment, the correspondence entirely exonerates Ross. He went between the lion and his wrath by warning Wilde in November 1896 that 'the deep bitterness of the feelings' he had expressed about Douglas might estrange the sympathies of others from him. Wilde devoted a whole letter in November to answering this hint. 'Do not think that I would blame *him* for my vices,' he said to Ross. 'He had as little to do with them as I had with his. Nature was in this matter a stepmother to each of us. I blame him for not appreciating the man he ruined.' He told Ross not to 'let Alfred Douglas suppose that I am crediting him with unworthy motives. He really had no motives in his life at all . . . He had passions merely.' Yet he felt it was incredible that Douglas should feel and express no remorse, and his letter – which foreshadows *De Profundis* – ended weakly: 'So in your letter tell me how he lives, what his occupations are, his mode of life.'[9] Ross let Douglas know how ineffectual his intercession on the latter's behalf had been, but Douglas replied sharply:

> You still seem to cling to the idea that Oscar does not want to see me. The wish is father to the thought. You probably overlook the fact that I am passionately devoted to him, and that my longing to see him simply eats at my heart day and night . . . You must, (in the course of your numerous adventures,) have had occasions when forcibly separated from somebody you were in love with by the intervention of kindly friends and relations, and I suppose you suffered then. That is my case, only multiplied by ten, in view of all the tragic circumstances. Then you make no allowance for jealousy, the most terrible of all sufferings. You have seen Oscar yourself, and can see him again as often as you like, and that is all you care.

The character of Douglas cast his actions into responses molded by others' actions. In his emotional life he was constantly importunate, and when thwarted infinitely resentful. As Wilde would tell him, 'By the terrible alchemy of egotism you converted your remorse into rage.'[10] His correspondence to others at this time shows only self-justification.*

Wilde was well aware, after three years and more of subjection to Bosie's moods, that he would be impenetrable to moral persuasion, but for the sake of his own sanity and self-respect he felt he must make the effort. Like Hamlet to his mother, he would say to Douglas, 'Look on that portrait, and on this.' He was embittered by Douglas's behavior before the prison sentence, and after it too, since no letter had come from him, though letters passed easily now in and out of the prison. Wilde could see a 'purple pageant' in which he was the noble stag hounded by the Marquess of Queensberry and his son: Douglas after his time and money, and Queensberry his reputation and liberty.

---

* An example is a letter Douglas sent to the French novelist, Rachilde, who had taken an interest in him:

> Toute tentative d'intervention entre quelqu'un qui aime et l'objet de son amour est une persécution . . . Je ne suis pas un monstre . . . je suis tout à fait sain et grec, et ce sont eux, *les autres*, les gens qui se disent normales qui sont des monstres, des dégenerés . . . Je ne suis pas un *Dorian Gray* pour avoir un portrait sur lequel se masqueraient les signes d'une âme corrompue . . . Si à 27 ans j'ai la figure d'un enfant de 18 ans, c'est que mon âme est saine et belle et serein, quoiqu'un peu fatiguée et martyrisée. [Every attempt to intervene between someone in love and the object of his love is a persecution . . . I am not a monster . . . I am quite healthy and Greek, and it is those other people, who call themselves normal, who are monsters, degenerates . . . I am no *Dorian Gray* with a portrait on which the signs of a corrupted soul are kept hidden . . . If at 27 I have the face of a child of 18, it is because my soul is healthy and beautiful and serene, though a little tired and martyred.][11]

Vicarious Confession

*Prison life makes one see people and things as they really are.
That is why it turns one to stone.*

De Profundis is a kind of dramatic monologue, which constantly questions and takes into account the silent recipient's supposed responses. Given the place where it was written, Wilde might have been expected to confess his guilt. Instead he refuses to admit that his past conduct with young men was guilty, and declares that the laws by which he was condemned were unjust.* The closest he comes to the subject of homosexuality is to say, impenitently, that what the paradox was for him in the realm of thought, sexual deviation was in the realm of conduct. More than half of *De Profundis* is taken up by his confession, not of his own sins, but of Bosie's. He evokes two striking images for that young man: one is his favorite passage from *Agamemnon*, about bringing up a lion's whelp inside one's house only to have it run amok. Aeschylus compared it to Helen, Wilde to Douglas. The other is Rosencrantz and Guildenstern, who have no realization of Hamlet's tragedy, being 'the little cups that can hold so much and no more.'

The main theme of self-recrimination is that he did not break with Bosie. But his letter is an attempt to restore relations. And while he admits to 'weakness,' he explains the weakness as due to his affection, good nature, aversion to scenes, incapacity to bear resentment, and desire to keep life comely by ignoring what he considered trifles. His weakness was strength. The gods, he has discovered, make instruments to plague us out of our virtues as well as our vices.

Wilde acknowledges that along with good qualities, he was 'the spend-thrift of my own genius.' But he passes quickly over this defect, and those that attend it. Much of *De Profundis* is an elegy for lost greatness. As he whips his own image, he cannot withhold his admiration for what that image was. Elegy generates eulogy. He heightens the pinnacle from which he has fallen:

> I was a man who stood in symbolic relations to the art and culture of my age. I had realised this for myself at the very dawn of my manhood, and had forced my age to realise it afterwards . . . Byron was a symbolic figure, but his relations were to the passion of his age and its weariness of passion. Mine were to something more noble, more permanent, of more vital issue, of larger scope.

---

* In 1894 he told an interviewer (Almy), 'Never attempt to reform a man. Men never repent. To punish a man for wrong-doing, with a view to his reformation is the most lamentable mistake it is possible to commit. If he has any soul at all, such a procedure is calculated to make him ten times worse than before. It is a sign of a noble nature to refuse to be broken by force.'[12]

The gods had given me almost everything. I had genius, a distinguished name, high social position, brilliancy, intellectual daring: I made art a philosophy, and philosophy an art: I altered the minds of men and the colours of things: there was nothing I said or did that did not make people wonder: I took the drama, the most objective form known to art, and made it as personal a mode of expression as the lyric or the sonnet, at the same time that I widened its range and enriched its characterisation: drama, novel, poem in rhyme, poem in prose, subtle or fantastic dialogue, whatever I touched I made beautiful in a new mode of beauty: to truth itself I gave what is false no less than what is true as its rightful province, and showed that the false and the true are merely forms of intellectual existence. I treated Art as the supreme reality, and life as a mere mode of fiction: I awoke the imagination of my century so that it created myth and legend around me: I summed up all systems in a phrase, and all existence in an epigram.

In prison, he says, he has at least learned humility. Humility is a slippery term in *De Profundis*. Wilde's only definition of it there is 'the frank acceptance of all experience.' The pursuit of pleasure must take into account the advent of sorrow. But in a way he has always known this. Still, much of the folderol of personality has receded in importance: as a young man he had often praised poses and masks, now he says, 'Those who want a mask have to wear it.' In America he announced that 'the secret of life is art.' Now he had found that 'the secret of life is suffering.'[13]

De Profundis moves from the discovery of pain to the discovery of consolation. Its climax, doubtless premeditated from the start, was a section dealing with Wilde's discovery in prison of Christ. This too is less humble than it seems, since Wilde not only describes Christ without recognizing his divinity, but blends Christianity with aestheticism, as long before he told André Gide he would do. Christ appears here as the supreme individualist, uniting personality and perfection, saying beautiful things, making of his life the most wonderful of poems by creating himself out of his own imagination. He sympathizes with sinners as Wilde in 'The Soul of Man under Socialism' sympathizes with criminals, and recognizes no morality but that of sympathy. Christ is a precursor of the Romantic movement, a supreme artist, a master of paradox, a type of Wilde in the ancient world. In this section of *De Profundis* Douglas is almost forgotten, but Wilde makes all he has learned about Christ into something he must impart to his friend. He cannot resist more particularization of the Queensberrys' misdeeds, but he reaches at last a Christlike conclusion: 'And the end of it all is that I have got to forgive you. I must do so. I don't write this letter to put bitterness into your heart, but to pluck it out of mine. For my own sake I must forgive you.'[14]

The most important thing about *De Profundis* is that it is a love letter. Wilde complains of neglect and arranges a reunion. He reminds Douglas, even at this late stage, that Douglas's family had promised to pay his court costs, but financial matters are forgotten as he evokes the thought of their meeting 'in some quiet foreign town like Bruges,' where Bosie, who had come to him once to learn the Pleasure of Life and of Art, may be offered tutelage in 'the meaning of Sorrow, and its beauty.' For no matter how badly Douglas behaved, he always loved Wilde in his fashion. As an apologia *De Profundis* suffers from the adulteration of simplicity by eloquence, by an arrogance lurking in its humility, and by its disjointed structure. But as a love letter it has all the consistency it needs, and must rank – with its love and hate, solicitude, vanity, and philosophic musings – as one of the greatest, and the longest, ever written. Wilde on 3 April 1897 asked permission to send the letter out, but cannily recognized that to send it to Douglas would be to anticipate its destruction. In that case there would be no record of what had brought him to prison. So he asked permission to send it to Ross, who was instructed to have it copied and send Douglas the original. The Home Office refused permission to send it to anybody, but said he could take it with him on his release.

The writing of *De Profundis* was regenerative. Wilde's repudiation of Douglas was complete enough for him to feel drawn towards him once more – a characteristic turnabout. His wife's behavior had turned about, too. For a time Constance rediscovered her love for her husband, but after their pathetic meeting in February of 1896, following his mother's death, she had not visited him again. Her letters, at first so sympathetic, became indignant. The bone of contention between them was not the divorce, which she gave up, but the life interest in her dowry. Wilde was entitled to half of it by the terms of the marriage settlement, and this half was offered for sale by the Official Receiver of his estate. It was rumored that Queensberry would bid for it, so as to make Wilde totally dependent upon him, but he did not. Constance Wilde's solicitor seems to have bid £25, but Ross and Adey bought it away from her for £75. Their object was to give Wilde something in case his wife should predecease him. They did not trust Constance's advisers. There were many complications, but Constance Wilde was convinced that her husband's friends were working against her. She had originally offered Wilde £200 a year as an allowance after his release, and, in case of her death, one-third the life interest, the rest to go to their sons. Now the offer was reduced to £150 and a third of the life interest. Wilde seems to have blamed Ross and Adey for interfering between himself and his wife and making her write unpleasant letters, but eventually he recognized that they had protected his interest, such as it was, and that Constance had misinterpreted their actions. He agreed to her terms early in 1897, and her solicitor Hargrove came to the prison in February 1897 to have Wilde sign papers turning over the custody of his children to his wife and Adrian Hope. Unknown to him, Constance Wilde had come with Hargrove, but remained outside the room as Wilde sat at the desk with Hargrove beside him. 'Let me have one last glimpse of my husband,' she asked the warder, and he moved away from the glass in the door so that she could look at the man she had loved. She left, in great emotion, in Hargrove's company.[15] The papers Wilde had signed contained a clause saying that his allowance would be cut off if he should visit her or the children without permission, or should live notoriously on the Continent. To return to Bosie Douglas would therefore mean financial disaster. And Adey's solicitor said that Queensberry had threatened to kill one or both of them if they reunited.

Reading's Rounds

Everything he [Ricketts] *said, including his remark that he supposed time went very fast in prison . . . annoyed me extremely.*

The final months of Wilde's prison life are recorded in part by a friendly warder. This was Thomas Martin, who knew him during his last months at Reading, which proved to be Martin's last months there as well. Because of his impending release, Wilde had the great privilege of being allowed to let his hair grow for five months. He felt more like himself, and soon had won Martin's heart. One day he remarked to him how keenly he felt the lack of a newspaper. 'When I come out,' he said, 'I shall be just like Rip Van Winkle.' Martin took the hint, and began to bring him the *Daily Chronicle* each morning. This produced a note which the warder treasured and kept:

My dear friend, What have I to write about except that if you had been an officer in Reading Prison a year ago my life would have been much happier. Everyone tells me I am looking better – and happier.

That is because I have a good friend who gives me the *Chronicle*, and promises me ginger biscuits!

At the bottom of this note Martin pencilled a reply, 'Your ungrateful I done more than promise.' Wilde said to him once, 'I know nothing about figures, except that two and two make five.' 'They don't,' said Martin, 'they only make four.' 'You see, I don't even know that,' said Wilde with a smile.[16]

One day in March Martin entered Wilde's cell to find him still in bed. 'I have had a bad night,' he explained, 'pains in my inside, and my head seems splitting.' He declined a visit from the doctor, but declared he would be all right once he had something warm to drink. Since his breakfast would not be brought for an hour, Martin decided to get him something. He heated some beef tea, poured it into a bottle, and put the bottle inside his jacket so it would not be observed. But on his way to

Wilde's cell he was accosted by the chief warder about some administrative detail, and was held in conversation so long that the hot bottle began to burn his chest. When he finally made his way to Wilde and told him what had happened, Wilde laughed. Martin was angry, and banged the cell door as he left. But by the time he brought his breakfast Wilde had become contrite, and said he would not touch it until Martin forgave him. 'Not even the cocoa?' asked Martin. 'Not even the cocoa,' said Wilde, looking at it poignantly. 'Well, rather than starve you, I'll forgive you.' 'And supposing I laugh again?' 'I shan't forgive you,' said Martin. The following morning Wilde gave him a formal 'Apology' written in his most highspirited vein. When Martin praised it, his prisoner said he had resolved never to laugh again, and never to write in that manner again. 'Then I thought it fitting when I had broken one vow to break the other also.' But he became grave: 'I am no longer the Sirius of Comedy. I have sworn solemnly to dedicate my life to Tragedy. If I write any more books, it will be to form a library of lamentation . . . I shall be an enigma to the world of Pleasure, but a mouthpiece for the world of Pain.'[17]

Wilde's fame spread among the warders, and they began to bring literary questions to him. As Wilde told Will Rothenstein, one man asked him, 'Excuse me, sir, but Charles Dickens, sir, would he be considered a great writer now, sir?' Wilde replied, 'Oh yes, a great writer, indeed; you see he is no longer alive.' 'Yes, I understand, sir, being dead he would be a great writer, sir.' And, on another visit, the same questioner asked: 'Excuse me, sir, but Marie Corelli, would she be considered a great writer, sir?' 'This was more than I could bear,' Wilde said to Rothenstein, 'and putting my hand on his shoulder I said: "Now don't think I've anything against her *moral* character, but from the way she writes *she ought to be here*."' 'You say so, sir, you say so,' said the warder, surprised but respectful.*[18]

Evidence of stranger behavior has been preserved. One day Wilde was walking in the yard during the exercise period, which he would dub 'The Fools' Parade.' Suddenly he saw one of the other prisoners stare at him meaningfully, and then join his arms over his forehead with the hands clasped together in a peculiar way. Wilde recognized the sign of the widow's son, which obliged any Mason who saw it to try to minister to the distress of the man making the sign. The problem bothered him to the extent that he asked for an interview with Major Nelson, to whom he explained his difficulty. Nelson was equal to the problem, and procured a pair of dark blue glasses for Wilde to wear during the exercise period, so that he would be unable to see the sign of the widow's son.[19]

Another day Wilde was walking the round when he heard somebody mutter, 'What are you doing in this place, Dorian Gray?' 'Not Dorian

---

* He would write to Leonard Smithers in December 1897, 'Half of the success of Marie Corelli is due to the no doubt unfounded rumour that she is a woman.'

Gray, but Lord Henry Wotton,' said Wilde. The man whispered, 'I was at all your first nights, and at all your trials,' as if they were comparable dramatic performances. Wilde found out the man's name and address, as he did of several other prisoners, so that he could send some gifts of money to them after his release. One of his letters to warder Thomas Martin indicates how he secured the information:

> You must get me his address some day – he is such a good fellow. Of course I would not for worlds get such a friend as you are into *any danger*. I quite understand your feelings.
>
> The *Chronicle* is capital today. You must get A S/2 to come out and clean on Saturday morning and I will give him my note then myself.

To Martin he spoke more frankly, when attendance at the prison chapel came up: 'I long to rise in my place and cry out, and tell the poor disinherited wretches around me that it is not so; to tell them they are society's victims, and that society has nothing to offer them but starvation in the streets, or starvation and cruelty in prison!'[20]

But all the same his irrepressible imagination played on Biblical stories. It was during these last months that he conceived new versions of the texts he had pored over during his first months in prison, when not much beside the Bible had been available. He reconstructed the story of Moses and the Pharaoh, in accordance with his own recent experiences:

> When the Pharaoh died, his daughter, who had rescued Moses in his ark of bulrushes from the river, was married to her own brother – the new ruler – in accordance with the law of Egypt. After a time Moses, bearing the words of Jehovah, came with his brother Aaron before the new Pharaoh. The great magician of the god of Israel transformed his rod into a serpent and covered with leprosy the hand with which he had sent out plagues over Egypt. Then the Queen entered, lamenting because her firstborn and heir to the throne had by command of the Eternal just died with all the first born of the men and beasts of Egypt. And Moses wept with her, for she had been like a mother to him, but she rebuffed him saying, 'When you were a little child I saved you from the river waters filled with crocodiles, and yet my child has been taken from me by your word. So I myself, in saving you, killed my firstborn. I have given my child life and I have taken it away, for each of us ends by killing what we love. May I be accursed for ever! Put upon me this leprosy which appears and disappears at your pleasure. Have the serpent which you rouse from the dead wood bite me.' And Moses answered her: 'O thou who wert to me like a mother, thou who saved me from the waters filled with crocodiles, no creature that suffers is out of harmony with the deepest secret of life, for the secret of life is suffering. Yes, it is hidden in all things. Because of thy son's death Pharaoh has recognized the might of the people of Israel and will permit them to go whither their destiny leads them. Because of thy son's death a predestined

487

son can be born. In the scales of life and death, only the Eternal knows the weight of souls. Bear in mind this truth among all truths: 'Worlds are built up out of suffering: there is suffering at the birth of a child as at the birth of a star.'

He told a different and livelier version of this story to Ricketts, perhaps when that artist visited him in prison in April 1897. Ricketts remembered a terrible moment when the new Pharaoh cried out to Moses, 'Praise be to thy God, O prophet, for he has slain my only enemy, my son!'[21] Wilde was well aware, through the Queensberry family, that the impulse to kill the father could dovetail with an impulse to kill the son. Both illustrated the propensity to kill the thing we love.

Two other stories, about betrayal, date from this period. The figure of Judas had always interested Wilde, from the time when he said, 'It is always Judas who writes the biography.' In one story, Judas was the most beloved of the disciples, until Jesus recruited John and James. John, because of his sweetness, became the favorite. Judas was madly jealous. 'And, because he loved Jesus and believed in him, Judas wished, even while he wrought his revenge, to allow him to fulfil the prophecies and to manifest his divinity. So it was that Judas betrayed because he had believed and because he had loved, for we always end by killing what we love.' The other story, which Wilde recounted to André Gide soon after his release from prison, ran somewhat like this:

After his treason, Judas was on his way to hang himself when some disciples came upon him, and perceiving his black look and anguish asked the cause. Judas answered them:—What dreadful people these priests are! They offered me ten pieces of silver to deliver up Christ.
—And what did you do, Judas?
—Of course I refused. But these priests are terrible. Then they offered me twenty pieces of silver.
—And what did you do, Judas?
—Of course I refused. But these priests are terrible, terrible. They then offered me thirty talents, and of course I accepted.
—Now we understand why you are about to hang yourself, for what you have done deserves worse than death.
—Oh, it's not for that, but the thirty pieces of silver they gave me were counterfeit![22]

Wilde's stories of this period grandly paralleled his conviction that he was being betrayed in money matters by Adey and Ross, by Ernest Leverson, and others, although they all seem to have behaved irreproachably. He continued his higher criticism of the Bible by reworking the story of Ahab and Jezebel, with the idea that it might be made into a play like *Salome*. In this version, Jezebel has Naboth (who has refused to sell his vineyard) killed not as in the Old Testament, by suborning witnesses against him, but by pretending he has made sexual overtures. After he is killed, she gloats over his vineyard. Wilde had learned about mercilessness.

As if to prove an old contention of his, that 'a truth in art is that whose contrary is also true,' he returned after this to his more sympathetic scenario about a woman, devised in 1894. He evidently conceived of returning to the stage with two plays, the one Biblical, the other contemporary. In the latter, the scene is a large house belonging to Mr and Mrs Daventry. As the revised version went, Mrs Daventry idolizes her husband, but it becomes clear to everyone but her, during a party, that Daventry is having an affair with the worthless wife of another man. After the guests leave Mrs Daventry falls asleep on a couch in the darkened drawing room, with only her blonde hair visible in the firelight. Daventry and his mistress enter, see no one, and embrace. Mrs Daventry wakes and makes an involuntary movement; the other woman is terrified, but Daventry assures her that it is only the Pekinese. There is a sudden knock on the door: the mistress's jealous husband has followed her. The lovers are nonplussed, with nowhere to hide, but Mrs Daventry gets up, goes to the door, and admits the husband, saying, 'We have been talking by the fire together.' Daventry, dazzled and relieved by his wife's sacrificial finesse, gives up his mistress.

It was the kind of story Wilde loved to tell about women. He used to recall how his mother behaved when his father was accused of seducing a patient, and also how she admitted a veiled woman to the sick room when he was dying. But most of all, the stories reflected Wilde's awareness of his wife's kindness in putting up with his thralldom to Douglas. That was why he called the play 'Constance.'

Prospects

I hope abroad to talk about lovely things.

Although composing unwritten works could assure him that his mind was unimpaired, Wilde had not come to any conclusions about his future life. When More Adey went to see him on 28 January 1897, Wilde said that as soon as he was released he would go abroad. He hoped to wake up 'the next morning in a little *appartement* in a French or Belgian town,' with some books about him, 'of course Flaubert's *Tentation de Saint Antoine* among them,' and some papers and pens, so that he might begin to write again at once. Adey suggested a seaside place in Brittany for the first few weeks. This Wilde declined. 'I shall have to face the world sometime and I intend to do it immediately,' he said. Adey reported him to be in excellent spirits. On 27 February Adey, Ross, and Leverson visited him, and again his health appeared improved, partly because they were giving him meat once a day and he had been sleeping better. It was probably on this occasion that the governor said to Ross, 'He looks well. But like all men unused to manual labour who receive a sentence of this kind, he will be dead within two years.'[23]

During April and May he adopted now one plan and now another. One was to settle in Brussels. On 7 April Frank Harris visited him in prison, and proposed that they drive through the Pyrenees to Spain. Harris was feeling affluent, having made thousands of pounds in South Africa, and promised to give Wilde £500 on the day of his release. But the promise faded in the following months, because Harris had unexpectedly heavy expenses, and because Wilde began to feel that a trip with Harris would be too exhausting in his present state. He withdrew from it, much to Harris's disappointment. The next plan was to go somewhere on the French coast: Boulogne was considered, but Douglas was there, so Le Havre was substituted, though in the end it was rejected too. Wilde also had another plan, put into his mind by Ross and Adey, both Catholics. This was to go first to a monastery, and then to Venice.

Wherever he was to go, he must be properly equipped. One of his requests in April was for his friends to provide him with books, some that they had written and others – by Flaubert and other favorites – which he did not feel he could do without. While he was still considering Harris's journey, he asked for some Spanish language books and plays. Clothing was another problem: what had happened to his fur coat which he had worn all over America? It had been left with Willie, unfortunately, and pawned along with two rugs, two portmanteaus, and a hatbox. He had himself measured for new clothes, and arranged with Ross to obtain an ulster and a blue serge suit from a tailor named Dore. Frank Harris offered other clothes. Wilde asked Adey to buy a brown hat from Heath, at Albert Gate, eighteen collars, two dozen white handkerchiefs and one dozen with colored borders, some dark blue neckties with white spots and other designs, eight pairs of socks ('coloured summer things'), size 8, some gloves (size 8! – 'as my hand is so broad'). From Pritchard, St James's, could be bought some good French soap such as Houbigant, kept for him there in the past. He must have scent, preferably Canterbury Wood Violet, and a hair tonic called Koko Marikopas, apparently intended to tint his greying hair a little. 'I want, for psychological reasons, to feel entirely physically cleansed of the stain and soil of prison life.'[24]

On 22 April Wilde petitioned the Home Secretary to allow him to leave prison on 15 May, instead of 20 May when his term came to an end. He hoped thereby to avoid the press, including the American newspaper which had offered him a thousand pounds for his reminiscences of prison life. On 7 May this, like all other such requests, was refused. Max Beerbohm proposed a decoy brougham which should be driven out of the prison-yard with blinds drawn down on each side to lure the journalists away.[25]

There were other last minute upheavals. Wilde grew increasingly incensed at Ross and Adey over the matter of his life interest, and began to think that Reggie Turner would be a more appropriate person to see on his release. But Turner said everything had been arranged with Adey and the Reverend Stewart Headlam, the latter as irreproachable at the end of Wilde's prison sentence as he had been before it began. Where to get money for the next months? Wilde urged that Lord Douglas of Hawick be approached and reminded of his earlier promises, but nothing came of this idea. The thousand pounds Adela Schuster had given Wilde two years before had been left with Ernest Leverson, but this money had almost all been spent in Wilde's interest, if not always with his consent. Yet amid much despair over destitution, Wilde experienced kindness from a number of people. Adey and Ross never ceased their efforts on his behalf. Turner gave him traveling bags initialed S.M., for Sebastian Melmoth, since Wilde had decided, at Ross's suggestion, to adopt the name of his favorite martyr and of his great-uncle's solitary wanderer. Constance sent him money to pay for food and traveling expenses. Ricketts gave him £100. It had been settled that the best place to go to for the moment was Dieppe, even though it was full of English people who would recognize him.

His last days in prison were clouded by two incidents. He had been aware for three months of a certain half-witted inmate, A.2.11, a soldier. It was clear to the other prisoners that he was demented, but the doctors regarded him as a malingerer, and some visiting justices sentenced him to twenty-four lashes. On Saturday, 15 May, Wilde heard from the basement prison 'revolting shrieks, or rather howls' and 'I knew that some wretched man was being flogged.' It was the soldier, whose name – as Martin informed him – was Prince. When Prince appeared at exercise the next day, he was in a still more wretched condition; the following day he did not appear; and when he did show himself, on Wilde's last day in Reading, 18 May, he looked close to insanity.

The other incident was the imprisonment of three children, convicted of snaring some rabbits, and unable to pay their fine. Wilde saw them as they were waiting to be assigned to cells. He knew only too well the terror they were feeling, and the hunger they would feel. He wrote to Martin on 17 May with something like desperation: 'Please find out for me the name of A.2.11. Also: the names of the children who are in for the rabbits, and the amount of the fine. Can I pay this, and get them out? If so I will get them out tomorrow. Please, dear friend, do this for me. I must get them out.' Martin was himself touched by their condition, and gave a biscuit to the smallest of them. For this he was dismissed from the service, as Wilde found out a few days later.[26]

Wilde was even more troubled by these incidents because he felt sure of the general benevolence of Major Nelson. He would have liked to mention the soldier and the children to him, on the assumption that he was not aware of them, but it did not seem appropriate to do so on his last evening at Reading. He was not inhibited from taking up the topic a few days later, in a fiery letter to the *Daily Chronicle*, where he excoriated prison injustice while praising Nelson.

For his departure, arrangements had been made so that he would not find himself being stared at as he had been at Clapham Junction on his transfer to Reading. He was allowed to wear ordinary clothes and was not handcuffed. Before he left, on 18 May, the warden handed him his momentous letter to Alfred Douglas. Two reporters had come to observe his departure, and to one of them he said, as quoted in the *New York Times*, that he 'coveted neither notoriety nor oblivion.' Then he and two prison officials took a cab to Twyford station. Wilde almost gave the game away when he opened his arms towards some budding bush saying, 'Oh beautiful world! Oh beautiful world!' The warder implored him to stop, 'Now, Mr Wilde, you mustn't give yourself away like that. You're the only man in England who would talk like that in a railway station.'[27]

EXILE

CHAPTER XXI

Prisoner at Large

It is always the unreadable that occurs.

The Visible World

From Twyford Wilde and the two prison officials took a train to London. At Westbourne Park they left it and traveled by cab to Pentonville, from which he was discharged the next morning. At 6.15 a.m., 19 May 1897, he officially completed his two-year sentence. There had been some discussion as to who should meet him. He had refused to have Ernest Leverson, and Frank Harris had refused to go. In the end More Adey and Stewart Headlam greeted him and put him into a cab. They avoided the press and drove to Headlam's house, where Wilde changed his clothes and had his first cup of coffee in two years. He talked of Dante. It was suggested that he might travel with Frank Harris. 'It would be a perpetual football match to be with him,' said Wilde. The Leversons arrived, and were shown into the drawing room. They felt ill at ease, but Wilde came in, as Ada Leverson recalled, 'with the dignity of a king returning from exile. He came in talking, laughing, smoking a cigarette, with waved hair and a flower in his buttonhole, and he looked markedly better, slighter, and younger than he had two years previously.' He greeted Ada Leverson by saying, 'Sphinx, how marvellous of you to know exactly the right hat to wear at seven o'clock in the morning to meet a friend who has been away! You can't have got up, you must have sat up.'

But he turned from this banter to say to Headlam, 'I look on all the different religions as colleges in a great university. Roman Catholicism is the greatest and most romantic of them.' He then wrote a letter to the Jesuits at Farm Street, asking for a six-month retreat. The messenger who took the letter was to wait for an answer. Meanwhile Wilde resumed the conversation. He talked of Reading as if it had been a resort: 'The dear Governor, such a delightful man, and his wife is charming. I spent happy hours in their garden, and they asked me to spend the summer with them. They thought I was the gardener.' Then, with a laugh, 'Unusual, I think? But I don't feel I can. I feel I want a change of scene.'

He went on, 'Do you know one of the punishments that happen to

495

people who have been "away"? They are not allowed to read the *Daily Chronicle*! Coming along I begged to be allowed to read it in the train. "No!" Then I suggested I might be allowed to read it upside down. This they consented to allow, and I read all the way the *Daily Chronicle* upside down, and never enjoyed it so much. It's really the only way to read newspapers.'

By now the messenger returned. Wilde opened the letter he brought and read a refusal: he could not be accepted on the spur of the moment; at least a year's deliberation was necessary. 'At this,' as Ada Leverson wrote, 'he broke down and sobbed bitterly.' But he recovered, as if resigned to accept secular life as a *pis aller*.[1] He talked with Arthur Clifton's wife (he had once given the Cliftons £120 so that they could get married) and other callers whom he insisted upon seeing. The result was that he missed the morning boat to Dieppe, so in the afternoon he went with Adey to Newhaven and crossed by the night boat.

On the Dieppe pier at 4 a.m. were Reggie Turner and Robert Ross. When they saw Wilde's boat coming they looked for him, and saw his heavy form as he walked with swaying gait in their direction. They too thought he looked well. As he joined them on the pier he handed Ross a bulky envelope, saying, 'This, my dear Bobbie, is the great manuscript about which you know.' The arrangement now was for Ross to keep the original and to send a copy to Douglas and one to Wilde at Dieppe. Then he laughed loudly, and talked and talked. His subject was Reading Gaol, and Ross noted that 'it had already become for him a sort of enchanted castle of which Major Nelson was the presiding fairy. The hideous machicolated turrets were already turned into minarets, the very warders into benevolent Mamelukes and we ourselves into Paladins welcoming Coeur de Lion after his captivity.' He went with his friends to the Hôtel Sandwich where he was ushered into a room filled with flowers, with all the books he had asked for arranged on the mantelpiece. Ross had raised £800 for him by subscription, which made for good spirits. There was a great deal more talk, till his friends were exhausted and went to sleep. Wilde wrote a letter to Ada Leverson, thanking her for her morning visit, and describing his present situation with an air of confiding great secrets. Traveling as Melmoth, he said, 'I have thought it better that Robbie should stay here under the name of Reginald Turner, and Reggie under the name of R. B. Ross. It is better that they should not have their own names.'[2]

So ended imprisonment. During the last eight months Wilde had contrived to live in his mind beyond the gaol, as he had not during the first sixteen months. He would have to discover whether he was in fact free, or still a prisoner. He felt as he had once predicted he would feel, like Rip Van Winkle. But he was also for the moment like Nathanaël in Gide's *Les Nourritures terrestres*, experiencing nature and life as if for the first time, rejoicing in all he could see, smell, hear, taste, and touch.

Return of Bosie

Always write to me about your art and the art of others. It is better to meet on the double peak of Parnassus, than elsewhere.

Much of the animus in the *De Profundis* letter to Douglas was dissipated by the time Wilde finished writing it. A solid remnant remained, but even this began to be modified between March 1897, when the letter was handed over to the governor of Reading, and 20 May when Wilde entrusted it to Ross on the pier at Dieppe. Bosie's image, however baleful, could not serve forever as whipping boy. On 13 May Wilde, raging with Adey and Ross over their supposed interference between him and his wife over his life interest in the marriage settlement, vengefully wondered aloud, in a letter to the hapless Ross, whether perhaps he had not been unjust to Douglas.[3] He forgot that Ross himself had pleaded Douglas's cause a few months before. The old lure was still in Wilde's thought, the love and pain that Douglas had aroused in him were ineradicable. He at once desired and dreaded the moment when Douglas would appear to hand him back his presents and letters. For the moment he could not face the tension of such an interview, and through Ross he instructed Douglas not to come to see him yet, though he was free to write.

Wilde had scarcely established himself in his hotel room in Dieppe when the first letter from Douglas arrived. It said that he had heard that Wilde had changed from loving him, and now hated him. His own attitude had not changed at all, and he asked for a meeting. Wilde's reply was intended to be Christian, but to Douglas sounded like cant. It said he did not hate Douglas but on the contrary still loved him very much; nevertheless they had better not meet for a time. This was the kind of provocation to which Douglas invariably responded: a few years later he would marry Olive Custance when he heard that she was engaged to a friend of his. He had had to put up with Ross's being a welcome visitor and correspondent, while he himself was unwelcome in either role, but he had always warned that when Wilde was released he would win him back. His jealousy, his competitive fury, and his awareness of his beauty, were roused by rejection. Perhaps fortunately, he had no idea of the detailed charges against him in the *De Profundis* letter, which because of its length Ross could not get typed – so that he could keep the original – until August. In a libel suit (the Ransome case) in 1913, during which the whole of *De Profundis* was read aloud, Douglas testified that he had received a copy of Wilde's letter from Ross. Having read Ross's note about it, he did not read the letter, but threw it in the fire. He asked Wilde how he had come to write such a letter to him, and Wilde replied, 'Please don't reproach me. I was mad with hunger, and in other ways.'[4] Still later Douglas denied that Ross had sent it to him.

Douglas knew how to wheedle, and how to wound. He denied that there was anything in his conduct to extenuate or excuse. He alone of all Wilde's intimates had stayed in London throughout the Queensberry trial, up to the eve of Wilde's own trial. So he berated Wilde for being 'unfair and ungrateful,' for behaving in a manner 'unworthy of him,' and for being deranged by his prison experience. The letters struck Wilde as 'revolting' and even 'infamous.' But Douglas could change his tone. He sent Wilde a poem, through More Adey, and this proved to be 'a love lyric.' Wilde was startled and commented, 'It is absurd,' without being altogether displeased: Bosie's obvious passion, though ferocious, was impressive. The two men exchanged letters frequently, but the prohibition on visits remained to nettle Douglas, who could remember how they had been together in Dieppe in the old days. Wilde smoothed him down, and Douglas then began on an opposite tack, begging Wilde to live with him for the rest of his life, and promising to atone by a lifelong devotion for the disaster that he and his family had brought about.[5]

Last Writings

The two long years of silence kept my soul in bonds. It will all come back, I feel sure, and then all will be well.

Wilde was seeking with some earnestness to reassemble his life. Of course he was badly in need of enjoying all that he had been deprived of for two years, but he still planned to do great things. The possibilities before him were all attended with difficulties, some arising from his temperament, some from his dubious status in the world. The plan of becoming a six-month penitent at a retreat had been thwarted. Then there was the plan to re-establish himself as artist. As Haldane had suggested to him long before, he wanted to write about the great subject of imprisonment. While he refused to exploit his prison reminiscences by paid journalism, within days of leaving Reading, he wrote his long letter to the *Daily Chronicle* about children in prison. He did not mind contradicting 'The Decay of Lying,' where he had criticized Charles Reade for 'a foolish attempt to be modern, to draw public opinion to the state of our convict prisons,' or his reproof of Dickens for trying 'to arouse our sympathy for the victims of the poor-law administration.' Now such subjects preoccupied him too. His friend Martin had been dismissed for kindness to child prisoners, and he took the occasion not only to defend him but to describe the harshness of prison for children. The letter carefully avoided details of his own sufferings, and Wilde – with his old hatred of autobiography – felt that if he was to describe prison at all, it must be obliquely. He envisaged three essays, of which two were to describe prison, and the third, as

Aspects of Wilde, by Max Beerbohm(*Ashmolean Museum, University of Oxford*)

Caricature of Wilde,
by Beerbohm

Sketch of Wilde in the dock,
by Ralph Hodgson (*Yorick*)

ABOVE: Playbill for *The Importance of Being Earnest*. BELOW: George Alexander as John Worthing and Rose Leclercq as Lady Bracknell in a scene from the original production, 1895 (*Courtesy of The Hyde Collection*)

Wilde, by Henri de Toulouse-Lautrec
(*Courtesy Guillot de Saix,*
H. Roger Viollet, Paris)

Berneval-Plage, prés Dieppe. · 13. - Marchands et Pêcheurs de Moules en 1900

Berneval, the village near Dieppe where Wilde stayed for several months
after leaving prison in 1897

ABOVE: Wilde and Lord Alfred Douglas in Naples, 1897 (*Courtesy of the William Andrews Clark Library*). BELOW: Wilde visiting the Royal Palace, Naples, 1897 (*Courtesy of the William Andrews Clark Library*)

In front of the equestrian statue of Marcus Aurelius in the Campidoglio, Rome, April 1900

Constance Holland in Heidelberg, 1897,
after changing her name

Wilde on his deathbed, photographed by Maurice Gilbert, 30 November 1900

Wilde's monument, by Jacob Epstein, in Père Lachaise Cemetery, Paris
(*photograph by Jack Oppenheim*)

foreshadowed in *De Profundis*, to deal with Christ as the precursor of the romantic movement in art. As in 'The Soul of Man Under Socialism,' Wilde would subsume prison and religion under one rubric. To mistreat the guilty, as to mistreat the innocent, was contrary to the canons of art as expressed by Christ the supreme artist and Wilde his prophet. These three essays were never written, and only a second letter to the *Daily Chronicle* the following year – Wilde's last work – discharged his obligation to speak for the prisoners in Pentonville, Wandsworth, and Reading.

There were plans to write a play, mentioned in his letters of 31 May and 2 June 1897. Either he would do his 'Pharaoh' or he would finish *A Florentine Tragedy*, the verse drama he had started long before. A letter he wrote to Douglas on 2 June, in which he urged the young man to write ballads, suggested that the idea of writing one himself had been gathering in his mind. Meanwhile he talked away other ideas: when a friend asked him on 22 June what he was doing, he answered that he was writing an essay entitled 'A Defence of Drunkenness,' to shock the English, the theme being 'that the soul is never liberated except by drunkenness in one form or another.' He went on, 'Here in a small place like Dieppe one's soul can listen to the words and harmonies and behold the colours of the Great Silence. But one is not always at Dieppe. And it is difficult to find the Great Silence. But a waiter with a tray will always find it for you. Knock, and the door will always open, the door of *le paradis artificiel*.'[6]

This was only Baudelairean high talk, probably necessary to him because, at the moment he was celebrating drunkenness, he was struggling to realize pathos. *The Ballad of Reading Gaol*, a name that Ross suggested, was occupying his thoughts. 'He owed his inspiration to Her Majesty's Government,' the judge in one of Douglas's libel actions said of it. Wilde had determined to focus it upon the trooper Wooldridge but to make clear that his own case and Wooldridge's were parallel:

> Like two doomed ships that pass in storm
>   We had crossed each other's way:
> But we made no sign, we said no word,
>   We had no word to say;
> For we did not meet in the holy night,
>   But in the shameful day.
>
> A prison wall was round us both,
>   Two outcast men we were:
> The world had thrust us from its heart,
>   And God from out His care:
> And the iron gin that waits for Sin
>   Had caught us in its snare.

The parallels were not limited to two men. Like Baudelaire, he would insist that his hypocrite reader was in the same image. As in his plays, sin was shown to be evenly distributed round the globe, though justice was not. The trooper had slit his wife's throat on the road (on the bed in his poem). Wilde daringly insists that all men commit the same crime of killing their love, whether by sword or kiss – that is, by brutality or cowardice. 'Treachery is inseparable from faith,' he wrote to Ada Leverson in 1894. 'I often betray myself with a kiss.' In his comedies the miscreants were always pardoned, but in the *Ballad*, while ultimately forgiven, they are treated vindictively by their fellows, who are equally guilty. The poem had a divided theme: the cruelty of the doomed murderer's crime, the insistence that such cruelty is pervasive; and the greater cruelty of his punishment by a guilty society.

By 8 July Wilde had started on the *Ballad* and by 20 July it was, he thought, nearly finished. He was to revise it with Ross's help in August, and to expand it later. The length of the poem was necessary, he said, to shake confidence in the penal system; he knew that it must fall between poetry and propaganda, but he was prepared to face some artistic imperfection for the sake of changing what was intolerable. 'Catastrophes in life bring about catastrophes in Art,' he told O'Sullivan. Ross always preferred its first, shorter version and Yeats, in the *Oxford Book of Modern Verse*, took much trouble to cut out almost all the message, feeling that the strength of the poem lay in its ballad narrative. But Wilde intended more. As he said to Chris Healy, 'It is the cry of Marsyas and not the song of Apollo. I have probed the depths of most of the experiences in life, and I have come to the conclusion that we are meant to suffer. There are moments when it takes you like a tiger, by the throat, and it was only when I was in the depths of suffering that I wrote [that is, conceived of] my poem. The man's face will haunt me till I die.'[7]

The *Ballad* is strongest when it concentrates on the trooper and prison conditions, weakest when it deals with capitalized abstractions like Sin and Death, and imports imagery from *The Rime of the Ancient Mariner*. At its best the sharp details and colloquial language carry conviction:

> I walked, with other souls in pain,
>   Within another ring,
> And was wondering if the man had done
>   A great or little thing,
> When a voice behind me whispered low,
>   *'That fellow's got to swing.'*
>
> With midnight always in one's heart,
>   And twilight in one's cell,
> We turn the crank, or tear the rope,
>   Each in his separate Hell,
> And the silence is more awful far
>   Than the sound of a brazen bell.

Wilde consciously imitates Coleridge, both in the stanza form* and in imagery, though his emphasis is on universal guilt rather than universal love:

> Dear Christ! the very prison walls
>   Suddenly seemed to reel,
> And the sky above my head became
>   Like a casque of scorching steel;
> And though I was a soul in pain,
>   My pain I could not feel.
>
> . . . . .
>
> The grey cock crew, the red cock crew
>   But never came the day
> And crooked shapes of Terror crouched,
>   In the corners where we lay:
> And each evil sprite that walks by night
>   Before us seemed to play.

or what he called 'out-Kipling Henley.'[8]

That the governor should have the 'yellow face of Doom,' or that none can tell 'to what red hell / His sightless soul may stray,' are among many purple passages. (The latter was added in a subsequent revision.) Yet if we grant that the poem is, as Major Nelson wrote when Ross – perhaps fearing legal trouble – let him see it in advance, 'a terrible mixture of good, bad and indifferent,' there is no doubt that Wilde had once again touched a great subject and left his fingerprints on it:

> He did not wear his scarlet coat,
>   For blood and wine are red,
> And blood and wine were on his hands
>   When they found him with the dead,
> The poor dead woman whom he loved
>   And murdered in her bed.

And if, as so often in life, he lacks restraint and bedizens his poem, a residue of it, as Yeats showed in his *Oxford Book*, is an almost great poem.[9] Once read, it is never forgotten.

This was the only creative work he was able to bring himself to write. He was uncomfortable about drawing the poem 'from personal experience, a sort of denial of my own philosophy of art in many ways. I hope it is good, but every night I hear cocks crowing . . . so I am afraid I may have denied myself, and would weep bitterly, if I had not wept away all my tears.'[10] But otherwise the poem was consistent in thought with his work from the beginning. In fact, the theme of *The Ballad of Reading Gaol* is closely similar to that of 'Humanitad' in his first book, the *Poems* of 1881.

* Coleridge's poem includes a number of six-line stanzas.

Writing the ballad had the virtue of restoring him to literature, and of showing that his creative powers remained intact in spite of their lack of exercise. He wrote one other thing that summer, a character of his sometimes friend Henley, to go with a drawing of Henley by Will Rothenstein. He served up some old and new witticisms in paradoxical form:

> He founded a school and has survived all his disciples. He has always thought too much about himself, which is wise; and written too much about others, which is foolish. His prose is the beautiful prose of a poet, and his poetry the beautiful poetry of a prose-writer. His personality is insistent. To converse with him is a physical no less than an intellectual recreation. He is never forgotten by his enemies, and often forgiven by his friends. He has added several new words to the language, and his style is an open secret. He has fought a good fight, and has had to face every difficulty except popularity.

Though Max Beerbohm liked the 'open secret' of Henley's style, and savored the rest, he concurred in Rothenstein's view that Henley would regard the evaluation as hostile, and would detect the author at once.[11]

Life in the Country

Civilisations continue because people hate them. A modern city is the exact opposite of what everyone wants.

Apart from the ballad and the 'character,' Wilde devoted himself to enjoying life. With no difficulty he succeeded in making heavy inroads on the £800 his friends had accumulated to help in his return. As always when his resources were limited, he dispensed money with liberality. No doubt he was bored at times, during intervals between visits of friends, and when they visited him he had to cope with silent reproach for idleness or patronizing sympathy for past sufferings. Wilde had dismissed too easily the importance of being married to Constance, with her stable affection and attention.

Even during periods of their marriage when he scarcely saw her for weeks on end, she had provided a structure outside which he could be truant. The devotion of his friends, especially Ross, touched him, but Ross could not offer more than bouts of company, having work in London and too small an income to neglect it. So Constance and his children came often into Wilde's thoughts. She was still his wife. On his first or second day in Dieppe Wilde wrote her a letter which was like the one he had written two years before, after three months in prison. Though the letter is lost, her description of it as 'full of penitence' cannot be doubted. The recognition of wronging her, and worse still, of cutting himself off from his children, preyed on Wilde's mind. Having failed to become a penitent, he dreamed of retreating into the role of husband and father. His letter begged for a meeting with her and their children, and Constance was touched and tempted. There had however been so much trouble over the life interest that she listened to her advisers, who could only warn her that Wilde might be no easier to manage now than before the *débâcle*. She therefore replied guardedly, not refusing but not agreeing, promising to visit him twice a year in any case, and mentioning a possible meeting between him and the boys. She had in mind a period of probation.[12] For Wilde, who had succeeded in pardoning Alfred Douglas, the postponement of absolution was intolerable. But for Constance, as for the Queensberry family, Douglas was a difficulty: a continent that contained both him and Oscar Wilde might well prove too small for a *vita nuova*. Still she wrote to her husband kindly every week, and did not reject the meeting for which he kept supplicating.

What Wilde could not guess from her letters, but learned privately from a letter sent him by their friend Carlos Blacker, was that Constance was in poor health. The spinal paralysis dating from her fall on the stairs at Tite Street had spread, so that a second operation was considered essential even though its results were problematic. In late July Wilde, perhaps not sure how unwell she was, proposed that she should bring Cyril and Vyvyan to Dieppe, after which he would return to live with them. Through Blacker, Constance asked him to wait until she had settled in a house in Nervi. Her letter made conditions, Wilde told Douglas afterwards, and Sherard says that one letter from her advisers to Wilde was 'slightingly worded.' Wilde felt keenly the contrast between Constance, all reluctance, and Bosie all avidity, as he tried to coax one into reconciliation and the other into delay.

With something of his old ability to rise beyond alternatives to a *tertium quid*, Wilde meditated another plan, entirely detached from wife and lover. This was to continue to live on the French coast. Dieppe, as he had feared, was not the best place for him. His friends might greet him effusively, other English tourists would not. He soon discovered that he could not rely upon the freemasonry of fellow artists, who could be as hypocritical as the inartistic in their gratuitous preference, as Wilde expressed it, for Messalina over Sporus, that is, for heterosexual debauchery over homosexual. As it happened, Dieppe was then full of artists, including three Englishmen and a Frenchman he had known well: Walter Sickert, Charles Conder, Beardsley, and Jacques-Emile Blanche. All were so eager to demonstrate that they were Bohemians that they became prigs. Sickert had reason to be grateful to Wilde for many acts of kindness to him and his family: now he shunned his old friend. Beardsley and Conder, walking with Blanche and aware that Blanche wished to show sympathy for Wilde, steered Blanche into a side street to prevent a meeting. Wilde may not have observed this cut, though one feels he observed every cut, but soon after, as he was sitting in front of the Café Suisse, he caught sight of Blanche, walking this time with Sickert, and beckoned to him. (Blanche had begun their friendship in 1883 by painting a picture of a young woman reading Wilde's *Poems*, and they had been on excellent terms for years.) But he ignored Wilde's signal and passed by as if he had not seen it. Wilde took great offense and made no further overtures.[13]

As for Beardsley, he had profited from Wilde's kindness, which he returned by insisting that Wilde should not be published in the *Yellow Book* if he were to illustrate it. At this time, moreover, he was being supported financially by André Raffalovich (whom he called 'Mentor'), and that sworn enemy of Wilde would have resented any friendship between them. Yet circumstances threw the two men together, and Beardsley was unable to resist at least one cordial meeting at a dinner party on 19 July 1897. On 3 August Wilde persuaded Beardsley to 'buy a hat more silver than silver.' Then Wilde invited him to dinner at Berneval, and Beardsley snubbed him by not showing up and by leaving Dieppe for Boulogne soon after, complaining of some members of the society there. 'It was *lâche* of Aubrey,' Wilde commented, playing snob to Beardsley's snub: 'If it had been one of my own class I might perhaps have understood it. I don't know whether I respect most the people who see me or those who don't. But a boy like that, whom I made! No, it was too *lâche* of Aubrey.'[14] 'To be spoken of, and not to be spoken to, is delightful,' he wrote ironically to Ada Leverson. But to the Ranee of Sarawak he sent a message, 'Tell her that horrible as are the dead when they rise from their tombs, the living when they come out from their tombs are more horrible still.'[15]

Of the four artists only Conder, after his first fluster and flutter, was amenable; he and Wilde saw each other often. Conder's conversation was 'like a beautiful sea-mist,' Wilde said.[16]* It was probably an invitation of Conder's, however, that subjected Wilde to another of the ordeals that awaited him in Dieppe. The proprietor of a restaurant, seeing Wilde among the four who were about to sit down at a table, approached them to say that he had food for three only, not for four, and they had to leave. A deputation of young French poets from Montmartre came to Dieppe to see Wilde, and were entertained at a lavish dinner at the Café des Tribunaux, which became so raucous that an official letter arrived from the sub-prefect warning Wilde that any public misconduct would lead to his expulsion from France.[18]

---

* Rothenstein says that Wilde was much taken with Conder's painted fans and wondered why people were not tumbling over one another to acquire them. Conder, always hard-up, was anxious to sell his work at any price. Wilde commented, 'Dear Conder! With what exquisite subtlety he goes about persuading someone to give him a hundred francs for a fan, for which he was fully prepared to pay two hundred!'[17]

But there were those who tried to make good the slights. A Norwegian landscape painter, Fritz von Thaulow, 'a giant with the temperament of Corot,' as Wilde described him, showed his sensitivity by booming at Wilde, who had just been insulted by some Englishmen, 'Mr Wilde, my wife and I would feel honoured to have you dine with us *en famille* this evening.' The Thaulow house, the Villa des Orchides, was always open to him. They had a party for him to which they invited among others the Mayor of Dieppe and the presidents of the city council and the chamber of commerce. It was sparsely attended. Another friend who rescued him from insult was Mrs Arthur Stannard, 'John Strange Winter.' Though her best-selling book, *Bootle's Baby*, was not to Wilde's taste – he mocked it to Ross as '*une oeuvre symboliste*' – he could not but approve of her courtesy. She made her husband call on Wilde soon after he arrived and ask him to dinner at the Pavillon de Berri where they lived. Soon after, observing him being snubbed by other English people, she crossed the street, took his arm, and said loudly, 'Oscar, take me to tea.'[19]

Wilde brought out the best as well as the worst in people living in Dieppe, but no courtesies could make up for the cuts. He was also conscious of another unpleasantness, that of being followed. Queensberry was determined that his son should not meet Wilde, and sent out a private detective to keep him informed. Wilde thought he might be freed from pursuit, as well as priggishness, if he moved out of Dieppe. Not being sure where to go, he hired a carriage and drove along the coast with Ross, who had stayed on after Adey left. By chance the white horse pulling the carriage was native to Berneval, and carried Wilde to that village five miles from Dieppe. Wilde knew the place slightly from previous visits, and decided to respect this equine hint. He moved to Berneval on 26 May. In so small a village the name of Sebastian Melmoth was a disguise which had a chance of working. In every other way he drew attention to himself. He took the two best rooms in the Hôtel de la Plage, and the delighted proprietor, one Bonnet, at once put up the rates. The hotel was comfortable, the cuisine – after Wilde had persuaded the chef not to serve him snake for dinner – quite good.

The experiment of Berneval seemed to work, and M. Melmoth thought of staying permanently. Bonnet, who dabbled in real estate, offered to find a piece of land and build a chalet to Wilde's specifications for £500. For a few days Wilde dreamed of becoming a small landed proprietor in Picardy. He wrote to Robert Ross, then serving as his treasurer but shortly to be relieved of the post, pointing out the advantages of such a step after his first play was finished. Ross responded soberly that Wilde might have difficulty keeping up the mortgage payments, and that in any case he was bound to spend most of his time in Paris rather than in Berneval.[20] To this Wilde protested that Paris would not suit him, that Berneval, so obscure and distant and tedious, was an ideal place for him to write. For the moment it did seem ideal, as the sun shone and he took his daily swim in the sea. (The weather and the mood changed in August.) Still, not having the £500 or the finished play, he gave up the idea of building a chalet and compromised by renting the Chalet Bourgeat, from 15 June 1897. He filled it with the books provided by his friends, asked Ross to send over his pictures, and made himself as comfortable as he could. He permitted himself a valet, but the problem of finding the right one gave him some amusement: 'He was very clever,' said Wilde of the first candidate. 'But he became impossible. It was my own fault; I am very unhappy about it. I gave him a blue uniform, a thing I ought not to have done. Of course he got conceited about it at once. He went to a ball, and made quite a hit with his blue uniform. Naturally he wanted to go to dances every evening. Then, of course, he wanted to sleep in the mornings. And I had to wait and wait for my hot water. One morning I got up myself and took him hot water. That helped for one day, but no more. Now he is dismissed and I have found another one. The next book I write will be about the effect of the colour blue on men.'[21]

Following the first week, when Adey and Turner left, then Ross, a series of people came to see the wounded lion of Berneval. Lugné-Poë, whose production of *Salome* in Paris in February 1896 had so splendidly signalled that Wilde was still a living author, wrote and asked if he might call. The response on 24 May was in Oriental style: '*L'auteur de* Salome *prie le Tétrarque de Judée de lui faire l'Honneur de déjeuner avec lui demain matin à midi.*' They talked of Wilde's next play, 'Pharaoh,' which Lugné-Poë was eager to produce. Wilde still hoped to make a comeback with a Biblical play in Paris. His enthusiasm paled, however, when it became clear there was no money to pay the playwright.[22]

On 3 June there arrived three men whom Wilde denominated as the Poet, the Painter, and the Philosopher. They were Ernest Dowson, Charles Conder, and Dalhousie Young. Young was more composer than philosopher, but he had written his *Apology for Oscar Wilde* which Wilde promoted (for the sake of a third *P*) to the status of philosophy. Young and his wife were so moved by Wilde's situation that they offered to pay for a chalet, at Bonnet's current price of £700.[23] Wilde apparently felt uneasy at so large a gift from a comparative stranger, and did not accept it. Dowson was the most congenial of the three: Wilde liked his verse and valued his company, which he enjoyed not only at Berneval but from time to time at Arques, where Dowson lived, and at Dieppe, where they sometimes met. The friendship moved quickly towards intimacy, tinged at least on Wilde's side with eroticism:

My dear Ernest, I arrived safe, under a cold white moon, at one o'clock in the morning ... There is a fatality about our being together that is astounding – or rather quite probable. Had I stayed at Arques I should have given up all hopes of ever separating from you. Why are you so persistently and perversedly wonderful?

Do I see you tomorrow? . . . Come with vine-leaves in your hair.

I suppose I shall see you in ten minutes from this. I am looking out for the green costume that goes so well with your dark hyacinth locks.

Dowson was his first hyacinth since Douglas. But this flower was wilting, and had not much longer to live. Another letter to Dowson said, 'You were wonderful and charming all last night.' This may have been the night that Dowson persuaded Wilde to try sexual relations with women again. On his return from a Dieppe prostitute Wilde said to Dowson with distaste: 'The first these ten years, and it shall be the last. It was like chewing cold mutton.' Then as an afterthought, 'But tell it in England, where it will entirely restore my reputation.'[24]

A week later, on 10 June 1897, Will Rothenstein and Edward Strangman came. Strangman worked in the office of the publisher Leonard Smithers. He asked Rothenstein about Ricketts and Shannon, and was told that they were doing much better and even making a little money. Wilde considered the matter for a moment and then said, 'When you go to sup with them, I suppose they have *fresh* eggs now.'[25] He took to Strangman at once, and after the two men left he wrote to him on 11 June to thank him for his visit, and then, four days later, to urge him, while in Paris, to meet Alfred Douglas. Wilde's description of that young man was not in tune with that in *De Profundis*: 'He is a most delicate and refined poet, and has a personality of singular charm. I have not seen him yet, but I am going to let him come and see me in a few days. Our lives are divided, but we love each other deeply and our souls touch in myriad ways through the estranging air.' Strangman and Douglas did become friends as well as creditor and debtor, for Strangman lent him money for gambling. (On 22 July Douglas was still apologizing for his inability to repay it.) Rothenstein stayed a day or two longer, and met another visitor, Arthur Cruttenden, fresh from Reading Gaol, where he too had been confined. Wilde was his host for a week, then sent him back to England with letters asking friends to help him find a job. Dowson paid a second visit later in June, this time for three days. On the 16th he took Wilde to lunch and Wilde brought him back to Berneval for dinner. Dowson found him in 'gorgeous spirits,' and wrote, 'I was amused by the unconscious contrast between his present talk about his changed position and his notions of economy and his practice, which is perversely extravagant. He does not realize in the least that nobody except himself *could* manage to spend the money he does in a *petit trou de campagne.* He is a wonderful man.'[26] A visit that Wilde paid to Aubrey Beardsley in Boulogne was less well received: Beardsley wrote requesting him not to repeat it.

On the 20th of the month, in the early evening, André Gide arrived unannounced. Wilde was away, so Gide had a taste of what life in Berneval was like, there being no one in the hotel with whom he could talk. But at 10.30 a carriage rolled up, and in came M. Melmoth, 'chilled through and through.' At first Wilde scarcely spoke to Gide: he was taken up with an overcoat he had somehow lost during the evening, a misfortune he blamed on his servant's having brought him a peacock feather the evening before. But after he had drunk some hot grog, he became his animated self, not swaggering as in Algiers in 1895 but simple as in Paris in 1891. Gide explained his visit to Wilde on the ground that, being the last of Wilde's French friends to see him, he wanted to be the first to see him again. He must have been curious to find out if Wilde, whom he chose to regard as Satanic, was still throning it now that he was in Hell. He was also curious to know what Wilde had made of what was obviously his portrait, Ménalque, in *Les Nourritures terrestres*, which Wilde pointed to in the bookcase.

As Wilde sat by the fire, Gide took in the redness and coarseness of his face and especially his hands, though he wore the old rings.* They talked of their last meeting in Algiers, and Gide reminded Wilde that he had then predicted his own catastrophe. Wilde replied, 'Oh, of course, of course! I knew that there would be a catastrophe, that way or another . . . It had to end that way. Just imagine: it wasn't possible to go any further, and it couldn't last.' As for his time at Reading, he described some of the injustices he had suffered, and then said 'Prison has completely changed me. I counted on it for that.' Their mutual friend Douglas, who came up often in the conversation, was in error in supposing that Wilde had been changed by friends in England, presumably by the Catholics Ross and Adey. No, it was prison that had wrought the change. He could not lead the same life as before. With something of his old manner he said, 'My life is like a work of art. An artist never starts the same thing twice.' He would go to Paris, but only when he had written a play and could present himself as playwright rather than convict.

Gide spoke of Dostoevsky, who had served a four-year penal sentence and had then written *From the House of the Dead*. Wilde said that he had come to admire the Russian writers for a quality totally lacking in Flaubert, their pity. This was a great change for him. It was pity, he said, that had kept him from killing himself, for he could not help pitying prisoners in the same misery. His friend Douglas could not understand this feeling, and wanted Wilde to be bitter and angry, but Wilde had purged himself of bitterness and anger. Still he could understand Douglas's position: 'I repeat to him in each letter: we cannot follow the same path; he has his, it's very beautiful. I have mine. His is that of Alcibiades, mine is now that of St Francis of Assisi.' When Gide proved to be knowledgeable about St Francis, Wilde asked him to send the best book he knew on the saint.

* Wilde was wearing two emeralds, engraved with cabalistic signs, one on the little finger of each hand. That on the left was the efficient cause of all joys, that on the right of misfortunes. Asked why he continued to wear the one on the right, Wilde said, 'One needs misfortunes to live happily.'[27]

They retired very late, for Franciscans, and in the morning Wilde took Gide to see the Chalet Bourgeat which he was beginning to furnish. It was here that he planned to write first his 'Pharaoh' and then his 'Ahab and Jezebel,' the plots of which he recounted 'marvellously.' They walked together to the train, and Wilde suddenly reverted to *Les Nourritures terrestres*, about which he had so far spoken only in general terms. 'Listen, dear,' he said to Gide, 'you have to make a promise now. *Les Nourritures terrestres* is fine ... it's very fine ... But dear, promise me from now on never to write *I* any more. In art, don't you see, there is no first person.'[28]

In such meetings Wilde passed June and July of 1897. Most of his friends paid for their *pension* in the Hôtel de la Plage, although Dowson not only failed to do this, but borrowed money from Wilde as well. It took months for one hard-up writer to retrieve the money from another. On the other hand, Wilde always defended Dowson. When someone said, 'It's a pity he drinks so much absinthe,' Wilde shrugged his shoulders as he replied, 'If he didn't drink, he would be somebody else. *Il faut accepter la personnalité comme elle est. Il ne faut jamais regretter qu'un poète est saoul, il faut regretter que les saouls ne soient pas toujours poètes.*'*[29] A young French novelist was allowed to remain for several weeks at Wilde's expense, and a French poet borrowed some money to get back to Paris and sent his creditor a sonnet instead of a cheque. The £800 gradually drifted away in such expenditures or in celebrations, such as the Diamond Jubilee of Queen Victoria on 22 June. Wilde, no doubt pining for his sons, invited fifteen small boys of the neighborhood, along with the curé, the postman, the schoolmaster, and other local worthies. He got Bonnet to decorate the banqueting room at the Hôtel de la Plage with colored lamps and English flags. The children were given strawberries and cream, apricots, chocolates, cakes, and grenadine syrup. A huge iced cake bore the words, *Jubilé de la Reine Victoria*, in pink sugar rosetted with green, encircled by a great wreath of red roses. Each child was allowed to choose a present; six chose accordions, five trumpets, and four bugles. The postman got an accordion. They sang the *Marseillaise*, danced a rondo, sang 'God Save the Queen.' Wilde proposed a toast to the Queen, then to France as '*la mère de tous les artistes*,' and finally to the Président de la République, after which the children cried, '*Vivent le Président de la République et Monsieur Melmoth.*'[30]

This enthusiasm for Queen Victoria was not new on Wilde's part. He had said that the three great personalities of the nineteenth century were Napoleon, Victor Hugo, and Queen Victoria. At Fritz von Thaulow's house the day after his party, he explained that it was not in her imperial character that he admired her, but as a person. Asked if he had ever met her, he replied that he had, and described with admiration her appearance

---

* 'Personality must be accepted for what it is. You mustn't mind that a poet is a drunk, rather that drunks are not always poets.'

('a ruby mounted in jet'), her walk, and her regal behavior.[31]* One effect of Wilde's prison sentence, as of Dostoevsky's, was to make him much less radical in politics, as he was to demonstrate at the time of the Boer War, when he enthusiastically supported England.

The visits continued into late July and August. Charles Wyndham came, anxious to contract with Wilde for a new play. If he did not feel like writing his own, he could adapt one by Scribe about society in the age of Queen Anne. He asked for a free hand in the adaptation, which Wyndham of course granted, but Wilde did not agree to anything, and in September he withdrew, saying he was not in the frame of mind to write comedy. He thought again of finishing *La Sainte Courtisane*, but could not. Other offers of work came in, one from Fernand Xau to do a weekly chronicle for *Le Journal*. But to persuade him Xau said, 'After all the brouhaha of your trial, the chronicles will have a great success.' Wilde put down his pen and said, 'My former successes will suffice me.'[33] As he told Vincent O'Sullivan, 'I would rather continue stitching sacks.' Vincent O'Sullivan was a young writer whom he had known only a little before, and at first they did not get on well, O'Sullivan being inclined as Wilde said to view everything from the perspective of the tomb. He also ventured to complain that Wilde had too many people of title in his plays. 'You would permit at least a Colonial Knight?' Wilde asked in irritation. But O'Sullivan did better when he remarked that Yeats had said to him that Wilde was meant to be a man of action. Wilde pondered before he replied, 'It is interesting to hear Yeats's opinions about one,' and then complained that English political life, which he had once considered entering, was too much a matter of catch-words.[34] He invited O'Sullivan to return, as he did.

Leonard Smithers was the next guest, and one destined to be of great importance to Wilde during the remainder of his life. Smithers had taken the place of John Lane as the principal publisher of Nineties work, and they had some discussion about Smithers' bringing out *The Ballad of*

* Many renderings of Wilde's conversation stultify his wit, and for the way he really talked one has to fall back on his letters. For example, this description of a pilgrimage which he sent to Ross:

'I am going tomorrow on a pilgrimage. I always wanted to be a pilgrim, and I have decided to start early tomorrow to the shrine of Notre Dame de Liesse. Do you know what Liesse is? It is an old word for joy. I suppose the same as *Letizia*, *laetitia*. I just heard of the shrine, or chapel, tonight, by chance, as you would say, from the sweet woman of the auberge, a perfect dear, who wants me to live always at Berneval! She says Notre Dame de Liesse is wonderful, and helps everyone to the secret of joy. I do not know how long it will take me to get to the shrine, as I must walk. But, from what she tells me, it will take at least six or seven minutes to get there, and as many to come back. In fact the chapel of Notre Dame de Liesse is just fifty yards from the hotel! Isn't it extraordinary? I intend to start after I have had my coffee, and then to bathe. Need I say that this is a miracle? I wanted to go on a pilgrimage, and I find the little grey stone chapel of Our Lady of Joy is brought to me.'[32]

Reading Gaol. Wilde was amused by the publisher's inveterate eroticism, in life involving 'first editions' of young girls, and in literature expressed in undercover pornography.

In August two old friends arrived, Robert Ross and Robert Sherard. For Sherard this visit did not go well: Wilde and Ross forgot to draw the curtains and he caught sight of them in sexual embrace, or so he said; and to make matters worse, there were telegrams and letters from Douglas arriving all the time to keep Wilde in a constant tremor of irritation and perplexity. The reconciliation with Constance, for which Sherard continued to hope, seemed farther off than ever. Wilde evidently caught Sherard's shift in tone, and treated him coolly in return. Back in London, Sherard met Smithers at the Authors' Club and alluded to homosexual behavior at Berneval; Smithers told Wilde, who wrote to Sherard with the utmost asperity. Though he followed up this letter with a conciliatory note sending him the *Ballad*, they never resumed their close friendship.

In the midst of winds and tides the firmest bond was that with Douglas. In no time, before May was over, Wilde's tone towards him changed from coldness and mute reproach to affection. 'Dear Bosie' became 'My darling Boy.' One element in the change was Wilde's consternation at hearing from More Adey that Douglas had given another of his interviews to the press, this time to *Le Jour* which published it on 28 May. Wilde was alarmed that Douglas was destroying him for a second time, and wrote to caution him. It may have been this letter – now lost – which Douglas returned to Wilde with two poems and a bitter letter of his own, in which he disclaimed the interview (as later he would disclaim his own article in *La Revue blanche*), and said that on reading it he had written to the editor to that effect, and also challenged the journalist to a duel. The interviewer responded that he had quoted Douglas accurately, but the duel did not take place.[35] Wilde was considerably flurried – by the article, until he got a copy and saw it was innocuous – and by the duel, both for Douglas's sake and his own. He asked Douglas to telegraph him about it. At the same time, in this complex mixture of terror, pleading, and high flown literary discourse, he said he did not greatly like Douglas's two new poems, and urged him to turn again to ballads.[36] This was his last genuine effort to judge Douglas's powers; after this he would always refer to his friend as the best of the younger poets, and brook no opposition.

Douglas's obsessive concern for him had touched Wilde. Douglas was the only person he knew who was not censorious, and who encouraged him to live in the way he lived before prison. As for Douglas's faults, *De Profundis* had already granted an official pardon for them. The alternation of fury and love, two sides of the same coin, was proving as overwhelming for Wilde now as in the old days. By 7 or 8 June he wrote to Lady Queensberry offering what she called 'conditions' for a possible meeting with Douglas and asking her consent. She wrote to More Adey on 9 June that she would not accept the conditions – presumably having to do with

Douglas's continued allowance – and that 'Mr Wilde must decide all matters concerned with seeing or not seeing Alfred entirely for himself and without making me responsible for his actions. Will you kindly show him this letter.' On 12 June, just three weeks after his debarkation at Dieppe, he issued an invitation to Douglas to visit him on the 18th. He must on no account come under his own name when he visited 'that strange purple shadow who is known as Sebastian Melmoth,'[37] but might well adopt that of Jonquil du Vallon. As a *nom d'amour* this was obviously preferred to Prince Fleur de Lys, against which Wilde had protested in *De Profundis*.

This idyllic reconciliation was not to take place. The solicitor Arthur D. Hansell, whom Wilde had engaged to protect his interest in the marriage settlement, got wind of it, and resigned on the spot. He may have found out from Queensberry's detective, from Queensberry himself, or from some other correspondent. Wilde had previously been warned that Constance would cut off his £150 allowance, and that Queensberry would descend on Dieppe with a revolver, if he and Bosie reunited. Now, on receipt of Hansell's letter, he wired in a panic to Douglas that a sudden terrific difficulty had arisen, to be explained by letter. Douglas scoffed when he learned that his father's arrival was threatened. At the same time, Wilde wrote a postcard to Ross: 'A.D. is not here, nor is he to come.' In a letter of the 23rd to Douglas, Wilde promised consolingly that when he had finished his play Bosie and he would meet and Wilde would once again be 'king of life.'[38]

Douglas was enraged by the contretemps and blamed More Adey for allowing such a clause to be included in Wilde's agreement with Constance. Adey was ill, so Ross replied that Adey had nothing to do with the insertion of the clause, which had been forced on them by events, and by the concern of all parties that Wilde should not resume his old life. He urged on Douglas the importance of encouraging Wilde to write a play. Douglas answered on 20 June accusing Ross of jealousy. An angrier letter came from Ross, saying that Douglas had much more money than he or Adey, though Adey had given Wilde a hundred pounds, and that since he was so casually proposing to lose Wilde £150 a year, he could easily settle the same amount on him. In that case, Wilde would 'have the added pleasure of your perpetual society and your inspiring temper for the future.' He enclosed an exact account of the stewardship, which showed that neither Ross nor Adey had initiated the offending clause.[39]

Incensed by this unaccustomed candor in an old friend, Douglas counterattacked in letters to Ross, Adey, and Wilde. His argument was that as an aristocrat he had a different attitude to money from Ross. It was as natural for him to gamble as for Ross to live within his means.[40] Wilde replied on 6 July with an eloquent defense of Ross, rejecting Douglas's claim of better blood. At this point Lady Queensberry, who had a suspicion that a meeting was about to take place between Bosie and Wilde, invited her son to Le Havre or Boulogne or wherever Wilde was not. She also sent £10 to Wilde by way of More Adey, in partial fulfillment of what Douglas had described as a debt of honor to Wilde for his court costs incurred by his brother Percy.

In August letters went thick and fast between Berneval and Paris. Douglas told Gide that Wilde wrote to him every day. Constance's weekly letter was overshadowed by this more pressing exchange. She could not bring herself to allow the meeting for which Wilde pleaded. According to More Adey's letter to Adela Schuster of 12 March 1898, she wrote to her husband '*too* late, saying that she could see him, as she had then got their children out of the way.' She felt that their lives could only be 'more ruined' by seeing him. He was so irritated by what he considered insensitivity, that contrary to the advice of his friends, he refused to go to her, and apparently wrote to the effect that he was utterly lonely, treated like a pariah and worn out with her perpetual procrastination, and was therefore going to live with the only person ready to give him his companionship, Alfred Douglas. He was blaming her (as she realized) for forcing him back to Douglas. Constance's reaction was recalled by her son, Vyvyan, who wrote to Frank Harris, 'I remember my mother's joy when he was supposed to be coming back, and I remember her misery when she found he had other claims upon his time.'[41] Wilde had managed to justify his momentous decision. He wrote to Douglas on 24 August offering to meet him at Rouen at the Hôtel de la Poste.

Douglas, at last sought not seeking, sent a surprising reply: he said he had no money and could not come. His power over Wilde restored, his wish to see him lessened. Wilde complained to Ross that this showed meanness and lack of imagination. Douglas thought better of it and telegraphed his acceptance of the rendezvous. They met at Rouen, almost certainly on 28 August. Wilde wept at the station, they held hands, they walked arm in arm. Bosie suggested that, since he had promised his mother that he would go with her and his sister to Aix-les-Bains, for a cure, they might meet in six weeks' time at Naples. They stayed overnight in Rouen and parted on the most affectionate terms. Douglas sent a loving telegram to Wilde and Wilde replied in a way that contradicted most of *De Profundis*, 'I feel that my only hope of again doing beautiful work in art is being with you. It was not so in the old days, but now it is different, and you can really recreate in me that energy and sense of joyous power on which art depends. Everyone is furious with me for going back to you, but they don't understand us. I feel that it is only with you that I can do anything at all. Do remake my ruined life for me, and then our friendship and love will have a different meaning to the world.'[42]

This was a second fall for Wilde. Ovid says '*Video meliora proboque; deteriora sequor* [I see the good and value it; I follow the bad].' But Berneval had failed Wilde, Constance had failed Wilde, all his friends had failed him, and there was only Bosie left. It seemed conceivable, for the moment, that the joy of life, which foggy Berneval had failed to disclose, might reappear in the Neapolitan sun.

CHAPTER XXII

The Leftover Years

DUCHESS: *They say the common field-flowers of the field*
Have sweeter scent when they are trodden on
Than when they bloom alone, and that some herbs
Which have no perfume, on being bruised die
With all Arabia round them.

Life with Douglas

Wilde's situation framed itself in terms of the Greek tragedies he knew so well. In *De Profundis* he had made Douglas the Helen of his tragedy, but he had also a sense of doom, early and late. The passions which his own life had allegorized were ambition and sloth, blending his character with his fate. His was not, like many tragedies, an allegory of mere pride, though in casual moments he would say, 'I had risen too high, and I fell sprawling in the mire.' But pride held its own in the chastened *De Profundis* as it had in his American tour.[1] He never abjured pride in his family or pride in his genius. Nor was he severe with pride's outward show, vanity, as displayed in his delight in clothing and appearance, in the turn of a phrase or the cut of a coat. What he regarded as his weaknesses were his inability to choose the greater pleasure over the lesser, and his proneness to give way to the most trifling of temptations. In him *hubris* had taken this seemingly innocuous form. He knew himself to be generous, sympathetic to the poor, the thwarted, the excluded, and his self-esteem valorized his guilt. He only felt apologetic, as a playwright, because there were fifty-five acts to his tragedy. In the United States, according to Samuel Beer, at least nine hundred sermons were preached against him between 1895 and 1900.[2]

As he yielded to the entreaties of Bosie to live with him, entreaties which echoed his own inclinations, Wilde could feel that the return was a *coup de théâtre* not calculated to propitiate the unseen directors who allot tragic parts. The fall in 1895 was spectacular; a second fall was of lesser importance. But the second fall confirmed the pattern of his destiny. Wilde's letters to his friends acknowledged the force of their disapproval, but saw no alternative. 'I daresay that what I have done is fatal,' he tells Robert Ross, who alone had read the whole of *De Profundis*, 'but it had to be done.' 'I love him as I always did, with a sense of tragedy and ruin.' 'My life cannot be patched up. There is a doom on it.' 'It is the result of the nemesis of character, and the bitterness of life. I was a problem for which there was no solution.' 'My going back to Bosie was psychologically inevitable; and, setting aside the interior life of the soul with its passion for self realisation at all costs, the world forced it upon me.'[3] Blame fell equally on the gods, the psyche, and the world, working towards a prearranged conclusion.

There is some evidence that the decision of Wilde and Douglas at the end of August to reunite was less wholehearted than either allowed the other to know. Douglas, moderating his earlier eagerness, specified a six-week delay before the reunion would take place. He had planned to spend three weeks in September with his mother at Aix-les-Bains, taking the waters for his rheumatism, and then to go on to Venice. So leisurely a convergence with Wilde implies some qualification of desire. He seems to have enjoyed himself at Aix, and in his *Autobiography* notes that it was there that he wrote his best ballad, 'The Ballad of St Vitus.' That poem is not about reconciliation with Wilde, but about reconciliation with Queensberry: it describes how Vitus regains his father's love by a miracle. Douglas was to seek consciously to be once more his father's son the next year. That he was irresolute is confirmed by his checking out of his hotel in Aix, and leaving a forwarding address of a hotel in Venice. He had evidently written to tell Wilde of this plan, for a letter from Wilde answers.

> My dearest boy: I hope to go to Naples in three days, but must try and get some more money. I see it costs £10 to go to Naples. This is awful. Of course, wait until your cure is finished. I hope you will have no more rheumatic horrors. I know how dreadful they are.
>
> As regards Venice, of course do just as you will, but the sooner you come to Naples the happier I shall be. At present I am wretched, and in low spirits. Come as soon as you can. The accumulated hotel bills were awful, and the proprietress, of course, turned out to be a Shylock. Ever yours, with love,
>
> OSCAR[4]

This letter may have decided Douglas; he wrote agreeing to an earlier meeting.

Wilde, for his part, was aware that returning to Bosie would outrage everyone. They all wanted him to see his wife first. He felt he had little choice. On going back to Berneval from Rouen, he had experienced that village in all its villagism, the company vying with the weather in being insufferable. And he was tired of the insufferable. He now went again to

Rouen, and according to Gertrude Atherton, whose account, though hostile, cannot be sheer invention, urged Reggie Turner, who was staying at her hotel, to come and live with him. Turner, after all, had a fixed income and could live wherever he liked; as a novelist, moreover, he shared Wilde's literary interests. But Turner rebelled at the prospect of committing himself, and confided his difficulty to Mrs Atherton; she urged him to escape to London, where Wilde could not follow him.[5] After three days Turner appears to have done just that. He would say much later that her report was full of lies, but visiting Wilde was one thing, living with him another; he wished to be a friend and not a *copain*.

When Turner failed him Wilde knew he had exhausted all the alternatives: he returned to Berneval, packed up his belongings, paid off M. Bonnet, arranged to have his books and other possessions sent on later (they arrived on 5 November), and on 15 September departed for Paris. Any thought of writing a play in Berneval had been dissipated. It may have been at this time that he ran into the journalist Chris Healy and said to him, 'I cannot say what I am going to do with my life; I am wondering what my life is going to do with me. I would like to retire to some monastery – to some grey-stoned cell where I could have my books, write verses, and reverently smoke my cigarettes.' Healy mentioned that Nordau's *Degeneration*, in which Wilde was a principal exhibit, treated all men of genius as mad. 'I quite agree with Dr Nordau's assertion that all men of genius are insane, but Dr Nordau forgets that all sane people are idiots,' was Wilde's reply.[6] From Paris he wrote to Douglas, and was encouraged to come on to Aix as soon as he had some money. Vincent O'Sullivan, whom Wilde saw again, was obliging. After listening to Wilde's plight over lunch, he went to his bank, withdrew the sum needed, and gave it to him.[7]

The two friends then met at Aix-les-Bains, neither of them quite so certain of enjoying the other's company as they pretended. Both looked forward to Naples; Douglas knew it well, and was acquainted with all the British community. He had no money, but regarded this as of no consequence. He and Wilde checked into the Hôtel Royal at Naples and ran up a bill of £60 on the strength of Douglas's being a lord. Then some lean days came. Douglas tried to raise money as usual from his mother, and probably also from his brother; but whatever handouts he received were grudging. Wilde was more resourceful: he had talked over with Dalhousie Young the possibility of writing a libretto for an opera about Daphnis and Chloe, for which Young would compose the music. Now Wilde declared he was ready to proceed at once if Young would advance £100. It was the first time since his release from prison that Wilde had asked for an advance on a work which he probably never planned to deliver, and was a step down in his rehabilitation. Still, he could scarcely afford old scruples now. Fortunately Dalhousie Young agreed. With his £100, and perhaps odd sums from Queensberry relations, Wilde and Douglas took the Villa Giudice, now 37 via Posillipo, in fashionable

Posillipo, north of the city of Naples, and moved into it before the end of September.

If Wilde meant at all seriously his letter saying that only with Douglas would he be able to write, he cannot have been pleased with the results. Douglas turned out a series of sonnets, which Wilde overpraised to Smithers and Ross as being 'ivory and gold' and 'quite wonderful.' (As Gordon Craig commented, 'To be kind was why he flattered – but woe to any fool who *accepted* the flattery.') Three of the sonnets, entitled by Wilde 'A Triad of the Moon,' were sent to Henley, of all people, who rejected them, as he had earlier rejected 'The Ballad of Perkin Warbeck.' One sonnet, on Mozart, was sent to the editor of a music magazine, who commented impertinently on its poor quality and was soundly rebuked for his pains by Wilde, on the grounds that the poem was a gift and not a submission.[8] These were feeble efforts to secure a few pounds and a little recognition, and did not work. Together, Wilde and Douglas produced a few lyrics for 'Daphnis and Chloe,' but not surprisingly Dalhousie Young gave up the project. More to the point, Wilde wrote a number of new stanzas for *The Ballad of Reading Gaol*; while they added to its cumulative effect, they did not otherwise improve it. Some additions were abysmal; he altered 'in God's sweet world again' to 'for weal or woe again.' Smithers made him restore the original phrase, which was a little better and not so archaic.[9] As for the projected plays, they remained unwritten, even unattempted.

Most of their time went in dawdling about the cafés or the beaches, good-humoredly competing for Neapolitan boys. When La Duse was performing in Naples, they went every night. Wilde wrote sending her *Salome* and begging her to produce it some day. She admired it.[10] The Villa Giudice proved to have rats, and Douglas had to move across the street until they called in a local witch who got rid of them. This was the same witch Wilde pointed out later to Vincent O'Sullivan with the words, 'Unless that old woman asks you for money, do not offer it to her. But if she asks you, be sure not to refuse.'[11] He was still in fear of the evil powers, though they had already indulged themselves at his expense. Once when Wilde received a £10 check from Smithers, he and Douglas went off to Capri for three days. The Swedish doctor Axel Munthe invited Bosie to dinner; Bosie said he could not come without Wilde, and Munthe urged him to bring Wilde, saying he had always thought his imprisonment unjust. They invited More Adey to stay with them in Posillipo, but he refused. They were not popular with the English set in Naples 'for some reason' (as Wilde said); one day Douglas met a man named Knapp, whom he had known at Oxford, and said to him, 'Oscar is here, do join us, or do you mind?' Knapp didn't mind, but the question showed that invitations could not be given without hesitation. One day the attaché from the British Embassy in Rome – where Bosie had spent the previous winter with his mother – came to Naples to warn him, in an apparently casual chat, that to share a house with Wilde was creating scandal. 'My existence is a scandal,' Wilde commented.[12] Still, if the English looked the other way, the Italians were friendly. So long as a little money trickled in, life at the villa was pleasant and sunny. There were four servants to reconcile them to their lot.

Elsewhere were only frowns and recriminations. Constance learned where her husband was, and with whom. On 29 September 1897 she wrote to him with unaccustomed forcefulness, 'I *forbid* you to see Lord Alfred Douglas. I forbid you to return to your filthy, insane life. I forbid you to live at Naples. I will not allow you to come to Genoa.' Wilde answered that he would never dream of going to see her against her will, or without assurance of her sympathy and pity. Her many refusals to meet had left him no alternative, he said, blaming her for his decision. For the rest, he only desired peace and to live his life as best he could. He did hope to winter in Naples. She wrote to her brother, 'Oscar has gone to Naples and consequently back to Lord A and has written me a horrid letter. If he prefers that life to living here with me – well, I am sorry for him but what can I do?'[13] To Carlos Blacker Wilde stated baldly that he had nowhere else to go, no one to live with, since Constance had spent three months fending him off. He said to Claire de Pratz, correspondent of *Le Petit Parisien* and *Daily News*, whose article on Loti he had published in *Woman's World*, 'Is there on earth a crime so terrible that in punishment of it a father can be prevented from seeing his children?'[14]

Constance did not reply to his letter directly, but through her solicitor she invoked the clause in their agreement which provided that his allowance would cease if he lived with a disreputable person. There followed a correspondence with Ross and Adey which is not without its comic side. Wilde and Douglas were quick to deny that Douglas was a disreputable person, and charged their friends in London with having meekly accepted this designation instead of challenging it. If Douglas was disreputable, then so were Adey and Ross; Ross had spent two months with Bosie on Capri the year before. (In fact, Constance had objected in 1895 to Wilde's seeing Adey in prison on exactly those grounds.) In another mood, Wilde allowed that Douglas was indeed 'a gilded pillar of infamy,' but not therefore disreputable.[15] Adey had to explain patiently that neither he nor Ross had ever said Douglas was disreputable; all they had acknowledged – and they had no alternative – was that Wilde and Douglas were living together. The designation of Douglas as disreputable had been made by Constance, and was the whole purpose of her having that clause inserted in the agreement. There was nothing they could do to save Wilde his three pounds a week, which was stopped in November.

Lady Queensberry was not to be outdone. She too saw that

> Love in a hut, with water and a crust,
> Is – Love, forgive us! – cinders, ashes, dust,

and was equally determined to separate Wilde and Douglas by financial means. She loathed Wilde as her son's corrupter as much as Constance loathed Douglas as Wilde's. The two women made common cause. Lady Queensberry knew that Bosie had no real source of money but herself, his allowance being £25 a week and whatever else he could wheedle from her. By thwarting his tastes for 'brandy, betting, and boys' she could bring him to heel. She wrote emphatically that until she had a pledge from both Douglas and Wilde that they would not live again under the same roof, her son would receive no more money. But if they would pledge themselves in writing, she was willing to pay whatever debts Douglas had contracted in Naples, and also pay Wilde £200 as a sort of compensation for his signature.[16]

Big spenders with little money, the friends discussed the matter, £200 being the golden bait. They agreed that they would never surrender their right to see each other, but with their present lack of means they were forced to envisage the possibility of living apart. By 23 November Wilde was writing to Ross to see if he thought Constance would be appeased if he and Bosie took separate quarters. Six days later Douglas wrote Edward Strangman a letter which indicated that they were still in doubt, but drifting toward decision:

> I am here with Oscar, we have been here two months. The whole thing has been a hand to mouth struggle, kept up by desperate telegrams to reluctant relations, and pawning of pins and studs. Now the struggle is quite over for Oscar's trustees have cut off his allowance on the ground that he has violated his agreement by living with me, and now my mother has cut off my allowance for the same reason. So that we are actually in view of positive starvation. Fortunately the rent of our villa is paid till the end of January. What we are going to do I don't know and don't much care being about as nearly desperate as is consistent with gentlemanly bearing . . . I suppose we (O and I) shall be forced to compromise the matter ultimately and separate at least for the present.[17]

The pace quickened. This same day or the next, Douglas wrote to his mother that he and Wilde were prepared to give her the written assurances she required. On 2 December 1897 he telegraphed that he was going to Rome next day and would send the assurance from there. But in Rome, on 3 December, he wrote that he felt miserable and wanted to go back to Wilde, and even more to defend his conduct. Had his mother expected him to write and say to Wilde:

> 'I cannot come and live with you now. I lived with you before and stayed with you and lived *on* you, but that was when you were rich, famous, honoured and at the summit of your position as an artist, now I am very

sorry of course, but you are ruined, you have no money, you have hardly any friends, you have been in prison (chiefly, I admit, on my account and through my fault), you are an ex-convict, it will do me a great deal of harm to be seen about with you, and besides that my mother naturally objects to it very strongly, and so I'm afraid I must leave you to get on as best you can by yourself.'

To do so would have been loathsome. He mentioned Munthe on Capri, and also a fashionable woman named Mrs Snow, who had entertained them both. Only his mother was inflexible.

Four days later his mood had changed violently, and he wrote to her from the Hôtel d'Italie in Rome on 7 December:

> I am glad, O so glad! to have got away. I am so afraid you will not believe me, and I am so afraid of appearing to pose as anything but what I am, but I am not a hypocrite and you must believe me. I wanted to go back to him, I longed for it and for him, because I love him and admire him and think him great and almost good, but when I had done it and when I got back, I hated it, I was miserable. I wanted to go away. But I couldn't. I was tied by honour.[18]

His promise to remain with Wilde for the rest of their lives had held him only until Wilde himself agreed that Douglas might as well go.

Their last weeks together can be pieced out. Douglas in his *Autobiography* attributes their drifting apart to the fact that at twenty-seven he was no longer the ever-young Dorian Gray. He was beginning to lose his looks. But Wilde's affections did not flag so quickly, and there is no evidence that he had become oblivious to that other bond between him and Bosie, that of the old sheep and the young butcher. In his letter to his mother Douglas probably comes closer to truth when he says that he had 'lost that supreme desire for his [Wilde's] society' which he had formerly had, and that he was also 'tired of the struggle and tired of being ill-treated by the world.' For after all, unlike Wilde, he had never committed what Ross called 'the supreme vulgarity of having been found out.' Wilde's place in the world was now fixed for good – no longer at its center, but always on its outskirts. Douglas had no vocation for dancing attendance upon an outcast. He wanted 'social recognition,'[19] and he felt he had done enough.

When their money ran out, as it did by early November, Wilde must have recalled his analysis of Douglas and money in *De Profundis*. Now the situation was repeating itself; Douglas was overspending Wilde's money as if he were Wilde and not Wilde's eternal dependent. Wilde did not recriminate. As Douglas acknowledged to Lady Queensberry, 'he has been sweet and gentle and will always remain to me as the type of what a gentleman and a friend should be.' But he admits in his *Autobiography* that they had several quarrels, and Bosie in quarrel has been described by Gide, a white face contorted with rage as he vented the insults guaranteed to wound.[20] He no doubt brought up again the risks he had taken to be by Wilde's side during the suit against Queensberry, when all his other friends had made off for the Continent; and he would not have been able to resist flaunting his self-sacrifice in consorting now with the pariah he had created. Wilde on his side clung tenaciously to his contention that the Queensberry family still owed him £500 for a debt of honor. Douglas replied that lots of gentlemen did not pay their debts of honor and were no less gentlemen therefore in the eyes of the world. But he devised or encouraged his mother's plan to send Wilde, if not £500, at least £200, and to promise to send the rest later. Wilde can hardly have urged Douglas to stay when his inclinations were to go, but while acquiescing in the separation, he did not take it easily. Douglas had offered him a sanctuary and then withdrawn the offer; his failure to find money was part of it. A letter to Ross of 2 March 1898 described Wilde's version of their stay:

> The facts of Naples are very bald and brief.
>
> Bosie, for four months, by endless letters, offered me a '*home.*' He offered me love, affection, and care, and promised that I should never want for anything. After four months I accepted his offer, but when we met at Aix on our way to Naples I found that he had no money, no plans, and had forgotten all his promises. His one idea was that I should raise money for us both. I did so, to the extent of £120. On this Bosie lived, quite happily. When it came to his having, of course, to repay his own *share*, he became terrible, unkind, mean, and penurious, except where his own pleasures were concerned, and when my allowance ceased, he left . . .
>
> It is, of course, the most bitter experience of a bitter life . . . it is better that I should never see him again. I don't want to. He fills me with horror.

Wilde never regarded the £200 paid by Lady Queensberry, of which Ross was fully informed, as anything but partial repayment of the debt of honor, and in no sense a reimbursement for supporting Bosie for three months or for being abandoned by him at the end of that time. (The money was paid through Adey, £100 to Wilde in December 1897 and £100 near the end of January 1898.)[21] Still, the horror he claimed to feel was perhaps intended to encourage Ross, who was writing to Constance urging her to renew the subsidy. That there was in fact no final rift is confirmed by a letter from Douglas to Wilde, still in Naples, on 8 January complaining of Paris prices and the 'unbridled chastity' – except on three occasions – he had practiced since he arrived.[22]

The Neapolitan interlude was as doomed to take place as to end. It could not have been drawn out much longer. Bosie may have been only half a monster, but by that half Wilde had once more been savaged. His relations with Constance, so far as they were personal, were just about finished by the three-month stay with Douglas, although she was too kindhearted ever to desert him, and even after officially withdrawing her subsidy, sent him money through Ross. Wilde did not offer her much excuse after Douglas had left on 3 December, except to say that he had loved too much, and that love was better than hate. She did not agree, and remarked to her brother that unnatural love was worse than hate. She wrote to Arthur Humphreys on 27 February 1898, 'his punishment has not done him much good since it has not taught him the lesson he most needed, namely that he is not the only person in the world.' Still, she could relent, and when Ross wrote to her in March a careful letter asking whether her husband's allowance might not be restored, since he was no longer living with Douglas, she complied, and added a codicil to her will to that effect. Her affection for him never ended, and she knew and wrote that if she saw him again, she would 'forgive everything.'[23]

Last Days in Naples

My life cannot be patched up. There is a doom on it.

From now on Wilde's abode changes, but the change is no longer significant. Once in a while he makes an effort to write something – the last act of his comedy is mentioned, for example – but nothing comes of it. He could still speak magnificently, but mostly repeating what he had said before. The essay he had planned which would have allowed pity into his aesthetic system, making explicit what he had always underplayed – the power of art to exorcise cruelty and to offer a perpetual Last Judgement in which the verdict was always merciful – never got written. He explained to Ross, 'I don't think I am equal to intellectual architecture of thought: I have moods and moments; and Love, or Passion with the Mask of Love, is my only consolation.'[24] He could not concentrate – his attention span was easily broken – and some sense that his literary life was over had come to him when he was writing some of the confessedly maladroit stanzas of *The Ballad of Reading Gaol.* If Bosie sought respectability ('social recognition'), Wilde knew it was no longer available for himself. The slights which occurred almost daily never lost their power to hurt. He had a constant uncertainty over whether people would acknowledge his existence or not. The dramatis personae of his earlier life returned as phantoms of his later life, some pretending not to see him, making him feel he was the phantom, from whom they fled. He was reliving his life as if it had all been a failure, not a success. In prison, he said, he had been 'buoyed up by the sense of guilt.' Outside, he was weighed down by the sense of exile. Vincent O'Sullivan, who visited Wilde in Naples for a few days after Douglas had left, witnessed treatment that had become almost standard. They were sitting in a restaurant when a crowd of people came in after the theatre. Some of them noisily pointed out Wilde to the rest. He was disturbed beyond O'Sullivan's expectation. 'He seemed to strangle,' O'Sullivan remembered, 'and then said in a thick voice, "Let us go."' They went some way in silence, then a beggar came up. Wilde gave him money, and murmured in English, 'You wretched man, why do you beg when pity is dead?' He told O'Sullivan that in Naples there was a garden where people who wanted to kill themselves went. 'I never thought seriously of that as a way out. What I felt was that I must drain the chalice of my passion to the dregs. But one night when there were no stars I went down to that garden. As I sat there absolutely alone in the darkness, I heard a rustling noise, and sighing and misty cloud-like things came round me. And I realised that they were the little souls of those who had killed themselves in that place, condemned to living there ever after. They had killed themselves in vain. And when I thought that such would be the fate of my soul too, the temptation to kill myself left me and has not come back.' O'Sullivan asked, 'How could you imagine spending all your life after life in Naples?' 'No,' replied Wilde, laughing, 'The cooking is really too bad.'[25]

British officialdom took some notice of his situation when the Consul, E. Neville-Rolfe, wrote to Lord Rosebery, who had a villa at Naples, and had once had his own involvement with the Douglas family, on 30 December 1897,

> Oscar Wilde calling himself Mr Sebastian Nothwell [sic] is in a small villa at Posillipo fully two miles from you. He and Alfred Douglas have definitely parted and Wilde lives a completely secluded life. He came here as Mr Nothwell for some business and I let him suppose that I did not know him by sight.
>
> He looks thoroughly abashed, much like a whipped hound.
>
> He has written a volume of poems, but no one in London would publish them and I hear he is printing them at his own expense.
>
> I really cannot think he will be any trouble to you, and after all the poor devil must live somewhere.[26]

Needless to say, they did not meet.

After O'Sullivan left, Wilde was persuaded by a Russian Elder to accompany him to Taormina. While there he met Baron von Gloeden, who photographed naked boys and sold the photographs to homosexuals. The trip is unrecorded but not its sequel, Wilde's return to Posillipo to find that a servant left in charge of the villa had run off with all his clothes. Nothing was left except those books carefully gathered by his friends at the time of his release. Wilde did not take them, and twenty-five years later a visiting Englishwoman who rented the villa found them still there.[27] Wilde would refer to their loss afterwards as of no consequence, but it meant that he had forsworn his place beside his favorite authors.

He stayed through January in Naples. In February 1898, perhaps because of the expense of maintaining the Villa Giudice, he moved to 31 Santa Lucia, the Palazzo Bambino.[28] Necessity made him resourceful:

Graham Greene tells how his father and another schoolmaster were sitting in a Naples café when a stranger, hearing them speak English, asked if he might join them over coffee. He looked vaguely familiar, but they did not recognize him during the hour and more that they were charmed by his conversation. He left them to pay for his drink which was 'certainly not coffee.' The elder Greene used to tell of this meeting with Wilde and conclude, 'Think how lonely he must have been to have expended so much time and wit on a couple of schoolmasters on holiday.' But as Graham Greene comments, Wilde 'was paying for his drink in the only currency he had.' His plight was so serious that *Le Journal* in Paris solicited contributions for him early in December, but these, if any were received, were meagre.[29]

A Last Triumph

It is my chant de cygne, *and I am sorry to leave with a cry of pain – a song of Marsyas, not a song of Apollo.*

It must have been a satisfaction to Wilde to know that all the time people were speaking of him with contempt at Naples, his *Ballad* was nearing completion and publication. Perhaps it would prove an earnest of future masterpieces; this hope never quite left him. Smithers had proved cooperative about the design of the book, and both had agreed that the author's name should appear on it only as C.3.3. Wilde had quieted Smithers' fears of a possible libel action by prison officials. He had written a dedication which was to run:

> When I came out of prison some met me with garments
> and with spices and others with wise counsel
> You met me with love

This was probably intended to allow Wilde to say to Douglas as well as to Ross, Adey, and perhaps others that the dedication was to each of them. Ross was convinced that it would do no good, either to the poem or to them; Smithers and eventually Wilde agreed. There was no dedication. The book was to be published on 9 February 1898, and this date probably spurred Wilde to return from Naples to Paris, where he could at least hear promptly about the poem's reception. He arrived on 13 February, and took a room at one of those cheap hotels where he was to spend most of his remaining days. This one was the Hôtel de Nice in the rue des Beaux-Arts, the street that would eventually serve as his final address, at the Hôtel d'Alsace.

He was greeted by good news: *The Ballad of Reading Gaol* was selling as no poem had sold for years. One shop sold fifty copies on the morning of publication. Smithers had only risked printing 400 out of a projected 800 copies in January, but early in February he ordered 400 more, and the same month had to print another thousand.

In March there was a deluxe edition of ninety-nine copies signed by the author (with his real name), and then two more printings, of 1,200 and 1,000 copies. In May a sixth impression was printed, of 1,000 copies. It was not until the seventh regular printing, in June of 1899, that at Smithers' suggestion Wilde inserted his own name as the author, in brackets beside C.3.3 on the title page.

Wilde sent copies to many old friends, with suitable inscriptions. Ada Leverson's read, 'To the Sphinx of Pleasure from the Singer of Pain Oscar Wilde,' Major Nelson's, 'Major Nelson from the author in recognition of many acts of kindness and gentleness Feby '98,' and there was one for 'Alfred Bruce Douglas From the Author.'* Constance read about the book in the *Daily Chronicle*, and, on receiving an uninscribed copy, wrote, 'I am frightfully upset by this wonderful poem of Oscar's ... It is frightfully tragic and makes one cry.'[30] Robert Sherard's copy was accompanied by a letter, 'I am sending you a copy of my Ballad – first edition – which I hope you will accept in memory of our long friendship. I had hoped to give it to you personally, but I know you are very busy, tho' I am sorry you are too busy to come and see me, or to let me know where you are to be seen.'[31]

Cunninghame Graham, who had been in prison himself, wrote Wilde a letter full of praise, and Wilde, in thanking him, replied, 'I . . . wish we could meet to talk over the many prisons of life – prisons of stone, prisons of passion, prisons of intellect, prisons of morality and the rest. All limitations, external or internal, are prisons – walls, and life is a limitation.'[32] He was moving toward a generalized and impersonal point of view, detaching himself from his poem.

There were many notices of the *Ballad*. Most expressed reservations but recognized that a literary event of importance had occurred. None of the reviewers mentioned Wilde by name, although everyone knew he had written the poem. The attention it received was too much for Henley, whose own book of verse had done less well: he dismissed the *Ballad* in the *Outlook* on 9 March as a jumble 'of excellence and rubbish,' complained that the details lacked veracity (one of his own claims to distinction in his hospital poems), and concluded that 'the trail of the Minor Poet is over it

* Wilde also inscribed copies: 'Ernest Dowson from his friend and admirer the author Feby 98 Naples,' 'Lionel Johnson from Oscar Wilde: 1898 Miserere Deus scriptori amico meo,' 'To Laurence Irving with the compliments of the author Naples '98 Feb,' 'To York Powell with the compliments of the author Naples '98,' 'R. C. Tillingham from the author in gratitude and affection Oscar Wilde Paris '98,' 'Robert Buchanan, from the author, in admiration and gratitude. Paris '98.' Copies also went to Ross, Turner, Adey, Rowland Fothergill, Fritz von Thaulow, Will Rothenstein, Charles Ricketts, Walter Sickert, Beerbohm, O'Sullivan, Shaw, Archer, Henry Harland, and Headlam.

all.' Wilde replied but his letter is lost. Henley's review was sandwiched between one in the *Academy* on 26 February, which pronounced the poem to be good if not great literature, one in the *Daily Telegraph* of the 27th which spoke of it as 'moving,' and a handsome notice by Arthur Symons in the *Saturday Review* for 12 March. Symons had not until then been one of Wilde's friends – there had been jokes about the productive Symons as a joint stock company in which Wilde proposed to take shares – but Symons was not jealous or meanspirited like Henley. He said of the poem that it 'had the value of a document'; and that it was 'not really a ballad at all, but a sombre, angry, interrupted reverie; and it is the subcurrent of medi- tation, it is the asides, which count, not the story.' He delighted Wilde with his praise for the poem's insistence that all men kill the thing they love: 'This symbol of the obscure deaths of the heart, the unseen violence upon souls [a phrase Wilde particularly liked], the martyrdom of hope, trust and all the more helpless among the virtues, is what gives its unity, in a certain philosophic purpose, to a poem not otherwise quite homogeneous.' It was an idea that was 'singularly novel,' and yet arose naturally from the experience described. On 19 March the *Pall Mall Gazette* said the *Ballad* was 'the most remarkable poem that has appeared this year,' with 'beautiful work in it.'

The publication of his poem in England, followed by its publication in Paris by the *Mercure de France* late in the year in a translation by Henry Davray, could have given Wilde the impetus he needed. Robert Ross faithfully sent him handsome copybooks in which he could write, but Wilde began to say, with ominous repetitiveness, that he no longer felt the inclination. He even said he had a '*cacoethes tacendi*' (an incurable itch not to write). He did tell Mrs Weldon he would translate *Ce qui ne meurt pas* by the aged dandy Barbey d'Aurevilly. Robert Ross says he never did, though a translation was published and has sometimes been attributed to him.[33] He was persuaded to have Smithers publish two of his own plays which, because of his disgrace, had never been printed, *The Importance of Being Earnest* and *An Ideal Husband*. The proofs of *Earnest* show Wilde very much in command of himself and of the play. As he corrected them he said to a friend, 'I can write, but have lost the joy of writing.'* He took

---

* He un-italicizes some italicized words, he changes 'woulds' to 'shoulds.' Speeches were improved. Instead of Jack saying, 'I was very nearly offering a reward,' he is made to say, 'I was very nearly offering a large reward,' and when Algernon attempts to claim it, he replies, 'There is no good offering a large reward when the thing is found.' Algernon, instead of saying, 'poor Bunbury is a horrible invalid,' says, 'poor Bunbury is a dreadful invalid.' Gwendolyn originally said, 'Yes, but men often propose for practice. I know my brother Gerald does. He tells me so.' Wilde revised it to, 'All my good friends tell me so.' Lady Bracknell's impressive speech had read, 'Fortunately, in England, at any rate, education produces no effect whatsoever. If it did, it would prove a serious danger to the upper classes, and probably lead to acts of violence.' Wilde retouched it by adding to the last sentence, 'in Grosvenor Square.'

account of Robert Ross's praise of this play by saying, 'There are two ways of disliking my plays. One is to dislike them, the other is to like *Earnest*. To prove to posterity what a bad critic you are I shall dedicate the play to you.' When it appeared in February 1899, the dedication ran:

> To Robert Baldwin Ross
> in appreciation
> in affection

An Ideal Husband, published in July 1899, bore a dedication to another old associate:

> To Frank Harris
> A slight Tribute to his Power and Distinction as an Artist
> His chivalry and nobility as a friend.

These publications brought Wilde a little money.

Sociability and Solitude

Why is it that one runs to one's ruin? Why has destruction
such a fascination?

Wilde had only enough energy to live out the day, or rather the night, for like his mother he did not get up till afternoon. Increasingly he sought assistance from stimulants, the favorite being the Dutch liqueur Advocaat, though he then switched to brandy and absinthe.* They did not make him drunk, but they offered consolation. So did the young men he picked up. 'How evil it is to buy love,' he remarked to a friend, 'and how evil to sell it! And yet what purple hours one can snatch from that grey slowly moving thing we call Time.'[35] One long-lasting favorite was Maurice Gilbert, a young soldier in the marine infantry. They played many games of bezique together. Wilde was seen embracing Gilbert by Jacques Daurelle, of *L'Echo de Paris*, who accused him of having '*retourné à son vomissement*.' Wilde merely replied, '*Il est si beau. Regardez-le. Il a le profil de Bonaparte*.'

---

* His attitude to absinthe varied. 'It has no message for me,' he told Bernard Berenson. But to Arthur Machen he said, 'I never could quite accustom myself to absinthe, but it suits my style so well.' Gradually he warmed to it, and said in Dieppe, 'Absinthe has a wonderful colour, green. A glass of absinthe is as poetical as anything in the world. What difference is there between a glass of absinthe and a sunset?' And, 'I have discovered,' he said, 'that alcohol taken in sufficient quantity produces all the effects of drunkenness.'[34]

Yet the lonely moments, intensified by sporadic penury, multiplied. An old friend, Carlos Blacker, fell away after an unpleasant sequence of events. Blacker, whom Wilde had regarded as 'the best dressed man in London,' and with whom he had often heard the chimes of midnight, remained loyal after the prison sentence. During the first summer of Wilde's freedom Constance went to stay with the Blackers at Freiburg. None of them liked Wilde's going to Naples with Douglas, but when Wilde came to Paris in February 1898 Blacker visited him a number of times and they exchanged letters. Early in May Wilde asked him for a loan, which Blacker gave; but something went wrong towards the end of the month. Ross heard from somebody – Wilde suspected it was Blacker – that the authorities were forcing Wilde to leave Paris. Evidently Blacker had shown signs of disapproval of Wilde's behavior in Paris, which made Wilde think he had spread the '*canard.*'

The immediate cause may well have been the acquaintance Wilde had struck up, soon after he came to Paris, with Commandant Ferdinand Walsin-Esterhazy, the man who had actually done the spying of which Alfred Dreyfus was wrongfully convicted. The Dreyfus case and the Wilde case had been tried within a few months of each other, and Dreyfus was sent to Devil's Island about the time Wilde was sent to Pentonville. So Wilde had a particular interest in what all France was buzzing about. Esterhazy had succeeded in being whitewashed by a court martial on 11 January 1898. Two days later Wilde's sometime friend Zola published his letter, '*J'accuse,*' in *L'Aurore*. In February, just as *The Ballad of Reading Gaol* was being published, Zola was convicted of libel and sentenced to a year's imprisonment, but later escaped to England.

Esterhazy was one of those dubious criminal figures who continued to fascinate Wilde. At one of their meetings the Commandant said to him, in a Dantesque dialogue, 'We are the two greatest martyrs of humanity – but I have suffered the most.' 'No,' Wilde replied, 'I have.' 'At the age of thirteen,' Esterhazy went on, 'I had a profound conviction that I would never be happy again.' 'And he never was,' said Wilde in recounting the conversation.

Wilde wrote to Blacker about this meeting, not perhaps considering how much his friend had at heart the injustice Dreyfus had undergone. Since 1897, when the first reports of Dreyfus's innocence reached Blacker, he had worked indefatigably to free him. By now he had learned from the Italian military attaché in Paris that the traitor was Esterhazy. In context, Wilde's letter to him could hardly have been more maladroit. Epigrams such as Wilde is reported to have tossed off in conversation – 'Esterhazy is considerably more interesting than Dreyfus who is innocent. It's always a mistake to be innocent. To be a criminal takes imagination and courage' – were all very well, but here was a man suffering on Devil's Island.

Wilde and Esterhazy met several more times. At the climactic session

Frank Harris claimed to have been present, but it seems likely that Rowland Strong – the correspondent of the *New York Times* and the London *Observer* – was there instead. Esterhazy fell into his usual denunciation of Dreyfus. Wilde leaned across the table and said, 'The innocent always suffer, Monsieur le Commandant; it is their *métier*. Besides, we are all innocent until we are found out. It is a poor, common part to play and within the compass of the meanest. The interesting thing surely is to be guilty and wear as a halo the seduction of sin.' Esterhazy, so weary of his own falsehoods that he swallowed Wilde's bait, suddenly said, 'Why should I not make my confession to you? I will. It is I, Esterhazy, who alone am guilty. I put Dreyfus in prison, and all France cannot get him out.' To his surprise his dinner companions merely laughed.[36]

But the next day Strong sent an article dated 29 March to the *New York Times*, revealing certain Dreyfusard plans to expose Esterhazy's guilt. Its publication was preceded by a letter signed 'Un Diplomate' in *Le Siècle* on 4 April, to the same effect, which Blacker was assumed by the anti-Dreyfusards to have written. They launched a smear campaign against him in their newspapers. Blacker thought that Wilde had informed them of his work behind the scenes, and it is possible that he had spoken indiscreetly about Blacker's business activities in England. Then Blacker wrote two letters to Wilde. The first objected to his continuing to associate with Douglas. Wilde did not reply. The second accused him of writing the anonymous attacks on Blacker. Wilde wrote at once 'a strong letter' demanding an apology. None came. It was the end of a long friendship.

There were not many people on whom Wilde could depend for companionship. Gide, a likely candidate in view of their long acquaintance, saw him only twice. The first time was by accident, when he heard a voice call, and saw it came from Wilde, sitting outside a café. Gide went over, intending to sit facing Wilde, with his back to the passersby; but Wilde insisted he sit beside him: 'I'm so alone these days.' After a pleasant conversation, Wilde suddenly said, 'You must know – I'm absolutely without resources.' Gide gave him some money and they arranged another meeting. That time Gide reproached him for having left Berneval without, as he had promised, writing a play. Wilde replied, 'One should not reproach someone who has been *struck*.' They did not meet again.[37]

Other incidents fill in a sorry sequence. Henry Davray, Wilde's translator, passed in front of the Café de Flore one day in May 1898 when Wilde beckoned to him and insisted on his sitting down for a moment. Davray thought his appearance so broken down and harassed that he yielded, though he was in a great hurry to keep an appointment. Wilde said he had fled the boredom of his hotel room. He became less troubled when Davray sat down, and talked about all sorts of things, at the same time insisting that Davray should not go away and leave him. In the end Davray had to telephone to cancel his appointment. Wilde was so afraid of being alone that when Davray got up to go he went with him to the Luxembourg, walked through the gardens with him and made him sit down at another café on the boulevard Saint-Michel. At last he confessed his embarrassment: 'I haven't a sou,' he said, then laughed. 'I'll give you security for some money,' and he took from his pocket a copy of Webster's *The Duchess of Malfi*, which he inscribed to his friend. Another writer, Frédéric Boutet, tells how in July 1899 he and a friend were walking along the boulevard Saint-Germain, and came upon Wilde seated at a café in torrential rain, which poured down on him, turning his straw hat into a candle-snuffer and his coat into a sponge, for the waiter, anxious to be rid of his last customer, had not only piled up the chairs but wound up the awning. Wilde could not leave because he could not pay for the three or four drinks he had taken to avoid going back to his squalid lodgings. As he wrote to Frances Forbes-Robertson, 'Like dear St Francis of Assisi I am wedded to poverty, but in my case the marriage is not a success. I hate the bride that has been given to me.' And to Frank Harris, 'A hole in the trousers may make one as melancholy as Hamlet, and out of bad boots a Timon may be made.'[38]

He could still turn his plight to farce. His friend Jean-Jacques Renaud heard from him how one night, after having gone as usual from the Calisaya to a series of other cafés, he was walking home through the Paris streets. Crossing the Pont des Arts, he stopped to look at the green water rivering enticingly below. Suddenly he noticed a poorly dressed man near him, also looking down at the river. '*Hein, mon pauvre, êtes-vous désespéré?*' he asked. '*Non, monsieur*,' came the answer, '*Je suis coiffeur*.'*[39] But to Maurice Maeterlinck and Georgette Leblanc, who invited him to dine with them in May 1898, he said he was in mourning for his life. 'I have lived. Yes, I have lived. I drank the sweet, I drank the bitter, and I found the bitterness in the sweetness and the sweetness in the bitterness.' He added, 'The cruelty of a prison sentence starts when you come out.' Maeterlinck mentioned that Huysmans had entered a monastery, and Wilde said approvingly, 'It must be delightful to see God through stained glass windows. I may even go to a monastery myself.' When Maeterlinck offered him a wine not to be found in England, Wilde commented wryly, 'The English have a miraculous power to change wine into water.'† In

---

* 'Hey, my poor man, are you desperate?' 'No, sir, I'm a hairdresser.'

† Another story of miracles explained the persecution of the early Christians in Rome. 'You know, Nero was obliged to do something. They were making him ridiculous. What he thought was: "Here everything was going on very well, when one day two incredible creatures arrived from somewhere in the provinces. They are called Peter and Paul, or some unheard-of names like that. Since they are here, life in Rome has become impossible. They collect crowds and block the traffic with their miracles. It is really intolerable. I, the Emperor, have no peace. When I get up in the morning and look out of the window, the first thing I see is a miracle going on in the back garden."'

prison, he told them, he was happy, 'because there I found my soul.' What he had written there, he said, would one day be read by the world, 'the message of my soul to the souls of men.'

But for Hugh Chesson he had a more melancholy fable: 'A man saw a being, which hid its face from him, and he said, "I will compel it to show its face." It fled as he pursued, and he lost it, and his life went on. At last his pleasure drew him into a long room, where tables were spread for many, and in a mirror he saw the being whom he had pursued in youth. "This time you shall not escape me," he said, but the being did not try to escape, and hid its face no more. "Look!" it cried, "and now you will know that we cannot see each other again, for this is the face of your own soul, and it is horrible."'[40]

A Widower

It is difficult for me to laugh at life, as I used to.

Constance Wilde submitted to a second operation on her spine at the beginning of April 1898 and on the 7th she died, at the age of forty. Douglas came to console her husband, who told him, 'I dreamt she came here to see me, and I kept saying, "Go away, go away, leave me in peace."' The next day he had learnt that she was dead. His reaction was complicated: he begged Robert Ross to come over because he was 'in great grief,' but proved not to be when his friend arrived. On the other hand, he said to Frank Harris with elegiac finality, 'My way back to hope and a new life ends in her grave. Everything that happens to me is symbolic and irrevocable.'[41] Access to his sons was not granted. He now received £150 a year from her estate without conditions. If he had not had a taste for luxury, it might have been enough to live on. A letter from Ross to Smithers, written during his Paris visit, gives a sense of Wilde at this time, still capable of resilience, still unable to launch out into any future:

> My dear Smithers, I ought to have written to you ages ago, but it is quite impossible with Oscar to get anything done . . . You will have heard of Mrs Wilde's death. Oscar of course did not feel it at all. It is rather appalling for him as his allowance ceases and I do not expect his wife's trustees will continue it. He is in very good spirits and does not consume too many. He is hurt because you never write . . .
>
> Oscar has only seen Douglas once. I went to see his lordship. He is less interested in other people than ever before, especially Oscar. So I really think that alliance will die a natural death.
>
> Oscar is very amusing as usual but is very abstracted at times. He says that The Ballad of Reading Gaol doesn't describe his prison life, but his

life at Naples with Bosie and that all the best stanzas were the immediate result of his existence there.[42]

Ross was relieved to find that Wilde and Douglas were living apart, but Wilde's relations with all his friends, including Ross, were less close. Ross remarked to Frank Harris after Wilde's death that he had never felt that Wilde really liked him. His own attitude towards Wilde was equally complicated. There would be periods during the next three years when Ross kept his distance, as when in September and October of 1898 he and Reggie Turner took a trip to Florence, Rome, and Naples, during which they avoided stopping to see Wilde in Paris. Fortunately Charles Conder had Wilde visit him at Chantemerle, near La Roche Guyon (Seine-et-Oise) in late September. Conder wrote to Mrs Dalhousie Young,

> For some time after I saw you it was very difficult to do anything for a good many people came and Oscar stayed here some time. I think some people were rather annoyed at my bringing him – but he turned Chantemerle into a charming little state made himself king and possessed himself of Blunt's boat – for his barge – and got little boys to row him from Chantemerle to La Roche every day there he took his aperitif and returned laden with duck-ham & wine usually which served as extras to the frugal dinners we get here.
>
> He is much more serious than when we saw him in Dieppe – very depressed at times poor fellow.
>
> He says with so much sorrow this [sic] he can never go into society again and feels I think that he is rather old for the volatile poets of the '*quartier*.'[43]

The only one in the group permanently resident in Paris was Alfred Douglas, and Wilde was very glad of what company he could get from him. In May 1898 he had an operation on his throat, the nature of which is unknown, but during this month he saw much of Douglas. To furnish Douglas's new flat in the avenue Kléber, Wilde went to the Paris branch of Maples and with £40 bought suitable furniture, including a green bed. Douglas managed this outlay, but otherwise he kept himself poor by gambling on the races with the money he got from his mother. 'He has a faculty of spotting the loser,' Wilde wrote, 'which, considering that he knows nothing at all about horses, is perfectly astounding.'[44] He told Claire de Pratz that one day he got into the Montparnasse-Etoile tram to go to Alfred Douglas, in the avenue Kléber. He suddenly realized that he had forgotten his wallet, or spent his last sou. On the tram he loudly confessed it and asked, 'Will anybody lend me 30 centimes?' Total silence followed. Then he made the driver stop, got down, hailed a cab, and sat down in triumph while he waved ironically to the tram passengers, knowing that Douglas's porter would pay his coachman. 'The moral of the story,' said Wilde, 'is that people have more confidence in someone who takes a cab than in someone who uses a public conveyance.' Saix also reports a story of Wilde that perhaps dates from this time. 'A young man in London contracted large debts and was living a dissolute life. His friends resolved to rescue him. They joined in paying his bills and gave him a hundred pounds with which he promised to go to Australia and get a fresh start. Two months later one of his friends came upon the young prodigal in Piccadilly, and said indignantly, "You here? You took a hundred pounds to go to Australia, and you're still here! You're breaking your word." The other replied by asking only, "Tell me, old boy, if you had a hundred pounds, would you go to Australia?" '[45] He was perhaps recalling his father's unsuccessful effort to pack Mary Travers off to that country.

During this spring of 1898 Douglas spent about half his time at Nogent-sur-Marne, where the hôtelier indulged the delay in paying his bills. A letter from Douglas to Wilde on 22 July attempts to extract a louis from him. In June and July Wilde went there too. Douglas had with him the Napoleonesque Maurice Gilbert, now his lover but who fascinated all the group, the darling of Ross and Turner in London as of Douglas and Wilde in Paris. In August and September Douglas went with his mother to Trouville and then to Aix, where once again he lost all his money gambling. In this year he published a book of nonsense verse, and seems to have thought the moment was propitious for his rehabilitation in England. He sounded out the authorities, and was sufficiently encouraged to go back in November.

He now made his supreme effort at reconciliation with his father. He wrote a letter to a cousin, Algernon Bourke, saying he was ready to express contrition. He clung to shreds of his old friendship: 'I cannot undertake not to see Wilde from time to time. I can, however, give you and my father my word that my relations with him are entirely harmless and only dictated by my feeling that I cannot abandon him now that he is poor and broken after being his friend when he was rich and flourishing.' He gave Wilde money when he could, but he had promised his mother never again to live under the same roof with him. He asked his father to 'consider the sort of dog's life I have had for the last few years and to meet me half way.' Bourke showed the letter to Queensberry, and within a day reported to Bosie that his father would be happy to see him.[46]

Queensberry's own life had been much affected by the Wilde trials. His initial pride at having won a glorious victory over subverters of morality, over a son and a son's defiant lover, had soured as lifelong friends began to avoid his company. The Marquess's brief spell of respectability as defender of public morals bore no relation to his career as prizefighter, gambler, adulterer, and atheist. His money troubles had increased: Wilde had gone bankrupt but Queensberry had had to sell his great house at Kinmount, where Bosie had grown up, his paintings by Kneller, Lely, Stubbs, Reynolds, Gilbert Stuart and others, and other property. He was on wretched terms with all his children except Edith, who had been married in April 1898 to St John Fox-Pitt. His first wife and he had not spoken for years. Bosie's letter sounded sincere, and his father agreed to meet him in the smoking-room of Bailey's Hotel, where he was living. It was a scene of high emotion, with Bosie contrite and the Marquess calling him 'my poor darling boy,' embracing him with tears, and promising to restore his allowance. He even wrote on the spot a letter to his financial manager arranging it. But he had second thoughts: the bitterness of the old quarrel was not so easily blotted out, and a week later he wrote saying he would not give Bosie a penny until he knew exactly what his relations were with 'that beast Wilde.' Bosie, irascible when in health, doubly so because of influenza, retorted that there could be no peace between them, and renounced the allowance as he had done four years before.

Months afterward he saw his father in a cab, looking so haggard that he was seized with compunction. From friends he learned that his father thought that the 'Oscar-Wilders' were persecuting him, shouting abusive epithets at him and driving him out of various hotels. Bosie wrote to his sister Edith's husband declaring that he felt nothing but kindness and affection for his father and regretted the feverish letter he had written. This letter was shown to the Marquess, who may well have felt that there was too much bad blood to mop up; he made no comment.

Wilde had his own black days to record. First there was Beardsley, dead at twenty-five on 16 March 1898. Wilde, shocked, wrote to Smithers, 'There is something macabre and tragic in the fact that one who added another terror to life should have died at the age of a flower.' The next death was his brother Willie, on 13 March 1899, the news of which reached Wilde in Switzerland. He expressed sympathy for Willie's wife, but could not bring himself to mourn his brother. Dowson's death on 23 February 1900 hurt him more. 'Poor wounded wonderful fellow that he was: a tragic reproduction of all tragic poetry, like a symbol, or a scene,' he wrote to Smithers. 'I hope bay-leaves will be laid on his tomb, and rue, and myrtle too, for he knew what love is.'[47] His sense of the Nineties coming to a doomed end was sharpened by these deaths.

Homelessness

But all is right: the gods hold the world on their knees. I was made for destruction. My cradle was rocked by the Fates.

During Douglas's absence in London, Wilde was approached by Frank Harris with a renewed proposal for a trip. He had refused to go with him to the Pyrenees, and when Harris took offense, wrote to him, 'You are a man of dominant personality . . . you require response, or you annihilate. The pleasure of being with you is in the clash of personality, the intellectual battle, the war of ideas. To survive you one must have a strong brain, an assertive ego, a dynamic character. In your luncheon-parties, in old days, the remains of the guests were taken away with the *débris* of the feast. I have often lunched with you in Park Lane and found myself the only survivor.'[48] He told Mrs Weldon, 'His [Harris's] treatment of the women of Shakespeare would have made Falstaff weep.' Now Harris reminded him that he had said he could not write in Paris during the winter months, but that he would write as naturally as the bird sings in a warmer climate. Harris was about to sell the *Saturday Review* for £40,000, and offered to treat Wilde to three months on the Côte d'Azur. When he arrived in Paris in mid-December and proposed to leave in three days' time, Wilde stalled for three extra days, repeatedly asking Harris for money to pay his 'debts.' On Sunday night at the Gare de Lyon he kept his rendezvous with Harris, but was romantically inconsolable at having had to part with Maurice Gilbert for whom he had bought a nickel-plated bicycle with Harris's money. This incident set the tone for many discussions during the next weeks, Wilde insisting that male beauty was finer than female, women being dumpy as Schopenhauer had said, while Harris defended the Venus de Milo against Antinous. Wilde now spoke habitually for 'Uranian' love, and he does so redundantly in his letters to Ross, as well as in the conversations reported by Harris. The best defensive aphorism was, 'A patriot put in prison for loving his country loves his country, and a poet in prison for loving boys loves boys.'[49]

Such were the themes as the two friends in December 1898 talked at the Hôtel des Bains at La Napoule, on the sea near Cannes. Harris's idea was that La Napoule would be quiet and restful, and good for concentration, while Cannes would be only ten miles away to relieve ennui. In the end, Harris spent much of his time in Monaco, buying a hotel and a restaurant, so Wilde was left to his own devices. He formed a close association with an Englishman, Harold Mellor, who delighted in his conversation. On one of his infrequent visits to La Napoule, Harris overheard Wilde say to Mellor that his own place in society had been quite different from Harris's, that Harris was proud of having met Balfour, while Balfour was proud of having met Wilde. It was the kind of social boasting that Wilde stooped to even in better days, with his constant insistence on playing gentleman.[50]

Wilde did not attempt to be anything but idle. As he had said to Laurence Housman in Paris, 'I told you that I was going to write something: I tell everybody that . . . It is a thing one can repeat each day, meaning to do it the next. But in my heart – that chamber of leaden echoes – I know that I never shall. It is enough that the stories have been invented, that they actually exist, that I have been able, in my own mind, to give them the form which they demand.'[51] There were two memorable meetings. One was with Sarah Bernhardt at Cannes: she was playing in *La Tosca*, and Wilde and Mellor went backstage to see her. She threw her arms around Wilde and wept, and he wept, 'and' – as he said – 'the whole evening was wonderful.' The second meeting was less pleasant: Wilde was walking near the sea when George Alexander appeared on a bicycle. 'He gave me a crooked, sickly smile and hurried on without stopping. How absurd and mean of him!'[52]

Wilde lolled about with young men. As he wrote to Smithers, 'Yes: even at Napoule there is romance: it comes in boats, and takes the form of fisher-lads, who draw great nets, and are bare-limbed: they are strangely perfect: I was at Nice lately: romance there is a profession plied beneath the moon.' When Harris urged Wilde to write something, he replied that he had in mind a counterstatement to *The Ballad of Reading Gaol*, which he planned to call 'The Ballad of the Fisher-Boy.' He would celebrate liberty instead of prison, joy instead of sorrow, kissing instead of hanging. The three stanzas he quoted from the unwritten poem were not unpromising, and Harris urged him to write them down. Wilde refused. He could write no more. He told Rothenstein, 'The intense energy of creation has been kicked out of me.'[53] Harris retorted abruptly that he could not go on indefinitely holding up an empty sack. Wilde was afraid that this meant an immediate withdrawal of financial support, but Harris promised to see his three-month commitment through to the end.

When it was over, Mellor invited Wilde to come as his guest to Gland in Switzerland. On the way Wilde stopped briefly in Nice, and then went out of his way to spend a day in Genoa. He wanted to bring flowers to Constance's grave, in a cemetery at the foot of hills that become mountains around the city. The inscription on the stone seemed to him altogether 'tragic': 'Constance Mary, daughter of Horace Lloyd, Q.C.' Wilde was not mentioned. It was as if he had never existed.* 'I was deeply affected –,' he wrote to Ross, 'with a sense, also, of the uselessness of all regrets. Nothing could have been otherwise, and Life is a very terrible thing.'[54]

With this memory he went on to Mellor, who as a host had none of Harris's openhandedness. Rather than let his hospitality be abused by Wilde, he constantly lowered its level. Inexpensive Swiss wines were served, then, probably in response to Wilde's rate of consumption, beer. No loans of money were forthcoming. 'If I ask him to lend me five francs, he grows yellow and takes to his bed.' At last Wilde could bear no more indignities, and said goodbye. Mellor recognized his guest's displeasure, and apologized to him; but Wilde went off down the Ligurian coast, settling on 1 April 1899 at Santa Margharita; he wrote to Ross, 'In Paris I am bad: here I am bored: the last state is the worse.' He remained in acute boredom till Ross came over in May, paid his debts, and brought him back to Paris.[55] By 7 May 1899 he was installed at the Hôtel de Néva, then at

---

* 'Wife of Oscar Wilde' has since been added to the stone.

the Hôtel Marsollier. Ross succeeded in frightening him out of drinking for six months.

This was a season when Douglas, again in Paris, was happy. Late in May 1899 he made his official claim to be a poet, though he could not put his name on the title page, with *The City of the Soul*, published by Grant Richards in London. It included twenty-five poems from the 1896 Paris volume, thirteen being omitted, and eighteen new poems. An equally anonymous review in the *Outlook* greeted his work as that of a poet among poetasters. It was by his cousin Lionel Johnson, though Douglas did not know that at the time. James Douglas wrote an anonymous eulogy in the *Star*. Bosie took Wilde out to a lavish dinner to celebrate. Not all the response was favorable: the President of Magdalen College, Herbert Warren, wrote to him, 'I regret I cannot accept this book from you.'[56] The second edition, in which Douglas was named as author, did not sell at all.

Wilde's life continued at much the same tempo as before. He occasionally indulged himself in little trips, and one of them brought him to Fontainebleau. He sat down at a café near the palace gates and was observed by a scientist he had known in London, Peter Chalmers Mitchell. Mitchell told the two English friends he was drinking coffee with that it was Wilde, and they left. But Mitchell went over to Wilde and said, 'Mr Wilde, I don't suppose you remember me, but a long time ago Ian Thynne introduced me to you at the Café Royal.' 'Ian Thynne. Yes! Isn't he dead?' 'I think so. It is years since I've heard anything from him. Robbie Ross is a friend of mine.' At this Wilde said, 'Ah! Robbie, with the face of Puck and the heart of an angel. Would you care to sit with me?' When Mitchell had sat down, Wilde said, 'Of course I remember you. We talked and talked and I asked you how to get rid of the body. I used you in *Dorian Gray*, but I don't think you would be easy to blackmail. Ian! In the days when I made phrases I called Ian "exquisitely corrupt."'' They talked of poetry and prisons, and Wilde impressed Mitchell as he had before. At last Mitchell rose and asked Wilde to dine with him, but he refused, saying, 'Your friends would not stand it. I am going back to my little inn where they don't know me. Good-bye. Thank you.'[57]

Between such excursions were moments when he could go nowhere. The opera singer Nellie Melba, who had known him in London, was walking along the streets of Paris one morning. A tall shabby man lurched around the corner, his collar turned up to his neck. 'Madame Melba,' said a voice, 'you don't know who I am? I'm Oscar Wilde, and I am going to do a terrible thing. I'm going to ask you for money.' She took all she had in her purse and gave it to him; he muttered his thanks and went. She remembered their first meeting long ago, when he had said, 'Ah, Madame Melba, I am the Lord of Language and you are the Queen of Song, and so I suppose I shall have to write you a sonnet.' Ellen Terry and Aimée Lowther also saw him in Paris, looking into the window of a pastry shop, biting his fingers. They invited him to a meal. He talked splendidly, as of old, but they never saw him again.[58]

A letter from the journalist Morton Fullerton, a friend of Henry James, suggests the kind of nastiness to which Wilde exposed himself by his importunities:

> 35 Bld des Capucines
> 23 June 1899

My dear Melmoth

I am distressed to have left your touching appeal unanswered for so long. But I have been on congé in the *patrie* of Stendhal, and had cognizance of your *gêne* only yesterday.

You do me too much honour in asking me to come to the rescue of an artist such as you. And if I could have known of the situation 3 weeks ago when I had money in my pocket I should not have hesitated for a moment, especially as I had just received your play [*Earnest*] and was in the state of mind of one who says of a thing without thinking: 'it is worth its weight in gold.' But at present, after an expensive journey, I am unable, with the best good-will in the world, to seize the event and to accept the *rôle* in this particular comedy – I use the word in its Hellenic and Gallic sense, *bien entendu*, in the sole sense in which it exists for the admirers of *Lady Windermere's Fan* and of *The Importance of Being Earnest*. The maker of those masterpieces has too much delicacy and *esprit* not to sympathize sincerely with the regret of a man obliged to reply thus to an appeal which certainly he could not have expected and for which it was impossible for him to prepare, but which is none the less precious for that. I grope at the hope that meanwhile the stress has passed, and that you will not have occasion to put, *malgré vous*, either me or any one else again into such a position of positive literal chagrin.

> Yours sincerely
> W.M. FULLERTON

Wilde only replied, 'In so slight a matter, my dear Fullerton, sentiment need not borrow stilts.'[59]

In *T. P.'s Weekly* T. P. O'Connor says his friend John O'Connor, once a prominent Irish M.P., recognized Wilde at a restaurant and was moved to speak to him by the sight of his front teeth gone and no plate to replace them. Wilde replied, 'You don't know me, sir,' meaning that he was not a man to be recognized by his countrymen. His Oxford friend Bodley came by, and Wilde pretended not to recognize him. Bodley persisted and invited him to his house. But on learning that Bodley's family was there, Wilde hesitated, then fled. He said to Max de Morès, 'I am a vagabond. The century will have had two vagabonds, Paul Verlaine and me.'[60]

One day, on the boulevard des Italiens, Wilde was passed by Edouard de Max, whom he had known long ago. 'So, Monsieur de Max, you too fail to recognize me here.' '*Oh, maître, mon cher maître,*' said de Max as he stopped and was on the verge of tears, 'I swear I didn't recognize you.' In full view of the boulevard, he took the poet's hands and kissed them.

Louis Latourette met Wilde coming out of the bar Calisaya after his throat operation. Wilde said, 'I want to show you Dorian Gray's photograph,' and he took out a photograph of a young Englishman he had met in Rome. 'That's the way I imagine Dorian. I didn't find or see him until after I described him in my book. You see, my idea is right, that art inspires and directs nature. This young man would never have existed if I hadn't described Dorian.' Latourette says they passed over the Pont Neuf, and saw a woman throw herself into the water. A sailor rescued her. Wilde watched anxiously. 'I could have rescued that woman. But this act was forbidden me. Yes, it's so. It's horrible. I would have seemed to be seeking attention for myself. Heroism would just have made for scandal. Since my trial, heroism and genius are forbidden me. You've heard how I made a feeble effort to enter a monastery. That would have been the best end. But I would have created a scandal. Pity me. And remember that I could have rescued that woman.'[61]

A happier occasion was a night at the theatre, when Emma Calvé in the audience recognized the back of the man in front of her. She waited until the interval to say 'Mr Wilde.' Wilde wheeled round. He remembered that he had met her at the great party in London when he had approached the hostess to know whether he might bring in a French poet who had been in prison – the hostess agreed and he had presented Paul Verlaine and had read one of his prison poems. Now he took Calvé's two hands in his and said, in a way she found heartbreaking, 'Oh Calvé! Calvé!'[62]

Ghosts

To be spoken of, and not to be spoken to, is delightful.

There were other meetings, other non-meetings. It was all *déjà vu*, like a bad play. Sir Edward Carson almost pushed a large man into the gutter when, about to apologize, he recognized him as Wilde. Oscar Browning, driving in a cab, passed Wilde, then realized too late who he was. 'The sudden pain in Wilde's eyes was unforgettable.' Stuart Merrill, Mendès, and Barrès, 'those Parisians who licked my conqueror's boots only ten years ago,' pretended not to see him.[63] Whistler and Wilde met as they were both entering a restaurant, and in the audible silence Wilde remarked to himself how old and weird the painter looked. 'My sentence and imprisonment raised Jimmy's opinion of England, and the English. Nothing else would have done so,' he commented later. Whistler said, with more nastiness than wit, 'Wilde is working on *The Bugger's Opera*.'[64] The palmist Cheiro saw him one night at a restaurant and came over to him. 'How good of you, my dear friend,' said Wilde, 'everyone cuts me now.' He had often thought of Cheiro's prophecy of five years before. Will Rothenstein and his wife took Wilde out to dinner, only to have him choose a restaurant where he was clearly making up to one of the musicians. The next time they came to Paris they decided to avoid him, but he was unavoidable on the *grands boulevards*, and he looked hurt as he realized that they would have liked to elude him.[65]

Wilde was as infamous as he had been famous in the early Nineties. In America a set of photographs in a scarlet cover, entitled *The Sins of Oscar Wilde*, was hawked about American colleges. Young men were being warned of the peril he represented. A college freshman named Armstrong was sitting with a bottle of white wine in the Café de la Régence when a voice asked, 'Have you a match?' He looked up, to see a large man with powder or ointment on his face (Wilde had a skin rash). Wilde called for a glass, Armstrong ordered another bottle. Then a friendly onlooker dropped a card saying, 'That is Oscar Wilde.' Armstrong blushed. Wilde looked at a silver watch, rose, and said, 'I remove the embarrassment.' By chance, however, they met again. Armstrong was on the Pont de la Tournelle painting the river when Wilde strolled up. He launched into a defense of formal art. Water, he declared, could not be painted; Greek and medieval painters were right in showing water as mere jags and curves of line. Then he spoke of historic scenes in Paris, of St Bartholomew, Catharine de Medici, King Henry III. Hearing that Armstrong was from Arkansas, he asked if there were springs there. 'Yes, Hot Springs,' said Armstrong. 'I would like to flee like a wounded hart into Arkansas,' Wilde told him. Then he went silent, suddenly swayed a little and said, 'Thank you for listening. I am much alone.' When Armstrong wrote to his mother that he had seen Oscar Wilde, he was ordered home by the next boat.[66]

The gloom was occasionally lightened by acts of kindness. Wilde contracted debts at the Hôtel Marsollier, and the proprietor refused to let him have his belongings until the bill was paid. Jean Dupoirier, who ran the Hôtel d'Alsace, liked Wilde and advanced the money. From August 1899 to 2 April 1900 he stayed at Dupoirier's hotel. Then in April 1900 Harold Mellor persuaded Wilde to go with him to Palermo and Rome, saying he would stake him to an upper limit of £50. In spite of the stinginess of the invitation Wilde accepted. They went first to Palermo and stayed there eight days before going to Naples for three days. They arrived at Rome on Holy Thursday, and Wilde could recall his visit twenty-three years before when he had had his interview with Pius IX. He was amused to see Grissell, Hunter Blair's friend, still a papal chamberlain, and on Easter Day – Grissell looking on in dismay – Wilde stood in the front ranks of the pilgrims and received the Pope's blessing. 'My walking stick showed signs of budding,' he wrote mockingly to Robert

Ross, and explained that he had got a ticket to the occasion through a miracle, for which he had paid thirty pieces of silver. He claimed that the skin rash from which he had been suffering for some months had been cured by the Pope's blessing. He managed to be blessed by the Pope six times more during his stay in Rome, but the miraculous cure did not last. Wilde was amused also to see his old disciple, John Gray, now a seminarist in Rome at the expense of André Raffalovich. As Edith Cooper heard the story, Gray was walking with his fellow-seminarists when he passed 'a large form planted as if to waylay him. There was complete silence – but mockery dangled it.'[67] They did not meet again.

After ten days at Gland with Mellor, Wilde returned to Paris, and to the Hôtel d'Alsace. The hotel was officially tenth category, but the proprietor Dupoirier thought it entitled to be fifth category. Dupoirier made Wilde as comfortable as he could: he brought him breakfast (coffee, bread and butter) at 11, and at two in the afternoon a cutlet and two hard-boiled eggs. He also provided four or five bottles a week of an excellent Courvoisier, at 25 and then 28 francs. At five Wilde went to the Café de la Régence, then dined at the Café de Paris, usually until two or three in the morning.[68] He was often at the Calisaya, too, where Ernest La Jeunesse, Jean Moréas, and others joined him.

He remained determinedly extravagant. Renaud says that one evening he called for cigarettes. A waiter brought him a pack of Marylands, which he rejected. 'No, blonde ones.' Nazirs were brought. 'No, with gold tips.' A groom brought some from the desk of the Grand Hôtel. Wilde gave him a louis, which the groom took to get changed. Meanwhile Wilde lit one up and said, 'Peuh!' When the groom returned with the money, he said, 'No, keep it. That way I'll delude myself into thinking these cigarettes are good.'[69]

There was news about the Queensberrys. The Marquess was dying in January 1900, and wished to see only his first wife, telling her he had always loved her. His son Percy, heir to the title, came to see his father, who gathered himself to spit at him. Bosie did not risk the same treatment. Before his death on 31 January Queensberry was said to have renounced his agnostic views, professed his love for Christ 'to whom I have confessed all my sins,' and received conditional absolution by a Catholic priest. Soon after Douglas and Percy, now the tenth Marquess, came to Paris in deepest mourning and the highest spirits. Queensberry's will freed his heirs to spend everything that was left without entail, as if he had decided that his profligate sons should be allowed to destroy themselves.* They

---

* Queensberry's will was faithful to his principles. It concluded, 'At my death I wish to be cremated and my ashes put into the Earth enclosed in nothing earth to earth, ashes to ashes, in any spot most convenient I have loved. Will mention places to my son. Harleyford for choice. I particularly request no Christian mummeries or tomfooleries be performed over my grave but that I be buried as a Secularist and an Agnostic. If it will comfort anyone there are plenty of those of my own faith who would

did. But Douglas now had a fortune of almost £20,000. Ross urged Wilde by letter to ask Douglas to settle money on him so he could have an assured income in addition to his wife's bequest of £150 a year. He broached the matter at the Café de la Paix, but Bosie was furious and indignant. 'I can't afford to spend anything except on myself,' he announced, and when Wilde mildly persisted, he accused him of wheedling 'like an old whore.' Wilde said, 'If you do not recognise my claim there is nothing more to be said.' He confided to Harris, 'He has left me bleeding.'[70] Douglas was spending so lavishly on a racing stable in Chantilly and on high living, that his inheritance was running through his fingers. He was confident that at any moment he could pick an American heiress from the many waiting for his proposal. Douglas felt that Wilde had no claim upon him, and while he was glad to give the odd handout, he detested the idea that he had anything to be remorseful over.

It was only one more bitter moment for Wilde. He was a man waiting for something, perhaps a miracle, only to find that it is death. During the summer of 1900 he had a new consolation, the International Exhibition. With Maurice Gilbert he visited Rodin's studio, and the great sculptor himself showed Wilde his 'dreams in marble,' *The Gates of Hell*. With Paul Fort, whom Louÿs had introduced to him in 1891, Wilde walked to the wrestling matches, following especially the fortunes of one Raoul le Boucher.[71] He also patronized all the cafés of different nationalities, and took a childish pleasure in everything. 'The Cloister or the Café – there is my future. I tried the Hearth, but it was a failure.' At the Calisaya one night in August he ran through all his stories like a last display of fireworks, as his friend Ernest La Jeunesse remarked. Another night, at the Spanish café his mother's friend Anna de Brémont was sitting with friends when she saw Wilde coming towards her. She feared his effect upon her friends, and put up her fan. Yet one friend said to her after Wilde had gone, 'I should have liked to meet him and find out what sort of monster he is.' The comtesse was staggered by this comment, and passed a sleepless night. In the morning she rose early and walked along the Champs-Elysées to the Pont de la Concorde, where on impulse she embarked on one of the *bateaux-mouches* which took passengers to Saint-Cloud. On the way she heard a voice: 'Good morning, are you surprised to see me? Surely not. You are not the only restless spirit in this great Paris.' He had seen her the night before but had not wished to speak to her before strangers. 'Life held to my lips a full flavoured cup, and I

---

come and say a few words of common sense over the spot where my ashes lay. Signed, Queensberry, January 23rd/95. Places to lay ashes. The summit of Craffed, or Queensberry, Dumfriesshire, the end of the Terrace overlooking the New Lock, Harleyford, Bucks. No monument or stone necessary or required, or procession, as ashes can be carried in one person's hand. Failing these places any place where stars shall ever shed their light, and sun still gild each rising morn.'

drank it to the dregs,' he said to her as to Maeterlinck, 'the bitter and the sweet. I found the sweet bitter and the bitter sweet.' 'Why do you not write now?' she asked. 'Because I have written all there was to write. I wrote when I did not know life, now that I know the meaning of life, I have no more to write.' Then, less penitently, he said, 'I have found my soul. I was happy in prison because I found my soul.' Anna de Brémont felt close to tears, but they had reached the pier, and he said, 'Contessa, don't sorrow for me,' and left her.[72]

During this summer George Alexander, who had snubbed him at Cannes, came to see him with an offer of help. At the bankruptcy sale of Wilde's effects, Alexander had bought the acting rights to *The Importance of Being Earnest* and *Lady Windermere's Fan*, and he now proposed to make Wilde some voluntary payments on these plays, which were beginning to be staged again, and to bequeath the rights to Wilde's sons. Wilde was touched. He was offered a novel form of charity by Frank Harris, who said to him, 'If you can't write your play, why not let me do it for you, and we can share the royalties?' Wilde signed an agreement to that effect, but did not tell Harris that he had signed agreements for the play with Charles Frohman on 4 October 1899, with Ada Rehan about 7 February 1900, and with Smithers. Harris efficiently put together the play, or a play, and *Mr and Mrs Daventry* was staged in the autumn of 1900 in London with some success. Wilde said, 'You have not only stolen my play, you have spoiled it,' and when he demanded his share of royalties, Harris explained that he had had to settle the claims of the others who had advanced money to Wilde on the unwritten play. Wilde agonized over what he considered Harris's perfidy, though Harris as always was being generous to him.[73] Harris's perfidy replaced Douglas's as something to ruminate about as the autumn proceeded.

Decline

I did not know
It was such a pain to die: I thought that life
Had taken all the agonies to itself . . .

Everyone is born a King, and most people die in exile – like most Kings.

The other subject which became alarming in these months was his health. The mussel poisoning – as he persisted in calling it – which had begun in the summer of 1899 had brought great red splotches on his arms, chest, and back. It was impossible not to scratch himself, and he said to Ross, 'I am more like a great ape than ever, but I hope you will give me a lunch and not a nut.' One doctor thought it was neurasthenia, not mussel poisoning. There was little time left for diagnosis. It was not syphilis, for syphilitic rashes do not itch. But Wilde's final illness was almost certainly syphilitic in origin. By late September 1900 he was bedridden, if his own calendar of events is accurate. Maurice a'Court Tucker, the thirty-two-year-old Embassy doctor, entirely misunderstood Wilde's case, according to Ross, though in the last days he diagnosed it more precisely. But he was attentive, and made sixty-eight visits to his patient beginning on 27 September, as his bill dated 5 December 1900 shows. Wilde wrote to Harris on 26 September, 'It is outrageous your leaving me as I am, ill in bed, operated on twice a day, in continuous pain, and without a penny.'[74] Dr Tucker advised an operation on his ear. This time Wilde hesitated because he had no money to pay, but on being warned that further delay might be dangerous, he borrowed from friends and had it performed by a surgeon named Cleiss, in his hotel room on 10 October. It may have been, as a modern surgeon suggests, paracentesis of the eardrum or removal of polyps. Although Ross spoke of it as a minor operation, Wilde – perhaps to exaggerate his plight – spoke of it to Harris as a 'most terrible' operation, which required a male nurse day and night, a doctor in the hotel, and much medication. Sir William Wilde had written in *Aural Surgery* (1853) 'So long as otorrhoea [discharge from the ear] is present, we never can tell how, when or where it will end, or what it may lead to.'[75] The ear was dressed daily by a man named Hennion. Wilde telegraphed the news of the operation to Ross, always his faithful friend in emergencies, and asked him to cross the Channel: 'Terribly weak. Please come.' He had written to Harris sometime before, 'The Morgue yawns for me. I go and look at my zinc bed there.'[76] He had in fact visited the morgue. Thoughts of death were never far away, and his friends could not distinguish his real fears from his pleas for their sympathy. 'One should live as if there were no death,' he had written. 'One should die as if one had never lived.' But such prescriptions were easier to make in health.

Ross had planned to come at the end of the month, but on learning Wilde's condition hurried over from London on 16 October, Wilde's birthday. He found his friend in good spirits, speaking of his sufferings as dreadful, but laughing abut them. 'Ah Robbie,' he said, 'when we are dead and buried in our porphyry tombs, and the trumpet of the Last Judgment is sounded, I shall turn and whisper to you, "Robbie, Robbie, let us pretend we do not hear it."' [77] Fortunately just at this time he had plenty of company: Reggie Turner was in Paris, and Ross's brother Alex. To Willie's widow, Lily, and her new husband Teixeira de Mattos, Wilde said, 'I am dying beyond my means. I will never outlive the century. The English people would not stand for it. I am responsible for the failure of the Exhibition:* the English went away when they saw me there so

* The Paris Exhibition of 1900, which ran from 14 April to 5 November.

well-dressed and happy. The English know this too, and they will not stand me any more.' Lily remarked, a little unfeelingly, that her first husband Willie had made similar prognostications on his deathbed. To Alice Rothenstein Oscar remarked, 'I can't even afford to die.' He had always said that in the life of Napoleon St Helena was 'the greatest theme of all,' and to St Helena he had come. He told Ross his drama had lasted too long.[78]

At midday on 29 October Wilde for the first time in weeks left his bed; the doctor had told him he might do so sooner. After dinner in his room in the evening, he insisted on taking a walk with Ross. With some difficulty he made his way to a café, where he drank absinthe, then walked laboriously back. Wilde said to Claire de Pratz, 'My wallpaper and I are fighting a duel to the death. One or the other of us has to go.' Ross said, 'You'll kill yourself, Oscar. You know the doctor said absinthe was poison for you.' 'And what have I to live for?' Wilde asked.[79] Next day, as Ross had feared, he had a cold and complained of great pain in his ear. Dr Tucker, the Embassy doctor, thought a drive in the Bois in the mild weather would do him no harm, but during their ride he told Ross he felt giddy, and they returned at once. His ear developed an abscess; he had otitis media. This the doctor now diagnosed, according to Turner, as a 'tertiary symptom of an infection he had contracted when he was twenty.' It led directly to meningitis, the legacy, as Ross said, of an attack of tertiary syphilis. The wound dresser (*panseur*) warned Ross that Wilde was getting worse. Ross arranged to see Dr Tucker privately on 6 November, and was somewhat reassured by his cheerful manner. But that afternoon Wilde declined to listen to the doctor's views, and was greatly agitated. He said he did not care if he had only a short time to live; he asked Ross to pay off a portion of his debts, which came to £400, after his death. He asked him to see that *De Profundis* was one day published, as he felt it would to some extent put him right with the world. He felt he was having a relapse. The morphine which had been prescribed, and injected by Dupoirier, no longer helped him; only opium and chloral had any effect.[80] He also drank champagne by day. The pain in his ear had increased, and the wound-dresser poulticed the wound against Tucker's orders.

Wilde said to Reggie Turner and Ross, who were in almost constant attendance, 'I dreamt I was supping with the dead,' to which Turner replied 'My dear Oscar, you were probably the life and soul of the party.' Wilde became high spirited again and almost hysterical, but Ross was growing anxious. On 2 November he had gone to Père Lachaise; Wilde asked if he had picked out a burial place for him. Ross wrote a letter to Douglas on 6 November saying that Wilde was very ill, and troubled by his debts. On the following Monday, 12 November, Ross went to say goodbye to Wilde, having promised his mother to meet her in the south of France. Wilde begged him not to go away, saying that in the last few days he had felt a great change, and would never see Ross again. When Ross said he had to go, Wilde said, 'Look out for some little cup in the hills near Nice where I can go when I am better, and where you can come and see me often.'[81] He also talked about his children, about Vyvyan who had suddenly said to his tutor, 'I am a Catholic.'

Reggie Turner took Ross's place at Wilde's bedside, and it became clear in ten days that Wilde was getting no better. A consultation on 25 November held out little hope; the doctors feared that the inflammation would go to his brain. They stopped the morphine, though they kept up a pretense of injecting it. On 27 November the doctors thought Wilde's mind was gone, but he gathered himself to talk coherently again and seemed better.* 'Poor Oscar has ceased to worry about anything except Tucker,' Turner reported. From 26 to 28 November there were periods of delirium, and nonsense spoken in English and French. He suffered Turner to apply an ice pack to his head, but after forty-five minutes asked, 'You dear little Jew, don't you think that's enough?' He said suddenly, 'Jews have no beautiful philosophy of life, but they are *sympathique*.' He was less cooperative about mustard plasters on his feet, which he would not allow anyone to apply. 'You ought to be a doctor,' he said to Turner,

---

* The doctors' report of that day has survived:

> Les médecins soussignés, ayant examiné M. Oscar Wilde, dit Melmott, le Dimanche 15 Novembre, ont constaté des troubles cérébraux importants résultant d'une ancienne suppuration de l'oreille droite d'ailleurs en traitement depuis plusieur années.
>
> Le 27 les symptomes se sont beaucoup aggravés. Le diagnostic de méningo encéphalite est admis sans conteste. En l'absence de tout indice de localisation on ne peut songer à une trépanation.
>
> Le traitement conseillé est purement médical. L'intervention chirurgicale semble impossible.
>
> Paris le 27 Novembre 1900
> DR PAUL CLEISS
> A' COURT TUCKER, M.D.
>
> En l'absence de la famille, qui sera prévenue sur notre demande, assistaient à la consultation MM. Turner et Dupoirier.
>
> REGINALD TURNER
> J. DUPOIRIER hôtelier

['The undersigned doctors, having examined Mr Oscar Wilde, called Melmott, on Sunday 15 November, established that there were significant cerebral disturbances stemming from an old suppuration of the right ear, under treatment for several years.

'On the 27th, the symptoms became much graver. The diagnosis of encephalitic meningitis must be made without doubt. In the absence of any indication of localization, trepanning cannot be contemplated.

'The treatment advised is purely medicinal. Surgical intervention seems impossible.   Paris etc . . .

'In the absence of the family, who are to be notified at our request, Messrs Turner and Dupoirier were present at the consultation . . .']

'as you always want people to do what they don't want to.' A further operation was out of the question, and he was taking no nourishment. He asked Turner if he would get a Munster to cook for him and added that one steamboat was like another. The *Munster* was one of the ships that plied between Holyhead and Kingstown, so Wilde was imagining a return to Ireland. On the 27th Turner wrote to Ross:

Today he asked for paraffin – finally we learned that he meant *Patrie*. When he got the newspaper he was overjoyed to see the picture of Kruger in a fur coat. He mispronounces certain words now. It is very hard to tend him, since he refuses to obey the doctor's orders.

On the 28th he appeared slightly better, and declared that his unwritten play was worth fifty centimes.[82] Turner would recall how in his last conversation he spoke of Gertrude Atherton's novel *Senator North*, which Turner had put in his hands the week before. 'This is a fine study of the American politician,' he said, 'and possesses the quality of truth in characterisation. What else has the lady written?'[83] His temperature was very high, and Turner wired to Ross, 'Almost hopeless.' Ross caught an express from the south of France and arrived on the morning of the 29th to find Wilde thin, his flesh livid, his breathing heavy. He had a fortnight's beard. He tried to speak to Ross and Turner, but could only press their hands. He put his own hand into his mouth to keep from crying out with pain.

Robert Ross hesitated about bringing a priest to his dying friend. He was not at all sure what Wilde's wishes were. Long before Wilde had said, 'Catholicism is the only religion to die in.' And three weeks before his death he had said to a correspondent for the *Daily Chronicle*, 'Much of my moral obliquity is due to the fact that my father would not allow me to become a Catholic. The artistic side of the Church and the fragrance of its teaching would have cured my degeneracies. I intend to be received before long.' (He had told Latourette the same thing.) Ross knew that Wilde had 'kneeled like a real Roman' to a priest in Notre-Dame in Paris, to another in Naples, as to the Pope in Rome.[84] But his views were scarcely orthodox. He said to Percival Almy that Christ was not divine: 'It would place too broad a gulf between him and the human soul.' He told George Ives that he hoped we would have tremendous passions in the next world. When another friend talked of life in the spirit, he replied, 'There is no hell but this – a body without a soul, or a soul without a body.'[85] Shortly after leaving prison, he said to Turner, 'The Catholic Church is for saints and sinners alone. For respectable people the Anglican Church will do.' And when Ross fervently declared that Catholicism was true, Wilde said in an avuncular tone, 'No, Robbie, it isn't true.' Wilde had known of Ross's anxieties about conversion, and on one occasion asked to see a priest. But Ross decided he wasn't serious, and was thereafter dubbed 'the cherub with the flaming sword, forbidding my entrance into Eden.'[86]

The sight of Wilde's pathetic state now decided Ross. As he later told Max Meyerfeld, when Wilde was unconscious, he made up his mind to get him a priest so there could be formal obsequies and a ceremonious burial. Otherwise the body might be taken to the morgue and an autopsy performed. He rushed to the Passionist Fathers and brought back Father Cuthbert Dunne.* Ross asked Wilde if he wished to see Dunne, and Wilde, unable to speak, held up his hand. Dunne asked him if he wished to be received and he once more held up his hand. On this sign Dunne gave him conditional baptism, and absolved and anointed him. 'He was never able to speak and we do not know whether he was altogether conscious,' said Ross. 'I did this for my own conscience and the promise I had made.'[87] The application of sacred oils to his hands and feet may have been a ritualized pardon for his omissions or commissions, or may have been like putting a green carnation in his buttonhole.

At 5.30 a.m., to the consternation of Ross and Turner, a loud, strong death rattle began, like the turning of a crank. Foam and blood came from his mouth during the morning, and at ten minutes to two in the afternoon Wilde died. (The death certificate says the time was 2 p.m. on 30 November.) He had scarcely breathed his last breath when the body exploded with fluids from the ear, nose, mouth, and other orifices. The debris was appalling.†[88] Dupoirier laid Wilde out, clothed in a white night shirt and with a white sheet over him. Dunne put a rosary in his hand and palm branches over him. At Ross's request, Maurice Gilbert took a flashlight photograph.

Douglas, to whom Ross had telegraphed, arrived on 2 December. He was chief mourner at the funeral, *'un enterrement de 6e classe.'*‡ The coffin was cheap, and the hearse was shabby. There were a number of wreaths, from Douglas, Adey, Turner, Ross, Adela Schuster, Clifton, Maurice Gilbert, Louis Wilkinson, Mellor, Teixeira de Mattos and his wife, Dr Tucker, and even from Dupoirier, 'À mon Locataire.' The *Mercure de France* also sent a wreath. At the funeral itself were Stuart Merrill, Paul Fort, Armand Point, Jean de Mitty (editor of Stendhal), Charles Lucas, Marcel Bataillant, Charles Gibleigh [?], Marius Boisson, Ernest La Jeunesse, Michel Tavera, Henry Davray, Frédéric Boutet, Léonard

---

* Ross's visiting card has survived, and bears the words: 'Can I see one of the fathers about a very urgent case or can I hear of a priest elsewhere who can talk English to administer last sacraments to a dying man?'

† Turner – perhaps out of self-censorship – was later to deny that this had happened, but Augustus John says he heard about it from Ross and Turner.

‡ In *The Importance of Being Earnest*, Jack says of his supposedly dead brother, 'He seems to have expressed a desire to be buried in Paris,' and Mr Chasuble comments, 'In Paris!,' shaking his head. 'I fear that hardly points to any very serious state of mind at the last.'

Sarluis, Henri Davenay. Raymond de la Tailhède and Jehan Rictus are said to have come every day to see Wilde in his last illness, and La Tailhède was at the funeral. Boutet says an American painter named Peters was there. Also attending were Dr Tucker, Ross, Turner, Pierre Louÿs (who had not seen Wilde for years), Anna de Brémont and her maid, an old servant girl of Constance, Mme Stuart Merrill in a heavy veil, an American woman, Miriam Aldrich, and a few journalists. The Reverend Cuthbert Dunne said the requiem mass at St Germain-des-Prés, only a side door being opened for the mourners. Four carriages followed the hearse. (It bore the number 13.) The first was occupied by Ross, Douglas, Turner, and Dupoirier; the second by a priest and a choir boy; the third by Mme Stuart Merrill, Paul Fort, Davray and Sarluis; the fourth by people Ross did not know. Gunnar Heiberg says he was at the grave. Gide said seven people followed the coffin, but Miriam Aldrich said there were fourteen, including herself.[89] At the graveside there was an unpleasant scene, which none of the principals ever described – perhaps some jockeying for the role of principal mourner. When the coffin was lowered, Douglas almost fell into the grave.[90] John Gray, who was not there, wrote a poem in 1931, 'The Lord Looks at Peter,' which is a kind of elegy for Wilde:

> A night alarm; a weaponed crowd;
> One blow, and with the rest I ran,
> I warmed my hands, and said aloud:
> I never knew the man.[91]

He was buried in the eleventh grave in the seventh row of the seventeenth section at Bagneux on 3 December. A simple stone, with an iron railing around it, bore the inscription from the Book of Job:

> Oscar Wilde
> RIP Oct 16th 1854 – Nov 30th 1900
> Job xxix Verbis meis addere nihil audebant et super illos
> stillebat eloquium meum.

That is, 'To my words they durst add nothing, and my speech dropped upon them' (Douai Version). Ross wrote to one of Wilde's friends, 'He was very unhappy, and would have become more unhappy as time went on.'[92] Wilde's humiliations were at an end.

Epilogue

*. . . The men who have realised themselves, and in whom all
Humanity gains a partial realisation.*

Wilde had to live his life twice over, first in slow motion, then at top speed.
During the first period he was a scapegrace, during the second a
scapegoat. For the three and a half years he lived after his release from
prison, he saw pass before him, mostly in dumb show, a multitude of
people he had known earlier, who evaded him. His wife kept him away and
then died. He did not know where his sons were. There were terrible
confrontations with old adversaries like Whistler and Carson in which,
after having stared at each other, neither spoke. The people whose lives he
had helped to make forgot him: though Lillie Langtry pretended in later
life that she had sent him money in his last years, she did not. Aubrey
Beardsley, after some hesitation, spurned Wilde. Max Beerbohm was
sympathetic, but kept his distance. Sherard and Wilde did not speak to
each other any more. It was ostracism – more or less – by two groups,
those who could not bear his homosexuality and those who could not bear
his requests for money. Douglas gave him dribs and drabs, then snubbed
him when he asked for more. Ross and Turner were not capable of
passing him but did pass Paris to avoid him. Frank Harris wrote Wilde's
play for him – and only distressed him. Wilde was as conspicuous in defeat
as in triumph, and as well known in Paris – he said – as the Tour Eiffel.
There were moments of grace. But these were rare, and brief.

No wonder he drooped. Or that he had a constant sense of ill being,
checked but not eliminated by absinthe and brandy. No wonder that he
stayed in bed longer and longer, until he discovered he was bedridden.
His body had its reasons, his mind also. Ross was cheering himself up
when he contradicted his earlier statement by saying that Wilde's last
years had not been so bad: though he had continued to find young men, to
talk, eat and drink, all these familiar activities took place in a desolate
environment, the memory of what he had been and the sense of what he
had become, the trivial debts at which he had once laughed and now could
only cry, the snubs and insults which every day brought. English law had
misdone him by punishment, and English society finished him off by
ostracism.

When Wilde died, the relations between him and Douglas came to a
kind of ending. But there was a posthumous connection as tumultuous as
any in life. This came about through *De Profundis*. Ross felt bound to
publish it in an abridged form and the 1905 edition omitted all reference
to Douglas. But it was clear that Douglas had been an *amour fatale*. A

551

vague reference to this effect in Arthur Ransome's book on Wilde in 1912 made Douglas sue for libel. (He had already begun to have some success in forcing apologies and out-of-court settlements.) Ross now felt he must disclose the missing portions of *De Profundis*, and at the request of Ransome's counsel, the whole letter was read out in court. Douglas was in the witness box at the time, but left during the reading. He could not bear to listen to Wilde's reference to his verse as undergraduate, to his stature as low, to his disposition as sponging, to his nature as shallow. Within months he had got his reply ready in *Oscar Wilde and Myself.*

Douglas disclaimed the book later, but in 1919 he republished it with a new preface, declaring that he had been 'born into this world chiefly to be the instrument, whether I would or not, of exposing and smashing Wilde's cult and the Wilde myth,' and that he was a poet and an honest man. Much the same account appears in his *Autobiography* (1928). The books insist that he had never participated in homosexual acts. Homer shows how Helen, back from Troy, blamed Venus for the elopement with Paris, and insisted that she had always longed to be back with her husband.

Douglas now began, in his father's manner, to write letters attacking Ross to Ross's friends, until the pressure became so great that Ross, as Wilde before him, had to sue for libel. On the witness stand Douglas proved too much for him, and though Ross escaped prosecution he felt harried until his death in 1918. It seemed to many people that Douglas had hounded him into his grave. Douglas found other targets: for a criminal libel of Winston Churchill he was sent to Wormwood Scrubs for six months, and during that time composed his sonnet sequence, *In Excelsis*, as a riposte to *De Profundis*. He said in it that England was being led by Wilde, as the lord of abominations, to black night. His father would have been proud of him.

In the late 1920s he began to change his views about Wilde. By the time he wrote his *Autobiography*, he had become ardently Catholic, and while his marriage ended in a predictable divorce, he had not, or said he had not, resumed homosexual practices. He tried to achieve detachment and forgiveness, though the name of Ross could still drive him to distraction. In his later years he managed a daily bet on the races. On his deathday he placed two bets instead of one, and lost both.

Douglas's love had a fierceness that prevented Wilde from throwing him off, but also from living in contentment. Yet his most brilliant work, *The Importance of Being Earnest*, pretends that the course of love can run quite smooth. It is a record of Wilde's emotions in that it excludes them, and defiantly demonstrates they are excludable. Douglas left a record too, in his *Autobiography*. It is a grimly intent work, but unconsciously funny too. Though the book is overtly opposed to homosexuality, Douglas feels that God led him to 'a most beautiful little boy with an angelic face and smile,' who told him where he could find a witness to testify against Ross.

And he himself looks forward to being a boy again in Paradise, where he says one can be any age one likes.

Even more than the hopeless loves of Yeats or Dowson or A. E. Housman, Wilde's love affair provides an example of berserk passion, of *Vénus toute entière à sa proie attachée*. It could have occurred only in a clandestine world of partial disclosures, blackmail, and libel suits. He was obliged by the trial to broadcast his love to the world, but could not contemplate pleading guilty, denied everything, and refused to let Douglas disclose their relations, or to disclose them himself. His behavior destroyed Constance. After first meditating and offering a confession (in French), Douglas adopted the same mode of reticence, holding back for years before finally telling, if not all, all but all, and then only in the character of a reformed profligate. But of course he never really changed. For twenty-seven years he was also Bosie the irresistible, the beloved object of a great writer. The history preserves in amber his beauty and his greed, rage, and cruelty.

After the death of Constance Holland in 1898 and of Oscar Wilde in 1900, their sons, Cyril and Vyvyan Holland, were befriended by Robert Ross, who as literary executor paid off Wilde's debts and recovered his copyrights for them. Cyril volunteered for combat duty in the First World War, and was killed. Vyvyan wrote books, married, and had one child, Merlin, who lives in London, is married, and has a son, Lucian. Willie Wilde and his wife Lily had one child, a daughter, Dolly, well known in Paris in the circle of Natalie Clifford Barney, the famous 'Amazon.'

Wilde's remains were moved from Bagneux to Père Lachaise, when the celebrated funerary monument by Epstein was placed there, in 1909. Mrs Carew, mother of Sir Coleridge Kennard, paid for the monument. When Ross died in 1918, his will directed that his own ashes be put into the tomb. This was done. The monument bears an inscription from *The Ballad of Reading Gaol*:

> And alien tears will fill for him
> Pity's long-broken urn,
> For his mourners will be outcast men,
> And outcasts always mourn.

'There is something vulgar in all success,' Wilde told O'Sullivan.[1] 'The greatest men fail, or seem to have failed.' He was speaking of Parnell, but what was true of Parnell is in another way true of Wilde. His work survived as he had claimed it would. We inherit his struggle to achieve supreme fictions in art, to associate art with social change, to bring together individual and social impulse, to save what is eccentric and singular from being sanitized and standardized, to replace a morality of severity by one of sympathy. He belongs to our world more than to Victoria's. Now, beyond the reach of scandal, his best writings validated by time, he comes before us still, a towering figure, laughing and weeping, with parables and paradoxes, so generous, so amusing, and so right.[2]

NOTES

Works frequently cited are referred to by author only, or by author and abbreviated title, after the first full citation. Where no author is given the work cited is by Oscar Wilde. The place of publication is London unless otherwise indicated. See the Acknowledgements at p. xi for a full list of sources of unpublished material referred to below in abbreviated form.

BEGINNINGS

Chapter I

1 Walter Hamilton, *The Aesthetic Movement in England*, 3rd edn (1882), 97.
2 *The Biograph* IV (1880): 130–5.
3 *Selected Letters of Oscar Wilde*, ed. Rupert Hart-Davis (1979), 1. The letter is quoted in a Stetson sale catalogue (1920).
4 Robert Sherard, *The Life of Oscar Wilde* (N.Y., 1906), 104.
5 Michael Field, *Works and Days*, ed. T. Sturge Moore (1933), 139.
6 Henriette Corkran, *Celebrities and I* (1902), 137; Lord Rathcreedan, *Memories* (1932), 51.
7 Robert Sherard, *Oscar Wilde: The Story of an Unhappy Friendship* (1902), 73.
8 R. Ross, letter to Leonard Smithers from Hôtel Voltaire, Paris, 17 Apr 1898 (Texas).
9 Lady W, letters to H. W. Longfellow, 30 Nov 1875 and 11 May 1878 (Houghton).
10 Lady W, letter to W. Carleton in D. J. O'Donoghue, *The Life of William Carleton*, 2 vols (1896), II: 138–9: Carleton to Lady W, 1849 (NLI, MS. 13993).
11 Brian de Breffny, 'Speranza's Ancestry,' *Irish Ancestor* IV (1972), no. 2: 94–103. Frances was the name of Jane Elgee's elder sister, born 1816, who died at the age of three months.
12 Horace Wyndham, *Speranza: A Biography of Lady Wilde* (N.Y., 1951), 23.
13 W. B. Yeats, *Thomas Davis Centenary Address* (Oxford, 1947), and Catherine Hamilton, *Notable Irishwomen* [1904], 176.
14 Terence De Vere White, *The Parents of Oscar Wilde* (1967), 82.
15 Charles Gavan Duffy, *Four Years of Irish History, 1845–1849* (1883), 94.
16 Sir William Hamilton, letter to Aubrey De Vere, quoted Wyndham, 56; Gavan Duffy to Jane Elgee (Wilde), n.d. [1849], letter in my possession.
17 Jane Elgee (Wilde), letters to unnamed Scottish correspondent, June [? July] 1848 and 7 Apr 1858 (Reading).
18 See C. Hamilton, *Notable Irishwomen*, 181.
19 Lady W, letter to unnamed correspondent, 1850 (Reading); Lady W, *Notes on Men, Women, and Books* (1891), 42.

555

20 Lady W, letter to Lotten von Kraemer, 19 Mar 1859 (copy, NLI).

21 'Mr. Pater's Last Volume,' in *The Artist as Critic: Critical Writings of Oscar Wilde*, ed. Richard Ellmann (Chicago, 1982), 230.

22 Lady W, *Social Studies* (1893), 13.

23 Lily Yeats's Scrapbook, 1889 (courtesy of W. M. Murphy).

24 Wyndham, 70.

25 Coulson Kernahan, 'Wilde and Heine,' *Dublin Magazine*, n.d., 22; Anna de Brémont, *Oscar Wilde and His Mother* (1911), 77.

26 Lady W, MS notes in NYPL: Berg.

27 H. Corkran, *Celebrities and I*, 138; W. B. Yeats, *Autobiography* (N.Y., 1965), 92.

28 Lady W, letter to Wilde, n.d. [1876] (Clark 2299).

29 Lady W, 'To Ireland' and 'Who Will Show Us Any Good?,' in *Poems* (1864). Not all her friends agreed. The feminist Mona Caird, protesting against Lady W's strictures on her novel *The Wing of Azrael* (1871), in which the heroine kills her husband when he tries to rape her, wrote: 'I do not share your admiration for the woman who is "sacrificial." . . . I do not agree with you in thinking that women have to prove themselves heroines and devotees of duty before they have a right to claim the fullest opportunity for development and life. They claim this right as human beings . . . Again you say "take woman as she is meant to be": I deny that she is "meant to be" anything in particular. She is as she makes herself, as the forces and conditions of life make her. The "inspiration of humanity" she may still be, and in my opinion is much more likely to be, when she ceases to be afraid, ceases to worship morals, ceases to see the "divine" only where she has been hitherto taught to see it in submission, sacrifice, "duty" (so-called) and general self-destruction.' (Letter of 27 June 1889 in my possession.)

30 Lady W, *Men, Women, and Books*, 175; letter to unnamed correspondent, 1852 (Reading).

31 Lady W, letter to Lotten von Kraemer, [Nov] 1862 (copy, NLI).

32 Yeats, *Autobiography*, 92; G. B. Shaw, 'My Memories of Oscar Wilde,' in Frank Harris, *Oscar Wilde, His Life and Confessions* (Garden City, N.Y., 1932), 388; J. B. Yeats, letter to W. B. Yeats, 13 June 1921 (W. M. Murphy papers).

33 T. G. Wilson, *Victorian Doctor* (N.Y., 1956), 109.

34 A. H. Sayce heard this story from J. P. Mahaffy: Sayce, *Reminiscences* (1923), 135.

35 Shaw, in Harris, 393–4; J. B. Yeats, letter to W. B. Yeats, 13 June 1921 (Murphy papers).

36 William M. Murphy, *Prodigal Father: The Life of John Butler Yeats* (Ithaca, N.Y., and London, 1978), 31; W. H. Chesson, 'A Reminiscence of 1898,' *Bookman* XXXIV (Dec 1911): 389–94.

37 Lady W, letters to unnamed correspondent, 1852, 22 Nov 1854 (Reading).

38 Lady W, letter to Mrs Rosalie Olivecrona, 1 Jan 1865 (copy, NLI).

39 Lady W, letter to unnamed correspondent, 1858 (Reading).

40 Information from Eileen O'Faolain, citing a tradition in Glenmacnass.

41 J. B. Yeats, *Letters to His Son . . .* , ed. Joseph Hone (N.Y., 1946), 277.

42 Murphy, *Prodigal Father*, 551. J. B. Yeats's letter of 30 May 1921, about this episode, was misread in Hone's edition.

43 Lady W, letter to Mrs Olivecrona, 1 Jan, 23 Mar 1865 (copy, NLI).
44 De Vere White, *The Parents of O.W.*, 210–11.
45 Rathcreedan, *Memories*, 52.
46 Lady W, letter to unnamed correspondent, *c.* 21 Nov 1852 (Reading).
47 Letter to unnamed correspondent (Reading).
48 Douglas Sladen, *Twenty Years of My Life* (1915), 109.
49 Coulson Kernahan, *In Good Company*, 2nd edn (1917), 208.
50 Vincent O'Sullivan, *Aspects of Wilde* (1936), 80.
51 *Pall Mall Budget*, 10 Jan 1895.
52 Wyndham, 52.
53 Lady W, letter to unnamed correspondent (Reading).
54 Sherard, *Life of O.W.*, 5–6 (on authority presumably of Ross).
55 Luther Munday, *Chronicle of Friendship* (1912), 95–6.
56 Thomas Flanagan, *The Irish Novelists, 1800–1850* (N.Y., 1959), 325.
57 Lady W, letter to Lotten von Kraemer (copy, NLI).
58 Lotten von Kraemer, 'Författaren Oscar Wilde's Föräldrahem i Irlands
    Hufvudstad,' *Ord och Bild* (1902), 429–35; translation by Alice Pederson.
59 Robert Sherard, *The Real Oscar Wilde* (n.d. [1917]), 163.
60 Ross, quoted in Hesketh Pearson, *The Life of Oscar Wilde* (1946), 20–1.
61 Reginald Turner, letter to A. J. A. Symons, 26 Aug 1935 (Clark).
62 Letter to the editor of the *Irish Times*, 28 Aug 1954, from Murroe Fitzgerald.
    In 1919, he says, he prepared a claim for a woman who had been nannie for
    both the Wilde children and Edward Carson at Dungarvan when she was
    fifteen years old, in 1859.
63 Wyndham, 56.
64 Rev. L. C. Prideaux Fox, 'People I Have Met,' *Donahoe's Magazine* (Boston)
    LIII, no. 4 (Apr 1905): 397.
65 Stuart Mason, *Bibliography of Oscar Wilde* (1914), 118.
66 William Morris, MS note in *Sidonia the Sorceress* (Clark).
67 See Isobel Murray, 'Some Elements in the Composition of *The Picture of
    Dorian Gray*,' *Durham University Journal* XXXIII (1972): 220–31.
68 Reminiscences of Claire de Pratz in Guillot de Saix, 'Souvenirs inédits sur
    Oscar Wilde,' in undated issue of *L'Européen* (Reading).
69 Lady W, letter to Lotten von Kraemer (copy, NLI).
70 Harris, 21.
71 Lady W, letter to unnamed correspondent, 22 Nov 1954 (Reading).
72 Lady W, letters to Mrs Olivecrona, 13 Feb 1865, and to Lotten von
    Kraemer (copies, NLI).
73 J. Glover, *Jimmy Glover, His Book* (1911), 17.
74 Sherard, *Life of O.W.*, 108.
75 Slason Thompson, *Eugene Field, a Study in Heredity and Contradiction*, 2 vols
    (N.Y., 1901), I.213; W. B. Maxwell, *Time Gathered* (1937), 142–3.
76 Sir Edward Sullivan in Harris, 18; Louis Claude Purser, 'Wilde at Portora,'
    a MS sent to A. J. A. Symons in 1932 (Clark).
77 Harris, 19.
78 [Jean Paul Raymond and] Charles Ricketts, *Oscar Wilde: Recollections*
    (1932), 18.
79 Epigrams in Hyde Collection.
80 Harris, 17–18.

81 Letters to Lotten von Kraemer, July 1867 and 3 Apr 1870 (copies, NLI).

82 Mason, 295.

83 Purser, 'Wilde at Portora' (Clark).

84 Reginald Turner, letter to A. J. A. Symons, 20 Aug 1935 (Clark); H. Montgomery Hyde, *Oscar Wilde* (N.Y., 1975), 13; Edward Marjoribanks, *The Life of Lord Carson* (1932), 13.

85 W. B. Stanford and R. B. McDowell, *Mahaffy* (1971), 60.

86 'Aristotle at Afternoon Tea' (review of Mahaffy), *Pall Mall Gazette*, 16 Dec 1887.

87 'Mr Mahaffy's New Book,' *Pall Mall Gazette*, 9 Nov 1887.

88 Oliver St John Gogarty, letter to A. J. A. Symons, 10 Sept 1935 (Clark); Gogarty, 'The Most Magnificent Snob I Ever Knew,' *Irish Times*, 10 July 1962.

89 Walter Starkie, *Scholars and Gipsies* (1963), 100.

90 *The Letters of Oscar Wilde*, ed. Rupert Hart-Davis (1962), 338; Lady W, letter to Wilde [1882] (Clark).

91 Commonplace Book (Clark).

92 Gogarty in *Irish Times*, 10 July 1962.

93 J. P. Mahaffy, *Social Life in Greece from Homer to Menander* (1874), 308.

94 Mrs Tyrrell, letter to Robert Ross, 20 Apr [1914] (Hyde).

95 Sherard, *The Real O.W.*, 148.

96 Lloyd Lewis and Henry Justin Smith, *Oscar Wilde Discovers America* (N.Y., 1936), 8–9.

97 The Suggestion Book is at TCD.

98 Sullivan in Harris, 26; Wilde's copy of Swinburne's *Poems and Ballads* is in the Library of King's College, University of London.

99 So Wilde wrote in 1876 in an apparently unpublished review of the Second Series of Symonds's *The Greek Poets* (1876). The MS is at Clark. *Letters*, 25.

100 Sold by James W. Borg, a Chicago bookseller, n.d.

101 G. F. Sims Catalogue no. 79.

102 *Letters*, 25; 'Ben Jonson', *Pall Mall Gazette*, 20 Sept 1886.

103 J. A. Symonds, *Studies of the Greek Poets* (1873), 416–17.

104 Wilde's copy of Symonds's *Shelley* was sold at Sotheby's in 1985.

105 Harris, 26.

106 Journal of J. E. Courtenay Bodley (Bodleian).

107 Ross makes this statement in his Introduction to the German edition of Wilde's works.

108 Lady W, letter to Lotten von Kraemer, 6 May 1875 (copy, NLI).

109 Edith Cooper, letter of 30 Nov 1900 (BL).

110 Ross, Introduction to the German edition of Wilde's works.

111 Douglas Ainslie, *Adventures* (1922), 93.

112 Lady W, letter to Mrs Olivecrona, 1874 (copy, NLI).

113 Mason, 498.

114 Stanford and McDowell, *Mahaffy*, 39, slightly varies the phrasing.

Chapter II

1 A letter from Bunbury (1878) is at Clark.

2 Review of '*Henry the Fourth* at Oxford,' *Dramatic Review*, 23 May 1885; Henry James, *Persons and Places* (1883), 246; *Letters*, 772.

3 [J. E. C. Bodley], 'Oscar Wilde at Oxford,' *New York Times*, 20 Jan 1882.

4 Michael J. O'Neill, ed., 'Unpublished Lecture Notes of a Speech by Oscar Wilde at San Francisco,' *University Review* (Dublin) I (Spring 1955): 29–32; Seymour Hicks, *Between Ourselves* (1930), 79; W. B. Yeats, *Autobiography*, 87.

5 G. T. Atkinson, 'Oscar Wilde at Oxford,' *Cornhill Magazine* LXVI (May 1929): 562.

6 Atkinson, 563.

7 Oliver St John Gogarty, 'A Picture of Oscar Wilde,' in *Intimations* (N.Y., [1950]), 50; Atkinson, 561.

8 Lord David Cecil, *Max: A Biography* (1964), 70.

9 Gelett Burgess, 'A Talk with Mr Oscar Wilde,' *The Sketch*, 9 Jan 1895, p. 495; E. F. Benson, *As We Were: A Victorian Peep-show* (1930), 246.

10 Oxford examinations (Bodleian).

11 David Hunter Blair, *In Victorian Days* (1939), 123.

12 Stanford and McDowell, *Mahaffy*, 31.

13 Atkinson, 561.

14 Lewis R. Farnell, *An Oxonian Looks Back* (1934), 57.

15 Atkinson, 561; Sladen, 109; Sherard, *Life of O.W.*, 138.

16 Sladen, 109; Pearson, *Life of O.W.*, 36.

17 Sir Frank Benson, *My Memoirs* (1930), 137–8.

18 Letter to me from Ward's daughter, Cissie, 1977.

19 *Letters*, 32.

20 Written in Wilde's copy of *Aurora Leigh* (Magdalen), for Ward's benefit.

21 *New York Tribune*, 8 Jan 1882.

22 Oscar Browning, letter to the editor of *Everyman*, 1 Nov 1912, and letter to Frank Harris, 25 Sept 1919 (Texas).

23 Archives of the Vice-Chancellor's Court (Bodleian).

24 Atkinson, 560.

25 Hunter Blair, 115–43; Yeats, *Autobiography*, 91.

26 Lady W, letter to unnamed correspondent, [5 May] 1875 (Reading).

27 Review of '*As You Like It* at Coombe House,' *Dramatic Review*, 6 June 1885; *Letters*, 471.

28 *The Works of John Ruskin*, ed. E. T. Cook and Alexander Wedderburn (1903), IV: 35–6; XXV: 122–3.

29 Walter Pater, Preface to *Studies in the History of the Renaissance* (1874 and later edns).

30 Atkinson, 563; H. W. Nevinson, *Changes and Chances* (1923), 55.

31 H. Kingsmill Moore, *Reminiscences and Reflections* (1930), 18.

32 Wilde gave this account of his work on the road often: *Home Journal* (N.Y.), 19 Oct 1881; *Nation*, 12 Jan 1882; *Indianapolis Journal*, 14 Jan 1882; *The World*, 4 Feb 1882. Bodley questions it in his unsigned article in the *New York Times*, 20 Jan 1882; but Alon Kadish, who has made a study of the subject, assures me that Wilde was one of the roadbuilders.

33 Kingsmill Moore, 45; Atkinson, 561–2.

34 *Letters*, 218.

35 *Letters*, 61.

36 *Letters*, 482.

37 Ruskin, *Works*, XXII: 235–6; XX: 91.

38 Stuart Merrill, essay on Wilde 20 Sept 1912 (Hart-Davis) at Clark; *The Artist as Critic*, 351; Max Beerbohm's notes on Wilde (NYPL: Berg).
39 Eduard J. Bock, *Oscar Wildes persönliche und frühste literarische Beziehungen zu Walter Pater* (Bonn, 1913), 26. Bock is quoting a letter to him from Robert Ross.

Chapter III

1 Hunter Blair, 126.
2 Harris, 33.
3 *The Picture of Dorian Gray*, ed. Isobel Murray (1974), 132.
4 Lord Ronald Gower, *My Reminiscences*, 2 vols (1883), II: 134.
5 Mason, 62–4.
6 Lady W, letter to Wilde [Mar 1876) (Clark).
7 Hunter Blair, 134–5; *The Biograph* IV: 133.
8 *Letters*, 24.
9 Both letters at Clark.
10 *Letters*, 16.
11 W. W. Ward, 'An Oxford Reminiscence,' in Vyvyan Holland, *Son of Oscar Wilde* (N.Y., 1954), 219.
12 Bodley journal (Bodleian); *Letters*, 31.
13 Julian Hawthorne, diary 18 Feb 1880 (courtesy of Michael Bassan).
14 Source unknown: perhaps to Harold Boulton (see *Letters*, 62–3).
15 Geoffrey Faber, *Jowett, A Portrait with Background* (1957), 96.
16 Information from Alon Kadish, based on contemporary letters; Bodley journal (Bodleian).
17 'A Batch of Novels,' *Pall Mall Gazette*, 2 May 1887.
18 Marc-André Raffalovich, *Uranisme et unisexualité* (Lyon and Paris, 1896), 245.
19 *Letters*, 23.
20 Oscar Browning papers (Eastbourne).
21 Copy in Hyde Collection.
22 Atkinson, 562; Berenson papers (courtesy of Prof. Ernest Samuels); 'Phrases and Philosophies for the Use of the Young,' *Chameleon*, Dec 1894.
23 Oxford examinations (Bodleian).
24 *Letters*, 14.
25 Sladen, 110.
26 Ainslie, 93; Chesson, 394.
27 *Letters*, 15; Frank Benson, *My Memoirs*, 137–8.
28 *Letters*, 18.
29 Copy in Hyde Collection.
30 *Letters*, 20; *The Artist as Critic*, 341.
31 *Letters*, 20.
32 Letter signed 'Le T', misdated 1 Nov 1877 (for 1 Nov 1876; Thursfield was proctor from 1 Jan 1876 to 1 June 1877) (*Oxford University Register*).
33 Atkinson, 561.
34 *Letters*, 30–1.
35 In Catalogue no. 429 of Ivor L. Poole, Ltd. (1951), item 415 is a letter from Wilde at Magdalen requesting photographs of these paintings.

36 *Letters*, 31.
37 *Letters*, 34.
38 Shane Leslie papers (TCD); G. A. Macmillan, letter to his father from Genoa, 28 Mar 1877, in possession of his grandson, W. S. G. Macmillan: Stanford and McDowell, *Mahaffy*, 41.
39 *Letters*, 35.
40 G. A. Macmillan, letter to his father, 28 Mar 1877.
41 G. A. Macmillan, letter to Margaret Macmillan, 29 Mar 1877 (courtesy of W. S. G. Macmillan).
42 *Letters*, 35.
43 A. Teixeira de Mattos, 'Stray Recollections,' in *Soil, A Magazine of Art* (N.Y.), Apr 1917, 156.
44 Charles Ricketts, *Self-Portrait*, comp. T. Sturge Moore, ed. Cecil Lewis (1939), 425.
45 [G. A. Macmillan], 'A Ride Across the Peloponnese,' *Edinburgh Monthly Magazine*, May 1878, 551–2, 561, 563.
46 George Fleming [pseud. of Constance Fletcher], *Mirage*, 3 vols (1877), II: 94; *Lady's Pictorial* (London), 7 July 1883.
47 Hunter Blair, 132–4.
48 Mason, 86.
49 *The Biograph* IV: 134.
50 W. W. Ward, in V. Holland, *Son of O.W.*, 220.
51 George Fleming, *Mirage* II: 91–2, 93; III: 26.
52 *Mirage* I: 93; II: 16–17; II: 91.

Chapter IV

1 President's Minute Book, Magdalen College.
2 [Raymond and] Ricketts, 35.
3 'The Grosvenor Gallery,' *Dublin University Magazine*, July 1873.
4 'The Grosvenor Gallery'; Henry James, *The Painter's Eye*, ed. John L. Sweeney (1956), 142.
5 'Secret Diary of a Lady of Fashion,' *Evening News*, 15 Nov 1920.
6 *Letters*, 39.
7 *Letters*, 40; Ruskin, *Fors Clavigera*, 2 July 1877.
8 *Letters*, 36–7.
9 Lord Alfred Douglas, *Oscar Wilde and Myself* (1914), 205.
10 *Letters*, 37–8.
11 Lord Houghton, letter to Wilde, 20 May 1877; W. M. Rossetti, letter to Wilde, 3 Aug 1877, both from a bound volume, 'Copies of 100 Letters to Oscar Wilde,' in my possession.
12 Pater's letters to Wilde are at Clark.
13 Quoted by Wilde in 'Mr Pater's Last Volume,' *The Speaker* I, no. 12 (22 Mar 1890): 319–20.
14 Letter to Ernest Radford, n.d., in unspecified Sotheby catalogue (item 555); Michael Field, 35; *The Artist as Critic*, 229–30.
15 [Bodley], *New York Times*, 20 Jan 1882.
16 *More Letters of Oscar Wilde*, ed. Rupert Hart-Davis (1985), 82.
17 Letter at Brasenose College, Oxford (courtesy of Bernard Richards).

18 [Raymond and] Ricketts, 37; Ross quoted in Bock, *Oscar Wildes ... Beziehungen zu ... Pater*, 11.
19 William Rothenstein, *Men and Memories* (N.Y., 1931), 139; O'Sullivan, 130; Michael Field, 121.
20 Thomas Wright, *The Life of Walter Pater*, 2 vols (1907), II: 126.
21 Lady W, letter to Wilde, n.d. (Clark).
22 *More Letters*, 26.
23 *Letters*, 23.
24 Sladen, 109; cf. Ainslie, 93.
25 Rhoda Broughton, *Second Thoughts* (1880), 187, 207, 9, 10, 188.
26 Wilde's partial authorship of this article in the *Athenaeum* is marked in the files of that periodical.
27 Raffalovich, 245–6.
28 *Letters*, 20–1. Wilde's copy of Mallock is now in the library of King's College, University of London.
29 *Letters*, 21; P. H. W. Almy, 'New Views of Mr Oscar Wilde,' *Theatre* n.s. XXII (Mar 1894): 119–27.
30 The copy of *Aurora Leigh* presented to Ward is at Magdalen. Cf. ch. II, n. 20.
31 *Letters*, 52.
32 Mason, 394–9.
33 Hunter Blair, 137–8.
34 *Letters*, 31.
35 In 1953, Maggs Catalogue no. 812 listed item 121 as a poem by Wilde, said to be 'probably' addressed to 'the prostitute from whom he caught syphilis.' It was included in a folio of letters belonging to the Queensberry family.
36 Lionel Johnson, copy of letter (Hart-Davis).
37 The Revd H. S. Bowden, letter to Wilde, 15 Apr 1878 (Clark).
38 André Raffalovich, 'Oscar Wilde,' *Blackfriars* VIII (1927), no. 92.
39 *The Picture of Dorian Gray*, ed. Murray, 132; O'Sullivan, 65.
40 Atkinson, 562; Ainslie, 93.
41 Robert Forman Horton, *An Autobiography* (1917), 44.
42 Margaret L. Woods, 'Oxford in the Seventies,' *Fortnightly* CL (1941), no. 282: 281–2.
43 Lady W, letter at Clark.
44 See article in the *Academy*, 17 Feb 1906.
45 *Letters*, 53.
46 [Bodley], *New York Times*, 20 Jan 1882.
47 Ethel Smyth, *Impressions That Remained*, 2 vols (1919), I: 115–17.

ADVANCES

Chapter V

1 *Letters*, 54, 74.
2 [Mrs] H. M. Swanwick (Helena Sickert), *I Have Been Young* (1935), 64–5.
3 Gower, *My Reminiscences* II: 320.
4 *Letters*, 720.
5 Farnell, *An Oxonian Looks Back*, 70–1.

6 Letter to A. H. Sayce, 28 May 1879 (Bodleian).

7 Wilde as reported in *New York Telegram*, 13 Jan 1882. Benson does not credit Wilde with any part in the undertaking.

8 *Letters*, 59

9 *Athenaeum*, 4 Sept 1880, 301–2: the section of the review identified as by Wilde (see above, ch. IV, n. 26) runs from 'Mr Jebb's article' to 'Athens.' E. R. Dodds's comment is from a letter to me.

10 *Letters*, 63.

11 *Letters*, 61.

12 Robert Sherard, *Twenty Years in Paris* (1905), 347.

13 Louise Jopling, *Twenty Years of My Life, 1867 to 1887* (1925), 79; Frank Benson, *My Memoirs*, 138; Mrs Julian Hawthorne in *Harper's Bazaar*, 18 June 1881.

14 *Letters*, 475.

15 Elizabeth Robins, *Both Sides of the Curtain* (1940), 9.

16 *Letters*, 62; Mrs Claude Beddington, *All That I Have Met* (1929), 34.

17 Beddington, 34–5; cf. Laura Troubridge, *Life Among the Troubridges*, ed. Jacqueline Hope-Nicholson (1966), 152.

18 Shane Leslie, *J. E. C. Bodley* (1930), 26.

19 Edwin A. Ward, *Recollections of a Savage* (1923), 111.

20 Lady Randolph Churchill, *Reminiscences* (1908), 105.

21 'Mrs Langtry as Hester Grazebrook,' *New York World*, 7 Nov 1882.

22 Noel B. Gerson, *Lillie Langtry* (1971), 54; Wilde reported in *Halifax Morning Herald*, 10 Oct 1882.

23 Bodley journal (Bodleian).

24 Lillie Langtry, *The Days I Knew* (1925), 86–7.

25 Gower, *My Reminiscences* II: 153.

26 [Raymond and] Ricketts, 29.

27 Raffalovich in *Blackfriars* (1927).

28 O'Sullivan, 175–6, and see *Some Letters of Vincent O'Sullivan to A. J. A. Symons* (Edinburgh, 1975).

29 Langtry, 97.

30 Langtry, 97.

31 *Letters*, 66n.

32 (Walford) Graham Robertson, *Time Was* (1931), 70.

33 Langtry, 96.

34 Langtry, 143.

35 Heinrich Felberman, *The Memoirs of a Cosmopolitan* (1932), 125.

36 Atkinson, 562.

37 'Should Geniuses Meet?', *Court and Society Review* IV (4 May 1887): 413–14.

38 From 'Copies of 100 Letters to O.W.', in my possession.

39 Jopling, 78.

40 Ada Leverson, 'The Last First Night,' *New Criterion*, Jan 1926, 148–53.

41 W. W. Ward, in V. Holland, *Son of O.W.*, 220.

42 Violet Hunt, *The Flurried Years* (1926), 13.

43 Sherard, *O.W.: Story of an Unhappy Friendship*, 13.

44 'Literary and Other Notes,' *Woman's World*, Jan 1888.

45 Langtry, 123.

46 [Raymond and] Ricketts, 16.
47 (James) Rennell Rodd, *Social and Diplomatic Memories, 1884–1893* (1922), 22–5.
48 V. Hunt, *Flurried Years*, 13; Walter Sichel, *The Sands of Time* (1923), 125.
49 Mason, 281.
50 *Letters*, 148.
51 *The Artist as Critic*, 308.
52 Denys Sutton, *Walter Sickert* (1976), 30.
53 Mason, 254.
54 Mme de Steiger, 'Oscar Wilde and His Mother,' *T.P.'s Weekly*, 25 Apr 1913.
55 *Letters*, 227–8n.
56 Wyndham, 107.
57 Max Beerbohm, *Letters to Reggie Turner*, ed. Rupert Hart-Davis (1964), 63; Cecil, 85.
58 Lady Augusta Fane, *Chit Chat* (1926), 103.
59 E. Smyth, *Impressions That Remained* I: 115.
60 *Jimmy Glover, His Book*, 15–16.
61 Mrs Julian Hawthorne in *Harper's Bazaar*.
62 *More Letters*, 33–4.
63 W. Schrickx, 'Oscar Wilde in Belgium', *Revue des langues vivantes* (Brussels), XXXVII (1971), nos 2/3, 117–256.
64 Wilde's 'Envoi' to Rennell Rodd, *Rose Leaf and Apple Leaf* (Phila., 1882), and Rodd's poem, 'Une heure viendra qui tout paiera,' p. 65.
65 Rodd, *Social and Diplomatic Memories*, 24.
66 *Letters*, 73; 'Envoi' to Rodd, *Rose Leaf and Apple Leaf.*
67 Sherard, *The Real O.W.*, 286.
68 Review in *Saunders's Irish Daily News*, 5 May 1879.
69 W. Rothenstein, 114; E. R. and J. Pennell, *The Whistler Journal* (Phila., 1921), 34.
70 Ellen Terry, *Memoirs*, ed. Edith Craig and Christopher St John (1933), 231.
71 Whistler, two undated letters to Wilde in 'Copies of 100 Letters to O.W.', in my possession; 'Oscar Wilde MSS,' *Pall Mall Gazette*, 5 July 1911.
72 Sladen, 65.
73 Pearson, *Life of O.W.*, 97.
74 Lewis and Smith, 46.
75 *New York World*, 8 Jan 1882.
76 E. R. and J. Pennell, *The Life of James McNeill Whistler* (1911), 724; Leonée Ormond, *George du Maurier* (1969), 468–9.
77 Hesketh Pearson, *Gilbert, His Life and Strife* (1957), 110.
78 Rodd, *Social and Diplomatic Memories*, 22.
79 Margot Asquith, *More Memories* (1933), 120.
80 Mason, 285.
81 Mrs Julian Hawthorne in *Harper's Bazaar*.
82 Said during his American tour.
83 Richard Le Gallienne, 'Mr Wilde's Whim,' *Daily Chronicle*, 23 May 1892; *Punch*, 23 July and 12 Nov 1881.
84 Rodd's view, expressed in a letter of the time, is somewhat modified in his

Social and Diplomatic Memories, 22. Oscar Browning's review is in the *Academy* XX (30 July 1881): 103–4.

85 J. A. Symonds, draft of a letter to Wilde [1881], sold by a bookseller.
86 Henry Newbolt, *My World as in My Time* (1932), 96–7.
87 *More Letters*, 37, 102–3.
88 Letter at Clark.
89 Sherard, *The Real O.W.*, 110–11; also a MS (Hyde).
90 *Frank Harris, His Life and Adventures* (1947), 303; E. A. Ward, *Recollections of a Savage*, 110–11.
91 Frank Miles, letter to Mrs Boughton, [1886] (Clark).

Chapter VI

1 W. F. Morse, 'American Lectures,' in *The Works of Oscar Wilde*, Edition De Luxe (Boston and N.Y., 1909), in the unnumbered volume containing *His Life*, 73–5. The letter from Morse is at Morgan.
2 *Jimmy Glover, His Book*, 20.
3 *The World*, 30 Nov 1881.
4 TS copy at Clark.
5 *The World*, 30 Nov 1881; James McNeill Whistler, *The Gentle Art of Making Enemies* (1904), 243; 'Oscar Wilde MSS,' *Pall Mall Gazette*, 5 July 1911.
6 Sherard, *The Real O.W.*, 288.
7 James Russell Lowell, *Letters*, ed. M. de Wolfe Howe (New Haven, Conn. and London, 1932), 262.
8 Rodd, *Social and Diplomatic Memories*, 22–5.
9 Lewis and Smith, 209.
10 *The Picture of Dorian Gray*, ed. Murray, 95.
11 *Philadelphia Press*, 17 Jan 1882.
12 *New York World*, 3 Jan 1882.
13 *Letters*, 509.
14 *New York World*, 3 Jan 1882.
15 Ann Thwaite, *Edmund Gosse* (1985), 211.
16 Mrs Thomas Bailey Aldrich, *Crowding Memories* (1921), 246.
17 Clara Barrus, *The Life and Letters of John Burroughs*, 2 vols (Boston, 1925), II: 106.
18 Maud Howe Elliott, *Uncle Sam Ward and His Circle* (N.Y., 1938), 602–9: Sam Ward Papers, p. 444 (NYPL); *New York Times*, 6 Jan 1882.
19 Lewis and Smith, 382.
20 Helen Potter, *Impersonations* (N.Y., 1891), 195–7.
21 *Cincinnati Daily Gazette*, 21 Feb 1882.
22 Mark Edward Perugini, *Victorian Days and Ways* (1932), 244.
23 Sherard, *The Real O.W.*, 336.
24 *Letters*, 86.
25 *Philadelphia Press*, 17 Jan 1882; for Wilde on Poe, see *The Artist as Critic*, 28.
26 Whitman letters at Texas.
27 *Philadelphia Press*, 19 Jan 1882.
28 *Cincinnati Daily Gazette*, 21 Feb 1882; *Philadelphia Press*, 19 Jan 1882.
29 Ainslie, 96. See also Whitman, letter to Henry Stafford, 25 Jan 1882, in

Whitman, *The Correspondence*, ed. E. H. Miller, 5 vols (N.Y. 1961–9): III, 1876–1885, 264.

30 Horace Traubel, *With Walt Whitman in Camden* (N.Y., 1914), 11.
31 *The Swinburne Letters*, ed. Cecil Y. Lang (New Haven, Conn., 1960–2), IV: 255; quoted *Letters*, 99–100.
32 George Ives journal, 6 Jan 1901, p. 4305 (Texas).
33 From a bookseller's catalogue (Hart-Davis).
34 'The Gospel according to Walt Whitman,' *Pall Mall Gazette*, 25 Jan 1889; Traubel, *With Whitman in Camden*, 284.

Chapter VII

1 Letter at Clark.
2 Archibald Forbes, letter to Miss Flossie, 15 Jan 1882 (Clark).
3 *Letters*, 89; Morse in *Works*, 80.
4 *Letters*, 89.
5 Lewis and Smith, 205.
6 *Washington Post*, 21 Jan 1882; *New York Times*, 23 July 1883.
7 *The Artist as Critic*, 276.
8 *Letters*, 102.
9 *Swinburne Letters* IV: 166; quoted *Letters*, 100n.
10 Mrs Bodley, 'For Remembrance' IV, pt. i: 648–9 (Bodleian).
11 *Philadelphia Press*, 13 June 1882; O'Sullivan, 176.
12 Mrs Henry Adams, *Letters*, ed. Ward Thoron (1937), 338.
13 Leon Edel, *Henry James: The Middle Years* (Phila., 1962), 31.
14 Edel, *H. J.: The Middle Years*, 31; Ernest Samuels, *Henry Adams: The Middle Years* (Cambridge, Mass., 1958), 164; Mrs Henry Adams, *Letters*, 342.
15 *Cincinnati Daily Gazette*, 21 Feb 1882.
16 *Our Continent*, 15 Mar 1882; *Washington Post*, 21 Jan 1882.
17 *More Letters*, 47; and cf. Maud Howe Elliott, *This Was My Newport* (Cambridge, Mass., 1944).
18 *Letters*, 94n; Chris Healy, *Confessions of a Journalist* (1904), 130–8.
19 *Boston Sunday Herald*, 29 Jan 1882.
20 Letter to John Boyle O'Reilly, n.d. (Hart-Davis).
21 Morse in *Works*, 81.
22 Morse in *Works*, 82; Ross's correction to Harris (Hyde).
23 *Letters*, 122n.
24 Lewis and Smith, 155–6.
25 *Rochester Democrat and Chronicle*, 8 Feb 1882.
26 *Boston Sunday Herald*, 25 Jan 1882.
27 Letter to Miss Selwyn, Oct 1887, Frances Edwards Catalogue no. 560 (Ledger-Ross Collection, Bodleian).
28 *Iowa State Register* (Des Moines), 27 Apr 1882.
29 Thompson, *Eugene Field* I: 171–2; Charles H. Dennis, *Eugene Field's Creative Years* (N.Y., 1924), 213.
30 *Omaha Weekly Herald*, 24 Mar 1882.
31 Account book in the Arends Collection, NYPL.
32 Letter at Yale.
33 'Oscar Wilde,' *Chicago Tribune*, 14 Feb 1882; *Omaha Weekly Herald*, 24 Mar

1882; *Freeman's Journal* (Dublin), 11 July 1883; *New York Times*, 24 Mar 1883.

34 *New York Herald*, 10 Feb 1882; *Boston Globe*, 10 Feb 1882.

35 *New York Tribune*, 12 Feb 1882.

36 *New York World*, 18 June 1882: *St Paul Globe*, 18 June 1882.

37 Hyde, *Oscar Wilde*, 71; *Philadelphia Press*, 9 May 1882.

38 *Daily Examiner* (San Francisco), 27 Mar 1882.

39 *Irish Poets of the Nineteenth Century*, ed. Robert D. Pepper (San Francisco, 1972), 33.

40 Unidentified clipping at Clark.

41 *Saratoga Weekly Journal*, 20 July 1882; *Atlanta Constitution*, 5 July 1882; *Letters*, 122.

42 Lewis and Smith, 180; *Cincinnati Daily Gazette*, 21 Feb 1882.

43 Lewis and Smith, 256, 261.

44 Kevin O'Brien, *Oscar Wilde in Canada* (Toronto, 1982), 67; Lewis and Smith, 362.

45 Martin Birnbaum, *Oscar Wilde, Fragments and Memories* (1920), 28–9.

46 See Sherard, *The Real O.W.*, 169, Brookfield on the incident.

47 *Swinburne Letters* IV: 312.

48 *New York Times*, 20 Sept 1882; *Andrew's American Queen*, 23 Sept 1882.

49 *Boston Globe*, 16 Oct 1882; *Times and Transcript* (Moncton), Diamond Jubilee, July 1954.

50 *New York Tribune*, 29 Dec 1882; *New York Times*, 29 Dec 1882. Letter to John Boyle O'Reilly sold Parke-Bernet, 6 Mar 1945 (Hart-Davis).

51 Sherard, letter to A. J. A. Symons, 13 May 1937 (Clark).

52 *Atlanta Constitution*, 6 July 1882.

53 *Letters*, 115.

54 *Letters*, 115.

55 George E. Woodberry, letter to Charles Eliot Norton, 25 Apr 1882 (Houghton).

56 *Letters*, 108.

57 M. H. Elliott, *This Was My Newport*; *Andrew's American Queen*, 17 June, 15 and 29 July 1882.

58 Isabel Field, *This Life I've Loved* (1937), 139–44.

59 *Letters*, 111–14; *Impressions of America*, ed. Stuart Mason (Sunderland, 1906), 30–3; *The World*, 7 Mar 1883.

60 *Letters*, 119.

61 Birnbaum, photograph opp. p. 26.

62 Lady W, letter to Wilde, [Oct?] 1882 (Clark).

63 O'Brien, *O.W. in Canada*, 128.

64 Langtry, 93.

65 Birnbaum, 27.

66 *New York Tribune*, 31 Oct 1882.

67 Ledger papers (Bodleian); *The Bookfellow* (Australia), 15 Nov 1914.

68 'Mrs Langtry as Hester Grazebrook,' *New York World*, 7 Nov 1882.

69 Undated item in *Society*.

70 Mary Anderson, *A Few More Memories* (1926), 20; *Letters*, 125, 126.

71 Letters to Steele Mackaye in Percy Mackaye, *Epoch: The Life of Steele Mackaye* (N.Y., 1927), 444, 445–6.

72 Mackaye, *Epoch*, 446; letter to Steele Mackaye, [11 Oct 1882] (Taylor Collection, Princeton).
73 Edgar Saltus, *Oscar Wilde, An Idler's Impressions* (Chicago, 1917), 14–15; Lewis and Smith, 410.
74 Saltus, 15.
75 O'Sullivan, 11; *New York Tribune*, 28 Dec 1882, 10 Jan 1883, 4 Feb 1883.

Chapter VIII

1 Letter to Waldo Story, [31 Jan 1883] (Manuscript Room, NYPL).
2 Rodd, *Social and Diplomatic Memories*, 25; Birnbaum, 14; Sherard, *Life of O.W.*, 215–16; *Letters*, 144.
3 Sherard, *The Real O.W.*, 51.
4 Sherard, *O.W.: Story of an Unhappy Friendship*, 25, 58.
5 Wilde's notes (NYPL: Berg); Birnbaum, 14; Sherard, *O.W.: Story of an Unhappy Friendship*, 24.
6 *The Artist as Critic*, 30.
7 Sherard, *The Real O.W.*, 22–5, 67.
8 Sherard, *O.W.: Story of an Unhappy Friendship*, 59, 20.
9 Sherard, *The Real O.W.*, 36.
10 Sherard, letter to A. J. A. Symons, 3 June 1937 (Clark); Robert Pepper called this to my attention.
11 Louis Latourette, 'Dernières heures avec Oscar Wilde,' *Nouvelles Littéraires*, 5 Dec 1928.
12 Augustus John, *Chiaroscuro: Fragments of Autobiography: First Series* (1952), 433–4.
13 Sherard, letter to A. J. A. Symons, 31 May 1937 (Clark).
14 Letter from W. R. Rodgers (Hart-Davis); Sherard, letter to Symons, 31 May 1937 (Clark); Raffalovich in *Blackfriars* (1927).
15 Sherard, *The Real O.W.*, 251.
16 Wilde's notes (NYPL: Berg).
17 Walter Sickert, *A Free House!* . . . (1947), 44.
18 Sherard, *The Real O.W.*, 200.
19 *The Artist as Critic*, 325.
20 Jopling, 80.
21 Wilde's notes (NYPL: Berg).
22 E. Terry, *Memoirs*, 253; *Truth*, 4 Oct 1883.
23 Sherard, *O.W.: Story of an Unhappy Friendship*, 72.
24 Robert Merle, *Oscar Wilde* (Paris, 1984), 83–4, compares the verse form of 'The Sphinx' to a serpent.
25 O'Sullivan, 231.
26 *Letters*, 139.
27 Swanwick, 66–7.
28 Sherard, *The Real O.W.*, 238.
29 Mary Anderson, letter to Wilde, n.d. (owned by the Players) (Hart-Davis).
30 Sherard, *O.W.: Story of an Unhappy Friendship*, 68.
31 Wilde's notes (NYPL: Berg).
32 *Letters*, 145; Wilde's notes (NYPL: Berg).
33 Sherard, *O.W.: Story of an Unhappy Friendship*, 50.
34 *More Letters*, 53.

Chapter IX

1 Mackaye, *Epoch*, 452; original letter is at Dartmouth.
2 *Letters*, 147–8; *The World*, 23 May 1883.
3 Violet Hunt, draft of her autobiography (Hart-Davis); letter to Wilde, July 1881 (Hyde Collection); Douglas Goldring, *South Lodge* (1943), 187.
4 Harry Phillips, son-in-law of Charlotte Montefiore, letter to Sir Rupert Hart-Davis, 14 Sept 1960.
5 *T.P.'s Weekly*, 30 May 1913.
6 Unidentified clipping.
7 Otho Holland (Lloyd), letter to A. J. A. Symons, 27 May 1937 (Clark).
8 Constance Lloyd, letter to Otho Lloyd, 7 June 1881, in *Letters*, 152n.
9 Lady W, letter to Wilde, [Dec 1882] (Clark).
10 *Letters*, 143.
11 *New York Herald*, 21–26 Aug 1883.
12 *The Globe* (London), 2 July 1882; *Lady's Pictorial*, 7 July 1883.
13 *New York Herald*, 12 Aug 1883.
14 Kenneth Rose, *Superior Person* (1969), 72.
15 *New York Times*, 12 Aug 1883.
16 *New York Times*, 28 Aug 1883.
17 *New York Times*, 29 Aug 1883.
18 Morse in *Works*, 165.
19 Constance Lloyd, letter to Wilde, 11 Nov 1883 (Hyde).
20 Constance Lloyd, letters to Otho Lloyd, 23 and 24 Nov 1883, in *Letters*, 152–3.
21 Constance Lloyd, letter to Otho Lloyd, 26 Nov 1883, in *Letters*, 153.
22 Otho Lloyd, letter to Wilde, 27 Nov 1883, in *Letters*, 153n.
23 Constance Lloyd, letter to Wilde, n.d. [1883] (Hyde).
24 *Letters*, 154.
25 Otho Lloyd, Holland family papers; Constance Lloyd, letter to Wilde, n.d. [early Dec 1883] (Hyde).
26 *Letters*, 155.
27 Constance Lloyd, letter to Wilde, 4 Jan 1884 (Hyde).
28 Otho Holland (Lloyd) to A. J. A. Symons, 27 Nov 1937 (Clark).
29 Willie Wilde, letter to Constance Lloyd; Lady W, letter to Wilde, both 27 Nov 1883 (Clark).
30 Sir Johnston Forbes-Robertson, *A Player Under Three Reigns* (1925), 110.
31 Sherard, letter to A. J. A. Symons, 3 June [1937] (Clark).
32 *Morning News*, article headed 'Paris, Tuesday June 10, 1884' (Clark).
33 *Life* (London), 19 June 1884.
34 Vernon Lee (pseud. of Violet Paget), *Letters*, ed. I. C. Willis (1937), letter of 8 June 1884 to her mother, p. 143.
35 Robert Baldick, *The Life of J.-K. Huysmans* (Oxford, 1955), 88; *Morning News*, 20 June 1884 (Clark).
36 Raffalovich, 246.
37 E. A. Brayley Hodgett, *Moss from a Rolling Stone* (1924), 130.

Chapter X

1 W. Rothenstein, 358; 'Phrases and Philosophies for the Use of the Young,' *Chameleon*, Dec 1894.

2 L. B. Walford, *Memories of Victorian London* (1912), 147–53, 230–3.
3 Jopling, 79, 82.
4 Hyde, *O.W.*, 121–3; a fuller account by him is in the Hyde Collection.
5 'A Handbook to Marriage,' *Pall Mall Gazette*, 18 Nov 1885.
6 Kernahan, 217.
7 A. de Brémont, *O.W. and His Mother*, 89; *Life Among the Troubridges*, 169.
8 Jopling, 80.
9 Hyde Collection.
10 Trevor Blackmore, *The Art of Herbert Schmalz* (1911), 43–4.
11 *Staffordshire Sentinel*, 6 Nov 1884.
12 *Edinburgh Courant*, 22 Dec 1884.
13 *York Herald*, 10 Oct 1884.
14 Hunter Blair, 138.
15 *Letters*, 295.
16 *Letters*, 165.
17 Harris, 337–8.
18 Beddington, 41.
19 *Letters*, 180; '*As You Like It* at Coombe House,' *Dramatic Review*, 6 June 1885.
20 J. H. Badley, *Memories and Reflections* (1955), 78–9; *Letters*, 181, 184–5; 'Literary and Other Notes,' *Woman's World*, Jan 1888.
21 Don C. Seitz, *Whistler Stories* (N.Y., 1913), 66–7; Pearson, *Life of O.W.*, 96.
22 [Raymond and] Ricketts, 29.
23 *Letters*, 170–1 and n.
24 *Letters*, 191 and n.; 'Mr Oscar Wilde at Mr Whistler's,' *The Bat*, 29 Nov 1887.
25 Reginald Turner, letter to A. J. A. Symons, 26 Aug 1935 (Clark).
26 Letter in Manuscript Room, NYPL.
27 Osbert Sitwell, *Noble Essences* (1950), 100.
28 A. J. A. Symons, letter to Reginald Turner, 28 Aug 1935; Turner to Symons, 26 Aug 1935 (both at Clark); Arthur Ransome, *Oscar Wilde: A Critical Study* (1912), 32.
29 *Letters*, 720.
30 Ada Leverson, *Letters to the Sphinx from Oscar Wilde and Reminiscences of the Author* (1930), 48–9.
31 J.-J. Renaud, 'Oscar Wilde tel que je l'ai "entendu,"' *Carrefour*, 8 Oct 1904.
32 Otho Holland (Lloyd), letter to Arthur Ransome, 28 Feb 1912 (Hart-Davis).
33 Jopling, 82.

EXALTATIONS

Chapter XI

1 'Should Geniuses Meet?', *Court and Society Review* IV, no. 148 (4 May 1887): 413–14, in Mason, 38.
2 Raffalovich in *Blackfriars* (1927).
3 Marc-André Raffalovich, *A Willing Exile*, 2 vols (1890), I. 88–9.
4 Jopling, 79, 82; *Letters*, 277.

5 Sir Isaiah Berlin told me of hearing these remarks by Wilde from Bernard Berenson, and Prof. Ernest Samuels confirmed that Berenson had noted them down.

6 *Pall Mall Gazette*, 17 Apr 1888.

7 Anne Clark Amor, *Mrs Oscar Wilde* (1983), 72, 76–9; Jopling, 305.

8 Chatterton lecture, poem by Chatterton (MS Clark; additional punctuation for the sake of clarity).

9 'A Note on Some Modern Poets,' *Woman's World*, Dec 1888.

10 'The Poet's Corner,' *Pall Mall Gazette*, 6 Apr 1888.

11 'Mr Pater's Imaginary Portraits,' *Pall Mall Gazette*, 11 June 1887.

12 Almy, 'New Views of Mr O.W.' in *Theatre* (1894), 124.

13 G. B. Shaw, letter to Frank Harris, 7 Oct 1908 (Texas). Shaw's diary indicates that the discussion with Wilde on socialism took place at the home of Fitzgerald Molloy, and Mrs Belloc Lowndes dates it. Sir Bernard Partridge, letter to Hesketh Pearson, 30 Sept 1943 (Holroyd), describes the scene.

14 R. Ross, letter to Frank Harris, 2 May 1914 (Texas).

15 N.F., 'Oscar Wilde as Editor,' *Cassell's Weekly*, n.d. (Clark); Yeats, *Autobiography*, 87–8.

16 Harris, 337–8.

17 Quoted in Beddington, 41.

18 '*As You Like It* at Coombe House,' *Dramatic Review*, 6 June 1885.

19 Cf. *Letters*, 185.

20 'Mr Whistler's Ten O'Clock,' *Pall Mall Gazette*, 21 Feb 1885.

21 E. F. Benson, *As We Were*, 244–5.

22 Swanwick, 66.

23 M. Asquith, *More Memories*, 116.

24 Ross, correction to Harris (Hyde).

25 Yeats, *Autobiography*, 87–8; MS draft of *Four Years* (family papers).

26 Epigrams in Hyde Collection.

27 Yeats, *Autobiography*, 181.

28 See Yeats's inscription in John Quinn's copy of *The Land of Heart's Desire* (NYPL: Berg). That Wilde 'all but saw the Grail' is from an interview by Sybil Bristow, 'Mr W. B. Yeats, Poet and Mystic,' *Daily Mail and Record*, 4 Apr 1913.

Chapter XII

1 Richard Le Gallienne, quoting Wilde, in a review of *Intentions*, *Academy*, 4 July 1891.

2 Michael Field, 136–7.

3 *The Artist as Critic*, 351; Michael Field, 139; Walter Pater, 'A Novel by Mr Oscar Wilde,' *Bookman*, Nov 1891.

4 W. Rothenstein, 187.

5 [Raymond and] Ricketts, 28; Frank Liebich, 'Oscar Wilde,' a TS at Clark.

6 Lionel Johnson, letter of 5 Feb 1891 (Hart-Davis); Ernest Dowson, *Letters*, ed. Desmond Flower and Henry Maas (1947), 182.

7 *Shaw: An Autobiography*, selected from his writings by Stanley Weintraub (1970), 50.

8 Lionel Johnson, letter to Arthur Galton, 18 Feb 1890 (Hart-Davis).
9 Anon., 'Wilde as I Saw Him,' *Book Lover*, 1 Dec 1914.
10 Leverson, 42.
11 Maxwell, *Time Gathered*, 97.
12 Notes (NYPL: Berg).
13 [Raymond and] Ricketts, 17.
14 Pearson, *Life of O. W.*, 145.
15 A. Conan Doyle, *Memories and Adventures* (1924), 78–80.
16 Sir Peter Chalmers Mitchell, *My Fill of Days* (1937), 183–4.
17 *The Picture of Dorian Gray*, ed. Murray, 246–7.
18 See the valuable introduction and notes to Isobel Murray's edition of *The Picture of Dorian Gray*.
19 'Ainsi ses tendances vers l'artifice, ses besoins d'excentricité, n'étaient-ils pas, en somme, des résultats d'études spécieuses, de raffinements extra-terrestres, des spéculations quasi théologiques; c'étaient, au fond, des transports, des élans vers un idéal, vers un univers inconnu, vers un béatitude lointaine, désirable comme celle que nous promettant des Écritures.' J.-K. Huysmans, *A Rebours* (Paris, 1965), 114.
20 David Bispham, *A Quaker Singer's Recollections* (N.Y., 1920), 150; Lady W, letter to Wilde, [June 1890] (Clark).
21 Elizabeth Longford, *A Pilgrimage of Passion: The Life of Wilfrid Scawen Blunt* (1979), 290–1; Harris, 306–7.
22 *Letters*, 257–70 *passim*.
23 Desmond Chapman-Huston, *The Lost Historian: A Memoir of Sir Sidney Low* (1936), 68–73.
24 Original title from a note in Hyde Collection.
25 *Letters*, 343, 288.
26 Kernahan, 213.
27 Robert Sherard, 'Aesthete and Realist,' *Morning Journal*, 22 Mar 1891; Max Beerbohm, 'Oscar Wilde,' *Anglo-American Times*, 25 Mar 1893.
28 D. S. MacColl, 'A Batch of Memories – Walter Pater,' *Week-end Review*, 12 Dec 1931; Walter Pater, 'A Novel by Mr Oscar Wilde,' *Bookman*, Nov 1891, 59–61.
29 Lionel Johnson, 'In Honorem Doriani Creatorisque Eius,' *Complete Poems*, ed. Iain Fletcher (1953), 246.
30 Lord Alfred Douglas, letter to A. J. A. Symons, 8 July 1930 (Clark); *Letters*, 281.
31 *Daily Telegraph*, 18 Apr 1913.
32 Henry D. Davray, *Oscar Wilde: la tragédie finale* (Paris, 1928), 19.
33 Frank Harris, letter to Wilde, offered as item no. 1139, in Maggs Catalogue (1951).
34 Sichel, *Sands of Time*, 125; George Lukàcs, *The Meaning of Contemporary Realism* (1963), 132.
35 A letter from Constance Wilde to the editor, *Pall Mall Gazette*, 21 Nov 1891, says, 'I should be very much obliged if you would insert a paragraph in your paper denying the assertion that any of our silver has been identified amongst the spoil of the burglaries on view at the King's-Cross Police Station. I receive many letters on the subject but unfortunately I get nothing else.'

36 E. Robins, *Both Sides of the Curtain*, 12–22.
37 *More Letters*, 85–6.
38 Harris, 97.
39 Hesketh Pearson, letter to Rupert Croft-Cooke, 18 June 1962, says Ross told him about stopover at Selby on the way back from Windermere (Texas).
40 'Wilde as I Saw Him,' *Book Lover*, 1 Dec 1914.
41 '*The Cenci*,' *Dramatic Review*, 15 May 1886.
42 George Alexander, quoted in *Evening Standard*, 29 Nov 1913, and *Liverpool Echo*, 8 Dec 1913.
43 Frederic Whyte, *William Heinemann* (1928), 83–5.

Chapter XIII

1 André Gide, *Oscar Wilde* (Paris, 1938), 14.
2 *Letters*, 287–8.
3 Whistler's letter to Mallarmé of 2 Nov 1891, and telegram of 3 Nov, from *Mallarmé-Whistler: Correspondance*, ed. C. P. Barbier (Paris, 1962), 98–9, 102–3.
4 Eileen Souffrin, 'La Rencontre de Wilde et de Mallarmé,' *Revue de Littérature comparée* XXIII, no. 4 (Oct–Dec 1959), 533; Guy Chastel, *J.-K. Huysmans et ses amis* (Paris, 1957), 263.
5 *Letters*, 298n.
6 Gédéon Spilett, *Gil Blas*, 22 Nov 1897.
7 Ross, preface to *Salome* (1912), xxiii.
8 Rose, *Superior Person*, 151.
9 Mrs Edgar Saltus, notes at Clark; O'Sullivan, 146; Saltus, 20.
10 Yvanhoe Rambosson, 'Oscar Wilde et Verlaine,' in *Comédia*, n.d. (Bibl. de l'Arsenal).
11 Ross, 'A Note on *Salome*,' in *Salome* (1912), xii.
12 Enrique Gomez Carrillo, *En Plena Bohemia*, in his *Obras Completas* (Madrid, n.d. [?1919–22]), XVI: 190ff.
13 Jean Lorrain, 'Salomé et les Poètes,' *La Journal* (Paris), 11 Feb 1896; Pierre Léon-Gauthier, *Jean Lorrain* (Paris, 1962), 370–1.
14 André Salmon in Louise Thomas, *L'Esprit d'Oscar Wilde* (Paris, 1920).
15 O'Sullivan, 33.
16 Gomez Carrillo, XVI: 214.
17 Guillot de Saix, 'Oscar Wilde chez Maeterlinck,' *Les Nouvelles Littéraires*, 25 Oct 1945.
18 Jules Renard, *Journal* (Paris, 1925), Dec 1891, p. 131; Jean Lorrain, *Sensations et souvenirs* (Paris, 1895).
19 Pierre Champion, *Marcel Schwob et son temps* (Paris, 1927), 99; O'Sullivan, 75–6.
20 Léon Daudet, *Memoirs*, ed. and trans. A. K. Griggs (N.Y., 1925), 200.
21 Philippe Jullian, *Oscar Wilde* (Paris, 1967), 246.
22 Stuart Merrill, *Prose et vers: Oeuvres posthumes* (Paris, 1925), 142–5; G. Spilett in *Gil Blas*, 22 Nov 1897.
23 Ernest Raynaud, *Souvenirs sur le symbolisme* (Paris, 1895), 393–7.
24 Ainslie, 178; Jean Lorrain, *Sensations et souvenirs*.
25 E. Raynaud, *Souvenirs sur le symbolisme*, 398–9.

26 Bungalow Catalogue no. 4, item 387, n.d. (Ross Collection, Bodleian).
27 Shane Leslie, *J. E. C. Bodley*, 18; W. Rothenstein, 93.
28 J.-J. Renaud, preface to his translation of *Intentions* (Paris, 1905), viii–xii.
29 Mrs T. P. O'Connor, *I Myself* (1910), 238; Coulson Kernahan, 'Oscar Wilde as I Knew Him,' TS at Clark.
30 Jean Lorrain, *Sensations et souvenirs*.
31 Inscribed copy of *The House of Pomegranates* (Hart-Davis).
32 Jules Renard, *Journal*, 107.
33 André Gide, *Oeuvres complètes* (Paris, 1932–9) XIII: 57. See also Richard Ellmann, *Golden Codgers* (1973), 81–100.
34 Gide, *Oeuvres complètes* III: 476–7.
35 Wilde's remark to Berenson is in the Berenson papers (courtesy of Prof. Ernest Samuels); that about creation was made to George Ives, who recorded it in his journal (Texas).
36 Gide, *Oeuvres complètes* III: 482.
37 Guillot de Saix, 'Souvenirs inédits', in *L'Européen*, n.d., 141.
38 Yeats, *Autobiography*, 91.
39 Jean Lorrain, *Heures de casse* (Paris, 1905), 31.
40 Edmond Jaloux, *Les Saisons littéraires* (Paris, 1950), 170–1.
41 André Gide, *Journal 1889–1939* (Paris: Pléiade edn, 1939), 28.
42 *Letters*, 476; Gide, *Journal*, 49.
43 Kernahan, 222–3.
44 *The Artist as Critic*, 270; and see *Letters*, 476–80.
45 Gide, *Oeuvres complètes* II: 84.
46 Quoted in *The Times* (London), 19 Jan 1922.

Chapter XIV

1 Sherard, *The Real O.W.*, 321; Hesketh Pearson, *The Pilgrim Daughters* (1961), 185, on the basis of information from Sherard.
2 *Letters*, 331–2.
3 Graham Robertson, 135.
4 *New York Times*, 28 Feb 1892; Leon Edel, *Henry James: The Treacherous Years* (1969), 39–40.
5 *Letters*, 313.
6 Harris, 98–9; Shaw, letter to Wilde, quoted in Sotheby Catalogue, 27 July 1911, item 220.
7 Richard Whittington-Egan and Geoffrey Smerdon, *The Quest of the Golden Boy: The Life and Letters of Richard Le Gallienne* (1960), 181.
8 Jopling, 81.
9 J.-J. Renaud, preface to *Intentions*, xv.
10 Royal General Theatrical Fund, report of speech 26 May 1892, George Alexander in the chair (NYPL: Berg).
11 Charles Hawtrey, *The Truth at Last*, ed. W. Somerset Maugham (1924), 221–7.
12 Beerbohm quotes this in *Letters to Turner*, 287.
13 *Letters*, 834; unidentified interview with Bernhardt, 8 July 1892 (Hyde). The copy of Wilde's *Poems* inscribed to her is in the Taylor Collection, Princeton.
14 Ross, letter to *Saturday Review*, 27 May 1895.
15 [Raymond and] Ricketts, 53.

16 Graham Robertson, 125–7.
17 *Pall Mall Budget* XL (30 June 1892); *New York Times*, 18 July 1892; Maurice Sisley, 'La *Salomé* de M. Oscar Wilde,' *Le Gaulois*, 29 June 1892.
18 Beerbohm, *Letters to Turner*, 22–3, 38.
19 *Pall Mall Budget*, 30 June 1892.
20 *Letters*, 333.
21 From 'Copies of 100 Letters to O.W.,' in my possession.
22 W. Rothenstein, 184; Squire Bancroft, *Empty Chairs* (1925), 112–13; Beerbohm, *Letters to Turner*, 36.
23 Robert Ross, *Aubrey Beardsley* (1909), 88; [Raymond and] Ricketts, 51–2.
24 Douglas, *O.W. and Myself*, 73.
25 H. Montgomery Hyde, ed., *The Trials of Oscar Wilde* (1948), 213.
26 Jopling, 81.
27 Michael Holroyd, *Lytton Strachey: The Unknown Years* (1967), 319.
28 Lady W, letter to Wilde, n.d. [1893] (Clark 2381).
29 Hesketh Pearson, *Beerbohm Tree: His Life and Laughter* (1956), 65.
30 [Raymond and] Ricketts, 54.
31 O'Sullivan, 20–1; Julia Neilson, *This for Remembrance* (1941), 131.
32 Pearson, *Life of O.W.*, 237.
33 Beerbohm, *Letters to Turner*, 37.
34 *Boston Evening Transcript*, 11 Jan 1922; Guillot de Saix, 'Souvenirs inédits'.
35 Cheiro [Count Louis Hamon], *Cheiro's Memoirs: The Reminiscences of a Society Palmist* (Phila., 1913), 152–3.
36 *Letters*, 475, 577.
37 Guillot de Saix, 'Souvenirs inédits'.

Chapter XV

1 *Letters*, 281; the second inscribed copy of *Dorian Gray* is in the Taylor Collection, Princeton.
2 Ives journal (Texas).
3 Beerbohm, *Letters to Turner*, 38–9, 90–1.
4 *Daily Telegraph*, 18 Apr 1913.
5 *The Bat*, 15 and 22 Dec 1885.
6 Hyde, ed., *Trials of O.W.*, 298.
7 *Letters*, 311–12.
8 André Gide, *Si le grain ne meurt* in *Journal 1939–1949. Souvenirs* (Paris: Pléiade edn, 1966), 583.
9 Raffalovich in *Blackfriars* (1927).
10 Leverson, 19–20.
11 *Letters*, 334–5; H. P. Clive, *Pierre Louÿs, 1870–1925* (Oxford, 1978), 91.
12 Beerbohm, letter to R. Ross, n.d. (Hyde).
13 G. P. Jacomb-Hood, *With Brush and Pencil* (1924), 116.
14 Edmond and Jules de Goncourt, *Journal*, 4 vols (Paris, 1956), IV: 395.
15 P. Louÿs, letter to Wilde, 25 May 1893 (Bibl. Doucet, courtesy of H. P. Clive).
16 Gide, *O.W.*, 30–3.
17 A. Hamilton Grant, '"The Ephemeral": Some Memories of Oxford in the Nineties,' *Cornhill Magazine* LXXI (Dec 1931): 641–53. I have slightly abridged Grant's renderings of Wilde's stories.

18 Theodore Wratislaw, memoir of Wilde (Clark).
19 See *Letters*, 431.
20 *Letters*, 432–3.
21 Aubrey Beardsley, *Letters*, ed. Henry Maas, J. L. Duncan and W. G. Good (1970), 58.
22 Douglas, letter to John Lane, [Nov 1884] (Rosenbach).
23 Beerbohm, *Letters to Turner*, 84.
24 Oscar Browning, letter to Frank Harris, 3 Nov 1919 (Texas); Ross testimony during Crosland trial, *Daily News and Leader* (London), 2 July 1914; Beerbohm, *Letters to Turner*, 84.
25 *Davos Courier*, 13 Jan 1894.
26 *Letters*, 434–5.
27 Emma Calvé, *My Life* (1922), 97–8.

Chapter XVI

1 *Letters*, 358; Lady W, letter to Wilde, 29 Mar 1894 (Clark).
2 Wilfrid Scawen Blunt, *My Diaries*, Part I (N.Y., 1921), 145–6.
3 *Letters*, 352.
4 Ricketts, *Self-Portrait*, 124.
5 Arthur Roberts, *Fifty Years of Spoof* (1927), 64.
6 The scenario of *The Cardinal of Avignon* is given in Mason, 583–5. An earlier version, written in 1882, is at Dartmouth.
7 Swanwick, 68.
8 C. Dyett, 10 Glycena Road, Lavender Hill, [London] S.W., letter to Wilde, 28 Apr 1891 (Clark); Saltus, 18; Gertrude Pearce, letter in a Wilde notebook owned by Malcolm Pinhorn.
9 George Santayana, *The Middle Span* (N.Y., 1945), 60.
10 See Ross, letter to Frank Harris, 17 May 1914 (Texas).
11 *Letters*, 435.
12 Rupert Croft-Cooke, *Bosie* (Indianapolis and N.Y., 1963), 97.
13 *Letters*, 446.
14 Croft-Cooke, 98.
15 *Letters*, 445.
16 Berenson papers (courtesy of Prof. Ernest Samuels).
17 Gide, *O.W.*, 29.
18 *Letters*, 446; unidentified newspaper clipping (Ross Collection, Bodleian).
19 *Letters*, 438, 446; Harris, 132.
20 Douglas, letter to Ross quoted in *Daily Telegraph*, 19 Apr 1913.
21 [Raymond and] Ricketts, 15; P. P. Howe, *Dramatic Portraits* (1913).
22 Ross, interview with Wilde, *More Letters*, 196.
23 Cecil, *Max*, 321.
24 Leverson, 31.
25 *Letters*, 373.
26 Constance Wilde, letters to Arthur Humphreys in the Hyde Collection.
27 Queensberry letter in my possession.
28 *Letters*, 438.
29 *Letters*, 379.
30 Ives journal (Texas).

31 O'Sullivan, 106.
32 Charles Wyndham, letter to [H.A.] Jones, 18 Feb 1895 (Hart-Davis); *Letters*, 418–19 n.
33 *Letters*, 381; *More Letters*, 129.
34 Gide, *Si le grain ne meurt*, 581–96; Daniel Halévy, *My Friend Degas* (1966), 84–5.
35 Pearson, *Life of O.W.*, 257.
36 Beerbohm's copy of *The Importance of Being Earnest*, with his MS notes, is in the collection of Sir Rupert Hart-Davis.

DISGRACE

Chapter XVII

1 *Letters*, 509.
2 Marguerite Steen, *A Pride of Terrys: Family Saga* (1962), 206.
3 I am grateful to R. E. Alton for his study of Queensberry's handwriting, which enabled him to read for the first time correctly the message on Queensberry's card.
4 *Letters*, 526.
5 *Letters*, 384.
6 *Letters*, 493, 524; Ross, statement of evidence in his libel suit against Douglas, 1914.
7 Lord Alfred Douglas, *Autobiography* (1929), 59.
8 Marie Belloc Lowndes, *Diaries and Letters 1911–1947*, ed. Susan Lowndes (1971), 14.
9 Reginald Turner, letter to G. J. Renier, 22 Mar 1933 (Clark).
10 Marjoribanks, *Lord Carson*, 202: Sir Travers Humphrey, Foreword to Hyde, ed., *Trials of O.W.*, 8.
11 Ives journal (Texas).
12 F.A.K. Douglas, *The Sporting Queensberrys* (1942), 156.
13 Harris, 132–40.
14 Henri Perruchot, *Toulouse-Lautrec*, trans. Humphrey Ware (N.Y., 1966), 227.
15 Ralph Hodgson, *Poets Remembered* (Cleveland, O., 1967), 11.
16 Marjoribanks, *Lord Carson*, 230.
17 This account is based upon Hyde, ed., *Trials of O.W.*

Chapter XVIII

1 Oscar Browning, letter to Frank Harris, 3 Nov 1919 (Texas).
2 Ives journal, 7 Jan 1903, p. 4849 (Texas).
3 *Le Temps*, 7 Apr 1895.
4 *Letters*, 386.
5 Henry Harland, letter to Edmund Gosse, 5 May 1895 (Hart-Davis).
6 *Le Figaro*, 13 avril 1895, p. 59:
   On nous demande de différents côtés quels étaient les gens que fréquentaient M. Oscar Wilde durant ses séjours à Paris.
   Nous ne saurions renseigner nos correspondants que sur ses relations

577

purement littéraires, ce qui, peut-être, ne satisferait qu'imparfaitement leur curiosité. La vérité, c'est que M. Oscar Wilde était trés fêté dans plusieurs centres.

Ses familiers étaient, croyons-nous, dans le monde des lettres et des arts, MM. Jean Lorrain, Catulle Mendès, Marcel Schwob et autres écrivains subtils.

Le Figaro, 14 avril 1895, p. 1:

Il a paru, dans notre dernier *Supplément littéraire*, sous la signature de notre collaborateur M. Jules Huret, absent en ce moment, une note où notre éminent confrère, M. Catulle Mendès, était signalé comme ayant été l'un des 'familiers' de M. Oscar Wilde durant son séjour à Paris.

Il y a là une erreur de fait. M. Catulle Mendès n'a jamais eu de relations d'amitié avec M. Wilde, dont le talent ne lui inspirait au surplus qu'une fort mince estime. On nous dit que M. Catulle Mendès s'est montré fort irrité de cette note, en raison des circonstances où elle a été publiée.

Notre excellent confrère peut se rassurer: il est de ceux que certaines plaisanteries et certains malentendus ne peuvent atteindre.

Le Figaro, 16 avril 1895, p. 1:

Par l'écho que nous avions inséré dimanche et qui contenait les protestations de M. Catulle Mendès à l'encontre d'une note parue dans la *Petite Chronique des lettres* du samedi de notre collaborateur Jules Huret, nous avions espéré mettre fin à un regrettable malentendu causé par une boutade purement littéraire.

M. Catulle Mendès ayant adressé à M. Huret et publié le même jour, dans un journal du matin, la dépêche suivante, il est de notre devoir de reproduire, avec cette dépêche, la réponse de notre collaborateur.

Voici la dépêche de M. Mendès:

Monsieur,
Si vous avez voulu faire du reportage, vous êtes bien mal informé;
Si vous avez voulu être plaisant, vous êtes un imbécile.

CATULLE MENDÈS

13 avril 1895

M. Jules Huret a répondu:

Lundi, 5 heures

Monsieur,
J'arrive à l'instant de la campagne, et je trouve votre dépêche.

Dans ma *Petite Chronique des lettres* de samedi je n'avais cru parler que des rapports littéraires établis entre M. Oscar Wilde et vous.

Puisqu'il vous plaît de les interpréter d'une façon plus large, je ne saurais m'élever contre une opinion dont vous savez mieux que moi le fondement: vous êtes un homme d'esprit.

JULES HURET

Le Figaro, 18 avril, p.2:

Voici les procès-verbaux de la rencontre d'hier:

A la suite d'une lettre adressée par M. Jules Huret à M. Catulle Mendès, dans le *Figaro* du 16 avril, et jugée offensante par M. Mendès, ce dernier a prié MM. André Corneau et G. Courteline d'aller demander à M. Jules Huret une réparation par les armes.

M. Jules Huret a constitué pour témoins MM. Jules Guérin et Gaëtan de Méaulne.

Tout essai de conciliation ayant été reconnu inutile, une rencontre a été jugée nécessaire. En conséquence, elle aura lieu demain, 17 avril, à trois heures de l'après-midi. L'arme choisie est l'épée de combat, avec gant de ville à volontè.

Les corps à corps et l'usage de la main gauche sont interdits.

Les reprises ne pourront excéder une durée de deux minutes.

Paris, le 16 avril 1895

Pour M. Catulle Mendès: *Pour M. J. Huret:*
André Corneau,   Jules Guérin,
G. Courteline.   Gaëtan de Méaulne.

Conformément au procès-verbal ci-dessus, la rencontre a eu lieu aujourd'hui, dans les environs de Paris, à quatre heures de l'après-midi.

Au premier engagement, M. Mendès ayant été atteint, à la partie moyenne de la région postérieure de l'avant-bras, d'une plaie de trois centimètres de largeur environ avec section d'une grosse veine sous-cutanée, qui a déterminé une hémorragie abondante, les témoins, sur l'avis des médicins, ont aussitôt arrêté le combat, M. Mendès se trouvant dans un état d'inferiorité évident.

M. le docteur Constant cousin assistait M. Catulle Mendès, M. le docteur Raïchline assistait M. Jules Huret.

Paris, le 17 avril 1895

Pour M. Catulle Mendès: *Pour M. J. Huret:*
André Corneau,   Jules Guérin
G. Courteline.   Gaëtan de Méaulne.

7 Reprinted in Octave Mirbeau, *Les Ecrivains, 1885–1910* (Paris, 1926), 39–44.

8 William T. Ewens, *Thirty Years at Bow Street* (1924), 52–3.

9 *Letters*, 448–50.

10 Jerusha McCormack, unpublished thesis on John Gray; Douglas, *Autobiography*, 111.

11 Beerbohm, *Letters to Turner*, 103.

12 *New York Times*, 7 Apr 1895.

13 Beerbohm, *Letters to Turner*, 102.

14 Beerbohm, *Letters to Turner*, 102–3.

15 *New York Times*, 5 May 1895; T. M. Healy, *Letters* (1928), 416. George Ives, in his journal for 21 May 1928, p. 2912 (Texas), says Asquith told Rosebery that, if he let Wilde off, he would lose the next election.

16 Yeats, *Autobiography*, 191; Sherard, *Life of O.W.*, 358.

17 Sherard, *O.W.: Story of an Unhappy Friendship*, 165, 179.

18 Yeats, *Autobiography*, 192, 193; Harris, 200; Sherard, *O.W.: Story of an Unhappy Friendship*, 170, and *Life of O.W.*, 366; Leverson, 41.

19 Croft-Cooke, 127.

20 Harris, 196–9.
21 Yeats, *Autobiography*, 191; Harris, 203–8; Leverson, 41; *Reynolds's News*, 2 June 1895.
22 Leverson, 39–40.
23 Yeats's note (NYPL: Berg).
24 Yeats, *Autobiography*, 191; *Collected Letters of W. B. Yeats*, ed. John Kelly (Oxford, 1986–), I: 465–6.
25 Leverson, 41–2.
26 *Letters*, 398; Yeats, *Autobiography*, 192.
27 *Letters*, 397; Douglas, *Autobiography*, 121, 112; letter to Wilde, May 1895 (Texas).
28 Ransome case 1913, clippings at Bodleian.
29 Sherard, *O.W.: Story of an Unhappy Friendship*, 194.
30 Marquess of Queensberry and Percy Colson, *Oscar Wilde and the Black Douglas* (n.d.), 66; Brian Roberts, *The Mad Bad Line* (1981), 252.
31 C. H. Norman, letter to Sir Rupert Hart-Davis (Hart-Davis), says *Reynolds's News* was sympathetic to Wilde because R. W. Anderson of its staff had learned from police officers about the sums paid to the boys.
32 *Letters*, 502; *More Letters*, 171.
33 Hyde, ed., *Trials of O.W.*, 291.
34 H. Montgomery Hyde, letter to Rupert Croft-Cooke, 19 Sept 1962 (Texas), says Sacheverell Sitwell heard this from Douglas.
35 Hodgson, *Poets Remembered*; Sherard, *O.W.: Story of an Unhappy Friendship*, 199; Yeats, *Autobiography*, 193.

Chapter XIX

1 Kernahan, 235.
2 Croft-Cooke, 133.
3 The Revd. H. S. Bowden, letter to More Adey, 11 June 1895 (Hyde).
4 *Journal du Havre*, 1 Aug 1895, quoted in Raffalovich, 279 (my translation); Guillot de Saix, 'Souvenirs inédits.'
5 [Raymond and] Ricketts, 22.
6 *Letters*, 495.
7 *Letters*, 722; Harris, 230.
8 Hugues Rebell, 'Défense d'Oscar Wilde,' *Mercure de France*, Aug 1895, 184.
9 Marie Belloc Lowndes, *The Merry Wives of Westminster* (1946), 174.
10 Shane Leslie, *Sir Evelyn Ruggles-Brise: A Memoir of the Founder of Borstal* (1938), 136.
11 Richard Burdon Haldane, *An Autobiography* (1929), 164–7.
12 Major O. Mytton Davies, 'Prison Life of Notorious Criminals,' *Sunday Express*, n.d. on clipping at Clark.
13 *Letters*, 871–2.
14 Douglas, letter to Ada Leverson, 13 Sept 1895 (Clark)
15 *Letters*, 391.
16 Sherard, *O.W.: Story of an Unhappy Friendship*, 206.
17 *Letters*, 453, 455.
18 Douglas, 'Oscar Wilde,' from a TS at Clark.
19 *Letters*, 453–5.

20 Sherard, *O.W.: Story of an Unhappy Friendship*, 214.
21 Lady Queensberry, letter to Douglas, n.d. [1895] (Hyde).
22 *Letters*, 459–60.
23 Oscar Browning papers (Eastbourne).
24 Sherard, *O.W.: Story of an Unhappy Friendship*, 209–10; Constance Wilde, letter to Hannah Whitall Smith, 15 Oct 1895 (courtesy of Barbara Strachey).
25 More Adey draft petition at Clark; *Letters*, 390–1n.; Stuart Merrill, 'Pour Oscar Wilde: Epilogue,' *La Plume*, Jan 1896.
26 Croft-Cooke, 138; Douglas, *O.W. and Myself*, 177.
27 Home Office files.
28 Harris, 232–3, 235.
29 'In the Depths: Account of Oscar Wilde's Life at Reading. Told by His Gaoler,' *Evening News and Evening Mail*, 1 Mar 1905; *Bruno's Weekly* (N.Y.), 22 and 29 Jan 1916; *Letters*, 691.
30 Dowson, *Letters*, 343.
31 Healy, *Confessions of a Journalist*, 130–8; Gide, *O.W.*, 42.
32 Chesson, 390.
33 Henry S. Salt, *Seventy Years Among Savages* (1921), 181–2, summarizing Warder Martin's recollections.
34 'The Story of Oscar Wilde's Life and Experiences in Reading Gaol,' in *Bruno's Weekly*, 22 Jan 1916; O'Sullivan, 63.
35 *Letters*, 398; Lady W's notebook (NYPL: Berg).
36 Willie Wilde, letter to More Adey, 4 Feb 1896 (Clark).
37 Harris, 249; H. Corkran, *Celebrities and I*, 142; Lily Wilde, letters to More Adey, 5 Feb and 13 Mar 1896 (Clark).
38 *Letters*, 543, 399, 499.
39 *Letters*, 399n.
40 V. Holland, *Son of O.W.*, 48–9.
41 Ross, letter to More Adey, May 1896, in Margery Ross, *Robert Ross, Friend of Friends* (1952), 39.
42 Harris, 234.
43 Ross, letter to Adey, in M. Ross, *Friend of Friends*, 41.
44 *Letters*, 400–1; *Daily Telegraph*, 25 Nov 1921 and 18 Apr 1913.
45 Raffalovich, 248.
46 [Lord] Alfred Douglas, *Oscar Wilde et quelques autres* (Paris, ?1932), ch. 29.
47 *Letters*, 401–5; Home Office records.
48 Lord Alfred Douglas, *Without Apology* (1938), 48.

Chapter XX

1 O'Sullivan, 36.
2 Leon Edel, letter to Sir Rupert Hart-Davis, n.d. (Hart-Davis).
3 Harris, 234.
4 Chesson, 390.
5 The book has since been sold at Sotheby's.
6 *Letters*, 424n.
7 E. V. Lucas claims to have suggested the title to Ross.
8 Douglas clipping (Bodleian).

9 *Letters*, 413.
10 *Daily Telegraph*, 25 Nov 1921; *Letters*, 437.
11 JD Sales Catalogue in Ross Collection (Bodleian).
12 Almy, 'New Views of Mr O.W.,' in *Theatre* (1894).
13 *Letters*, 466, 473.
14 *Letters*, 465.
15 'The Story of O.W.'s Life and Experiences in Reading Gaol,' *Bruno's Weekly*, 5 Feb 1916.
16 *Reynolds's News*, 28 June 1903.
17 Warder Martin in Sherard, *Life of O.W.*, 397.
18 W. Rothenstein, 310–11.
19 *Letters*, 565.
20 *Letters*, 528; Warder Martin in Sherard, *Life of O.W.*, 391–2.
21 Guillot de Saix, 'Moïse et Pharaon,' in *Le Chant du cygne* (Paris, 1942), 52–5; [Raymond and] Ricketts, 48.
22 Guillot de Saix, 'Jean et Judas,' in *Le Chant du cygne*, 113–14; 'Les Trente Deniers,' in the same work, 120–3, offers a variant of Wilde's other story.
23 More Adey, letter to Adela Schuster, 16 Mar 1897 (Clark). Ross repeated the governor's remark to Osbert Sitwell, who quotes it in *Noble Essences*, 13.
24 *Letters*, 534–5.
25 Beerbohm, letter to Ross [Spring, 1897], in M. Ross, *Friend of Friends*, 48.
26 *Letters*, 568–74, 554.
27 *New York Times*, 19 May 1897; Shane Leslie, 'Oscariana,' *National Review*, 15 Jan 1963.

EXILE

Chapter XXI

1 More Adey, letter to Adela Schuster, 12 Mar 1898 (Clark); F. G. Bettany, *Stewart Headlam* (1926), 152; Sitwell, *Noble Essences*, 142; Leverson, 44–6.
2 *Daily Telegraph*, 13 May 1962; Ross, unfinished preface to Wilde's letters to him, 1911 (Clark); Turner to Beerbohm in *Letters to Turner*, 117–18n.; *Letters*, 564–5, 566. For Wilde's name of Sebastian Melmoth, see Ross's letter to the editor of *T.P.'s Weekly*, 4 Nov 1910.
3 *Letters*, 597.
4 Testimony of Douglas, 19 Apr 1913, in Ransome case.
5 *Letters*, 577, 579, 828.
6 Christian Krohg, *I Smaa Dagsreisck til og fra Paris* (Christiania, 1897), trans. Barbara Bird, *New Age*, 10 Dec 1908.
7 *Letters*, 654, 666; O'Sullivan, 97; Chris Healy, 'Oscar Wilde and Zola,' *To-Day*, 26 Nov 1902.
8 *More Letters*, 150.
9 Major J. O. Nelson, letter to Ross, 12 Jan 1898, in M. Ross, *Friend of Friends*, 49–50; W. B. Yeats, ed., *The Oxford Book of Modern Verse* (Oxford, 1936), vi–vii.
10 *More Letters*, 153.
11 *Letters*, 631, 632–3.

12 A. C. Amor, *Mrs O.W.*, 210–14.

13 Jacques-Emile Blanche, *Portraits of a Lifetime* (1937), 98; John Rothenstein, *The Life and Death of Conder* (N.Y., [1938]), 137.

14 The dinner party on 19 July 1897 was at the home of Fritz von Thaulow. *More Letters*, 151; O'Sullivan, 87; J. Rothenstein, *Conder*, 138.

15 Leverson, 64; Mrs Belloc Lowndes, *Merry Wives of Westminster*, 174.

16 Dowson, *Letters*, 385.

17 J. Rothenstein, *Conder*, 148.

18 Simon Pakenham, *Sixty Miles from England: The English at Dieppe 1814–1914* (1967), 166.

19 J. Rothenstein, *Conder*, 118; Pakenham, *Sixty Miles from England*, 168.

20 *Letters*, 585.

21 C. Krohg, trans. in *New Age* (1908).

22 *Letters*, 588–9.

23 *Letters*, 596–7.

24 Sherard, letter to A. J. A. Symons, 8 May 1935 (Hyde).

25 W. Rothenstein, 312.

26 Dowson, *Letters*, 16 June 1897, p. 287.

27 G. Spilett in *Gil Blas*, 22 Nov 1897.

28 Gide, *O.W.*, 34–46.

29 C. Krohg, trans. in *New Age* (1908).

30 Alin Caillas, *Oscar Wilde tel que je l'ai connu* (Paris, 1971).

31 C. Krohg, trans. in *New Age* (1908).

32 *Letters*, 582.

33 Sherard, *Life of O.W.*, 278–9.

34 O'Sullivan, 28.

35 *Letters*, 589, 591, 592.

36 *Letters*, 599.

37 Lady Queensberry, letter to More Adey, 9 June 1897 (Clark); Douglas, *Autobiography*, 151.

38 *Letters*, 697; Gide, *O.W.*, 47.

39 Ross, letter to Douglas, 1897 (Hart-Davis).

40 *Letters*, 624.

41 Gide, *O.W.*, 47; More Adey, letter to Adela Schuster, 12 Mar 1898 (Clark); V. Holland, letter to Frank Harris, 9 May 1926 (whereabouts unknown).

42 *Letters*, 635, 637.

Chapter XXII

1 G. Spilett in *Gil Blas*, 22 Nov 1897; Harris, 367, quotes Wilde as saying that Douglas drove him like the Oestrum of which the Greeks wrote, to disaster.

2 *Letters*, 741; Samuel Beer, *The Mauve Decade* (1926), 129.

3 *Letters*, 649, 638, 695, 685, 644.

4 Douglas, *Autobiography*, 152; letter to Edward Strangman, 29 Nov 1897 (sold at Sotheby's 1984); Douglas clippings, n.d. (Ross Collection, Bodleian).

5 Gertrude Atherton, *Adventures of a Novelist* (1930), 44–7.

6 C. Healy in *To-Day*, 8 Oct 1902.

7 O'Sullivan, 196–7.

8 *Letters*, 649, 651, 657; Gordon Craig, *Index to the Story of My Days* (1957), 148.

9 *Letters*, 755–6, 730n.

10 *Letters*, 695.

11 O'Sullivan, 64.

12 Douglas, *Without Apology*, 299; Croft-Cooke, 162; *Letters*, 673.

13 *Letters*, 685; Constance Wilde, letter to Otho Holland (Lloyd), 7 Oct 1897 (Hart-Davis).

14 Claire de Pratz in Guillot de Saix, 'Souvenirs inédits.'

15 *Letters*, 693.

16 *Letters*, 696–8.

17 Douglas, letter to Edward Strangman, 29 Nov 1897 (sold at Sotheby's).

18 Douglas, *Without Apology*, 297–8, 302–5.

19 Douglas, *Autobiography*, 138; *Letters*, 719.

20 Croft-Cooke, 168; Douglas described by Gide in *Si le grain ne meurt*.

21 *Letters*, 709–10. Wilde always regarded the sum received from Lady Queensberry as part payment (and part only) of the 'debt of honor' that the Douglas family had contracted when he prosecuted Queensberry.

22 Quoted in *Daily Telegraph*, 25 Nov 1921.

23 Constance Wilde, letters to Otho Holland (Holland TSS); to Carlos Blacker, 10 Mar 1898 (courtesy of J. Robert Maguire); to Arthur Humphreys, 27 Feb 1898 (Hyde); to Mrs Carlos Blacker, 26 Mar 1898 (Maguire); to Arthur Humphreys, 18 Feb 1898 (Hyde).

24 *Letters*, 766.

25 O'Sullivan, 162, 69–70.

26 Joseph O. Baylen and Robert L. McBath, 'A Note on Oscar Wilde, Alfred Douglas, and Lord Rosebery, 1897,' *English Language Notes* 23 (Sept 1985), 42–3.

27 Catalogue of The Bungalow, Spring 1922, item 579 (Ross Collection, Bodleian).

28 Pamela Matthews told me this.

29 Graham Greene, *A Sort of Life* (1971), 26; *New York Times*, 15 Dec 1897.

30 Constance Wilde to Otho Holland (Lloyd), 1897 (Hart-Davis).

31 Sherard, *O.W.: Story of an Unhappy Friendship*, 261–2.

32 *More Letters*, 165.

33 *Letters*, 813; Mason, 350.

34 Berenson papers (courtesy of Prof. Ernest Samuels); Arthur Machen, letter to Colin Summerford (courtesy of Roger Dobson); C. Krogh, trans. in *New Age* (1908); Léon Lemonnier, *La Vie d'Oscar Wilde* (Paris, 1931), 232.

35 *Letters*, 828.

36 Vance Thompson, 'Oscar Wilde: Last Dark Poisoned Days in Paris,' *New York Sun*, 18 Jan 1914; C. Healy in *To-Day*, 8 Oct 1902; Chesson, 391. J. Robert Maguire provided information on the Esterhazy episode.

37 Gide, *O.W.*, 49–51.

38 Henry Davray, letter to Walter Ledger, 26 Feb 1926, in Ross Collection (Bodleian); Frédéric Boutet, 'Les Dernières Années d'Oscar Wilde' (clipping from unidentified newspaper, 3 Dec 1925, at Clark); *Letters*, 803, 809.

39 J.-J. Renaud, 'The Last Months of Oscar Wilde's Life in Paris,' TS of a broadcast (Clark).

40 Guillot de Saix, 'O.W. chez Maeterlinck,' *Les Nouvelles Littéraires* (1945); O'Sullivan, 67; Chesson, 394 [*Letters*, 790].

41 Lord Alfred Douglas, *Oscar Wilde: A Summing Up* (1962), 90; *Letters*, 729–30; Frank Harris, *Contemporary Portraits* (1915), 90–118.

42 *Letters*, 729–30n.

43 Charles Conder, letter to Mrs Dalhousie Young, n.d. (Hart-Davis).

44 *Letters*, 732.

45 Claire de Pratz, quoted in Guillot de Saix, 'Souvenirs inédits'; G. de Saix, 'La Cruelle Charité,' in *Le Chant du cygne*, 249–50.

46 Croft-Cooke, 177–8.

47 *Letters*, 816.

48 *Letters*, 608.

49 *Letters*, 705.

50 Harris, 351.

51 Laurence Housman, *Echo de Paris: A Study from Life* (1923), 34. Housman said this part of his book recorded actual statements of Wilde.

52 *Letters*, 772.

53 *More Letters*, 178; W. Rothenstein, 314.

54 *Letters*, 783.

55 *Letters*, 790, 794, 794n.

56 Croft-Cooke, 174.

57 Chalmers Mitchell, *My Fill of Days*, 183–4.

58 Dame Nellie Melba, *Melodies and Memories* (1925), 74–5; M. Steen, *A Pride of Terrys*, 206n.

59 W. M. Fullerton, letter to Wilde, 23 June 1899 (Clark); *Letters*, 804.

60 'T.P.'s Table Talk,' *T.P.'s Cassells Weekly*, 27 Oct 1923; Leslie, *J. E. C. Bodley*, 18; Max de Morès in G. de Saix, 'Souvenirs inédits.'

61 Latourette, 'Dernières Heures avec O.W.,' in *Les Nouvelles Littéraires* (1925).

62 E. Calvé, *My Life*, 96–8.

63 Marjoribanks, *Lord Carson*, 231; Louis Marlow [L. U. Wilkinson], 'Oscar Wilde . . . ,' *New Statesman*, 3 Jan 1914; Latourette in *Les Nouvelles Littéraires* (1925).

64 *Letters*, 731; Stanley Weintraub, *Whistler* (N.Y., 1974), 306.

65 *Cheiro's Memoirs*, 56–61; W. Rothenstein, 361–2.

66 Beer, *Mauve Decade*, 130–3.

67 Edith Cooper, *Works and Days* (BL Add. MS 46798, f. 202).

68 Dupoirier, quoted by Latourette in *Les Nouvelles Littéraires* (1925).

69 J.-J. Renaud, preface to *Intentions* (1905), xxii.

70 *Letters*, 828–9, 831; Harris, 361, 364.

71 *Letters*, 831; Paul Medina, 'Zum 25. Todestag Oscar Wildes am 30 November, Ein Gesprach mit dem "Dichterfürsten" Paul Fort, dem letzten Freund Oscar Wildes,' *Die Literarische Welt* (Berlin) I, no. 8 (17 Nov 1925): 1–2.

72 *Letters*, 828; A. de Brémont, *O.W. and His Mother*, 178–88.

73 *Letters*, 832, 837–44, 859, 860.

74 Harris, 372. Dr Tucker's bill is in the Hyde Collection. *More Letters* 186.

75 Terence Cawthorne, 'The Last Illness of Oscar Wilde,' *Proceedings of the*

Royal Society of Medicine LII, no. 2 (Feb 1959): 123–7; *Letters*, 837; Wilson, *Victorian Doctor*, 211.

76 *Letters*, 708.
77 [Raymond and] Ricketts, 59.
78 *St. James's Gazette*, 6 May 1905; [Raymond and] Ricketts, 59; A. [Douglas], 'Oscar Wilde's Last Years in Paris. II,' *St. James's Gazette*, 3 Mar 1905; Housman, *Echo de Paris*, 32; M. Ross, *Friend of Friends*, 153.
79 Claire de Pratz, in G. de Saix, 'Souvenirs inédits'; Harris, 572.
80 *Letters*, 861, 840; Ross, deposition in Ransome case. Turner states the medical diagnosis in his letter to Sherard, 3 Jan 1934 (Reading), and Ross is given as the source for Ransome's statement, *O.W.*, 199.
81 *Letters*, 849.
82 *Letters*, 852.
83 Reginald Turner, letter to Ross, 26–28 Nov 1900 (Clark).
84 Douglas, *Without Apology*, 255; *Daily Chronicle*, 3 Dec 1900; *Letters*, 825.
85 Almy, 'New Views of Mr O.W.,' in *Theatre* (1894); Ives journal, 4 Mar 1905 (Texas); Chesson, 393–4.
86 Reginald Turner, letter to T. H. Bell, n.d., in Bell's unpublished MS on Wilde (Clark); Ives journal, 4 Mar 1905 (Texas); letter from 'Sacerdos', *St. James's Gazette*, 1 Mar 1905.
87 Max Meyerfeld, '*Gedenkblätter*, Robert Ross,' in *Das Literarische Echo* XXI (4 Jan 1919): 779–85; Ross's visiting card, copy in NLI.
88 *Letters*, 854; Reginald Turner, letter to R. S. Meickeljohn, 31 Dec 1936 (Hart-Davis); John, *Chiaroscuro*, 396.
89 Cecil Georges-Bazile, 'Oscar Wilde et Paris,' *Paris Soir*, 29 Oct 1925 (based on Ross); Gunnar Heiberg, *Set og Hørt* (Christiania, 1917), 162–7.
90 Paul Fort interview by Paul Medina, *Die Literarische Welt*, 17 Nov 1928.
91 Iain Fletcher, 'The Poetry of John Gray,' in *Two Friends*, ed. Brocard Sewell (1963), 68.
92 Ross, letter to Louis Wilkinson, 10 Dec [1900] (LC), in M. Ross, *Friend of Friends*, 61.

Epilogue

1 O'Sullivan, 222.
2 See Jorge Luis Borges, 'About Oscar Wilde,' in *Other Inquisitions 1937–1952* (N.Y., 1966), 84.

SELECT BIBLIOGRAPHY
Principal published sources cited or quoted

(The place of publication is London unless otherwise stated.)

The Artist as Critic: Critical Writings of Oscar Wilde, ed. Richard Ellmann (Chicago, 1982)
The Letters of Oscar Wilde, ed. Rupert Hart-Davis (1962)
More Letters of Oscar Wilde, ed. Rupert Hart-Davis (1985)
Oscar Wilde, *The Picture of Dorian Gray*, ed. Isobel Murray (1974)

Anne Clark Amor, *Mrs Oscar Wilde* (1983)
G. T. Atkinson, 'Oscar Wilde at Oxford,' *Cornhill Magazine* LXVI (May 1929)
Max Beerbohm, *Letters to Reggie Turner*, ed. Rupert Hart-Davis (1964)
E. F. Benson, *As We Were: A Victorian Peep-show* (1930)
Sir Frank Benson, *My Memoirs* (1930)
Martin Birnbaum, *Oscar Wilde, Fragments and Memories* (1920)
David Hunter Blair, *In Victorian Days* (1939)
[J. E. C. Bodley], 'Oscar Wilde at Oxford,' *New York Times*, 20 January 1882
Anna de Brémont, *Oscar Wilde and His Mother* (1911)
W. H. Chesson, 'A Reminiscence of 1898,' *Bookman* XXXIV (December 1911)
Rupert Croft-Cooke, *Bosie* (Indianapolis and New York, 1963)
Lord Alfred Douglas, *Autobiography* (1929)
　　　　　　　　Oscar Wilde and Myself (1914)
　　　　　　　　Oscar Wilde: A Summing Up (1962)
　　　　　　　　Without Apology (1938)
André Gide, *Oscar Wilde* (Paris, 1938)
Frank Harris, *Oscar Wilde, His Life and Confessions* (New York, 1930)
Vyvyan Holland, *Son of Oscar Wilde* (New York, 1954)
H. Montgomery Hyde, *Oscar Wilde* (New York, 1975)
　　　　　　　　ed., *The Trials of Oscar Wilde* (1948)
(John) Coulson Kernahan, *In Good Company: Some Personal Recollections*, 2nd edn (1917)
Lillie Langtry, *The Days I Knew* (1925)
Ada Leverson, *Letters to the Sphinx from Oscar Wilde and Reminiscences of the Author* (1930)
Lloyd Lewis and Henry Justin Smith, *Oscar Wilde Discovers America [1882]* (1936)
Stuart Mason, *Bibliography of Oscar Wilde* (1914)
Kevin O'Brien, *Oscar Wilde in Canada* (Toronto, 1982)
Vincent O'Sullivan, *Aspects of Wilde* (1936)
Hesketh Pearson, *The Life of Oscar Wilde* (1946)
[Jean Paul Raymond and] Charles Ricketts, *Oscar Wilde: Recollections* (1932)
(James) Rennell Rodd, *Social and Diplomatic Memories, 1884–1893* (1922)
Margery Ross, *Robert Ross, Friend of Friends* (1952)

587

William Rothenstein, *Men and Memories* (New York, 1931)

Edgar Saltus, *Oscar Wilde, An Idler's Impressions* (Chicago, 1917)

Robert (Harborough) Sherard, *The Life of Oscar Wilde* (New York, 1906)

Oscar Wilde: The Story of an Unhappy Friendship (1902)

The Real Oscar Wilde (n.d. [1917])

Mrs H. M. Swanwick [Helena Sickert], *I Have Been Young* (1935)

Terence De Vere White, *The Parents of Oscar Wilde* (1967)

Horace Wyndham, *Speranza: A Biography of Lady Wilde* (New York, 1951)

W. B. Yeats, *Autobiography* (New York, 1965)

APPENDIX A

The extraordinary productivity of the Wilde parents can be seen in the following list:

Sir William Wilde (1815–1876)		Lady Wilde (1821–1896)
Narrative of a Voyage to Madeira, Teneriffe, and along the shores of the Mediterranean . . . (Dublin: William Curry, Jun.)	1839	
The same, second edition	1840	
Austria: Its Literary, Scientific, and Medical Institutions . . . (Dublin: William Curry, Jun.)	1843	
The Closing Years of Dean Swift's Life . . . (Dublin: Hodges and Smith)	1849	Translation of William Meinhold, *Sidonia the Sorceress* (London: Reeves and Turner, 2 vols.)
The Beauties of the Boyne and Blackwater (Dublin: James McGlashan)		
The same, second edition	1850	Translation of Alphonse de Lamartine, *Pictures of the First French Revolution*
Essay on the Epidemic Ophthalmia which has prevailed in . . . Tipperary and Athlone . . . (Dublin: James McGlashan)	1851 (Marriage)	Translation of Lamartine, *The Wanderer and His Home*
Census		
Irish Popular Superstitions, dedicated to Speranza (Dublin: James McGlashan)	1852 (Willie born)	Translation of Alexandre Dumas *père*, *The Glacier Land*

[Sir William Wilde]		[Lady Wilde]
Practical Observations on Aural Surgery and the Nature and Treatment of Diseases of the Ear (London: Churchill)	1853	
On the Physical, Moral and Social Condition of the Deaf and Dumb (London: Churchill)	1854 (Oscar born)	
A Descriptive Catalogue of the Antiquities . . . in the Museum of the Royal Irish Academy, Vol. I (Dublin: The Academy)	1857 (Isola born)	
A Descriptive Catalogue, Vol. II	1861	
A Descriptive Catalogue, Vol. III	1862	
An Essay on the Malformations and Congenital Diseases of the Organs of Sight (London: Churchill)		
	1863	Translation of M. Schwab, *The First Temptation or 'Eritis Sicut Deus'* (London: T. Cautley Newby)
	1864	*Poems* (Dublin: James Duffy)
	1866	*Poems: Second Series: Translations*
Lough Corrib: Its Shore and Islands . . . (Dublin: McGlashan and Gill)	1867 (Death of Isola)	
	1871	*Poems* (Glasgow: Cameron & Ferguson)
Lough Corrib, second edition	1872	
	1874	Translation of Emmanuel Swedenborg, *The Future Life*

1876 (Death of Sir William)	
1880	*Memoir of Gabriel Beranger* (London: Richard Bentley and Son)
1884 (Marriage of Oscar and Constance Lloyd)	*Driftwood from Scandinavia* (London: Richard Bentley and Son)
1888 (Birth of Cyril 1885 and Vyvyan 1886)	*Ancient Legends, Mystic Charms, and Superstitions of Ireland* (London: Ward and Downey)
1890	*Ancient Cures, Charms, and Usages of Ireland* (London: Ward and Downey)
1891 (Marriage of Willie and Miriam Leslie)	*Notes on Men, Women, and Books* (London: Ward & Downey)
1893 (Divorce of Willie and Miriam)	*Social Studies* (London: Ward & Downey)
1894 (Second marriage of Willie, to Lily Lees)	
1896 (Death of Lady Wilde)	
1898 (Death of Constance Wilde)	
1899 (Death of Willie Wilde)	
1900 (Death of Oscar Wilde)	

APPENDIX B

For an impression of how Wilde talked, especially on the lecture platform, the best guide is the American, Helen Potter, whose book *Impersonations* (New York: Edgar S. Werner, 1891) offers a detailed account of his way of accenting and pausing:

LECTURE ON ART.

A Study of Oscar Wilde. *

(–) Everything made by the hand of man | is either ₒug°ly | or (/) ₒbeauti°ful; (–) and it might as well be beautiful as (/) ₒug°ly. (–) Nothing that is made | is °too ₒpoor [pooah], | or °too (/) ₒtrivi°al, | (–) to be made with an idea [ideah], | of pleasing the aesthetic ₒeye.

°Americans, | ₒas a class, | °are not (/) ₒpractical, (–) though you may laugh | at the (/) ₒassertion. (–) When I enter [entah] a room, | I see a carpet of (\) vulgar [vulgah] (/) ₒpattern, | (–) a cracked plate upon the (/) ₒwall, | (–) with a peacock feather stuck °be₀hind °it. (–) I sit down | upon a badly glued | machine-made (/) ₒchair [chăah], | that creaks | upon being (/) ₒtouched; | (–) I see | a gaudy gilt horror, | in the shape | of a (/) ₒmirror, | (–) and a cast-iron monstrosity | for a °chande₀lier. (–) Everything I see | was made to (/) ₒsell. (–) I turn to look for the beauties of nature [nātyah] | in (/) vain; | (–) for I behold only muddy streets | and (\) ugly (/) ₒbuild°ings; (–) everything looks (\) second (/) class. (–) By second class | I mean | that | which constantly *decreases* °*in* (/) ₒ*value*. (–) The old Gothic cathedral is firmer [firmah] and (/) stronger [strongah], | and more [mōah] beautiful ₒ*now* | than it was | years [yeahs] (/) ₒago. (–) There is one thing worse | than °*no* (/) ₒart | and that is | ₒ*bad* °art.

(–) A good rule to follow | in a house | is to have nothing therein | but what is useful | or (/) ₒbeautiful; | (–) nothing that is not pleasant to use, | or was not a pleasure | to the one | who (/) ₒmade °it. (–) Allow no machine-made ornaments | in the house | at (/) ₒall. (–) Don't paper your [youah] halls, | but have them (/) ₒwain°scoted, | or provided | with a (/)

* Key to symbols used: '*Sounds of letters*: ē as in eve; ā as in ale; ă as in at; ī as in rice. *Signs for pitch, force and time*: (°) high pitch; (ₒ) low pitch. *Signs placed before, and applying to, words and phrases*: | bar, means a halt, or short rhetorical pause; (–) monotone, to the next bar or change; (/) rising pitch, to the next bar or change; (/) downward pitch, to the next bar or change; (◡) go up, down and up on the phrase or sentence. Any one of these signs over a word or syllable applies to that word or syllable only.'

₀dado. (–) Don't hang them with pictures, | as they are only | (/) ₀passage°ways. (–) Have some definite idea [ideah], | of ₀color [culah], (–) some dominant | keynote | of (/) ₀color [culah], (–) or exquisite gra₀da°tion, | like the answering calls | in a symphony of (/) ₀music. There are symphonies | of color [culah], | as (\) well as of | (/) ₀sound. I will describe | one of Mr Whistler's | symphonies in color – (–) a symphony | in *white*. A picture [pictchah], representing | a gray and white sky [skēī]; a gray sea, flecked with the white crests of (\) °dancing (/) ₀waves; | a white (/) ₀balco°ny | with two little children in white, | leaning over [ovah] the (/) ₀rail°ing, | (–) plucking | with white (/) ₀fingers (finggahs], | the white petals | of an almond tree | (/) in bloom.

(–) The truths of art | cannot (/) be *taught*. (–) They are revealed | only | to natures [nātyahs] which have made themselves receptive | of all | (\) °beautiful (/) ₀impressiŏns | by the study, | and the worship of | all | beautiful | (/) ₀things. (–) Don't take your [youah] critĭc | as any sure [shuah] test | of (/) ₀art; for artists, | like the Greek gods, | are only revealed | to one (/) ₀another [anothah]. The true critic | addresses | °*not* the (/) ₀artist | (/) *ever*, | but the public. *His* work | is with (/) ₀them. Art | can have no other [othah] aim | but her own °per₀fec°tion.

(–) Love art | for its own sake, | and then | all these things | shall be (/) ₀added °to yōu. (–) This devotion to beauty | and to the creation of beautiful things, | is the test | of all | great | °civil₀za°tiŏns. (–) It is what makes the life | of each citizen | a sacrament | and °not | a °specu₀la°tiŏn; for beauty | is the only thing | time | cannot harm. Philosophies may fall away | °like the (/) ₀sand; creeds | follow one °an₀oth°er; | but what is beautiful | is a joy for all seasŏns, a possession | for all | °e₀tēr°nitў. (–) National hatreds | are always strongest | where culture [cultchah] is (/) ₀lowest; but art | is an empire | which a nation's enemies | cannot | take (/) ₀*from* °her.

(–) We | in our Renaissance | are seeking to create a sovereignty | that shall °still be (/) ₀England's | when her yellow leopards | are weary of wārs [wahs], | (–) and the rose | on her shield | is crimsoned °no (/) ₀more [mōah] | with the blood | of (/) ₀bat°tle. And °you | ₀tōō, | (–) absorbing | into the heart of a great people | this pervading artistic (/) ₀spirit, will create for your[youah]selves | °such ₀richēs | as you have never [nevah] yet | °cre₀a°tēd, | though your [youah] land | be a network of (/) ₀railways, | and your [youah] cities | the harbors | of the gallēȳs | of the (/) ₀world.

. . . This disciple of true art speaks very deliberately, and his speech is marked by transitions, as marked by the small signs (₀) (°) throughout the text; the closing inflection of a sentence or period is ever upward.

INDEX

W = Wilde

594

music, W hears yodelers at Oxford, 39; at W's Magdalen open house, 44; W at London performances, 75; Willie W composes for piano, 122; Rigo's music and *Salome*, 324–5

Music Hall (Boston), W's lecture in, 173; Harvard students mock W in, 173

Musset, Alfred de, as cuckold, 206

myth, W's aphorism on, 284; *Dorian* a myth for aestheticism, 293

Naples, W and Bosie in, 517–23; take villa in Posillipo, 517–18; rats removed by witch, 518; W shunned by English set, 518–19; money troubles, 519–21; quarrels described, 521–2; W's version of life in, 522; W remains after Douglas's departure, 523–5; W with Mellor in, 541

Napoleon I, Emperor, as cuckold, 206; Gilbert's profile Napoleonic, 528; St Helena greatest theme, 546

Napoule, La, W's sojourn at, 536

Narcissus, bronze figure of, 242; in Tite Street, Chelsea, house, 242; W's parable on, 336–7; Gide's book on, 339

Nation (Dublin), Lady W's essays in, 120

National Review, Lady W's patriotic poem in, 4

nature, views are for bad painters, 131n; W prefers social life to, 210; W detests, 329

Nebraska, W visits state penitentiary at Lincoln, 191

Nechayev, S. C., 'Catechism of a Revolutionary', 117

Nelson, J. O., Major, becomes Reading Warden, 476; kindly treatment of W, 476–9; W's interview with, 486; predicts W's death, 490; W's praise for, 491–2; inscribed copy of *Ballad* to, 526

Nemesis, W's pervasive sense of doom, 89, 410; 515–16; ominous inscription at Tournai, 124; Rodd's dedication to W, 125; sense of doom in *Salome*, 326; palmist forecasts W's ruin, 360; presages of disaster, 387; W's 'imagination of disaster', 406; 1890's come to doomed end, 535

Nerval, Gérard de, W traces Paris routes of, 207

Nettleship, R. L., Balliol classics tutor, 58

Neville-Rolfe, E., Consul at Naples, 524

Nevinson, H. W., W described by, 47

Newbolt, Henry, accuses W of plagiarism, 140

New College, Oxford, W's friendships at, 291

Newdigate Prize (Oxford), W's age at winning, 7; and W's entry into Ravenna, 69; results announced, 93; won by Rodd, 100

Newgate Prison, W taken to, 450

Newman, John Henry, Cardinal, founds university, 32; apostasy of, 51; W sends 'Rome Unvisited' to, 55; and receives praise from, 55n; W reads books of, in Ireland, 63; honorary Oxford fellowship, 88; W's dream of conversion and, 88

New Orleans (Louisiana), W's Confederate uncle in, 185

Newport (Rhode Island), W plans to visit, 227; W's visit to, 229

News of the World, praises verdict against W, 450

newspapers, *see* press, *and under individual papers*

Newton, Sir Charles, Mrs Langtry hears lectures of, 109

New York City, W treated as *petit roi* in, 153; first lecture a sellout, 156; reception follows lecture, 159; W ends American tour in, 177; W tricked by confidence man in, 190; W's visit to Wall Street, 190; W's post-lecture stay in, 195

New York Herald, reviews *Guido Ferranti*, 313

New York Mirror, calls *Vera* marvelous, 228

New York Sun, calls *Vera* a masterpiece, 228

New York Times, Bodley's account of W in, 37, 169, 220; reports *Vera* cancellation, 146; courteous treatment of W, 168; on W's appearance, 196; reports W's arrival, 227; Marie Prescott's letter to, 228; pompous review of *Vera*, 228; reports W's wedding, 234; W's letter on marriage and, 237; review of *Guido Ferranti* in, 313; praises *Lady Windermere*, 345; reports Willie W's mockery of W, 358; praises *Importance of Earnest*, 406; on W's first trial, 435; article on Dreyfus affair, 530

New York Tribune, says W spoke in hexameters, 151; worst enemy of W, 168; mocks W's misadventure, 190; calls American tour failure, 199; calls W a changed man, 228; reviews *Guido Ferranti*, 313

New York World, W's sonnet to Bernhardt in, 113; on W's enunciation, 151; Joaquin Miller letter in, 175; W's new clothing described in, 177n; W's review of Mrs Langtry in, 197; Theodore Child writes for, 202; reports W's wedding, 234

Niagara Falls, W's visit to, 185; in W's London lecture, 225

Nicholson, Dr (Wandsworth prison doctor), reports on W's health, 476

'Nightingale and the Rose, The', W's new story, 269

Nihilism and Nihilists, Turgenev invents term, 116, 213; called boring in *Vera*, 223, 228

Nineteenth Century (review), W hopes to publish in, 79; 'Decay of Lying' in, 282, 284; W's 'Value of Criticism' in, 289; 'Critic as Artist' in, 307

Nittis, Giuseppe de, Paris painter, 213; W guest of, 214

Nobes, Warden, W sees Nebraska penitentiary with, 191

Noble, Revd William, W's uncle, 24

Nogent-sur-Marne, W's sojourn at, 534

Nordau, Max, W mentioned in his *Degeneracy*, 517

Norton, Charles Eliot, W's letter of introduction to, 170; hospitable to W, 172;

Pre-Raphaelites – *cont.*
workmanship, 158; precursors of aestheticism, 197; W loses interest in, 246, 265

Prescott, Marie, W explains *Vera* to, 116; and rewrites play for, 212, 223; selects vermilion gown for, 224, 227; opens in New York, 227; distressed by poor reviews, 228. *See also Vera*

press, coverage of W's American tour, 149; W's friends in English press, 149; W meets American reporters, 150; English press hostile to tour, 152, 168; Baltimore papers attack W, 167; Forbes attack on W and, 168; W's battle with American press, 171; Boucicault and treatment of W, 173; W discounts press malice, 176; W's lectures printed verbatim in, 183; discussing W's trial for weeks, 430, 435, 437, 444, 444n, 445n, 446, 446n, 450. *See also* journalism *and individual papers*

'Priest and the Acolyte, The', Bloxam's homosexual story, 403–4; in W's cross-examination, 421

Prince (prisoner), flogged in Reading Gaol, 491

Prince of Wales Theatre, *The Colonel* plays at, 128

Prince's Hall, Piccadilly, W's London lecture in, 225; Whistler to lecture in, 255

prison, W sentenced to, 449; W resigned to, 442–3; W's fictional treatment of, 451–2; petitions for clemency, 452; in 'Soul of Man', 454; W's life in Pentonville, 454–7; W asks for books, 455; effect on W's health, 462, 464n, 465, 468–9, 475–6; W's infraction of rules, 466; W petitions for release, 471–2; many prisons of life, 474; wave of prison reform, 474–5; more books approved, 475–9; W petitions Home Office, 476, 490; turns one to stone, 481; W plans for future life, 489–91; W's sentence completed, 495; W wants to write about, 498–500; has completely changed W, 508; makes W less radical, 510; W on cruel after-effects of, 531; 'there I found my soul', 532, 544; Douglas in Wormwood Scrubs, 552

prison reform, Prison Act of 1865, 474; Prison Commission and, 475; and 1898 Prison Act, 475

progress, heading in W's Commonplace Book, 41

prose, Pater urges W to write, 80

Proust, Marcel, his *Sodome et Gomorrhe*, 261; *Dorian* and, 301; W meets through J.-E. Blanche, 327; W's first encounter with, 327–8; W invited to dinner by, 328

Psychical Society, W cites, 236

Punch, Burnand editor of, 128; du Maurier's caricatures in, 130, 229, 352; hostile to *Poems* (1881), 138; on W's discard of mannerisms, 208; calls W a 'Mary-Ann', 220; W misquoted in, 255

Purser, Louis Claude, and W's *viva voce* at Portora, 21; at Trinity with W, 25; W's

competition with, 28; candidate for Trinity fellowship, 33

Puvis de Chavanne, Pierre, W gives painting to Sherard, 204

Queensberry, Marchioness of (Sybil Montgomery Douglas), Alfred Douglas's mother, 363; meeting with W, 363; wins divorce, 366; W's letter to, 381–2; sends Douglas to Cairo, 383; insists on break with W, 390–1; sends W Douglas's address, 392; overindulgent to Bosie, 410; concern for son, 444–5; provides companions for Bosie, 452; and W's meeting with Douglas, 511; forestalls Bosie meeting W, 512; cuts off money, 519–21; sends W £200, 522; Douglas at Trouville with, 534

Queensberry, 9th Marquess of (John Sholto Douglas), character and temperament, 365–6; rebuffed by Scottish lords, 365; divorced, 366; relations with son Alfred, 366; contests suit for annulment, 381; second marriage of, 381; writes to son in Cairo, 391; briefly charmed by W, 393; threatens to disinherit son, 394; confronts W at Tite Street, 396, 420–1; W shaken by threats of, 396–7; reads *Green Carnation*, 400; second marriage annulled, 402; plans theatre disruption, 403, 406; a very rich man, 409; leaves insulting card at W's club, 412; W begins libel suit against, 15, 412, 413–14; pleads justification, 414, 416–18; appears in court, 417; his letters as evidence, 423; acquitted, 425, 427; will not prevent W's flight, 428; letter to *Star*, 449n; victory dinner, 449; challenged to duel, 457; sets detective on W, 505; Douglas reconciled with, 534–5; death of, 542–3; his will, 542n–543n. *See also* Drumlanrig

Queensberry, 10th Marquess, *see* Douglas, Percy

Quilter, Harry, takes over Whistler's house, 126; W's strictures on, 248; on Royal Academy Committee, 257

Rachilde (Marguérite Eymery), theme of variable sexuality in, 85; her *Monsieur Vénus*, 266; Douglas's letter to, 481n

racism, W's valet evicted from Pullman, 191

Radford, Ernest, W's correspondence with, 80

Raffalovich, Marc-André, hostile to W, 59, 238; takes name Brother Sebastian, 68; Fr. Bowden and, 91; hears W on woman's reputation, 107; W's comment on verse of, 206; W reviews poems of, 248; gives lavish entertainments, 266; his novel, *A Willing Exile*, 266; affair with John Gray, 369, 542; his green carnation sonnet, 401; publishes pamphlet on trial, 438n; W's sworn enemy, 504

Rambosson, Yvanhoe, Verlaine's comment on W, 322

626